T5-ARZ-460

International's Series in

ECONOMICS

MONEY, BANKING, AND INCOME

Theory and Policy

MONEY, BANKING, AND INCOME
Theory and Policy

PHAM CHUNG

Department of Economics
The University of New Mexico

INTERNATIONAL TEXTBOOK COMPANY
An Intext *Publisher*
Scranton, Pennsylvania 18515

ISBN 0 7002 2287 1

Printed in the United States of America by The Haddon Craftsmen, Inc. Scranton, Pennsylvania. Library of Congress Catalog Card Number: 74-117419.

To

Huynh-Hoa, Duong-Hung, and Phuc-Hoa

Preface

This book may be used for a one-semester course in Money and Banking, or a two-semester course. The organization of the book, in general, is conventional, but there are innovations in the selection and integration of materials.

The book consists of six parts. Part I is on the general nature and functions of money and credit, monetary standards, and the relative importance of money in different economic systems. Part II deals with the operations of institutions that create money, and Part III, with the operations of institutions that control money. Part IV is on money and income theory. It is devoted to the analysis of the relationships between money and such economic variables as the level of prices, the level of income and employment, the rate of interest, and the integration of these variables in models to show the interdependence between monetary variables and real variables. Part V is concerned with the relation between theory and policy, the objectives of economic policy, the major tools of economic policy, and the application of these tools in the light of American experiences in recent decades. Part VI is on money in international transactions and international monetary problems.

The primary purpose of the book is to introduce students to theoretical principles in Money and Banking and their uses as guides to intelligent policy decisions. It is more theoretical than most texts in the field, but the way theoretical concepts are presented, they are, I believe, within the grasp of the "average" student. In discussing theoretical principles I always begin with simple models and move graudally to slightly more complex models, supported by geometrical illustrations and easy numerical examples. Historical and institutional materials are by no means played down. They are, however, presented not for their own sake but primarily to support theoretical discussions or to show the influences of the past on present developments and arrangements.

A relatively greater emphasis is given to the treatment of some subjects that I believe to be of special interest yet inadequately discussed in most texts on Money and Banking. The discussion on central banking, for example, is not only concerned with American central banking but also with the scope and role of central bank control in less developed countries. This would give students insights into how central banks in such countries modify traditional control instruments and develop new control techniques to meet problems arising from the monetary and financial institutional environment of underdevelopment. Considerable attention is given to the discussion on international monetary problems such as international liquidity, gold and the U.S. dollar, international monetary cooperation, and international monetary reforms.

Those students who wish to know the derivation of various formulas in the text will find mathematical discussions in footnotes helpful. Each chapter of the book is followed by questions for discussion and/or problems. Answers to selected problems are also included. Some of my colleagues may question the advisability of including answers to problems on the grounds that students would look at the answers before they work on the problems. On this, my view is different. It seems to me that since it is not possible for the instructor to go over these numerical examples in class, especially when the course is given in one semester which appears to be the current practice in a good number of institutions, providing answers to selected problems is giving students the means to check the results of their exercises. This would encourage them to work on the problems. It is true that they may look at the answers before working on the problems, but I believe that half a loaf is still better than none. Without the answers to problems, they might not even look at the problems as there is no way for them to verify their answers.

The people who have made the preparation of this book possible are numerous. To express my gratitude to all of them would probably leave no space for anything else. I wish, however, to express special thanks to my colleagues in the Department of Economics of the University of New Mexico, namely, Sanford Cohen, Ralph d'Arge (now with the University of California at Riverside), David Hamilton, and Alfred Parker for having read parts of the manuscript, and especially to Oliver Wood, Jr. of the University of South Carolina, whose comments and suggestions have led to improvements in a number of chapters. Last but not least I wish to thank David Gabriel and John A. Wargo, and their staff at International Textbook Company, for their cooperation and assistance.

Pham Chung

Albuquerque, New Mexico
February, 1970

Contents

part I

MONEY, CREDIT, AND MONETARY STANDARDS

chapter 1

The Economic Role of Money

Nearly all aspects of economic life in modern societies involve the use of money. The purchase of goods, services, and claims, the settlement of debts, and payment of taxes are generally effected with the agency of money. Our individual economic well-being depends upon the amount of money income we receive for the goods we produce or the services we render, and the goods and services our money income will buy. For payment purposes, we always carry with us some money in the form of coins and notes, or checkbooks with which we can order the transfer of deposit money that we have in commercial banks. Money is indeed familiar to every one of us. Yet its functioning and the control of its flow remain complicated problems of modern economic analysis and policy.

The economic importance of money cannot be overemphasized. The use of money immensely facilitates the exchange process and makes possible market expansion and specialization which are among the essential ingredients in the development of advanced industrial societies. Working with other nonmonetary cooperating factors, the availability of money may help monetize untapped resources and unemployed labor, make chimneys smoke and factories run. But while it is a powerful device enabling societies to accomplish progress which would be impossible to realize under pure barter exchange, money may become a source of economic chaos and social disorder when it is seriously out of control.

BARTER EXCHANGE

The main concern of economic life is the production and exchange of goods and services. The exchange of goods and services can be effected with or without the agency of money. Direct or barter exchange, however, involves several problems. First, for a barter transaction to be successfully completed, a perfect coincidence of wants of the parties involved in the transaction is required. For example, if one unit of product x could be traded for two units of product y, the owner of one unit of x who wants two units of y has to find an owner of y who wants one unit of x in exchange for his product. To reach such a coincidence of wants is obviously a difficult arrangement. When products to be bartered have different qualities or when they cannot be divided into smaller units, trading seems more difficult to carry out. Given the exchange ratio between goats and rabbits—one goat for, say, 10 rabbits—trade would not be practical should the owner of rabbits want to sell only two rabbits. It would be rather difficult for the owner of the goat to find on the same market day people who are willing to pool their rabbits in exchange for his goat.

In a monetary economy, wages, salaries, interest, rent, and other obligations calling for future payments are written in contracts expressed in terms of money. In barter-exchange societies there is no primary unit of value measurement in terms of which these contracts can be written. They have to be expressed in terms of specific commodities and services. The conclusion of such contracts would run into several hurdles. It would be difficult for the parties involved in a contract to agree on the specific goods acceptable to both for repayment. Since commodities are hardly homogeneous, to arrive at an agreement as to the quality of commodities for repayment purposes presents another contractual difficulty.

In a monetary economy we compare the values of goods and services by referring to the ratios of their money prices. Under barter exchange, in the absence of a common standard of value in terms of which values of goods and services can be quoted, each good, instead of carrying one price, would have to be quoted in terms of the remaining goods for sale on the market. For instance, if there were 100 goods on the market, each good would carry with it 99 exchange ratios which indicate its value relative to the remaining ones. The total number of exchange ratios to be reckoned with is then 4950.[1] Bookkeeping under such conditions would be too cumbersome. We can imagine problems encountered by a store in making up a balance sheet, in keeping scores of receipts and disbursements—all in goods and services and claims of various kinds, involving large numbers of relative barter rates. Producers could hardly know if a productive undertaking would be an economic proposition, as they would have little information on production costs and probable receipts from the sale of their products. Individuals would find it difficult to make decisions regarding the selection of various types of work, and the allocation of their incomes in kind between consumption, saving, and investment.

Individuals do not spend all the incomes they earn on current consumption. Portions of their incomes would be saved for things they need later, for a "rainy day" and unanticipated future consumption requirements. Money, most of the time, serves well the purpose of a "store of general purchasing power." People can hold part of their incomes in money which can be very easily exchanged for

[1] If there are n commodities to be bartered, the value of each is expressed in terms of the n - 1 remaining goods. Since the relative value of two commodities is expressed by one exchange ratio and its reciprocal, the total number of exchange ratios to be reckoned with in the case of n commodities would be $T = \frac{n(n-1)}{2} = \frac{n^2 - n}{2}$. In our example, $n = 100$, hence $T = \frac{100\,(99)}{2} = 4950$.

things they need. In barter societies incomes in kind would have to be stored for future consumption needs. While this is practical in the case of nonperishable products, they would require large storage spaces and costs. Perishable goods would be out of the question since they cannot be stored for long. Furthermore, holders of these incomes in kind may not in times of need, be able to exchange them quickly for the goods and services they want.

In view of these difficulties, barter exchange is inconsistent with an economic society which has achieved any substantial degree of specialization. It could prevail only in very primitive societies with very small populations and little or no economic integration, in which each individual family would be primarily a self-sufficient economic unit producing mostly for its own consumption.

MONEY, MARKET EXPANSION, AND SPECIALIZATION

The introduction of money facilitates the exchange process and simplifies value calculations. Individual goods and services on the market each carries a price tag which is its value in relation to money. They are exchanged for money which is in turn exchanged for goods and services. The addition of one intermediate stage in the exchange process, commodity–money–commodity, eliminates the need for a coincidence of wants and the considerable amount of time and effort that would have to be spent in direct exchange. Comparison of values is much easier to make. The accounting of receipts and payments of individuals and business is much simplified. Guided by the money prices of both inputs and outputs, producers would be able to select combinations of input factors for the production of commodities which would maximize profit–that is, the difference between what they pay out in wages, salaries, interest, and rent, and the sale receipts of their outputs; consumers would be able to spend their money incomes on combinations of goods and services which are most preferable to them. The use of money thus promotes economic efficiency, providing producers with a greater incentive to produce for exchange, since their products can be more easily marketed through the money medium.

Increases in production for exchange enlarge the size of the market. Market expansion in turn helps to promote greater production through specialization or division of labor. The expansion of the market not only permits individuals to specialize at particular jobs for which they are best suited, but also makes it possible for business enterprises to engage in particular lines of productive activity. Thus manufacturers of automobiles can depend on a network of suppliers of materials such as rubber, glass, paint, batteries, and so on, and a network of dealers to deliver automobiles to individual buyers. All these economic activities are linked together by money payments. As a consequence of specialization, goods and services are made available to consumers in larger quantity, with greater variety and better quality. Division of labor, stimulated by market expansion, leads to more specialization and higher productivity as a result of the introduction of new production techniques made possible by specialization in the first place. Subsequently, further market expansion is stimulated. Money, market expansion, and division of labor are parts of a cumulative process which has made possible the development of highly industrialized societies where individuals enjoy ever-rising standards of living.

The use of money alone, however, is not a sufficient condition for the emergence of market expansion and production specialization, which are essential requirements for the formation of modern economic societies. A highly productive economy requires in addition such nonmonetary cooperating factors as the size and skill of the labor force, the general level of education, and the endowment of natural resources which are readily accessible, among other things. In underdeveloped economies the extent of the market is still very limited, and the degree of specialization of the economic function is still negligible, although in most of these areas money has been in use for centuries. Production in these places is pretty much for self-consumption, not for exchange, and the standard of living there remains at the subsistence level.

TECHNICAL FUNCTIONS OF MONEY

Money performs several important technical functions. It serves as a unit of account, a medium of exchange, a store of value, and a standard of deferred payments. And like any other technical device, the money device performs its functions well when it is in order.

Money as a Unit of Account

Money serves as a unit of account—that is, a unit in terms of which the relative values of goods and services can be expressed. The unit of account is also interchangeably referred to as standard of value, unit of value, common denominator, or money of account. Each monetary system has a unit of account. In the United States, the unit of account is the dollar; in France, the French franc; in Germany, the mark; in Russia, the ruble, and so on. Expressed in terms of the unit of account, each commodity has a money price which is its monetary value: the number of monetary units which it will exchange for. The ratios of money prices of commodities and services indicate their value in relation to one another, their relative prices. The process of economic calculation is immensely simplified by the system of prices resulting from the denomination of the value of goods and services in terms of money.

The money of account is by no means the only unit of measurement used in economic activity. In addition to money, there are other units of measurement, such as meter and yard for the measurement of distance, pound and kilogram for the measurement of weight, and so on. While these units of physical measurement remain constant as time and economic conditions change, the money of account, being a unit of value, unfortunately does change with changing times and economic conditions. It may appreciate or depreciate in its value in terms of goods and services. The value of the dollar today is not the same as it was, say, in 1930. Nor do we expect it to be the same in 1980 as it is today.

Normally for each monetary system there is one unit of account. But dual units of account were not uncommon in the monetary history of nations. This was either the result of inflationary conditions or the strength of customs and the attachment of people to a popular monetary unit of the past. In the United States during the Civil War period, the gold dollar, even though it had disappeared from circulation, continued to serve as a standard of value for some accounts in addition to the "greenback" which was losing its value rapidly as a result of inflation. Also during the colonial period it was a common practice to keep accounts in terms of the English pound and shillings, although very few of these were in actual circulation. In Germany, during the period of inflation of the early 1920's, accounts were kept and contracts written in terms of foreign currencies instead of the official unit of account, the mark. In England, dual units of account still exist, the pound sterling and the guinea—the latter being a "ghost" unit.

Money as a Medium of Exchange

This function is rather obvious. We receive money in payment for the goods we produce or for the services we render. We in turn use money for the purchase of things we need and are produced by others. We are willing to accept money for our goods and services because we are confident that other people will accept money in exchange for their goods and services. Irrespective of the physical substance of the things used as money, so long as it is accepted by all of us in exchange for goods and services, it serves as a common means of payment. The existence of such a common circulating medium (which decomposes the single barter transaction into separate transactions of buying and selling, thereby eliminating the double coincidence of wants) is essential to functional specialization. It enables the individual to devote his time and effort in one particular occupation and employment, and to exchange part of his money receipts for the goods and services he wants and are produced by others.

As a medium of exchange, money represents "generalized purchasing power" or "bearer of options," giving its holders great freedom of choice. We are indeed free to spend our money income the way we want. With money, we can purchase practically any good or service that is available for sale, provided we have enough money for this purpose. We can spend all the money income we earn or save portions of it for future consumption. We are free to select the time and place to spend our money. The extent of this freedom, of course, depends on the amount of commodities and services available. The greater the amount of goods and services, the greater the range of the commanding power of money, and the greater the freedom of spending choice. In highly developed societies where millions of products are available, holders of money certainly have wider freedom of choice than do people in underdeveloped areas with far fewer commodities and services.

Each country has its own medium of exchange. What is a medium of exchange in one country is usually not a means of payment in other countries. But holders of domestic money can easily spend it on foreign products when currencies of nations are freely convertible into each other, or when the money concerned is internationally accepted. For instance, holders of United States dollars can spend them not only on American products but also on foreign commodities as well—since the United States dollar, in addition to being a national monetary unit, is also an international means of payments serving trade between nations, an international reserve for a large number of central banks throughout the world.

Money well serves its function as a medium of exchange when its value is kept relatively stable. When its purchasing power is subject to frequent fluctuations, it is bound to cause economic hardships to various groups in the economy. When it loses too much of its value, it may be rejected altogether by the public as a circulating medium. This is rare, but it has happened, as in periods of hyperinflation, political revolution and social disturbance, when the public lost confidence in its monetary unit.

Money as a Store of Value

We have mentioned that money represents generalized purchasing power. It can be exchanged at any time for any good or service. For this reason alone, money is worth holding. Under normal conditions, we always hold certain amounts of money on hand, first of all, in order to bridge the gap between receipt and payment resulting from the fact that the dating of our expenditures does not coincide with that of our income receipts. In addition to money held for exchange purposes, we also hold money in order to provide for a "rainy day," to meet emergency spending requirements, and to take advantage of economic opportunities which may present themselves in the future, such as the opportunity to purchase something offered at a special discount price. Money is therefore a store of value, an asset in which wealth can be held.

Money is by no means the only store of value. In addition to money, our wealth can be held in real assets such as land, houses, automobiles, appliances, and financial assets such as corporate bonds and government securities. The portion of our wealth held in these alternative wealth-holding forms at any given time depends primarily upon their relative economic merits, which tend to change with changing economic conditions, and expectations. If we expect prices, in general, to decrease in the future, i.e., an increase in the value of money, then money is relatively a better store of value. We will be induced to move from real assets to money and fixed-value financial claims (such as savings accounts). On the other hand, if our expectation is that prices in general will increase in the future—that is a decrease in the value of money—then real assets and financial claims become relatively more desirable stores of value in relation to money. We will then be induced to move from money to other assets. It follows that for money to perform its function well as a store of value, it is essential that its value be relatively stable over time.

Under normal conditions, we hold money, and are willing to sacrifice income that could be obtained by holding real assets and income-yielding claims, mainly because of its liquidity[2]—that is, its ability to be gotten rid of quickly without loss in value. We hold money because it is a liquid store of value.

Money as a Standard of Deferred Payments

Money also serves as a standard of debt or deferred payments. This function of money follows from the preceding one. Since money is a store of general purchasing power with relatively stable value, we are willing to accept future money payments for the goods we currently produce, for the services we currently perform, and for the loans we currently make to other people. Contracts calling for future money payments are essential to the process of production and distribution of goods and services. Charge accounts, real estate mortgages, government securities, corporate bonds, wage and salary contracts—to name a few—are all contracts involving future payments of money. Indeed, we can purchase goods from stores or automobiles from car dealers, and stretch the payments over a period of weeks, months, or years by using charge accounts. A producer of a commodity can borrow money from a commercial bank to pay for raw materials, hired labor, other production costs, and to finance his own consumption until his products are ready for sale on the market. A corporation can raise additional funds by selling bonds to the public to finance its capital expansion. All these are contracts promising to pay future sums of money. They are accepted because, among other things, money received in the future is expected to have roughly the same purchasing power as that of money currently parted with in making loans or acquiring securities. If this expectation fails to materialize, then either lenders or borrowers will suffer, depending on the direction of the change in the value of money. If the value of money increases, as in the case of deflation, the victims are debtors who have to pay off their debts with money of considerably higher value. On the other hand, if the value of money decreases as a result of inflation, the burden is on creditors as they are repaid with money of substantially less purchasing power.

Here again a relatively stable value of the monetary unit is a necessary condition for money to fulfill its function as a standard of debt. When money continuously loses its value in terms of goods and services as a result of inflation, people would be reluctant to accept contracts involving future payments of money, especially long-term contracts, unless they contain an "escalation clause" to make up for the expected loss in the value of money.

[2]More details on money and liquidity are presented in Chapter 2.

DYNAMIC FUNCTIONS OF MONEY

In a free market economy, money is something more than a technical device serving as a standard of value, a medium of exchange, a store of value, and a standard of deferred payments. Money does exert important dynamic influences on the economic process. The change in the quantity of money and the speed of its motion may affect the behavior of such vital economic variables as output and employment. And when its flow is out of control, money may become a source of serious economic as well as social troubles.

Money, Output, and Employment

The total volume of output produced by an economy and the degree of utilization of its labor and other resources are directly related to the flow of money spending. The effect of the money flow on output and employment can be seen by first looking at a simple closed economy with two sectors: household and business.[3] Family households sell productive services to the business sector and receive in return a flow of income payments in wages and salaries, interest, and rents, which are in turn spent on consumption goods produced by business firms. The flow of consumption spending from households to firms provides the latter with funds to pay for households' wages and salaries and so on. There are thus two continuing flows through the economy in opposite directions: one real, the other monetary (see Fig. 1-1). The productive services from households to firms and consumers' goods from firms to households make up the real flow. The income payments from firms to households and the resulting consumption expenditure from households to firms constitute the money flow. Let us concentrate on the flow of monetary expenditure and the stream of consumers' goods. If the spending flow is adequate to sustain the stream of consumers' goods which business firms are capable of producing, using all productive services and assets owned by households, there would be no great changes in employment, production, sales, or prices. As population grows, technology changes; as new resources and materials are discovered, the flow of consumers' goods can be increased. If increases in output are sustained by equivalent increases in consumption spending, then the economy continues to enjoy full employment of labor and resources, relatively stable prices, and steady growth of real outputs.[4]

According to classical thinking, the two flows are always in balance at full

[3] More details on this are given in Chapter 18 on the accounting and composition of national income.

[4] The magnitude of these two flows would not be changed with the inclusion of savings by households and accumulation of producers' goods by firms if savings of households are channeled back to firms through financial intermediaries for investment spending. What is changed is the composition of the flows. The expenditure flow is now made up of consumption and investment spending and the output flow of both consumers' and producers' goods. So long as the stream of consumers' and producers' goods is sustained by the flow of consumption and investment expenditure at high and stable levels, both expanding as population grows and technology is improved, full employment and relatively stable prices and growing outputs would prevail.

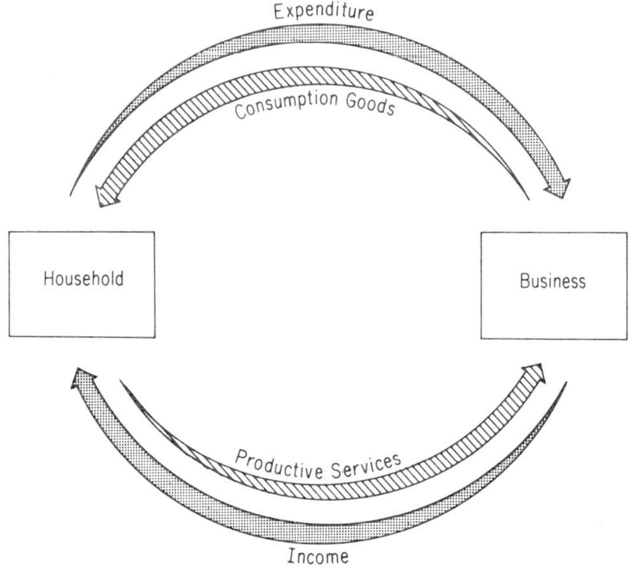

Fig. 1-1.

employment of labor and resources. The flow of real output is in no way affected by money which is considered simply as a technical device whose sole function is to facilitate trade. Just like oil, money only helps lubricate the economic machinery. It is neutral, having no effect on the economic process. Such real variables as employment, output, wages, and so on are not affected, but rather are obscured by the money "veil." Under that veil, goods are exchanged for goods, just as under barter. Since money is a transaction device having no inherent utility of its own, people have no desire to increase or decrease money balances for purposes other than those facilitating the exchange between commodities. Balances over and above those required for transactions will return to the expenditure flow. Hence there is no possibility of "clots" in the expenditure flow resulting from the hoarding and speculation in money; the function of money as an asset, as an alternative form of wealth holding, is not considered. The classical assumption regarding the nature and function of money is exemplified in John Stuart Mill's statement:

> There cannot . . . be intrinsically a more insignificant thing, in the economy of society, than money; except in the character of a contrivance for sparing time and labor. It is a machine for doing quickly and commodiously, what would be done, though less quickly and commodiously, without it; and like many other types of machinery, it only exerts a distinct and independent influence of its own when it gets out of order.[5]

[5] J. S. Mill, *Principles of Political Economy*, Book III, Chap. 7, p. 3.

Though aware of possible short-run independent influence exerted by the monetary mechanism when it is out of order, as indicated in Mill's statement, this short-run instability appears to be deemphasized by classical analysis which is concerned primarily with long-run equilibrium conditions in wages, prices, output, and employment. As prices and wages are assumed to be completely flexible upward as well as downward, according to classical thinking, the effect of an increase or decrease in the quantity of money is merely reflected by a corresponding increase or decrease in all prices. The structure of relative prices—that is, relative values of goods and services—remains unaffected, as does output, employment, and other real variables.

Contrary to "classical" thinking, however, short-run instability is frequently generated by the almost perennial malfunctioning of the money mechanism. In modern economic analysis, short-run instability occupies an important place as it affects short-run fluctuations in income and employment, and hence the long-run achievement of economic development and growth, among other things.

The classical assumption concerning the nature and function of money underlined Say's "Law of Market" which was a foundation of classical thinking. This law stated that "it is production which creates market for goods" or what amounts to the same thing, "supply creates its own demand." Commodities which producers bring to the market for sale are their means of payment for goods that they want from others, their real purchasing power. They supply their goods because they want the goods offered by others. The supply of goods generates the demand for goods. With regard to the economy as a whole, aggregate supply is identical with aggregate demand. It follows that general overproduction, hence general unemployment, is not possible. To be sure, according to Say's law, it is possible that there may be temporary overproduction in particular industries resulting from misjudgment of demand by producers, but oversupply in some industries is always to be accompanied by undersupply in some other industries.

Under barter exchange, Say's law necessarily holds. A producer brings his products to the market in order to exchange them for goods produced by others. The supply of his goods corresponds to his demand for a given amount of commodities which he wants from other producers. Suppose that he is not able to find someone who is willing to trade the goods that he needs for his own products. There is, then, an oversupply of goods that he produces. But at the same time there is a supply deficiency of goods for which he demands. Under monetary exchange, in order for Say's law to hold, money receipts must return to the spending stream as monetary expenditure. But this is not always the case. Money is not only a medium of exchange but also a store of value, an asset in which people can hold part of their wealth. The existence of money, which makes possible the extension and separation over time of sales and spending decisions, renders unnecessary the simultaneity of sale and purchase by the same spending unit as would prevail under pure barter exchange. In other words, under monetary exchange, for a given spending unit, a sale is not necessarily followed by a purchase, or vice versa. Suppose that family households decide to hoard a portion of their money receipts obtained from selling productive services to firms. This withdrawal of purchasing power from the spending stream, unless offset by equivalent addition of new purchasing power, will cause a contraction in the expenditure flow. A surplus of goods would follow—prices drop, inventories pile up, profits dwindle, production is cut back, workers are laid off, unemployment rises, income declines; the decrease in income will lead to further decreases in consumption demand, further decline in prices, and smaller outputs. These are symptons of deflation or recession.

On the other hand, substantial increases in the flow of money spending at times when the economy could not significantly increase the flow of goods and services lead to inflationary pressures. Prices rise. People rush from money to goods. "Too few" commodities are then chased by "too much" money. This can happen when there is overexpansion of bank loans to consumers and firms for consumption and investment spending, when the government prints large sums of money to finance its budget deficits while firms are already operating at "capacity" and resources are fully employed. However, until the economy reaches its output and employment potential, increases in the expenditure flow, whether they reflect spending decisions of households and firms or actions taken by men in authority, are expected to exert healthy influences on the economy as a whole, as they can sustain greater flows of goods and services. With greater demands for their products, business firms are in a position to increase production, expand their plants, hire more workers, pay more wages and salaries, interest, and dividends. Income and employment rise. In such a situation, injections of more money into the spending stream indeed may help "monetize" unemployed labor, unused resources, and make factories run.

Money is thus a dynamic element, participating actively in the economic process. But we should definitely not allow ourselves to believe that money alone can accomplish all this. The dynamic nature of money lies primarily in the fact that it can create an environment conducive to employment and output changes. It is a cooperating factor working with other nonmonetary cooperating factors to increase the flow of goods and services. But the flow of real output which an economy is capable of depends largely on such factors as the skill and creativeness of its work force, the rate of growth of its population, its endowment of natural resources, its geographical location, its stock of capital equipment, and so on. The material well-being of a nation as a whole will not necessarily be improved by simply increasing the volume of money.

Money Troubles

We have seen that so long as the expenditure flow, which is determined by the quantity of money and its rate of turnover, is adequate to sustain a high and stable stream of goods and services, there would be no great changes in prices, employment, production, and sales. The balance between the two flows at high levels of employment and output is not automatic but requires proper monetary

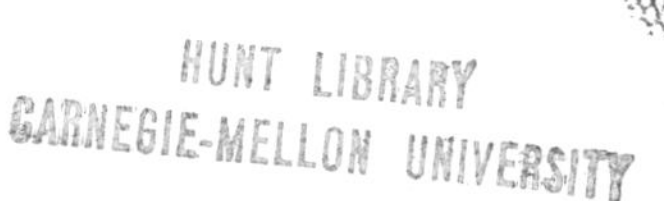

and fiscal control measures. The art of controlling the money flow, at this stage of its development, is unfortunately still imperfect. When money is out of order, it is bound to cause economic and social troubles. The seriousness of money troubles of course depends upon how badly the money mechanism is out of control.

When the spending stream is substantially out of balance with the flow of outputs, we have symptoms of either inflation or deflation, and money starts its troublesome course. As illustrated earlier, increases in aggregate spending at a time when there could be little or no further increases in outputs will inevitably result in inflation. A significant decline in the value of money as a result of inflationary pressures can cause serious economic hardships to creditors and persons whose incomes are fixed. Creditors are repaid for their loans with money of substantially less value; workers with fixed wage and salary contracts and retired people find themselves much poorer as the real purchasing power of their fixed money incomes declines.

In the case of runaway or hyperinflation, money becomes a disruptive force causing economic chaos which could lead not only to the breakdown of the monetary mechanism but also could affect the existing political system and social order. In modern times, several countries have gone through the frightening experiences of hyperinflation. Such an instance was Germany during the early 1920's. Defeated by the Allied Forces, Germany had to shoulder the heavy burden of the payments of war reparation. As domestic taxes were inadequate to sustain reparation payments as well as heavy reconstruction spending, the German government had to cover its ever-widening budget deficits by resorting to central bank borrowings which gave rise to tremendous increases in the volume of paper marks in circulation. This took place at a time when the German economy was operating at capacity. As a consequence, prices increased rapidly. At the same time funds were flowing freely from commercial banks to firms for carrying stocks, for speculative operations, as their profits were enhanced by tremendous price increases. The government found it necessary to print more and more paper marks to cover its increasing costs resulting from rising prices. The German economy was then following the self-propagating process of galloping inflation. In late 1923 the volume of paper marks reached astronomical figures—and so did prices. The volume of paper marks in circulation in December increased to 496.8 quintillion marks.[6] Notes were issued in 1,000, 2,000, 5,000, 10,000 and 100,000 billion denominations, printed only on one side! The index of consumer prices increased from 3.66 billion in October to 1,247 billion in December.[7]

[6]One quintillion = $(1{,}000{,}000)^3$ or (1,000,000,000,000,000,000) (the United States and French systems).

[7]In late November 1923, the price in Berlin of one kilogram of butter was reported to be 5,600 billion marks; a newspaper, 200 billion; a kilogram of bread, 428 billion. Thirty paper mills were engaged in the production of paper for printing bank notes. As the printing facilities of the Reichsbank were inadequate to turn out necessary amounts of notes, more than one hundred private printing presses were engaged in stamping notes. Costantino Bresciani-Turroni, *The Economics of Inflation* (London: Allen & Unwin, 1953), pp. 25, 35, 82, 440, 442.

With prices skyrocketing and money becoming practically worthless, people rushed from money to goods as fast as they could. Workers spent their money incomes as soon as they were received. People bought whatever they could, regardless of whether the things they acquired were of any use to them since, under such conditions, anything was better than money. In the second half of 1923 the situation was hopeless. The German economy was disorganized, and the distribution process was in complete chaos. Unable to keep accounts of receipts and payments as a result of astronomical price increases which occurred from one hour to the next, shops discontinued their sales. Food products and industrial goods became scarce–nobody wanted to sell them for money that was worthless. Factories had to close down for lack of raw materials. Unemployment rose. The mark was altogether rejected by the public, which turned to foreign currencies and devices created by private firms as means of payments.

The grave monetary and economic crisis in which several years of galloping inflation had culminated was finally relieved by a thorough monetary reform. In 1923-24 a new currency was issued in exchange for the old at the rate of one new mark for one trillion of the old marks. Government spending was cut back. The budget was balanced. The tax system was overhauled; new taxes were introduced, and existing taxes were raised. Bank credit was kept under control. Payments of reparation were scaled down by the Allied governments. Public confidence was restored. Inflation was finally put to an end.

The German hyperinflation did cause serious political and social consequences. Holders of debentures and bonds issued by the central and local governments, mortgage bonds and other fixed-value financial claims, retired people, and government employees whose wages and salaries did not keep pace with runaway price increases, all suffered greatly as their wealth was wiped out. The enrichment of great industrialists, financiers, and profiteers, who took advantage of the situation at the expense of the impoverishment of the masses, was a source of bitter resentment which encouraged a change in the public's political and social attitude in the years which followed–a reaction against democracy. The new Democratic–Liberal party continually lost supporters who turned to extreme political organizations. In the words of L. Robbins, the depreciation of the mark "destroyed the wealth of the more solid elements in German society; and it left behind a moral and economic disequilibrium, an apt breeding ground for the disasters which have followed. Hitler is the foster-child of the inflation."[8]

Germany by no means had a monopoly on hyperinflation! During and after two world wars, a large number of countries went through the same frightening experiences: Austria, Poland, and Russia, after World War I; Greece, Hungary, and Rumania during and after World War II; and Germany again in 1946-47. China's wartime and postwar inflation (1937-49) was believed to be one of the primary factors which caused the downfall of the Nationalist government and the conquest of the mainland by the Chinese Communist Party. In the United States, the expression "not worth a continental" is still a reminder of the night-

[8]Lionel Robbins' Preface to Costantino Bresciani-Turroni, *The Economics of Inflation, op. cit.*

mare of galloping inflation in the American colonies during the War of Independence.

At the other end of the scale lies economic depression. One such instance was the Great Depression of the early 1930's which was both economically and socially disastrous. The United States, for instance, had witnessed a drastic decline in the flow of money spending during the period. This had resulted in sharp decreases in income, prices, production, and rising unemployment. Thus, from the peak of prosperity in 1929 to the bottom of the depression in 1933, gross national product shrank from $104.4 billion to $56.0 billion. The index of prices decreased from 100 to 77 during the same period. Masses of workers were laid off. The rate of unemployment rose from 3 percent in 1929 to a quarter of the work force in 1933. Depositors ran on banks. Banking institutions went bankrupt, carrying in their wake the bankruptcy of hundreds of firms. Shops were deserted. Factories were idle. Unemployed workers roamed the streets. Debtors were not able to pay their debts, and thousands of property mortgages were foreclosed. The economy practically stood still. The period witnessed a change in government from Republican to Democrat. Not until the late 1930's when more aggressive measures taken by the government were coupled with changes in the international situation did the economy recover. Similar experiences also prevailed in other countries during this period of the world depression.

Between these two extremes, the nightmare of hyperinflation and the destitution of prolonged depression, money always affects the functioning of the economic process, though in a considerably less spectacular fashion. Changes in the quantity of money and the speed of its motion, which affect the flow of money spending, may at times cause inflation, at times recession. As the value of money changes, it alters the distribution of income between various groups in the economy, causing hardship to some and enriching others. Despite all these troubles, we still stick to money as it is indispensable to the operation of the modern economy. Indeed, without money, the development of highly industrialized societies such as ours, with ever-rising standards of living, would hardly be possible.

MONEY AND ECONOMIC SYSTEMS

The allocation of scarce resources in the production and distribution of goods and services for the satisfaction of human wants is the ultimate goal of all economic societies. But the way by which resources are allocated for the achievement of this goal differs in different economic systems with different economic institutions and processes. In an economic system in which economic decisions are left largely to the initiative of the individual, money plays a considerably more important role than in a system in which economic activities are directed and controlled by the state.

Money and the Capitalistic Free-Enterprise System

In a capitalistic free-enterprise system such as our own where individual initiative, private property, competition, and the profit-motive prevail, money and the price and market mechanism play a vital role in the economic process. They serve as guides to the allocation of resources, as an integrating force coordinating all component parts of the whole system into one interdependent whole. While we are all aware of governmental intervention in the economic process—minimum wages and banking control, to name a few—what we tend to take for granted is that tens of thousands of goods and services are produced and distributed every day by millions of individuals and firms without control or direction from the government. Economic decisions are made independently by individuals and firms for their own economic gains, yet they are all coordinated and reconciled with each other primarily by the price and market mechanism operating through the money medium. Most of the things we want, provided we have adequate purchasing power to back them up, are always made available to us by producers in proper amounts. The information on what we want and do not want is automatically transmitted to producers via money and the price system which registers price variations, signaling, among other things, changes in our preferences for goods and services.

Suppose we want more strawberries and less grapes. We then start buying more strawberries and reducing our purchase of grapes. This will raise the price of strawberries and lower the price of grapes. The increase in the price of strawberries will induce growers to grow more of this fruit. On the other hand, the decline in the price of grapes will make grape growers cut back their production. In time, the production of strawberries will increase to meet the increase in demand, and the supply of grapes will drop as the demand decreases. By trial and error, prices will settle at levels at which the quantities supplied are in balance with the quantities demanded. This adjustment process between prices and production works itself out via the price system operating through the money medium without conscious control exercised by any central intelligence. It is the "brain" for the whole system, receiving impulses of economic changes, transmitting these changes throughout the system, recording price changes, coordinating changes in production activities to create, if left undisturbed by other stimuli, a new equilibrium position where what the consumers want is balanced with what producers are willing to produce and sell.

Individuals are free in their economic pursuits. The freedom of consumers' and workers' choices is the foundation of the system which responds to them through competitive pricing that controls the economic process. With money prices serving as points from which they can take their bearings, consumers shop around for combinations of products which are compatible with their budget resources and best satisfy their desires and wants. Workers shop around for jobs that promise high rewards for their productive services; business firms employ least-cost combinations of inputs to produce goods most wanted by consumers for best profits. In a perfectly competitive system the checks and balances of competition always assure that prices reflect on the one hand the relative wants and preferences of the consumers, and the relative productivity and scarcity of productive agents on the other.

Admittedly our system is not a perfectly competitive one. It is mixed, in that there are elements of both competition and imperfection of competition. Where imperfection of competition prevails, money spending and the price mechanism serve as a less efficient guide to the allocation of productive resources. Prices then may be manipulated by some groups for their own interests without being checked by opposing forces. Nor is it that in our own system money and the price mechanism are the only coordinating and integrating forces. We know that the control of the economic process is shared by decisions of private individuals and firms as well as by public authorities. Decisions made by the government sometimes do interfere with the free play between supply and demand, of free-market forces such as the imposition of minimum wages, maximum interests, price ceilings, and the like. There are, however, decisions made by the government sector which tend to strengthen, instead of obstructing, the operation of the price and market mechanism, such as measures taken to prevent monopoly, to reduce extreme inequality of income distribution, not to speak of the maintenance of law and order which is essential to the smooth functioning of a free-enterprise economy. In sum, money and the price and market mechanism still serve as basic guides to the allocation of productive resources in our mixed capitalistic free-enterprise system.

Money and the System of Centralized Economic Planning

Money and the price mechanism is by no means the only coordinating and integrating force. In alternative economic systems with different economic institutions, the coordination and integration of economic activities can be accomplished by channels other than the price and market mechanism. Thus under a system of centralized economic planning such as that of the Soviet Union, Communist China, and other Communist countries, almost all economic activities are controlled by the state, which has the sole ownership of all natural resources and large-scale industrial equipment. For instance, in Russia economic activities are coordinated primarily by central planning authorities in accordance with long-range economic plans—five-year or seven-year plans. The overall planned economic goals to be achieved over each planning period are broken down for all segments of the Soviet economy. Each segment is assigned specific planned goals. The fulfillment of these planned goals is the primary responsibility of economic management at all levels. The monetary mechanism is but a component part of the centralized planning machinery. The basic function of monetary and financial institutions, owned and controlled by the state, is to provide whatever monetary and financial means are necessary for the attainment of the goals.

The unconscious control over the economic process by a system of relatively free prices and competitive markets is replaced by economic planning. Instead of letting the system respond to decisions of individuals through competitive pricing which guides the allocation of productive resources, aggregate social ends are determined by the central authority, which then uses the money and price mechanism to achieve these planned goals. Prices do not necessarily reflect either the relative preferences and wants of the consumers or the relative productivity and scarcity of productive resources, but rather priority decisions of the planning authority. Money and the price and market mechanism no longer play a major role in guiding the allocation of resources.

The use of money, nevertheless, is still indispensable to the functioning of the Soviet economy. It performs its major technical functions as a standard of value and a medium of exchange. Without the use of money, it would be hardly conceivable that the Soviet economy would be able to attain its present status in industrial development and growth. Attempt indeed had been made by Soviet leaders during the period of "War Communism" (1917-20) to abolish the use of money–ideologically considered as an institution of capitalism–and to provide citizens free of charge with necessities of life. The attempt did not appear to be a deliberate policy of the then Soviet government to effect the transition to a moneyless Communistic economy, but rather was the result of chaotic economic conditions arising from hyperinflation at that time. At any rate, the attempt failed and money was again brought into use. Despite talks by Soviet leaders and theoreticians concerning the future abolition of money and the transition to transactions in terms of commodities, the scope of monetary transactions has grown continuously. Wages and salaries of farmers in collective farms (representing about two-thirds of the agricultural sector of the Soviet economy), which had been paid primarily in kind prior to the reform of 1958, have been paid in money ever since, the same as workers in state enterprises and state farms.

Money and the price system still serve as a guide for economic calculations. On the basis of labor and commercial contracts (negotiated in terms of the nation's economic plan and materials allocation priorities) regarding the purchases of machinery, equipment, materials, parts, and the sales of products of enterprises, records of current operations of these enterprises are kept in the accounting terms of money receipts and payments. Comparison between money receipts and payments is an indication of whether enterprises are proceeding according to, ahead of, or behind planned schedules. The lag of receipts behind payments is a sign of possible maladjustment and requires management attention. As accounts of enterprise are consolidated into accounts of industries which are in turn integrated into accounts of higher economic divisions, the resulting consolidated balance sheet of the economy as a whole reveals the overall performance of the economy in relation to planned targets. Guided by this aggregate account, necessary corrective actions are taken by the central authority.

As economic activities are controlled by the state, money only plays its passive role as a technical device used to facilitate exchange and simplify economic calculations. Its dynamic reaction is "suppressed." Monetary factors which are partially responsible for fluctuating economic activities in free market economies do not operate in Russia's centrally planned economy. The unbalance between savings and investments, considered as one of the primary factors accounting for income fluctuations in free market economies, does not exist in a centrally planned system, as decisions on both savings and investments are made by one policy-making body, the state. Total savings are always matched with total investments. There is, however, a price to be paid for this apparent stability: production inefficiency which has for years plagued Russia as well as other Communist countries. Since prices do not reflect the relative consumers' wants and preferences and relative factors' productivities, the planned outputs sometimes are not those most wanted by consumers. As consumers' reactions are not allowed to operate in the USSR as a corrective measure of production, maladjustment via "autonomous" price variations, as under a free monetary economy, especially in the field of consumer goods, it is not uncommon that unsold surpluses exist side by side with tremendous scarcities.[9]

With a view of reducing waste and improving efficiency, reform proposals have been made by Soviet leaders and economists to allow greater use of "profit" as a criterion for judging the performance of enterprises, to give more room to the operation of money and the price mechanism.[10] How far the Soviet government will go in its reform movement remains to be seen. The answer to the question appears to depend to some extent on the success or failure of the initial experiments which have been undertaken. At any rate, in present-day Soviet Russia although the extent of consumers' and workers' freedom is still restricted and the scope of the operation of money and the price mechanism still limited, they are, nevertheless, broader than ever before since the introduction of centralized economic planning.

SUMMARY

Money plays an important economic role in all societies. It renders invaluable economic services without which the development of modern industrialized societies would hardly be possible. As a unit of account, a medium of exchange,

[9]For an account of the reform movement and concrete examples of production inefficiency in the USSR and other Communist countries, see Ernest Conine "Communism's New Economics," *Harvard Business Reviews* (May-June 1965), pp. 53–61.

[10]Profitability can serve as an efficient criterion of performance only when it is based on a system of pricing which more or less reflects not only the relative desires and wants of the consumers but also the relative productivities and scarcities of factors. It is hardly conceivable how such conditions could be approximated in a system of centralized economic planning. Such a pricing process can exist only when prices are competitively determined by independent competing sources of supply and demand. This, however, is not possible in a centrally planned economy in which the state, in principle, owns all productive resources (other than labor) and at the same time has the complete monopoly in nearly all output markets.

a store of value and a standard debt, money facilitates trade, simplifies value calculations, and creates conditions favorable to market expansion and production specialization—essential ingredients of highly productive economies. In addition to its technical services, money does exert dynamic influence on the economic process. Changes in the magnitude and composition of the flow of money spending may give rise to changes in output and employment and other real variables. The allocation of productive resources, in free-market economies, is guided primarily by the price mechanism operating through the money medium without conscious control exercised by men in authority. In a system of centralized economic planning, money is still indispensable. However, as economic activities are directed and controlled by the state, money and the price system no longer play the role of a coordinating and integrating force as under a capitalistic free-enterprise system.

PROBLEMS

1. Explain some of the inconveniences and difficulties which you believe would be encountered under pure barter exchange.
2. The use of money is a necessary but not a sufficient condition for market expansion and production specialization. Do you agree? Why or why not?
3. Comment on this statement: "In some respects, the effects of monetary changes are more than nominal and money is more than a veil."
4. Why is money still indispensable in a system of centralized economic planning such as that of the Soviet Union?
5. What are necessary conditions under which money and the price mechanism may serve as an efficient guide to the allocation of productive resources?

chapter 2

Money: Nature, Classification, and Evolution

We have discussed the economic importance of money, but we have not defined what we mean by money. In this chapter we shall define money and discuss the concepts of near-moneys, money supply, the relation between money, assets and liquidity, different types of money, and the evolution of money.

DEFINITION OF MONEY

For analytical purposes, we shall define money in terms of its economic function. Functionally, money can be defined as anything that is generally accepted as a medium of exchange within a given economic society. This definition stresses the exchange function of money as its basic characteristic. This is not to say that other functions of money are not important, but only that they are not its main characterization. It is quite possible to have a standard of value that does not correspond with the monetary unit, that does not exist in any monetary form. The guinea in Great Britain is an example of a unit of account that does not exist in monetary form. It is also possible to state contracts in terms of commodities, other assets, and foreign currencies in place of the domestic monetary unit. It is true that the asset function of money is important, especially in the context of monetary analysis; still, it is not a basic characteristic of money. When something is accepted as a medium of exchange it is also invariably used as a store of value. But a store of value which is not generally accepted as a means of payment is not money. Each of these functions could be performed by a different good. They are closely connected, however, and under normal conditions they are all fulfilled by money, the exchange medium.

General acceptability is the *sine qua non* of money. The acceptability by the public of something as money is a matter of faith, a social convention. When this confidence in money is lost, it ceases to be money. The granting of legal tender power by the government may enhance the general acceptability of money, but, as will be seen, this is neither a necessary nor a sufficient condition. The physical substance of money also has little or nothing to do with its acceptability. In fact, demand claims against commercial banks, which constitute the bulk of money in highly industrialized societies, hardly have any physical constitution at all. They represent no more than numbers in the books of commercial banks.

Therefore, the question as to whether something is money or not depends on whether it is generally accepted by the public as a means of payment. If it is, then it is money; otherwise, it is not. In the United States, currency in the form of coins (issued by the Treasury) and Federal Reserve Notes (issued by Federal Reserve Banks), and demand deposits in commercial banks are money. They are accepted by the public as means of payment. Currency is a claim on the government and demand deposits are claims on commercial banks. The latter are promises of banks to pay currency on demand. They are paid in currency on demand by banks, but they are not to be confused with currency placed in commercial banks by depositors. Currency holdings of banks are a part of their assets, while demand deposits are their (demand) liabilities. The former usually represents a very small proportion of banks' assets and liabilities.

Demand deposits (or deposit money or bank money) are transferred by means of checks. Checks, which are means of transferring money, are not money. When a person purchases something he can pay for it by writing a check on his account with his bank. Instead of paying money directly, he orders his bank to pay a given sum of money to the seller by using a check. It may happen that the personal check presented by the buyer is refused by the seller. This, however, does not mean that the latter does not accept demand deposits as money. His refusal perhaps reflects the fact that he does not know for sure if his customer has adequate funds in his checking account. Our seller refuses the personal check because it is an inadequate transfer technique. In this case, if a check of higher quality is used, such as a certified check, a cashier's check, or a traveler's check, it is very unlikely that the seller would refuse.

On the other hand, he may refuse the check because of the difference between the amount of purchase and the amount of the check. Suppose that the amount of purchase is five dollars and the amount of the check is five hundred dollars. He may refuse it because he does not have enough currency for change or he needs the amount of currency on hand for dealing with other customers. The refusal of the check in this case is concerned with the quantity, not with the quality, of demand deposits as money. This can also happen in the case where payment is made in currency. Suppose the amount of purchase is 25 cents and the buyer presents a hundred-dollar bill in payment. The seller may refuse the $100 bill simply because he does not have enough change. Again, the refusal is in connection with the quantity, not the quality, of currency as money.

Currency is generally more convenient for small transactions, especially retail transactions, and demand deposits transferred by checks are more convenient for larger transactions. It would be very inconvenient indeed to a seller to accept a payment of $10,000 in $1 and $2 bills, not to speak of half dollars and quarters. It would also be rather inconvenient (and costly) to the buyer to pay a sum of 20 cents in check. There are many advantages in using checks. They eliminate the need for people to keep larger quantities of currency on hand to make payments. They are safer. Stealers of currency have no difficulty in spending it, but would have some trouble cashing stolen checks. Also, canceled checks serve as receipts of payments. These are some of the reasons which account for the widespread use of checks in most advanced nations where up to 90 percent of the total volume of transactions is effected by means of checks drawn against commercial banks' demand liabilities. Yet some individuals still hold nothing but currency. This may be because they fail to realize the advantages of using checks for payment purposes or because of their distrust of banks resulting from, say, personal experiences with banks which failed in the past. It follows that, depending upon individual tastes and experiences and the various types and sizes of transactions, either currency or deposit money may be preferable. But in general both currency and banks' demand liabilities are equally acceptable to the public as means of payment.

Quasi-Moneys

There are claims which are not conventionally considered as money because they are not generally accepted as means of payment, but they closely resemble money in that they are, in general, available for immediate spending. Savings deposits at commercial banks are such claims. They are liabilities of banks, just like demand deposits. While the latter are obligations which have to be honored by banks on demand, the former are their time liabilities. In principle, holders of savings deposits are required to give advance notice to banks concerning savings withdrawals and wait for the notice period to run off before withdrawals can be made. This optional delay in paying currency to savings depositors is usually waived by banks so that their depositors can withdraw funds any time during banking hours. On the basis of their availability for immediate spending, savings deposits appear to be very close to demand deposits. They nevertheless differ from each other in several respects. While savings deposits are created when banks receive currency or checks in deposit from savers, the bulk of demand deposits at banks is created primarily through their lending and investing operations.[1] Perhaps the major difference between demand and time deposits is that while the former are transferrable by checks, the latter are not. For payment purposes, holders of time deposits have to convert them into currency or transfer them to checking accounts first. Strictly speaking, then, savings deposits are not money. But since they are very close to money, they are referred to as quasi-moneys, money substitutes, or near-moneys. Similarly, deposits in mutual savings banks and "shares" in savings and loan associations are also considered as near-moneys.

When money is defined as a medium of exchange, the demarcation line between money and quasi-moneys is rather clear; but if it is defined in terms of its asset function–for instance, a store of value which is readily available for im-

[1] The process of deposit creation is explained in detail in **Chapter 8**.

mediate spending–the line between money and near-moneys is blurred. The definition of money on the basis of its exchange function facilitates the analysis of the various motives behind the holding of money which is a noninterest-bearing claim, and near-moneys which are income-yielding assets. On the other hand, the inclusion of near-moneys may be justified from the standpoint of the analysis of the influence of "money" on the expenditure flow, since, just like money, near-moneys do affect the flow of aggregate spending. It follows that the definition of money is a matter of analytical convenience.

MONEY AND LIQUIDITY

Wealth can be held in money, real assets, and financial claims. Money, as an asset, differs from real assets and income-yielding claims in two respects. Holders of real assets, such as land and buildings and financial claims such as government securities and corporate bonds, are entitled to a flow of income receipts in the form of rent and interest. On the other hand, the holding of money balances does not produce incomes. Money is a noninterest-bearing claim. But for payment purposes, holders of real assets and financial claims have to convert them into money first. The conversion of these assets and claims into money–especially real estate and long-term financial assets–may cause considerable capital losses to their holders, in addition to the amount of time and effort involved in selling them. The extent of these potential capital losses depend on the market conditions of these assets at the time when the holders wish to sell them, the intensity of their needs for money, and the number of buyers interested in the assets offered. These problems would not occur to holders of money balances. Money as a store of generalized purchasing power is always acceptable at full value, always exchangeable for any asset or claim. It is this property which makes money the most liquid of all assets.

Inasmuch as other assets and claims would for spending purposes, have to be first converted into money, we can define the liquidity of an asset or claim in terms of its ability to be converted into money. The degree of liquidity of various assets can be measured by the speed with which they can be sold for money and the amount of capital loss involved in the conversion process. This capital loss is represented by the difference between the selling price and face value in the case of financial claims and appraised value in the case of real assets. According to these criteria, an asset is highly liquid if it can be exchanged for money promptly and without loss. It is illiquid if it can be sold for money only with substantial loss and considerable delay.[2] Thus savings deposits in banks and

[2]To measure the degree of liquidity of various assets and claims, this way is no different from measuring the liquidity of liquids with different degrees of thickness by putting them in different glasses and pouring them, all at once and with the same degree of inclination, into other glasses. The liquidity of each liquid is indicated by the amount of time which it takes each glass to empty itself and the amount of liquid residual remaining in each glass. The pouring speed is analogous to the speed of converting assets and claims into money and the amount of liquid residue in each glass to the amount of capital loss in the conversion process from assets into cash.

shares in savings and loan associations and fixed-price government securities are almost as liquid as money, for they are readily available for payment purposes without any loss.[3] Treasury bills, short-term commercial obligations, though less liquid than near-moneys, are still highly liquid assets because they can be sold quickly for money. Long-term securities and bonds are less liquid. Commodities, real estate, and special machinery and equipment are least liquid of all. It would be unlikely for the owner of a piece of land with an appraised value of $20,000 to obtain that value if he is to sell it immediately.

Since money is readily available for spending at any time, we are willing to hold part of our wealth in money, forsaking interest incomes which could be earned by moving from money to interest-bearing claims. The interest incomes sacrificed are the prices which we pay for the liquidity of money.

MONEY AND WEALTH

The money balance held by an individual is part of his wealth, just like real assets and other financial claims. If we subtract from his total assets what he owes others—his liabilities—what is left is his net worth or wealth. Suppose that Mr. X owns a $10,000 house, a $2,000 automobile, $1,000 in furniture and appliances, $500 in government securities and corporate bonds, a $200 savings account, a checking account of $300, and $100 in currency. His total assets are then $14,100. Assume that his total liabilities are $4,100; his net worth is then $10,000. It is clear that when we compute the net wealth of an individual, we include both real assets and financial claims. They are all components of his wealth. But what is wealth to an individual economic unit may not be wealth with regard to the community as a whole. The corporate bonds, checking accounts, and currency held by an individual which constitute part of his assets are the liabilities of the issuing business corporations, banking institutions, and the government, respectively. By the same token, the promissory note given by a borrower to a bank is the evidence of his debt; it is at the same time an earning asset of the lending bank. It follows that in the community, to each financial claim, there corresponds a financial liability. If we consolidate the assets and liabilities of all sectors of an economy, then internally held financial claims, including money, will be washed out in the resulting consolidated balance sheet of the economy as a whole.[4] What is left of the aggregation is its stock of real

[3]It is true that when one converts time deposits into cash, there is a loss of interest income which could otherwise be earned on these deposits. This loss is a price to be paid for the higher liquidity of money. This loss is not what we are concerned with when we say that these deposits can be converted into cash without loss. We refer to the fact that a given amount of time deposits in commercial banks is convertible into an equivalent amount of currency or demand deposits.

[4]This does not apply to externally held claims and liabilities. In the aggregation process, external claims have to be added to, and external liabilities subtracted from, the aggregate net wealth of a community. Thus foreign government securities and corporate

assets, machinery, equipment, building, factories, and so on. Modern moneys—which are financial claims, (central bank notes, and demand deposits)—like other financial assets, are claims on wealth, but are not part of the net wealth of the community.

The netting out of money and financial assets in the process of aggregation is illustrated by Balance Sheet I, the consolidation of the three balance sheets of the three sectors of a hypothetical economy, the business, household, and banking sectors (Table 2-1). The banking sector, which makes loans and issues money

TABLE 2-1
Sectoral Balance Sheets

Business Sector		Household Sector		Banking Sector	
Assets (a)	Liabilities	Assets (b)	Liabilities	Assets (c)	Liabilities
Money = 50 Tangible = 100	Borrowing from (c) = 60 Net Worth = 90	Money = 50 Tangible = 50	Borrowing from (c) = 40 Net Worth = 60	Loans = 100	Money = 100

Consolidated Balance Sheet (I)

Assets	Liabilities
Tangible Assets = 150	Accumulated Savings = 150

to the household and business sectors, holds no tangible assets. The business and household sectors hold tangible assets as well as financial claims and liabilities. In the consolidated balance sheet, money and financial claims (100) all disappear. The aggregate net wealth of this community is the stock of tangible assets (150).

The aggregation shows what constitutes the net wealth of the community as a whole. But since internal claims and liabilities are all washed out in the aggregation process, the aggregation eliminates a good deal of information which is essential to the analysis of the working of the economy, of the effects of the change in the volume and structure of claims and liabilities on aggregate spending which is the basic determinant of the rate of production of real assets, among other things.

THE MONEY SUPPLY

The concept of money supply, money stock, or quantity of money will be used frequently in later chapters dealing with commercial banking operations, central banking operations, and the analysis of the relationships between money

bonds and foreign currencies and deposits held by Americans are part of the aggregate net wealth of the United States. They represent American claims against foreign resources. On the other hand, United States Government securities and United States currency and deposit balances held by foreigners have to be subtracted from American net wealth as they represent foreign claims on American resources.

and other economic variables. We know that money consists of currency and demand deposits. But the money supply does not encompass all currency and demand deposits. The money supply as defined by the Federal Reserve is the sum of (1) demand deposits at all commercial banks other than those due to domestic commercial banks and the U. S. Government, less cash items in process of collection; (2) foreign demand balances at Federal Reserve Banks; and (3) currency outside the Treasury, the Federal Reserve Banks, and vaults of all commercial banks.

The exclusion of currency holdings of the central bank, the Treasury, and the commercial banks is usually justified on the ground that they are money-issuing institutions and their holdings serve as reserves to meet the currency demand of financial institutions and the public at large. These funds are not available for spending by the public. Moreover, to include commercial banks' cash holdings in the supply of money would involve double counting, inasmuch as currency deposited by the public in checking accounts is already counted in the deposit component of the money supply. Interbank demand liabilities and cash items in process of collection are excluded because their inclusion would also involve double counting.[5]

The exclusion of government deposits, however, is debatable. They are part of the general funds immediately available for spending by the government the same as deposits of state and local governments which are included in the money stock. The argument that the spending of Treasury deposits is influenced by motives different from the public, in general, does not seem to be very satisfactory, as this can also be referred to deposits of state and local governments.

The existence of minimum compensating balances presents another difficulty. This refers to the practice by which commercial banks require borrowers to maintain certain minimum or average balances on which they are not free to draw. Since these balances are not available to borrowers for spending purposes, they should be excluded. Yet, they are counted as part of adjusted demand deposits.

A more far-reaching view on the composition of the supply of money includes not only currency and demand deposits held by the public but also savings deposits in commercial banks and savings banks. This broad definition of the money supply appears to stress the analysis of the effects of money and near-moneys on the expenditure flow. At the same time, however, it tends to blur the analysis of the various motives behind the holding of money balances as

[5] "Cash item in process of collection" arises because of the time lag involved in the process of clearing checks. The following example illustrates its meaning. Suppose that X draws a check on his account with bank A in New York in payment to Y who subsequently deposits the check in his bank B in San Francisco. Y's account increases by the amount of the check. But because of the delay in the process of collection, X's account with his bank is not simultaneously debited. Until the check is received by X's bank and his account debited, the amount of the check is a "cash item in process of collection." If it is not subtracted, the amount of demand deposits available to the public for making payments is overstated. The same thing is in fact counted twice.

distinguished from those behind the holding of other liquid financial assets and claims.

Like the definition of money, the definition of the money supply is also a matter of analytical convenience. Depending on the objectives of problems under investigation, we may include near-moneys in, or exclude them from, the "supply of money." In this book we shall use the Federal Reserve's definition of money supply. Any deviation from this definition will be explicitly noted.

CLASSIFICATION OF MONEY

Moneys in use in the past, as well as modern moneys, are of various kinds. They are different with respect to the relation between the value of their alternative uses or their legal status. Moneys of early times were primarily commodity moneys which were either consumable goods or stones and precious metals. They were just as valuable in their commodity usage as in their monetary usage. Modern moneys are mostly noncommodity moneys. They have no other value than their monetary value. Moneys are also different with regard to their legal character. Some kinds of money are "legal tender," legally enforceable in the discharge of money obligations. Certain kinds of money have no such legal status. We can thus classify moneys on the basis of the relation between the values of their alternative uses or their legal property.

Full-Bodied Money

Full-bodied money is the type of money whose monetary value is equal to the commercial value of its component material. Commodity moneys, such as tobacco as used in the past, were full-bodied. Their monetary value was equal to their commodity value as a result of the free substitution between their monetary and commodity uses. For example, owners of corn were free to use it as money or to sell it on the market as a food product. Should the money value of corn be lower than its market value, corn would then move from its monetary to commodity use. The subsequent increase in the supply of corn as a food product would reduce its market value until it would again be equal to its monetary value. Any deviation between its monetary value and market value would be corrected by market forces. Circulating gold and silver coins in countries which were on the gold and silver standard were also full-bodied. The United States gold dollar prior to 1933 was full-bodied, as its monetary value was equal to the market value of its metallic content of 23.22 grains of pure gold. So were the pound sterling and the French franc before 1914. The equality between the monetary value and the commodity value of these full-bodied coins was maintained as a result of the free coinage of gold coins and the freedom of holders of coins to melt them down for sale by weight should their commodity value be higher than their monetary value.

It is not uncommon for some kind of money to be full-bodied at one time, to cease to be full-bodied at another time, and then become full-bodied again as a result of the variation in its market value in relation to its monetary value brought about by changing demand and supply conditions and by coinage restrictions. The standard silver dollar of the United States offers an example. It was full-bodied late in the eighteenth century. In the late 1870's, however, because of the continuous decline in the value of silver arising from the decrease in the demand for silver and the increase in silver production, and the subsequent restriction of silver coinage, the silver dollar ceased to be full-bodied. It circulated with a monetary value much higher than its commodity value. After 1963 the silver dollar again became full-bodied as the tremendous increase in the demand for silver for industrial use and for coinage purposes caused silver to increase rapidly in value. At the price of $1.2929 per ounce pegged by the Treasury, the market value of the silver content of the silver dollar was equal to its monetary value.

The equality between the monetary value and the commodity value of a full-bodied money does not necessarily mean that its value in terms of goods and services—its general purchasing power—would remain the same. The latter would increase, decrease, or remain stable, depending upon the rate of change in the volume of money and the rate of change in the production of goods and services, among other things.

Representative Full-Bodied Money

The handling of full-bodied gold and silver coins was rather cumbersome, especially for payments involving large sums. For payment convenience, "warehouse receipts" were issued against the deposit of gold and silver coins or gold and silver bullion for payment purposes. At the discretion of bearers, these receipts or certificates were fully convertible into standard gold and silver coins or gold and silver bullion. They were therefore called representative full-bodied money. They themselves had no commodity value, but they were freely exchangeable for full-bodied moneys. Gold certificates, issued by the United States Treasury before 1933, were representative full-bodied money. A $10 gold certificate was freely convertible into one "gold eagle," or a weight of gold of 232.2 grains, which also had a market value of $10.

Token Moneys

These are moneys that have only monetary value, or those kinds of moneys whose value as money is substantially higher than the market value of their commodity contents. Modern moneys are mostly token moneys. In the United States, coins issued by the Treasury, such as half dollars, quarters, and dimes, are token coins. Federal Reserve notes and demand liabilities of commercial banks are purely token moneys. They have no commodity value whatsoever. The latter are simply banks' book entries. These moneys are sometimes referred to as "credit money," since they represent liabilities of the government and the commercial banks, respectively.

They are accepted at full value by the public mainly by faith, by confidence. To sustain that faith requires a relative stability in their value. The stability in the value of money in modern economic societies depends primarily on the responsibility of central monetary authorities in controlling the flow of money and credit in relation to the flow of goods and services.

Legal Tender Money

Moneys are different not only on the basis of the relationship between their monetary usage and commodity usage but also from the standpoint of the law. Certain kinds of money are granted "legal tender" power by the government. They are legal tender moneys, legally recognized for the purpose of discharging obligations calling for deferred money payments. When legal tender money is offered by a debtor in fulfilling his money obligations, the creditor has no legal right to refuse it.

When there is only one kind of money in use, its legal tender status is not necessary as deferred money obligations will be discharged with this only—the kind of money acceptable to both parties involved in a contract. However, when there are several kinds of money in circulation at the same time, the designation of certain kinds of money as legal tender is a necessity. It protects the interest of the creditor in that, aside from legal tender, he does not have to accept in payment the type of money not acceptable to him. It also protects the interest of the debtor in that he may not be required to pay moneys which are less convenient or desirable to him. The designation of a legally enforceable means of payment would also prevent unnecessary and costly litigations between creditors and debtors with regard to a particular type of money used for repayment.

The legal tender status given by the government to a certain kind or kinds of money may be limited or unlimited. in the United States, prior to 1933, gold coins were full legal tender. Standard silver dollars were full legal tender "except where otherwise stated in the contract." Gold certificates were full legal tender after December 1919. Silver certificates were not legal tender until May 1933.[6] United States notes or "greenbacks" were legal tender except for the payment of interest on the public debt, for the payment of import duties and for contracts between private parties which specified payments in coin or bullion. National Bank notes, Treasury notes of 1890, Federal Reserve Bank notes, and Federal Reserve notes which were receivable "for all taxes, customs, and other public dues" were not legal tender in transactions between private parties. Silver and nonsilver subsidiary coins were made legal tender up to a limited amount in one payment.[7]

[6]Arthur Kemp, *The Legal Qualities of Money* (New York: Pageant Press, 1956), p. 108.

[7]The act of February 21, 1853 limited the legal tender quality of silver and nonsilver subsidiary coins to five dollars in one payment. The act of February 12, 1873, later limited the legal tender status of nonsilver minor coins to twenty-five cents in one payment. And the act of March 14, 1900, extended the legal tender quality of subsidiary silver coins to ten dollars in one payment.

After June 5, 1933, all circulating currencies were made full legal tender. A provision of Public Resolution No. 10 of that date states:

> All coins and currencies of the United States (including Federal Reserve notes and circulating notes of the Federal Reserve Banks and National Banking Association) heretofore or hereafter coined or issued, shall be legal tender for all debts, public and private, public charges, taxes, duties and dues, except that gold coins, when below the standard weight and limit of tolerance provided by the law for the single piece, shall be legal tender only at valuation in proportion to their actual weight.

In common law when legal tender money is offered by a debtor in proper amount in payment of his debt and is refused by the creditor, the payment of interest on his obligation is discontinued. This refusal on the part of the creditor, however, does not mean that he forfeits his credit, and the debtor's obligation is discharged. If a lawsuit is brought against him by his creditor, he can offer to pay off his debt in court in legal tender.[8]

The legal tender quality of some kind(s) of money may enhance its general acceptability. But this is by no means an essential condition for acceptability. In highly industrialized societies, the volume of central bank notes in circulation represent no more than 10 percent of the total money stock. Yet they are legal tender. Demand deposits which represent the remaining proportion of the stock of money are not "legal money." In the United States, in the late 1870's, silver certificates, which were not legal tender, were much preferred to standard silver dollars which were—regardless of efforts made by the government to promote the circulation of silver dollars. Continental currency, which was made legal tender by the Continental Congress in 1777, was rejected outright by the public in 1781. As we have mentioned, during the crisis of Germany during the early 1920's, the mark was rejected by the public, which then used foreign currencies and other devices as means of payment.

EVOLUTION OF MONEY

The question as to how money came to be used has received no clear-cut explanation either from economic historians or anthropologists. The popular explanation is that the necessity of overcoming the inefficiency and difficulty of barter exchange had led to the invention of money. This appears to be a rational-

[8]In the past, refusal to accept legal tender at face value or in payment of debt gave rise to heavy fines and sometimes severe punishment. Thus Henry VIII imposed fines and imprisonment on those who refused to accept his coins at face value. In the United States, during the period of the War of Independence, a person who refused to accept Continental currency was subject to various penalties varying from being publicly declared an enemy of his country, forfeiting his credit to imprisonment, and sometimes the loss of his ears! In ancient China, Chinese emperors were known to have imposed the death penalty on those refusing imperial coins. Roman emperors were also known to have levied heavy fines and punishments on those who refused legal tender moneys.

ization made in the light of experiences under monetary exchange. Some economists explain the emergence of money on the basis of the customary use of various commodities by people in primitive societies for noncommercial purposes, such as official tribal ceremonies and religious sacrifices. The frequent use of these commodities for noncommercial purposes gradually led to their acceptance as means of commercial payment. At any rate, regardless of *how* money came into being, it *did* and, since its introduction, money has gone through a long process of evolution before reaching the present stage of development.

In early times, a great variety of commodities and cattle had acquired the quality of being accepted as moneys. A list of ancient moneys is a long one. It suffices to mention but a few: wool, corn, rice, woven mat, leather, cocoa, the great stone wheels of yap, goat, and water buffalo. Gold and silver were used as money in more recent history. In comparison with nonmetallic commodity moneys and "cattle moneys," the use of gold and silver offer definite advantages. They are homogeneous and are completely divisible into smaller units, thus making possible the designation of a standard unit of a given weight, and its multiples and fractions become very suitable for various sizes of transactions. Because of their high value, owing to their relative scarcity, units of small weight of gold or silver could be exchanged for much larger quantities of goods. Gold and silver moneys are more convenient to handle. They are less bulky. They are easy to store, to transport, and are highly durable. Since the production of gold and silver can change only very slowly, the value of gold and silver moneys is relatively stable. Moreover, their bright and shiny look would make them more attractive than nonmetallic commodity moneys. Owing to these advantages, gold and silver ultimately emerged as the most popular form of money.

Gold and silver, which were initially used for monetary purposes, were in the form of bars and ingots of different weights and standards. As they came to be used increasingly as money, they were made into coins by private businesses to differentiate their monetary usage from their commodity usage. These privately issued gold and silver coins were also of different weights and standards. They were all circulated at the same time and their monetary value was determined primarily by the commercial value of their fine metallic content. Under such conditions it would be rather difficult for users of coins to verify their weights and standards, which could be falsified by private issuers. To avoid this, among other things, the coinage of metallic money was soon taken over by public authorities as an exclusive right. Each government then designated a given weight of gold or silver as the standard unit. Multiples or fractions of this unit could be issued with their weights equal to a multiple or a fraction of the weight of the standard money. At the legally fixed weight of gold or silver, the coinage of gold coins and silver coins was free to holders of gold or silver bullion.

Sometimes government authorities did exactly what they prohibited private merchants from doing by monopolizing the right of coinage: "falsifying" coins. The metallic content of coins—especially silver and other relatively plentiful metals such as copper—was deliberately reduced, and the resulting profits went to the government as additional revenue. This could be achieved only by restricting coinage. Otherwise those profits would go to private holders of silver and copper. The circulation of these debased coins could be voluntarily accepted by the public because of customary usage or scarcity of coins or, to some extent, forced upon the public with heavy fines and penalties to those who refused to accept. The practice of debasement was rather popular with Roman emperors, European monarchs, and ancient Chinese emperors in the past as a means of obtaining additional revenues to finance wars.

Gold and silver coins privately issued, as we have mentioned above, were different in weights and standards. Merchants had to bring their coins to goldsmith's shops to have their weights and standards ascertained. For safekeeping, merchants as well as wealthy people also deposited their surplus funds and gold and silver bullion in the shops of goldsmiths who issued in return "certificates" promising to pay in coin or bullion on demand. These certificates gradually came to be accepted as means of payment as a result of improvements in their issuance and payment techniques. Payments by these certificates were more convenient since they precluded the transfer of large quantities of gold or silver coins. As these certificates were not frequently presented for payment in specie, goldsmiths began making loans to merchants by issuing "notes" to them, backed by coins and bullion of depositors which remained idle in their vaults. As this business expanded, many goldsmiths gave up their traditional business to become bankers, specializing in receiving in deposits gold and silver in coins and bullion and making loans to merchants. They issued to borrowers as well as to depositors of coins and bullion bank notes which were redeemable in gold or silver. In issuing notes against some promises to pay money in the future by borrowers, banks created money out of thin air. This possibility of creating money, initially uncontrolled, sometimes led to overissuance of notes which resulted in frequent failures of banks as they were not able to redeem their notes in specie. Remedial actions led initially to governmental controls over the volume of bank notes which could be issued by private banks and ultimately to governmental monopoly in note-issue. When central banking institutions were developed, they were granted the exclusive right to issue notes. Central bank notes which were redeemable in specie at various times in the past have become purely paper claims in modern times. They are fiduciary moneys. Thus notes issued by the Federal Reserve system, the Bank of England, or the Bank of France, are all fiduciary currencies.

Commercial banks do not issue notes. Instead, they issue demand deposits which are promises to pay currency on demand when they receive currency or checks "in deposit," make loans, or purchase financial claims. Banks' demand deposits transferrable by checks were initially of limited acceptability. They were used primarily for transactions between firms and financial organizations, and not by the general public (which is still the case in most underdeveloped areas). With the passage of legislation in various industrial nations limiting the note issue of banks which prompted a rapid development of the cheque system, deposit money has developed into the predominant form of money of modern times, as attested by the fact that from 70 to 80 percent of the money stock in most advanced nations is made up of demand deposits.

Through its long process of evolution, money has thus assumed numerous forms. It has changed from concrete commodities, having both monetary and commodity values, to representative claims convertible into commodity moneys, to pure paper claims and abstract numbers in the books of commercial banks. In brief, it has changed from commodities to numbers. But this is not the end of the evolution of money. It is likely to continue its evolution. In the next generation or so, as the use of bank credit cards becomes widespread, payments by bank credit cards would eliminate to a large extent the use of checks as well as currency. Supermarkets, department stores, drug stores, and others which receive credit card payments from customers will collect them from banks issuing credit cards. Eventually, it is believed that the monetary system will be completely computerized in view of the rapid advance in the use of electronic computers. Individuals, governments at all levels, banks, business enterprises, nonprofit organizations, and so on, will all be issued specific account numbers which will be handled by a national computer center. Income receipts and payments will be added to or subtracted from these accounts by pushing a button. This sounds incredible, perhaps, but with the tremendous development of modern sciences and technology, what is incredible in one generation becomes commonplace in the next.

SUMMARY

Money is commonly defined as anything which is generally accepted by members of a given economic society as a means of payment for goods and services and for the discharge of other money obligations. Near-moneys are those financial assets which can be substituted for money as they are readily available for spending purposes. The money stock is defined by the Federal Reserve as the sum of currency and demand deposits held by the public and foreign demand balances at Federal Reserve Banks.

Money is the most liquid asset since it is accepted at full value at any time for any good or service. It is used as a yardstick to express the liquidity of other assets which represents their ability to be converted into money. The degree of liquidity of an asset is measured in terms of the speed with which it can be converted into money and the amount of loss involved in the conversion process. Modern money is a financial claim. It is a part of the wealth of individual economic units, but it is not an integral part of the aggregate net wealth of the community.

Moneys in use in the past and modern moneys are of various types. Full-bodied moneys are moneys whose monetary value is equal to the market value of their component materials. Representative full-bodied moneys are paper claims fully convertible into full-bodied moneys. Modern moneys are mostly token moneys. They have only monetary value and little or no commodity value. Moneys are also different from the standpoint of the law. Some kinds of money are legal tender. They are legally enforceable means of payments. Some other kinds of money do not have such a legal status, and creditors may legally refuse them when offered in payment of debts by debtors.

Money has gone through a long process of evolution. It has changed from commodities of various types to pure paper claims and deposit money which represents nothing more than abstract numbers on the books of commercial banks.

PROBLEMS

1. The definition of money and the money stock is largely a matter of analytical convenience. Do you agree? Why or why not? Explain.
2. What is the liquidity of an asset? Why do you define the liquidity of assets in terms of money?
3. Money is part of the wealth of the individual spending unit, but not of the aggregate net wealth of the community. Does this apply to all kinds of money or certain kinds of money only? Explain.
4. The granting of the legal tender power by the government to some kind (or kinds) of money is neither a necessary nor a sufficient condition of its general acceptability. Do you agree? Why or why not? Use examples to support your arguments.
5. What is full-bodied money? Representative full-bodied money? What accounts for the equality between the monetary value and commodity value of full-bodied money? What is the difference between full-bodied money and token money? Was the U.S. standard silver dollar a full-bodied coin in the 1960's?
6. Sketch the major stages in the evolution process of money.

chapter **3**

Monetary Standards

The monetary standard of a country represents the set of rules which govern the nature and conditions of the issuance of its standard money and the relations between the standard money and various forms of money in circulation. Standard money is the basic unit of the system, the type of money in which money-issuing institutions and agencies would have to discharge their obligations. If the standard money in use in a country is a commodity such as gold or silver, then it is on a commodity standard. If the standard money is paper money, then it is on a paper standard. The popular standards which have been used have been commodity standards of various types and paper standards.

COMMODITY STANDARDS

We shall describe the nature and operating mechanisms of such popular commodity standards as the gold standard, the silver standard, and bimetallism.

The Gold Standard

A country is on the gold standard when circulating currency of any form is freely convertible into the standard money which is defined in terms of a fixed weight of gold with a fixed degree of fineness; when the government is prepared to accept gold bullion for coinage (or for other forms of money at the discretion of holders of gold) at the legally fixed rate in unlimited amounts; and when holders of gold coins are free to melt down their coins for sale by weight as a commodity. The free exchangeability between currency and gold assures the equality between the monetary value of the standard unit and the market value of its fixed weight of gold, and any deviation between them is corrected by the operation of market forces. This is illustrated by Fig. 3-1(a) and (b). In the initial equilibrium position, we have the equality between the monetary value of gold (say, per ounce) represented by OV_0 in (a) and its commodity value, OC_0 in (b). Of the existing total stock of gold, OA is used for coinage, and OB as a commodity. Suppose that there is an increase in the commodity demand for gold (say, for industrial usage) reflected by the upward shift in the demand curve from DD to D_1D_1 (b). As a consequence, the market value of gold increases to OC_1 which is of course higher than its monetary value fixed by law at OV_0. As

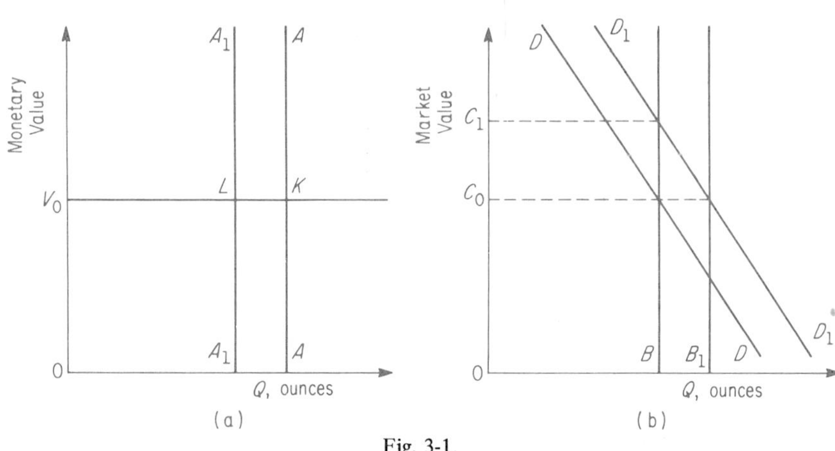

Fig. 3-1.

the market value of the gold content of gold coins is now higher than their monetary value, holders of gold coins would melt them down for sale by weight. This contributes to increasing the commodity supply of gold which would eventually bring the market value of gold into line with its monetary value again. At equilibrium, the increase in the commodity supply of gold is indicated by the change from OB to OB_1. Assuming that there is no change in the total stock of gold, the increase in the commodity supply of gold is met by an equivalent contraction of gold coinage from OA to OA_1.[1] The value of gold coins being melted down is represented by the rectangle $AKLA_1$. The analysis is reversed when there is an increase in the commodity supply of gold resulting from, say, an increase in gold production. Gold will then move into coinage until its market value rises to equality with its monetary value.

The gold standard comes in various versions, depending upon the form of the interconvertibility between currency and gold. When circulating currency in a country is fully convertible into standard gold coins, it is on a *gold-coin standard.* The United Kingdom, before 1914, and the United States, before 1933, among other countries, were on a gold-coin standard. The pound sterling was then defined in terms of 113 grains of fine gold, and the British mint accepted gold for gold coins or notes at the fixed price of 3.17s 10 1/2d per fine

[1]It should be noted that a substantial decrease in the supply of money resulting from the melting down of coins and the conversion of other currency into gold would tend to cause expenditures, incomes, and prices to decrease. The decrease in the production cost of gold (and costs in general) as a consequence of declining prices, and the increase in the buying power of money, could stimulate the production of gold. The increase in the supply of gold from both the melting down of coins and increase in gold production would bring the commodity value of gold back into line with its monetary value. Also note that in drawing Figs. 3-1(a) and (b), we assume away minting and melting costs.

ounce. The United States dollar was defined in terms of 23.22 grains of pure gold, that is, the price of gold was fixed at $20.67 per ounce by the government.[2] The coinage of gold was unlimited and there was full convertibility between circulating currency and gold.

When circulating currency of a country is convertible only into gold bullion with a minimum amount of currency determined by law, it is said to be on a *gold-bullion standard.* Under such standard, no gold coins are coined and put into circulation. The gold-bullion standard enables a country to be "on gold," to tie its money stock to the gold stock, among other things, even though it does not have adequate gold for a gold-coin system. France in 1928 and Great Britain in 1925 were among countries on a gold-bullion standard.

Another version of the gold standard is the so-called *gold-exchange standard.* This form of the gold standard enables a country to be on gold, with little gold of its own, by simply tying its currency to a foreign currency fully convertible into gold. The Philippines and India at one time in the past were on such a standard. The Philippine peso was defined in terms of, and fully convertible into, the United States dollar. Her reserves consisted primarily of United States dollar balances and short-term United States Treasury obligations. The Indian rupee was tied to and fully exchangeable for pound sterling. India's reserves were made up primarily of sterling balances in London. One of the arguments in favor of the gold exchange standard was that it made it possible for a country with little gold of its own to benefit from the (alleged) advantages of being on gold. But in making its currency a satellite of a foreign currency, the gold-exchange standard country would be directly affected by monetary policy decisions of foreign monetary authorities. In the event of a devaluation of the foreign currency, the country which is on a gold-exchange standard could be subject to substantial gold losses as a result of the decrease in the gold value of its foreign exchange reserves.

The gold standard, under various forms, was widespread all over the world from the turn of the second half of the nineteenth century until the beginning of World War I and during the late 1920's. It totally collapsed in the early 1930's with the Great Depression which witnessed a world-wide departure from gold. In no country in the modern world does gold circulate as money. Modern media of exchange represent primarily deposit money, central bank notes, and token coins. Gold, however, is still the foundation of the international monetary system. It is still the most important international means of payment; it is accepted without qualification in international transactions. The United States dollar, being a national as well as an international currency, has served as a vehicle for international payments, but the accumulation of dollar balances by foreign countries resulting from the United States' continuous payments deficits ulti-

[2]There are 480 grains in a troy ounce, hence 480/23.22 = $20.67.

mately will have to be honored in gold (assuming that the United States Treasury continues its policy of convertibility of official foreign balances into gold). Since the volume of international means of payment is still closely tied to the gold stock of the world, the volume of international trade remains pretty much governed by gold. (More details on this point will be discussed in Chapter 30 on international financial problems.)

The Silver Standard

Silver is another metal which has been widely used as standard money. The operating mechanic of the silver standard is similar to that of the gold standard. The difference is that the standard money is defined in terms of a given weight of silver at a fixed fineness. Again, there is unlimited coinage of silver coins and interconvertibility between currency and silver. The silver standard had been very popular in countries in the East and Far East, as well as in European countries, up to the first half of the nineteenth century, particularly in Mexico and China. However, beginning with the second half of the nineteenth century, silver gradually fell into disrepute as its value began to decline with respect to gold. As their currencies continued to depreciate in terms of gold currencies, countries "on silver" abandoned the white metal in favor of gold or inconvertible paper money. This, coupled with increases in silver production resulting from the discovery of new silver deposits, tended to speed up the downward movement in the value of silver. Mexico and China, traditionally on silver, finally were forced to abandon the silver standard. With the departure from silver by these two countries, the doom of the silver standard was sealed. Nowadays, where silver is used for monetary purposes it is mostly in the form of subsidiary token coins.

Bimetallism

A monetary system based on two metals as standard moneys which are freely exchangeable for one another at a legally fixed ratio, and which allows the free coinage of the two metals, constitutes a bimetallic standard, or "bimetallism." Circulating currency under such a system is fully convertible into either standard money at the discretion of holders. In principle any two metals such as copper and zinc, can serve as a foundation for bimetallism. The two metals popularly used, however, were gold and silver. The mere fact that a country uses silver and gold for monetary purposes does not mean that it is on a bimetallic standard. From ancient times until the end of the eighteenth century, silver and gold had been used as media of exchange. But this was not bimetallism, as these gold and silver currencies were not minted and put into circulation at a legally fixed ratio. Their relative value was determined primarily by the commercial value of their metallic contents. The necessary condition for a country to be on a bimetallic standard is that gold and silver have to be freely exchangeable at a fixed ratio referred to as the mint ratio—the ratio of the fixed weights of gold and silver at which they are freely accepted for coinage.

The mint ratio may be at variance with the market ratio (the ratio of the market values of the two metals). Suppose that the mint ratio is 15 ounces of silver to one ounce of gold and the market ratio is 16 to 1. In this case, silver is overvalued with respect to gold at the mint (or what amounts to the same thing, gold is undervalued). As silver is overvalued, a profit can be made by bringing 15 ounces (or any multiple of this amount) to the mint in exchange for an amount of gold coins made from one ounce of gold. The gold coins will be melted down for sale by weight on the market for 16 ounces of silver which will be brought back to the mint for a greater amount of gold coins, and so on. Should the discrepancy between the mint ratio and the market ratio persist, gold coins would completely disappear from circulation, and only silver coins would remain.

The theoretical argument behind bimetallism is that if the discrepancy between the mint and market ratios is small, then the operation of free market forces would react to bring the market ratio into line with the mint ratio following the movement of silver and gold into and out of the mint. For example, when gold is undervalued with respect to silver, it would cease its monetary use and convert to commodity use, as its monetary value is lower than its market value. On the other hand, silver would move from commodity to monetary use as its market value is below its monetary value. As a consequence, the commodity supply of gold increases, thereby reducing its market value with respect to silver. At the same time, the commodity supply of silver decreases, thus raising its market value in relation to gold. The free substitution between the monetary usage and commodity usage of both gold and silver would eventually bring the market ratio into equilibrium with the mint ratio.

This adjustment process operates only if the domestic mint ratio is close to the market ratio on the one hand, and the mint ratios prevailing in foreign countries, on the other. The holding of gold must be adequate to sustain the movement of gold from the mint so that the increase in the supply of the gold commodity is large enough to depress its value in terms of silver. Moreover, the movement of silver to the mint must not be hindered by high transportation costs and minting delays; otherwise, there would be no substantial decrease in the commodity supply of silver to raise its market value. These conditions did not appear to have been satisfied in some of the countries which have been on bimetallism in the past. Either gold or silver was overvalued at one time or another. Another major difficulty was the inequality of the mint ratios in different countries adopting the bimetallic standard. The discrepancy between the mint and market ratios could then persist in some countries. The country with large gold and silver reserves could remain on bimetallism whereas in the country with small reserves, only silver or gold (depending upon which one is overvalued) would remain in circulation.[3]

The disappearance from circulation of the undervalued metal is one aspect of the operation of the so-called Gresham's law which, in its traditional form, states that "bad money drives out good." If silver is overvalued with respect to gold, it is supposed to be "bad money," and gold is "good." The terms "good" and "bad" are misleading. There is nothing "bad" about silver coins in domestic circulation; they are money. Gold, being undervalued, is hardly "money," as it is withdrawn from circulation into commodity usage. Gresham's law embodies the idea that monetary objects which have alternative uses would tend to be used where they command the highest value. Thus when gold is undervalued by the mint, it disappears from circulation simply because its commodity value is higher than its value as money. Silver coins remain in circulation because their monetary value is either above or equal to the commercial value of their metallic contents.

Bimetallism was advocated on the basis of the argument that the use of two metals together would give a broader base to the currency and credit system. But, attempts to broaden the currency basis by putting into circulation both gold and silver at legally fixed ratios had met with failure in the United States and some other countries following the operation of Gresham's law as a consequence of deviations between the market values and mint values of the two metals.

INCONVERTIBLE PAPER STANDARDS

A country is on a nonconvertible paper standard when the standard money is paper money, and circulating currency is not exchangeable for any commodity money but only other forms of paper currency. In the past, paper money was issued in large quantities in various countries, mostly to meet the financial requirements of war. The issuance of such paper money was considered to be temporary. Once the emergency was over, efforts were made by governments to restore the convertibility between circulating currency and standard commodity

[3]This can be illustrated by the following example. Suppose the mint ratio in country A is 14 ounces of silver to 1 ounce of gold and the ratio in country B is 14.5 ounces to 1, and the market ratio is 15 to 1. There is free movement of gold and silver between A and B, and, for the sake of simplicity, transportation and minting as well as melting costs are assumed away. Gold is undervalued in both A and B by the mint. In both A and B gold would move out of the mint, and silver would move into the mint. This movement of gold out of the mint and silver into coinage would raise the market value of silver and lower the commodity value of gold. When the market ratio is brought into line with the mint ratio in B, gold is still undervalued in A. If A has a small holding of gold, it might not be able to sustain the gold drain even before the market ratio came close to the mint ratio in B. A would be forced to go on a *de facto* silver standard. If A has a larger holding of gold, the movement of gold would drive the market ratio closer to its mint ratio. Then B would be on a *de facto* gold standard.

money. Since the Great Depression of the early 1930's, however, paper money has been the monetary institution in most countries of the world.

Internally, modern paper moneys have one thing in common: they are not convertible into full-bodied moneys. Externally, however, they are different in different countries. Paper moneys of some nations, though domestically inconvertible, are still defined in terms of gold and are externally convertible into gold bullion. The United States dollar, for example, is defined in terms of gold; and dollar balances held by foreign central banks and governments are freely convertible into gold at the Treasury at the fixed price of approximately $35 per ounce. It follows that the United States, though domestically on paper, is internationally on gold.

Moneys of some countries, though defined in terms of gold, are neither domestically nor internationally exchangeable for gold or foreign currencies. For instance, the ruble of the Soviet Union is defined in terms of gold, but it is not convertible into gold within Russia, nor has it been used in international trade which has been carried on in terms of gold or foreign exchange. Russia is basically on a managed paper standard, pure and simple. Similarly, the Dong-Viet of the Democratic Republic of Viet Nam is also defined in terms of gold. But it is a managed paper money internally as well as externally. The gold definition of these moneys does not seem to serve any practical purpose except for propaganda value.

GOLD VERSUS PAPER

The question of "gold versus paper" has been one of the most controversial monetary issues. The controversy arises basically from the divergence of viewpoints on monetary policies and the extent of discretionary central bank control. It centers largely on the alleged advantages and disadvantages of "gold" and "paper" relative to the accomplishment of certain objectives of economic policy.

The adherence to the gold standard has advantages, but it also involves serious shortcomings. According to the proponents of the gold standard, one of the arguments in favor of the gold standard is that it tends to promote not only foreign exchange rate stability but also domestic stability as well.[4] Under the international gold standard, the exchange rates between national currencies are indeed stable, as their variations are strictly limited by gold movements. For example, prior to 1914, the pound sterling represented 113 grains of pure gold, and the United States dollar, 23.22 grains; the mint parity, that is, the ratio of the fixed weights of gold at which the British and American mints accepted gold for coinage, was therefore 4.866 U.S. dollars to the pound sterling (113/23.22 = 4.866). The rate of exchange between the pound and the dollar on the London and New York exchange markets could not deviate from the mint

[4]The rate of foreign exchange is the price of a unit of foreign money in terms of domestic money.

parity by more than the transportation cost of gold between London and New York, so long as gold could be shipped between the two centers for payment purposes. The main advantage of the stability of exchange rates between national currencies is that it enabled more reliable short- and long-run planning and forecasting of production costs, prices, and profits by enterprises specializing in foreign investments. International transactions could be carried out with confidence since there is little or no risk of exchange losses.

Under the gold standard, the stock of gold coins into which other circulating currency is fully convertible is governed by the gold stock. It can increase only when there is an increase in the gold stock or a decrease in the commodity demand for gold. To maintain the interconvertibility between currency and gold requires the holding of gold reserves which represent a certain proportion of the total money stock. Any downward deviation from that proportion would mean a risk of redemption failure. Under gold, the operation of the monetary mechanism is therefore more or less "automatic," because the money supply can expand or contract only with the expansion or contraction of the stock of gold. There is little room for the exercise of discretionary control by monetary authorities. There is little room for overissue of bank notes or overexpansion of credit. The gold standard is thus considered as a barrier against inflationary developments.

Another advantage of the international gold standard is that it provides an automatic mechanism for the adjustment of imbalances in a country's international receipts and payments via gold movements and income and price variations. When a country is buying more than it is selling abroad, the settlement of the "import" surplus would result in an outflow of gold. The consequent contraction of the supply of money and credit would cause expenditures, income, and prices to decline. The decrease in income would reduce expenditures on both domestic products and imports. The decrease in domestic prices relative to foreign prices, on the other hand, would stimulate exports. The latter would also be stimulated by the increase in domestic and import expenditures in foreign countries, with increases in income generated by payment surpluses. The increase in exports and the decrease in imports would eventually restore equilibrium in the country's international payments position.[5]

Critics of gold hold that the maintenance of interconvertibility between gold and circulating currency, which is the primary objective of the gold standard, sometimes can be achieved only at the price of unemployment and deflation, since policy measures taken to promote full employment and economic growth may at times be in direct conflict with those called for to maintain the gold convertibility of currency. For example, currency convertibility would require a contraction of the flow of money and credit consequent upon a loss of gold resulting from trade deficits, but this would give rise to more serious deflation and unemployment should this take place at a time when the economy is already operating with declining income and employment. Under the gold stan-

[5] More details on this are given in Chapter 28 on the balance-of-payments equilibrium and exchange-rate systems.

dard, the tying of the money stock to the stock of gold would subject the economy to the vagaries of gold which could cause undesirable inflationary pressures or deflation. When the supply of gold and the supply of money failed to increase to levels required to sustain higher levels of income and employment, the economy would be subject to deflationary pressures. Similarly, an increase in the commodity demand for gold for hoarding or for industrial use could cause serious deflationary implications, since this would cause a decline in the monetary gold stock and the supply of money and credit. Conversely, at times when the economy is already operating at capacity with full employment of labor and resources, an increase in the money stock brought about by an increase in gold production as a result of new techniques of gold mining and processing, or an inflow of gold resulting from trade surpluses, then the economy would inevitably be subject to inflationary pressures. Economies of nations in the past were indeed subject to such vicissitudes of gold changes.

Advocates of paper money argue that the advantages of the gold standard could be achieved under a well-managed system of paper money without suffering from its disadvantages. True, foreign exchange rates between currencies of nations "on paper" are subject to fluctuations. A substantial degree of exchange stability, however, could be achieved through international financial cooperation and through exchange stabilization operations. Under a managed system of paper money, discretionary monetary measures could be taken by central banking authorities to keep the rate of change in the stock of money approximately at levels required to sustain price stability consistent with full employment and maximum economic growth. Suppose that a rate of change in the money stock of a certain percentage per year is necessary to sustain a certain rate of growth of output which is considered consistent with price stability and full employment. To achieve such rate of change in the supply of money requires decisions by monetary authorities. It does not just happen.

It is argued that under the paper standard, since the supply of money is not subject to any physical limitation, there is a greater possibility of overissuance of bank notes and overexpansion of bank credit; there is greater room for political manipulation of the currency. An unscrupulous government thus could overspend by overborrowing, which would lead to inflationary pressures. But whether currency manipulation is good or bad depends upon the purposes for which such manipulation is intended. If the currency is manipulated for economically unsound expenditures, then it is undesirable. But if the flow of money and credit is manipulated in such a manner as to promote economic recovery, to expand demand, to bring about increases in production, profits, higher levels of employment, and fuller utilization of resources, then there is nothing bad about it. It is true that most periods of serious inflation in the past were associated with paper money. But it should be noted that during those periods the gold standard broke down and the job had to be done by paper money. The gold standard could keep its steady course only in "calm water" and quiet times.

When the sea was rough, gold "abandoned ship" and paper money took over. The ship was wrecked, and paper money was to blame.

The international gold standard indeed provided an automatic mechanism for balance of payments adjustment. But this adjustment process can operate without causing deflationary pressures only when there is an automatic adjustment in the structure of domestic wages and prices. Otherwise, deflation and unemployment would follow a substantial outflow of gold resulting from payment deficits. As a consequence of the downward inflexibility in prices and wages, monetary authorities in countries with payment deficits did take deliberate actions to offset the deflationary implications of gold losses even during the golden days of the international gold standard. Similarly, gold inflows were deliberately "sterilized" by countries with trade surpluses to avoid inflationary developments.[6]

The main virtue of the gold standard appears to be exchange rate stability. But the price of this stability may well be recession, unemployment, and slow rate of growth. When the main objectives of economic policy are full employment, stability, and a high rate of economic growth, the operation of the monetary system cannot be left to the vagaries of gold. The achievement of these goals requires a system of paper money which is intelligently and responsibly managed. Recent experiences have indicated the versatility and flexibility of paper money. It has been operating successfully in various countries of the West which have enjoyed unprecedented economic prosperity after World War II.

The day of the gold standard, in its classical form, is considered by many as over. As economic conditions change, monetary institutions also have to change. If the gold standard befitted conditions of the past, managed paper money is the monetary institution under modern economic conditions and development. It is unrealistic to believe that the classical gold standard would work under modern conditions, as it did in the second half of the nineteenth century and the early decades of the twentieth century. There are, nevertheless, champions of gold advocating a return to the old gold standard. Since a great deal has been learned in the art of fiscal and monetary controls in the promotion of economic stability as well as development and growth, it would appear undesirable to return to a monetary system in which the flow of money and credit is closely tied to a commodity stock, the changes of which are not reflective of the changing monetary and credit requirements of the economy.

MONETARY STRUCTURE AND STANDARDS OF THE UNITED STATES

Historical Background

Prior to the passage of the Coinage Act of 1792, the monetary situation in the United States was rather confusing. There was in circulation a great variety of foreign coins, such as English shillings, French louisdors, Spanish dollars,

[6] See Sir Charles Morgan-Webb, *The Rise and Fall of the Gold Standard* (New York: Macmillan, 1934).

Mexican dollars, Dutch ducats, all of which were legal tender. Because of the scarcity of these foreign coins in relation to the monetary requirements of trade expansion in the various colonies, such commodities as wampum, beaver skin, moose skin, tobacco, corn, and rice were used as media of exchange. Most of these commodities were legal tender. For example, tobacco was legal tender in Virginia; corn in the Massachusetts Bay Colony; and tobacco in Maryland. The scarcity of foreign coins was later supplemented by domestic coins consisting of pine-tree shillings which were first coined by the mint of the Colony of Massachusetts in 1651, and paper money was issued by various colonial governments, private banks, and associations of merchants.

The confusion became chaos at the outbreak of the War of Independence. The Continental Congress had to issue paper money, the Continental currency, to sustain the war effort. The substantial increase in the volume of Continental currency from $2 million in mid-1775 to more than $240 million at the conclusion of the war caused it to depreciate very rapidly. By 1780, it became practically worthless. By 1781, it ceased to function as money and was bought by speculators as a speculative commodity at rates up to 1,000 to one.[7] The end of the Continental currency came with the Refunding Act of 1790, allowing its redemption at 100 to 1. The nightmarish experience of the Continental currency and the rapid depreciation of paper money issued in large quantities by various states after the war, prompted the prohibition by Congress of the issuance of money by state governments. Coinage became an exclusive right of the federal government. To reorganize the monetary situation and establish a systematic currency for the whole country, the Coinage Act of 1792 was passed, the first coinage under the Constitution of the United States. From 1792 up to the passage of the Gold Standard Act of 1900, the monetary story of the United States was pretty much a story of the operation of Gresham's law.

Legal Bimetallism, De Facto Silver: 1792-1834. The Coinage Act of April 2, 1792, provided for the establishment of the Mint and the issuance of gold and silver coins. The act defined the dollar in terms 24.75 grains of pure gold, or 371.15 grains of pure silver. The mint ratio between the two metals was thus 15 to 1 (371.25/24.75). At this legally fixed ratio, the Treasury accepted gold and silver for coinage without limits and circulating currency was freely exchangeable for standard gold or silver coins.

The monetary system intended by the act was therefore bimetallism. It failed, however, in practice following upon the operation of Gresham's law. The mint ratio of 15 to one was not as close to the market ratio as the mint ratio of 15.5 to one prevailing in France and other countries. Gold, undervalued, was not brought to the Mint. In terms of the act, its monetary value was below its value as a commodity. As a consequence, only silver flowed to the Mint for coinage when it started operations in late 1794, and only silver coins were issued. The United States was then on a de facto silver standard.

But, silver coins did not stay long in circulation in the country. Since

[7]The speculation was based primarily on the expectation of the eventual redemption of the Continental currency in specie, since in principle Continental currency promised payment in gold, silver, or specified foreign coins.

American silver dollars were then accepted at par in the West Indies with Spanish and Mexican dollars which had a slightly higher content in pure silver, they were exported to the West Indies by American traders for Spanish and Mexican dollars which were melted down and brought back to the United States for sale by weight or for coinage into American dollars to be reexported. The only dollars which remained in circulation in the United States were worn-out Spanish and Mexican dollars. The flow of American silver dollars abroad prompted the suspension of the coinage of silver dollars by President Jefferson in 1806. The coinage of half dollars, however, continued. Most of them remained in domestic circulation as their export involved higher cost.

Legal Bimetallism, De Facto Gold, 1834-62. To keep the country on legal bimetallism, to keep both gold and silver coins in circulation, the obvious remedy was to raise the value of gold with respect to silver so that the mint ratio was in line with the market ratio. Consequently, in 1834, the mint ratio was changed to 16 to one. In other words, the dollar, in terms of gold, represented 23.22 instead of 24.75 grains of pure gold. (The silver definition of the dollar remained unchanged.) Unfortunately, the new mint ratio overvalued gold, since it was slightly higher than those in French and Latin countries (the French mint ratio remained at 15.5 to one) which expressed more or less the market ratio at that time. Gold now flowed to the Mint for coinage, while silver dollars disappeared from circulation, melted down and exported–since the new mint ratio understated their monetary value with respect to the market value of their metallic content. Instead of legal bimetallism, the United States was on a de facto gold standard.

In the late 1840's the coinage situation became worse, following the discovery of new gold, which tended to depress further its value in relation to silver. This made it profitable for American traders to export silver half dollars and other subsidiary silver coins which had remained in circulation after the revaluation of 1834, with the exception of old foreign coins and copper one-cent and half-cent pieces (authorized by the act of 1792), The American public was left with inadequate small change. To overcome this shortage, the public then used postage stamps for small change.

With a view to improving the subsidiary coinage system, Congress in 1853 authorized the issue of token silver subsidiary coins on the government's own account. The free coinage of small silver coins was discontinued. The coinage of the full-bodied standard silver dollar remained free, but no silver was brought to the mint as it was worth more as commodity than as money. The passage of the Act of 1853 was to a considerable extent influenced by the successful experience of the copper one-cent and half-cent pieces which were of course token coins and the monetary usage of postage stamps which hardly had any commodity value. In 1857 the supply of silver subsidiary coins was adequate for domestic demand, and the legal tender status of foreign coins was withdrawn. They subsequently disappeared from the scene.

Period of De Facto Paper, The Civil War. The act of February 15, 1862, empowered the treasury to issue noninterest-bearing United States notes, popularly referred to as "greenbacks." These notes were legal tender for all payments with the exception of interest on the public debt and duties on imports. The purpose of the act was primarily to provide revenue for the federal treasury to finance the war, tax resources and borrowings being inadequate. The redemption of the currency in gold was suspended, and the country was on a de facto paper standard.

As the war progressed and the volume of greenbacks increased from the initial amount of $150 million to almost half a billion near the end of the war, greenbacks depreciated rapidly with respect to gold. Gold coins consequently disappeared from circulation. Gold was bought and sold primarily as a commodity for the payment of import duties, for the purchase of foreign exchange, and for hoarding purposes. The rapid depreciation of greenbacks also raised the commodity value of subsidiary silver coins above their monetary value. As a result, the fractional silver coins were also withdrawn from circulation. The country again faced an even more serious shortage of fractional coins. The gap was partially filled by fractional notes issued by banks, special postage stamps were issued by the government, and copper one-cent pieces were minted to the order of business organizations. For some reason, the government did not authorize the issuance of silver subsidiary coins with reduced metallic content. This appeared to be a simple and systematic remedy.

After the war, efforts were made by the government toward the redemption of greenbacks in specie. The volume of greenbacks outstanding was reduced as greenbacks offered in payment of taxes were retired. This, however, met with strong opposition on the grounds that it would cause undesirable deflationary pressures in the economy. The law of May 1878, fixed the volume of greenbacks outstanding at about $347 million.

In the late 1870's the value of greenbacks rose gradually in terms of gold, as a result of the slow rate of increase in the supply of money relative to trade expansion at that time. From a low value of about 39 cents in 1864, the value of greenbacks with respect to gold increased to nearly 90 cents in 1876, and afterward slowly approached parity with gold. The condition was then favorable for a return to full convertibility.

Return to Convertibility and the Emergence of Gold, 1879-1900. The Specie Resumption Act, enacted in 1875, provided that, beginning in January 1879, the convertibility of greenbacks into gold should be restored. In 1879, the greenback was fully convertible into gold, and the country was back to de facto gold.[8]

[8]Since, in terms of the act of May 1878, the amount of greenbacks outstanding was required at $347 million, when they were offered for redemption, they were reissued by the Treasury. Against these greenbacks, the Treasury was required to hold a gold reserve of less than 50 percent.

The passage of the Coinage Act of February 12, 1873, however, had already sowed the seed of monetary controversy in the late 1870's. The act, purportedly a general revision and codification of coinage laws, authorized the coinage of one-dollar gold pieces weighing 25.8 grains of gold 9/10 fine (or 23.22 grains of pure gold) and gold coins which were multiples of the one-dollar piece, with the double eagle of $20 as the largest denomination. The act also provided for the coinage of a "trade dollar," representing 420 grains of standard silver 9/10 fine (or 378 grains of pure silver), for circulation in the East and Far East in competition with the Spanish dollar and Mexican dollar, but not for domestic circulation.[9] No provision was made, however, for the coinage of the standard silver dollar as defined by the acts of 1792 and 1834 (412 1/2 grains in gross weight). The act was passed without fanfare. The omission was in fact intended for the suspension of the free coinage of silver, but nobody was greatly disturbed by it, since neither gold nor silver was in circulation at that time. Silver interests were satisfied with the market price of silver, which was at that time much higher than its mint value. The possibility of being adversely affected by the suspension of the free coinage of silver appeared remote.

After 1875 the situation was not the same, however. The value of silver, which had remained relatively stable with respect to gold, began its downward course—a result of the increase in silver production because of discoveries of new, rich silver deposits, and the decrease in the demand for silver after the abandonment of silver in Europe and other countries of the world in favor of gold. The decline in the value of silver began to adversely affect those who had vested interests in silver. The suspension of the free coinage of silver meant the loss of a constant source of demand for their product, further tending to depress its price. A campaign was initiated to restore free silver coinage. The campaign was soon joined by debtors and farmers whose vested interests were in generally rising prices. One of the main arguments of the free-silver movement was that the restriction of silver coinage would restrict the supply of money, thereby causing deflationary pressures. The campaign resulted in some concessions by Congress, reflected by the passage of the Bland-Allison Act of 1878 and the Sherman Silver Purchase Act of 1890.

The Bland-Allison Act authorized the Treasury to purchase between $2 and $4 million of silver bullion each month to be coined into standard silver dollars (as defined by the act of 1792). The act also provided for the issuance of "silver certificates" against the deposit of silver dollars with the Treasury. From 1878 to 1890, the country could be said to have been on a "limping standard," in view of the limited coinage of silver, the free coinage of gold, and the absence of a provision to keep silver at par with gold.

The Bland-Allison Act was replaced by the Sherman Silver Purchase Act of 1890. This act authorized the Treasury to issue Treasury notes against a monthly purchase of 4.5 million ounces of silver. These notes were redeemable in gold or silver at the discretion of the Treasury.

[9]The coinage of the "trade dollar" was suspended in 1878.

The uncertainty regarding the future of gold and the fear of the possibility of a return to silver, created by the Silver Act of 1890, prompted the liquidation of foreign investments and the conversion of currency into gold, both by domestic and foreign holders, either for hoarding or export. The withdrawal of funds following the liquidation of foreign assets, the flight of gold, and the uncertain outlook of business, among other things, contributed to the Panic of 1893, a result of which was the repeal of the Sherman Silver Purchase Act in 1893.

The economy recovered during the late 1890's. The gold reserve of the Treasury increased substantially following increases in the country's exports. This, coupled with the defeat of William Jennings Bryan, the champion of silver, paved the way for the legal adoption of gold. In March 1900, the Gold Standard Act, legalizing the gold standard, was passed. By virtue of the act, the standard money became the gold dollar, representing 25.8 grains of gold 9/10 fine. The coinage of gold was unlimited and circulating currency was fully convertible into gold. The act, for the first time, instituted the legal gold standard in the country. It marked the end of a long period of monetary controversy and agitation, during which the operation of Gresham's law defied the monetary laws of Congress!

The Reserve Act of 1934 and the Present Monetary Standard

The United States was firmly on gold until the Great Depression of the early thirties, following which a world-wide collapse of the gold standard occurred. The United States was deep in depression. The main prescription recommended by experts to the Roosevelt administration for economic recovery was an increase in the general price level which, according to the experts, could be achieved by simply raising the dollar price of gold.[10] This recommendation was accepted and followed by President Roosevelt. In April 1933, the redemption of currency in specie was suspended, and gold coins were withdrawn from circulation. The Treasury began buying gold at increasing prices—from $31.36 in late 1933 to $34.45 per ounce in early 1934. This was, in effect, a de facto devaluation of the dollar, since in terms of the Gold Standard Act of 1900, the buying and selling price of gold by the Treasury was supposed to be $20.67 per ounce. This de facto devaluation was legalized by the Gold Reserve Act of January 1934. Under the authority of the Act, the President proclaimed a new gold definition of the dollar at 1/35 of a fine ounce, or approximately 13.7 grains of pure gold. The coinage of gold coins was to be discontinued, and existing coins were to be melted into bullion. Gold certificates were to be issued only to the Federal Reserve Banks as reserves against Federal Reserve notes and deposit liabilities. Private holding of gold was prohibited. The Secretary of the Treasury was authorized to buy and sell gold at his discretion and at prices which he might consider most "advantageous to the public interest." The Treasury has sold gold to domestic users for industrial and artistic purposes on a limited basis.

[10] An analysis of the theoretical arguments behind the proposed remedy is given in Chapter 16.

It has, however, sold gold freely to foreign central banks and governments for dollars at about $35 per ounce.

The present monetary standard of the United States may be classified in two ways. In as much as the Treasury is committed to convert freely into gold dollar balances held by foreign monetary authorities, the United States may be considered to be internationally on gold. But this could be changed overnight as the sale of gold is a matter of discretion of the Treasury. Domestically, the United States is on a managed paper standard, pure and simple, following the passage of the Act of Congress of March 18, 1968 eliminating the gold reserve requirements for Federal Reserve notes (and for United States notes and Treasury notes of 1890) thereby severing the last link between the dollar and gold.[11]

MONETARY STRUCTURE

The structure of money in the United States is rather complex both in terms of issuing institutions and the composition of circulating currency.

Deposit Money. Demand liabilities of commercial banks transferrable by checks represent the dominant form of money in the country. They constitute more than 80 percent of the total money stock. A more detailed discussion on bank deposits will be given in Chapter 6 on commercial banking operations.

Currency. Circulating currency consists of various types, some of which are remnants of past monetary legislation and are now in process of retirement.

Silver Certificates. Silver certificates were issued by the Treasury in exchange for standard silver dollars, or against free silver bullion—that is, silver which was not required against silver certificates already outstanding. After mid-1961, silver certificates were retired by the Treasury in order to free silver for the coinage of subsidiary silver coins.

United States Notes. United States notes, or "greenbacks," were originally authorized by the act of February 1862. They were also issued by the Treasury. The amount of greenbacks outstanding, as noted earlier, was fixed at $347 million by the act of 1878, and it is still in force.

Federal Reserve Notes. Federal Reserve notes are issued by the Federal Reserve banks. They constitute the bulk (almost 90 percent) of total currency in circulation. Federal Reserve notes are issued in denominations of $1, $5, $10, $20, and up to $10,000. After 1945, however, notes of more than $100 were not issued, as there was little demand for notes of the larger denominations. Before 1963 the Federal Reserve Banks were not authorized to issue notes in denominations of less than $5. They have, since then, been authorized to issue one-dollar Federal Reserve notes to replace one-dollar silver certificates being retired by the Treasury. The Reserve Banks were required to hold a reserve in

[11]The gold reserve requirements against the deposit liabilities of the Federal Reserve Banks were eliminated in March 1965.

gold certificates equal to at least 25 percent of their notes outstanding. The reserves for the remaining 75 percent of notes outstanding were made up of United States obligations and such discounted or purchased paper as eligible under the terms of the Federal Reserve Act of 1913 and its various amendments.

Notes in Process of Retirement. There are other types of paper money issued in the past that are now in the process of retirement. They consist of Federal Reserve Bank notes (different from Federal Reserve notes), national bank notes, and Treasury notes of 1890. National Bank notes are those issued by national banks authorized under the National Bank Act of 1863, and as amended in 1864. Since national banks failed to redeem their notes, they were made an obligation of the Treasury; the Treasury redeemed these notes through Treasury bonds pledged by national banks for the privilege of issuing bank notes. Federal Reserve Bank notes were issued by the Federal Reserve banks during World War I to offset the decrease in silver certificates withdrawn by the Treasury following the sale of silver to England. They were also issued for emergency purposes during the banking crisis of the early 1930's and during World War II to provide additional paper money required by the war. The Federal Reserve Banks were in a less restrictive position to issue Federal Reserve Bank notes since a gold reserve of only 5 percent was required against these notes. Treasury notes are those authorized by the Sherman Silver Purchase Act of 1890.

Circulating Coins. Circulating coins are standard silver dollars, subsidiary coins which consist of half dollars (50 cents), quarters (25 cents), dimes (10 cents), and minor coins in denominations of five cents (nickels) and one cent. Coins are issued by the Treasury (the Director of the Mint) and distributed through the Federal Reserve Banks, in accordance with the demand for coins by the public.

In the early 1960's the country witnessed a serious shortage of coins, attributed to the tremendous increase in the demand for coins generated by economic expansion, population growth, the greater use of coin-operated vending machines, and the increasing business (and hobby) of collecting coins on the one hand and inadequate minting facilities on the other. The shortage was more or less relieved in the mid-1960's after an expansion of minting facilities. But the coin shortage overshadowed an even more serious problem: a world-wide shortage of silver, which led to the passage of the Coinage Act of July 23, 1965, reducing the silver content of the half dollar and eliminating silver in the coinage of quarters and dimes.[12]

The Treasury had accumulated, throughout the years, a huge stockpile of silver as a result of past silver legislation. The bulk of the silver stock was used in coins and mostly as a reserve against outstanding silver certificates. The remaining portion was "free silver," available for additional coinage and for sale to

[12]The silver content of subsidiary silver coins prior to the act of 1965 is as follows: half dollar, 173.61 grains of pure silver; quarter, 86.805 grains; and dime, 34.722 grains.

industries to fill the gap between silver consumption and silver output which had prevailed after 1950. The silver situation tightened after 1958. The gap between the silver demand and silver production widened, increasing from 64 million ounces in 1958 to more than 440 million ounces in 1965. This reflected the tremendous increase in the demand for silver for industrial use—especially in photography, electronics, and jewelry—and the rising requirement of silver for coinage, as mentioned above. The increase in the sale of silver to industry, coupled with a greater use of silver for new coins, finally reduced the Treasury's stock of free silver to a low level in 1961. To protect the amount of free silver available for new coinage, the sale of silver to industry was discontinued by the Treasury in November, 1961. In addition, to increase the volume of free silver, the Treasury began retiring $5 and $10 silver certificates and, after mid-1963, $1 certificates as well.[13]

In the meantime, the discontinuance of the sale of silver by the Treasury drove its price up to $1.2930 per ounce in September 1963. At that price the market value of the commodity content of the standard silver dollar became equal to its monetary value (480/371.25 = 1.2930) and the silver dollar became full-bodied. In order to prevent further increases in the price of silver, which could induce the melting of silver dollars and coins, the Treasury was forced to resume the sale of silver to industries against silver certificates at the monetary value price. So long as the Treasury sold silver at that price, the market price of silver could not increase further. Had no action been taken and should the price of silver have risen to, say, $1.40 per ounce, it would have been profitable to melt down not only standard silver collars but also quarters and dimes for sale by weight: their commodity value would have been higher than their monetary value. This situation would have aggravated the already serious shortage of coins and would have been very detrimental to the general economic welfare of the country.

The sale of silver to industrial users, coupled with the increase in silver required for coinage, would eventually have exhausted the Treasury's stockpile of silver, already down to around 1 billion ounces in late 1965. Since silver output was inadequate to meet even the industrial demand, the exhaustion of the silver stock of the Treasury would inevitably have produced a more acute and chronic shortage of silver for subsidiary coins. To avoid any such development, the Coinage Act of July 23, 1965, was passed, reducing the fine silver content of the half dollar (77.16 grains of pure silver instead of 173.61 grains), and eliminating silver in 25-cent and 10-cent pieces.[14] The new coins have been

[13]It should be noted that for each $1 silver certificate retired, 371.25 grains of pure silver was freed for the coinage of subsidiary coins.

[14]There appears to be no monetary justification for the maintenance of silver in the coinage of the half dollar. It is a luxury, a waste of silver. This seems to reflect primarily political influence of silver interests in Congress, as does the omission regarding the status of the standard silver dollar. Should the commodity demand for silver decline in the future, the monetary demand for silver for the coinage of these coins would serve as a buffer against sharp decreases in silver prices.

produced since late 1965, and have been accepted without qualification by the public. The silver requirement for the new half dollar was estimated to be no more than 15 million ounces per year, which would be met for quite some time from the existing stockpile of silver, and eventually from current output.

The reduction in the silver requirement for coinage would allow the Treasury to maintain the price of silver at its monetary value for a longer period of time, thereby preventing the possible melting of silver coins while the new coins were still in short supply. In mid-1967, as the production of new coins was considered adequate to meet the demand for coins by the public, the Treasury decided to abandon its policy of pegging the silver price at its monetary value by offering to sell silver at what the market would bear. Once the lid was opened, the price of silver rose sharply. In late July 1967 it was as high as $1.87 per ounce. As the market value of silver was substantially higher than its monetary value ($1.29 per ounce) it would be profitable to melt down old silver coins—dollars, half dollars, quarters, and dimes—for sale by weight.[15] Such withdrawals of silver coins from circulation for the recovery of silver, however, would not exert any detrimental influences on economic activities since the production of new coins was adequate to meet the demand for coins by the public.

SUMMARY

Popular commodity standards in use in the past were the gold standard, the silver standard, and bimetallism. The silver standard was popular the world over until late in the nineteenth century. Afterward, it fell into disrepute as a result of frequent changes in its value. Gold became the "standard money" in place of silver until the outbreak of World War II. Attempts by nations to broaden their currency and credit basis by adopting bimetallism had failed as a result of the operation of Gresham's law. After the Great Depression of the early 1930's, inconvertible paper money became the monetary institution of most countries of the world. Advocates of commodity standards emphasize their merits as exchange rate stability and domestic price stability. Proponents of managed paper, on the other hand, hold that an intelligently and responsibly managed system of paper money helps promote not only relative stability of domestic prices and foreign exchange rates but also full employment and high rates of economic growth.

In the United States, efforts made toward establishing a working bimetallic standard had been thwarted by the operation of Gresham's law. Legal bimetallism was officially abandoned in 1900 in favor of gold, which was in operation until 1933. Her present monetary standard is rather difficult to classify. On the

[15]Since the new half dollar contains only 77.16 grains of pure silver (as compared with 173.61 grains of the old half dollar), it is profitable to melt it down for sale by weight only when the market price of silver rises above $3.20 per ounce. It should be noted that it is not legal to melt down coins. But the enforcement of the law against the melting of coins when this is profitable is a different matter!

basis of the inconvertibility between currency in domestic circulation and gold, she can be considered to be on a managed paper standard. However, as official foreign-held dollar balances have been freely convertible into gold, the U.S. may be considered to be on gold internationally.

PROBLEMS

1. Discuss the theoretical arguments behind bimetallism. What are conditions which you would consider as necessary for a working bimetallic system?
2. Explain and compare the advantages and disadvantages of the gold standard and the managed paper standard.
3. The choice between commodity standards and nonconvertible paper money is primarily a matter of choice of specific economic objectives and the extent of the discretionary control of monetary authorities. Do you agree? Explain.
4. Monetary legislation in the United States in the past was sometimes influenced by the political influence of special-interest groups. Do you agree? Why or why not? Use examples to support your arguments.
5. How would you classify the present standard of the United States? Is it conflicting to say that she is domestically on paper and internationally on gold?
6. Some people believe that since the new subsidiary coins contain less silver, or no silver at all, they would drive existing silver coins out of circulation. Do you agree? Explain some possible events which might put Gresham's law into operation.
7. Explain the major factors responsible for the shortage of coins in the United States in the early 1960's and various measures taken to overcome that coin shortage. Is it correct to say that the passage of the Coinage Act of July 23, 1965 was prompted primarily by the world-wide shortage of silver? Why or why not?

chapter 4

Credit and Credit Instruments

To understand the working of the monetary system, it is important to understand the operation of the credit system, since money and credit are closely intertwined and are superimposed on each other. Currency, as we have seen, is a claim on the government. Bank money is a claim on commercial banks. Money is created mostly as a result of the extension of credit; and the extension of credit, in most cases, will give rise to money payment. Credit or debt arise from the lending or borrowing activitites between individuals, business enterprises, financial institutions, and the government. We shall discuss the nature and function of credit or debt, various types of instruments used in the transfer of credit, arrangements for the transaction of these instruments, and the structure of their prices.

CREDIT AND DEBT

The terms *credit* and *debt* represent something of a paradox—a subject of mixed and conflicting emotions. Few individuals want to be in debt. It is a "burden," "the prolific mother of folly and crime." Credit, on the other hand, is "good" and "desirable." Yet credit and debt represent exactly the same thing, the same transaction seen from opposite viewpoints. It is credit to the lender, and it is debt to the borrower. Credit is simply the right of the lender to receive money in the future, in return for his obligation to transfer the use of his funds to the borrower; and debt is the obligation of the borrower to pay money in the future in exchange for the privilige to use the lender's money. Credit is debt, and to grant credit is to incur debt. It is impossible to think of a debt owed by somebody without a corresponding credit owned by somebody else. Credit is a claim on the incomes and assets of the borrower. It is an asset of the lender. For example, the sum of money which the X corporation borrows from a commercial bank is its debt. The promisory note given by the borrowing corporation to the bank is the latter's earning asset. The corporate bonds owned by John are part of his wealth. But they are debts of the issuing corporation, and so on.

The foundation of credit is faith—faith of the lender in the borrower's ability and willingness to honor his obligations. The ability and willingness of the borrower to pay off his debt is essentially governed by his character, capacity, and capital. Character refers to the moral integrity of the individual or institutional borrowers. To the individual, his character reflects his mode of living, his reputation, his record of past and current dealings with other creditors, etc. The "character" of a borrowing enterprise reflects the integrity of its management, the stability and development of its business, and the reputation of its owners, among other things.

Capacity is concerned primarily with the earning power of the borrower. It indicates whether the debtor would be able to earn sufficient income in the future to repay his debt—both principal and interest. The capacity of the individual borrower to honor his obligation is reflected by his current and future income, which is determined by his educational training, his health, the type of employment which he has, and whether his job is a steady one or he has to move frequently from one job to another. The earning power of a business firm is reflected by records of its past and current performances. It depends upon such factor as the competency of its management, its capital structure, and particularly, its growth potential in the industry in which it is operating.

Capital represents the various types of assets owned by the debtor. They consist of real estate, personal property, and financial claims owned by the individual; in the case of business enterprises, they consist of current assets and fixed plant and equipment. Should the borrower be unable to honor his obligation, the creditors would have prior claim on the liquidation proceeds of these assets. The greater the liquidity, marketability, and value of these assets the greater the protection for the creditors. Which is the more important factor in the granting of credit by lenders: character, capacity, or capital? This is a matter of the lenders' own judgment. With regard to some borrowers, all these factors are simultaneously satisfied; with regard to others, they are not. It is possible that an individual or a business firm may have a good "character," but a poor capacity to earn income, or may be a poor capital risk due to illiquid and nonmarketable assets. The willingness to pay is one thing, and the ability to pay is another thing. The special factors which are taken into consideration by lenders would depend upon the size and types of loans and the kinds of borrowers involved. Character appears to be the more important factor in the granting of loans by banking institutions to well-known and regular customers. Similarly, character and capacity seem to be the basic consideration in loans granted by retailers to their customers in the form of charge accounts, credit cards, and installment plans.

The faith in the ability and willingness of the borrower to honor his obligation alone often does not offer adequate protection to the lender. Therefore, credit is usually secured by pledging of assets by the borrower as collateral for loans. With collateral, the lender is provided with more protection. In the event that the borrower fails to pay off his debt, the lender can dispose of those assets put up as collateral to recover his own credit. On the other hand, the use of collateral provides the borrower with added incentives to honor his obligation, as this is the only way by which he can recover his collateral assets.

THE IMPORTANCE OF CREDIT

We may have an idea about the importance of credit by considering the following example concerning the financing of a productive undertaking. Suppose that Mr. Smith went into business for the production of a commodity with a new production method that he invented. With a loan of, say, $200,000 from a financial institution which was impressed by the potential growth of his business, he was able to lease a small factory building, purchase machines and equipment hire skilled and unskilled workers, acquire materials and office supplies, and finance the expenditures of his family before the sales of his products, which were ready for the market only one year after production started. His business was a success. The earnings from his enterprise not only enabled him to pay off gradually his debt but also allowed him a handsome profit. It is clear that credit is vital to this productive enterprise. Without credit, it would be impossible. The availability of credit enabled this individual to use his talents for his own benefit, to create new job opportunities for workers, to provide new outlets for firms producing machines, equipment, and materials, and created new lending opportunities for financial institutions. These activities, in turn, created more jobs and incomes for others.

Indeed, credit plays a vital role in the functioning of a free market economy—it is based on credit and is sustained by credit. The development of modern industrial societies would hardly be possible without developed credit systems. Almost all aspects of modern production and distribution processes involve the use of credit in one form or another. Business firms borrow to meet their working capital needs. Those enterprises which desire to acquire machines and equipment for the expansion of their production facilities may obtain additional funds, either from financial intermediaries or banking institutions or individuals. The government borrows to fill the gap between current expenditures and tax receipts, to cover spending deficits, and to finance long-term public work projects, such as the construction of highways, public schools, or hospitals. Family households borrow money to purchase real estate, household furniture and appliances, automobiles, and other goods and services. Financial intermediaries, in turn, borrow from banking institutions which borrow from the public and the central bank. Households, financial institutions, business firms, and the government are thus involved in an intricate system of credit and debt, both as borrowers and as lenders. In this never-ending process of lending and borrowing, new credits are created and old debts are paid off. And both borrowers and lenders stand to gain. Borrowers have the funds necessary for the purchase of goods and services which they need, or for the acquisition of capital equipment for productive operations. Lenders, on the other hand, are given opportunities to earn more income by putting to work their idle funds or newly-created funds.

The flow of credit or debt between the various sectors of the economy is just like the flow of blood through organs of the human body—so long as it flows smoothly and expands at rates as required for steady growth of output, it would make possible rising income, employment, production, and sales. Should this flow be contracted, or "clotted," then, like a blood clot, it would cause serious damage to the economy, or even economic collapse. We can imagine the drastic decreases in income and employment following a drastic contraction in charge accounts, installment credit, bank credit and public borrowings. But the expansion of credit is not always desirable. Excessive expansion of credit at a time when the economy is operating at full employment would inevitably result in inflationary tensions, as existing productive capacity cannot sustain the swelling spending stream. The responsibility of central banking authoritites is to avoid too much or too little credit, to control the flow of credit so that it is in line with credit requirements for stability, high levels of employment, and growth. This, as will be seen, is not an easy task.

TYPES OF CREDIT

Credit comes in various forms. We can classify the various types of credit on the basis of maturity, collateral, and usage.

Credit by Maturity

With respect to its maturity, a loan can be a demand, short-term, medium-term, or long-term loan.

Demand Credit. This is the type of credit which is subject to repayment on demand. Demand deposits in commercial banks are an example of this type of credit, as it is payable in currency on demand. The call loan, granted by banking institutions to security dealers and brokers to finance stock and bond transactions, is another example. It is repayable "on call." Although there are cases where call loans were outstanding for quite some time, this type of credit is used mostly by firms whose operations generate regular flows of cash, as they may be called upon at any time to honor their obligations.

Short-term Credit. This is the type of credit whose maturity is one year or less. Short-term credit is used primarily to meet seasonal financial requirements. Wholesalers and retailers need short-term funds to carry stocks of goods in anticipation of, say, Thanksgiving and Christmas sales. Business firms also use short-term credit to cover their current production expenses. The cost of short-term credit is relatively low, since the lender is expected to receive payment in the near future; hence, the risk involved is also relatively small. But as the borrower has to pay off the loan in a short period of time, he may be faced with difficulties, especially when short-term obligations come due at a time of financial strain or adversity.

Long-term Credit. This represents credit whose maturity is five years or more; this type of credit is used mostly by business firms for the acquisition of factory buildings, machines, and other assets of long durability. The financing of these assets requires long-term funds as it would take them years to generate enough earnings for repayment purposes. This type of credit is also used by individuals for the purchase of homes and other real estate.

Medium-term Credit. Medium-term credit is the class of credit with maturity of more than one year and less than five years. This kind of loan is used when the financial requirement is for a period too long for short-term credit and too short for a long-term loan. For instance, a firm which needs credit for three years would find a medium-term loan more appropriate. A short-term loan in this case would inevitably require negotiation for renewal, whereas a long-term loan would be costly in interest payments.

Medium-term credit may be obtained either by direct negotiation between the borrower and the lender or a small group of lenders, or by the sale of bonds of intermediate-term maturity. When a medium-term loan is directly negotiated between the borrower and the lender, the loan is referred to as a "term loan." The term loan is highly flexible. The direct negotiation between the borrower and a lender (or a few lenders) makes possible the "tailoring" of credit to meet the requirements of both parties involved in the loan agreement. It also makes it relatively easier to alter the terms and conditions of the contract later on, such as the shortening or lengthening of its maturity. This would be difficult to do with regard to alternative financing devices which would involve hundreds or thousands of individual lenders. Moreover, the costs of term-loans are often relatively lower than those of other means of financing,–for example, the issuance of stocks and bonds which would have to meet the conventional standards of public security markets.

Term loans are used mostly by business firms to finance the purchases of relatively durable business assets. This kind of credit is of recent origin. It is a product of the Depression of the 1930's. Business enterprises, in need of funds for replacement investments, obtained credit by directly negotiating with banks and other financial institutions which had ample idle resources because of inadequate lending opportunities during the Depression. Moreover, the cost of conventional financing, particularly for small firms, was prohibitive, owing to unstable conditions in financial markets at that time.

Most medium– and long-term loan contracts contain provisions for periodic repayments of principal and interest over the life of the loan instead of a lump-sum repayment at maturity.

Credit by Collateral

On the basis of collateral, loans are either secured on unsecured.

Unsecured Loans. Unsecured loans, as we have mentioned, are extended primariliy on the basis of the confidence which the lender has in the ability and willingness of the borrower to honor his obligation.

Secured Loans. These are loans collateralled by various types of assets. Valuables which are put up by borrowers as collateral for their loans are commonly government securities, stocks, bonds, mortgages, life insurance policies, warehouse receipts, trust receipts, or real estate. The amount of the loan is usually a fraction of the market value of the assets used as collateral. The difference is referred to as "margin." Thus a margin of 30 percent means that the amount of the loan is 70 percent of the market value of the collateralled assets. Sometimes, however, loans are secured not by valuable properties or financial assets but by the guarantee of a cosigner or a comaker in the loan agreement. A comaker is a party involved in the contract, and who is, therefore liable for the whole amount of the loan. The cosigner is not a party in the loan contract but only acts on behalf of the borrower in guaranteeing the repayment of the loan. He would be called on to honor the contract should the borrower be unable to comply with the loan agreement.

Credit by Usage

Credit is used for various purposes, such as consumption, investment, or commercial operations.

Consumer Credit. This form of credit is used by family households for consumption purposes, for the purchase of durable goods (automobiles, refrigerators, and other household appliances), for the payment of hospital bills, utility bills, and the like. One important feature of consumer credit is that consumption requirements which give rise to borrowings do not by themselves generate incomes for the repayment of loans. The repayment of consumer loans depends primarily on expected incomes of the borrowers, a greater savings effort on their part, in the future. Not all family households which borrow money for consumption purposes, however, are deficit-spending units. Some hold surplus funds such as savings accounts and other financial assets but elect to borrow instead of withdrawing savings or selling financial claims to cover their consumption needs; they may find this to be the most profitable financing alternative, especially when borrowing is on short-term basis. But there are holders of surplus funds who borrow although they may have to pay interest rates which are substantially higher than those earned on savings deposits and other income-yielding claims simply because they fail to realize the costs involved.

Commercial Credit. Commercial credit is the class of credit used by commercial firms to finance their current operations, such as the marketing of goods and the carrying of inventories. The need for such credit arises from the fact that payments of current expenses are not synchronized with cash flows generated by the sales of products. Thus, an importer borrows from a bank to pay for imported goods and later repays the loan with the sale proceeds of imported commodities. A retailer buys goods on credit from a wholesaler and pays off his debt after the goods are sold. In contrast with consumer credit, commercial credit is self-liquidating, since the commercial operations which necessitate credit generate funds for the repayment of loans, assuming that such operations are successful.

Investment Credit. This kind of credit is used by firms for the acquisition of durable business assets in order to expand their production capacities, etc. Unlike commercial credit which is mostly short-term, investment credit is mostly long-term, as years will elapse before adequate earnings are accumulated for loan repayment. Investment credit, like commercial credit, can be considered as self-liquidating; the earnings from the uses of these assets are expected to be sufficient for the gradual retirement of loans.

Maturity, collateral, and usage are among the possible bases for credit classification. Credit can also be classified on the basis of types of borrowers, such as public and private debts, and sources of funds, such as individual savers, banking institutions, financial intermediaries, and government lending agencies. There is, indeed, a good deal of overlap in these various forms of credit classification. Each, however, befits special purposes of special investigations on problems of credit and debt.

CREDIT INSTRUMENTS

There are several forms in which credit is granted or debt is contracted. The granting of credit may be in the form of oral agreements, open-book accounts, or written contracts. When the loan agreement is written in proper form, the contract is a credit instrument which is simply a written evidence of the transfer of funds between the lender and the borrower.

Open-book credit is simple and informal. It consists of nothing more than entries in the books of the selling and buying firms. They are the seller's accounts receivable and the buyer's accounts payable. Although, at the retail level, buyers are required to sign sales documents, such practice is not common in the wholesale business. To encourage prompt payment on the part of the buyers, in open-book credit, wholesalers usually allow a certain rate of discount if payment is made within a specified period of time. The common practice is that buyers are allowed a 2 percent cash discount if payment is made within 10 days after goods are delivered. Open-book credit is a simple, convenient form of credit, but the absence of written evidence specifying the terms and conditions of credit may give rise to disputes between lenders and borrowers as to the amount and time of payment.

Oral credits, as the term indicates, is concluded by simple understanding between the parties involved. With no document evidencing the granting of credit, should the borrower refuse to honor his obligation, the lender would have a hard time proving the existence of debt. Because of these inconviences, open-book credit is used mostly among firms which have long-standing commercial relations with one another, and oral credit, by individuals well-known to one another.

These problems would not arise when credit or debt is evidenced by a written document specifying the amount of principal, interest, and maturity, that is, when it is represented by a credit instrument. Credit instruments come in various forms. They can be classified on the basis of their maturities—short-term and long-term credit instruments—or in terms of promises to pay and orders to pay.

Promises to Pay

Promises to pay include such instruments as promissory notes, certificates of time deposits, bonds, and Treasury securities.

Promissory Notes. A promissory note is a written document given by the borrower to the lender, promising to pay a given sum of money at a fixed future date. Sometimes interest is specified in the note; sometimes it is not specified. In the second case, the note is discounted, that is, the amount of interest is deducted in advance from the original amount of the loan. Depending upon whether a note is interest or noninterest-bearing, there may be a difference between the nominal rate of interest and the effective rate. When a person borrows against a promissory note, \$10,000 at 5 percent per annum for one year, and repays \$10,500 at maturity date, the moninal rate is the same as the effective rate, that is, 5 percent. But when the note of \$10,000 is discounted at 5 percent, the actual amount of loan received by the borrower is only \$9,500. The effective rate is then $\frac{500}{9500} \times 100 = 5.26$ per cent.

It should be noted that various kinds of currency issued by the Treasury and the Federal Reserve Banks are special noninterest-bearing promissory notes payable on demand. They are promises to pay on demand other kinds of currency at the discretion of holders, say, five brand-new \$1 bills for a worn-out \$5 bill!

Certificates of Time Deposit. These are short-term notes of banks promising to pay holders fixed sums of money plus interest on the dates specified on the certificates. The maturity of certificates of time deposits ranges from three months or longer. Unlike interest rates on other kinds of promissory notes, the maximum rate of interest which could be paid by banks on certificates of time deposits is determined by the Federal Reserve authorities. The use of certificates of time deposits, although of recent origin, has been widespread in the United States. They are held by business firms, state and local governments, and individuals, as well as foreign financial institutions.

Bonds. A bond is a written promise to pay, by the issuing corporation, a given sum of money at a specified future date and at a fixed rate of interest, payable either annually or semiannually throughout the life of the bond, which can run up to 20 years and more. A bond is thus a long-term promissory note. Interest rates on the face of "bearer bonds" are referred to as coupon rates, since bond holders have to clip coupons attached to these bonds and present them to the issuers or agents acting as their trusts for interest payments. The number of coupons depends upon the number of periods of interest payments. For example, a ten-year, 5 percent bond, which pays interest semiannually, would carry 20 such coupons.

Bonds may be secured or unsecured. Bonds issued by corporations, which are not secured by any types of collateral, are referred to as "debentures," or "debenture bonds." Holders of debenture bonds are general creditors of the issuing firms. In order to attract buyers and to enhance the marketability of their bonds, corporations frequently secure their issues with various types of collateral. When bonds are secured by real estate, the bonds are referred to as "mortgage bonds." Since the same property can be mortgaged more than once, we have first, second, and third-mortgage bonds. When bonds are collateraled by stocks and bonds owned by the issuing firms, they are called "collateral trust bonds." Since these bonds are unconditional promises to pay by the issuers, their inability to pay interest on these bonds on due dates means violation of contract, which usually leads to bankruptcy. There are, however, special types of bonds whose interest payments are not mandatory, but rather are optional. Interest on these bonds is paid only when the earnings of the issuers are adequate for such purposes. These bonds are referred to as "income bonds." They are usually issued by firms which were subject to reorganization, and relieve them of the burden of mandatory interests.

Treasury Securities. These are various types of promissory notes issued by the Treasury, such as Treasury bills, notes, and bonds. Treasury bills are short-term promissory notes used to raise short-term funds to cover the gap between current government expenditures and tax revenues. The maturity of Treasury bills runs from 90 days to one year. They are not interest-bearing. They are sold by auction at a discount. Treasury notes and bonds are securities of medium-term and long-term maturity. The maturity of notes is from one to seven years, and that of bonds, longer. They are used to obtain funds for capital and other spending purposes. Bonds are also issued by state and local governments to raise long-term funds for the financing of public work projects.

Orders to Pay

These include checks of various types and drafts or bills of exchange.

Checks. A check is a written order drawn by a depositor on his bank, ordering it to pay on demand a given sum of money, either to himself or to a specified third party. It is the instrument, most familiar to everyone, for the transfer of money. The use of checks is both safe and convenient. It precludes the necessity of carrying large quantities of currency. Cancelled checks serve as receipts of payment. Personal checks, although widely accepted, sometimes are refused, such as when an individual is not well known to the payee. In these cases, checks of superior quality, such as certified checks or cashier's checks, may be used. A certified check is one which bears indication by the bank on which it is drawn that it will be honored in full when presented for collection.

To assure that funds are available in the drawer's account for payment, when the check is certified by the bank, the amount of the check is immediately debited to the account of the person drawing the check. A cashier's check is a check which is drawn by the bank against itself. This type of check is used mostly by banks in payment of their expenses, or by bank customers in payment to others who do not wish to accept other kinds of checks. Another variety of check is a bank draft–simply a check drawn by a bank on its correspondent bank. Cashier's checks and bank drafts are more acceptable than personal checks since the makers are not individuals but banking institutions. Banks' depositors and others who wish to use cashier's checks and bank drafts have to pay certain fees for the services rendered.

Drafts or Bills of Exchange. A draft or bill of exchange is a document drawn by the seller demanding payment of a given sum of money from the buyer. The demand for payment may be on sight or at a fixed future date. When the payment is on demand, the draft is referred to as a demand or sight draft. When the payment is to be made at some future date, it is called a time draft. For example, A sells goods to B; he draws a draft directing B to pay for the goods, say, in 60 days after sight. To be sure that the draft will be honored at the due date, A can ask B to accept the draft. If B agrees to accept the draft, the document is called a trade acceptance. If the draft is accepted by B's bank, it is referred to as a bank acceptance.

Bills of exchange are used mostly in international trade. For instance an American importing firm in New York wishes to purchase goods from a firm in Paris. It asks its New York bank (e.g., The First National City Bank) to issue a letter of credit to the foreign firm, in which details of shipment and credit terms are specified. The First National City Bank, in agreeing to issue the letter of credit, assumes the obligation to accept the draft from the Paris firm when it is presented. The Paris firm, upon receipt of the letter of credit, ships the goods to the American importer and draws a draft on the First National Bank, ordering it to pay the amount involved in, say, 30 days after sight. Assume that he sells the draft to a Paris bank, with the bill of lading (an evidence of ownership of goods in transit issued by the shipping company) and other documents attached. The Paris bank sends the draft and other documents to its office in New York, and they are presented to the First National Bank. The latter accepts the draft (stamps "accepted" on the face of the draft) and receives the bill of lading and attached documents. The office of the Paris bank can collect the amount of the draft from the First National Bank at maturity or sell it to a dealer in bankers' acceptances. The First National Bank forwards the bill of lading to the importing firm and receives in return a trust receipt (an evidence of ownership of the sale proceeds of goods). With the bill of lading in hand, the importer obtains the goods from the shipping company, sells them to other firms, and pays the First National Bank with the sale proceeds of the goods.[1]

[1] More details on this are discussed in Chapter 27 in the section on the mechanism of international payments.

NEGOTIABILITY OF CREDIT INSTRUMENTS

Credit instruments may be negotiable or nonnegotiable. The title of a nonnegotiable instrument is transferred from one holder to another by assignment. There are risks involved in the transfer of titles by assignment, since all the defects contained in the ownership of nonnegotiable instruments are also transmitted to new owners. For instance, a person who obtains a nonnegotiable instrument by assignment would have no title to it should the instrument turn out to be a defective or stolen one, even though the assignee was not aware of this. To avoid this possible impairment of title of credit instruments which could hamper the flow of credit necessary for commercial and production operations, laws were passed defining conditions for credit instruments to be negotiable, to be transferable freely to new owners without the latter worrying about defects involved in previous ownership.

To be negotiable, a credit instrument must satisfy the following requirements: (a) it has to be in writing; (b) it must be signed by the maker; (c) it must be an unconditional promise or order to pay a specified sum of money; (d) it must be payable either on demand or at a fixed future date; and (e) it must be payable to order or bearer. A "holder in due course" of a negotiable credit instrument has perfect title to it, regardless of any infirmity or defect in previous ownership. For example, the buyer of a stolen instrument, without any knowledge that it was stolen, has complete title to it, although the previous owner did not legally own it. The transfer of a negotiable instrument to "a holder in due course" thus gives him rights which might not be in the possession of the previous owner. A credit instrument is transferred to a holder in due course only when (a),it was complete and regular on its face (there is no indication that it has been altered, such as erasing marks); (b) it was acquired before it was overdue and without any knowledge that it had been previously dishonored; and (c) it was acquired for value in good faith and without any knowledge of any title defects.

Negotiable credit instruments are transferred by delivery or endorsement. If the instruments are payable to bearers, the transfer only requires delivery. When credit instruments are payable "to order," they are transferred by endorsement. For example, checks are transferred by endorsement. The individual who endorses the transfer is liable to the individual for whom the instrument is endorsed should, for some reason or another, the drawee fails to honor his obligations. There are several forms of endorsement. The endorsement is called "blank" when the holder signs his name on the back of the check. The check then becomes an instrument payable to bearer. The endorsement is sometimes "special," which is in this form: "Pay to the order of *X*," with the signature of the holder. The new holder, in turn, would endorse the check when it is presented to the bank for collection. Endorsement may be restrictive. When the holder desires to make the instrument payable to a designated individual and to him alone, the endorsement would be as follows: "Pay to the order of *X* only":

the instrument then ceases to be negotiable. It is of value to no one but the individual for whom the check is endorsed. Likewise, when a depositor sends by mail a check to his bank for deposit, for safety, he would make the endorsement restrictive by writing "For Deposit Only" on the back of the check.

Negotiable credit instruments give lenders as well as borrowers several advantages. Business enterprises are in a position to raise large amounts of funds necessary for productive undertakings by selling, say, bonds to a large number of financial institutions and individual savers. Individuals and institutional investors would not have to wait until maturity for the conversion of securities into money. They can sell these financial assets on financial markets to meet their liquidity needs whenever such needs arise. The existence of a large variety of credit instruments of various maturities enables investors to space the maturity distribution of their assets to meet their liquidity needs and to diversify their investment portfolios to reduce credit risks. The uses of negotiable credit instruments help widen the scope of credit markets which in turn enhance the marketability, and, hence, the liquidity of credit instruments. These are among factors which facilitate the mobilization of financial resources necessary for the financing of the operations of business enterprises.

PRICES AND YIELDS OF CREDIT INSTRUMENTS

The value on the face of a credit instrument is its face value; it is the amount which the issuer is to pay at maturity. The rate of interest thereon is a contractual rate which remains unchanged throughout the life of the credit instrument. The market price and the market rate of interest or yield of the credit instrument, however, changes with changing maturity and market conditions. We shall discuss the relationship between the price, yield, and maturity of a credit instrument. But first, we would have to familiarize ourselves with such concepts as present value (or discounted value) and accumulated value, and the formula for their computation. Assuming that at the beginning of the year we invest an amount P at an interest rate i compounded annually for n years. At the end of the first period, the interest earned is iP and the total amount (principal plus interest) is $P + iP = P(1 + i)$. At the end of the second period, it amounts to $P(1 + i) + P(1 + i)i = P(1 + i)(1 + i) = P(1 + i)^2$. It amounts to $P(1 + i)^2(1 + i) = P(1 + i)^3$ at the end of the third period, and so on. It is clear that at the end of the nth period, the total amount is $A = P(1 + i)^n$. The formula indicates that the initial principal P invested at the rate i for n years accumulates to the value A. A is called the *accumulated value*, and $(1 + i)^n$ the accumulation factor. The value of $P = A(1 + i)^{-n}$ is called the present value (or discounted value) of the amount A due n years hence when the rate of interest is i per annum. The factor $(1 + i)^{-n}$ is called the *discount factor*. In the above formula, when the values of any three of A, P, r, n, are given, the value of the remaining can be calculated.[2] For example, when $P = \$1{,}000$, $i = 0.05$, and $n = 8$ years, then $A = 1{,}000\,(1 + 0.05)^8 = 1{,}000 \times 1.478 = \$1{,}478$.

Yield and Price of a Security of Infinite Maturity

A security with infinite maturity is a promise to pay a fixed sum of money in perpetuity. The "Consols" issued by the British government are an example. Suppose that a security promises to pay a fixed sum R per year forever. What is the present value of this security when the prevailing market rate is i? The present value of this security is the sum of the discounted values of the series of income receipts from holding this security spread over an infinite period of time. Formally, its present value is:

$$P = R(1+i)^{-1} + R(1+i)^{-2} + \cdots + R(1+i)^{-n} \text{ or}$$
$$= R\left[(1+i)^{-1} + (1+i)^{-2} + \cdots + (1+i)^{-n}\right] = R\frac{1}{i}$$ [3]

For example, if the fixed income from holding a perpetual bond is \$100 a year and the market rate is 5 percent, the market price of this bond would be $P = \frac{100}{0.05} = \$2{,}000$. This is easy to understand. At an interest of 5 percent, in order to earn \$100 a year, we would have to invest \$2,000. Since the bond pays \$100 a year, its market value would be \$2,000. Assuming that the market rate of interest decreases to 2.5 percent, the market value of the bond would be \$4,000. Again, if we do not hold the bond, we would have to invest \$4,000 at 2.5 percent to earn \$100 a year.

[2] The values of P, A, n, and i can be found by using logarithms, or interest tables. For example, from $A = P(1+i)^n$, we have $n = \frac{\log A - \log P}{\log(1+i)}$ or $\log(1+i) = \frac{1}{n}(\log A - \log P)$ and so on. They can also be found by using interest tables which give the value of the accumulated amount of 1 in n periods, that is, the accumulation factor $(1+i)^n$. For instance, to find A, we find the value of $(1+i)^n$ from the interest tables and multiply it by the given value of P. In the above example, 1.478 is the accumulated value of 1 in 8 years at $i = 0.05$. It should be noted that in the formula $A = P(1+i)^n$, i is interest paid once a year, and n is the number of years. This formula is for compound interest. In the case of simple interest, calculated on the original principal throughout the life of the loan, the formula is $A = P + Prm = P(1 + rm)$ where A is the amount received n periods hence; P, the principal; r, simple interest, and m, the number of periods.

[3] The series in brackets is an infinite geometric series whose sum is

$$\frac{(1+i)^{-1}}{1-(1+i)^{-1}} - \frac{(1+i)^{-n-1}}{1-(1+i)^{-1}} = \frac{1}{i} - \frac{(1+i)^{-n-1}}{1-(1+i)^{-1}}$$

Since $\frac{1}{1+i} < 1$ the limit of the series is $\frac{1}{i}$ (that is, $(1+i)^{-n-1} \longrightarrow 0$ as $n \longrightarrow \infty$, hence

$$\frac{(1+i)^{-n-1}}{1-(1+i)^{-1}} \longrightarrow 0\text{).}$$

Yields and Prices of Securities with Fixed Maturities

Let us first consider the relation between the price and yield of a bond which is a promise to pay a given sum of money at a specific date in the future and a given rate of interest payable either annually or semiannually. The amount on the face of the bond is its face value. The rate of interest on it is called "coupon rate." It is a contractual rate which remains constant throughout the life of the bond. Different from the coupon rate, the market yield (or yield rate or market rate) of the bond has to be computed. As will be seen, it varies inversely with the market price, that is, when the market price increases, the market yield decreases, and vice versa. The purchase price of the bond may be greater than, smaller than, or equal to its face value. When the market price in equal to the face value, the bond is said to be sold at par (in this case, the coupon rate is equal to the market rate); when the market price is greater than the face value, the security is said to be sold at a premium (in this case the coupon is higher than the market rate); and when the market price is less than face value, the security is said to be sold at a discount (in this case the coupon rate is lower than market rate).

As an example, consider a 20-year, $1,000-bond, with a coupon rate of 5 percent payable annually, and which sells for $900. The current or running yield of the bond is $\frac{1{,}000 \times 0.05}{900} \times 100 = 5.6$ percent, which is higher than the coupon rate as the bond is sold at a discount. This running yield is a very rough approximation of the market yield, since, in our example, in addition to an interest income of $50 a year, the buyer will make a capital gain of $100 (the difference between the purchase price and the face value) if he holds it to maturity. His average capital gain is then $\frac{100}{20} = \$5$ per year. In order to find the effective yield or yield to maturity, we have to include in our calculation this accumulation of discount. A rough approximation of the effective yield is $\frac{50 + 5}{900} \times 100 = 6.11$ percent. This is also a rough approximation, since the accumulation of discount does not average to $5 a year. It is smaller than $5 for the initial periods and rises to more than $5 as the bond approaches maturity. A more accurate rate can be obtained from bond tables, or by using the following formula for the relation between bonds' prices and yields.

Since a bond is a contract to pay to the holder a given sum of money at a future date and periodic interest until maturity, its price is the sum of the present value of the principal to be paid n periods hence and the present value of the series of interest income. The present value of the principal is $Vp = S(1 + i)^{-n}$ where S is the principal; Vp, the present value; i, the market rate, and n the number of periods. The present value of the series of interest payments is the sum of the discounted values of interest income for each period, that is:

$$V_a = R_1(1+i)^{-1} + R_2(1+i)^{-2} + \cdots + R_n(1+i)^{-n}$$

where V_a is present value and $R_1 = R_2 \ldots = R_n$ is the interest income per period, which is simply the product of the coupon rate and the face value of the bond. We then have

$$\begin{aligned} P = Vp + V_a &= S(1+i)^{-n} + R(1+i)^{-1} + R(1+i)^{-2} + \cdots + R(1+i)^{-n} \\ &= S(1+i)^{-n} + R\,[(1+i)^{-1} + (1+i)^{-2} + \cdots + (1+i)^{-n}] \\ &= S(1+i)^{-n} + R\left[\frac{1-(1+i)^{-n}}{i}\right] \end{aligned}$$

For example, the present value of a bond paying $1,000 after 20 years and an annual interest payment of $50 at a market yield of 6 percent is

$$P = 1{,}000(1+0.06)^{-20} + 50\left[\frac{1-(1+0.06)^{-20}}{0.06}\right] = \$885$$

An eight-year, $100 bond, with a coupon rate of 4 percent payable semiannually, sold at $110.82, yields a market rate of 2.5 percent. While the coupon rates on bonds remain constant throughout their life, their market prices and yields change with changing maturities. It is these price changes which bring different coupon rates of securities into line with their changing market rates. Thus, at a market rate of 6 percent, a bond carrying a coupon rate of 5 percent with, say, 20 years to go, would be sold at a discount so that to the buyer, the accumulation of discount plus the fixed interest income on the bond per period is consistent with earnings which he could obtain in alternative investment opportunities at the market rate of 6 percent. If the redemption value of the bond is $1,000, the discount would be $1{,}000\ (0.06 - 0.05) \times \left[\frac{1-(1+0.06)^{-20}}{0.06}\right] = 10.00 \times 11.5 = \$115$; hence[4] its price is $1{,}000 - 115 = \$885$. The buyer of the bond would receive an income of $50 per period. But at the market rate of 6 percent, the earnings of $885 would be $53.10, which is $3.10 more than the income on the bond. This amount is the "accumulation of the discount" to be added to the book value of the bond to bring its value to the face value at maturity. This

[4]The formula for the discount is

$$D = S(i-r)\left[\frac{(1-(1+i)^{-n}}{i}\right]$$

and that for the premium is

$$Q = S(r-i\left[\frac{1-(1+i)^{-n}}{i}\right]$$

where S is the face value, i the market rate, r, the coupon rate, and n, the number of periods, assuming that the bond is redeemed at face value.

amount plus \$50 earned on the bond is consistent with the amount of earnings which the investor could obtain should he invest \$885 in alternative opportunities at 6 percent interest. On the other hand, when the market rate is lower than the coupon rate, the bond would be sold at a premium. The "amortization of premium," when subtracted from the interest income on the bond, would leave the buyer a net earning consistent with earnings from comparable obligations at the prevailing market rate. In the above example, at the market rate of 4 percent, the bond would be sold at a premium, \$1,136. At 4 percent, the income earned on \$1,136 would be \$45.44, as compared with \$50 per period earned from the bond. If we subtract from the amount of earning of the bond the amortization of the premium of \$4.56 for the first period, the holder of the bond would be left with a net earning of \$45.44.

There are credit instruments which do not bear interest rates on their face. These are sold at a discount and the interest represents the difference between their market prices and face values. Treasury bills are such instruments. For example, a Treasury bill of a one-year maturity, with a face value of \$100, sold for \$96.15, would yield 4 percent ($96.15(1 + i) = 100$; hence $i = 3.85/96.15 = .04$). When its market yield rises to, say, 6 percent, its market price falls to \$94.34. Conversely, when its yield falls to 2 percent, its market price rises to \$98.04. Similarly, the market price of a 90-day Treasury bill would be \$99 at 4 percent; \$99.5 at 2 percent, and \$98.04 at 8 percent; and so on.

Yields, Prices, and Maturities

The above examples show that the prices and yields of securities move in opposite directions. When the market yield decreases from 4 to 2 percent, the market price of a perpetual bond with an annual income payment of \$100 increases from \$2,500 to \$5,000. The price of a 20-year bond, with a coupon rate of 5 percent, rises from \$885 to \$1,136 when the market rate drops from 6 to 4 percent, etc. These inverse relations can be seen in the expression for the present value of a perpetuity ($P = R/i$) and that for the present value of a given accumulated value $P = A(1 + i)^{-n}$ Given R, A, and n, the higher the value of i, the lower the value of P, and vice versa.

The magnitude of the price and yield variations of securities depends upon their maturities. Given the change in the market rate from 5 to 4 percent, the market price of a 5 percent coupon, \$1,000 bond, would rise to \$1,010 when it is due one year hence; \$1,081 in 10 years; \$1,136 in 20 years; \$1,215 in 50 years; and \$1,245 in 100 years. The market price of a 3-month Treasury bill would increase from \$98.77 to \$99, and that of a 6-month bill, from \$97.56 to \$98.04. It is clear from these examples that, given a change in the market rate, the longer the maturity of a security, the greater the variation in its price. On the other hand, given a change in the market price of a security, its market rate tends to vary inversely with its maturity. For example, when the market price of a \$1,000 bond with a coupon rate of 5 percent drops to \$950, its market rate would increase approximately to 6.15 percent if it matures in 5 years; 5.65 percent in 10 years; and only 5.40 percent, in 20 years. This is not difficult to understand. When a bond is sold at a discount, the accumulation of discount is spread over a period of several years, thereby reducing the yearly yield effect. But in the case of a short-term obligation, say, a security of one year's maturity, the entire accumulation of discount is computed for one period, thereby causing its yield to rise substantially.

SUMMARY

Credit and debt represent the same transaction looked at from opposite viewpoints. Credit is the lender's right to receive money, and debt is the borrower's obligation to pay money, in the future. Credit plays a vital role in production and distribution processes. It is the lifeblood which sustains the functioning of the economic system. Nevertheless, too much credit may cause undesirable inflationary pressures. The extension of credit may be in the form of oral agreements, open-book accounts, or written documents. Credit instruments are written evidences of debt. They are either negotiable or nonnegotiable. Nonnegotiable instruments are transferred by assignment, and negotiable instruments are transferred by delivery or endorsement. While the face value and contractual rate on a credit instrument are fixed, its market price and yield change with changing supply and demand and maturity. The market prices of securities vary inversely with their market yields. The variation in the prices of securities tend to increase as their maturities lengthen, but the fluctuations in their market yields become wider as their maturities shorten.

PROBLEMS

1. What is credit? Why is credit so important in a free market economy? Is the expansion of credit always desirable?

2. Is debt a blessing or a burden? In what sense is it a blessing and in what sense is it a burden? Explain your own viewpoints.

3. "Debt is the prolific mother of folly and crime" (Benjamin Disraeli). Do you agree? Why or why not? If you do agree, how would you reconcile this statement with the following: "Let us all be happy and live within our means, even if we have to borrow the money to do it," (Artemus Ward).

4. What are differences between consumer credit, commercial credit, and investment credit? In your opinion, what would be the major factors which lenders take into consideration when they grant these various types of credit?

5. Explain briefly: (a) cashier's check, (b) bank draft, (c) trade acceptance, (d) bank acceptance, (e) Treasury bill, (f) certificate of time deposit, (g) corporate bond.

6. (a) What would be the market price of a 20-year, 5 percent coupon, $1,000 bond, when the market yield is 8 percent; (b) 6 percent; and (c) 4 per-

cent? (d) How would you reconcile the difference between the coupon rate and market yields?

7. (a) What is the present value of a perpetual bond paying $100 a year when the market rate of interest is 4 percent? (b) 2 percent? (c) Is this computation applicable to the calculation of the market price of a security with fixed maturity?

8. (a) Find the market value of a $100 Treasury bill due in 60 days and that of a 4 percent coupon, $1,000 bond, due in 15 years, when the market rate of interest is 6 percent. (b) What is the variation in the prices of the bill and the bond when the market rate decreases from 6 to 3 percent? (c) What observation would you have regarding the behaviour of the prices of these securities with respect to their maturities? Is this of any importance to investors? Explain.

chapter 5

The Money and Capital Markets

Money may be raised either through direct arrangements between borrowers and lenders or through the sale of securities in the money and capital markets, which may be broadly referred to as financial markets. Transactions in these markets are impersonal in that there are no personal relationships between borrowers and lenders. A national corporation which borrows through the flotation of bonds in financial markets would hardly know the ultimate holders of its obligations. Inasmuch as newly issued securities floated in these markets represent only a fraction of the total value of securities transacted therein, these markets are essentially secondary markets for the trading of outstanding securities. The existence of these secondary markets, which promotes the saleability and liquidity of credit instruments, immensely facilitates the flow of funds from surplus to deficit spending units both directly and, more importantly, indirectly through financial institutions which act as intermediaries between ultimate lenders and borrowers.

WHAT ARE THE MONEY AND CAPITAL MARKETS?

Credit instruments are bought and sold either on the money market or the capital market, depending upon their maturities. The capital market is commonly defined as an organization for the borrowing and lending of long-term funds through the use of such long-term credit instruments as corporate bonds and other long-term obligations, and the money market, as arrangements for dealing in short-term, highly liquid obligations, such as Federal Funds, Treasury bills, and other short-term government securities, certificates of deposit, and short-term commercial paper.

Admittedly in some cases there is no clear-cut line between the money market and the capital market. If some credit instruments are transacted exclusively in the capital market, and others in the money market, there are credit instruments which represent borderline cases. Their transactions may be included either in the money market or capital market. Furthermore, as the maturity of credit instruments changes over time, the sale and purchase of a credit instrument may belong to the long-term market at one point in time and to the short-term market at another point in time.

There are close relationships between the money market and the capital market. Funds flow between these markets in accordance with the income and liquidity preferences of individual and institutional investors, on the one hand, and the financial needs and liquidity requirements of business firms and others, on the other. Factors which tend to affect prices and yields in the capital market also tend to affect prices and yields of money market instruments, and vice versa.

Borrowing in the money market and capital market serves different purposes. While the capital market is a place where long-term funds are made available to business firms and other borrowers for long-term investment purposes, the money market offers short-term credit facilities to enterprises, financial institutions, and others, to meet their liquidity needs which arise from their current operations. While an enterprise sells stocks and bonds in the capital market for funds to acquire durable machines and equipment, it obtains short-term funds from the money market for seasonal working-capital requirements. The money market is thus concerned with the short-term phase of business operations, while the capital market underwrites capital formation. It is the latter which finances the growth of the economy's capital stock, the basic variable in the long-term growth of income and employment. The money market also serves as the primary point of impact of central banking operations. The effects of central bank controls are first felt in the money market reflected by changes in the cost and availability of short-term credit, which, in turn, affect the cost and availability of credit in other sectors of the economy.

The money and capital markets are financial organizations, and like other financial organizations, they change with changing economic and financial conditions and developments. These changes are reflected by the creation of new instruments, the introduction of new techniques, the development of new practices, the decline of the relative importance of old instruments, etc. The more developed the money and capital markets, the more complicated their structure and organization.

MONEY-MARKET STRUCTURE[1]

A highly developed money market is characterized by a highly developed and organized banking system, a large volume and great variety of credit instruments transacted, and a large number of other institutions which actively participate in money-market dealings. A developed money market is made up of several divisions, and in each division, arrangements for the issuance, trading, and redemption of short-term obligations are highly specialized. Thus the New York money market is an integration of several major divisions: the market for trans-

[1]For a detailed treatment of the New York money market and its mechanics, see Carl H. Madden, *The Money Side of "The Street"* (Federal Reserve Bank of New York, 1963).

actions in Federal Funds, the market for dealings in Treasury bills, the market for various types of commercial paper, and the certificates of deposit market.

The Federal Funds Market

The Federal Funds market represents various arrangements for the sales and purchases of Federal Funds which are reserve balances held by member banks with the Federal Reserve Banks. Inasmuch as most of these balances are required reserves—reserves required against member banks' deposit liabilities—the stock in trade of this market consists essentially of excess reserves—reserves over and above the legal requirements. Banks with reserve deficiencies can make the adjustment by purchasing Federal Funds, and banks with excess reserves can put them to work by offering them to others. Transactions in the Federal Funds market are typically one-day transactions. They are effected generally in units of $1 million and in multiples of $1 million. Smaller transactions are sometimes made by large banks as an accommodation to their small correspondent banks, but they are rarely less than $200,000. The average daily volume of trading in Federal Funds has been estimated to be about $800 million to $1.1 billion during the 1955-57 period, and more than $1.5 billion in the early 1960's. Active participation in the Federal Funds market has been limited to no more than a couple of hundred large banks in money centers throughout the country. More than half the dollar volume of trading is made by New York City banks, however. Buyers and sellers of Federal Funds are brought together by a few money market banks in New York, which buy and sell Federal Funds not only to adjust their own money positions but also to accommodate their correspondent banks, and by a number of New York brokerage firms of which Garvin, Bantel and Company is by far the most important. The firm usually offers these brokerage services free of charge to its customers in return for the business which it receives from them.

The Treasury Bills Market

The Treasury bills market is a major component of the money market. The stock in trade of this market is Treasury bills having a maturity of one year or less. Newly issued bills are offered weekly and quarterly by the Treasury on a discount basis to government securities dealers, banks, and other subscribers, largely through competitive bidding. Bills are allotted to the highest bidders who may tender them for their own accounts, for their customers, or for resale to other investors. New issues of bills, which vary in size from $1+ billion to $2+ billion, represent a small fraction of total bills outstanding. For instance, during the four weeks from October 6, 1966 to October 31, 1966, the average amount of bills "auctioned" was $2.302 billion, whereas the amount of bills outstanding in October of 1966 was $62.3 billion. Outstanding bills are bought and sold mainly by commercial banks, nonbank financial institutions, foreign central and commercial banks, nonfinancial business corporations, the Federal Reserve Banks, and individual investors, mostly through government security dealers who buy and sell at bid and asked prices. The bills market is an alternative earning outlet for holders of temporary idle funds and an alternative means for sellers to meet their short-term liquidity requirements.

As for the Federal Reserve Banks, they operate in the Treasury bills market primarily to inject funds into, or withdraw them from, the money market to keep the flow of money and credit in line with the flow of goods and services. The bills market, in particular, and the United States Government securities market in general, has experienced a tremendous rate of growth over the years. This has been fostered by the growing volume of public debt generated by deficit financing required during the depression and during the war and postwar periods. Thus, the volume of securities issued by the government increased from $41.6 billions in December 1941 (of which $2 billion were Treasury bills, $6 billion were notes, and $33.6 billion were bonds) to $296.6 billion in March 1969 (of which $77.5 billion were Treasury bills, $78.2 billion were notes, and $140.9 billion were bonds, both marketable and nonmarketable).[2]

The Market for Bankers' Acceptances

The Bankers' acceptance market was developed in the 1910's, following the passage of the Federal Reserve Act (providing for the establishment of the Federal Reserve System), which authorized member banks to accept bills of exchange (arising from foreign trade, domestic shipment of goods, domestic and foreign storage of readily marketable commodities, and dollar exchange drafts of foreign banks drawn on and accepted by United States banks) and the Federal Reserve banks to purchase and rediscount acceptances offered by member banks. Bankers' acceptances are particularly attractive to foreign central banks and foreign commercial banks because of relatively high yields, their familiarity with acceptance financing, and the tax advantage as incomes earned by foreigners on their holdings of acceptances are exempt from Federal income taxes.

Domestic banks are also buyers of bankers' acceptances. They buy both bills which they have accepted ("own bills") and bills accepted by other banks ("bills bought"). In addition to domestic banks, business corporations also have been interested in the acceptance market. The Federal Reserve was an active buyer of acceptances during the 1915-34 period. From 1934 to 1955, its participation in the market was irregular, but since 1955, it has again been a regular buyer of acceptances, not only to carry out credit policy but to promote greater interest in and wider participation in the market for acceptances. There are a few dealer firms operating in the acceptance market, but the main line of their businesses is dealings in United States Government securities and other securities. They usu-

[2]The total volume of gross debt, which is the sum of marketable and nonmarketable securities, and special issues held only by U.S. Government agencies and trust funds increased from $57.9 billion to $359.5 billion in the same period.

ally sell acceptances immediately after buying them and rarely hold sizable inventories of acceptances overnight.

The importance of this component of the money market has changed over the years. After attaining a peak of $1,732 million in 1929, the volume of bankers' acceptances declined drastically during the Depression of the early 1930's, following depressive international trade and during the war and postwar years, as a consequence of trade restrictions and exchange controls. Since the late 1950's, however, the market has regained importance, as attested by the substantial increase in the volume of banker's acceptances outstanding from $1,307 million in 1957 to $4,420 million in February 1969. This reflects the substantial increase in the volume of international trade in the 1950's and 1960's promoted by the elimination and liberalization of trade and exchange controls, the return to the free convertibility between the United States dollar and key European currencies, the restoration of confidence in the trade relations between nations, and the position of the U.S. dollar as an international reserve currency, among other things.

The Commercial Paper Market

"Commercial paper" represents mostly notes issued and sold in the open market by finance companies and business corporations, especially manufacturing firms, wholesalers, chain stores, and department stores, all of very high credit standing. These are typically unsecured, single-name, promissory notes payable to the bearer, with maturities running from 30 days to as long as 18 months. The denominations of these notes range from $5,000 to $1 million or more. They are noninterest-bearing notes and are sold at a discount. The major investors in commercial paper are commercial banks and nonfinancial corporations.

Until recently, the common practice of borrowing firms has been to discount their notes with commercial paper dealers who in turn resell them to other investors. Since the early 1960's, although most small finance companies continue to market their notes through commercial paper dealers, large finance companies have developed the practice of selling their notes directly to investors. The volume of directly placed notes has increased sharply. They are attractive to investors as they can be tailor-made to suit their own needs. Thus, of the total volume of commercial paper outstanding of $12,094 million in July 1966, $9,723 million were directly placed notes, and $2,361 million were marketed through commercial paper dealers. The commercial paper market, like the bankers' acceptance market, has its ups and downs. After reaching a peak of $1,296 million in 1920, the market declined in the 1920's as firms substituted bank loans and other sources of short-term credit for open market borrowing to meet their seasonal liquidity requirements. Since the 1950's, however, with the rising demand for consumer installment credit (generated by economic expansion and economic prosperity), among other things, the market has increased substantially in importance, as indicated by the sharp increase in the volume of paper outstanding from $929 million in 1950 to $22.865 billion in early 1969.

The Certificates of Deposit (CD's) Market

The market for certificates of deposits was developed in the early 1960's following the offering of negotiable certificates of deposit by New York money-market banks to large business corporations which, for additional earnings, have developed the practice of investing their temporarily idle balances in such short-term earning assets as Treasury bills, commercial paper, and other money-market obligations, thereby causing adverse drains of bank reserves. Since the ceilings on maximum rates of interest which could be paid by commercial banks on certificates of deposits have been raised by the Federal Reserve authorities, making them competitive with other money-market instruments and attractive to buyers, the market for certificates of deposits has achieved a phenomenal rate of growth. Thus from 1961 to early 1969, the volume of certificates of deposit outstanding increased from $1 billion to $14.6 billion.

Although certificates of deposit are not payable until maturity, holders can resell them to other investors in the secondary market through brokers and dealers. These certificates of deposit issued by money market banks in New York City are commonly denominated in $500,000, $1 million, and up to $10 million. They are bought mostly by large business corporations, state and local governments, foreign governments, insurance companies, and other non-bank financial institutions as an investment outlet for temporarily idle funds while awaiting long-term investment opportunities or in anticipation of expenditures. The denomination of certificates issued by banks in smaller cities, however, is usually $100,000 and less, which makes them accessible to smaller investors.

These various submarkets of the money market are closely integrated. Changes in the supply and demand conditions in each and every submarket would generate forces which cause changes in other components of the money market as well. This reflects, among other things, the high degree of shiftability on the part of buyers and sellers among the various types of short-term obligations traded.

In addition to intrarelations between various components of the money market, there are also close connections between money-market centers. For example, the New York, Chicago, and San Francisco money centers are closely connected. Funds flow between these money centers in accordance with the demand for and supply of short-term funds in each market in relation to conditions in other market centers. The excess supply of short-term funds in one market would find employment in another center where the supply is deficient. This interflow of short-term funds would tend to reduce interest differentials which would otherwise exist in different money-market centers.

One important feature of the money market is that trading in money-market obligations takes place not in organized exchanges but primarily in "over-the-counter" markets, or more properly, "over-the-telephone" markets, as dealings therein are ordinarily concluded by telephone.

CAPITAL-MARKET STRUCTURE[3]

Business corporations in need of additional funds may obtain loans from commercial banks or other nonbank financial institutions, may sell stocks and bonds directly to investors, or offer them to investment banking houses which serve as "underwriters," buying these securities wholesale for resale to the public. While new issues of securities of business corporations are usually underwritten by investment bankers, trading in outstanding securities ("secondary securities") takes place either on organized securities exchanges or over-the-counter markets, which are essentially secondary markets. The middlemen for buyers and sellers in these secondary markets are brokers and dealers. Brokers act as agents for buyers and sellers and receive commissions for their services. Dealers buy and sell securities for their own accounts with customers and other dealers, their income being the "spread" between the "bid" price (what they will pay) and the "ask" price (what they will take to sell).

The Organized Exchange

An organized securities exchange is a market in which trading is open only to members who operate primarily as brokers between buyers and sellers of securities permitted to be traded therein. There are several organized securities exchanges in the country. These include the New York Stock Exchange, the American Stock Exchange, and exchanges of other major cities such as Chicago, Boston, San Francisco, and Los Angeles. The New York Stock Exchange is by far the largest and most important organization. It is a national center in which stocks and bonds of national and international importance are traded.

The New York Stock Exchange, like other exchanges, is a voluntary association whose membership is acquired by purchase from a retiring member, subject to a favorable vote of the committee on admission. Each member may be associated with many partners as "allied" members and representatives located in various cities across the country. Securities traded on the floor of the exchange are listed securities. A corporation may apply for the listing privilege which requires full disclosure of its financial history and submission of copies of its charter and bylaws, among other things. Participants in the organized exchange as buyers and sellers include individuals and such institutional investors as life insurance companies, savings and loan associations, pension funds, trust companies, personal trust departments of commercial banks, and investment companies.

Trading practices and procedures on the organized securities exchanges are subject to the control and supervision of the Securities and Exchange Commission, created in 1934 to administer and enforce the Securities Act of 1933 and the Securities Exchange Act of 1934, which were purported to protect the

[3]For more details on the capital market and its structure, see for example, H. G. Guthman and H. E. Dougall, *Corporate Financial Policy* (Englewood Cliffs, N.J.: Prentice Hall, 1962).

public against malpractices in securities market transactions. "National" securities exchanges are required to register with the commission and to comply with the law and the commission's rules and regulations. Exchange members are subject to disciplinary action or expulsion for violation of trading rules and regulations. The partners and representatives of members are also subject to the control of the commission. The commission is also responsible for the enforcement of the margin requirements fixed both for banks and brokers by the Board of Governors of the Federal Reserve. A buyer of stock on margin pays a certain percentage of the purchase price of stock in cash and borrows the remaining balance from a broker, using the stock as collateral. The broker, in turn, can borrow from a commercial bank, using the stock as security. The percentage of the purchase price of stock which is to be paid by the buyer in cash, or the margins, is determined by the Federal Reserve Board, which, in principle, can be as high as 100 percent.

The "Over-the-Counter" Market

The "over-the-counter" or "off-board" market encompasses all transactions outside the organized securities exchanges. Trading in these markets is concerned not only with unlisted securities but also listed securities as well. These include the stocks of most banks and insurance companies, bonds of state and local governments (which are usually unlisted), securities of smaller business corporations, most corporate bonds, of which some major issues are listed. Although the bonds of the federal government are listed, almost all their trading is over-the-counter. While the trading in listed common stocks ordinarily takes place in the organized exchanges, the distribution of new issues is effected by investment bankers in the over-the-counter markets. Participating in the over-the-counter markets are a large number of dealer and broker firms (more than 3,000), which includes commercial banks, investment banks, bond houses, and stock exchange members which operate "over-the-counter" departments. They are members of the National Association of Security Dealers, Inc., an organization which sets standard practices and procedures for members. The Association operates in close cooperation with the Securities and Exchange Commission.

INSTITUTIONS IN THE MONEY AND CAPITAL MARKETS

As we have seen, the money and capital markets are arrangements for the issuance and trading of short-and long-term obligations, respectively. A large number of institutions participate actively in money and capital market transactions. Although all these institutions operate both as lenders and borrowers, some of them are predominantly lenders, while some others are predominantly borrowers. Of the lending institutions, aside from the central bank and the commercial banks which operate with newly created funds (currency in the case of the central bank and deposit money in the case of commercial banks), other lending institutions, such as savings banks, savings and loan associations, and life insurance companies operate largely with savings accumulated by individuals which are passed on to such borrowers as the government and business corporations.

Commercial Banks

The commercial banks represent the most important group of participants in the money market, both as borrowers and lenders, though mostly in the capacity of lenders. They constitute the major source of supply of short-term credit to business firms, financial intermediaries, and the government. Although most commercial banks buy and sell money market obligations, the number of banks which take part actively and regularly in money market transactions is rather small. They are primarily money market banks in New York City and large commercial banks in major cities, such as Chicago, Los Angeles, Philadelphia, and San Francisco, which operate either for their own account, or for the account of their correspondents and other customers. Banks also appear in the money market as borrowers, mostly for the adjustment of their liquidity requirements. Although they confine their operations mostly in the money market, commercial banks also participate in the capital market as suppliers of long-term funds. Their participation in the capital market is not as important as their holdings of bonds, mortgages, and other long-term obligations, as will be seen, are strictly regulated by banking supervising authorities. It should be noted that foreign central banks, commercial banks, and international financial institutions holding dollar balances with New York money-market banks also particpate actively in money market transactions. These dollar reserves are mostly invested in United States short-term obligations.

The United States Treasury

The U.S. Treasury is the preeminent borrower of short-term funds in the money market. The use of Treasury bills as an instrument for short-term borrowing has been expanding very rapidly and has become a money-market instrument of major importance, as indicated by the sharp increase in the volume of Treasury bills outstanding from nearly $30 billion in 1951 to almost $64 billion in late 1966. The Treasury is also active in the long-term market as a demander for long-term credit through the issuance of long-term Treasury bonds.

The Federal Reserve System

The Federal Reserve operates in the money market as a lender or borrower in order to ease, tighten, or "keep even" conditions in the money market in accordance with its monetary policy objectives. Its activity is mostly confined to the Treasury bill component of the money market. To ease money-market conditions, the Federal Reserve can buy Treasury bills or increase its advances to, and discounts for, commercial banks. It can also engage in repurchase agreements with security dealers, a technique by which the Federal Reserve buys securities from dealers with their agreement to repurchase them after a short period of time. Although the Federal Reserve System operates in the money market, it sometimes finds it necessary to operate in the long-term market, especially to bring about a direct change in long-term money rates to promote the expansion of private domestic investments, income, and employment.

Security Dealers

Security dealers are mostly borrowers of short-term funds to finance the purchase of carrying of securities for their accounts or accounts of their customers. Loans extended to dealers are mostly call loans, as their repayment is made on call. The call loan market, which used to be a major component of the New York money market and the major source of secondary reserves for banking institutions, is not as active and important as other sectors of the money market, as those for Treasury bills and Federal Funds, for instance.

Business Enterprises

Business firms are at the same time borrowers of short and long-term funds, thereby operating both in the money and capital markets. They borrow short-term funds mostly to meet their working capital requirements. But firms with temporary idle funds appear in the money market as suppliers of funds. For example, a firm with idle balances, such as reserves for tax payments and accrued wages, can purchase Treasury bills, certificates of time deposits, and other short-term obligations for additional earnings. When cash is needed, these liquid assets can be liquidated quickly for money.

In the capital market, business corporations are demanders of long-term funds. Firms which need capital funds for the acquisition of durable business assets raise those funds by issuing stocks and bonds and other long-term obligations. It is to be noted that foreign enterprises also participate in the capital market. It is not uncommon for foreign firms to raise long-term funds by floating bonds and stocks in the New York capital market.

Financial Intermediaries

Such intermediaries as life insurance companies, savings and loan associations, and mutual savings banks operate primarily in the capital market as suppliers of long-term funds, investing mostly in stocks, bonds, and mortgages. They also appear in the money market as suppliers of short-term funds, their idle balances waiting for long-term investment opportunities. Investment banking firms operate in the capital market largely as underwriters for stocks and bonds issued by business corporations or as intermediaries selling securities for the issuing firms for commissions. It is through these financial institutions that the bulk of the long-term credit demand in the capital market is accommodated.

Individuals

Individuals do not significantly participate in money market transactions. They do participate directly in transactions in the long-term market, but the volume of their direct participation is relatively small. The savings of individuals are mostly entrusted to financial institutions offering a relatively low yield but highly liquid claims (savings deposits in savings banks and commercial banks and share accounts in savings and loan associations). Furthermore, financial market outlets directly available to individuals are limited. Dealers in government securities are wholesalers to whom individuals have access only through banks and brokers. First claim on new corporate and municipal offerings is enjoyed by institutional buyers, if in fact they are offered to the public at all; only when an entire new issue is not absorbed by institutional investors are retail sales efforts made by underwriters.

STRUCTURE OF MONEY RATES

Short-term Rates

We have seen that short-term obligations are bought and sold in the money market. Just like the determination of prices of commodities on commodity markets, the prices of money market obligations are determined by supply and demand. The determination of the prices of these obligations in turn reveals the levels as well as structure of short-term money market rates. The supply of–and the demand for–money market obligations reflects the liquidity preferences of lenders, on the one hand, and the liquidity needs of borrowers, on the other. Changes in the liqudity perferences of lenders and the liquidity needs of borrowers will cause the structure of money rates to change. Since buyers and sellers can easily shift between various types of short-term obligations, so long as the differentials between money rates are such that it is preferable and profitable for them to shift, we would expect changes in the structure of money rates to be more or less in the same direction.

Table 5-1 shows the structure of money rates and their unison variations over time. The table also shows a variety of rates, which reflect differences in the maturity, liquidity, and risk of various money market obligations. For instance, 90-day Treasury bills and Federal Fund rates are low relative to others, as they represent the most liquid and safest money market instruments.

Within the structure of money market rates, some rates are more sensitive than others. The most sensitive of all money market rates is usually the Federal Fund rate which changes from day to day. It is considered as the barometer for the daily conditions in the money market. Like the Federal Fund rate, the Treasury bill rate also serves as an indicator of money market conditions. It is considered as the basic rate for short-term credit. Commercial paper rates are relatively less sensitive than Treasury bill rates, but they are more so than call-

TABLE 5-1
Money Market Rates (1962–69)
(Percent Per Annum)

Period	Prime Commercial Paper 4–6 Months	Finance Company Paper Placed Directly 3–6 Months	Prime Bankers' Acceptances 90 Days	Federal Funds Rate	U. S. Government Securities (Taxable)			
					3 Month Bills	6 Month Bills	9–12 Month Bills	3–5 Year Issues
					Market Yield	Market Yield	Market Yield	Market Yield
1962	3.26	3.07	3.01	2.68	2.77	2.90	3.01	3.57
1963	3.55	3.40	3.36	3.18	3.16	3.25	3.30	3.72
1964	3.97	3.83	3.77	3.50	3.54	3.68	3.74	4.06
1965	4.65	4.60	4.55	4.32	4.37	4.54	4.56	4.77
1966	5.55	5.42	5.36	5.11	4.85	5.06	5.07	5.16
1967	5.10	4.89	4.75	4.22	4.30	4.61	4.71	5.07
1968	5.90	5.69	5.75	5.66	5.33	5.48	5.45	5.59
1969*	8.65	7.53	8.41	8.61	6.98	7.23	7.14	7.02

Source: Federal Reserve Bulletin, 1969.
*July

loan rates (loans extended by banks to brokers and dealers subject to repayment on call) which appear to be less responsive to money market conditions. For example, from 1961 to 1965, despite variations in other money market rates, the call-loan rate remained more or less unchanged.

Long-term Rates

In the capital market, the prices of long-term obligations are determined by the supply of, and the demand for, long-term funds. These prices in turn reveal the levels and structure of long-term rates. Like the structure of short-term rates, long-term rates also display a sympathetic movement which reflects the substitutability between the various types of long-term obligations by investors and various kinds of long-term funds by borrowers. The movement of some long-term rates is shown in Table 5-2.

TABLE 5–2
Bond Yields (1962–69)
(Percent Per Annum)

Period	Government Bonds		Corporate Bonds by Group		
	United States (Long-Term)	Total	Industrial	Railroad	Public Utility
1962	3.95	3.30	4.47	4.86	4.51
1963	4.00	3.28	4.42	4.65	4.41
1964	4.15	3.28	4.52	4.67	4.53
1965	4.43	3.34	4.79	4.91	4.82
1966	4.66	3.90	5.30	5.37	5.36
1967	4.85	3.99	5.74	5.89	5.81
1968	5.25	4.48	6.41	6.77	6.49
1969*	6.07	5.79	7.29	7.50	7.49

Source: Federal Reserve Bulletin, 1969.
*July

Ordinarily, long-term rates are higher than short-term rates. This reflects, on the one hand, the fact that lenders prefer liquidity to illiquidity. Since short-term lending is liquid, lenders are willing to make short-term loans at relatively low rates of interest, since long-term lending is not only illiquid but also is much riskier than short-term lending. On the other hand, borrowers are willing to borrow short-term funds only at low rates of interest since they are faced with the risk of illiquidity resulting from recurring loan repayments. They are willing to pay higher interest rates for long-term loans inasmuch as–to them,–the longer the maturity of a loan, the smaller the illiquidity risk. It is to be noted, however, that sometimes the demand for short-term funds is such that short-term rates are driven above long-term rates. For instance, during the 1955-57 period, the sharp increase in the demand for short-term credit forced money market rates above long-term rates.

Relationships Between Short-term and Long-term Rates[4]

Short-term and long-term money rates are closely related. Figure 5-1 shows the sympathetic movement between short-term and long-term rates of interest, although the cyclical variations in long-term rates are not as wide as those of short-term rates. This sympathetic movement is accounted for, among other things, by the shiftability between long- and short-term obligations by both borrowers and lenders. Changes in either long-term rates or short-term rates would generate forces which cause changes in other rates until a new equilibrium pattern between long- and short-term rates is established, that is, a position in which there is no longer any tendency on the part of the lenders and borrowers to switch between short- and long-term obligations. The "switchability"between long- and short-term obligations would depend upon the nature of the operations of the lenders and borrowers, the relative advantages of changes in interest differentials, and expectations regarding future interest changes. For example, assume that long-term rates are rising to levels substantially above those considered as "normal" by investors and are expected to decline. Holding of long-term obligations then would appear more attractive, as investors would benefit not only from current high rates but a greater probability of capital appreciation, that is, increases in securities prices resulting from expected declining future rates. Investors would sell part of their short-term obligations in order to acquire long-term claims. Borrowers, on the other hand, would be inclined to move to the short-term market and postpone long-term borrowings. The resulting increases in the demand for short-term funds and increases in the supply of long-term credit (the increase in the supply of short-term obligations and the increase in the demand for long-term claims) would drive up the short-term rates and lower the long-term rates until the differentials between them is such that it is no longer preferable for both lenders and borrowers to switch between short- and long-term markets.

The more developed the money and capital markets, the more rapid the transmission of the impulses of changes between long- and short-term money rates. The reactions between the two markets, however, may not be as rapid as those taking place within the structure of money market rates or within the structure of rates in the capital market. This is due, among other factors, to some degree of specialization of institutions operating in the money and capital markets. For example, a change in either Treasury bill rates or commercial paper rates could cause banks to change the compositions of their holdings or short-term obligations. But, increases in rates in the capital market may not induce banks to liquidate a substantial amount of their short-term holdings for investing in long-term obligations, since this may not be consistent with the nature of commercial banking. On the other hand, institutions whose opera-

[4]This section is a somewhat crude treatment of the relationships between short-term and long-term money rates. A more refined treatment will be given in Chapter 21, section on the term-structure of rates.

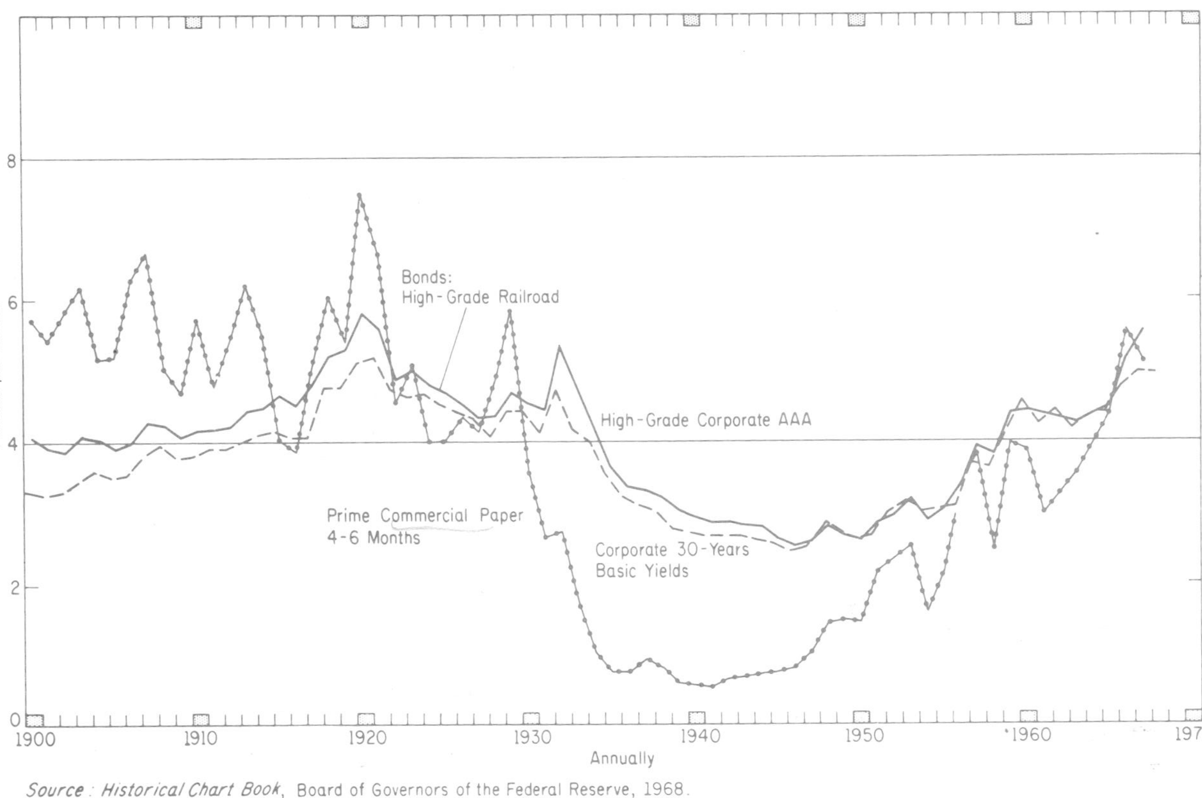

Source: Historical Chart Book, Board of Governors of the Federal Reserve, 1968.

Fig. 5-1. Long- and short-term interest rates.

tions are confined primarily to the long-term markets may not switch to short-term obligations should short-term rates rise relatively to long-term rates. Moreover, because of the nature of the credit needs of borrowers, they may not move easily between the money market and the capital market. It is true that business firms can borrow short-term funds to finance their medium and long-term credit requirements, but the risks and inconveniences involved in such practice may discourage them from switching freely between the two markets. Conversely, to borrow long-term funds to finance short-term credit needs may be too costly.

SUMMARY

Credit instruments, depending upon their maturities, are either traded in the money market or the capital market. The money market is concerned with dealings in short-term, liquid, low-risk obligations. A developed money market is an integration of several submarkets, and in each submarket, arrangements for the issuance and redemption of the obligations traded therein are specialized. The capital market represents the complex of arrangements for the issuance and trading of long-term securities. Borrowing in the money market is mostly for the adjustment of liquidity needs, whereas borrowing in the capital market is largely for capital investment purposes.

There are large numbers of institutions which actively participate in the money and capital markets. Of these institutions, commercial banks, and such financial institutions as savings banks and savings and loan associations, are predominantly lenders, whereas the government and business corporations are predominantly borrowers.

The prices of securities traded in the money market and capital market and the structure of short- and long-term money rates are determined by supply and demand which reflect, among other things, the income and liquidity preferences of the buyers, and the liquidity and credit requirements of the sellers. The structures of money rates changes with changing market conditions. Changes in the structure of rates in the money and capital markets tend to be in the same direction; this reflects the shiftability of funds between the various sectors of these markets.

PROBLEMS

1. Define money and capital markets. Is the definition of these markets largely a matter of analytical convenience? Why or why not? What are the purposes of borrowing in these markets? Why are they referred to as impersonal markets?

2. What are the characteristics of a highly developed money market? Describe some of the major subdivisions of the New York money market.

3. What is an off-board market? What is an organized exchange? What kinds of securities are permitted to be traded in the organized exchange? Is trading in

the organized exchange subject to control and supervision? What is the agency responsible for the supervision of practices in organized exchanges?

4. What is the instrument of major importance in the money market? What accounts for the growth of its relative importance?

5. What is the bankers' acceptance market? Why are bankers' acceptances particularly attractive to foreign banks?

6. What are the major participants in the money and capital markets? What are the sources of funds in these markets? Why is the direct participation of individuals in these markets relatively not important?

7. What are the relationships between short- and long-term money rates? Why are long-term rates normally higher than short-term rates? What accounts for the sympathetic movement of the structure of money rates?

part II

COMMERCIAL BANKING

chapter 6

Commercial Banking Operations: Sources of Funds

There are several types of banks in operation—commercial banks, savings banks, and investment "banks." We are concerned only with the operations of commercial banks. The Amercian commercial banking system is composed of more than 13,500 banks, operating more than 20,000 banking offices throughout the United States. They vary greatly in size. Some banks, especially banks in rural areas and small business communities, are very small—with assets of one million dollars or less. Some banks are very large, particularly banks in New York City, Chicago, and the major cities, with assets and deposits of billions of dollars. About three-fourths of them are unit banks, or banks that operate with one office, and the remaining ones are branch banks. Less than half of all commercial banks are members of the Federal Reserve System, but almost all of them are insured by the Federal Deposit Insurance Corporation. Slightly more than one-third of these banks are chartered by the U.S. Government; the remaining are chartered by the banking authorities of individual states.

Commercial banks are distinguished from other financial institutions in that they have the ability to create deposit money through their loan and investment operations. It is this unique ability of commercial banks which makes them institutions of major importance in the nation's monetary and credit system. In this chapter, we shall describe some important functions of commercial banks, their organization and management, and their major sources of funds. Bank assets, the process of money creation, and portfolio management, is discussed in the next three chapters. Chapter 11 is devoted to the discussion of the functions, operations, and the role of nonbank financial intermediaries in the economy.

COMMERCIAL BANK FUNCTIONS

The major functions of commercial banks consist in creating, lending, and transferring money. Commercial banks accept currency and checks from depositors and credit the latter's checking accounts with demand claims. These claims or demand deposits are promises of banks to pay currency on demand. Depositors, in holding demand claims on banks instead of currency, are motivated by several considerations. In the first place, they want the safety, convenience, and prestige that go with bank accounts. Second, it would probably be easier for depositor-customers to obtain credit accommodations from banks whenever they need additional funds. The third and probably most important consideration is that they want to use the payment facilities of the banking system. Demand deposits, which are the most widely accepted means of payment in the country, are created when currency is received in deposit, loans are granted, or investment securities are purchased by commercial banks.

Commercial banks are the major suppliers of credit in the economy—they are predominant lenders to consumers, commercial and industrial firms, as well as to the government. The money-creating and lending functions of commercial banks are closely intertwined. It is in the process of lending and investing that banks create deposit money. The importance of the credit function of commercial banks is indicated by the volume of loans and securities held by banks in relation to those of other financial institutions. In late July 1968, for example, the loans and securities held by commercial banks amounted to $376 billion, as compared with $136 billion of savings and loan associations, $184 billion of life insurance companies, and $67 billion of mutual savings banks. The total assets of the banks—$456 billion—were more than the combined total assets of $402 billion of these other financial intermediaries.

Demand deposits, or "bank money," are transferred by means of checks. Generally, we make payments to others by drawing checks on our checking accounts with banks, ordering them to effect the transfers. When checks are drawn on some banks in payment to customers of other banks, funds are transferred not only between individual depositors but also between individual banks. The payees deposit checks in their banks which collect them from banks on which they are drawn. The drawee banks, in turn, deduct the amounts of checks from the accounts of makers. Commercial banks, together with the Federal Reserve System, provide an efficient mechanism for the clearing and collection of checks. In fact, it is the collection efficiency which promotes the widespread acceptability of demand deposits as means of payment. In addition to the transfer of funds by means of checks, banks also provide the public with other transfer facilities, such as cable transfers and bank money orders.

Apart from these basic functions, commercial banks render a host of other services to their customers. For instance, most large banks operate trust departments which hold trust accounts for individuals. They also provide safey deposit facilities, hold securities and other valuables for safekeeping for their customers, and give them advice on financial matters. Although some of the auxiliary services are rendered by banks to their customers in order to promote customer relations and to attract deposits, they also yield sizable incomes to banks.

Because of the multitude of services performed by banks for their customers and the wide variety of their loan and investment operations, banks are referred to as "financial department stores," a title appearing to be more appropriate than the term "commercial bank," which was applied to these institutions in the past when their operations were confined mostly to short-term, "self-liquidating" commercial loans.

ORGANIZATION AND MANAGEMENT

Bank Incorporation

Banks can be incorporated under state laws or federal laws. Banks which are organized under national laws are referred to as national banks. Banks which are organized under state laws are called state banks. Applications for national bank charters are considered by the office of the Comptroller of the Currency, which is in charge of chartering and supervising national banks. Applications for state bank charters are considered by the superintendent of banks of the respective individual states.

The chartering of a bank, whether a national bank or a state bank, is not a mere formality in the sense that once the organizers satisfy all the legal banking laws and requirements they will be granted a charter. To obtain a charter it is necessary to show that there is a real need for additional banking facilities in the community in which the proposed bank is to operate, and that its management will be in the hands of competent and honest management.

The Balance Sheet

Assume that a group of organizers succeed in securing from the Comptroller of the Currency a charter for a national bank, called the Second Bank of Albuquerque. With the charter in hand, they sell 2,000 shares of common stock (the par value of $100 per share) at $120 each. Of the $240,000 received from stockholders, $100,000 is spent in bank building and equipment, $7,200 is used for the paid-in subscription to the capital stock of the district Federal Reserve Bank, equal to 3 percent of the capital and surplus of the new bank, and the remaining $132,800 is held as cash reserve. The initial balance sheet of the Second National Bank of Albuquerque is as follows:

Balance Sheet

Assets		Liabilities	
Cash	$132,800	Capital stock	$200,000
Stock of Federal Reserve Bank	7,200	Surplus: paid-in	40,000
Bank building and equipment	100,000		
Total assets.	$240,000	Total liabilities + capital	$240,000

Assume that a few weeks after the opening celebration of the new bank, attended by the mayor of the city, members of the local chamber of commerce, and a large number of prominent local businessmen, the bank has received $1,500,000 of demand deposits and $800,000 in savings deposits from the public, on which the bank has lavished a large quantity of free souvenirs. Demand depositors are provided with books of checks with which they can order the bank to make payments. Savings depositors are provided with passbooks, to be presented to the bank's savings department for deposits or for cash withdrawals. The bank has a total cash reserve of $2,432,000, of which $2,300,000 has been provided by customers and $132,800 is the remainder of capital funds subscribed by shareholders. This enables the bank to create demand deposits and make loans and investments. Suppose that the bank keeps $50,000 on deposit with other commercial banks and $200,000 with the Federal Reserve Bank, grants $1,500,000 of loans to local businesses and individuals and purchases $532,800 of government securities and other short-term obligations. Just as the receipts of demand and savings deposits of the bank cause the cash reserves of other banks in the area to deplete, its loans and investments result in losses of reserves consequent upon the checking out of loan proceeds by borrowers or the sale proceeds by sellers of investment securities. Assume that following our bank loans and investments, it loses $2,032,800 of reserves to other banks. The balance sheet of the bank is then as shown.

Balance Sheet

Assets			Liabilities	
Cash and due from banks		$400,000	Demand deposits	$1,500,000
Vault cash	150,000		Savings deposits	800,000
Reserve balance at Federal Reserve Bank	200,000		Capital accounts:	
Balances from banks	50,000		Capital stock	200,000
			Surplus: paid-in	40,000
Loans		$1,500,000		
Investments		532,800		
Stock of Federal Reserve Bank		7,200		
Bank premises		100,000		
Total assets		$2,540,000	Total Liabilities and capital	$2,540,000

Assume that at the end of the year the total deposits of our bank have remained unchanged and it has earned a gross income of $150,000, derived mostly from interest receipts on loans and investments and service charges. Of this amount, $100,000 has been used to cover the bank's expenses–interest on savings deposits, and wages and salaries of bank officers and employees. The bank is left with a net profit of $50,000. This amount of net income has been held by the bank as retained earnings, of which $20,000 has been transferred to the surplus account and $30,000 held in the undivided-profits account. No dividend has been declared since the net earnings are needed by the bank to build up its capital account. The bank's total assets increase by the same amount, reflected in the increase in the stock of the Federal Reserve Bank by $600 (3 percent of the increased surplus account of $20,000) and in the investment account of $69,400 (this portion of the net earnings is assumed to have been invested in government securities). The balance sheet of the bank at the end of the year is shown.

Balance Sheet

Assets			Liabilities		
Cash and due from banks		$400,000	Demand deposits		$1,500,000
Vault cash	150,000		Savings deposits		800,000
Reserve balance of Federal Reserve Bank	200,000		Capital accounts:		
			Capital Stock		200,000
			Surplus:		60,000
			paid-in	$40,000	60,000
			earned	20,000	
Balances from banks	50,000		Undivided profits		30,000
Loans		$1,500,000			
Investments		582,200			
Stock of Federal Reserve Bank		7,800			
Bank Premises		100,000			
Total assets		$2,590,000	Total liabilities + capital accounts . .		$2,590,000

The items in this hypothetical balance sheet are the major accounts which appear in the statements of condition of all commercial banks, large as well as small. However, in addition to these major accounts, we can find in the balance sheet of a large bank which engages in the acceptance business such items as "customer's acceptance liabilities," on the asset side, and "acceptances outstanding," on the liability side. Acceptances outstanding show the value of bills of exchange accepted by a bank in behalf of its customers and payable to those who draw them when they come due. "Customers' acceptance liabilities," on the other hand, represent the claims of a bank on customers in whose behalf it has accepted bills of exchange.

The balance sheet, or statement of condition of a bank, is simply an accounting summary of the various phases of its operations at a given point in time. Unlike the income or profit-and-loss statement, showing the flow of income earned and the expenses incurred during a given period, the balance sheet is a snapshot of the bank's financial situation. The fundamental identity of the balance sheet is:

Assets = Liabilities + Net Worth

The assets represent the value of all that is owned by the bank as a legal entity. Liabilities represent the claims of creditors, and net worth (or capital accounts) represents the residual claims of shareholders on the bank's assets. In the preceding balance sheet of the Second National Bank of Albuquerque, of its total assets of $2,590,000, the depositors have a claim of $2,300,000 and the shareholders have a residual claim of $290,000. In the event of liquidation, after all the claims of creditors are satisfied, what is left goes to the owners. Owing to the nature of their operations, banks prepare statements of condition daily, since the knowledge of the day-to-day changes in their reserve and deposit positions is essential to the conduct of the banking business.

Management

The overall management of a bank is administered by a board of directors elected by stockholders. Members of the board of directors have to be American citizens. They also have to satisfy certain residence requirements, as well as other requirements, before they can be elected. Bank directors are frequently selected from well-known, experienced businessmen or industrialists who would provide bank mangement with professional advice and guidance. They are, however, sometimes chosen from prominent retired government officials who know very little about the banking business. They are elected mostly for the magic of their names, which are expected to attract more depositors, more customers. While the overall administration of a bank is in the hands of the board of directors, its daily operations are carried out by the president, vice-presidents, and other officers appointed by the board of directors. Since banks are institutions which uniquely affect the public interest, they are subject to strict regulations by public authorities. These regulations are aimed primarily at maintaining safe and sound banks. Decisions made by bank directors and officers regarding banking operations have to be formulated within the framework of the rules and regulations established under either federal laws or state laws.

With this brief account of the bank's balance sheet and management, we now proceed to discuss the major sources of funds of commercial banks, mainly, bank deposits and capital funds.

BANK DEPOSITS

Bank deposits are the main source of funds of commercial banks. The total volume of bank deposits depends primarily upon the nation's overall economic condition and the monetary policy of central banking authorities which affect the volume of reserves available to banks for credit and deposit expansion. Bank deposits are made up of two components: demand deposits and time deposits.

Demand Deposits

Creation. Demand deposits constitute about half the total liabilities of commercial banks. They are obligations of the banks to pay currency on demand to holders of checking accounts. A bank creates demand deposits when it receives in deposit currency or checks drawn on other banks or when it makes loans or purchases securities. Demand deposits which are created as a result of the inflow of cash are referred to as "primary" deposits. Those created as a consequence of the loan and investment operations of the bank are called "derivative" deposits.

Let us consider the case of an individual, Mr. X, who pays $1,000 in currency into his checking account with Bank A. Bank A pays for the currency by crediting X's account with $1,000, on which X can draw checks to make payments. The transaction leads to an increase in both the assets and liabilities of the bank. The bank creates a demand claim on itself in exchange for the currency. X, on the other hand, instead of holding $1,000 in currency, which is a claim on the government, exchanges it for a demand claim on the commercial bank, which is also money. The change in the balance sheet of Bank A is as follows:

Balance Sheet

Assets	Liabilities
Cash + 1,000	Demand deposits + 1,000

The transaction increases the volume of commercial bank money. It, however, does not cause the money supply to change immediately. The money supply, we may recall is the sum of currency in circulation and demand deposits held by the public, $M = C + D$; since the increase in demand deposits of $1,000 is offset by an equivalent decrease in currency in circulation; therefore, there is no immediate change in the money supply.

In this example the commercial bank plays a purely passive role in creating demand deposits. It simply reacts to the decision of the customer to hold commercial bank money instead of central bank money (currency). These are primary deposits, created as a result of currency payments into the banking system. The bank, with added reserves, is in a position to grant more loans to its customers or to purchase more securities, and the banking system as a whole, as will be seen, will be able to create a greater volume of deposit money.

Derivative deposits, on the other hand, are created consequent upon the granting of loans or the acquisition of securities by banks. Assume that a bank purchases $10,000 of securities offered by an individual. It pays for the securities by drawing a check against itself, payable to the order of the seller. If the seller is one of the bank's customers, he would deposit the amount of the check in his account. The change in the bank's balance sheet is then as follows:

Balance Sheet

Assets	Liabilities
Investments + 10,000	Demand deposits + 10,000

If the seller is not a depositor of this bank but is a customer of another bank, he would deposit the amount of the check in his bank. The transaction then results in an increase in the assets and liabilities of the seller's bank by $10,000 and a change in the composition of the buying bank's assets.

Balance Sheet

A	Buying bank	L	A	Seller's Bank	L
Cash − 10,000 Securities + 10,000			Cash + 10,000		Demand deposits + 10,000

There is a transfer of cash reserves from the buying bank to the seller's bank. Although the volume of central bank money in the banking system as a whole remains the same, the gain or loss of reserves of individual banks as a result of their daily operations presents important problems regarding banking management. The bank which gains cash reserves is in a position to expand credit and deposits. The bank which loses reserves, on the other hand, may have to call back loans or reduce investments—should the decrease in reserves cause it to be deficient in required reserves.

Let us consider the case of a bank which grants a loan of $10,000 to a customer against the latter's promissory note. The account of the borrower is then credited with the amount of the loan. In the balance sheet of the lending bank, both assets and demand liabilities increase by $10,000. In the last two examples, the money supply increases immediately by $10,000, as the increase

Balance Sheet

Assets	Liabilities
Loans + 10,000	Demand deposits + 10,000

in deposit money is not offset by any change in currency in circulation. These are derivative deposits. It is the bank which makes the decision whether to create deposit money to pay for the note or securities. The bank is obviously a dealer in debts, trading claims on itself (demand deposits) for the income yielding claims of others. The bank has "monetized" debts, as the acquisition of these earning assets results in the creation of demand deposits, which are money. The creation of derivative deposits therefore follows the monetization of nonmonetary assets.

As demand deposits are created following the receipt of currency or checks by banks or their loan and investment operations, they are destroyed as a result of currency withdrawals, loan repayments, or reduction in investment. When Mr. X withdraws $1,000 in currency from his Bank A, demand deposits decrease by the same amount:

Balance Sheet

Assets	Liabilities
Cash - 1,000	Demand deposits - 1,000

Note that this case, like the case of currency deposit, does not cause any immediate change in the money supply. The decrease in demand deposits of $1,000 is offset by an equivalent increase in currency in circulation. By the same token, the repayment of a loan by a customer also reduces demand deposits and the volume of loans of the bank. This case, however, unlike the previous example, leads to a decrease in the supply of money.

Assets	Liabilities
Loans - 1,000	Demand deposits - 1,000

Ownership. Demand deposits are held by individuals, nonfinancial corporations, the Treasury, financial institutions, state and local governments, and so on. Figure 6-1 shows the growth of demand deposits in insured commercial banks and major holders for the 1959-68 period. As can be seen, the bulk of demand deposits is held by individuals, partnerships, and corporations.

Demand deposits are held primarily as working balances. Some demand balances, however, have the nature of time balances in that transactions in relation to these accounts are few and irregular. Demand balances held by financial institutions and business enterprises are most active, and are subject to much wider fluctuations. Deposits or withdrawals by this class of depositors are usually in large amounts. Balances held by individuals, on the other hand, are more or less stable. Balances held by the Treasury with commercial banks, referred to as "tax and loan accounts," do not serve as working balances. Payments by the Treasury are made by checks drawn on its accounts with the Federal Reserve Banks, not on its accounts with commercial banks. To increase its deposits with the Federal Reserve Banks, the Treasury may direct the former to transfer funds from its accounts with the commercial banks to its accounts

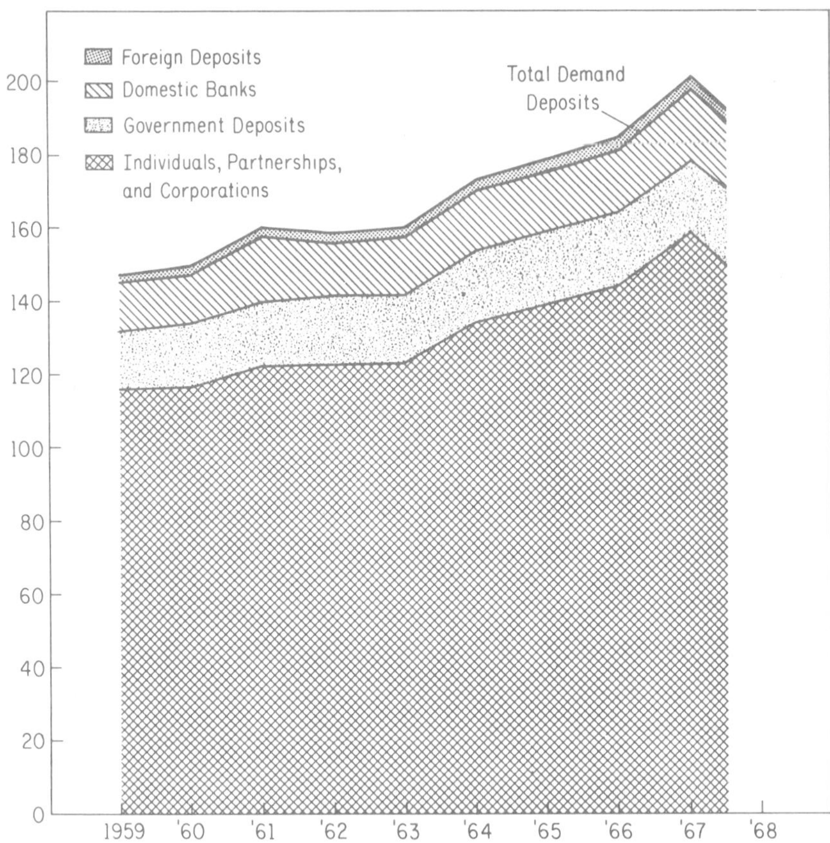

Source: Annual Reports, FDIC, 1959–67, and *Report of Call,* FDIC, No. 82, 1968.

Fig. 6-1. Major holders of demand deposits in insured commercial banks, 1959–1968 (billions of dollars).

with the Federal Reserve Banks. The latter effect the transfer by simply crediting the specified amounts to the accounts of the Treasury and debiting them to the reserve accounts of member banks. This will result in losses of reserves by the banks, which are subject to such transfers. When payments are made by the Treasury, deposits will flow back to the banking system. It is unlikely that banks which are subject to such losses would receive all these deposits in the return flow. In order to minimize adverse effects of withdrawals of funds by the Treasury, banks are usually given advance notice by the Treasury regarding eventual transfers of deposits so that they may have enough time to adjust their reserve positions.

Depositors receive monthly statements from their banks showing the volume of transactions on, and the balances of, their accounts. In terms of the Banking Act of 1933, interest payments on demand deposits are prohibited, as this practice may lead to unsound competition between banks and unsound banking practices which may have to be used by banks to make up for interest costs on demand deposits. In order to attract deposits, commercial banks, instead, use "nonprice" competitive devices, such as greater advertising efforts, more imposing bank buildings, the appointment of persons of reputation as members of boards of directors, better services, and contributions to public services in the community in which they are located. The granting of credit to depositors with specified minimum balances is another device used by commercial banks to attract deposits. Suppose that the minimum balance required is $300 and a depositor has a balance of $700 at the time the monthly statement is prepared; he will be given a credit of, say, $0.25 per $100 balance, a total of $1.75 which is deducted from maintenance and service charges. This can be considered as a form of *de facto* interest payment. But, it is to be noted that should the amount of credit thus given be greater than the maintenance and service charges, the excess could not be credited to the account of the depositor.

Time Deposits

These represent another major source of funds of commercial banks. The growth of time deposits in insured commercial banks and major holders during 1959-68 are indicated in Fig. 6-2. Like demand deposits, the bulk of time deposits is also held by individuals, partnerships, and corporations. Time deposits consist of savings deposits, time accounts, and certificates of deposits. Savings deposits are represented by savings books. They are held by individuals and nonprofit organizations for savings purposes or as liquidity reserves which can be quickly converted into cash when such a need arises. In principle, savings deposits are withdrawable upon advance notice on the part of depositors. But, in practice, this option is usually waived by commercial banks, and holders of savings accounts can withdraw their funds by simply presenting their savings books and withdrawal slips. Savings deposits constitute the bulk of banks' total time deposits.

Business firms, which are not permitted to hold regular savings deposits, may hold time accounts, evidenced by negotiable or nonnegotiable certificates of deposit. As we have mentioned, certificates of time deposits are banks' promises to pay to holders given sums of money plus interest at some fixed future date. The maturities of certificates of deposit may vary from 30 days to 90 days, and longer. They are devices used by banks to attract idle funds from individuals and business firms which would otherwise use them for the acquisition of Treasury bills and other money market obligations. Certificates of deposit are issued in large denominations: $500,000 and $1 million or more by money-market banks, and $100,000 or less by smaller banks. The offering of negotiable certificates of deposit by New York money market banks since 1961 and the subsequent development of secondary markets for these certificates have made them money-market instruments of major importance.

Interest rates paid by member banks on time deposits are subject to maxi-

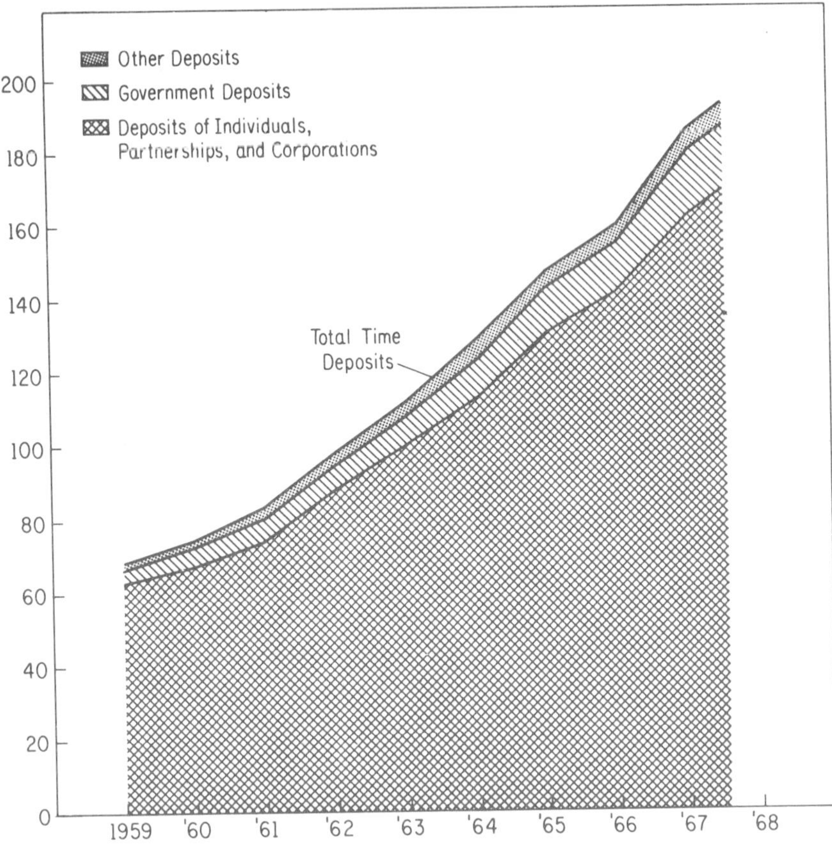

Source: Annual Reports, FDIC 1959–61, and *Report of Call*, FDIC, No. 82, 1968.

Fig. 6-2. Major holders of time deposits in insured commercial banks, 1959–1968 (billions of dollars).

mum limits determined by the Board of Governors of the Federal Reserve System. Maximum rates payable by insured nonmember state banks, on the other hand, are fixed by the Federal Deposit Insurance Corporation. Table 6-1 shows the maximum rates which member banks have been allowed to pay on savings and time deposits. While commercial banks compete for "cash deposits" in checking accounts, they compete not only between themselves but with other financial institutions such as mutual savings banks and savings and loan associations for savings funds. Since the above two federal agencies have from time to time raised the maximum rates, commercial banks have been able to pay on time deposits rates which have been competitive with rates paid by mutual savings banks on savings deposits, rates paid by savings and loan associations on savings and loan "shares," and rates on money market obligations. It is the relatively

TABLE 6-1
Maximum Interest Rates Payable on Savings and Time Deposits
(per cent per annum)

Rates January 1, 1962–July 19, 1966

Type of Deposit	Effective Date			
	Jan. 1 1962	July 17 1963	Nov. 24 1964	Dec. 6 1965
Savings deposits:				
12 months or more	4	4		
Less than 12 months	3½	3½	4	4
Other time deposits:				
12 months or more	4	}		}
6 to 12 months	3½	} 4	4½	}
90 days to 6 months	3½	}		} 5½
Less than 90 days	1	1	4	}

Rates Beginning July 20, 1966

Type of Deposit	Effective Date		
	July 20 1966	Sept. 26 1966	April 1 1968
Savings Deposits:	4	4	4
Other time deposits:			
Multiple maturity*			
90 days or more	5	5	5
Less than 90 days	4	4	4
Single maturity:			
Less than $100,000	5½	5	5
$100,000 or more	}		
30 to 59 days	}		5½
60 to 89 days	} 5½	5½	5¾
90 to 179 days	}		6
180 days and over	}		6¼

Source: *Federal Reserve Bulletin*, 1969.

*Multiple maturity time deposits include deposits that are automatically renewable at maturity without action by the depositor and deposits that are payable after written notice of withdrawal.

attractive rates paid by commercial banks which have partly accounted for the rapid rate of growth of time deposits, as compared with a much slower rate of growth of demand deposits, on which no interest is allowed by law. For example, during the two decades from 1945 to 1965, the volume of time deposits of all banks increased by more than 380 percent, as compared with the increase of demand deposits of only 40 percent.

It should be noted that these maximum rates are only applicable to domestic time deposits. In terms of the Act of Congress of July 1965, amending Regulation Q regarding maximum rates payable on time deposits, commercial banks may pay higher interest rates on foreign time deposits. One of the main purposes of this legislation is to avoid heavy withdrawals of time deposits held by foreign holders, which would result in heavier deficits in our international payments and greater losses in our gold reserve. As rates paid by domestic banks on foreign deposits are competitive with rates prevailing in other international money-market centers—such as London and Paris—foreign commercial banks, foreign central banks, and governments have more incentives to hold their balances with U.S. banks.

CAPITAL

Structure

The capital account of a bank represents its liability toward its owners. It is made up mostly of capital stock, surplus, and undivided profits. The relative size of a bank's capital funds indicates its ability to absorb losses resulting from decreases in asset values. The capital account or net worth of a bank is a residual item of its balance sheet. Given its liabilities to depositors and other general creditors, any increase in the value of its assets results in a corresponding increase in the size of its net worth. Likewise, a decrease in asset value reflects an equivalent decrease in the value of the capital account. So long as losses do not exceed the sum of all the capital accounts of a bank, its depositors are fully protected. A bank's capital funds, therefore, constitute a "cushion" on which depositors can fall in periods of financial stress.

The capital stock account of a bank consists of the par value paid in by its stockholders when it was organized and additional increases which may be made by the issuance of new shares or by a declaration of stock dividends (dividends paid in the form of additional shares). The establishment of a bank requires minimum capital which varies according to the location as well as to the class of bank. The minimum capital required for a national bank is $50,000 in places whose total population is up to 6,000, $100,000 where the population is from 6,000 to 50,000, and $200,000 where the population is over 50,000. The capital stock of a bank is impaired when the value of its net worth is smaller than the par value of all shares outstanding. This obviously can take place only when other accounts (such as surplus and undivided profits) all vanish. A national bank with impaired capital is required to restore impairment in capital by assessment upon the shareholders pro rata for the amount of common stocks held by each. This is referred to as the "assessment liability" of shareholders. A bank which fails to remove the deficiency in capital stock after a stated period may be placed under receivership and liquidated.

The surplus account consists of two components: paid-in surplus and earned surplus. Paid-in surplus represents the excess over par value of shares sold by a bank. For example, when a bank sells 2,000 shares of common stock with a par value of $100 each at a 50 percent premium, its capital stock is $200,000 and its paid-in surplus is $100,000. In addition to minimum capital requirements mentioned above, in order to start their operations, national banks are required to have a paid-in surplus equal to 20 percent of their capital stock. Earned surplus, on the other hand, represents sums transferred by banks from their undivided profits account to the surplus account.

The undivided profits account represents the part of a bank's earnings which is not paid out as dividends to shareholders. Until its surplus account is built up to 100 percent of its common capital, no dividends may be declared by a national bank. In the above example, the bank has to transfer earnings to the surplus account until the latter increases by another $100,000 before dividends can be paid. The sum of bank's capital stock, surplus, and undivided profits represents the bulk of their total capital funds, as indicated in Table 6-2.

TABLE 6-2
Capital Accounts of All Insured Banks
(in millions of dollars)

Type of Accounts	December 30, 1961		December 31, 1964		December 31, 1967	
	Amount	Percent of Total	Amount	Percent of Total	Amount	Percent of Total
Capital notes, preferred stock, and debentures	37	0.1	853	2.7	2,071	6.1
Capital stock	6,585	25.9	7,887	25.3	9,254	27.2
Surplus	13,068	51.5	15,552	50.0	14,983	44.1
Undivided profits	4,871	19.2	5,873	19.0	6,611	19.4
Reserves	842	3.3	1,004	3.0	1,087	3.2
Total	25,403	100	31,169	100	34,006	100

Source: FDIC, *Annual Report*, 1965–1967.

The reserve account of the banks' capital consists of funds set aside for special purposes. This account is made up of several components, such as reserves for contingencies, reserves for dividends, and reserves for losses on loans. Reserves for contingencies are funds set aside by banks to meet such liabilities as those arising from the default of obligations for which they are contingently liable. Reserves for dividends represent amounts to be used for the payment of stock dividends or cash dividends on common and preferred stock not yet declared. "Reserves for losses," or "valuation reserves," are amounts set up on specific assets or groups of assets for possible losses in their values.

It is true that the separation of such accounts as undivided profits and reserves for losses are merely different ways by which the same values on the books of the banks are presented. It is useful in that it helps avoid overstating profits, which may lead to more pressure from shareholders and boards of directors for unduly high rates of dividend payments.

In addition to these capital funds which may be referred to as "owned capital," commercial banks also use "borrowed capital" in the form of capital notes and debentures. This type of capital, as indicated in Table 6-2, represents a very small percentage of total banks' capital funds. It shows a rising trend, however, from slightly more than 0.1 percent in 1961 to almost 3 percent at the end of 1964, and 6 percent in December 1967.

The Problem of Capital "Adequacy"

The capital funds of a bank, as noted earlier, serve as a protective margin of safety to depositors. But how much capital is "adequate" for this purpose and for safe banking operations? This problem of capital adequacy is a difficult one. It is determined primarily by rule of thumb and by banking experience. A rough indicator of the degree of capital adequacy is the ratio of deposits to capital funds which relates the number of dollars of deposit to the dollar of capital. The ratio of 10 to 1 was the popular guideline until the 1930's. Without additional information on the composition and liquidity structure of a bank's assets and investment portfolio, little is revealed by this ratio, however. A bank with a high ratio does not necessarily mean that its capital is more adequate and its operations safer than those of another bank with a relatively lower ratio. Since the relative size of a bank's capital funds indicate its ability to absorb asset losses, another measurement of the "capital cushion" is the ratio of capital funds to total assets. Again, without information on the structure of banks' assets, the ratio sheds little light on the adequacy of its capital. A bank with a low ratio may nevertheless offer more adequate capital protection than does another one with a higher ratio, if a greater proportion of the latter's loans represents substandard and poor loans.

Apparently, the capital requirements of a bank have to be related to various classes of assets. Such assets as cash, balances due from banks, U.S. Government securities, such as Treasury bills and other short-term Treasury notes, hardly require any capital funds at all. Other money market obligations, long-term U.S. Government securities, and adequately secured loans would call for less capital requirements than high-risk assets such as private long-term obligations, substandard loans, stocks, and fixed assets. Thus another raw but better indicator of the adequacy of the capital cushion is the ratio of capital funds to risk assets. Risk assets represent the difference between total assets and the sum of cash assets and U.S. Government securities. The greater the value of the ratio, the greater is supposed to be the ability of the bank to absorb asset losses. During the 1935-67 period, this ratio for all commercial banks was declining from 27 to 10.9 percent. So were the ratios of capital to deposits and capital to total assets, which decreased from 16 and 14 percent to 8.5 and 7.5 percent, respectively. This declining trend was accounted for by the fact that the rate of growth of bank deposits and bank assets was much faster than the rate of growth of capital funds. For example, in 1960-68, total assets and total deposits increased by more than 90 percent, whereas capital funds increased by only 75 percent. This seems to indicate a deterioration in the capital position of banks in general. This, however, does not necessarily mean that banking is less safe today than it was during the past decade, or that protection of depositors is less adequate. As we have mentioned, the safety of banking and the protection of depositors not only depend on the relative size of capital funds but also on the quality of bank management, the relative liquidity structure of bank assets, and the structure of deposits, among other things. The development of financial markets which enhances the marketability of financial assets, and hence their liquidity, coupled with banks' holdings of a relatively greater proportion of low-risk assets, would justify lower capital requirements.

Too small a capital cushion, however, may undermine the confidence of depositors—one of the essential elements of successful banking operations. Moreover, banks with low ratios of capital to risk assets may find themselves in difficulty during periods of financial stress. In addition, since the size of capital funds serves as a legal limit for certain types of loans which can be made by banks, the expansion of these loans requires the expansion of capital. For example, the general limit on loans to any one borrower from a national bank is 10 percent of its unimpaired capital stock and surplus. The total volume of conventional real estate mortgage loans is limited to 100 percent of banks' unimpaired capital and surplus. Obviously, banks cannot increase the volume of these loans unless they increase their capital funds.

THE CLEARING AND COLLECTION OF CHECKS

Demand deposits, as we already know, are transferred by means of checks. It is estimated that more than 90 percent of the total volume of transactions in our economy is effected by checks. There are several ways by which checks can be collected. When the maker of a check and the payee are depositors of the same bank, the payment of the check is effected by that bank. But, in a multibank system, a large percentage of checks are drawn on some banks in payment to customers of other banks. Then, depending upon the location of the banks on which checks are drawn (the paying or drawee banks) and that of the banks receiving these checks on deposit (the collecting banks), they can be collected either through the local clearing house, the Federal Reserve Banks, or correspondent banks.

Intrabank Clearing

When a check is drawn by an individual in payment to another individual banking with the same bank, the check is paid by the transfer of deposits from the account of the one who draws to the account of the payee by the bank. Suppose that X draws a check for $1,000 on his account with the Chase Manhattan Bank in payment to Y, who also has an account with the Chase Manhattan Bank. When Y deposits the check in the bank, the latter transfers deposits from X's account to that of Y.

A	Chase Manhattan Bank L
	X's account − 1,000 *Y*'s account + 1,000

Intracity Clearing and Collection

When the makers of checks and the payees bank with different banks located in the same city, the collection of these checks can be effected through the local clearing house. Once a day, or oftener, representatives of banks that are members of the local clearing house meet and exchange checks received in deposit by each on other banks. Claims of banks against each other are then offset or "cleared," and the net balances due to each are settled. A bank has a clearing surplus when the total value of checks it receives in deposit is greater than the value of checks drawn on it in favor of other banks. It has a deficit balance when the value of checks deposited with it is smaller than the value of checks drawn on it and deposited with other banks. Net clearing balances are settled by credits and debits on the books of the clearing house. In Reserve Bank cities, the settlement of balances is effected by the Federal Reserve Bank of the district which, upon receipt of a list of clearing balances due between banks from the clearing house, credits the reserve accounts of banks with favorable clearing balances and debits the accounts of banks with clearing deficits. The table shows hypothetical clearing balances between four banks. Bank A and D

Hypothetical Clearing House Balances

Bank	Value of Checks Received in Deposit	Value of Checks Drawn on Each Bank in Favor of Others	Clearing Balances
A	+ $65,000	− $51,000	+ $14,000
B	+ $70,000	− $74,000	− $4,000
C	+ $74,000	− $90,000	− $16,000
D	+ $76,000	− $70,000	+ $6,000

have surplus clearing balances of $14,000 and $6,000 respectively. Their reserve balances with the Federal Reserve Bank increase by these amounts. Banks B and C, on the other hand, have unfavorable clearing balances of $4,000 and $16,000. Their reserve balances with the Federal Reserve Bank decrease accordingly, as shown by the following balance sheet.

A	Balance Sheet of the Federal Reserve Bank	L
		Balances of A + 14,000
		Balances of B - 4,000
		Balances of C - 16,000
		Balances of D + 6,000

The example indicates that the existence of clearing house facilities helps minimize the cash payments between banks. Although the total value of checks drawn amounts to $570,000, the amount of reserves which actually changes hands between the banks for the settlement of clearing balances is only $20,000.

In a city where there is no clearing house, bank representatives meet at a local bank to exchange checks and net balances due to each other; these are paid by drawing on their balances with the Federal Reserve Bank of the district, or its branch, and on their balances with correspondent banks.

Intradistrict Collection

When the drawee banks and collecting banks are located in different cities in the same reserve district, checks can be collected through the District Federal Reserve Bank. Banks which deposit checks with the Federal Reserve Bank receive credit in their reserve accounts. The Federal Reserve Bank sends the checks to the drawee banks for payment and charge the amounts to their reserve balances. Suppose Mr. X at Lubbock draws a check for $1000 on his Lubbock bank in payment to Mr. Y, in Dallas. Mr. Y deposits the check with his Dallas bank. The Dallas bank credits the checking account of Mr. Y and sends the check to the Federal Reserve Bank of Dallas. The Reserve Bank of Dallas credits the reserve account of the Dallas bank, sends the check to the Lubbock bank, and debits its reserve balance the same amount. The Lubbock bank, upon receiving the check from the Federal Reserve Bank of Dallas, deducts the amount of the check from X's checking account. The balance sheet changes of the Reserve Bank of Dallas, and the Lubbock bank are as shown.

A	Dallas Federal Reserve Bank	L
		Reserve balance of Dallas Bank + 1,000
		Balance of Lubbock Bank - 1,000

A	Dallas Bank	L
Reserve balance at Dallas Reserve Bank +1,000		Y's checking account +1,000

A	Lubbock Bank	L
Reserve balance at Dallas Reserve Bank - 1,000		X's checking account - 1,000

Interdistrict Collection

When the depositing banks and drawee banks are located in different Federal Reserve Districts, checks are collected through the twelve Federal Reserve Banks and the Inter-District Settlement Fund, which serves as a clearing house for the Federal Reserve Banks. Suppose that Mr. X draws a check for $10,000 on his New York bank in payment to Mr. Y, who banks with a Chicago bank. Mr. Y deposits the check with his bank. The Chicago bank credits the amount of the check to Y's account, and sends it to the Federal Reserve Bank of Chicago for collection. The Reserve Bank of Chicago sends the check to the Federal Reserve Bank of New York and credits the reserve account of the Chicago bank. The Reserve Bank of New York in turn sends the check to the New York bank, the drawee bank, and debits the latter's reserve account. The New York bank then debits the amount of the check to Mr. X's account and eventually sends the canceled check to him. The settlement of balances between the Federal Reserve Banks is effected by the Inter-District Settlement Fund. The Fund is a pool of gold certificate credits held by the Treasury for the Federal Reserve Banks.

Each day the Federal Reserve Banks inform the Fund of the net balances due to each other as a result of the national collection of checks. Positive balances are added to, and negative balances subtracted from, the accounts of the Federal Reserve Banks with the fund, which is administered by the Board of Governors of the Federal Reserve. In our example, the Federal Reserve Bank of Chicago is a creditor to the Federal Reserve Bank of New York and its account with the Fund is credited, and that of the Reserve Bank of New York is debited.

Correspondent Collection

Not all out-of-town checks are collected through the Federal Reserve Banks. They can also be collected through correspondent banks. This collection process is sometimes faster and more convenient. For instance, a bank in Phoenix, Arizona, can collect checks drawn on banks in San Francisco by sending them to its San Francisco correspondent, say, the Second San Francisco National. The latter will credit the account of the Phoenix bank and collect from other San Francisco banks through the local clearing house. Through correspondent banks, nonmember banks can participate indirectly in the collection facilities of the Federal Reserve by depositing checks drawn on out-of-town banks with their reserve city and other member banks which, in turn, collect these checks through the Federal Reserve Banks. (State nonmember banks can also benefit directly from the collection facilities of the Federal Reserve by agreeing to hold "clearing balances" with the Federal Reserve Banks and to pay the face values of checks presented to them for collection.) Checks drawn on nonpar banks, it should be noted, cannot be collected through the Federal Reserve System. They have to be collected through correspondent banks. Nonpar banks are those banks which do not pay the face values of checks drawn on them. The difference between the face value of a check presented to these banks for collection and the amount remitted is referred to as "exchange charge." These banks settle their balances with other banks by drawing on their accounts with correspondent banks. They are mostly banks located in rural areas where the absence of banking competition enables them to impose the exchange charge. The number of nonpar banks represents a small fraction of commercial banks operating in the country. For instance, in December 1965, of 13,804 banks, 12,312 were parbanks, and 1,492 were nonpar banks. The par collection requirement for membership in the Federal Reserve, among other things, is probably one of the important deterrents for these banks to join the system, since the exchange charges constitute a sizeable portion of their earnings.

SUMMARY

Commercial banks are different from other financial institutions in that they have the ability to create money. Creating, lending, and transferring money are among the important functions performed by commercial banks. Deposits constitute the major source of funds of commercial banks. They are made up of demand deposits and time deposits. Demand deposits are bank money. They are convertible into currency (central bank money and Treasury money) on demand at the discretion of depositors. Demand deposits are created when banks receive currency in deposit or when they make loans or purchase securities. They are destroyed when currency is withdrawn by depositors and loans are repaid to the banks by borrowers. Demand deposits are transferred by means of checks. Checks are cleared and collected either through local banks, local clearing houses, the Federal Reserve System, or the system of banking correspondence.

Time deposits consist mostly of regular savings deposits and certificates of time deposits. In principle, savings deposits are withdrawable only after advance notice. In practice, however, they are withdrawable upon presentation of passbooks. Certificates of time deposits are convertible into cash only at maturity.

Banks are not allowed to pay interest on demand deposits. They can pay interest on time deposits, but the rates payable on time deposits by member banks are subject to maximum limits determined by the Board of Governors of the Federal Reserve.

Demand deposits are held by the public mostly as working balances. Time deposits, on the other hand, are held mostly for savings purposes or as reserves which could be used for future liquidity requirements.

The capital account of the banks represents the residual claims of the owners on the bank's assets. It is composed of several components, such as capital notes and debentures, capital stock, surplus, and undivided profits. The capital account is a protective margin of safety for depositors. It serves as a cushion to absorb losses in the value of bank assets. How much capital is adequate is rather difficult to determine. It depends upon the experiences of the individual banks, the composition of their liabilities, and the liquidity structure of their assets, among other things.

PROBLEMS

1. What are the major functions of commercial banks? Why are they called "department stores of finances?" Explain.

2. What is the difference between primary deposits and derivative deposits? Use examples to illustrate the difference.

3. Commercial banks are dealers in debts. Do you agree? Why or why not? Use examples to illustrate your answers.

4. What is the difference between demand and time deposits? Are all customers of commercial banks permitted to hold savings deposits? What are factors which, you believe, account for the rapid rate of growth of time deposits as compared with demand deposits? Are rates on interest payable by commercial banks on time deposits subject to control? If so, which government agencies control them?

5. Explain briefly: capital stock; paid-in surplus; earned surplus; undivided profits; reserves for contingencies; reserves for dividends; reserves for loan losses.

6. What do you understand "capital adequacy" to mean?

7. Show the following transactions in terms of balance-sheet changes of the parties involved (use a balance sheet for each transaction).

(a) Bank A purchases $1,000 of securities from Mr. X, a customer.
(b) Bank B lends $1,000 to Mr. Y.
(c) Mr. Z withdraws $1,000 in currency from Bank C.
(d) Bank D (a member bank) borrows $1 million from the Federal Reserve Bank.
(e) Bank E received $1,000 in currency on deposit from Mr. R.
(f) Bank F sells $10,000 of governement securities to the Federal Reserve Bank.
(g) Mr. M repays a $1,000 loan to Bank *G*
(h) Mr. N opens a $1,000 savings account with Bank *H*

8. Mr. *X* draws a check for $1,000 on his account with the Houston Bank (a member bank) in payment to Mr. *Y* in Dallas. Mr. *Y* banks with the Dallas Third National Bank. (These two banks belong to the Dallas Federal Reserve District.) Show the balance sheet changes of the Houston Bank, the Dallas Bank, and the Dallas Federal Reserve Bank when the collection process is completed.

9. Mr. *Z* in Philadelphia, makes a check for $10,000 on the Philadelphia Fourth National Bank in payment to Mr. *R* in Chicago. *R* banks with the Chicago Third National. Show the balance sheet changes of all parties involved in the collection of the check.

10. The following items appeared on the balance sheet of the ABC National Bank on December 31, 1966 (in thousands of dollars).

Acceptances Outstanding	500
Balance with Federal Reserve Bank	19,000
Balances with Other Banks	1,500
Bank Premises and Equipment	8,000
Business and Commerical Loans	80,460
Customers' Acceptance Liability	700

Common Stock	14,000
Consumer and Real Estate Loans	30,000
Demand Deposits	100,000
Obligations of State and Local Subdivisions	25,000
Other Assets	6,000
Other Liabilities	2,000
Savings and Time Deposits	90,000
Stock of Federal Reserve Bank	840
Surplus	14,000
Undivided Profits	2,000
U.S. Government Securities	47,000
Vault Cash	4,000

Arrange these items into a proper balance sheet.

chapter 7

Commercial Banking Operations: Uses of Funds

The composition of the assets of banks show ways in which banks use their funds. Banks have to structure their assets so that they are in a position not only to meet their demand obligations toward depositors but also the liquidity requirements of the community which they serve. To satisfy their own liquidity needs, banks keep part of their assets in the form of cash reserves, which are nonearning assets. On the other hand, they meet the liquidity requirements of the public through their lending and investing operations. Loans and investments are earning assets from which banks derive their income. Changes in the volume and composition of bank assets affect both the composition of output and the level of economic activity.

BANK RESERVES

In the normal course of their operations, some banks gain, and others lose, cash reserves. The losses of cash reserves of a bank may arise from the excess of cash withdrawals over cash deposits, and from the excess of claims by other banks over its claims on them. The loss of reserves resulting from the excess of cash withdrawals over cash deposits represent over-the-counter deficit balances. The loss of reserves resulting from the excess of checks drawn on a bank over the value of checks it receives represent unfavorable clearance balances. To be able to meet adverse over-the-counter balances and clearing balances, banks have to hold cash reserves.

Total Reserves

The sum of all cash reserves available to individual banks to meet currency demands and to settle unfavorable clearing balances represent their total reserves, which consist of vault cash (currency and coin held in their vaults), reserve balances with the Federal Reserve Banks (as in the case of member banks), and demand balances held with other commercial banks. In banks' statements of condition, these items are usually grouped under "cash and due from banks." The relative size of total cash reserves maintained by individual banks is determined primarily by their experiences, the liquidity structure of their assets, the nature of the business community in which they are operating, and the character of bank management, among other things. Banks which are more liquidity minded would hold relatively larger reserves than do banks which are overly income-minded. Banks which hold a relatively large portion of their total assets in the form of liquid assets, such as Treasury bills, certificates and other short-term money market obligations, are in a position to hold a relatively smaller amount of cash reserves, as these assets can be quickly converted into cash should their cash reserves prove insufficient to meet currency withdrawals by depositors.

Required Reserves

Commercial banks which are members of the Federal Reserve System are required to hold minimum legal reserves against their demand and time liabilities. The legal reserve ratios—that is, ratios of required reserves to deposits—vary according to types of member banks and classes of deposits. Thus reserve city banks are required to hold minimum reserves varying from 10 to 22 percent of their net demand deposits (the difference between gross demand deposits and cash items in process of collection and balances with other banks). Country banks are likewise subject to legal reserve ratios, varying from 7 to 14 percent of net demand deposits. With respect to time deposits, the legal reserve ratio is from 3 to 10 percent for both reserve city banks and country banks.[1] Between these upper and lower limits, the effective legal reserve ratios are determined by the Board of Governors of the Federal Reserve System (see Table 7-1). The

TABLE 7-1
Reserve Requirements of Member Banks

Legal Reserve Ratios	Net Demand Deposits (a)				Time Deposits (b) (All Classes of Banks)		
	Reserve City Banks		Country Banks		Savings Deposits	Other Time Deposits	
	Under $5 million	Over $5 million	Under $5 million	Over $5 million		Under $5 million	Over $5 million
Ratios in effect Mar. 31, 1969 . . .	16½	17	12	12½	3	3	6
Minimum	10		7		3	3	3
Maximum.	22		14		10	10	10

Source: *Federal Reserve Bulletin*, 1969.

[1] Prior to September 1966, the maximum limit of the legal reserve ratio for time deposits was 6 percent. The Act of Congress of September 21, 1966 (Public Law 89-597), raised the maximum limit to 10 percent.

minimum legal reserve requirements are computed on the basis of weekly average reserves for both reserve city banks and country banks.

The legal reserve ratios against the deposit liabilities of state nonmember banks are determined by state banking authorities. They vary from state to state, but the most common ratios are 15 percent for demand deposits and 5 percent for time deposits. In some states, the legal reserve requirements for nonmember banks are as strict as those on members of the Federal Reserve System, but in most states they are less so.

Legally required reserves are more or less immobilized funds. They are available to banks to meet their liquidity needs only to a limited extent. The imposition of minimum legal reserve requirements is therefore not to assure the liquidity of banks, although it was originally so intended; it is primarily a central-bank control device used to affect the volume of banks' excess reserves, hence, their ability to expand credit and deposit money.

Legal Reserves, Excess Reserves, and Free Reserves

Legal reserves are those assets that may count toward meeting Federal Reserve or states reserve requirements. With regard to member banks, legal reserves consist of vault cash and reserve balances held with the Federal Reserve banks.[2] The composition of legal reserves of state nonmember banks vary in various states. In most states, legal reserves of nonmember banks consist of vault cash and balances held with other commercial banks. In some states United States Government securities and sometimes state and local government obligations are also included in the computation of required reserves, in addition to vault cash and demand balances due from banks.

The difference between legal reserves and required reserves is excess reserves. This is an important variable. It indicates the potential lending power of banks. Other things being equal, as will be seen, the greater the volume of excess reserves available to banks, the larger the volume of bank credit and demand deposits which can be created.

While some banks have excess reserves, other banks may be deficient in required reserves and have to borrow to meet minimum reserve requirements. The difference between excess reserves and borrowings at Federal Reserve banks is referred to as "free reserves." This may be either positive or negative. The variation in excess reserves and free reserves is an indicator of changing money market conditions. As shown in Table 7-2, the declining trends in excess reserves and

[2] The reserve balances which each member bank is required to maintain on deposit with the Federal Reserve Bank of its district are prescribed by the Board of Governors of the System. For example, effective as of September 15, 1966, a member bank not in a reserve city was required to maintain reserve balances at the Federal Reserve Bank equal to 4 percent of its savings deposits, plus 4 percent of its other time deposits up to $5 million and 6 percent of such deposits in excess of $5 million, plus 12 percent of its net demand deposits. For a reserve city bank, the ratios were the same for savings and time deposits, but the ratio of reserve balances on deposit with the Federal Reserve Bank to its net demand deposits was higher, 16½ percent.

TABLE 7-2
Legal Reserves, Excess Reserves, Borrowed Reserves and Free Reserves of Member Banks, 1960-1969.
(in millions of dollars)

Year-End	Legal Reserves (1)	Required Reserves (2)	Excess Reserves (3)=(1)-(2)	Borrowings at F.R. Banks (4)	Free Reserves (5)=(3)-(4)
1960	19,283	18,527	756	87	669
1961	20,118	19,550	568	149	419
1962	20,040	19,468	572	304	268
1963	20,746	20,210	536	327	209
1964	21,609	21,198	411	243	168
1965	22,719	22,267	452	454	- 6
1966	23,830	23,438	392	557	-165
1967	25,260	24,915	345	238	107
1968	27,221	26,766	455	765	-310
1969*	27,079	26,776	303	1,249	-946

Source: Federal Reserve Bulletin, 1969. *As of August.

free reserves indicate the tightening reserve and liquidity positions of commercial banks, reflecting the rapid expansion of bank credit to meet the rising credit demands of booming businesses of the 1960's.

Working Reserves

Inasmuch as required reserves are available to banks to meet their liquidity requirements only to a limited extent, banks have to maintain reserves over and above the minimum legal reserve requirements. Bank reserves over and above legally required reserves are referred to as working reserves, which consist of vault cash (which is also part of legal reserves), legal excess reserves, and demand balances held with other commercial banks. Working reserves are usually kept to a minimum necessary for current operations. During periods of declining business activity, however, working reserves may accumulate to above the minimum level as a result of the lack of lending and investing opportunities. These excess balances are not working reserves in the true sense of the term; they are purely idle funds.

Banks need vault cash for their daily cash operations. Since under normal conditions cash withdrawals are more or less offset by cash deposits, the amount of vault cash held by banks is very small—no more than 10 percent of total reserves and slightly more than 1 percent of total deposits. Banks subject to loss of vault cash, as a result of adverse over-the-counter balances, may replenish it by drawing on their balances with the Federal Reserve banks (the case of member banks) or on their balances with correspondent banks (the case of nonmember banks). On the other hand, banks with excess vault cash resulting from favorable over-the-counter balances may use them to replenish their reserve balances with the Federal Reserve Banks or with correspondent banks, to pay off their borrowings from the Federal Reserve banks or to increase their earning assets. The size of vault cash varies from season to season. For example, during Easter and Christmas, banks are expected to increase their currency holdings in anticipation of heavy cash withdrawals.

The amount of time which it would take banks to obtain additional cash from the Federal Reserve banks and correspondent banks is another important factor determining the size of vault cash. Reserve city banks and banks located near their correspondent banks hold relatively smaller vault cash since, should their vault cash be considered inadequate to meet currency demands, they could obtain additional cash very quickly from the Federal Reserve banks or reserve city correspondent banks. Banks located far from Reserve Banks or reserve city correspondent banks hold relatively larger vault cash, since it would require a substantial amount of time to acquire additional cash reserves. This, among other things, accounts for the larger holdings of currency by small country banks, especially banks located in rural areas.

Excess legal reserves held by member banks with the Federal Reserve banks are used mostly in the settlement of unfavorable clearing balances. As we have mentioned, the collection of checks through the Federal Reserve System results in the transfer of reserves from the accounts of banks with adverse clearing balances to the accounts of banks with clearing surpluses.

Demand balances held with other banks are another important component of working reserves. They are also part of the legal reserves of nonmember banks, as noted earlier. The holding of interbank balances serves several purposes. Small country banks have balances with city banks; they can collect checks drawn on banks in cities where their correspondent banks are located by sending checks to them for collection and having their accounts credited. Also, they can effect payments to other banks by simply drawing on balances with their correspondent banks. With these balances, moreover, they can make loans and purchase securities through the facilities of their city correspondent banks, or can participate in their lending and investing operations.

THE MONEY MARKET AND THE ADJUSTMENT OF RESERVES

The adjustment of reserves is very important in commercial banking management. Banks which experience heavy unfavorable over-the-counter balances and adverse clearing balances have to replenish their reserves not only to meet the liquidity requirements of their current operations but also to meet the minimum legal reserve requirements.

The money market, with a great variety of credit instruments traded therein, offers several alternative means by which commercial banks can adjust their reserve positions. Banks which are deficient in required reserves may purchase federal funds, which are excess reserves held by other banks with the Federal

Reserve banks. When the buying and selling banks are located in the same reserve city—for instance, New York—the transaction, which can be arranged through a stock exchange broker, can be effected by an exchange of checks. For example, bank A sells $10 million of federal funds to Bank B for one day at 3½ percent interest. Bank A gives bank B a check for $10 million drawn on its reserve account with the Federal Reserve Bank of New York. Bank B in turn gives bank A a check for $10,000,972 (the amount bought plus $972 interest for one day). B presents the check to the Federal Reserve Bank of New York and receives immediate credit in its reserve account which helps remove the deficiency. The following day, A presents the check to the Clearing House and has its reserve account credited. The reserve account of bank B is at the same time debited. If bank B is located in a different reserve city (say, Chicago) then, after the arrangement is made with bank A, A tells the Federal Reserve Bank of New York to make a wire transfer of $10 million to bank B through the Federal Reserve Bank of Chicago. The reserve account of B with the Reserve Bank of Chicago is credited with the amount, and the reserve account of A with the Reserve Bank of New York is debited. The following day, bank B tells the Federal Reserve Bank of Chicago, to make a wire transfer of $10 million to bank A in New York through the Reserve Bank of New York. Bank A's reserve account with the Reserve Bank of New York is credited, and the reserve account of B with the Reserve Bank of Chicago is debited. Bank B can pay the interest of $972 by either drawing on its reserve balance with the Reserve Bank of Chicago or on its balance with a New York correspondent bank. The check is sent through the mail.

Transactions in federal funds can be disguised in the form of "repurchase agreements," whereby the borrowing banks sell securities to lending banks and agree to repurchase them at the same prices plus interest on a specified date. The payments are effected in federal funds. In the above example, where banks A and B are New York banks, B can sell $10 million of short-term government securities to bank A, which pays for them by drawing on its reserve account with the Federal Reserve Bank of New York. Bank B represents the check to the Reserve Bank and receives immediate credit. Next day, bank B repurchases the securities from A by drawing a check for $10 million plus $972 interest on its reserve account with the New York Reserve Bank. Bank A presents the check to the Reserve Bank. Its reserve account is credited, and that of bank B is debited. One of the advantages of "repurchase agreements" is that the lending banks are not subject to the "ten percent rule" which prohibits a national bank from lending to any one borrower by more than ten percent of its capital and unimpaired surplus. A small bank which desires to lend a substantial amount of federal funds can also avoid the "ten percent rule" by requiring the borrowing bank to secure the loan with short-term government securities. Owing to the inconvenience arising from changing title to securities, federal funds borrowing between large banks are largely straight or unsecured borrowings.

In addition to borrowing federal funds, member banks can obtain additional reserves by borrowing from the Federal Reserve banks. Borrowing from the Federal Reserve banks can be effected in the form of advances or discounts. In the case of discount, member banks sell at a discount eligible paper to the Federal Reserve banks, such as short-term commercial and agricultural paper. Instead of discounting, they can obtain short-term advances from the Federal Reserve banks against their own promissory notes secured by United States Government securities and other acceptable obligations. Banks can also adjust their money positions by selling Treasury bills and other short-term money market obligations.

Any one or any combination of these alternative methods of adjusting reserves can be used by banks. The methods to be used depend upon the duration and extent of the needs for reserves and the relative costs involved. If the duration of such needs is very short, then funds can be obtained at low cost by purchasing federal funds or using repurchase agreements or borrowing from the Federal Reserve banks. But banks which consider borrowing an indication of financial weakness may elect to sell securities for additional reserves, even though the cost involved may be relatively higher than the cost of other alternative devices.

It should be noted that these alternative methods have different effects on the volume of reserves of individual banks and that of the banking system as a whole. For example, the withdrawal of demand balances held with other banks or the purchase of federal funds increase the reserves of the individual banks, but they have no effect on the overall reserve position of the banking system. The increase in reserves of some banks is offset by the decrease in reserves of some other banks. This can be illustrated by the following balance sheet changes resulting from the transaction of federal funds between two member banks A and B, B being the buyer, and A, the seller.

A — Bank B	L
Balances with the Federal Reserve Bank+	Borrowings +

A — Bank A	L
Balances at the Federal Reserve Bank– Loans +	

A — Federal Reserve Bank	L
	Balances of A – Balances of B +

On the other hand, borrowing at the Federal Reserve "discount window" not only increases the reserves of borrowing banks but also the total reserves of the banking system, as indicated by the balance sheet change of bank B borrowing from the Federal Reserve Bank:

A	Bank B	L	A	Federal Reserve Bank	L
Balances with the Federal Reserve Bank +		Borrowings at Federal Reserve Bank +	Loans to member banks +		Balances of B +

The sale of securities by banks may or may not affect the volume of reserves of the individual banks and that of the banking system, depending upon to whom the securities are sold. If the buyers of securities are depositors of the selling banks, there would be no change in their reserves but only decreases in their demand liabilities offset by equivalent decreases in their securities holdings. Although there are no changes in reserves, the decreases in demand deposits would reduce the amounts of required reserves to be met by banks deficient in reserve requirements. If they are not depositors of the selling banks, but are of other banks, then the reserves of the selling banks increase, but there is no change in the aggregate reserves of the system, as the increases in reserves of the selling banks are offset by losses of reserves of other banks as the buyers draw checks on these banks in payment for the securities. If the securities are sold to the Federal Reserve Banks, then both the reserves of the selling banks and the aggregate reserves of the banking system increase.

BANK LOANS

Bank loans and discounts involve the sale of credit by the banks to their customers. The granting of credit is referred to as a "loan" or "discount," depending upon the form of the borrower's note. When the note is interest-bearing, the transaction is a loan; the borrower receives the full amount of the note and promises to repay this amount plus interest at maturity. When the note is not interest-bearing, it is discounted—that is, the interest is deducted in advance from the face value of the note. The transaction is called a discount. When the note is discounted, the effective rate of interest paid by the borrower, as noted earlier, is higher than the nominal rate. For instance, a person borrows $1,000 at 6 percent interest for one year and repays $1,060 at maturity; there is no difference between the nominal and effective rate of interest. When the note of $1,000 is discounted at 6 percent, the borrower receives only $940 of credit and repays $1,000 at maturity. The effective rate of interest is then 6.3 percent, which is higher than the nominal rate.

Bank loans normally constitute the bulk of the earning assets of the banks, and are the major source of their incomes. Figure 7-1 shows the major components of bank loans and their growth during 1959-68. There are several bases for the classification of bank loans. They may be classified in terms of maturity, collateral, or types of borrowers. We shall classify them in terms of major purposes, namely, business loans, consumer loans, real estate loans, and farm loans.

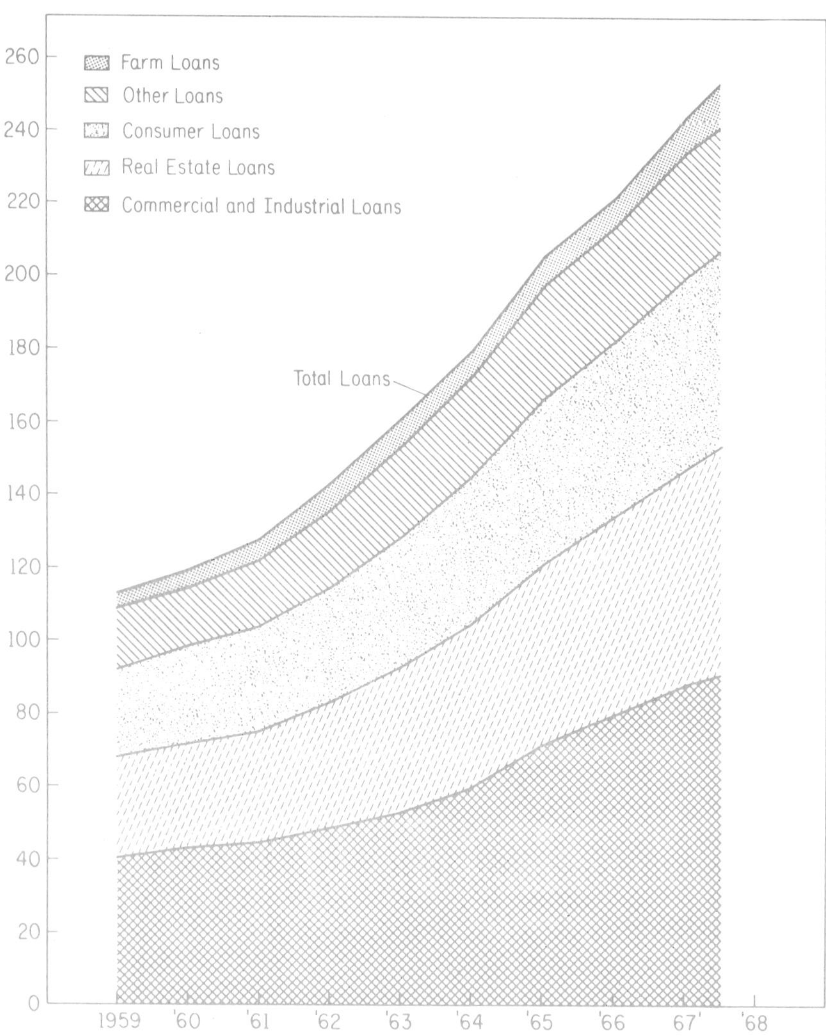

Source: Annual Reports, FDIC, 1959–67, and *Report of Call*, FDIC, No. 84, 1968.

Fig. 7-1. Major components of bank loans, 1959–1968 (billions of dollars).

Business Loans

Commercial banks are one of the most important sources of loans to businesses. Banks make loans to all types of businesses, including among others industrial and commercial firms, public utilities, securities dealers, and other financial institutions. Business loans granted by commercial banks are mostly short- and medium-term in nature.

Short-Term Loans. These are loans granted to businesses with maturities of one year or less. Business firms borrow short-term funds from commercial banks for a variety of purposes, such as to meet their seasonal financial needs or their working capital requirements. For example, a manufacturing firm may need short-term funds for the purchase and processing of unfinished goods and other current expenses before their products are available for sale. Commercial firms such as department stores borrow short-term funds to carry larger stocks of goods in anticipation of greater sales during Easter, Thanksgiving or Christmas seasons. Financial institutions also need short-term funds from commercial banks to finance their current operations. For example, investment banking firms which underwrite securities issued by business enterprises need short-term loans to carry them while they are in process of being distributed to other investors. Government securities dealers need short-term funds to finance securities transactions either for their own accounts or for the accounts of their customers. Construction firms may borrow short-term loans from banks for such current expenses as payment for construction materials, wages and salaries, and so on.

Short-term commercial and productive loans are said to be self-liquidating since the production or commercial operations which necessitate the loans would generate sufficient funds for their repayment. For instance, a store which borrows short-term funds to carry inventories of goods pays off the loan with the sales proceeds of the goods.

Term Loans. Term loans are loans with maturities ranging from more than one year to less than five years. If business firms borrow short-term funds to finance their working capital needs and seasonal financial requirements, they borrow medium-term loans mostly to finance the acquisition of business assets of long durability. The source of funds used for the repayment of these loans are earnings generated by the uses of these assets. Almost all types of businesses borrow term-loans from the commercial banks. Public utilities, and firms producing metals and metal products, coal, petroleum, chemicals and rubber, are the most important customers of the banks with respect to term loans. They alone account for almost half of the total term loans made by commercial banks.

The granting of term loans usually involves one lending bank. When the volume of loans is large, the loan can be made by the participation of a group of banks or by banks and other financial institutions. In terms of dollar amounts, a large portion of term loans is granted to large businesses. But in terms of the number of term loans, a large percentage of the total goes to small businesses. This is accounted for, among other things, by the fact that small business firms do not have adequate internal funds for the purchase of fixed assets and it would be costly or impossible for them to raise intermediate and long-term funds in the capital market through the flotation of stocks and bonds.

Term loans, as noted earlier, are a product of the depression of the early 1930's when firms which were in need of funds to replace their business assets negotiated directly with commercial banks for term loans. Commercial banks at the time had ample idle resources, lending and investing opportunities being inadequate. Term loans are a popular form of borrowing by businesses. Their costs are relatively lower than the cost of alternative financing devices. The terms and conditions of term loans can be "tailored" to suit the needs of both the borrower and lender. They are more flexible than other types of loans. Since the number of lenders involved is small, the terms and conditions of these loans can be modified by either lengthening or shortening of maturities. Since the maturity of term loans involves several years, commercial banks usually protect themselves partly by requiring certain restrictive features in the term-loan agreements, such as the requirement of minimum working capital, the restriction on the amount of earnings which could be paid out as dividends, and limitations on the amount of additional funds which could be borrowed by the borrowing firm.

Most term loans are amortized and call for periodical repayments of both principal and interest, either on a monthly or quarterly basis rather than a lump-sum payment on the maturity date.

Security of Business Loans. The granting of business loans, just like other types of loans, involves investigation by the banks on the character, capacity, and capital of the borrowers. They would look into the records of repayment of past debts by the borrowing businesses, the integrity of their management, their past, current and prospective earnings, their liquidity positions, their capital structures, and especially their potential growth. Unsecured loans are available to business firms with good earnings and loan repayment records. These are mostly large firms which are regular customers of banks for short-term loans as well as term loans. Firms with relatively weak financial conditions or erratic earning records would have to secure their loans.

With regard to short-term business loans, more than 50 percent of the overall total consists of secured loans. Assets used as collateral for loans by commercial and industrial firms are usually accounts receivable, securities, such as stocks and bonds, plant and equipment, real estate, and inventories. The latter could be pledged under trust receipts (documents in terms of which the borrower acts as a trustee to the lender in selling the goods and repaying the loan), factor liens (documents assigning inventories, raw materials, unfinished goods to the lender by the borrower), and warehouse receipts.

In the case of term loans, a higher percentage of total term loans represents secured loans, since the risk involved is relatively greater as a result of their longer maturities. Most secured term loans are granted to small business firms. The assignment of title to plant, equipment and real estate is the most common form of security of term loans.

Sometimes loans are secured not by assets but by comakers and cosigners. A comaker, as noted earlier, is a party involved in the loan agreement and is liable for the whole amount of the loan. A cosigner, on the other hand, is not really a party in the loan but acts as an endorser or guarantor of the loan on behalf of the borrowing firm. The cosigner is usually a larger firm, well known to the lending bank, and who usually holds stocks of the borrowing company.

Consumer Loans

Commercial banks are relatively new in the field of consumer financing. Banks in the past were reluctant in lending to consumers. Such lending was considered to be relatively more of a risk than other types of loans, since consumer loans, unlike business loans, were considered not self-liquidating.

During the depression, commercial banks began to venture in the field of consumer lending as an outlet for their idle funds; lending opportunities to businesses were scarce. Owing to the profitability and relative safety of consumer loans, as they found out, banks participated increasingly in lending to consumers and eventually emerge as the main source of consumer credit.

Consumers borrow both short- and medium-term loans from commercial banks for a variety of purposes, such as the purchase of automobiles, household appliances, home repair and modernization, and for such personal expenditures as vacations and medical expenses. Automobile loans constitute almost half the total of banks' consumer loans. For example, in late 1968, of the total consumer loans of $44 billion, $20 billion represented automobile loans.

On the basis of repayment, consumer credit is divided into installment and noninstallment credit. Installment credit accounts for more then 80 percent of the total. Commercial banks are the most important holders of installment credit. In late 1968 they held 45 percent of the total volume of installment credit, as compared with 21 percent by sales finance companies, 12 percent by credit unions, and 8 percent by consumer finance companies. Banks are also the major holder of noninstallment consumer credit, with a total of more than $7 billion in late 1968 in comparison with slightly more than $1 billion held by other financial institutions, and $1.5 billion by other retail outlets. Noninstallment credit is granted mostly on a short-term basis (less than 12 months), and involves relatively small amounts. Installment loans, especially those incurred for the purchase of automobiles and home repair and modernization, are of longer maturities and involve larger amounts.

Consumer loans may be granted either directly or indirectly. Direct loans are those directly negotiated between the banks and the individual borrowers. Indirect loans, on the other hand, are made through the purchases of paper from dealers of commodities—for example, the purchase of automobile papers from automobile dealers. Consumers who anticipate financial requirements in the future may apply for a "revolving check credit" from the bank. It is a predetermined line of credit on which the borrower, if granted the credit, can draw checks to make payments up to a specified maximum amount. Consumers can also obtain credit in the form of "charge credit account." It is a technique by which banks issue credit cards to a number of selected customers enabling them to charge purchases at stores which have entered into agreements with the banks.

The selling stores present the sales slips to the banks for collection. The latter in turn collects from the holders of credit cards.

In granting consumer credit, the bank is primarily concerned with the character and capacity of the individual borrowers. Their incomes and the types of employment which they have are among important determinants of the maximum amounts of loan which they can borrow.

Interest rates on consumer loans are usually higher than those on other types of loans, since the amounts of loans are relatively small and the handling costs are high.

Real Estate Loans

Real estate loans are those loans granted for the acquisition of real estate, and are secured by either residential and business properties or farm land. A real estate loan is evidenced by a note and a mortgage which is a legal document conditionally transferring the title to the property to the lender or mortgagee as security for the loan. Should the borrower, for some reason or other, default his obligation, the mortgagee could foreclose the mortgaged property to recover the loan. Most real estate mortgage loans are amortized, which calls for repayment of principal and interest in a number of equal monthly payments.

Commercial banks in the past were reluctant to make real estate loans.[3] These loans were considered illiquid, due to their long maturity (10 to 25 years or more), the limited marketability of real estate mortgages as a result of the lack of a secondary market for these credit instruments, the limited saleability of mortgaged properties, and the fact that these loans were repaid in one single payment at maturity. The attitude of banks toward real estate loans, however, was changed later on following the creation of the Federal Housing Administration (FHA) and the Veteran Administration (VA) to insure and guarantee residential mortgage loans; the establishment of the Federal National Mortgage Association (FNMA), for the purpose of providing a secondary market for secured mortgages through regular sales and purchases of these instruments, therefore enhancing their marketability and liquidity; and the introduction of the amortization feature regarding monthly repayments of principal and interest which enable banks to receive a continuous flow of loan repayments. These developments, coupled with the rapid growth of the volume of time deposits whose low rate of turnover made it possible for banks to lengthen the maturities of their loans, enabled them to increase the volume of real estate loans. The growth of the banks' real estate loans was remarkable. During the two decades from 1945 to 1965, real estate mortgages held by member banks increased by 840 percent, from less than $5 billion to almost $47 billion. They constitute an important component of the total assets of the banks, second only to commercial and industrial loans.

[3] National Banks were prohibited from making real estate loans by the National Banking Act. It was not until the late 1920's that restrictions on real estate loans which could be made by national banks were broadly liberalized.

More than 60 percent of real estate loans made by banks consist of residential mortgage loans. For example, in the second quarter of 1965, of the total real estate loans of $47 billion, more than $30 billion represented residential real estate loans. The amount of FHA-insured and VA-guaranteed loans accounted for only 34 percent of total residential loans, and the remaining consisted of conventional real estate loans—that is, loans that are neither insured nor guaranteed. The relatively higher rates of interest on conventional loans, their larger down payments, hence shorter maturities, the informality in granting these loans as compared with the granting of FHA-insured and VA-guaranteed loans, which has to be in conformity with uniform standards, among other things, appear to account for the lion's share of conventional real estate mortgages. Real estate loans made by banks to business firms for the acquisition of business and other properties represent another major component of banks' real estate loans, about 27 percent of total. Real estate loans to farmers for the purchase of farm land and buildings are relatively small—about 6 percent of total.

Farm Loans

The volume of loans to farmers is relatively small, about 4 percent of total bank loans. Farm loans (exclusive of loans on farm real estate) made by banks are mostly short- and medium-term in nature. Because of the nature of farming operations, short-term farm loans are relatively longer than short-term business loans. Farmers borrow short-term funds from commercial banks mostly for current and seasonal farming expenses. Farmers need short-term funds for the purchase of seeds, fertilizer, fuel, for the payment of wages to farmhands and other expenses involved in the preparation of crops. At harvest time, they also borrow to pay for expenses associated with the harvest. After the harvest, loans are repaid from the sales of crops. A cattle grower may borrow short-term funds for the purchase of feed to fatten his cattle before they are brought to the market.

Intermediate-term loans are needed by farmers for the purchase of farm machines and equipment—tractors, trucks, harrowers, and harvesters and the like. These loans are secured by equipment and machinery which are acquired through the use of the loans. They are repayable on an installment basis.

BANK INVESTMENTS

Bank investments differ from bank loans in several respects. Loans are made mostly on a personal basis—that is, they result from the negotiation between the banks and the borrowers. Investments, on the other hand, are impersonal in that they are mostly acquired on the open market, with no "personal" relation between the issuers of securities and the buying banks. While loans are initiated by the borrowers, investments are made at the initiative of the banks.

The term "bank investments" refers loosely to the securities held by the commercial banks. The major components of bank investments and their growth

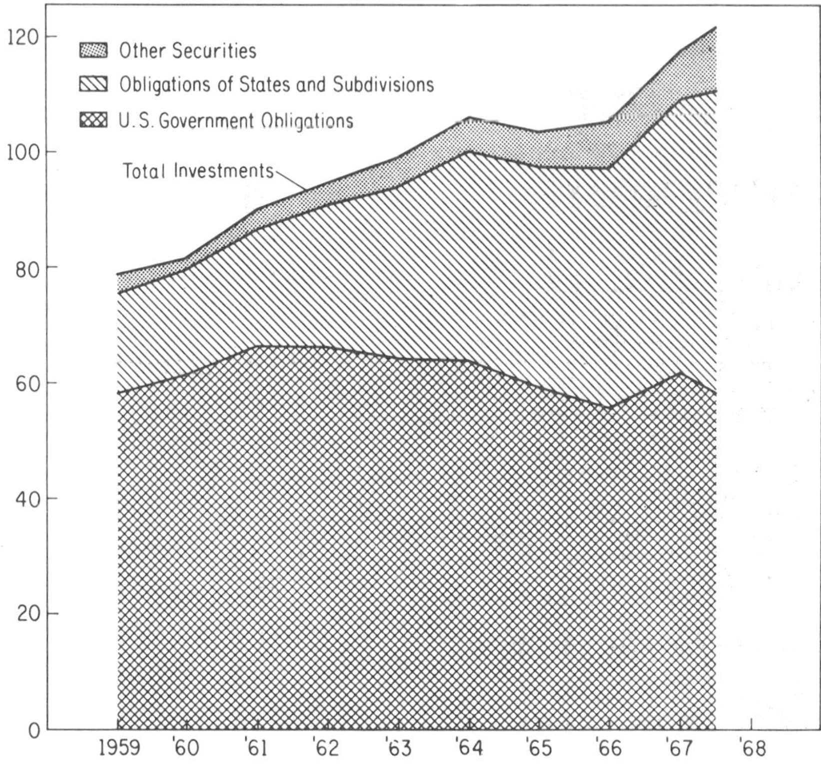

Source: Annual Reports, FDIC, 1959–67, and *Report of Call,* FDIC, No. 84, 1968.

Fig. 7-2. Bank investments, 1959–1968 (billions of dollars).

during 1959-68 are shown in Fig. 7-2. Bank investments may be divided into two broad categories in accordance with their purposes: investments for liquidity, and investments for income.

Investments for Liquidity

As already mentioned, to meet adverse over-the-counter balances and unfavorable clearing balances, commercial banks have to maintain working reserves in the form of vault cash, reserve with the Federal Reserve Banks, and balances with other commercial banks. These are their primary reserves, the first line of defense of their operations. In addition to primary reserves, in order to be able to meet unseasonal or abnormal demands for currency, banks hold highly liquid assets which can be converted quickly into cash should their cash reserves prove inadequate. These liquid assets constitute the secondary reserves or "investments for liquidity" account of the banks, consisting mostly of Treasury bills, certificates, and notes maturing in one year or less. The holding of these securities not only provides the bank with a second source of liquidity but also with additional income. The size of the investments for liquidity accounts depends upon the proportion of cash reserves held by the banks. A relatively large proportion of cash reserves would allow a relatively small proportion of investments for liquidity, and vice versa.

Investments for Income

These constitute the Investment Account Proper of the banks. Securities included in this account are acquired for interest income. The Investment Account Proper is essentially a residual account. After arrangements are made for adequate cash reserves and investments for liquidity, banks' resources are allocated in loans and discounts which constitute the major and more profitable earning assets of the banks. The remainder is used in the Investment Account Proper. Securities which make up this account include medium- and long-term government securities, obligations of state and local governments, securities of Federal agencies and private corporations, other bonds, notes, and debentures. U.S. government bonds and obligations of state and local subdivisions account for the lion's share of total investments for income. For instance, on June 29, 1968, these obligations accounted for $104.8 billion of the total "investments for income" portfolio of $116.2 billion of insured banks.

The dividing line between the investment for liquidity and investment for income accounts, however, is not clear-cut. It shifts with the changing maturity distribution of the assets of the banks. For instance, a long-term government bond is part of the Investment Account Proper. When it is within one year or less of its maturity, it would be considered as part of the investments for liquidity account. Although long-term securities are held primarily for income, at times they serve equally well the liquidity purposes of the banks, especially in periods during which the prices of government securities are supported by central banking authorities. For example, during the postwar period, since the prices of government securities were "pegged" by the Federal Reserve authorities, long-term government securities were as liquid as short-term securities because they could be offered at any time to the Federal Reserve banks for additional reserves at fixed prices.

Because of its residual nature, the Investment Account Proper tends to increase when outlets for bank loans are inadequate, and tends to decrease when loans and discounts expand. Thus, during the Depression, the accumulation of idle funds was invested in government securities. The volume of securities held by the banks then far exceeded their loans and discounts. During World War II, as funds needed by firms having contracts with the government were more or less provided by governmental lending agencies and retained earnings of businesses were more or less adequate, among other things, commercial banks again invested their excess funds in government securities which were highly liquid as a result of the "support" policy of the Federal Reserve System. In 1945 the volume of securities held by all commercial banks was almost four times the volume of bank loans. During the postwar period, the rising demand for loans by businesses and individuals witnessed rapid increases in bank loans and a gradual liquidation of securities for lending purposes. Bank investments, however continued to exceed bank loans until 1955. During the business expansion of the 1960's, bank loans, on the other hand, were almost twice the volume of bank investments ($256 billion of loans against $130 billion of securities in March 1969).

BANK EARNINGS

The earnings of banks, just like the earnings of other businesses, are an indicator of the performance of their management. To stay in business, banks not only have to maintain adequate liquidity to meet their obligations vis-à -vis depositors and other creditors, but also have to earn sufficient earnings.

Commercial banks derive their incomes from several sources. Interest on loans and securities constitutes their main source of earnings, which is more than 65 percent of total current operating revenue (see Table 7-3). The rate of return on the dollar of loan is higher than the rate of return on the dollar of investment. This is indicated by the fact that while bank loans account for slightly more than 60 percent of total loans and investments, interest on loans represents almost 80 percent of total income from loans and investments.

With regard to expenses, interest on savings and time deposits, wages, salaries, and related expenses constitute the bulk of total current operating expenses—more than 70 percent. Net operating earnings, which are the difference between current operating revenue and current operating expenses, amount to slightly more than one percent of total assets.

When recoveries and transfers from valuation reserves are added to net operating earnings, and when loan losses, charge-offs, transfers to valuation reserves, and Federal and State income taxes are subtracted from them, the net income available for interest on capital notes and debentures, and for dividends on preferred and common stock, amounts to less than 0.65 percent of total assets. The profitability of capital funds, however, is much higher. For instance, for 1967 the ratio of net current operating earnings to total capital funds was 15.37 percent and that of net income after taxes to capital was 9.23 percent, of which 4.19 percent was paid out as cash dividends and 5.04 percent was transferred to the capital account. This reflects the high degree of "leverage" with which banks operate, that is, they operate primarily with funds they themselves create and funds entrusted to them by customers. Thus in late 1967 the ratio of invested funds to total assets was less than 8 percent, which means that more than 92 percent of their total assets were acquired through "created" funds and other people's money.

SHORT-TERM BUSINESS LOANS AND THE COMMERCIAL LOAN THEORY

A popular banking theory of the past held that commercial banks should confine their operations to short-term, self-liquidating commercial loans. This theory is referred to as the *commercial-loan theory,* or "real bills" doctrine, or sometimes, as the "needs of trade" theory. The granting of loans against bills used in the financing of inventories of finished or unfinished goods, according to the theory, would assure the liquidity of commercial banks. Bank liquidity is assured, since the loans are always repaid from the sales proceeds of goods. The granting of such loans, furthermore, would result in a proper, elastic supply of bank credit and money–that is, the supply of money and credit is just what is needed to meet trade requirements. Thus in periods of business loans, greater short-term loans are needed by businesses to finance increases in the production and inventories of goods. The expansion of credit is accompanied by the greater production and inventories. In periods of declining business activities, on the other hand, bank credit is contracted as production is cut back and inventories are reduced. Old debts are paid off and fewer new loans are needed. Banks therefore play a completely passive role, expanding or contracting credit in accordance with the expansion or contraction of business activity. Since the volume of credit so granted is what is required for the "needs of trade," the general price level, according to the theory, is also expected to be relatively stable. It should be noted that the theory assumes that banks make short-term loans to businesses to meet their working capital requirements only. Long-term loans, necessary for capital expansion, are supposed to come from voluntary savings channeled through financial intermediaries.

Plausible in appearance, the theory contains several shortcomings. With regard to individual banks, short-term production and commercial loans may or may not be self-liquidating. Modern production processes are undertaken in anticipation of consumers' demands. If the goods produced are what the consumers want, then the borrowers are in a position to pay off their loans from the proceeds of the sales of their goods. If the goods are not what the consumers want, their producers will not be able to sell their goods, their inventories will pile up, and they may not be able to honor their obligations. The commercial-loan theory presupposes that the production and commercial operations which necessitate bank loans are successful in generating adequate funds for loan repayments. While this may be the case of a business world in which firms operate with perfect foresight, it certainly is not the case of the real business world in which firms operate amid uncertainty and risk.

In addition, if short-term commercial loans are self-liquidating with respect to individual banks, they may not be so with respect to the banking system as a whole. To infer that if such loans are self-liquidating for individual banks they are also self-liquidating for the banking system is to commit a fallacy of composition; what is true for the individual bank may not be true for the whole banking system. An individual bank holding "real" commercial bills may liquidate them quickly on the money market for cash to meet its liquidity requirements. But if all banks try to liquidate their holdings of commercial bills at the same time to meet their liquidity needs, the liquidation process may be a difficult and painful one. The outcome of such an attempt may be substantial decreases in securities prices and asset losses which can cause bank illiquidity and "insolvency." The liquidity of banks is therefore not necessarily assured by lending against short-term commercial bills. The ultimate source of liquidity for the banking system is the central bank, since it is only the central bank which can increase the liquidity position of the whole banking system by buying securities from the public and banks to make credit facilities more readily available to them.

The argument of the theory regarding the proper amount of bank credit and money and the relative stability of the price level requires among other things a perfect synchronization between the time schedules of the movements of goods and the time schedules of loan repayments. In other words, the flow of goods must move at the same rate as the opposite flow of loan repayments. Thus for a given volume of inventories, there must be one and only one loan outstanding. But this is not always the case. It is possible that there may be several loans outstanding for the same volume of inventories. The theory also appears to neglect autonomous changes in the velocity of circulation of money which, as will be seen, is capable of producing variation in the price level. The variation in the supply of bank money and credit is not in accordance with the changing needs of trade, as the theory holds. It is instead self-sustained or cumulative in its movement, upward as well as downward. The fallacy of the theory lies in its assumption that the volume of bank credit and money is regulated by the value of commercial bills of exchange used in the financing of inventories. It does neglect the fact that the value of commercial bills and inventories is, in turn, influenced by the volume of bank money and credit. Hence, increases in prices in periods of rising business activity would cause the value of inventories and commercial bills to rise. This would make possible a greater volume of bank credit and money. The increase in the supply of credit and money would give rise to higher prices and higher value of inventories, and so on. The reverse holds in periods of declining business activity, of recession and depression. The stability of prices and elasticity of the supply of money and credit do not necessarily depend upon the granting of particular types of loans by the commercial banks, as advocated by proponents of the theory. In fact, it is the discretionary control operations of the central banking authorities which partly help promote price stability and the elasticity of the supply of money.

The theory, fallacious in its foundation, is no longer in vogue in modern banking. It did, however, influence the thinking of central bankers and commercial bankers alike in the past. It left its marks in the writing of the original Federal Reserve Act which allowed the Federal Reserve Banks to rediscount only "short-term, self-liquidating agricultural, industrial, or commercial paper which was originally created for the purpose of providing funds for producing, purchasing, carrying, or marketing of goods."

Modern bankers depart substantially from the commercial-loan theory. This is evidenced by the fact that short-term commercial and industrial loans account for a small percentage of the total assets of the commercial banks. Real estate loans, and other long-term obligations which constitute a major portion of the banks' earning assets, are certainly not in compliance with the "real bills" doctrine. Consumer loans are another important component of banks assets. Yet they are not "self-liquidating" loans. Bank liquidity is of course a basic problem of banking management. But the problem is approached not in the light of the commercial-loan theory. Modern banks rely mostly on their holdings of short-term government securities, such as Treasury bills, and certificates, for liquidity purposes rather than on short-term commercial obligations.

BANK ASSETS AND THE LEVEL OF ECONOMIC ACTIVITY

Credit in general and bank credit in particular play a vital role in modern production and distribution processes. Bank loans and investments, which are the earning assets of the banks, represent the liquidity they supply to the economy. The creation of purchasing power (bank money, through bank loans and investments), enables households to acquire such consumer durables as automobiles and appliances ahead of their income receipts, the undertaking of income and employment-generating productive operations. The expansion in consumption, production, income, and employment, promoted by the expansion of bank credit and money, among other things, in turn enable further increases in consumption and production which require further expansion of bank credit and money, and so on. Production, consumption, income, employment, bank credit, and money are closely interwoven in a reciprocal process; one influences and is in turn influenced by others.

Bank credit and money created through bank loans and investments, while playing an important role in promoting fuller utilization of labor and resources and higher levels of income, is also an important source of economic instability. During periods of prosperity when the economy is operating more or less at capacity, when prices are relatively high and profits are relatively adequate, even for marginal firms, banks are more eager to expand credit to business firms which need more funds for inventories of materials, for unfinished products and finished goods, for capital expansion and to consumers who are more disposed to acquire consumer durables. The expansion of bank loans at such times would tend to inflate the flow of aggregate spending, thus giving rise to heavier inflationary pressures. As a result of restrictive measures taken by monetary authorities to limit the volume of reserves available to banks for credit and deposit expansion, banks can expand loans through reserves obtained by liquidating their investment holdings. The sales of securities to holders of idle balances release reserves for lending purposes. Increases in bank loans would lead to greater pressures on total spending and the levels of prices. On the other hand, during periods of declining business activity, banks are less eager to lend as declining profits and incomes reduce the ability of businesses as well as individuals to repay loans. It is true that the contraction of bank loans in periods of recession and depression reflects mostly declining demands for bank credit by businesses and individuals, but the unwillingness of banks to make loans to customers who are in need of funds and are in weak financial condition tends to slow down economic recovery. The overexpansion of bank loans in periods of prosperity and the unwillingness of banks to lend in times of economic recession therefore tend to magnify the amplitude of business fluctuations.

SUMMARY

Bank assets represent the uses of bank funds. Bank assets are composed mostly of reserves, loans and discounts, and investments. Reserves are needed for banks to meet the legal reserve requirements imposed by law, to meet normal over-the-counter unfavorable balances or deficit clearing balances as well as seasonal and abnormal demands for currency by depositors. Since reserves are nonearning assets, banks usually keep them to a minimum necessary for their operations only. Funds in excess of what is needed for reserves are available for loans and investments which are banks' earning assets.

Loans constitute the major asset component of the banks and their main source of income. Banks make various types of loans: business loans, consumer loans, real estate loans and agricultural loans. Short-term and medium-term loans, both secured and unsecured, are granted to businesses for their seasonal financial needs, for working capital purposes as well as for the purchase of business machinery and equipment. The theory that banks, by confining their operations to short-term self-liquidating commercial loans, would assure not only their liquidity and solvency but also the elasticity of the supply of money and the relative stability of prices, appears fallacious. Modern bankers depart substantially from this commercial loan theory—as indicated by the wide variety of loans made by banks other than short-term commercial loans, among other things.

Banks are also a predominant source of credit to consumers who borrow mostly for the acquisition of automobiles, appliances, and for home repair and modernization. Most consumer loans are secured loans. Real estate loans constitute another important component of total bank loans. They are needed for the purchase of land, for land improvements, houses and buildings. They are secured by mortgages on residential and business properties and land. Banks also make short-term and intermediate-term loans to farmers for current farming expenses and for the acquisition of farm equipment. While short-term loans represent mostly single-payment loans, intermediate and longer-term loans call for periodic repayments of both principal and interest.

Investments are another major component of total bank earning assets. Investments are divided into two accounts–investments for liquidity, and investments for income. The investment for liquidity account consists mostly of Treasury bills and other short-term U.S. obligations which can be quickly converted into cash to meet liquidity requirements. The investment for income account, on the other hand, consists of long-term securities, such as government bonds, and state and municipal obligations. They are held primarily for income purposes.

Bank loans and investments represent the liquidity which they supply to the economy. Although bank credit is essential to growth and development, it may at times become a source of economic instability as well.

PROBLEMS

1. Explain why it is necessary for banks to hold cash reserves? Is the purpose of minimum legal reserve requirements to insure the liquidity of banks? If not, why?

2. What is the commercial-loan theory of banking? What are the basic shortcomings of this theory? Was it a popular theory in the past? Do commercial bankers nowadays observe closely this theory of banking?

3. Is it true that the central bank is the ultimate source of liquidity of the banking system? Explain your answer in detail.

4. Explain why it is necessary for banks to make adjustment in their daily money positions? What are the various methods available to banks for this purpose? Does the use of these methods have the same effects on the reserves of the individual banks and the banking system as a whole?

5. Explain why the lending and investing operations of banks may magnify the amplitude of business fluctuations? If this is the major source of economic instability, how would you propose to correct it? Give your own opinions.

6. What are the various purposes served by the investment account of a bank? Why is the investment-for-income account considered as residual account? If it is a residual account, what would be its behavior in times of prosperity and recession?

7. Following is the balance sheet of the Fourth National Bank on December 31, 1966 (millions of dollars).

Assets

Vault Cash	$ 50
Reserve Balance at the Reserve Bank	370
Demand Balances Due from Domestic Banks	20
Loans	3,050
Investments	1,641
Federal Reserve Bank stock	9
Bank Premises and Equipment	20
Other assets	10
Total Assets	$5,170

Liabilities and Net Worth

Total demand deposits	$1,800
Time deposits	1,500
Other liabilities	
Net Worth	20
Capital Account	350
Total Liabilities + Capital	$5,170

Find the legal reserves, required reserves, and excess reserves of this bank, assuming that the legal reserve ratio is 20 percent for demand deposits and 5 percent for time liabilities.

8. Show the changes in the balance sheets of the parties involved in the following transactions.

(a) Bank A sells $1 million of securities to bank B which pays for the securities by drawing on its reserve account with the Federal Reserve Bank (A and B are member banks).

(b) Bank A transfers $100,000 from its demand balance with bank B to its reserve account with the Federal Reserve Bank.

(c) Bank A increases its cash holdings by drawing on its account with the Reserve Bank.

(d) Bank A sells $1 million of securities to the Treasury which pays for them with a check drawn on its account with a Reserve Bank.

(e) Is there any change in the total volume of reserves of the banking system as a consequence of each of the above transactions?

chapter 8

Commercial Banking Operations: The Process of Deposit Creation

The creation of deposit money has been mentioned in Chapter 6. In this chapter we shall discuss in more detail the deposit creation process of individual banks and the banking system as a whole. We shall begin with simple models based on simplified assumptions. We then drop these assumptions one by one in order to approximate actual conditions of banking operations.

Reserves play an important role in the process of money creation by commercial banks. The reason commercial banks have to keep cash reserves is that in the normal course of their operations they do have to make payments in currency, the type of money which they cannot by themselves create. There would be no need for cash reserves should the means of payments consist solely of deposit money.

Deposit Creation in a Noncash System

We can show the significance of cash reserves by first considering the creation of money in a hypothetical closed economy in which there is only one bank, the Big Bank, and bank money is the only means of payment. In this economy, there are no limits to the ability of the bank to create deposit money. It acquires earning assets such as loans and securities by crediting the accounts of sellers. Suppose that the Big Bank grants a loan of $10,000 to X and purchases $20,000 worth of securities from Y. The change in its balance sheet will be:

Assets	Balance Sheet of Big Bank — Liabilities
Loans + $10,000	Account of X + $10,000
Investments + $20,000	Account of Y + $20,000

Assume that X draws a check for $1000 on his account in payment to Z who, in turn, deposits the check in the bank. The transaction would result in the transfer of deposits from X's account to Z's account as follows:

A	Balance Sheet of Big Bank	L
Loans + $10,000		Account of X + $ 9,000
Investments + $20,000		Account of Y + $20,000
		Account of Z + $ 1,000

On the other hand, money is destroyed when loans are repaid and securities are sold by the bank. The repayment of loans by borrowers and the payment for securities by buyers are effected by drawing on their accounts with the bank.

In our example, there is no limit to the ability of the Big Bank to create money because it has to make payments only in money which it can create. The quantity of bank money is determined largely by general economic conditions and the availability of lending and investing opportunities in the economy.

Let us now assume that in addition to the Big Bank there are other banks—among them, the Little Bank. Since we have several banks in operation, payments made by customers of the Big Bank are not likely to return to the same bank. In the above example, suppose that Z is a customer of the Little Bank. When X draws a check for $1,000 in payment to Z, the latter deposits the check in his bank, the Little Bank. This leads to an increase in both the assets and liabilities of the Little Bank and the following balance-sheet changes of the Big Bank.

A	Big Bank	L
Loans + $10,000		Account of X + $ 9,000
Investments + $20,000		Account of Y + $20,000
		Balances due to Little Bank + $1,000

A		Little Bank	L
Claim on Big Bank	+$1,000	Account of Z	+$1,000

As a result of the claims of the Little Bank on the Big Bank, its assets increase by $1,000. On the other hand, the liability of the Big Bank with regard to X decreased by $1,000, which is offset by an equivalent increase in its liability toward the Little Bank. This may be partially or entirely canceled by claims of the Big Bank on the Little Bank, resulting from payments made by customers of the latter to customers of the former. The loan and investment operations of banks and the payments between their customers would give rise to claims of banks on each other which are more or less canceled. If the mutual claims between banks are so canceled that no bank has a net claim on the others, then there is no limit to the ability of the banks to grant credit and create money. Otherwise the ability of each bank to create deposit money depends largely on the willingness of other banks to hold claims on it and its holdings of assets acceptable for the settlement of claims due to other banks.

Cash Reserves in a Mixed-Payment System

In the above hypothetical closed economy, since there is no use for cash, there is no need for commercial banks to hold cash reserves. But we know that in our economy, means of payment consist of both demand deposits and currency. It is a mixed-payment system. While demand deposits are created by the commercial banks, currency is issued by the Federal Reserve and the Treasury. Cash and demand deposits are used interchangeably by the public. Since commercial banks cannot create cash, and their demand liabilities are convertible into cash at the option of depositors, they have to hold cash reserves in order to be able to meet their demand obligations. Cash reserves held by the banks to meet their liquidity requirements therefore serve as a limit to their ability to expand credit and deposit money. A bank which overexpands credit and deposit money faces the risk of being unable to meet the currency demand of its depositors.

As noted earlier, in the normal course of their operations, since currency withdrawals are more or less offset by currency deposits, banks usually keep cash reserves as a small fraction of their deposit liabilities to meet adverse clearing balances and unfavorable over-the-counter balances as well as seasonal currency demands by depositors. In some countries, this fraction of reserves is determined largely by convention, by banking experiences, and the standard of banking prudence. In other countries, such as the United States, for instance, banks are required by law to hold minimum legal reserves. The legal reserve ratio—the ratio of required reserves to deposit liabilities—is the ultimate limit to the ability of the banks to create money. They can expand credit and deposit money only up to the legal reserve ratio. An overexpansion of deposit money by banks would cause them to be deficient in required reserves.

THE INDIVIDUAL BANK AND DEPOSIT EXPANSION

Let us start with the following simplified initial balance sheet of a bank, say Bank A.

A	Balance Sheet of Bank A		L
Reserves	$20,000	Demand deposits	$100,000
Loans and Investments	$80,000		

Since we are concerned with the relationship between reserves, loans and investments, and demand deposits, we shall omit other asset and liability items on the balance sheet of the bank. With an assumed legal reserve ratio against demand deposits of 20 percent, bank A is said to be "loaned up" with no excess reserves.

Its cash reserve is just equal to 20 percent of its demand liability: (0.20) ($100,000 = $20,000. Bank A is in an "equilibrium" position. It cannot increase its earning assets and demand deposits unless it acquires additional reserves. Suppose that our bank receives in deposit a check for $10,000 from Mr. M, a government securities dealer, who sold securities to the central bank.[1] Bank A pays for the check by creating a demand claim on itself in favor of Mr. M, a depositor. The transaction leads to an increase in the assets and liabilities of the bank by $10,000. Since the increase in demand deposits of $10,000 requires an increase in required reserves of only $2,000, our bank has an excess reserve of $8,000. The balance sheet change of our bank is as follows:

A	Balance Sheet of A	L
Required reserves + $2,000		Demand deposits + $10,000
Excess reserves + $8,000		

If we assume that our bank is the only bank in the system, a monopoly bank, that lending and investing opportunities are available for it to be "loaned up" with no excess reserves, that in the process of deposit expansion through loan and investment operations, our bank suffers no loss of cash to the nonbanking sector, that is, loan proceeds checked out by borrowers are redeposited in the bank, then our bank would be in a position to expand credit and deposit money by another $40,000. The $8,000 of excess reserves of our bank becomes required reserves. The final balance sheet change of our bank looks somewhat like the following:

A	Balance Sheet of A (Assumed to be a monopoly bank)		L
Required reserves	+$10,000	Demand deposits	+$50,000
Excess reserves	0		
Loans and investments	+$40,000		

Our bank is once again "loaned up" with no excess reserve. There is an increase in the total demand liability of our bank of $50,000. Of this amount, $10,000 was passively created as a result of the initial currency deposit of Mr. M, and $40,000 were derivative deposits as they were actively created by the bank through its loan and investment operations.

In a system in which there are in operation thousands of commercial banks,

[1]This is but one source of additional reserves. The analysis applies to any source of changes in reserves, such as those resulting from the purchase of gold and silver by the Treasury, the increase in the borrowings of the banks from the central bank, or the decrease in currency holdings of the public. We are not concerned with the transfer of reserves from one bank to another bank. In this case, since there is no net addition to the reserves of the banking system, there will be no net expansion of credit and demand deposits.

it is unlikely that loan proceeds checked out by borrowers of a bank in payment to others would return in full to the same bank. Most of these payments would go to other banks. If our bank is only one bank in a multibank system, it can safely grant loans equal to its excess reserves only. Should the loan proceeds be used by the borrowers in payment to customers of other banks, our bank would not be embarrassed by being caught short of required reserves. Suppose[2] Bank A grants a loan of $8,000 to Mr. X. His account is credited with $8,000. Assume that Mr. X draws a check for $8,000 in payment to Mr. Y, who is a customer of Bank B. Mr. Y deposits the check in his bank. When the check is collected, Bank A loses its excess reserves. Its balance sheet change in this case is:

Balance Sheet of A
(An individual bank)

A			L
Required reserves	+$2,000	Demand deposits	+$10,000
(Excess reserves	+$8,000)	(Demand deposits	+$8,000)
(Excess reserves	- $8,000)	(Demand deposits	- $8,000)
Loans and investments	+$8,000		

As far as Bank A is concerned, this is the end of the process. Together with Mr. M, it has created $10,000 of deposit money. In a multibank system, this is approximately the experience of the individual bank. It cannot create deposit money several times the initial reserve. It usually loses cash reserves to other banks (and to the public) when it makes loans or purchases securities. It would be erroneous, however, to say that the bank lends its cash or excess reserves. Definitely not. It acquires the earning asset, the promissory note from the borrower, by creating a demand claim on itself, which is money. The promissory note, a nonmonetary asset, is monetized by the bank. The borrower exchanges his promissory note for the right to draw on the bank up to $8,000 for payment purposes. Whether the bank loses cash or not depends upon to whom payments are made by the borrower. If part of the loan is used in payment to another customer of the lending bank, then it will not lose as much as $8,000 of cash. This is usually the case when the borrower uses the loan for local payrolls, or for the purchase of goods and services supplied by local businesses. In the example, Bank A loses $8,000 of reserves because the loan is used by the borrower in payment to a customer of a different bank. The loss of reserves by Bank A as a result of its loan operation does not enable it to expand further credit and deposit money. But what it loses is gained by other banks. With added reserves, they are in a position to create more credit and deposit money. As will be seen, the banking system as a whole can create much more deposit money than can an individual bank, given an increase in reserves.

[2]The analysis remains the same if instead of lending, the bank purchases securities or uses a combination of loans and investments.

DEPOSIT EXPANSION BY THE BANKING SYSTEM: THE MONEY-CREATION MULTIPLIER

We continue to assume that the availability of profitable lending and investing opportunities enables banks to be "loaned-up," that there is no loss of cash by the banks to the nonbanking sector in the process of deposit expansion, and that loan proceeds are checked out by borrowers in payment to customers of other banks.

With regard to Bank A, after the loan is checked out by X in payment to Y it is again in "equilibrium" with no excess reserves. But what about Bank B? It receives a check for $8,000 in deposit from Mr. Y. Both its reserves and demand liabilities increase by $8,000. This increase in demand deposits calls for an increase in required reserves of 0.20 x 8,000 = 1,600. Hence, it has an excess reserve of $6,400. It grants a loan of $6,400 to Mr. Z by crediting his account with that amount. The latter uses the loan to pay for the goods which he purchased from Mr. H, who banks with Bank C. When the loan is checked out, Bank B loses $6,400 of reserve. Following is its balance-sheet change.

A	Balance Sheet of B		L
Required reserves	+1,600	Demand deposits	+8,000
(Excess reserves	+6,400)	(Demand deposits	+6,400)
(Excess reserves	- 6,400)	(Demand deposits	- 6,400)
Loans and investments	+6,400		

Bank B, together with Y, is able to create $8,000 of deposit money. Bank C now acquires an additional reserve of $6,400 from Mr. H, whose account is credited with that amount. This requires an increase in required reserves of (0.20) x (6400) = $1,280. Its lending potential thus increases by $5,120. It makes a loan of $5,120 to Mr. S, who checks out the loan in payment to Mr. G who banks with Bank D. The balance-sheet change of Bank C is:

A	Balance Sheet of Bank C		L
Required reserves	+ 1,280	Demand deposits	+ 6,400
Loans and investments	+ 5,120	(Demand deposits	+ 5,120)
(Excess reserves	+ 5,120)	(Demand deposits	- 5,120)
(Excess reserves	- 5,120)		

Again, Bank C loses $5,120 of reserve. It creates $6,400 of deposit money. Bank D, in turn, receives in deposit a check for $5,120 from Mr. G. Its reserves and demand liability increase by $5,120. Its required reserves increase by $1,024 and excess reserves by $4,096, which enables it to make a loan of $4,096 to a borrower who checks it out in payment to another individual who banks with another bank, and so on. The process of deposit expansion thus continues with each successive bank at each stage receiving smaller and smaller amounts of reserve and creating smaller and smaller amounts of deposit money. The change in demand deposits created by the banking system as a whole as a result of an initial increase of reserve of \$10,000 is the sum of deposit money created by each individual bank at each stage. Let Δ D be the change in total deposit money. It is equal to the sum of deposit money created by Bank A, which is \$10,000; by Bank B which is \$8,000; by Bank C, \$6,400; by Bank D, \$5,120; etc. We have

$$
\begin{aligned}
\Delta D &= \$10{,}000 + 8{,}000 + 6{,}400 + 5{,}120 + \cdots + \\
&= 10{,}000 \times \left[1 + (1 - 0.20) + (1 - 0.20)^2 + \cdots + (1 - 0.20)^{n-1}\right] \\
&= 10{,}000 \times \left[\frac{1}{1 - (1 - 0.20)}\right] = 10{,}000 \left[\frac{1}{0.20}\right] \\
&= 10{,}000 \times 5 = \$50{,}000
\end{aligned}
$$

With an initial increase in reserve of \$10,000 and the legal reserve ratio of 20 percent, the banking system as a whole can create a maximum amount of deposit money of \$50,000, five times the initial increase in reserves. The final balance sheet change of the banking system is:

A	Balance Sheet Change of Banking System		L
Required reserves	+ \$10,000	Demand deposits	+ \$50,000
Loans and investments	+ \$40,000		

The extent of the creation of deposit money by the banking system is the same as that of Bank A when it is assumed to be a monopoly bank. The only difference is the amount of time involved in the expansion process. In the case of the monopoly bank, it can immediately increase its loans and investments by another \$40,000. In the case of the multibank system, on the other hand, the speed with which the expansion process works itself out depends upon the amount of time involved in the clearance and collection of checks at various stages of the process. It should also be noted that the change in the supply of money contributed by the banking system is \$40,000. Although the volume of deposit money created by the banking system is \$50,000, it has to hold \$10,000 of required reserves transferred from the nonbank public, which is a decrease in circulating currency.

From the above example, we can derive the general expression for the expansion of deposit money by the banking system. Let ΔR be the increase in reserve and r, the legal reserve ratio; then the formula for the expansion is:[3]

$$\Delta D = \Delta R \left[\frac{1}{1-(1-r)}\right] = \Delta R \times \left(\frac{1}{r}\right) \tag{1}$$

The total change in deposit money which can be created by the banking system as a whole is equal to the product of the initial change in reserve (ΔR) and the multiplication factor $\frac{1}{r}$. This $\frac{1}{r}$ is referred to as the *money-creation multiplier*, which is simply the reciprocal of the legal reserve ratio. In our numerical example, the multiplier is $\frac{1}{0.2} = 5$. It indicates the extent of the change in total demand deposits resulting from a given change in reserve. From formula (1) it can be seen that given ΔR, ΔD varies inversely with r. With $r = 0.10$, the money creation multiplier is 10 and the amount of deposit money which can be created by the banking system is $\Delta D = 10{,}000 \times \frac{1}{0.10} = 10{,}000 \times 10 = \$100{,}000$; on the other hand, with $r = 0.50$, ΔD is only \$20,000. Therefore, given the initial

[3] We may also derive that expression as follows: note that when each bank is "loaned up," its reserves are required reserves which are a fraction of its deposit liabilities. Let S_i be the required reserves of the ith bank, and d_i, its demand liability, then we have:

$$d_1 = S_1 \left(\frac{1}{r}\right)$$

Similarly,

$$d_2 = S_2 \left(\frac{1}{r}\right)$$

and

$$d_n = S_n \left(\frac{1}{r}\right)$$

Let

$$D = d_1 + d_2 + \cdots + d_n$$

and

$$R = S_1 + S_2 + \cdots + S_n$$

we have

$$d_1 + d_2 + \cdots + d_n = (S_1 + S_2 + \cdots + S_n)\left(\frac{1}{r}\right)$$

or

$$D = R\left(\frac{1}{r}\right) \tag{1}$$

Let R change by ΔR; we have

$$D + \Delta D = R\left(\frac{1}{r}\right) + \Delta R\left(\frac{1}{r}\right) \tag{2}$$

Subtracting (1) from (2), we obtain

$$\Delta D = \Delta R\left(\frac{1}{r}\right)$$

change in reserves, the lower the legal reserve ratio, the greater the size of the money-creation multiplier; the greater the size of the multiplier, the larger the change in demand deposits which can be created by the banking system.

The total change in loans and investments of the system is equal to the sum of the change in the loans and investments of each individual bank at each stage. We know that Bank A increases its loans and investments by \$8,000, Bank B, by \$6,400, Bank C, by \$5,120, and so on. Let ΔL be the change in the system's loans and investments; we have:

$$\begin{aligned}\Delta L &= 8{,}000 + 6{,}400 + 5{,}120 + 4{,}096 + \cdots + \\ &= 10{,}000 \times [(1 - 0.20) + (1 - 0.20)^2 + \cdots + (1 - 0.20)^n] \\ &= 10{,}000 \left[\frac{(1 - 0.20)}{1 - (1 - 0.20)}\right] = 10{,}000 \times 4 = \$40{,}000\end{aligned}$$

The change in loans and investments is \$40,000, four times the initial increase in reserves, as already indicated in the preceding balance sheet of the system. From this example, we have the following general expression for maximum credit expansion:[4]

$$\Delta L = \Delta R \left(\frac{1 - r}{1 - (1 - r)}\right) = \Delta R \left[\frac{(1 - r)}{r}\right]$$

The term $\frac{1 - r}{r}$ can be referred to as the credit-expansion multiplier.

[4]We know that each bank can make loans or purchase securities until it is "loaned up" with no excess reserves. Let l_i be the volume of loans and investments of the ith bank, then

$$L_1 = S_1 \left(\frac{1}{r}\right) - S_1 = S_1 \left(\frac{1 - r}{r}\right)$$

Similarly,

$$L_2 = S_2 \left(\frac{1 - r}{r}\right)$$

and

$$L_n = S_n \left(\frac{1 - r}{r}\right)$$

Let

$$L = L_1 + L_2 + \cdots + L_n$$

and again

$$R = S_1 + S_2 + \cdots + S_n$$

We have

$$L = R \left(\frac{1 - r}{r}\right)$$

Hence

$$\Delta L = \Delta R \left(\frac{1 - r}{r}\right)$$

From the foregoing analysis, it is obvious that only under a fractional reserve banking system is multiple deposit expansion possible. With a legal reserve ratio of 100 percent, the process of money creation does not work. For each dollar of deposit money, the banks have to keep one dollar of central bank money. Under 100 percent reserve,the balance sheet change of Bank A in our example would be:

A	Balance Sheet of Bank A	L
Required reserves + 10,000	Demand deposits + 10,000	

The acquisition of $10,000 of reserve permits the bank to create the same amount of demand deposits (the money-creation multiplier is one). There is no change in the supply of money contributed by the banks. The change in the supply of money of $10,000 in this case resulted from the creation of money by the central bank when it purchased securities from the public. The nonbanking sector, instead of holding $10,000 in currency, elected to hold it in the form of demand deposits. Under such a system, the supply of money would be affected by the operations of the central bank, not by those of commercial banks. The latter would acquire earning assets with funds obtained from the public through the sales of stocks, capital notes and debentures, and borrowings from the central bank.

DEPOSIT EXPANSION AND CASH LEAKAGE

Up to this point, we have assumed that the initial increase in reserve remains in the banking system—that is, the loss of reserves of an individual bank as a result of its lending activity is gained by another bank, but that there is no loss of cash by the banking system to the nonbanking sector in the expansion process. This assumption is more or less unrealistic and is now abandoned. While the ratio of cash to demand deposits held by the public slightly varies from year to year, it is fairly reasonable to assume that the cash held by the public bears a fairly constant ratio to deposit money. Indeed, during the last two decades or so, the ratio of currency to demand deposits was approximately 27 percent. Since cash bears a fairly constant ratio to demand deposits, an increase in demand deposits as a result of the expansion of the loan and investment operations of the banks is expected to induce an increase in the currency holdings of the public.[5] The withdrawal of currency induced by deposit expansion is referred to

[5]Following are some cash to deposit money ratios between 1947 and 1965 (computed from Federal Reserve Bulletins):

Mid-Year	Ratios of Cash to Demand Deposits	Mid-Year	Ratios of Cash to Demand Deposits
1947	27+	1960	26
1951	27+	1963	26+
1955	26+	1965	28
1957	26		

as cash leakage or cash drain. As a portion of the initial increase in reserves is lost to the nonbanking sector, the volume of deposit money which can be created by the banking system will be smaller, since a smaller amount of excess reserves can support only a smaller volume of loans and investments.

Assume that the induced increment in currency in circulation (ΔC) is directly proportional to the increment of demand deposits (ΔD)—that is, $\Delta C = c \cdot \Delta D$ (where $0 < c < 1$, the factor of proportionality). The ratio $c = \Delta C/\Delta D$ indicates the change in currency in circulation resulting from a dollar change of deposit money. Suppose that $c = 0.20$. This means that for each dollar change of deposit money, there is a change in currency in circulation of 20 cents. With the existence of cash leakage, the initial reserve is used up not only to meet the minimum reserve requirements ($r \cdot \Delta D$) but also the cash loss ($c \cdot \Delta D$). Hence

$$\Delta R = r \cdot \Delta D + c \cdot \Delta D = \Delta D(r + c), \text{ or}$$

$$\Delta D = \Delta R \left(\frac{1}{r + c}\right) \tag{2}$$

With cash leakage, the money-creation multiplier becomes $\left(\frac{1}{r + c}\right)$. When $c = 20$ percent, the maximum amount of deposit money which can be created by the banking system in the above example is

$$\Delta D = 10{,}000 \left(\frac{1}{0.20 + 0.20}\right) = 10{,}000 \times 2.5 = \$25{,}000$$

As a result of the cash drain, the volume of deposit money which can be created by the system is only \$25,000 (the multiplier is 2.5) as compared with \$50,000 in the case when $\Delta C = 0$ (the multiplier is 5). From expression (2), it can be seen that, other things being equal, the greater the value of c, the smaller the value of ΔD. The effect of the cash leakage on deposit expansion is not different from that of an increase in the legal reserve ratio. The maximum amount of earning assets which can be acquired by the banking system in this example is:[6]

$$\Delta L = \Delta R \left(\frac{1 - r}{r + c}\right) = 10{,}000 \left(\frac{1 - 0.20}{0.20 + 0.20}\right) = 10{,}000 \times 2 = \$20{,}000$$

The expansion of bank credit, hence deposit money, is associated with rising economic activity, rising income and expenditure. The increases in cash transactions as a result of the increase in general expenditure would require a larger holding of currency by the public. The demand for currency therefore tends to increase with the expansion of deposit money.

[6]In the case of cash leakage, the total volume of loans and investments of the banking system is equal to the difference between total deposits and reserves, the latter being equal to initial reserves less the cash drain. We have

$$L = R\left(\frac{1}{r + c}\right) - r \cdot R\left(\frac{1}{r + c}\right) = \left(\frac{1 - r}{r + c}\right) \cdot R$$

Hence

$$\Delta L = \Delta R \left(\frac{1 - r}{r + c}\right)$$

The final balance sheet change of the banking system is as follows:

A	Balance Sheet of System		L
Required reserves $(r \cdot \Delta D)$	+ 5,000	Demand deposits (ΔD)	+ 25,000
Loans and investments (ΔL)	+ 20,000		

It should be noted that with cash leakage, the total change in the supply of money is greater than the net change in the money supply contributed by the banking system through credit expansion by the volume of cash drain. In our example, the net change in the supply of money resulting from the credit expansion of the banking system is \$20,000 (although total deposit expansion is \$25,000, the banks have to keep a cash reserve of \$5,000 transferred from the nonbank sector) and the total change in the money supply is \$20,000 + \$5,000. The second term represents the induced cash leakage.

TIME-DEPOSIT CHANGES AND DEPOSIT EXPANSION

We have been concerned with the expansion of deposit money and have implicitly assumed away time deposits. But we know that in addition to demand deposits, banks also hold time deposits. The expansion of demand deposits may induce a larger holding of time deposits by the public, as those who receive payments from borrowers from commercial banks and have no immediate use of demand balances may desire to transfer part of the funds from their checking accounts to their savings accounts for additional interest income. The change of demand deposits to time deposits further limits the ability of the banks to expand deposit money as part of the reserves which would otherwise be available to support demand deposits now has to be used to support increased time deposits.

Assume, for simplicity, that the change in time deposits (ΔT) induced by the expansion of deposit money is proportional to the latter, $\Delta T = a.\ \Delta D$ where $0 < a < 1$. The ratio $a = \dfrac{\Delta T}{\Delta D}$ shows the change in time deposits resulting from a dollar change of demand deposit. For instance, $\Delta T/\Delta D = 0.50$ means that for a dollar increase of deposit money, the public increases its holdings of time deposits by 50 cents. Let the legal reserve ratio against time deposits be h; an increase in time deposits, $\Delta T = a \cdot \Delta D$ requires an increase in required reserves of $h \cdot \Delta T = ah \cdot \Delta D$. The initial increase in reserve is now "used up" to meet the required reserves against increases in demand deposits, $(r \cdot \Delta D)$, cash drain, $(c \cdot \Delta D)$, and reserves required against time deposits, $(ah \cdot \Delta D)$ as well. We have the following relation:

$$\Delta R = r \cdot \Delta D + c \cdot \Delta D + ah \cdot \Delta D = (r + c + ah)\Delta D$$

It follows immediately that

$$\Delta D = \Delta R \left(\frac{1}{r + c + ah} \right)$$

The money-creation multiplier is now $\left(\frac{1}{r + c + ah} \right)$. Again, assume that ΔR = 10,000, r = 0.20, c = 0.20, a = 0.50, and h = 0.20. The maximum amount of deposit money which can be created by the banking system is

$$\Delta D = 10{,}000 \left(\frac{1}{0.20 + 0.20 + 0.10} \right) = 10{,}000 \times 2 = \$20{,}000$$

The money-creation multiplier is 2 and the increase in deposit money is $20,000 in this case, as compared with the multiplier of 2.5 and ΔD = $25,000 in the previous case where there is no induced change in time deposits. The change in the volume of loans and investments of the banking system is[7]

$$\Delta L = \Delta R \left(\frac{1 - r + a(1 - h)}{r + c + ah} \right) = 10{,}000 \left[\frac{1 - 0.20 + 0.50(1 - 0.20)}{(0.20 + 0.20 + 0.10)} \right]$$
$$= 10{,}000 \times 2.4 = \$24{,}000$$

In balance-sheet terms, the example can be presented as follows:

A	Balance Sheet of Banking System (I)		L
Required reserves ($r \cdot \Delta D + ah \cdot \Delta D$)	+ 6,000	Demand deposits (ΔD)	+ 20,000
		Time deposits ($a \cdot \Delta D$)	+ 10,000
Loans and investments (ΔL)	+ 24,000		
Total	30,000	Total	30,000

A comparison between this balance sheet (I) with the following balance sheet (II) of the case in which there is no induced change in time deposits reveals some interesting information.

A	Balance Sheet of the System with $\Delta T = 0$ (II)		L
Required reserves	+ 5,000	Demand deposits	+25,000
Loans and investments	+20,000		

[7]In this case, the total loans and investments of the banking system are the difference between total deposits (demand and time deposits) and total required reserves—that is,

$$L = \left(\frac{R}{r + c + ah} + \frac{aR}{r + c + ah} \right) - \left(\frac{r \cdot R}{r + c + ah} + \frac{ah \cdot R}{r + c + ah} \right) = R \left(\frac{1 - r + a(1 - h)}{r + c + ah} \right)$$

Hence

$$\Delta L = \Delta R \left(\frac{1 - r + a(1 - h)}{r + c + ah} \right)$$

In balance sheet (I), although the change in demand deposits is smaller than that in balance sheet (II) as a result of the diversion of reserves from the support of demand deposits to that of time deposits, the change in total deposits is greater in (I) than in (II), \$30,000 as compared with \$25,000. This reflects the fact that a smaller amount of deposit money would induce a smaller cash drain, hence a larger amount of reserves would remain in the banking system for the support of time deposits.[8] Thus in (I), the cash drain is only \$4,000 as compared with \$5,000 in (II). The change in loans and investments in balance sheet (I) (\$24,000) is greater than that of (II) (i.e., \$20,000), since the banks acquire earning assets by increasing both their demand and time liabilities.

EXCESS RESERVES AND OTHER QUALIFICATIONS

In the preceding sections, we have assumed that the banks are "loaned up" with no excess reserves, among other things. They expand their loans and investments until their excess reserves are all used up. This assumption does not appear to be too realistic. We have mentioned that required reserves are available to the banks to meet their liquidity requirements only to a very limited extent. Therefore, excess reserves are usually held as working balances to meet adverse clearing balances and currency demands of depositors. The assumption moreover implies that profitable lending and investing opportunities are always available for the banks to be loaned up. This, however, is not always the case. At times, the excess reserves of the banks pile up because of inadequate profitable loan outlets. This is the case of periods of declining business activity or recession. At such times business enterprises are less eager to borrow, owing to depressing profit expectations, and banks are less willing to lend, due to the limited ability of borrowers to repay their debts. When banks keep minimum excess reserves, the volume of deposit money which can be created by the banking system is smaller since the amount of reserves available to support credit expansion is smaller.

Assume that the minimum excess reserves held by the banks for liquidity purposes (E) is proportional to total demand deposits (D), that is $E = e \cdot D$. Hence, $\Delta E = e \cdot \Delta D$ indicates the increase in excess reserves held by banks as demand deposits increase by ΔD. With $\Delta C = 0$ and $\Delta T = 0$, the initial increase in reserves is used to meet required reserves and minimum excess reserves: $\Delta R = r \cdot \Delta D + e \cdot \Delta D = (e + r)\Delta D$. It follows that $\Delta D = \Delta R \dfrac{1}{r + e}$. With $\Delta R = 10{,}000$, $r = 0.20$ and $e = 0.05$, then

$$\Delta D = 10{,}000 \times \frac{1}{0.20 + 0.05} = 40{,}000$$

[8]It would appear erroneous to explain this in terms of the lower legal reserve ratio against time deposits. In the above example, assume that $h = 0.30$, which is greater than $r = 0.20$, the change in total deposits ($\Delta D + \Delta T$) is still approximately \$27,300, as compared with \$25,000 in the case in which there is no induced change in time deposits ($\Delta T = 0$).

If $\Delta E = 0$ then ΔD will be \$50,000. The effect of the holding of minimum excess reserves on the volume of deposit money which can be created by the banking system is therefore similar to that of a higher legal reserve ratio. But while required reserves have to be observed by the banks, the levels of minimum excess reserves held for operational purposes in fact vary according to the experiences of individual banks. These excess reserves could be used to support further credit and deposit expansion if this is considered safe and desirable by management.

In the preceding sections we also have assumed implicitly that the legal reserve ratio against demand deposits is the same for all commercial banks. While this is true in most foreign countries where commercial banks are subject to uniform minimum reserve requirements, it is not the case for the American commercial banking system in which reserve city banks are subject to higher legal reserve ratios than are country banks. With different reserve ratios applicable to different classes of banks, the volume of deposit money which can be created by the banking system, given an increase in reserves, is of course not the same as that indicated by the various expressions presented above. In addition, the requirement of the banks regarding the holding of compensating balances on the part of borrowers is another qualification of the expansion process which we have described. If, in terms of the loan agreements, borrowers are allowed to draw on their accounts up to certain specified percentages of the loan proceeds, then the reserves received by some banks as a result of the checking out of loans by borrowers of other banks would be smaller. Hence they would be in a position to create smaller amounts of deposit money.

In the light of these qualifications, it follows that the expressions discussed in the above sections only represent the maximum volume of deposit money which can be created by the banking system under given limiting assumptions.

DEPOSIT CONTRACTION

The money-creation multiplier works in either direction. We have seen the expansion of credit by a bank when it receives additional reserves, enabling the banking system to expand credit and deposit money by a multiple of the initial increase in reserves. Conversely, a loss of reserve when the system is fully loaned up would give rise to a cumulative contraction of demand deposits. The loss of reserves may result from the conversion of demand deposits into currency by depositors or the sale of securities by the Federal Reserve to the public. The bank which suffers the initial loss of reserves will have to make up for the reserve deficiency by recalling loans or selling securities. This will put pressure on other banks which in turn will have to recall loans or liquidate investments. The contraction of demand deposits so induced will go on until existing reserves of the banking system are adequate to meet the minimum legal reserve requirements.

To illustrate the contraction process, assume that the banks lose \$10,000 of cash reserves as a result of currency withdrawal by customers, and the legal reserve ratio is 20 percent. The initial balance-sheet change of the banking system is

A	Balance-Sheet Change of Banking System		L
Reserves	- $10,000	Demand deposits	- $10,000

The decrease in demand deposits of $10,000 would reduce required reserves by $2,000. But the loss of reserves is $10,000; the system is still deficient in required reserves by $8,000. To meet the minimum reserve requirements, further contraction of deposits is required. The overall contraction of deposit money is

$$\Delta D = \Delta R \cdot \left(\frac{1}{r}\right) = -10{,}000 \left(\frac{1}{0.20}\right) = -\$50{,}000$$

The loss of reserves of $10,000 thus has caused a contraction of $50,000 of deposit money. (It is assumed that $\Delta C = 0$ and $\Delta T = 0$). In balance sheet terms, the contraction is as follows:

A	Balance Sheet Change of System		L
Required reserves	-$10,000	Demand deposits	-$50,000
Loans and investments	- 40,000		

It should be noted that the decrease in the supply of money in this case is only $40,000, as the decrease in deposit money of $50,000 is partly offset by an increase in currency in circulation of $10,000. With induced cash flow, the contraction of demand deposits would be smaller than in the case in which there is no induced cash flow. The inflow of cash as a result of deposit contraction would help reduce the deficiency in required reserves, thereby reducing the magnitude of the contraction of deposit money. With $c = 0.20$, the contraction of demand deposits is

$$\Delta D = \Delta R \left(\frac{1}{r + c}\right) = -10{,}000 \left(\frac{1}{0.20 + 0.20}\right) = -10{,}000 \times 2.5 = -\$25{,}000$$

The induced cash inflow of $5,000 has reduced the net loss of reserves to only $5,000. This required only $20,000 contraction in loans and investments.

The process of deposit contraction is just the reverse of the expansion process. If one dollar of additional reserve can support the creation of several dollars of demand deposits, the loss of a dollar of reserve requires the destruction of several dollars of deposit money. The money-expansion multiplier is the same as the money-contraction multiplier. However, note should be taken of the following point. When the banks receive additional reserves either from the central bank or the public, there is an increase in their potential power to expand credit and money. Whether there is an actual multiple increase in demand deposits depends upon the willingness of the banks to lend, the disposition of the borrowers to borrow, and the availability of profitable lending and investing opportunities, among other things. If lending outlets are inadequate, the result could be an increase in idle reserves of the banks. On the other hand, when the central bank takes action to reduce the volume of reserves of the banks, such as the sale of securities to the public, the banking system will be forced to contract credit and demand deposits. Therefore it appears that the central bank has more power in reducing the supply of credit and money than in stimulating credit and deposit expansion. Indeed, in periods of declining business activity, efforts made by the central bank to increase the reserves of the banks for credit and deposit expansion may result only in more bank excess reserves.

SUMMARY

Under the system of fractional reserves, the banking system as a whole is able to expand credit and deposit money by a multiple of its reserves. Conversely, a given loss of reserves would cause a cumulative contraction of credit and demand deposits. Central bank money and Treasury currency which makes up the legal reserves of the banks is thus high-powered money. Each dollar of central bank money can support many dollars of commercial bank money.

The ability of the banks to expand credit and demand deposits depends upon the availability of reserves, the levels of the legal reserve ratios against demand and time liabilities, the amount of excess reserves which the banks desire to hold, and the size of the induced cash flow, among other things. The relative size of the induced cash flow does not vary substantially, as it is governed by relatively stable factors such as the habit of payments of the public. The amount of excess reserves held for operational purposes is determined by the banks. The availability of reserves and the legal reserve ratios, on the other hand, are determined by the Federal Reserve. By changing the availability of reserves and varying the legal reserve ratios, the Federal Reserve authorities are in a position to influence the flow of credit and money in accordance with the objectives of monetary policy. The various measures which can be used by the Federal Reserve to influence the supply of money and credit is discussed in some detail in Chapter 13 on the control functions of the Federal Reserve.

PROBLEMS

1. What is the ability of a monopoly bank to create money in a noncash closed economy? Is there any limitation on its ability to create money if this is an open-society in which payments may involve foreign money? Assume that there are several commercial banks in this cashless closed system; what are the necessary conditions for the banking system to create bank money without limits?

2. "For nearly a century following the rapid development of banking, which occurred early in the nineteenth century, bankers and economists argued about the character of bank loans. The economist's argument may be summed up in the statement, 'loans create deposits,' whereas the banker's case was enshrined in the seemingly contrary thesis, 'deposits permit loans;' in fact both statements are true but neither is complete." (W. T. Newlyn, *The Theory of Money.*) Do you agree? Why or why not? Explain.

3. Do you agree that "nonmonetary assets are monetized" by commercial banks? Use examples to illustrate your arguments.

4. Do banks lend out their cash or excess reserves? If not, what do they lend? Explain.

5. What are various qualifications to the process of money creation of the banking system other than induced cash leakage, induced time deposits changes, and banks' holdings of minimum excess reserves for working purposes?

6. Assume that Mr. X deposits in his bank, Bank A (one bank in a multibank system), $1,000 in currency which he has held in his wall safe. (a) Given the legal reserve ratio against demand deposits of 10 percent, what is the maximum amount of deposit money which can be created by the banking system? (b) Show the balance-sheet change of the banking system. (c) What is the change in the money supply?

7. In question 6 above, in addition to $r = 0.10$, assume that $\Delta C/\Delta D = 0.14$, $\Delta T/\Delta D = 0.20$, and the legal reserve ratio against time deposits is 5 percent. (a) What is the maximum amount of deposit money which can be created by the banking system? (b) Show the system's balance sheet change. (c) What is the size of ΔD when $\Delta T = 0$? (d) Explain the differences between the balance-sheet changes of the banking system in the cases in which $\Delta T = 0$ and $\Delta T > 0$.

8. Suppose that the Y corporation withdraws $1 million in currency from the banking system, and this takes place when the system is loaned up. (a) With $r = 0.10$, what is the maximum contraction in the demand deposits of the banking system? (b) Would the process of multiple deposit contraction operate if the system were able to sell $900,000 of securities to the Federal Reserve?

chapter 9

Commercial Banking Operations: Portfolio Management

We have discussed to this point the major assets and liabilities of banks and the process of money creation. We have not touched upon the ways by which banks select and manage various types of earning assets which make up their portfolios. This is important, since the success or failure of banks depends to a large extent on how these assets are selected and managed. In this chapter we shall discuss some problems of portfolio management, various variables to be considered in the selection of assets, some rules which can be used for portfolio selection, portfolio regulations, and the relationship between the money market and portfolio management.

LIQUIDITY, SOLVENCY, AND INCOME

Banks have different problems and policies with regard to their internal organization, personnel management, customer relations, loan and investment operations, among other things. There is, however, one basic problem common to all commercial banks, large as well as small: liquidity and solvency versus income. Banks would have to manage their funds so that they are not only in a position to meet their demand obligations toward depositors but also to earn adequate incomes to remain in business. The holding of cash assets helps a bank to meet its liquidity needs. The holding of earning assets helps it to earn incomes. But too much cash would mean unnecessary sacrifice of income. On the other hand, too little cash would mean the risk of illiquidity and failure.

The segments *OA* and *OB* in Fig. 9-1 represent the two extreme alternatives by which a bank can use its funds. It can keep all its funds in cash (*OA*) or use all of them to acquire earning assets (*OB*).[1] The outcome of these two opposite alternatives, however, is the same: the bank would be in trouble. It is either too liquid to be able to earn income or too illiquid to be able to meet its current obligations. Between these two extremes, *AB* represents an infinite number of

[1] Since earning assets represented by the *OX*-axis are expressed in terms of money, it follows that *OA* = *OB* and the straight line *AB* has a -1 slope (prices of earning assets are assumed to be constant).

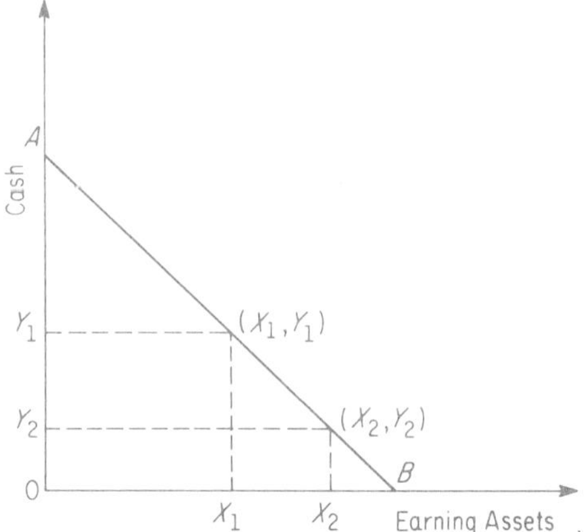

Fig. 9-1. Portfolio alternatives.

combinations of cash and earning assets which can be selected by bank management such as (X_1, Y_1) or (X_2, Y_2). Assume that combination (X_1, Y_1) is selected, the bank then keeps OY_1 of its total assets in cash and OX_1 in the form of income-yielding claims. Among these various combinations, there is one which is optimal in that it helps the individual bank to best meet its liquidity needs and at the same time to maximize its earnings. To approximate that optimal combination is the major challenge of bank management. The cash-earning-assets combination selected by an individual bank reflects, among other things, the attitude of management toward income and liquidity, the expected returns on available loans and investments, and the bank's anticipated short- and longer-term liquidity requirements.

The cash-earning-assets combination of a bank constitutes its portfolio. The proportion of cash held by a bank influences the composition and the maturity structure of its portfolio of earning assets. In general, a bank which holds a relatively large percentage of its assets in cash can lengthen the relative maturity distribution of its earning assets. A smaller proportion of cash would require the bank to hold a larger portion of its income-yielding claims in liquid forms.

Bank Liquidity

The liquidity problem is common to all enterprises, whether commercial banks, financial intermediaries, or commercial and industrial firms. To remain in business they all have to meet their obligations when they come due. The liquidity problem faced by commercial banks, however, is much more acute since almost all of its liabilities are payable either on demand or on short notice.

A bank is liquid when it is able to meet all its current liabilities. If it is not able to meet its demand obligations, then it fails. But bank liquidity is generally understood not only in the sense of its ability to meet its demand obligations but also its ability to satisfy the legitimate credit requirements of its customers.[2] The first type of liquidity can be referred to as "deposit liquidity"; and the second type, "loan liquidity." The deposit liquidity of the bank is of primary importance. Its inability to meet its deposit liquidity would inevitably result in failure. With regard to loan liquidity, the bank has some degree of control. It can either tighten or liberalize its credit policies at its own option. But a bank which is not able to satisfy the legitimate demand for credit of its customers would jeopardize its customer relations. This would adversely affect its long-run earning power. The ability of a bank to meet its "loan liquidity" needs, it should be noted, tends to reduce its ability to meet its deposit liquidity requirements. When a bank grants a loan to a customer, the checking out of loans could result in an adverse drain on its reserves.

No two banks have the same liquidity needs at any given time, and the liquidity needs of the same bank vary over time with the changes in its deposit flow and in customers' loan demands. The deposit liquidity of a bank is largely a function of the structure and behavior of its deposit liabilities. The greater the instability of its deposits, the greater the likelihood of deposit withdrawals, and hence the greater the proportion of liquid assets required for liquidity purposes. Demand deposits generally require a higher degree of liquidity than do time deposits, since the former are relatively more unstable than the latter. The same class of deposits, either demand or time deposits, public or private deposits, however, does not call for the same degree of liquidity. For example, special liquidity provisions are always required for large demand accounts, especially those of large corporations and public bodies, since these accounts are usually subject to a high degree of fluctuation. In terms of their "scientific cash management," holders of large demand accounts do not customarily keep them idle for extended periods of time. Business organizations which have large, temporarily idle demand balances usually convert them into such short-term earning assets as Treasury bills, certificates of deposit, and open-market paper for additional income. They will liquidate these assets for cash when their anticipated liquidity needs arise, such as the payment of taxes and other periodical expenses.

The loan-liquidity requirement of a bank, on the other hand, is related to the customers' demand for loans. The amount of funds needed for loan-liquidity purposes depends on the expected increases in deposits and in loan demands. If the increase in deposits is expected to be roughly the same as the increase in the demand for loans, then new loan requests can be satisfied out of new deposits. If loan demand is expected to rise faster than deposits, then bank management would have to hold sufficient liquid assets to meet anticipated future demands for loans. The close contacts between bank

[2] See Howard D. Crosse, *Management Policies for Commercial Banks* (Englewood Cliffs, N. J.: Prentice-Hall, 1962), Chap. 8.

officials and business customers, such as visits by bank officials with customers to learn about their future plans, enable bank management to approximate customers' future credit needs.

The overall liquidity requirements of an individual bank thus have to be related to the total demand for funds made upon it by both depositors and borrowers over time. The time pattern, both seasonal and cyclical, of its expected liquidity requirements determines both the form and maturity of assets which it must hold for liquidity purposes. While cash assets are needed by a bank to meet its immediate liquidity needs, and the minimum legal required reserves, short-term earning assets are held for future liquidity needs. A bank that holds cash assets for future liquidity needs would unnecessarily sacrifice incomes. Responsible management would have to space the maturity distribution of its assets so that they come to maturity approximately at the time when the expected liquidity needs arise. Forecasting, unfortunately, is still a developing art. While bank management has a fairly good idea about the pattern of seasonal deposit variations and liquidity needs, its forecasting of longer-term liquidity requirements is usually subject to wide margins of error. Additional reserves are therefore always needed to allow for these forecasting errors and unforeseen demands for loans.

The individual bank can correct forecasting errors regarding its liquidity requirements by borrowing either from the Federal Reserve, or from other commercial banks in the form of Federal Funds purchases or repurchase agreements, or by selling earning assets. The source of liquidity for the individual bank, however, may be different from that of the banking system as a whole. It is true that a bank can adjust its liquidity position through Federal Funds purchases, repurchase agreements, or the sale of earning assets, but this is not the case for the banking system. As we have mentioned, these transactions only represent the transfer of reserves between banks, but there is no change in the system's total reserves. Yet the overall liquidity position of the banking system can be improved only when there is a net increase in its total reserves. This can be brought about only by the Federal Reserve when it purchases securities either from the banks or the public and makes greater advance or rediscounting facilities available to them. For the banking system as a whole, the Federal Reserve is therefore the ultimate source of liquidity.

It would be of interest to note that several kinds of ratios can be used to measure the liquidity position of a bank—for example, the loan-to-deposit ratio, the ratio of cash to demand deposits (cash ratio) and the ratio of cash and governments to deposits. These ratios are usually referred to as liquidity ratios. The loan-to-deposit ratio varies inversely with the liquidity position of the bank. The higher the ratio is, the lower the bank's liquidity is supposed to be. This ratio is a crude liquidity measurement, however. Without information on the liquidity structure of a bank's assets, the composition and character of its deposits, very little can indeed be learned from this ratio. The cash ratio relates the cash position of a bank to its demand deposits which normally represent the unstable component of total deposits. Other things being equal, the higher the ratio, the greater is the ability of the bank to honor its demand obligations. Since the reserve assets of a bank can be quickly converted into cash for liquidity purposes, they should be included in the measurement of its liquidity. Therefore, a more reliable indicator of a bank's liquidity position is the ratio of cash and governments to total deposits. The ratio reveals the overall liquidity capability of the bank.

Bank Solvency

To remain in business, a bank has to be at once liquid and solvent. A bank is solvent when the value of its assets is adequate to cover all its liabilities. We know from the balance sheet identity that Capital Account (CA) = Total Assets (TA) − Total Liabilities (TL). So long as TA − TL = CA > 0, the bank is solvent. Then it is insolvent when the value of its assets is smaller than its liabilities, or TA − TL = CA < 0. In principle, a bank may be insolvent, yet liquid, or it may be illiquid, yet solvent. The following hypothetical balance sheet of Bank A indicates that it is liquid, but it is insolvent. Its total liabilities ($350,000) exceed the value of its assets ($340,000) by $10,000. The capital account of $20,000 is not adequate to absorb the loan and investment losses of $30,000. Had the capital account been $30,000, the bank would have remained solvent, however, barely. It follows that whether a bank is solvent or not depends to a considerable extent upon the size of its capital relative to its total liabilities. The greater the relative size of the capital account, the greater the ability of the bank to adsorb asset losses, and the smaller the risk of bank insolvency.

The immediate cause of bank insolvency is the decline in the value of bank assets. This can be accounted for by numerous factors. Asset losses may be due to irresponsible management which granted substandard loans to borrowers who subsequently defaulted their obligations, or to developments which adversely affected the ability of borrowers to pay off their debts such as strikes, declining prices, and profits. The decline in asset values which could cause banks to be insolvent may also be accounted for by capital losses experienced by a bank which was forced to sell part of its long-term assets to meet unexpected liquidity requirements. This indicates that although liquidity and solvency are two different problems, they are closely related. Liquidity and solvency go hand in hand. A liquid bank with sufficient liquid assets will not have to liquidate long-term assets at substantial losses in order to satisfy its liquidity needs. Again, responsible management would have to program the liquidity structure of its assets so that it does not have to liquidate illiquid assets to meet the liquidity test, which may cause it to fail its test of solvency.

A	Balance Sheet of Bank *A*		L
Cash and due from banks	\$ 60,000	Demand deposits	\$200,000
		Time deposits.	\$150,000
Loans and investments	\$250,000	Paid-in capital, \$20,000	
Building and equipment.	\$ 30,000	Less deficit -\$30,000	- 10,000
Total	\$340,000	Total	\$340,000

Income

Liquidity and solvency are but two major requirements for a bank to continue its operations. To stay in business, banks also have to earn adequate incomes. While liquidity represents the obligation of the bank toward its depositors and customers, to make profits is the responsibility of bank management toward the shareholders. Banks derive their incomes mostly from interest on loans and investments. There appears to be a conflict, at least in the short run, between liquidity and profitability. A bank can increase its earnings by lengthening the relative maturities of its loans and investments, as long-term assets usually yield higher returns. But by lengthening the maturities of its loans and investments for larger incomes, the bank faces an increasing liquidity risk, as it may be forced to liquidate these long-term assets to meet its liquidity needs with substantial delays and capital losses.

Since a defunct bank does not earn income, in order to make profits, a bank has to be a going concern, which requires that it be both liquid and solvent. In the long run, bank management would have to compromise between liquidity and earnings, selecting portfolios of loans and investments so that profits are adequate, on the one hand, and liquidity requirements are best satisfied, on the other.

VARIABLES TO BE CONSIDERED IN ASSET SELECTION

There are several variables which the management of a bank would have to consider in the selection of earning assets. It would have to consider the liquidity of various types of loans and investments, the various types of risk associated with these assets, their expected returns, among other things. These variables are closely related. High-yield earning assets are usually riskier and less liquid than low-income claims.

Asset Liquidity

The liquidity of an earning asset is its ability to be converted into cash promptly and without loss. Liquidity is largely a function of marketability and maturity. Generally speaking, between two assets which have the same maturity, the one having a greater marketability is the more liquid one, since it is more easily and quickly exchangeable for cash. The marketability of an asset depends upon the size of the market in which it is traded and the regularity of trading. A security which is regularly traded on a large market is more liquid than the one which is traded on an irregular and narrow market. On the other hand, between two assets which have the same degree of marketability, the one with a shorter maturity is more liquid since the capital loss, if any, involved in the sale of the short-term asset, will be smaller than the loss arising from the liquidation of the long-term security. The liquidity of an asset, as we have mentioned, is measured not only by the speed with which it can be converted into cash but also the capital loss involved in the conversion process. Liquid assets are usually short-term, highly marketable securities. But in some instances, a longer-term asset may be more marketable than a short-term one. Then the former may be more liquid, even though it has a relatively longer maturity.

Risk

There are two types of risks associated with loans and investments: credit risk and interest risk. The credit risk may arise from the inability of borrowers to repay their loans or the inability of issuers of securities to redeem their obligations at maturity. This risk is present in loans to private borrowers and securities issued by private corporations. This type of risk can be minimized by requiring adequate collateral, by loan and investment diversification, both geographical and by industry, and by careful investigation of the credit standing of the borrowing firm, the integrity of its management, the nature of its business, the stability of its earnings, its prospect for further growth and development. The credit risk is minimal when loans are extended to, or securities are bought from, a firm with a stable record of earnings, with a high degree of productive diversification, and a bright prospect of steady growth and expansion. In regard to the quality of investment securities, the judgment of bank management can be supplemented by reliable ratings of such rating organizations as Moody's Investors Service, Inc., or Standard & Poor's Corporation.

The interest risk, on the other hand, reflects the decline in the market prices of securities resulting from rising interest rates. This type of risk is not usually present in loan assets because these are mostly not marketable. The interest risk is inherent in both securities issued by private corporations and public bodies. The main difference is that while private corporate securities are subject to both the credit risk and interest risk, government securities are subject primarily to adverse changes in market prices. The probability of the federal government failing to redeem its obligations at maturity is practically zero. The risk of loss in the market value of securities reflects the inverse relationship between their market prices and yields, which we have already mentioned. The longer the maturity of an earning asset, the more it is susceptible to price fluctuations, and the greater the interest risk.

It is true that the variety of interest rates prevailing on the money and capital markets in the long run tend to move in the same direction, but this unison movement is not perfect. There are time lags in the movement of individual rates in relation to one another. Investment diversification, therefore, always helps to minimize the interest risk, especially when securities selected are not highly correlated with one another. A portfolio which consists mostly of highly correlated securities would, on the other hand, benefit the least from the advantage of diversification, as their market prices and yields tend to move closely together. It should be noted that the interest risk will materialize only when banks decide to liquidate their earning assets prior to their maturity date when interest rates are rising. This again indicates that the ability of bank management to forecast their future liquidity requirements and schedule the maturity distribution of their earning assets in accordance with these anticipated liquidity needs would help reduce probable capital losses resulting from forced premature sales of securities.

Expected Returns

In addition to liquidity and risk, bank management has to consider the net expected returns from the various types of loans and investments under consideration. Net returns represent the difference between gross earnings and costs. The costs of loans and investments are composed of their original costs (prices) and servicing expenses. Gross incomes consist of interest receipts plus discounts on securities bought below par (and held to maturity) and capital gains realized on securities sold before maturity. (Premiums on securities bought over par and capital losses are subtracted from gross income estimates.) It follows that the level of expected income is determined not only by the levels of interest rates prevailing at the time when securities are purchased, but also on the future changes in the levels and structure of interest which will give rise to either capital losses or gains. Since, with the exception of the coupon rates on securities and their purchase prices which are known, other determinants of gross receipts are estimates which depend on unknown future interest variations, estimates of gross income may be subject to wide margins of error. The difference between estimated incomes and realized incomes depends upon the extent of the deviation between the anticipated pattern of interest changes and actual interest changes.

Loan and investment costs, on the other hand, can be estimated rather accurately by banks. The initial costs of investments and loans are of course known to the banks. They also have good information on the servicing and handling costs involved in the acquisition of additional earning assets. Since the administrative cost of each individual loan or investment belonging to the same class is about the same, irrespective of its size, the larger the size of the loan or investment, the smaller the operating cost per dollar loaned or invested, or the greater the net income.

Tax Law

The federal income tax law is another important variable which bank management has to take into consideration in the formulation of portfolio policy. Commercial banks, like other business enterprises, have to pay federal income tax on their net income. The marginal rate of taxation can be as high as 48 percent. For a bank which is already subject to a high marginal tax rate, the tax-exempt income which can be earned on certain kinds of securities is an important consideration, inasmuch as a dollar of tax-exempt income is equivalent to several dollars of taxable income. Thus, for a bank which pays 48 percent in federal income tax on its net earnings, an interest income of \$3 per \$100 invested in state and municipal bonds, which is entirely exempt from all federal taxes, is equivalent to a taxable income of about \$5.8, which a bank earns on government securities or corporate bonds, for $3(1 - 0.48)^{-1} = 5.8$.

Another provision of the federal income tax law which has to be considered is the different treatment of capital losses and gains. According to the law, banks can charge capital losses against ordinary income, whereas profits realized from the sale of assets which have been held for more than six months are subject to the low capital-gains tax of only 25 percent. This provision sometimes enables banks to undertake losses in order to make profits. For example, during periods of prosperity when interest is high and prices of securities are below their "average" levels, banks subject to higher income tax rates may be willing to sell government securities at capital losses in order to release funds for the purchase of securities of longer maturities for anticipated higher prices of securities which will prevail in the next recession when interest declines. When the recession comes, they will sell long-term securities at higher prices for capital gains, and will purchase short-term obligations to avoid probable capital losses resulting from rising interest rates expected to prevail in the next boom. As an example, suppose that the capital loss experienced by a bank which sold securities at time t was \$10,000, the decrease of net income after taxes would be \$5,200, assuming that the bank was paying the 48 percent income tax rate. Suppose that by taking this capital loss, the bank was able to acquire securities which would promise a capital gain of, say, \$12,000, at time $t + 5$ (five years hence). Since the capital gain tax is only 25 percent, the expected increase in income after tax would be \$9,000. This taking of loss would be profitable should the present value of the net income of \$9,000, expected at $t + 5$, calculated on the basis of a subjective rate of discount (which reflects both the market rate at t and an allowance for the risk that the expected capital gains might not be materialized) be greater than the net income of \$5,200, which would have been obtained at t

had the capital loss not been taken. Assume that the rate of discount used is 10 percent. The present value of a net income of \$9,000 expected five years hence is \$9,000 $(1 + 0.10)^{-5}$ = \$5,589. It appears profitable for the bank to take the capital loss.[3]

RULES FOR PORTFOLIO SELECTION

The portfolio of a bank, as we have mentioned, represents the overall collection of its earning assets, both loans and investments. The loan component is sometimes referred to as loan portfolio, and the investment component as investment portfolio. Just like any other financial institutions and business corporations, the problem faced by a bank in its portfolio management is a constrained maximization problem. Given the amount of funds available for the acquisition of earning assets, the major challenge of bank management is to select a portfolio which is optimal from both the liquidity and profitability standpoints.

Inasmuch as the profitability and liquidity of a bank's portfolio are more or less in conflict with each other, its portfolio policy is mainly a compromise between these two basic considerations. Theoretically, an optimal portfolio can be considered as the one that, given its profitability, minimizes the liquidity risk; or alternatively, the one that, given the liquidity risk, maximizes earnings.

Since the liquidity problem is mainly a short-run concern, banks, in the short run, have to give primary consideration to their liquidity position. In order to meet their immediate liquidity needs as well as legal required reserves and unforeseen currency withdrawals, banks have to keep cash reserves. These are their primary reserves. They constitute their first line of defense. In addition to cash reserves, banks also hold liquid assets for future liquidity purposes. These assets consist of such assets as Treasury bills and other money market obligations. They are banks' secondary reserves. They form their second line of defense. After adequate provisions are made for primary and secondary reserves, banks are in a position to use their remaining reserves in loans and investments for income purposes.

The earnings of a bank are related to the size of its loans and investments. Assume that $X_1\ X_2, \ldots, X_n$ are the various types of loans and investments available, and Bank A wants to select among these earning assets, a combination which yields the greatest return. The earnings of the bank will depend on the amount of earning assets which it will require. Earnings then can be expressed as a function of $X_1, X_2, \ldots, X_n$ as follows:

$$E = E\,(X_1, X_2, X_3, \ldots, X_n)$$

[3]In general, let X_t be the capital loss taken at time t; τ, the corporation income tax rate; X_{t+n} the capital gain expected to be realized at time $t + n$; r, the capital gain tax rate; and i, the subjective rate of discount used, then it would be profitable to take capital loss if:

$$\frac{X_{t+n}(1-r)}{(1+i)^n} > |X_t\,(1-\tau)|$$

where E represents total earnings. Let $r_1, r_2, \ldots, r_n$ be the costs of $X_1, X_2, \ldots, X_n$ respectively, and C, the volume of funds available to the bank for loans and investments, we have the following equation showing the various ways by which the bank's funds can be allocated among the earning assets:

$$C = r_1 X_1 + r_2 X_2 + \cdots + r_n X_n$$

The problem which the bank faces is to select a feasible combination of $X_1, X_2, \ldots, X_n$ such that its earnings are maximum. By "a feasible combination of $X_1, X_2, \ldots, X_n$," we mean a combination which is well within the bank's financial capability. In order to maximize E, it will have to equate the marginal earnings of the dollar invested in all these assets—that is, it has to fulfill the following conditions:[4]

$$\frac{E_1}{r_1} = \frac{E_2}{r_2} = \frac{E_3}{r_3} = \because = \frac{E_n}{r_n} \tag{I}$$

[4]The earning function of the bank is $E = E(X_1, X_2, X_3, \ldots, X_n)$ and the financial restriction is $C = r_1 X_1 + r_2 X_2 + \cdots + r_n X_n$. To maximize E subject to C, we form a new function

$$V = E(X_1, X_2, \ldots, X_n) + \phi(C - r_1 X_1 - r_2 X_2 - \cdots - r_n X_n)$$

and set the first-order partial derivatives of V with respect to $x_1, x_2, \ldots, x_n$, and ϕ equal to zero, we have

$$\frac{\partial V}{\partial X_1} = E_1 (X_1, X_2, \ldots, X_n) - r_1 \phi = 0$$

$$\frac{\partial V}{\partial X_2} = E_2 (X_1, X_2, \ldots, X_n) - r_2 \phi = 0 \tag{1}$$

$$\frac{\partial V}{\partial X_n} = E_n (X_1, X_2, \ldots, X_n) - r_n \phi = 0$$

$$\frac{\partial V}{\partial \phi} = C - r_1 X_1 - r_2 X_2 - \cdots - r_n X_n = 0$$

From (1) we have $\frac{E_1}{r_1} = \frac{E_2}{r_2} = \cdots = \frac{En}{r_n} = \phi$ (which is condition 1 above) where $E_i = \frac{\partial E}{\partial X_i}$ is the marginal earnings of the ith security. The system of Equation (1) is the necessary condition for maximum E. Solve this system of equations for $X_1, X_2, \ldots X_n$, we would obtain a combination of earning assets which maximizes the earnings of the bank. The coefficient ϕ is the change in total earnings per dollar change of investible funds, that is,

$$\frac{dE}{dC} = \phi$$

We know that

$$dE = E_1 dX_1 + E_2 dX_2 + \cdots + E_n dX_n$$

and

$$dC = r_1 dX_1 + r_2 dX_2 + \cdots + r_n dX_n$$

$$= \frac{1}{\phi} (E_1 dX_1 + E_2 dX_2 + \cdots + E_n dX_n)$$

as

$$r_i = E_i \left(\frac{1}{\phi}\right) \text{ from (1), hence}$$

$$\frac{dE}{dC} = \frac{(E_1 dX_1 + E_2 dX_2 + \cdots + EndXn)}{1/\phi\, (E_1 dX_1 + E_2 dX_2 + \cdots + E_n dX_n)} = \phi$$

where Ei is the marginal earning of the ith security and ri as its price. The marginal earning of a security, say, security 1, represents the change in total earnings resulting in a unit change of that security. Since the price of security 1 is r_1, the ratio of E_1/r_1 indicates the marginal earning per dollar invested in that security. Unless the ratios of marginal earning to prices of all securities selected are the same, the bank can always improve its earnings by investing more in those securities promising the highest extra returns and less in those securities with lowest extra earnings.

This earning-maximization rule, while theoretically feasible, is hardly operational. While banks make portfolio decisions in the midst of uncertainty or risk, this rule, among other things, does not allow for risk or uncertainty.

An approach which appears to be promising in applicability is linear programming. By using linear programming models, a bank can find a combination of assets which not only maximizes profits but also satisfies such operational restrictions and requirements as the loan, investment, and capital cushion restrictions and the deposit-liquidity and loan-liquidity requirements. The following model is an oversimplified illustration of the possible use of linear programming in portfolio selection. In this model we assume among other things that a bank attempts to schedule the liquidity structure of its earning assets in relation to the liquidity structure of its deposits—that is, the greater the liquidity of deposits, the more liquid assets it would have to hold. When there is a shift in the liquidity structure of deposits, the bank also changes the liquidity structure of its earning assets. For example, when there is a shift from liquid to less liquid deposits (a shift from demand to time deposits), the bank can accordingly shift from liquid, low-yield assets to relatively less liquid, high-income-yielding claims.

Assume that the amount of funds available to Bank A is \$300,000, of which \$260,000 are deposits and \$40,000 are capital funds (retained earnings, proceeds from the sale of new capital notes and debentures, etc.). It is estimated by the bank that in order to meet its minimum needs for working reserves, it would have to hold at least 3 percent of total funds, or \$9,000 in cash assets (X_1), and the remaining amount of funds could be used for the acquisition of six different types of earning assets, such as Treasury bills (X_2), other U.S. Government securities (X_3), short-term business and commercial loans (X_4), medium-term loans (X_5), long-term investments (X_6), and long-term, high-risk, high-income loans (X_7). On the basis of past operating records, the bank groups its deposits into four classes, in accordance with their liquidity, as follows: (a) highly unstable deposits (about \$60,000), (b) unstable deposits (\$70,000), (c) relatively stable deposits (\$80,000), and (d) stable deposits (\$50,000). The future loan demand of the banks' customers, say, six months hence, is estimated to be at least \$60,000. Since \$60,000 of total deposits are considered highly unstable, at least that portion of funds available would have to be held in cash and secondary reserve assets only. The amount of funds which could be used in short-term business and commercial loans and U.S. Government securities should be no more than the unstable portion of total deposits. Likewise, the volume of long-term investments and intermediate term loans should be no more than the relatively stable portion of total deposits. And long-term, risky, high-income-yielding loans should be no more than capital funds and stable deposits.

To protect the interests of depositors, the bank also would have to assign capital funds requirements to each category of assets, with smaller requirements for short-term loans and higher requirements for long-term loans and investments. On the basis of these estimates and considerations, the following programming model is formulated by the bank:

$$E = 0.02X_2 + 0.03X_3 + 0.04X_4 + 0.05X_5 + 0.06X_6 + 0.07X_7 \qquad \text{(I)}$$

$$\begin{aligned}
X_1 &\geqslant 9{,}000 & (1)\\
X_1 + X_2 &\geqslant 60{,}000 & (2)\\
X_3 + X_4 &\leqslant 70{,}000 & (3)\\
X_5 + X_6 &\leqslant 80{,}000 & (4)\\
X_7 &\leqslant 90{,}000 & (5)\\
X_2 + X_3 &\geqslant 60{,}000 & (6)\\
0.10X_4 + 0.15X_5 + 0.20X_6 + 0.25X_7 &\leqslant 40{,}000 & (7)\\
X_1 + X_2 + X_3 + X_4 + X_5 + X_6 + X_7 &\leqslant 300{,}000 & (8)
\end{aligned} \qquad \text{(II)}$$

The bank wishes to select a combination of $(X_1, X_2, \ldots X_7)$ such that Equation (I) (the profit function) is maximized and at the same time all the restrictions and requirements in (II) are satisfied. In the profit function (I), E is expected net total earnings, and the coefficients of the terms on the right-hand side represent the net expected returns per dollar invested in these various kinds of earning assets. For example, for long-term investments, the net expected return is 6 cents per dollar invested.[5] In the system of inequalities (II), the first, second, and sixth inequalities represent the deposit-liquidity and loan-liquidity requirements. The liquidity of the bank is also promoted by inequalities, 3, 4, and 5, as these various categories of loans and investments do not exceed the portions of funds which could be safely used in these assets. Inequality 7 is the capital-cushion restriction. So long as the losses in the values of X_4, X_5, X_6, and X_7 do not exceed 10, 15, 20, and 25 percent of their value, respectively, then the losses would be completely absorbed by shareholders, the interests of depositors and other creditors would be fully protected, and the bank would remain solvent. The last inequality is the budget restriction, that is, the amount of funds used in the assets should not exceed the funds available for those loans and investments.[6] The solution of the above linear programming problem yields the following "optimum" combination of cash and earning assets:

$$\begin{aligned}
X_1 &= \$\ 9{,}000\\
X_2 &= 51{,}000\\
X_3 &= 9{,}000
\end{aligned}$$

[5]Note that vault cash (X) has no return.

[6]It should be noted that the nonnegative requirements of (II), that is $X_i \geqslant 0$ ($i = 1, 2, \ldots, 7$) (the bank is not allowed to sell earning assets at the time funds are allocated) are satisfied since the constant terms of the inequalities in (II) are all positive.

$$X_4 = 61{,}000$$
$$X_5 = 15{,}500$$
$$X_6 = 64{,}500$$
$$X_7 = 90{,}000$$

With this combination of earning assets, the maximum earnings of the bank are:

$$E = (0.02)(51{,}000) + (0.03)(9{,}000) + (0.04)(61{,}000) + (0.05)(15{,}500) + (0.06)(64{,}500) + (0.07)(90{,}000) = \$14{,}675$$

The use of linear programming in asset management can be useful in many ways. By formulating periodical programming models, banks would have insights into problems bearing on their operations. They would be able to measure the effects of changes in policy decisions by changing the various restrictions and requirements in the model, to test the efficiency of their performance. Portfolio decisions are made by banks in the face of uncertainty since they would have to forecast the future liquidity requirements of both depositors and borrower-customers, funds available, the direction of changes in the structure of interest rates at different phases of the business cycle, among other things. For each set of forecasted values of the various variables involved, a programming model can be formulated and its expected earnings calculated. On the basis of past records and experience, banks could assign a probability of occurrence to each of these various sets of forecasted values and allocated funds in accordance with the model that would yield the highest expected earnings.

Harry M. Markovitz has developed a promising theory which can be used by banks for portfolio selection, particularly their trust departments, which are especially interested in such investment securities as stocks and bonds. The theory is referred to as the "expected-return-variance-of-return" theory. Essentially, the theory seeks the selection of portfolios which, given the desired expected returns on invested funds, assume the least possible risk; or, alternatively, it seeks the selection of portfolios which maximize expected returns for a given level of risk. The theory thus does not yield a unique optimum asset portfolio but a set of "efficient" portfolios. For each desired portfolio's rate of return, it yields a portfolio which is the most efficient in that the risk of earning variations is minimum. For higher rates of return, the investors would have to content themselves with higher levels of risk, as indicated by the efficiency path *EE* in Fig. 9-2.

For the desired rate of return OX_0, the risk of not realizing that rate of return is minimum (OY_0) with portfolio E_0 on the efficiency path. Portfolio E_1, on the other hand, yields a higher rate of return (OX_1), but it also is riskier since to increase earnings, the investor would have to allocate a relatively larger proportion of total funds available in high-risk, high-yield securities. But for a given rate of return (or a given level of risk), the portfolio represented by a point on the efficiency path is most "efficient." Asset combination *G* is not efficient, since for

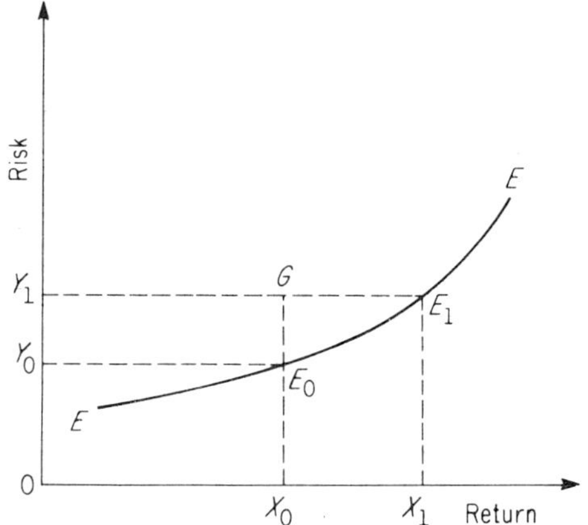

Fig. 9-2. Markovitz's efficiency path.

the same rate of return OX_0, the investor can minimize risk by selecting portfolio E_0, or for the same level of risk (OY_1), the investor can raise the rate of return from OX_0 to OX_1 by selecting portfolio E_1. The technical aspect of the theory is rather complicated to be presented here. An oversimplified illustration of the technique is presented in the footnote for interested readers, however.[7]

[7]The following example is concerned with three securities, but the theory applies to any number of securities. Let X_1, X_2, X_3 be the amounts of funds available which a bank wishes to invest in securities 1, 2, and 3; Y, the total amount of funds available; U_1, U_2 and U_3, the expected rates of returns from securities 1, 2, and 3; and E, the total expected returns of the portfolio. (X_1, X_2, X_3, Y, and E can be expressed either in absolute or relative terms. When they are expressed in relative terms, then $Y = 1$, X_1, X_2, X_3 represent the proportions of total funds invested in the three securities, and E, the portfolio's rate of return.) Let V be the variance of the portfolio and $S_{ij} = didjr_{ij}$, the covariance of returns between the ith and the jth securities (r_{ij} is the coefficient of correlation between returns from the ith and jth securities; d_i is the standard deviation of expected returns on the ith security. They are all calculated on the basis of the probability beliefs of management about expected returns. We have the following relations:

$$V = X_1^2 S_1^2 + X_2^2 S_2^2 + X_3^2 S_3^2 + {}_2X_1 X_2 S_{12} + {}_2X_1 X_3 S_{13} + {}_2X_2 X_3 S_{23} \quad (1)$$

$$X_1 + X_2 + X_3 = Y \quad (2)$$

$$U_1 X_1 + U_2 X_2 + U_3 X_3 = E \quad (3)$$

V, the variance of the portfolio, represents the risk of earning variation. We seek to minimize (1) subject to (2) and (3). We form a new function $W = V + \phi(\Sigma X_i - Y) + \lambda(\Sigma U_i X_i - E)$ and set the first-order partial derivatives of W with respect to X_1, X_2, X_3, ϕ and λ equal to zero, we have

$$\begin{aligned}
&X_1 S_1^2 + X_2 S_{12} + X_3 S_{13} + {}^1/_2\,\phi + {}^1/_2\,U_1\lambda = 0\\
&X_1 S_{12} + X_2 S_2^2 + X_3 S_{23} + {}^1/_2\,\phi + {}^1/_2\,U_2\lambda = 0\\
&X_1 S_{13} + X_2 S_{23} + X_3 S_3^2 + {}^1/_2\,\phi + {}^1/_2\,U_3\lambda = 0\\
&X_1 + X_2 + X_3 = Y\\
&U_1 X_1 + U_2 X_2 + U_3 X_3 = E
\end{aligned}$$

Admittedly, these various techniques, complicated as they are, only represent a somewhat oversimplification of the actual process by which banks make decisions regarding the selection of earning assets, which involves a large number of variables and a multitude of legal restrictions and operational requirements. But they can be useful in that they serve as theoretical guides to bank management in deciding how much of the total funds available to be invested in the portfolio should be invested in each security in order to obtain an optimum asset combination after it has made such decisions as to the specific objective of the portfolio and which securities are to be included in the portfolio from the list of possible candidates.

PORTFOLIO REGULATIONS

Commercial banks are institutions which uniquely affect the public interest as they are responsible for the creation of the bulk of money and credit in the

---

The solution of the system of Equation (I) will yield the combination of X_1, X_2, X_3, which, given the desired earnings E, minimizes the variance V. Assume that $U_1 = 0.05$; $U_2 = 0.08$; $U_3 = 0.06$; $S_2^1 = 0.02$; $S_{12} = 0.06$; $S_{13} = 0.008$; $S_2^2 = 0.08$; $S_{23} = 0.04$; $S_3^2 = 0.05$; $Y =$ \$100,000, and $E =$ \$6,000 (when X_1, X_2, X_3 are expressed in percentages, then $Y = 1$ and $E = 0.06$), we have

$$\begin{aligned} 0.02\,X_1 + 0.06X_2 + 0.008X_3 + {}^1\!/_2\,\phi + 0.025\,\lambda &= 0 \\ 0.06\,X_1 + 0.08X_2 + 0.04\,X_3 + {}^1\!/_2\,\phi + 0.04\lambda &= 0 \\ 0.008X_1 + 0.04X_2 + 0.05\,X_3 + {}^1\!/_2\,\phi + 0.03\lambda &= 0 \\ X_1 + X_2 + X_3 &= 100{,}000 \\ 0.05\,X_1 + 0.08X_2 + 0.06\,X_3 &= 6{,}000 \end{aligned} \qquad \text{(II)}$$

The solution of (II) yields:

$$X_1 = \$36{,}570$$
$$X_2 = \$18{,}290$$
$$X_3 = \$45{,}140$$

The solution shows that in order to earn an expected return of \$6,000 on the total investable funds of \$100,000, our bank has to invest \$36,570 in security 1, \$18,290 in security 2, and \$45,140 in security 3.

Given the desired return of \$6,000, this portfolio is most efficient as it minimizes risk. Should the bank wish a return of \$7,000, the efficient portfolio would be:

$$X_1 = \$\ 2{,}724$$
$$X_2 = \$51{,}360$$
$$X_3 = \$45{,}910$$

The second portfolio yields a higher return than the first one. It is also riskier. This can be verified by substituting the value of the two portfolios in Equation (1). For more information on this approach, see Harry M. Markovitz, *Portfolio Selection* (New York: Wiley, 1956); A. D. Martin, Jr., "Mathematical Programming of Portfolio Selections," *Management Science*, Vol. I, No. 2 (January 1954); and J. Fred Weston and William Beranek, "Programming Investment Portfolio Construction," *Analysts' Journal*, Vol. 11, No. 2 (May 1955).

economy. In order to avoid unsound banking practices, overexpansion of loans and investments which may jeopardize the safety of banking operations and the smooth functioning of the monetary and credit system, banks' lending and investing activities are closely regulated. Since portfolio regulations of state banks vary from state to state, we shall be concerned mainly with national banks which are subject to uniform portfolio regulations.

Loan Regulations

The lending operations of national banks are subject to several legal restrictions. A national bank is prohibited from extending loans to any one borrower in excess of 10 percent of its capital stock and surplus. This rule is referred to as the "10 percent rule." The main purpose of this provision is to promote the safety of operations through credit diversification. Heavy concentration of credit to a borrower could place the bank in difficulty should, for some reason or other, the borrowing firm be affected by adverse developments which make it unable to repay the loans when they fall due. The rule also prevents the possibility that bank officials could grant large loans to their friends or business firms in which they have financial interests, even though their credit standing is questionable. There are, however, exceptions to the 10 percent general limit on loans to individual borrowers. For example, the rule does not apply to loans secured by government securities and such commercial paper as bills of exchange used in the financing of foreign trade and domestic goods in transit. The limit on loans to any one borrower on state chartered banks generally varies from 15 to 20 percent of their capital and surplus.

A bank that is a member of the Federal Reserve is not permitted to grant loans to one affiliate in excess of 10 percent of its capital and surplus and 20 percent to all affiliates. It may make a loan not exceeding $30,000 to any executive officer if it is secured by a first lien on the officer's home.[8] It is prohibited from granting loans to bank examiners and their assistants. It is also not allowed to make loans to a subsidiary of a parent holding company of which the lending bank is also a subsidiary. These provisions were designed to guarantee against such malpractices as large loans granted to affiliates in financial difficulties, the abusive uses of bank funds by its officers for speculative purposes, the bias of bank examiners in favor of banks which granted them credit, and the monopolization of the resources of a bank by its parent holding company, among other things.

National banks are also subject to restrictions with regard to certain types of loans. For instance, the total volume of conventional real estate mortgage loans which can be made by a national bank, as already noted, is limited to 100 percent of its capital stock and surplus, or 70 percent of its time and savings deposits, whichever is greater. These loans have to be secured by first liens on real estate. In the case of "straight," or lump-sum real estate mortgage

[8]Public Law 90–44, approved July 3, 1967, ammended Sec. 22(g) of the Federal Reserve Act.

loans, they could be granted for five years, at not more than 50 percent of the appraised value of the real estate involved. With respect to amortized real estate mortgage loans, they may be granted for longer maturities, up to 25 years, and the size of the loan may be greater, from 66 to 80 percent of the real estate's appraised value. Government-insured real estate loans, such as FHA-insured and VA-guaranteed loans, however, are not subject to these general restrictions. Regulations on real estate mortgage loans of state chartered banks, in most states, are less restrictive than those applied to national banks.

In terms of the Securities Exchange Act of 1934, the Board of Governors of the Federal Reserve is empowered to regulate the amount of credit which can be extended by banks to borrowers for the purpose of purchasing and carrying stocks registered on a national securities exchange by determining the cash or margin requirements which represent that portion of the market value of securities to be paid in cash by borrowers. By changing the margin requirements, the Federal Reserve Board can either increase or reduce the volume of credit which can be made by banks to borrowers for security transactions. The main purpose of the regulation is to prevent excessive uses of bank credit in security speculation, one of the major factors responsible for the stock market crash of the late 1920's.

Investment Regulations

The investment securities held by a bank are subject to both quantitative and qualitative regulations. In terms of the Banking Act of 1935, the total amount of investment securities of any one obliger or maker held by a bank for its own account cannot at any time exceed 10 percent of its capital and surplus (the same 10 percent rule). This rule was, again, purported to reduce banking risk through investment diversification.

"Investment securities" refer to marketable obligations evidencing indebtedness, such as bonds, notes, and debentures. Securities eligible for bank investment but subject to the 10 percent rule include such securities as corporate mortgage or debenture bonds, notes, collateral trust securities, bonds issued by foreign governments and corporations, obligations of international financial instititutions, such as the International Bank for Reconstruction and Development and the Inter-American Development Bank. Exempted from the 10 percent restriction are securities issued or guaranteed by the United States Government, general obligations of state and political subdivisions, and obligations of federal agencies, such as the Federal Housing Administration, the Federal Land Banks, and the Federal Home Loan Banks.

Members of the Federal Reserve System are prohibited from acquiring for their own account shares of stock of any corporation. This prohibition appears to be based on the assumption that the holding of common shares is much riskier than holding obligations evidencing indebtedness, since the latter represent prior claims on the assets of the borrowers while the former are residual claims on the issuers' assets. Here again, there are several exceptions to this restriction, such as membership stock in the Federal Reserve Banks (equal to 6 percent of a member's capital and surplus, of which 3 percent is paid in); ownership of stock in small business investment companies (limited to 5 percent of capital and surplus); stock of corporations engaged in the safe-deposit business (limited to 15 percent of capital and surplus). Member banks are also prohibited from acquiring securities convertible into stock at the option of the issuer. With regard to stocks held by banks as a result of the default of the obligations of firms which had used them as collateral for loans, they would have to be "disposed of within a reasonable period of time."

For added safety of banking operations, the investment securities held by a bank are also subject to a certain degree of control in regard to their quality. According to the directive of the Comptroller of the Currency (in charge of chartering, examining, and supervising national banks, as will be seen later), national banks are not supposed to acquire securities which are "predominantly speculative " in nature. Marketability is the main criterion used in considering the quality of investment securities. The greater the marketability of a security, the higher its quality. Quality, however, is a relative concept. It tends to change over time with changing economic conditions. A security may be of high quality at one point in time but not at another point in time, because of changing market conditions.

For examination purposes, the investment securities held by banks are usually grouped in four basic groups in terms of their quality. The first group consists of highly marketable securities. The second group is made up of securities which are "speculative" in nature. The remaining two categories consist of securities in default and corporate stocks. Commercial banks, because of the nature of their operations, hold securities which are mostly included in the first group.

THE MONEY MARKET AND PORTFOLIO MANAGEMENT

Commercial banks are major institutions in the money market. The latter, we can recall, is a complex of arrangements for dealing in short-term, low-risk, liquid assets. The development of the banking system is a major factor in the development of the money market. The development of the money market, in turn, promotes banking development and facilitates banking management. A highly developed money market is a liquidity pool from which commercial banks can draw reserves to meet their liquidity requirements, or in which they can put to work temporarily idle reserves for additional income. A bank which is subject to heavy adverse over-the-counter balances or clearing balances can always replenish its reserves by going to the money market, either buying federal funds, selling Treasury bills, and other money market obligations. On the other hand, a bank with idle funds can use them for the acquisition of money-market securities, which can be promptly converted into cash later, either for liquidity needs or for more profitable loans and investments when they are available.

The existence of a highly developed money market thus helps bank management to improve earnings in at least two ways. In the first place, since banks can always turn to the money market for additional reserves to meet their liquidity requirements, they can reduce to some extent the proportion of cash reserves which are nonearning assets and increase the relative size of their earning portfolios. In the second place, the availability of highly liquid money-market instruments, such as Treasury bills, which are quickly convertible into cash, enables banks to increase the relative proportion of long-term assets for higher yields.

SUMMARY

Like any other enterprises, in order to stay in business, banks have to be liquid, solvent, and, at the same time, profitable. A bank is liquid when it is able to meet all its current liabilities. It is solvent when the realizable value of its assets is greater than the value of its total liabilities. It is profitable if in the long run, it can earn for its shareholders a return at least comparable to earnings which they could obtain by using their funds in other investment opportunities.

Liquidity and profitability tend to move in opposite directions. To meet their liquidity needs, banks need cash reserves which are not earning assets. Profits, on the other hand, are derived from loans and investments. The holding of unnecessary cash reserves means sacrifice of income. Too large a proportion of earning assets in relation to cash may increase the liquidity risk. The main problem of a bank's portfolio management is to select a combination of earning assets so that it is not only able to make a profit but to meet its future liquidity needs as well as legal restrictions and requirements. In the selection of earning assets, banks will have to consider their liquidity, risk, and returns. Several procedures have been suggested for portfolio selection. They are indeed oversimplified, but they do provide banks with some theoretical basis on which to make decisions.

Banks are subject to legal restrictions regarding the types and amounts of loans and investment which can be made. These provisions are purported primarily to maintain the safety of banking operations.

PROBLEMS

1. What do you understand by bank liquidity and solvency? Is it possible for a bank to be liquid, yet insolvent, or solvent, yet illiquid? Use examples to illustrate your discussion.

2. In the short-run, there appears to be a conflict between the objectives of liquidity and profitabaility. In what way would you say that in the long-run, they are perfectly consistent with each other? Explain.

3. What are the various types of risk associated with banks' earning assets? How to minimize them? Why is it that a portfolio of securities that are highly

correlated with one another would benefit the least from investment diversification? Explain your answer in some detail.

4. Why is it that federal tax law is sometimes an important consideration in the selection of earning assets? What are necessary conditions for a bank to take a profitable capital loss?

5. Why are commercial banks subject to more restrictive loan and investment regulations than are other financial institutions? Explain some of the important loan and investment regulations to which banks are subject.

6. In what way does the existence of a highly developed money market facilitate bank management?

7. Following is the balance sheet of Bank X on December 31, 1967:

Balance Sheet

Assets		Liabilities	
Cash and due from banks	20	Demand deposits	160
U.S. Government securities	40	Savings deposits	100
Corporate bonds	30	Other time deposits	30
Obligations of state and local subdivisions	60	Net Worth	
Business and commercial loans	80	Capital stock	10
Consumer loans	30	Surplus	10
Real estate loans	40		
Bank premises and other assets	10		
Total assets	310	Liabilities and capital	310

Compute the loan-to-deposit ratio; cash-to-demand deposits ratio; and cash and governments to deposit ratio. What is the significance of each of these ratios? According to you, which ratio is a good indicator of the bank's liquidity position?

8. Following are the two balance sheets of Banks A and B:

Bank A

Assets		Liabilities		
Cash and due from banks	20	Demand deposits		250
Loans	260	Time deposits		200
Investments	140	Net Worth		
Other assets	10	Paid-in capital	80	
		Less losses	___	___

Bank B

Assets		Liabilities		
Cash and due from banks	6	Demand deposits		100
Loans	100	Time deposits		95
Investments	90	Net Worth		
Other assets	4	Paid-in capital	10	
		Less losses	___	___

Which bank is insolvent? What is the capital position of the bank that is solvent? Of the one that is insolvent? Explain.

chapter 10

Commercial Banking: Structure and Development

We have so far been concerned with modern banking operations. But commercial banking, as we know it today, has its origins in the distant past. It has been subject to a long process of evolution, changing with the shifting patterns of commercial and industrial expansion, before reaching the present stage of development. The banking process will certainly continue to change, adapting itself to changing economic and technological environment, especially in the forms in which general banking services are performed. In this chapter, we shall discuss the origins and development of modern banking, the early development of American banking, the national banking system, banking structure and organization, bank supervision, and deposit insurance.

THE ORIGINS AND DEVELOPMENT OF MODERN BANKING

The development of banking traces back to ancient days. Some of the important functions performed by modern banks, such as safekeeping, transferring, and lending money were already carried on in ancient Greece, Rome, and China by money lenders and money changers, merchant houses, and various monastic and religious orders. For example, in ancient Greece, banking activities were practiced by money changers and priests whose temples served as safe depositories of money. They accepted funds in deposit, maintained accounts, made loans, and exchanged local and foreign coins. Banking operations, which included the acceptance of specie deposits and lending, were also highly active in Rome.

During the Middle Ages financial activities were dominated by various monastic and militant religious orders and by the Jews. From the eighth century to the eleventh century, the abbeys, or monasteries, with their great wealth, were the predominant financial group in the European continent. From the eleventh century to the end of the thirteenth century, the Knights Templar, one of several militant religious orders, emerged as the major financial power. Their activities were confined mostly to the acceptance of funds from merchants, nobles, and kings for safekeeping purposes, and for the transfer of funds between distant places. These religious orders, with their temples located throughout major financial centers of Europe, effected the transfer of funds on behalf of merchants and others through the use of bills of exchange, which helped avoid the risk and inconvenience of shipping large quantities of specie. A merchant in Venice who wished to purchase goods from a merchant in Amsterdam could effect the necessary payment by purchasing a bill from these religious orders drawn on their temple in Amsterdam and payable to the Amsterdam's merchant. A merchant in Venice who sold goods to a trader in Hamburg could draw a bill of exchange on the latter and sell it to another merchant who needed the foreign currency for payment of, say, goods purchased in Hamburg. The seller of the bill received local currency and the buyer had the foreign currency which he needed. In domestic trade, merchant houses in different cities where temples had branches could make payments to one another by means of book transactions with these temples acting as collecting and paying agents. These transactions were offset with one another and the net balances were settled by the shipment of specie. In addition to safekeeping and transferring money, the Knights Templar also engaged in lending operations directed mostly to merchants, princes, and kings.[1]

The Jews were also important bankers during the Middle Ages. Their activities covered all major trading centers of the European continent and England. They engaged mostly in the transfer of funds between cities of Europe, and in money changing and lending. Toward the end of the thirteenth century they fell into disrepute in England and were ordered to leave the country. Their place was then taken over by a group of merchant bankers from various parts of Italy, the Lombards, who remained active in banking in England until the fourteenth century.

The Renaissance, which marked the revival in the arts and learning, witnessed a flourishment in trade and commerce. The discovery of the New World, toward the latter part of the fifteenth century, was a major impetus to this expansion of commercial activities. The increasing monetary and credit requirements for the financing of trade expansion, coupled with the increasing demand for credit by monarchs to finance constant wars between them, then gave birth to "institutions" specializing in the lending business. The period witnessed the emergence of powerful private banking families, such as the Medici, Peruzzi, and Strozzi in Italy, Jacques Coeur in France, the Fuggers in Augsburg, Germany, and the Rothschilds; the latter remain a famous banking family in the twentieth century. These banking families were engaged mostly in the transfer of funds, acceptance of specie deposits, and money lending. Their customers ranged from kings, popes, bishops, and merchants.

The expansion of trade, especially international trade which resulted in the increased use of a great variety of foreign coins, gave rise to another problem:

[1]The Knight Templar Order was dissolved by Philip IV of France in 1207, who defaulted the royal debt to this order of more than 1/2 million gold livres.

money changing. Coins in circulation at that time, issued by different states, cities, and municipalities, were of different weights and standards. In order to avoid the incovenience and difficulty involved in verifying the weights and standards of these coins, which tended to hamper the functioning of commerce, "banks of deposit" were then established, and their sole responsibility was to receive in deposit both domestic and foreign coins from merchants and others, and in return provided them with "deposits" which were expressed in terms of the standard unit of account (of specified weight and fineness) of the territory in which these banks were located, and were evaluated on the basis of the pure metallic contents of the coins deposited.[2] These banks were to hold specie reserves equal to 100 percent of their deposits. Payments were effected by the transfer of these credits between the accounts of *payers and payees.*

Banks of deposits were established in Venice, Genoa, Hamburg, and Amsterdam during the period. The Bank of Amsterdam (1609) was the most important of these banks. After a period of successful operation, the bank began to lend out secretly the specie deposited with it. The discovery of such practice destroyed the confidence of the public in the bank and led to its dissolution in 1820.

In the seventeenth century, goldsmiths, particularly those in England, in addition to their traditional profession of making and selling gold and silver plates and jewels, began for a fee to accept funds from their customers for safekeeping, as they had facilities for storing their valuables. Those who entrusted specie to goldsmiths for safe custody received in return certificates which were the latter's promises to pay specie on demand. Merchants, instead of checking out specie for payment purposes, which was rather inconvenient, especially when large sums of money were used, soon developed the practice of assigning to one another goldsmiths' certificates as means of payment. Another method by which a merchant could withdraw money for payment was to draw a "note" requesting a given sum of money to be paid to a third party or to bearer. The amount was to be deducted from his account. These notes were the forerunners of modern bank checks.

Meanwhile, in order to facilitate the use of certificates, goldsmiths began to issue in standard denominations and made them payable to bearer on demand. For example, a merchant who deposited 100 gold sovereigns, would be given, instead of one single receipt of 100, say, 20 certificates denominated in five sovereigns each. These certificates were backed by 100 percent of specie reserves.

[2]It should be noted that the deposits of these banks were not like demand deposits of modern banks, which are mostly created by their lending and investing operations. These deposits were merely substituted for specie for the convenience of payment. Since the specie reserves held by these banks were always equal to their deposits, their deposit operations did not change the supply of money but simply promoted the efficiency in the use of money. Since the creation of money is considered as the essence of banking, these "banks of deposit" were not banks in the modern sense of the term.

With the widespread use of these certificates, those who received them from others held onto them as means of payment instead of presenting them for specie. Moreover, as the number of depositors increased, the withdrawals of specie by some customers were more or less offset by specie deposited by others. The result was the accumulation of large quantities of idle specie in goldsmiths' vaults. Goldsmiths soon realized that since their certificates were increasingly used as money, and specie withdrawals could be met out of new specie deposits, the volume of specie which they had in their vaults could support a much larger volume of certificates. They began to make loans to customers by using part of the specie deposited with them or by issuing notes to them against the latter's promissory notes. For example, when A borrowed £ 500 from a goldsmith banker, he was issued £500 worth of notes. The change in the balance sheet of the goldsmiths would be as follows:

Balance Sheet

Assets			Liabilities
Loans	+500	Notes	+500

The money supply increased by £500 as a result of the goldsmith's lending activity, since the notes which were used as money were not issued in payment for specie deposited, but for the claim on the borrower, the promissory note, which was not money. The goldsmith banker traded his own obligation, which was money, for the obligations of borrowers which constituted his earnings assets.[3] On the other hand, when the loan was repaid, notes returned to his shop and the supply of money decreased. The change in the balance sheet of the goldsmith banker would be

Balance Sheet

Assets			Liabilities
Loans	-500	Notes outstanding	-500

Money was thus created or destroyed by the goldsmith bankers through their lending and investing operations. They were engaged in fractional reserve banking operations: their specie reserves were reduced to certain fractions of their

[3]It should be noted that when the goldsmith lent out specie deposited with it instead of issuing notes, the money supply also increased. The balance-sheet change of the goldsmith, however, would be as follows:

Balance Sheet

Assets			Liabilities
Loans	+500		
Vault Cash	-500		

The increase in the supply of money in this case is a result of the increase in the volume of specie in circulation.

note and deposit liabilities. This was the beginning of modern banking, the essence of which is the creation of money.

It is quite obvious that under a fractional reserve system, if all holders of notes were to turn them in to the issuers for specie (i.e., if they ran on their banks), the latter would not be in a position to meet all their demand obligations. The operation of fractional reserve banking relies on the belief that the probability of occurrence of such an event is remote, since as long as holders of notes were confident that they could exchange them for specie at any time, they would use them for payment purposes. This is not to say that "runs on banks" did not take place. They did take place frequently in the past as a result of the loss of the confidence of the public in the ability of banks to convert their notes into specie. As a matter of fact, such an event did take place as early as 1667, consequent upon the defeat of the British fleet by the Duke of Chatham. Banking panics and failures resulting from "runs on banks" were not an uncommon scene in the history of American banking prior to the early 1930's.

Goldsmith banking was given added impetus in 1640 after Charles I, desperately in need for funds to defray the expense of war, seized gold and silver which had been stored by merchants in the Tower of London. They then turned to goldsmiths for banking as well as safekeeping services. The greater profits of banking operations prompted many a goldsmith to abandon their traditional craft and specialize in banking.

The second half of the seventeenth century witnessed another development: the growth of great chartered banks organized to meet the increasing banking needs of trade and economic developments of the time. Goldsmith banking was soon overshadowed by these organized banking institutions. The first of these chartered banks was the first Riksbank of Sweden, established in 1656. The bank played an important role in providing the country with a more efficient mechanism for the transfer of funds, and bank notes which were more convenient means of payment than specie. The overissue of bank notes by the bank, however, led to the suspension of specie payment and its reorganization in 1668. The reorganized bank, which discontinued its note-issuing operations because of the unfavorable experience with fractional reserves of the first bank, resumed the issue of bank notes in 1701. The overissue of notes once again led to suspension of specie payment in 1745, and eventually led to its reorganization in 1776.[4] The reorganized bank finally emerged as the central bank of Sweden.

In France during the early decades of the eighteenth century the monetary and financial situation was in chaos. Coins were scarce and state notes depreciated rapidly in terms of specie. The Duke of Orleans, in view of restoring the finances of the government, granted John Law, a brilliant Scottish financier, a

[4] After the suspension of specie payments, the bank continued to issue bank notes. These were fiat currency. Since the notes were not convertible into specie, they circulated at a discount vis-à-vis specie. These notes were redeemed at 50 percent of their face value by the reorganized bank of 1776.

charter to establish the first Bank of France in Paris in 1715. Law believed that so long as the issue of bank notes was confined to the financing of commercial transactions, the overissue of bank notes which would lead to inflation, to the loss of confidence of the public and hence the resulting suspension of specie payments and failure, would not prevail. Law's bank produced spectacular successes. The bank accepted bullion in return for bank notes which were fully convertible into specie. Credit was made available to businesses at rates much lower than those charged by existing lending organizations. Public confidence in the bank was widespread, and prosperity was restored. The magical performance of the bank prompted the king to convert it into the Royal Bank in 1718, through the purchase of shares from private shareholders.

Law was in charge of the new Royal Bank. In addition to banking, Law also promoted the establishment of other businesses, especially the organization of the "Compagnie des Indes." Thanks to Law's successful banking operations and the virtual monopoly of the company of France's foreign trade, among other things, the company's shares were soon sold at high premiums. The excessive speculation in the company's shares and the issue of a vast quantity of bank notes for the financing of speculative transactions, however, led to the collapse of the bank in 1720. The bank was unable to convert its notes into specie, as the public, losing faith in bank notes, turned them in for specie in wholesale numbers after the speculative boom reversed its course. The collapse of the bank led to the downfall of John Law, who could have been one of the greatest bankers in the world.

In England, during the last decade of the seventeenth century, the government, hard pressed by the financial requirements of the war with France, permitted the establishment of the Bank of England in 1694, which promised to lend the government £1.2 million in return for its charter. The activities of the bank, like those of goldsmith bankers, were mainly the acceptance of deposits, making loans, transferring money, and issuing bank notes which were fully convertible into specie. After an initial period of weakness, the position of the bank was gradually consolidated and strengthened, especially after the collapse of the South Sea Company, which was established in 1711 to engage in trade with Spanish America. At the beginning of the eighteenth century, the bank already occupied the predominant position in the banking system of England. The Bank of England survived the emergencies of 1763, 1772, and 1783. But it was forced to suspend specie payment in 1797 consequent upon the crisis triggered by the rumor of the invasion of England by Napoleon. The bank continued to issue inconvertible notes, which circulated at a discount. Specie payment was resumed in 1821. The bank gradually evolved into a central bank.

The existence of a multitude of banks which issued bank notes, while beneficial to commercial and industrial developments, frequently resulted in overissue of notes, leading to banking panics and failures with monetary losses to depositors and adverse economic consequences. This led to legal restrictions of the issue of bank notes, and finally, to the granting of the exclusive right of note-issue to central banking institutions. Thus the Bank of France (The Third Bank), established by Napoleon in 1800, was given the monopoly of note-issue in 1848. The Bank Charter Act of 1844, in England, restricted the issue of notes of commercial banks and regulated the note-issuing function of the Bank of England. The restriction of note-issue was an important impetus to the development of checkbook money, the major form of payment of modern times. Banks, in lieu of issuing bank notes convertible into specie, issued and held demand accounts convertible into either representative full-bodied or full-bodied moneys.

EARLY DEVELOPMENT OF AMERICAN BANKING

Loan banks and land banks were the types of banks which existed in the United States during the colonial period. The land banks issued notes secured by land, and the loan banks made loans by issuing notes against the borrowers' promissory notes secured by their property. These banks discontinued their operations when the act of 1720, regarding the issue of paper money of English banks following the monetary disorder caused by the collapse of the South Sea Company, was extended to the American colonies in 1740.

In 1781 the Bank of North America was established. It was chartered by the Continental Congress. The bank accepted specie deposits in exchange for bank notes and provided the government, as well as industry, with needed credit facilities. The conservative management of the bank enabled it to redeem and circulate its notes at par, while the continental currency issued by the Continental Congress was rapidly becoming worthless. Facing the uncertainty as to the power of the Continental Congress to charter banks, the bank's management requested and was granted a charter by the State of Pennsylvania. (The bank joined the national banking system in 1864. At present, the bank operates as the Pennsylvania Banking and Trust Company.)

Following the Bank of North America, other state banks were chartered in Massachusetts, New York, Maryland, and other states.

In 1791, upon the recommendation of Alexander Hamilton regarding the creation of a nationally chartered bank, Congress passed a law establishing the First Bank of the United States, with a twenty-year charter. The bank was capitalized at $10 million, of which $2 million was subscribed by the federal government. The bank was well managed and its operations were successful. It issued bank notes (not to exceed its capital), granted discount facilities to individuals and businesses, handled receipts and disbursements relative to the account of the government, and made loans to the government in anticipation of tax collections. The practice of the bank, in accumulating large sums of notes of state banks and presenting them to these banks for specie payments, deterred the overissue of notes by state banks, thus assuring a more sound currency system. Despite its successful operations, the bank had many opponents. Those having interests in state banks wanted their banks to be free from the restrictive banking practices used by the bank; others objected on the ground that the chartering of the bank by Congress was unconstitutional; that the bank constituted a step toward banking monopoly; that the bank was dominated by foreign interests.[5] The opposition succeeded in defeating the effort to renew the bank's charter in 1811.

A rapid development of state banks followed the dissolution of the First Bank of the United States. During the 1811-16 period, the number of state banks increased from 88 to 246. Many of these banks, which excessively issued bank notes, were soon forced to suspend specie redemption under the pressure of the War of 1812. The government, which had deposited funds in these banks was subject to heavy losses. The remedy of this monetary disorder led to the establishment of the Second Bank of the United States, with a capitalization of $35 million and a twenty-year charter by the federal government in 1816. The Second Bank performed essentially the same functions as the First Bank. During the initial period, the bank was riddled with serious mismanagement and fraud on the part of the bank's officials. Sound operations, however, were restored in 1823 under new management. Like the First Bank, the practice of the Second Bank to present large sums of notes to issuing state banks for specie gave rise to a "war" with state banks. President Andrew Jackson, antagonized by the political attitude of the bank's president, Nicholas Biddle, in 1833 ordered the transfer of all government deposits from the Second Bank to state banks, and began a campaign against the renewal of the bank's charter. Consequently, the bank was not rechartered in 1836.

The end of the Second Bank of the United States marked the beginning of a period of banking chaos. From 1835 to the outbreak of the Civil War in 1861, the number of state banks increased from 704 to 1,601. In addition to the dissolution of the Second Bank, which meant no more restriction on the note-issue of state banks, the passage of free banking legislation in many states was another important stimulus to this tremendous growth of state banking. Prior to 1837, the establishment of a state bank required an act of the state legislature, but this tended to foster corruption and favoritism. To avoid these abuses, a law was first enacted in Michigan, allowing anyone who satisfied certain legal banking requirements to start a bank. Similar laws were soon passed in New York and other states. While in some states, such as Michigan and New York, provisions were made for strict bank supervision, and restrictions were imposed on the volume of notes which could be issued by banks, in some other states, especially Western states, banking requirements were rather loose. The practice in some Western states of allowing the purchase of banks' shares by signing promissory notes made possible the establishment of banks with practically no paid-in capi-

[5] It should be noted that even though more than 70 percent of the shares of the bank were held by foreigners, particularly Englishmen, they could not vote by proxy in the selection of the bank's management.

tal at all. "Bankers" with handfuls of specie established their head office in an inaccessible location to avoid the redemption of their notes, which were put in circulation in large cities. Some banks even intimidated those who intended to present bank notes for specie.

The existence of a large number of state banks, each issuing its own notes, resulted in the circulation of thousands of different types of money. Notes issued by sound and well-known banks in the eastern seaboard, especially New England, were in circulation at par. Other notes were circulating at various and changing rates of discount, not to speak of thousands of notes of fraudulent banks and counterfeiters.

The monetary confusion at the time was such that traders had to resort to bank note periodicals for the values of various types of bank notes.

Inadequate banking supervision, superficial banking requirements, abusive uses of the note-issuing privilege, among other things, led to the failure of a large number of banks. The loss of money to the government, as a result of the failure of banks which had received government deposits prompted Congress in 1840 to establish the Independent Treasury System made up of a number of Treasury branch offices which served as depositories of funds, collecting taxes and making payments. The operations of the system, while preventing losses to the government, had disturbing effects on the banking and business community. The expansion or contraction of the supply of money reflected primarily the variation of the Treasury's cash flows rather than the changing credit requirements of businesses. The withdrawals of specie by the public for the payment of taxes resulted in the depletion of banks' specie reserves, causing unwarranted credit restriction and monetary contraction. Treasury disbursements, on the other hand, could cause unwarranted monetary and credit expansion. Following the establishment of the National Banking System in 1863, part of the government funds were deposited with approved national banks, but the operation of the Independent Treasury System was not discontinued until 1921.

THE NATIONAL BANKING SYSTEM

The passage of the National Banking Act of 1863, extensively amended by the Act of 1864, regarding the creation of the national banking system through the establishment of nationally chartered banks, was prompted by several considerations. In the first place, the creation of national banks would help meet the increasing financial requirements of the Civil War by providing a market for the sale of government bonds. Second, the act was intended to institute a more sound banking system through more restrictive banking requirements, stricter bank control, supervision and examination. Finally, the act was designed to provide the country with a uniform currency system replacing the hodge-podge of notes then in circulation, a major source of transaction confusion and difficulty.

Many provisions of the act are still in force. The act created the office of the Comptroller of the Currency, set up in the Treasury Department with the authority to charter, control, supervise, and examine all nationally chartered banks. The act retained the principle of free banking. Any group of not less than five individuals could obtain a national bank charter, provided they met certain legal requirements. State banks, of course, could become national banks by taking up national charters.[6]

In terms of the act of 1864, national banks were (and still are) subject to minimum capital requirements which vary from $50,000 for banks in areas with less than 6,000 inhabitants to $200,000 for banks in cities with populations of more than 50,000, as already noted. In order to start its operation, 50 percent of a national bank's capital had to be paid in, and the remaining balance could be paid at 10 percent per month. Stockholders were subject to the double-liability assessment in the event of the failure of their banks. This requirement was abandoned in 1937. There was, however, an amendment in the capital provision of the act which required (and this requirement still prevails) national banks to start with a paid-in surplus equal to at least 20 percent of the par value of its capital stocks (i.e., the initial shares have to be sold at premiums of at least 20 percent).

Each national bank was required to purchase and deposit with the Treasury government bonds of not less than one-third of its capital, with a minimum of $30,000. This provision constituted a new source of funds for the government to finance its war efforts. (When the war was over, the minimum was reduced to one-quarter of capital.) The Treasury, in return, issued to each national bank "national bank" notes to the extent of 90 percent of the face value of the bonds so deposited. (In 1900 this percentage was extended to 100 percent.) But in no case could the volume of notes issued to each bank exceed the amount of its capital. National bank notes, although they were issued to thousands of individual banks, were uniform in size, shape, and color, as they were all printed by the Bureau of Printing and Engraving of the Treasury Department. These notes, which were fully guaranteed by the government, were accepted at par by all national banks.

Each national bank was required to hold minimum legal reserve against its notes outstanding and deposit liabilities. National banks were divided into three classes for reserve purposes. Central reserve city banks (New York and later Chicago) were required to hold reserves in "lawful" money (United States notes and gold and silver coins) equal to 25 percent of their notes and deposits. The legal reserve ratio for reserve city banks (banks in some 16 other large cities) was

[6]It should be noted that as a consequence of the passage of subsequent banking legislation, free banking no longer prevails in practice. Thus the Banking Act of 1935, which amended the National Banking Act of 1864, authorized the Comptroller of the Currency to deny the chartering of a national bank if this is justified in the light of the credit and banking needs of the community in which the new bank is proposed, even though the promoters of the bank fulfill all the legal banking requirements.

25 percent, of which one-half had to be in "lawful" money held in their vault, and the remaining, in the form of demand balances with central reserve city banks. "Country banks" were subject to a low legal reserve ratio of 15 percent, of which two-fifths had to be in "lawful" money, and the remaining could be made up of demand balances with reserve and central reserve city banks.[7] In addition to legal reserves, in order to insure safe and sound banking practices, the National Banking Act subjected national banks to several operational restrictions and requirements, such as the prohibition of national banks from making real estate loans, which were considered too risky because of their long maturities. (This prohibition was not relaxed unitl the creation of the Federal Reserve in 1914.) The "ten-percent rule" which, as we have already discussed, is still in force; and submission of detailed financial statements to, and periodical examinations by, the Comptroller of the Currency.

It was hoped that the passage of the act would induce state banks to convert to national banks. In fact, the higher capital and legal reserve requirements for national banks, stricter supervision rules, and more serious operational restrictions provided no incentive for state banks. As state banks, they could issue notes and operate under more favorable conditions. This led to the passage of the amendment of 1865, imposing a 10 percent tax on notes issued by state banks after July 1865. Since lending bank notes was then the major source of income to state banks, the imposition of this prohibitive tax gave rise to a wholesale conversion of state banks to national banks. Thus, state banks, which numbered 1,089 in 1864, decreased to 247 in 1868. The number of national banks, on the other hand, increased from 467 to 1,640 during the same period.

However, with the increasing use of checks by businesses in making payments, it soon became apparent to state banks that demand balances held by customers in exchange for specie or bank notes could be effectively substituted for bank notes. Instead of lending bank notes to borrowers, they could pay for the borrowers' notes and other earning assets by crediting their accounts with demand claims payable in specie or other lawful money on demand. This, in addition to liberal state laws regarding banking organizations and operations, prompted a large number of national banks (which had been state banks) to regain their state status, as well as the establishment of new state banks. The issue of bank notes by state banks was completely discontinued after 1870. National banks then had the monopoly of issuing bank notes. But this became of secondary importance, as deposit money became increasingly accepted by the public.

Under the national banking system as intended by the act of 1863-64 and other amendments, several important accomplishments were realized. It provided the country with a uniform currency system which was a great improve-

[7]It should be noted that the classification of members of the Federal Reserve System for reserve purposes was a remnant of this division of banks under the National Banking Act. The classification of central reserve city banks was, however, dropped by the Board of Governors of the Federal Reserve after July 1962.

ment over the currency situation which prevailed during the 1836-65 heydey of counterfeiters and fraudulent banks. It also promoted safer and sounder banking operations by imposing stricter operational rules and regulations. The national banking system, however, suffered from several serious defects, and it was the correction of these defects, among other things, which prompted the establishment of the Federal Reserve System. These shortcomings are discussed in Chapter 12 on the American central banking system.

BANKING STRUCTURE AND ORGANIZATION

The structure and organization of American banking display some unique features. They reflect partly banking legislation enacted in the past, and practices developed by banks to adapt themselves to the continuous changes in the American economic and social environment.

Dual Banking

The incorporation of banks in the United States, as we have seen, may be granted either by the banking authorities of the individual states or by the federal government. "Dual banking" refers to the existence, side by side, of state and nationally chartered banks. Although the First and Second Banks of the United States were chartered by the federal government in 1791 and 1816, respectively, it was not until 1864 that the dual banking system was firmly established following the passage of the National Banking Act. The system is an outgrowth of the failure of the act of 1864 to win over state banks.

In terms of number, national banks represent no more than 35 percent of the total number of commercial banks, but they hold more than half of the total assets and total deposits of the commercial banking system (see Table 10-1).

TABLE 10-1
Classes of Banks, Assets, Deposits, Number of Banks in Each Class, and Bank Branches (June 29, 1968)

Classes of Banks	Total Assets, millions	Percent of Total*	Total Loans and Investments, millions	Percent of Total*	Total Deposits, millions	Percent of Total*	Number of Banks	Percent of Total*
National banks ...	$265,497	58	$212,344	57	$229,028	58	4,742	34
State banks	191,330	42	155,216	43	164,976	42	8,981	66
Member banks....	376,904	82	297,630	81	332,990	82	6,039	44
Nonmember banks	79,923	18	69,930	19	71,014	18	7,684	56
Insured banks.....	454,398	99	365,955	99	392,801	99	13,512	98
Noninsured banks	2,429	01	1,605	01	1,203	01	211	02

Source: Federal Reserve Bulletin, June 1968.
*For each class of banks.

Most large banks are national banks, but some of the largest banks in the country still prefer state charters.

The passage of the Federal Reserve Act of 1913, establishing the Federal Reserve System, added one more dimension to the dual banking system. In terms of the Reserve Act, nationally chartered banks are required to take up membership in the Federal Reserve, but state banks, if qualified, may elect to become members of the system. The stringent requirements for membership in the system, as compared with more liberal state banking requirements, however, provided little incentive to state banks to join the system. Of the 13,723 operating in the country in June, 1968, only 6,039 were member banks, of which 4,742 were national banks and 1,297 were state member banks. Since most large state banks elected to become members of the system if for no other reason than prestige, the assets and deposits held by member banks represent more than 80 percent of the total assets and deposits of the banking system (Table 10-1).

The establishment of the Federal Deposit Insurance Corporation in 1933, following a long period of disastrous banking panics and failures, added still another dimension to the dual banking system. All member banks are required to participate in the insurance plan, and qualified state nonmember banks may apply for insurance coverage. In June 1968 as shown in Table 10-1, all but 211 banks were insured by the corporation. They held 99 percent of the assets and deposits of all commercial banks.

The merits and weaknesses of "dual banking" remain a subject of discussion. One of the merits of the system frequently cited is the high degree of banking flexibility which is a result of the ability of banks to convert from state to federal charter and vice versa. But this very switchability appears to be one of the weaknesses of the system. It is believed that liberal state banking laws and supervisory rules may prevent the imposition of stricter rules and requirements designed to promote sounder banking operations on the part of the federal banking authorities. They may, in fact, induce looser federal requirements. An evidence of such a tendency appears to be the liberalization of national banking laws in order to enable national banks to "compete" more effectively with state banks.

Unit Versus Branch Banking

Banks in the United States are predominantly unit-banks—that is, banks having only one office. Of the 13,654 banks in operation in the country in 1967, 10,139 were unit banks, a large portion of which were banks located in some eighteen states where branch banking was prohibited. The remaining 3,555 banks were branch banks which operated 18,111 branch offices, located mostly in sixteen states which permitted state-wide branch banking, and in some sixteen other states which allowed limited area branch banking (branch offices are confined to the city where the head office is located). The extent of American branch banking is thus limited either within the boundaries of the individual states or within local areas where branch banking is prevalent. This is no comparison with the nationwide branch banking system of Canda, England, and European countries. But there is a strong tendency toward branch banking in the United States, which is reflected by the growth of branch offices from 10,605 in December 1960 to 18,111 in 1967, an average growth of more than 1,000 branch offices a year. This, among other things, appears to be a response to the growth and shifts of population and the creation and relocation of industries. The creation of new industries and the relocation and expansion of existing industries often create new working and residential communities with new needs for banking services and facilities. The movement of population from urban to suburban areas tends to shift the demand for banking facilities to these suburban areas. Through branching, banks may retain their competitive position in the industry by "moving with their customers." Without branching, urban banks would be deprived of their relocated customers.

There are several arguments in favor of branch banking. In the first place, branch banking makes possible loan and investment diversification, both geographically and by industry, which helps reduce banking risks; losses suffered by one branch in one community can be compensated for by the profits realized by branches in some other areas. Branch banking also enables the diversification of ownership of deposits which improves deposit stability. All this tends to improve the safety of banking operations. Unit banks, particularly banks located in communities dominated by a single industry, on the other hand, could find themselves in difficulty when this major industry is affected by adverse economic developments. Second, branch banking promotes the mobility and maximum utilization of funds, since the excess of funds of one branch can be used by branches in other areas where profitable lending and investing opportunities are available. Third, the establishment of large banks with several branch offices enables the specialization of banking functions, the use of automatic equipment which would result in economies of scale, and hence higher earnings for the banks, better services and lower costs to the public. Fourth, branch banks, with greater financial resources, are in a better position to cater to the credit needs of large commercial and industrial enterprises than small unit banks with limited funds. Finally, branch banks can better afford the high cost of training and attracting talented management.

Branch banking is also subject to several objections. First, it is argued that the close contact between unit banks and the business communities which they serve will be lost when branch offices are substituted for unit banks, owing to the rotation of branch officers who operate as "strangers," less well informed of, and less sympathetic to, local needs. This, however, may not always be the case. The successful operation of a bank, regardless of whether it is a unit bank or a branch office, requires a close touch between management and the local community. In fact, in some instances, branch banks can maintain even closer and more productive relationships with customers, especially large enterprises doing business with branch banks. Another objection to branch banking is that it leads to banking monopoly. The argument appears to neglect the fact that instead of competition between unit banks, under branch banking there will be competition between branches of different branch banks. If branch banking results in the increase in the number of banking offices, then it will increase instead of reducing banking competition. The prohibition of branch banking for fear of monopoly sometimes results in restraint of competition. Indeed, in some areas where branch banking is not permitted, banking is dominated by one or a few unit banks only. Furthermore, in communities where new branches might be able to operate profitably while new unit banks could not survive, the prohibition of branching would exclude potential competitive forces from these communities.

Branch banking could result in less competition when it takes the form of conversion of existing small unit banks into offices of branch banks through bank mergers or consolidation. But bank mergers do not necessarily lead to restriction of banking competition. It is true that mergers will give rise to large banks, but to identify size with monopoly appears erroneous. In selling credit, banks encounter not only competition among themselves but also competition with a great variety of other financial institutions, such as savings and loan associations, savings banks, finance companies, insurance companies, and various government lending agencies. The amalgamation of small and weak banks into stronger and larger banks would enable them to compete effectively not only with other large banks but also with nonbank financial intermediaries as well.

Bank Mergers and Bank Holding Companies

A bank merger or consolidation refers to a complete fusion of a number of formerly independent banks into a new bank with a new name or the absorption by a bank of a number of other banks with the absorbed banks ceasing to exist as independent banks. The fusion or absorption is usually accomplished through a stock exchange plan or direct acquisition of assets. A bank holding company, on the other hand, is a corporation that owns or controls a number of banks; the constituent banks in a holding-company system retain their independent existence.[8]

Bank mergers and bank holding companies are permitted as they may yield benefits to the banks and the banking public. These benefits may be in the form of improved customer services and convenience, more efficient and aggressive management, more effective competition, and prevention of probable failures of banks with serious asset and management problems through the assumption of their assets and liabilities by sounder banks.

Bank mergers and holding companies, however, involve serious risks, particularly the risk of restriction of competition through the concentration of economic power. Hence their permission is subject to regulatory approval and supervision.

[8] Constituent banks in a holding-company system, of course, may be merged.

Bank Mergers. Bank mergers are regulated by the Bank Merger Act of 1960. It provides for the approval of bank mergers either by the Comptroller of the Currency, the Federal Reserve, or the Federal Deposit Insurance Corporation (FDIC), depending on the status of the resulting bank. If it is a national bank, the approval of the Comptroller of the Currency is required. If it is a state member bank, approval is to be granted by the Board of Governors of the Federal Reserve. If it is an insured nonmember bank, then the approval of the FDIC is required.[9] The Attorney General was given a purely advisory role. He is to report to the Comptroller of the Currency, the Board of Governors of the Federal Reserve, or the FDIC, as the case may be, on the effect of a proposed merger on competition. And that is all. There is no provision that requires the banking regulatory agencies even to consider the Attorney General's report.[10] The Justice Department was of the opinion that it should have greater jurisdiction over bank mergers. The position of the Department was upheld by the Supreme Court in the Philadelphia National Bank and the Girard Trust merger case. The proposed merger between the Philadelphia National Bank and the Girard Trust Corn Exchange Bank was approved by the Comptroller of the Currency in early 1961. The merger was contested by the Justice Department on the grounds that it would result in greater concentration of economic power and restriction of competition.[11] The Supreme Court, in 1963, reversed the decision of the District Court (which had ruled in favor of the merger). It was the opinion of the High Court that the merger would constitute a violation of the Celler-Kefauver Act (an amendment to section 7 of the Clayton Act) which prohibits the acquisition of stock or assets the effect of which "may be substantially to lessen competition, or tend to create a monopoly."

The decision of the Supreme Court thus implied that any bank mergers could be halted by actions of the Justice Department on account of violation of antitrust laws,[12] even though they had been approved by the banking regulatory agencies. The conflict between the Justice Department and the various banking regulatory agencies in their decisions on bank mergers appeared to have been accounted for largely by the lack of a uniform set of criteria for actions. While the banking regulatory agencies, in approving a merger application, balanced their views on such factors as the effect of the transaction on competition, customer services and convenience, financial and managerial resources, and the

[9]It should be noted that prior to the Bank Merger Act of 1960, all bank mergers were subject to the approval of the Comptroller of the Currency.

[10]The Act also requires the approving agency to secure reports on a proposed merger from the other two agencies as well.

[11]It is to be noted that the Reports of the Federal Reserve and the FDIC were not favorable to the proposed merger.

[12]The Sherman Antitrust Act of 1890; the Clayton Act of 1914; and the Celler-Kefauver Act of 1950. Readers who wish to learn more about these Acts, they may read R. E. Slesinger and Asher Isaacs, *Business, Government, and Public Policy* (Princeton, N.J.: Van Nostrand 1968), or V. A. Mund, *Government and Business* (New York: Harper 1965).

needs of the community to be served, among other things, the effect on competition appeared to have been the sole criterion for actions of the Justice Department.

Consequently, an amendment to the Bank Merger Act of 1960 was approved in 1966 seeking to establish uniform standards to be taken into account by the banking supervisory authorities, the Department of Justice, and the courts with respect to their actions on bank mergers. Before granting approval, the regulatory agencies are required to consider all the relevant factors such as competitive effects, financial and managerial resources and future prospects, and convenience and needs of the community to be served. The Department of Justice is given 30 days to study a proposed merger and to take antitrust action. A merger that has anticompetitive effects thus may be approved by the regulatory agencies if they are clearly outweighed in the public interest by the probable effect of the transaction in meeting the convenience and the needs of the community involved. A good number of bank mergers have been approved in the light of these considerations.[13]

Bank Holding Companies. Bank holding companies are regulated by the Bank Holding Company Act of 1956. A bank holding company is a corporation that owns or controls 25 percent or more interest in each of two or more banks. This form of banking organization is partly used as a means to circumvent branch banking restrictions which prevail in several individual states. This appears to be supported by the fact that this occurs more frequently in unit-banking states than in states that permit branch banking.[14]

The supervision of bank holding companies is a responsibility of the Board of Governors of the Federal Reserve. The formation and expansion of bank holding companies requires the prior approval of the Board of Governors.[15] As in the case of bank mergers, consideration for approval includes such factors as anticompetitive potential, financial and managerial resources and future prospects of the bank holding company and the banks concerned, and the convenience and needs of the community to be served. Under the Bank Holding Company Act, a bank holding company is prohibited from acquiring shares of any company that is not a bank. This is motivated primarily by the preservation of

[13]See, for example, the case of the merger of the Island State Bank (Patchogue, N.Y.) with the First National Bank of Bay Shore (Bay Shore, N.Y.), *Federal Reserve Bulletin,* March 1969; the merger of the First State Bank of Ransom (Ransom, Kansas) with the Farmers State Bank (Ransom), and that of the Arapahoe Bank (Littleton, Colorado) with the Valley National Bank (Littleton), *Annual Report,* FDIC, 1967.

[14]*Annual Report,* FDIC, 1964, p. 140.

[15]For instance, unless approved by the Board, a bank holding company cannot acquire more than 5 percent of the voting stock of a bank. It follows that any acquisition up to 5 percent does not require the approval of the Board. Inasmuch as a bank holding company can have a great deal of influence over a bank by acquiring 5 percent or less of its voting stock, the Board of Governors has suggested that this provision be eliminated from the Bank Holding Company Act and the Board's prior approval be required for every acquisition of bank stock by a holding company.

competition and the soundness of banking.[16] The combination of banks and nonbank businesses in a holding company, if allowed, would involve numerous dangers. There is a possibility that banks in a holding company system may deny credit to firms that compete with the system's affiliated firms, or require other firms to do business with affiliated firms of the system as a condition for credit facilities; or they may make credit more readily available to customers of affiliated firms than to customers of nonaffiliated enterprises. There are, nevertheless, exceptions to this provision. Bank holding companies may be permitted by the Board of Governors to acquire shares of companies whose activities are "related" to banks, if the benefits to the public derived from such transactions, in the opinion of the Board, outweigh potentially adverse consequences.[17]

The Bank Holding Company Act of 1956 applies only to bank holding companies that own or control two or more banks, that is, "multibank holding companies." One-bank holding companies,—that is, corporations that own or control 25 percent or more of the voting shares of one bank,—are not covered by the Act. The question as to whether one-bank holding companies should be brought within the Bank Holding Company Act has been a subject of discussion in recently proposed legislation.[18] The exemption of one-bank holding companies from the Act presents an opportunity for banks to organize one-bank holding companies and undertake indirectly operations which they may not undertake directly under existing legislation. Then why the exemption? The answer was the preservation of small unit banks as most one-bank holding companies in the past owned small banks. The elimination of the exemption could result in the forced sale of these small banks and this would result in lesser instead of greater competition.

Things have changed, however. The economic power of one-banking holding companies is growing. Unless the loophole is closed by extending the Bank Holding Company Act to cover one-bank holding companies, their growth could neutralize to a considerable extent the effectiveness of laws designed to preserve competition. It does not appear to be consistent to require a nonbank corporation to liquidate its nonbank holdings if it acquires 25 percent or more of the voting shares of, say, two very small banks, and exempts it from the Act if it acquires 25 percent or more of the voting shares of a very large bank. The anticompetitive potential in the latter case is surely at least as great as in the former. To bring one-bank holding companies within the Bank Holding Company Act may render it difficult for individuals to continue to hold or form

[16]Thus, upon the passage of the Act in 1956, existing holding companies were required to divest themselves of nonbank activities.

[17]For example, companies whose activities are of financial, fiduciary, or insurance in nature.

[18]See statements of W. M. Martin, Chairman of the Board of Governors of the Federal Reserve, and J. L. Robertson, Vice-Chairman, before the Committee on Banking and Currency, House of Representatives, April 18, 1969; *Federal Reserve Bulletin,* April 1969. It is from these sources that most of the discussion on one-bank holding companies is drawn.

small, independent banks. But this may be avoided by granting exemption to small one-bank holding companies. The practical problem to be dealt with here is a matter of defining how small is a "small" one-bank holding company.

In discussing bank holding companies, perhaps a few words on chain banking are in order. Chain banking is another form of multiple office banking in which an individual or group of individuals own or control several banks. This form of banking organization is also popular, especially in states where branch banking is restricted. Chain banking has not been a direct subject of any regulatory legislation. It was believed that as "chain banks" were small banks owned or controlled by individuals, they would not involve any significant anticompetitive potential. Research literature on the recent growth of chain banking is relatively limited. But some recent investigations suggested a significant degree of chain banking concentration in a number of states and regions.[19] To the extent that the growth of chain banking is such that it may reduce the effectiveness of legislation enacted to preserve competition, then the question as to whether it should be brought directly within some regulatory legislation, perhaps the Bank Holding Company Act of 1956, should be considered.

Correspondent Banking

Banks in the United States, as we have mentioned are mostly small, independent unit banks, locally owned and locally operated. They are, however, closely tied together through a network of correspondent relationships which are necessary for the performance of such important banking services as the collection of out-of-town checks and lending and investing operations. Correspondent relationship is manifested in the holding of demand balances by banks with one another. Country banks hold balances with reserve city banks. The latter, in turn, hold balances with money market banks in New York, Chicago, and other important financial centers.

Prior to the establishment of the Federal Reserve System, the collection of checks drawn on banks in distant places could be effected only through the system of correspondent banking. With the creation of the central banking system, which provides clearing and collection facilities not only to member banks but to nonmember banks as well (clearing banks), correspondent banking declined in importance. This is reflected by the decrease in the proportion of interbank balances from about 25 percent of total bank deposits before 1914 to about 5 percent in the 1960's. But correspondent banking remains popular. Even with the collection facilities of the Federal Reserve System, an important portion of the total number of checks drawn each year is still collected through correspondent banks, since this collection process is sometimes much faster and more convenient. Moreover, checks drawn on nonpar banks (1,492 such banks

[19] See, for example, J. C. Darnell, "Chain Banking," *The National Banking Review* (March 1966), and "Determinants of Chain Banking," *The National Banking Review* (June 1967).

were in operation in December 1965) can be collected only through correspondent banks.

Aside from the collection of checks, correspondent banks provide their customer banks with a variety of other banking services, such as loan participation, arrangement for the sale and purchase of securities, international banking services, and security analysis and investment advices. Thus a small bank which is not in a position to make a large loan to a customer may request its correspondent banks to participate in the loan. With correspondent banking facilities, a small bank can remain fully invested as arrangements can be made with correspondent banks for, say, the sales of Federal Funds or the purchase of other earning assets with their temporarily idle funds. On the other hand, should it need additional reserves to meet its liquidity needs, it could arrange with correspondent banks for the purchase of Federal Funds, for the sale of reserve assets, or borrowing reserves directly from them. Banks in large cities are willing to act as correspondents for small banks because of the earnings which can be derived from the use of deposit balances of customer banks, among other things. These earnings are, in most cases, more than adequate to offset the costs incurred in providing correspondent banking services.

BANK SUPERVISION

Banks are institutions which greatly affect the public interest, as they are major suppliers of money and credit in the economy. Banks are, therefore, subject to special governmental supervision. The basic objective of bank supervision is to maintain liquid, safe, and sound banking institutions. Banks are required to observe special rules and regulations, to submit to supervisory authorities detailed statements of condition, and are subject to periodic examinations. Through bank examination, supervisory authorities are in a position to detect possible violations of banking rules and regulations, unsound banking methods, undesirable loan and investment operations, etc., and to take corrective actions when violations are discovered.

The establishment of new banks, the change in the capitalization of existing banks, the opening or closing of branches, all require the prior approval of supervisory authorities. This would help insure that banks are adequately financed, managed by qualified persons, and that the organization of new banks is desirable with regard to the banking needs of the communities in which they are to be established. These requirements and others tend to negate the free banking principle, as the supervisory authorities have the power to deny the establishment of new banks or new branches, even though they may be proposed by individuals who have met all the legal banking requirements.

Banks in the United States are subject to a multiplicity of supervisory authorities: the Comptroller of the Currency, the Federal Reserve System, the Federal Deposit Insurance Corporation, and the banking authorities of the individual states. There is, however, a division of labor between these authorities with regard to supervision. National banks and nonmember banks in the District of Columbia, about one-third of all banks, are supervised by the Comptroller of the Currency. Examination reports of the Comptroller of the Currency are made available to the Federal Reserve upon request. State member banks, approximately one-tenth of the total number of banks, are supervised by the Federal Reserve authorities (and state authorities). The examination of state member banks is made by the Federal Reserve banks, either independently or jointly with the state banking authorities. Nonmember state banks which are insured by the FDIC, about one-half of all banks, are supervised by the corporation and the respective state supervisory agencies. State banks which are not insured by the FDIC, slightly more than one percent of all banks, are not subject to federal supervisory authorities, but only to the respective state authorities.

This multiplicity of supervisory authorities sometimes gives rise to inter-agency friction and information delays which could result in harmful consequences. For example, the delay of one agency in making examination reports to another may result in the latter dealing with banks which are in financial difficulty. It also gives rise to differences in the interpretation, hence the application, of banking rules and regulations. For example, to apply the 10 percent rule, the Comptroller of the Currency allows the inclusion of capital notes and debentures as part of the aggregate amount of unimpaired capital and surplus. The Board of Governors of the Federal Reserve takes the contrary view on the ground that capital notes and debentures are evidences of debt, not "equity" interests in the assets of the banks. Likewise, there is a difference between the two agencies with regard to the inclusion or exclusion of undivided profits in the computation of capital and surplus.

Proposals have been made to bring all banks under one single federal control and supervisory authority. It is argued that since the banking business is concerned with the national interest, it should be put under federal supervision. According to these proposals, uniform federal supervision of banks can be achieved either by the Comptroller of the Currency, the Federal Reserve System, or the Federal Deposit Insurance Corporation. Supervision by the Comptroller of the Currency would require national charters for all banks. This would likely encounter opposition from those having interests in state banks which, in general, are subject to less restrictive banking requirements than national banks, among other things. Supervision by the Federal Reserve System, on the other hand, would require all commercial banks to take up membership in the system. One of the merits of this proposal, according to its proponents, is that as supervisory policies and monetary policies would be formulated by the same agency, the Federal Reserve can change supervisory rules and standards so as to strengthen its monetary control power, to the extent that such actions do not interfere with the safety of banking operations. One of the objections to such a proposal is likely to be the reluctance on the part of nonmember banks to join the system because of higher legal required reserves and the observance of the par-collection principle which would deprive many of these banks a substantial source of income. The proposal which appears to be most feasible is federal supervision under the Federal Deposit Insurance Corporation. Although subject to federal supervisory authority, each individual bank can retain its preferred status as a national bank, state member bank or state nonmember bank.

BANK FAILURES AND DEPOSIT INSURANCE

The establishment of the Federal Deposit Insurance Corporation for the insurance of deposits is an important landmark in the development of American banking. This followed a long period of banking crisis and failure which culminated in the early 1930's with the suspension of thousands of banks and deposit losses of billions of dollars to depositors.

Bank Failures

Bank failures cause more serious economic consequences than do the failures of other business enterprises. Since banks are the major suppliers of money and credit to all sectors of the economy, serious failures of banks would result in a drastic contraction in the flow of money and credit, causing difficulties to businesses which depend upon them for credit facilities and general disruption in the production and distribution process. Bank failures were frequent in the United States in the past. During the 1921-33 period, almost 15,000 banks were suspended. During the Great Depression alone, from 1930-33, more than 9,000 banks failed. The epidemic of bank suspension was then so paralyzing that a national bank holiday had to be declared by the Roosevelt administration.

It is true that in countries with nationwide branch banking, bank failures do occur, but the extent of bank failures in these countries is insignificant as compared with the scope of bank failures in the United States. In Canada, for example, there was no bank failure after the early 1920's. The magnitude of bank failures in the United States thus cannot be explained in terms of factors inherent in fractional reserve banking, but in terms of factors peculiar to the American banking system itself. One of the overriding factors frequently cited is the inherent weakness of a banking system dominated by small, independent unit banks. Many of these banks are too small to operate efficiently. Because of the limited extent of their loan and investment diversification, both geographically and by industry, small, independent unit banks, especially banks in rural areas and in small communities dominated by one industry, are more susceptible to failure in the face of adverse economic developments. Difficulty is also likely to occur with small unit banks as a result of the loss of business following the acquisition of local firms by national enterprises doing business with large branch banks. All this appears to be attested by the fact that banks which failed in the past were mostly small banks located in rural areas and in small business communities. Small unit banks continue to be plagued by failure. Most of the 470 insured banks which were either liquidated or reorganized during the 1934-67 period were banks which held deposits of $1 million or less at the time of closing. The vulnerability to failure therefore appears to be a special feature of a unit-banking system.

Liberal requirements for the organization and operation of state banks, unsound banking practices, unsafe and excessive loans and investments, and speculative operations of bank officials were also factors contributing to wholesale bank failures prior to 1934. "Overbanking" was another contributing factor. The passage of free banking laws in the past resulted in a tremendous increase in the number of commercial banks. From 1877 to 1921, the number of banks increased from 5,141 to 30,659. This reflected mostly the growth in state banks, which increased from 631 to 21,267 during the same period. It was then no uncommon occurrence for small rural communities with no more than a couple of thousands of inhabitants to have several banks. These banks were too small and too inefficient to survive adverse economic developments. Following the sharp decline in farm prices in the early 1920's, these small rural banks failed in large numbers.

The paralyzing effects of mass bank failures during the Great Depression led to drastic remedial actions. In order to improve the safety of banking operations, federal and state laws were passed imposing more restrictive banking rules and regulations. The payment of interest on demand deposits, which appeared to have led to unsound competition between banks was prohibited. The Federal Reserve was given greater authority to make greater advance and rediscounting facilities available to sound banks which are temporarily in difficulty. The major measure taken, however, was the creation of the Federal Deposit Insurance Corporation to protect depositors against losses in the event of bank failure. The corporation was also purported to promote a sounder money and banking system by generating confidence of the public in the safety of deposits through deposit insurance.

The FDIC and Deposit Insurance

The FDIC is by no means the first institution organized to insure bank deposits. It is, however, the first to be organized on a national scale. In the past, there were several schemes designed to guarantee state bank notes which were then the predominant form of payment. One such scheme was the New York Safety Fund, established in 1829. In terms of this plan, every state chartered bank in New York was required to pay an annual premium to the fund equal to one-half of one percent of its paid-in capital until the cumulative assessments amounted to 3 percent of the bank's capital. In case of failure, the fund would make up for the difference between the value of the insured bank's liquidated assets and its total liabilities. The fund was initially intended to protect noteholders as well as other creditors of insured banks. But, owing to the high costs of failures of banks during the early 1840's, after 1842 only noteholders were protected by the fund. The plan was abandoned in 1866. Plans similar to the New York Safety Fund were adopted in several individual states. Like the fund, the operation of these schemes were limited, as they were confined to individual states and state chartered banks. National bank notes which superseded state bank notes after 1865 were guaranteed by the federal government through its holdings of Treasury bonds pledged by national banks in return for the privilege of issuing national bank notes. But bank deposits which were to become the dominant medium of exchange were not guaranteed. The inability of banks to pay depositors specie on demand had resulted in the failures of a large number of banks. This led to the establishment of deposit insurance programs in several states, after 1907, to insure bank deposits. These deposit insurance schemes, limited in scope, were unable to withstand the shock of mass failures of the 1920's and early 1930's. The creation of a deposit insurance organization at the national level was then considered as a remedy to the situation. Consequently, the Banking Act of 1933 was passed, authorizing the establishment of the Federal Deposit Insurance Corporation (FDIC).

The FDIC began its operations in 1934. It is administered by a Board of Directors made up of three members: the Comptroller of the Currency and two members appointed by the President for six-year terms. Its original capital was provided by the government and the Federal Reserve Banks ($289 million). The successful operation of the corporation, subsequently enabled it to retire the whole amount of initial capital after 1948. Though the FDIC has no capital, it holds a surplus of more than $3 billion, referred to as the Deposit Insurance Fund. In addition, if need be, the FDIC has authorization to borrow up to $3 billion from the United States Treasury to meet its insurance obligations.

The FDIC insures more than 98 percent of all commercial banks. The maximum amount of insurable deposits for each depositor in each bank was initially $2,500. It was later increased to $5,000, then to $10,000 after 1950, to $15,000 after October, 1966, and to $20,000 beginning in December, 1969. A survey of the corporation on June 29, 1968 showed that 98.5 percent of the total number of accounts in all insured banks were fully protected by Federal deposit insurance. However, since the average size of the 1.5 percent of accounts not fully covered greatly exceeds the insurance maximum per depositor, only 60 percent of total deposits in insured banks were covered by Federal deposit insurance. The recent increase in the insurance maximum per depositor would of course increase the percentage of total deposits covered by the Corporation.

National banks and state banks which are members of the Federal Reserve System are automatically insured. Qualified state nonmember banks can also be insured upon application and approval by the corporation's Board of Directors. In granting insurance coverage to a bank, the corporation takes into consideration such factors as the record of the bank's past and current performance, the adequacy of its capital structure, its future earning prospects, the general character of its management, and so on. The corporation regularly examines insured state nonmember banks in order to discover and correct unsound banking practices or violations of laws and regulations. An insured bank which fails to comply with laws and regulations and fails to discontinue practices which are considered unsafe and unsound after a stipulated period of time may have its insured status withdrawn by the corporation.

When a bank fails, it may be liquidated or reorganized and merged with another stronger insured bank in the same community. When it is merged with another bank, its assets and liabilities are assumed by the new bank with additional funds made available by the corporation. Under this procedure, deposits are immediately made available to all depositors. In deposit "payoff cases," the bank is placed under receivership, with the corporation serving as receiver (in most cases) to liquidate the bank's assets. Depositors with accounts of no more than $20,000 are paid in full after offsetting their debts to the bank. Holders of accounts in excess of $20,000 would have a portion of their deposits cancelled by their debts to the bank, if any, and are entitled to share, pro rata, with other creditors the residual proceeds of the liquidated assets.

The corporation derives its income mostly from its holdings of government securities, assets of insured banks which failed, and regular assessments from insured banks which pay one-twelfth of one percent of their "adjusted" total deposits–that is, total deposits less 16 2/3 percent of demand deposits and one percent of time deposits. In terms of the act of 1950 amended in 1961, after deduction of the corporation's expense and insurance losses from such assessment incomes, 33 2/3 percent is credited to the corporation, and 66 1/3 percent is credited to the insured banks.[20]

The creation of the corporation was initially criticized in several respects. Some of these criticisms are legitimate, some are groundless. One serious criticism is concerned with the method of insurance assessment. Since the insurance premium represents a fixed percentage of total deposits, yet an individual account is insured only up to $20,000, banks with large accounts receive no insurance benefits for the assessment on deposits in excess of $20,000 per account. While deposits in small banks with small accounts are almost 100 percent protected, the insurance covers only from 25 to more than 50 percent of the deposits of large banks. In addition, the insurance assessment is not made in relation to insurance risks. Since small banks are more vulnerable to failure than large banks, a fixed percentage assessment amounts to making large banks pay for the mistakes of small banks. The creation of the corporation was criticized on the grounds that the insurance of deposits would lead to lax banking management. There appears to be no logical basis for this objection, since it is owners of banks who suffer the most loss in the event of failure.

In any case, the rather impressive record of the corporation appears to have

[20]It should be noted that because of the assessment credit, the effective assessment rate is much lower than the nominal rate of one-twelfth of one percent. For example, for 1965, the effective assessment rate was approximately 1/32 of 1 percent of assessable deposits.

dispelled doubts and to have quieted criticism. From 1934 to 1967 a total of 470 insured banks were suspended, most of which were small banks with deposits of less than $1 million. Of this total, 190 banks were reorganized and merged with other banks and 280 were liquidated. (Most of these banks failed during the early years of the corporation.) The total volume of deposits involved was $816 million, of which $790 million were fully recovered by depositors. The loss to depositors thus represented slightly more than 3 percent of total deposits. The insurance payments made by the corporation amounted to $430 million, of which $377 million were recovered from liquidated assets. The insurance losses were thus $53 million, less than 6 percent of total insurance disbursements.[21]

The corporation is certainly an important factor contributing to the stability of the banking sytem. It promotes the confidence of the public in the banking business and contributes to further banking development as the confidence in the safey of deposits generated by deposit insurance would likely attract people to banks who would otherwise stay away from them in the absence of insurance. The insurance coverage of deposits of the majority of depositors certainly helps reduce the probability of "runs" on banks, although elements of instability are still present, owing to the fact that a large portion of deposits of business firms, a class of deposits which is amenable to wide fluctuations, is not fully protected. The supervision and examination of insured banks by the corporation and other federal regulatory agencies tend to improve bank management. This, coupled with the readiness of the Federal Reserve System to make greater advance and rediscounting facilities to banks in difficulty, would make very improbable the recurrence of banking panics of the magnitude of those taking place prior to the creation of the corporation.

SUMMARY

Although some of the important functions of modern banks were already performed by various institutions and organizations in ancient past, the essence of modern banking—the creation of money—was not developed until early in the seventeenth century following the issue of bank notes by goldsmith bankers operating with fractional specie reserves. Late in the seventeenth century, the banking activities of goldsmith bankers were overshadowed by corporate banking institutions established to meet the increasing monetary and credit requirements of trade and industrial developments of the time. All these banks were engaged in the acceptance of deposits, issuing and lending bank notes, and transferring funds. The overissue of bank notes which caused frequent bank failures led initially to the restriction of note-issue and eventually to the granting of the note-issuing privilege exclusively to some of these banks which emerged as central banks. The prohibition of note-issue by commercial banks promoted the development of bank deposits which became the major means of payment in modern times.

[21] *Annual Report,* FDIC, 1967.

Loan banks and land banks were banks that existed in the United States during the colonial period. The First and Second Banks of the United States were the first two nationally chartered banks in the country, but they were short-lived. A tremendous growth of state chartered banks followed the dissolution of the Second Bank in 1836, reflecting mostly the passage of free banking laws in individual states and the liberal requirements regarding the organization and operation of state banks. Each bank issued its own notes. The result was the circulation of a great variety of bank notes. The overissue of notes by many of these banks resulted in recurrent banking crises and failures.

The increasing financial requirements of the Civil War, the need for a uniform currency and a sound banking system, prompted the passage of the National Banking Act of 1863-64, providing for the establishment of nationally chartered banks. Since the act failed to convert state banks which continued to issue their own notes, another act was passed in 1865, imposing a 10 percent tax on the notes issued by state banks. This was expected to induce state banks to join the national banking system. This did not materialize, however. The rapid development of bank deposits as means of payment enabled state banks to remain in business and flourish.

The structure of American banking is rather unique. It is dual in more than one sense. First, nationally chartered banks operate side by side with state chartered banks. Second, there are banks which are members of the Federal Reserve and banks which remain outside the system. Third, there are banks which are insured by the Federal Deposit Insurance Corporation, and banks which are not insured. Banks in the United States are organized mostly as small, independent unit banks. But the trend toward multiunit banking is running strong.

American banks are supervised by a multiplicity of supervisory authorities. National banks are supervised by the Comptroller of the Currency; state member banks are supervised by the Federal Reserve and state authorities; insured nonmember banks are supervised by the FDIC and the individual states; and noninsured state banks are supervised by the state banking authorities.

Banking panics and failures were a familiar scene in the United States in the past. Following the wholesale failures of banks during the Great Depression, a law was passed in 1933 establishing the Federal Deposit Insurance Corporation to protect depositors through the insurance of deposits, and to promote sounder banking operations. The operation of the corporation which generates confidence of the public in the safety of deposits is an important factor contributing to the stability of the whole banking system.

PROBLEMS

1. Would you consider such "banks of deposits" as The Bank of Amsterdam (1609) commercial banks in the modern sense of the term? Why or why not? Explain.

2. Explain in some detail the goldsmith banking principle. Is this the beginning of modern banking?

3. What are the major factors which accounted for the demise of the First and Second Banks of the United States?

4. Why was it necessary for Congress to establish the Independent Treasury System? What were the economic and monetary effects of the system?

5. Explain some of the major features of the National Banking Act. What prompted the passage of the act? Why did the amendment of 1865 fail to eliminate the state banking system? Explain in detail.

6. What is the "dual banking system?" Is the emergence of the dual banking system a historical accident? Why or why not? Explain.

7. What are the advantages and disadvantages of branch banking?

8. You know that competitive forces generated by freedom of entry in industries would cause productive resources to move to their best uses. One of the benefits of free competition is more goods and services are made available to the consumers at relatively lower prices. The banking industry, on the other hand, is strictly regulated since entry is controlled through the requirement of public charters. This entry restriction, among other things, could deprive the public of better banking facilities and services at relatively lower costs. Would you or would you not favor unrestricted entry into the banking industry? Why or why not? Discuss your answer in detail.

9. Why are the consequences of the failures of banks more serious than those of the failures of other business corporations?

10. What is the Federal Deposit Insurance Corporation? What are its purposes and functions?

chapter 11

Nonbank Financial Institutions

In addition to commercial banks, there are other financial institutions which supply credit to the economy. But unlike commercial banks, which create money in the process of lending and investing, these institutions either collect savings from the public or borrow funds from commercial banks and others and lend them to individuals and business enterprises. Since they act mostly as "intermediaries" between lenders and borrowers, they are referred to as financial intermediaries. These financial intermediaries fall into two broad groups: "savings intermediaries" and "borrowing intermediaries." The first group consists of savings institutions, whose source of funds represents mostly the savings which they receive from the public. Institutions in the second group, while they do not collect savings, nevertheless act as intermediaries between borrowers and lenders.

These private institutions, together with governmental credit organizations, play an important role in mobilizing financial resources for the financing of trade and industry, in the process of capital formation, which is the major motor generating economic development and growth. In this chapter, we shall describe the operations of some important financial intermediaries, both public and private, and their economic and monetary significance.

SAVINGS INTERMEDIARIES

These specialized financial institutions include mutual savings banks, savings and loan associations, life insurance companies, and credit unions. They compete with commercial banks in attracting savings from individuals, households, and others by offering them claims which are almost as liquid as commercial bank demand and savings deposits.

Mutual Savings Banks

These institutions are organized for the promotion of thrift among people of limited means. Mutual savings banks are mostly concentrated in the Eastern states, especially in the New England states, New York, Pennsylvania, New Jersey, and Maryland. They operate with no paid-in capital. Their only source of funds is savings deposits which they receive from individuals and nonprofit organizations. In principle, these deposits are withdrawable only after advance notice, but in practice, this requirement is usually waived and they can be withdrawn on demand. In some states the amount of deposits which a depositor can hold is limited by law. In New York, for instance, the maximum limit is $10,000.

Mutual savings banks invest the bulk of their funds in mortgage loans. They also invest in government securities, corporate bonds, and obligations of state and local governments. In April 1969, for example, of their total assets of $73 billion, $54 billion (73 percent) were held in mortgage loans, $11 billion (15 percent) were held in corporate bonds, securities of international organizations, and foreign governments, and $4 billion (5.4 percent), in U.S. government securities. Cash assets, on the other hand, represented about one percent of total assets and slightly more than one percent of total savings deposits. This cash ratio appears rather low as compared with that of commercial banks, but for mutual savings banks, it is adequate since deposits in savings banks are made primarily for savings purposes. They have a low rate of turnover.

The earnings of mutual savings banks are derived from their loans and investments. Part of their earnings is used in building up surplus and reserves, the remaining is paid out as interest to depositors. Mutual savings banks are under pressure to pay high interest on deposits in order for them to be competitive with commercial banks and savings and loan associations. The pressure of competition is also reflected in their efforts to enlarge the scope of their operations which include the offering of safe deposit and collection facilities for depositors, and the extension of commercial, industrial, as well as consumer, loans.

Mutual savings banks have had an excellent safety record. This reflects both their conservative management and the strict rules and regulations imposed on their operations by state laws. Indeed, very few mutual savings banks have failed. Even during the great depression, when thousands of commercial banks were suspended, no more than a dozen mutual savings banks were closed.

Mutual savings banks may join the Federal Reserve System, but few have elected to become members. They may also apply for insurance from the Federal Deposit Insurance Corporation. Of the 501 mutual savings banks in operation in the country in 1968, 331 banks with total deposits of $55 billion were insured. The remaining 170, with total deposits of $8 billion, were not covered. Savings banks in Connecticut and Massachusetts, however, are covered by state deposit insurance systems.

Savings and Loan Associations

These are savings institutions which specialize mostly in mortgage financing. Their source of funds is the savings entrusted to them by the public. When a person places his savings in a savings and loan association, technically, he does not make a deposit, as in the case of savings deposits in commercial banks. Instead, he buys a share account with the association. When he wishes to receive cash, he asks the association to repurchase his share or part of his share. The association is not legally obligated to honor the cash request on demand, since he is a shareholder, not a creditor of the association. In practice, however, savings and loan associations usually honor the cash requests of shareholders on demand so long as funds are sufficient for such "withdrawals." Some holders of savings and loan share accounts may not be aware of the fact that they are shareholders and believe that they are holders of savings accounts, just like savings accounts in commercial banks. This source of confusion comes mainly from the fact that the customers of savings and loan associations may purchase or sell any fraction of their share account, and the transactions are recorded in passbooks just like passbooks representing savings deposits in commercial banks.

Except for small proportions of cash assets and modest amounts of government securities and other obligations, the assets of savings and loan associations are made up mostly of mortgage loans. For instance, in April 1969, of their total assets of $156 billion, $134 billion (86 percent) were mortgages, and $10 billion were held in U.S. government securities. Cash assets represented slightly less than 2 percent of total assets.

Dividends are paid on share accounts out of earnings after allowance is made for surplus and reserves. Savings and loan associations are permitted to pay relatively higher rates of interest on their shares, as compared with rates paid by commercial banks on saving deposits. This, among other things, appeared to have given savings and loan associations a competitive advantage over commercial banks in attracting savings.

Savings and loan associations can be chartered under state law or federal law. Nationally chartered associations are called federal savings and loan associations. They are required to take up membership in the Federal Home Loan Bank system. State chartered associations may elect to join the system as they wish. In some respects, the Federal Home Loan Bank system is to member savings and loan associations what the Federal Reserve is to member commercial banks. The eleven Federal Home Loan Banks which make up the Federal Home Loan Bank system, supervise and control member associations in their respective districts. Member associations which are in need of additional funds to meet their liquidity needs can borrow from the Federal Home Loan Banks with mortgages or government securities as collateral. Member associations are also required to hold minimum reserve requirements against their savings and loan share accounts. The legal reserve ratio is fixed by the Federal Home Loan Bank Board. The reserves which can be used to meet required reserves are cash and government securities.

Both state and federal savings and loan associations are insured by the Federal Savings and Loan Insurance Corporation. The insurance status is compulsory for nationally chartered associations and optional for qualified state chartered associations. The Corporation insures individual share accounts up to $20,000 per account in each association. The FSLIC is to insured savings and loan associations what the FDIC is to insured commercial banks.

Life Insurance Companies

Life insurance companies constitute the second most important component of the financial sector of the economy after commercial banks. Their total assets amounted to $191 billion in March 1969, as compared with $483 billion of commercial banks, $156 billion of savings and loan associations, and $73 billion of mutual savings banks. The premiums which they receive from the sale of life insurance policies, annuity contracts, and other insurance contracts constitute their major source of funds. Except for term life insurance policies, the payment of premiums on nonterm life insurance policies, although it involves a purchase of protection, does represent an element of savings. This element of savings is represented by the cash-surrender value of contract. This cash value can be withdrawn by the policyholder.

Life insurance companies invest their funds mostly in mortgages, corporate bonds, and, to a much lesser extent, government securities and corporate stocks. For example, of their total assets of $191 billion in March 1969, $70 billion were held in mortgages, $70 billion in bonds, $11 billion in stocks, and $11 billion in government securities. The variety of investment assets which can be held by life insurance companies is regulated by the insurance departments of the individual states. Corporate bonds purchased by life insurance companies are mostly those issued by public utilities and other industrial enterprises. The volume of common stocks held by life insurance companies is limited by state laws. In New York, for instance, they are permitted to hold no more than 5 percent of their assets in common stock. The proportion of cash assets held by life insurance companies is relatively small. This reflects the predominantly long-term nature of their liabilities on the one hand, and the steady stream of insurance premiums which they receive from policyholders, on the other.

Credit Unions

Credit unions are savings institutions which operate for the benefit of their members. They are usually organized by groups of people having common economic or social bonds such as workers in the same plant, members of the same church, or residents in a community. Most credit unions in the country are organized by workers of industrial enterprises, however. Members place their savings in credit unions by purchasing membership shares. The proceeds of the sale of these shares constitute their operating funds. Credit unions only lend to members on their promissory notes. Sometimes, member borrowers are required to secure their notes by comakers or cosigners. Unlike mutual savings banks and savings and loan associations (and to a large extent life insurance companies, which are engaged mostly in mortgage financing), credit unions mostly make installment consumer loans to members for the purchase of automobiles, household appliances, and other consumer durables. Credit unions are the third most important source of consumer installment credit. For example, in April, 1969, the volume of installment credit outstanding of credit unions was $10.5 billion, as compared with $18.4 billion and $37.8 billion granted by sales finance companies and commercial banks respectively.

The operating costs of credit unions are rather low. This is accounted for by the fact that directors and officers of credit unions often serve without pay and that office space and clerical help are usually made available to them by business enterprises which regard the establishment of credit unions as a way to promote thrift and efficiency among their employees. Low operating costs enable credit unions to grant loans to their members at low rates of interest.

Although membership shares in credit unions are not insured like share accounts in savings and loan associations, or like deposits in mutual savings banks and commercial banks, the risk involved in holding credit union shares is rather small. The loan loss experienced by credit unions indeed has been extremely low. This is accounted for not only by the "esprit de corps" of members who, tied together by a common occupation or other common bonds, want to keep their organization in operation, but also by the loan collection method through their employer's payroll deduction plan, not to speak of the moral consequence of being expelled from their organization as a result of unjustifiable delinquency.

BORROWING INTERMEDIARIES

These institutions differ from savings intermediaries in that they do not receive savings from the public. Some of these institutions borrow mostly from other financial organizations and the public for their own lending operations. Others borrow to provide brokerage services for both lenders and borrowers. These borrowing intermediaries include, among others, investment banks, mortgage banks, finance companies, and investment companies.

Investment Banks

The term *investment banks* is rather misleading. They are not banks like commercial banks or savings banks. They do not accept deposits, nor do they engage in investment operations in the sense of holding securities for their own account. They are essentially "securities merchandisers," buying securities from business corporations wholesale and distributing them at retail to investors.

A business corporation which wants to raise additional funds and plans to offer a new issue of securities may enter into direct negotiation with an investment bank. The negotiated agreement between the issuer and the investment house will determine the type of securities to be offered to the public, the terms of the issue and the provisions for satisfying the requirements of the Securities Exchange Commission and other official authorities and agencies. Apart from direct negotiation, the issue may be offered to investment houses through competitive bidding. The issue will go to the highest bidder, that is, the one offering the highest price. When the size of the issue is large, groups of investment houses may be formed as syndicates to participate in the auction. Competitive bidding is required by state laws for securities issued by state and local governments, and by the Securities and Exchange Commission for securities of registered public utility holding companies and their subsidiaries.

The handling of securities by investment banks, either through direct negotiation with the issuer or through competitive bidding, requires a thorough investigation of the issuing corporation, especially its credit standing, its earning potential, its capital structure, and the proposed use of the new funds. The investment banker, as a merchandiser of securities, faces two groups of people with apparently opposing interests. The users of funds want high prices for their issue. The investors, on the other hand, wish to acquire securities at low prices. The terms of the issue—such as the price of stocks, interst, maturity, and redemption value of bonds and other features—have to be settled by the investment banker so that they suit the needs of the borrower and at the same time are attractive to potential investors.

The investment house may agree to sell the issue on a best-effort basis or to underwrite it. When it offers to sell the issue on a best-effort basis, the issuing corporation will have to take what the issue sells. If it can be sold only at a price lower than the one asked, the borrower may end up short of the funds which he needs. There is no risk involved on the part of the investment banker. He receives commissions from the borrower for his selling efforts. On the other hand, if the investment house agrees to underwrite the issue, it commits itself to purchase the issue at prices specified by the underwriting agreement for resale. If the underwriter can sell the issue to investors at high prices, he will make a profit. If he cannot sell the issue at profitable prices, he may elect to hold on to it and hope for the best. In any case he has to pay the issuer the amount specified in the underwriting agreement. The risk of loss is entirely on the shoulders of the underwriter. Underwriting operations thus require large amounts of borrowed funds, especially when investment houses are forced to hold on to securities which they cannot sell. These borrowed funds come mostly from commercial banks.

When the issue is very large, involving millions of dollars, it is usually underwritten by a syndicate which is made up of a number of participating investment houses. A syndicate member agrees to purchase a fixed portion of the issue. The privileges and obligations of each syndicate member are specified in the syndicate agreement. The manager of the syndicate is usually the originating house—that is, the investment house that originates the issue and negotiates the underwriting contract with the issuer. The formation of syndicates is a way to spread the risk involved in underwriting.

Whether investment houses can obtain higher prices for the securities which they underwrite depends to a considerable extent on their distribution efforts.

In the distribution of securities, the common practice is for syndicate members to sell securities through their own organization and their dealers. In order to secure a wider distribution of the issue, the underwriting syndicate sometimes sets up a "selling group" made up of most or all members of the buying syndicate and other investment houses and security dealers. They are allotted specific amounts of securities for sale. They are expected to take up that portion of their allotment which is not sold.

Mortgage Banks

The operations of mortgage banks in the market for new mortgages are similar to the operations of investment banks in the market for new corporate securities. They are essentially middlemen between mortgage borrowers and mortgage lenders. Builders and real estate dealers who need mortgage loans use the services of mortgage banks in securing loans. Institutional investors, such as life insurance companies and savings and loan associations, use the services of mortgage bankers all over the country for lending opportunities and for the geographical diversification of their mortgage portfolios. Mortgage banks also include in their operations the servicing of properties and the collection of interest payments for the lender.

Consumer Finance Companies

These institutions, sometimes referred to as personal finance companies or small-loan companies, are specialized in the field of consumer lending. They obtain funds by selling stock and bonds to the public, but mostly by borrowing from commercial banks. These companies grant loans to consumers primarily on an installment basis. The borrower repays the loan in a number of equal monthly payments which represent both principal and interest. Loans may be secured or unsecured. Secured loans are based on chattel mortgages on such consumer durables as furniture, other household appliances, and automobiles. Since the cost involved in the seizure and sale of such collateral is high, not to speak of the loss of good will, consumer finance companies rely mostly on the character and credit standing of the borrower for loan repayment. Loans of these companies are thus made primarily on unsecured notes of borrowers.

Consumer finance companies are not subject to usury laws applicable to other lenders. The interest which they can charge and the amount of loan which they can make are, however, strictly regulated. The maximum amount of loan is generally $500 or less. In some states, they are permitted to charge interest from 2½ to 3 percent per month. These rates are relatively high as compared with rates charged by commercial banks and other institutional lenders. They are still reasonable relative to rates charged by loan sharks, which can be as high as 20 percent per month and more. The high rates of interest charged by consumer finance companies reflect mostly the high costs of investigating and servicing small consumer loans and the relatively greater risk involved in consumer lending.

Sales Finance Companies

Unlike consumer finance companies which lend directly to the consumers, sales finance companies are specialized in the financing of installment sales contracts from such retail outlets as automobile dealers, department store, and furniture and appliance stores. They constitute the second most important source of consumer installment credit after commercial banks. As noted earlier, in April 1969, for example, they granted a total of $18.4 billion of installment credit as compared with $37.8 billion by commercial banks.

Sales finance companies range from national companies operating with a nationwide network of branch offices (e.g., General Motors Acceptance Corporation and Commercial Credit Company), to regional companies and local companies. They operate with their capital funds and funds borrowed from commercial banks. When they discount installment sales contracts from automobile dealers and other merchants, they collect the monthly payments directly from the customer. They are protected by conditional bills of sales or chattel mortgages signed by the purchasers until all payments have been made. Should the buyer of an automobile (or other consumer durables) default his obligation, the sales finance company could repossess the car and sell it in order to recover the balance of the contract.

Inasmuch as sales contracts are discounted, the effective charges on these contracts are much higher than the nominal charges. In some cases, they may be as high as 50 percent per year. These financial charges represent not only interest but also filing fees, insurance costs, and the like, which may be included in the monthly payments. In order to avoid excessive charges on the part of sales finance companies, laws have been passed in several states limiting the maximum charge which can be made by these companies.

In addition to discounting installment sales contracts, sales finance companies also provide funds to automobile dealers and other merchants to carry inventories. For instance, an automobile dealer may borrow from a sales finance company to pay the manufacturer when cars are delivered. The loan may be secured by a trust receipt signed by the dealer, giving the lender ownership on the proceeds of the sale of automobiles when cars are sold. The dealer can repay the loan in cash or can turn over an amount of automobile paper as agreed upon between him and the lender.

Investment Companies

These are institutions that raise funds by selling their stock to the public and use them in the purchase of stocks and bonds issued by other business corporations. One of the advantages of the investment company facilities is that by investing in these companies, investors with modest means are in a position to benefit from the safety of asset diversification since the large volume of funds which these companies receive from these investors enable them to acquire securities of a diverse number of business enterprises. Investors with a couple of thousand dollars are not likely able to achieve that kind of investment diversification. Furthermore, investors, regardless of the size of their participation in these companies, always have at their disposal the investment skills of the experts of investment companies.

There are two types of investment companies: open-end companies and closed-end companies. The former are sometimes referred to as mutual funds, and the latter, as stock funds. The majority of investment companies operating in the country are open-end companies. The basic difference between them lies mainly in the manner in which their shares are issued and sold. The open-end companies issue their shares in relation to the demand of the public. These shares may be purchased either directly from the companies or from security dealers. Holders of these shares can redeem them by simply selling them back to the issuing company. The number of shares outstanding of an open-end company thus depends upon the sale and redemption of shares. For instance, in 1968 the total sale of shares amounted to $6.820 billion and the value of shares redeemed was $3.841 billion. This resulted in net sales of $2.979 billion. Open-end investment companies were growing very rapidly during the last decade. Their assets (market value of assets less current liabilities) increased more than sixfold, from $7.819 billion in 1955 to $52.677 billion at the end of 1968.

Closed-end investment companies issue only a fixed amount of shares which are usually distributed through investment banks. Once they are distributed, they are bought and sold on the open market just like shares of industrial enterprises. Holders of these shares cannot redeem them by selling them back to the companies, as in the case of mutual funds. They have to sell them to other investors.

Investment companies differ significantly in their investment policy, which is reflected in the composition of their asset portfolios. Some companies have a "balanced" policy, reflected by a balanced selection of common, preferred stocks and bonds. Some companies are specialized in stocks, either stocks of reputable, stable, well-established firms, or stocks of companies which are less well-known, but show promising growth potential. Some companies invest their funds almost exclusively in bonds. It is true that the benefit of investment diversification in the companies which deal exclusively with particular types of securities, either stocks or bonds, is not as great as could be obtained in companies having balanced portfolios; the element of diversification is still there. A portfolio made up of, say, bonds of a diverse number of firms belonging to different industries offers relatively greater safety than a portfolio which is concentrated on the securities of a single business corporation.

THE GROWTH OF COMMERCIAL BANK AND NONBANK FINANCIAL INTERMEDIARIES

During the past few decades, there was rapid development and growth of commercial banks and nonbank financial institutions. New institutions emerged and existing institutions were multiplied and diversified. All this was in response to the continuously changing credit requirements of the economy, and the changing forms and sources of savings. The growth of banks and nonbank financial intermediaries was reflected by the tremendous increase in their assets. For example, during the 1951-68 period, the combined assets of the four major financial institutions—commercial banks, life insurance companies, savings and loan associations, and mutual savings banks, increased from \$308.4 to \$909.5 billion (See Fig. 11-1). This rapid growth was accounted for largely by rising

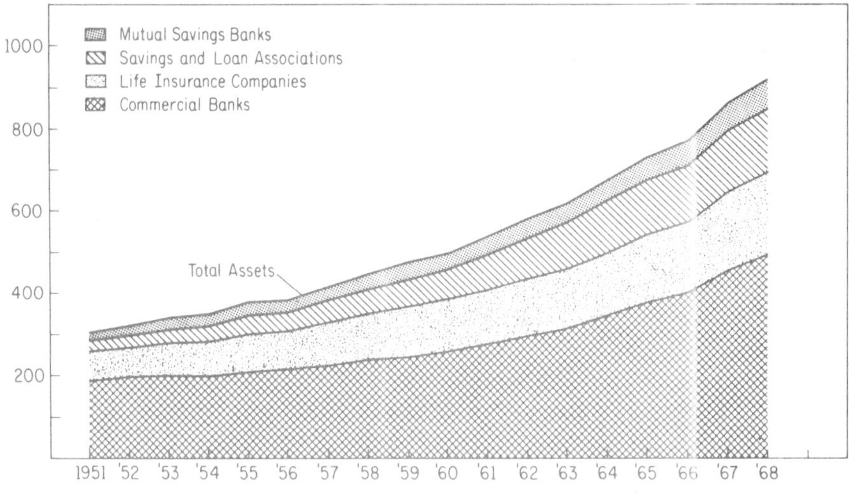

Fig. 11-1. Assets of commercial banks, mutual savings banks, life insurance companies, and savings and loan associations, 1951-1968 (billions of dollars).

personal incomes generated by the continuing growth of the economy, and the increase in the income share of wage and salary earners, the class of savers who prefer to put their savings in such safe and liquid assets as those offered by savings intermediaries. The relatively attractive interest rates offered by these institutions for savings funds, the establishment of institutions for the insurance of the liabilities of banks and some savings intermediaries, and the strict rules and regulations governing their operations constitute another important stimulus to the flow of savings from individuals and households to financial institutions.

While the assets of banks and nonbank institutions were growing during the past few decades, there were differentials in their rate of growth. From 1951 to 1968 the assets of savings and loans associations displayed an annual compound rate of growth of about 12.3 percent, as compared with about 5.8 percent of life insurance companies and commercial banks, and slightly more than 6 percent of mutual savings banks. While the assets of all these institutions were increasing remarkably, the relative share of the total assets of some institutions was rising; that of some other institutions was declining. Thus, of the combined assets of commercial banks, mutual savings, life insurance companies, and savings and loan associations, the share of mutual savings banks remained practically unchanged at 8 percent of the total, the share of life insurance companies slightly decreased from 23 to 20 percent, and the share of commercial banks declined substantially, from 61 percent in 1951 to only 54 percent at the end of 1968. The share of savings and loan associations, on the other hand, was rising sharply, from about 7 percent to 17 percent during the same period.

There was a sharp change in the share of these institutions in the flow of savings (see Fig. 11-2). In regard to the combined total savings in commercial

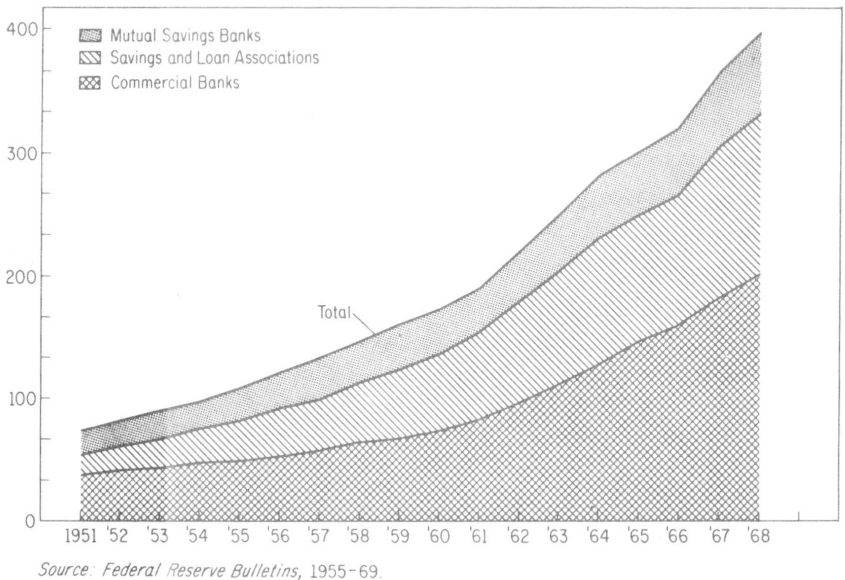

Fig. 11-2. Savings in commercial banks, mutual savings banks, and savings and loan associations, 1951–1968 (billions of dollars).

banks (time and savings deposits), mutual savings banks (saving deposits), and savings and loan associations (savings capital), the share of savings and loan associations increased substantially from 21 percent in 1951 to 38 percent in 1968 at the expense of commercial banks and mutual savings banks whose shares were declining from 51 to 46 percent and 28 to 16 percent respectively. This reflected, among other things, the relatively low rates of interest that could be paid by commercial banks on savings and time deposits as compared with rates payable by savings and loan associations.[1]

While the relative share of savings funds of these institutions is determined, to a considerable extent, by the relative rates of interest which they pay (and other nonprice competitive measures); their share of the aggregate savings of the community depends largely on the level of income and on the interest rates which they pay on savings deposits relative to the rates on other savings opportunities, such as United Savings bonds and other savings assets.

GOVERNMENTAL CREDIT INSTITUTIONS

Private financial institutions, while responsive to the credit needs of some sectors of the economy, are not so responsive to the credit requirements of other sectors, especially the small business and farming sectors, presumably due to the relatively risky nature of small business and farming operations, among other things. To fill this credit gap, several credit institutions have been established by the federal government to make credit facilities available to these special groups at low cost. The wholesale foreclosure of homes during the Great Depression, when owners were unable to honor their mortgage debts, also prompted the creation of several federal agencies to facilitate home financing.

Federal Home Loan Bank System

The structure of the Federal Home Loan Bank System is somewhat patterned on the Federal Reserve System. The objective of the system is to help facilitate home financing by making federal credit facilities available to, and insuring the liabilities of, savings and loan associations which are specialized mortgage-lending institutions.

The Federal Home Loan Bank Board, made up of three members appointed by the President of the United States, is in charge of supervising the operations of the Federal Home Loan Banks, the Federal Savings and Loan Insurance Corporation, and the federal savings and loan associations, which constitute the foundation of the system.

[1] It should be noted that following the increases in interest ceilings authorized by the Board of Governors of the Federal Reserve and the Federal Deposit Insurance Corporation after mid-1962 and the subsequent increases in rates that they paid, commercial banks were able to increase their savings share slightly, from 45 percent in 1963 to 47 percent at the end of 1965. With the change in regulation Q in December 1965 that allowed banks to pay up to 5 1/2 percent interest on certificates of time deposits, banks were able to compete effectively with savings and loan associations in attracting savings funds from the public. This was indicated by the fact that during the period from December 1965 to May 1967, savings and time deposits of commercial banks increased by more than 16 percent while the savings capital of savings and loan associations increased by slightly more than 5 percent. The position of savings and loan associations was improved after late 1967 following the increases in the maximum rates that they could pay on savings and loan share accounts. These were authorized by the Federal Home Loan Bank Board.

The Federal Home Loan Banks. There are eleven Federal Home Loan Banks located in eleven home loan bank districts. The main operation of the Federal Home Loan Banks is the extension of both short- and long-term advances to members. These advances are secured by first mortgages or government securities. The total advances outstanding by the Home Loan Banks in February 1969 were $5.298 billion, of which $4.940 billion were short-term and $358 million were long-term. The bulk of these advances was granted to savings and loan associations.

Institutions which are eligible for membership in the system include savings and loan associations, insurance companies, and cooperative banks. As we have mentioned, nationally chartered savings and loan associations are required to take up membership in the system, but qualified state chartered associations may elect to join the system at their own option. A member institution is required to subscribe to the capital of the Federal Home Loan Bank of its district equal to 2 percent of its total outstanding mortgage loans. The source of funds of the Federal Home Loan Banks is made up of the capital subscription of members, cash and government securities deposited by members, and the sale of their own obligation to the public.

The Federal Savings and Loan Insurance Corporation. The FSLIC is also under the jurisdiction of the Federal Home Loan Bank Board. The corporation was established in 1934 to insure savings and loan share accounts of savings and loan associations. The FSLIC thus gives savings and loan associations the same kind of protection as that provided by the FDIC to insured commercial banks. Federal savings and loan associations are required to participate in the insurance plan, and state chartered associations may choose to join the corporation, if qualified. As noted earlier, each individual share account in a savings and loan association is insured up to $15,000.

Like the FDIC, the FSLIC derives its income from insurance assessment of members and earnings on government securities which it holds. Each insured association pays an annual insurance premium equal to 1/12 of one percent of its share accounts and creditor obligations. The initial capital of the FSLIC, like that of the FDIC, was provided by the federal government. The corporation is required to retire gradually the government stock from part of its earnings, and the remaining income goes to the corporation's insurance fund. Should the insurance fund be inadequate for insurance payments, the corporation could borrow additional funds from the U.S. Treasury Department.

Federal Mortgage Insurance and Marketing Institutions

In order to encourage financial institutions to grant more mortgage loans to borrowers for home ownership, institutions have been established by the government to insure mortgage loans and to promote the marketability of mortgages. These institutions are: the Federal National Mortgage Association, the Federal Housing Administration, and the Veterans Administration.

The Federal National Mortgage Association. This institution, popularly known as "Fannie May," was organized in 1938. The basic purpose of the establishment of the Association is to provide a secondary market for secured mortgages and to stabilize their prices, rendering them more attractive to banks and other private financial institutions. The association derives the major source of its funds from the sale of notes and debentures to the public. These funds have been used by the association to stabilize the market for FHA-insured and VA-guaranteed mortgages. It enters the market as a buyer when the demand for these mortgages is weak and their prices low, and as a seller when supply is tight and prices are high.

The Federal Housing Administration. The FHA was created in 1934 (under the authority of the National Housing Act of June of that year) for the purpose of insuring mortgage loans which meet FHA rules and regulations. Thus, the agency is not a lending institution. It serves only as a guarantor of mortgage loans made by private institutions. The various provisions regulating the insurance of mortgage loans are subject to change by administrative regulation. The amounts of mortgage loans which can be insured, their maturities, and interest charges, are all subject to limits. Thus, in the 1960's, the maximum amount of loan which could be insured for a one-unit and two-unit family dwelling was $25,000. The maximum rate of interest which could be charged was 5 3/4 percent. FHA-insured mortgages have to be amortized by monthly payments. The FHA also provides for insurance of mortgage contracts for multifamily rental units, cooperative-housing loans, and slum clearance construction projects.

The Veterans Administration. The Veterans Administration was authorized by the Servicemen's Readjustment Act of 1944 to guarantee mortgage loans made to veterans for the acquisition of houses and business property. The program is rather similar to the FHA-insurance program.

During periods of rising business activity, the interest ceiling on insured mortgage loans, among other things, rendered them less attractive to financial institutions than conventional mortgages on which they could receive higher rates. For instance, during the 1960-68 period, while the volume of conventional mortgages increased from $131.7 to $270.7 billion, more than 100 percent, the volume of FHA-insured and VA-guaranteed mortgages increased by only about 50 percent, from $62.3 to $92.0 billion.

Federal Agriculture Credit Institutions

The farming sector, because of the nature of its credit needs and its operations, has limited access to the credit facilities of commercial banks. Its income is rather uncertain and is more susceptible to adverse economic developments than the commercial and industrial sectors. Its short-term credit requirements are usually longer than the short-term credit needs of commercial and industrial enterprises. Likewise, its medium and long-term credit requirements are usually longer than those of other businesses. In order to fill the gap between the credit requirements of farmers and what is made available to them by private financial institutions, various agricultural credit institutions have been created by the government to provide farmers with short, intermediate and long-term credit. These institutions are supervised and controlled by the Farm Credit Administration. We shall describe briefly some of the organizations under the jurisdiction of the Federal Farm Credit Board of the Farm Credit Administration.

Federal Land Banks. The Federal Land Banks were established in 1916. There are twelve such banks located in twelve land bank districts. They grant long-term loans to members of the National Farm Loan Associations. These associations are owned by member borrowers who are required to purchase an amount of stock in their association equal to 5 percent of the loans which they obtain from the Federal Land Banks. Loans granted by the Federal Land Banks have to be secured by first mortgages on farm property. They are made for periods ranging from 5 to 40 years, but the common maturity range is from 20 to 30 years. They are used mostly for the purchase of farm land, equipment, land improvement, farm construction buildings, fertilizer, and livestock.

Production Credit Corporations. There are twelve production credit corporations operating in the country. Basically, they are not lending agencies. Their major operation is supervising and assisting in the organization of production credit associations which are formed by groups of local farmers and stockmen to provide members with mostly short-term credit facilities. Loans are usually made for periods of one year or less, but sometimes they may be extended up to three years. Member borrowers are required to purchase stock in the associations. The major source of funds of these associations comes from the discounting of member-borrowers' notes with the Federal Intermediate Credit Bank. The production credit corporation assists in the formation of production credit associations by providing them with initial capital. The initial capital of the Production Credit Corporations was provided by the Federal Government.

Banks for Cooperatives. The system of Banks for Cooperatives is made up of the "Central Bank" for Cooperatives and twelve regional banks for cooperatives located in 12 farm credit districts. While the Central Bank for Cooperatives makes loans to large national and regional farmers' cooperatives, the district banks for cooperatives cater to the needs of small, local cooperative associations. Loans granted are short-term, intermediate, and long-term. They are used mostly for the marketing of farm products, the purchase of farm equipment, and product processing facilities. The Banks for Cooperatives obtain their loanable funds, by selling stock to cooperative associations, offering debentures to the public, and by borrowing from the intermediate credit banks and commercial banks. Their initial capital was provided by the federal government under the Agricultural Marketing Act of 1933.

Federal Intermediate Credit Banks. There are twelve Federal Intermediate Credit banks in the country. They were established in 1923. Their primary function is to grant advances to such organizations as Production Credit Associations and Banks for Cooperatives through the discounting of their notes. They also discount notes of farmers borrowing from commercial banks, agricultural credit corporations, and livestock loan companies, provided the loans are used for farming operations. The maturity of notes discounted by these Intermediate Credit Banks is usually one year or less, but sometimes it may run up to three years. These banks obtain part of their funds by offering short-term debentures to the public.

The Small Business Administration

Small businesses are somewhat handicapped in securing loans from private sources. If they have access to commercial banks for short-term credit, and to a lesser extent for medium-term loans, it is rather difficult for them to secure long-term funds. Where bank credit is available, the interest costs are usually high. This reflects not only the high administrative costs involved in small business loans but also the relatively greater risk in lending to small businesses. It is not practical for small businesses to raise long-term funds by directly offering their own obligations in the open market, since they are not widely known to investors. Nor is it practical for them to raise funds through investment banking firms, since the cost involved would be prohibitive, and investment houses are not likely to agree to handle the securities for unknown small firms. They usually deal with large, reputable, well-established business corporations. Thus, for long-term funds, small businesses rely mostly on the savings of friends and relatives. This source of funds is limited.

The major purpose of the Small Business Administration (SBA), established by the Small Business Act of 1953, is to render financial assistance to small businesses unable to obtain credit from private lenders. The agency makes short, intermediate and long-term loans to small firms for working capital purposes, for plant construction, and for the acquisition of land, equipment, raw materials, and other productive facilities. Any small firm can borrow up to $350,000 for a period of up to 10 years. The SBA can make loans either directly or in participation with private lending institutions, or may simply guarantee private loans. In the case of participation with private lenders, the participation of the SBA is not to exceed 90% of the total loan. The SBA also makes loans to victims of disaster areas.

In view of mobilizing private funds as a service to small businesses, Congress, in 1958 passed the Small Business Investment Act, authorizing the establishment of a system of "small business investment companies" to provide funds to small businesses. The Act is administered by the Small Business Administration. These companies obtain their loanable funds by selling stock to individuals as well as financial institutions. They may sell subordinated debentures to the SBA up to $700,000 and borrow from other private sources. They may grant loans to small business for periods of 20 years or more. A large number of such companies were being established after 1959.

FINANCIAL INTERMEDIARIES AND THE ECONOMY

The volume and quality of capital goods, such as machinery and equipment, which a country can produce determines its long run economic progress and its standard of living. The larger the volume of capital goods per worker, the greater will be the per capita output of goods and services, and the higher will be the standard of living.

The volume of capital goods which can be produced during a given period of time depends upon the amount of productive resources which are released from the production of consumption goods. In other words, it depends upon the magnitude of savings which is that portion of total income not spent on consumption. But savings alone does not automatically add to the productive capacity of an economy. In fact, savings without investment, in the sense of capital formation, would result in deflation, declining business activity, as businesses, unable to sell all their goods, would have to cut back production and lay off workers, thereby causing declining income and rising unemployment. For the formation of capital to take place, savings have to be accompanied by investment. Savings release productive resources from the production of consumption goods, and investment uses these facilities in the production of capital goods which will help increase the production of both consumer and capital goods in the future.

Savings is not automatically translated into investment. It is true that some business enterprises make both savings and investment decisions in that they acquire capital goods out of their own savings—depreciation allowance and retained earnings—but the bulk of savings is accumulated by people who do not directly make decisions regarding investment. The translation of savings into investment therefore requires a mechanism for the transfer of savings, which are claims on resources, to the users, business corporations, and others desiring to acquire additional productive facilities. This transfer mechanism is provided mostly by financial intermediaries which pool the savings resources of the public and channel them to businesses for the acquisition of capital equipment. Financial intermediaries thus play an important role in the savings-investment process,[2] in influencing the level of aggregate economic activity. In the absence of financial intermediaries which offer to the public savings and other facilities, a larger portion of its income would probably be spent on consumption. The resulting smaller amount of savings would probably be entrusted to commercial banks. Since banking operations are mostly confined to short and medium-term lending, a still smaller portion of total savings would be available for capital formation; hence the level of income in the future would be lower than otherwise would be possible.

The operations of financial intermediaries, important as they are in the

[2] A more detailed discussion on savings and investment is presented in Chapter 19 on the theory of income determination.

process of capital formation, do create economic problems. We have seen that people who entrust their savings to savings intermediaries receive in return such claims as savings deposits and savings and loan share accounts which are almost as liquid as money itself. Since these assets are money substitutes, changes in the volume of these liquid assets affect the velocity of circulation of money (the speed at which money changes hands) through their effect on the demand for money balances. The following example shows the relation between the change in the liquid assets created, say, by savings and loan associations and the turnover rates of money. Assume that Mr. X has a demand account of $5,000 in the banking system, of which about $2,000 remains idle most of the time. Attracted by the high rate of interest paid by savings and loan associations on their share accounts, he decides to purchase a share of $2,000 in a savings and loan association and pays for it by drawing on his account with the banking system. The savings and loan association deposits the check in its bank and receives credit in its demand account. The change in the balance sheet of the banking system and the savings and loan association is shown by transactions (1) of the two balance sheets:

A		Banking System	L
		Deposits of X −2,000	(1)
		Deposits of the Savings and Loan Association +2,000	(1)
		Deposits of the Savings and Loan Association −2,000	(2)
		Deposits of borrower +2,000	(2)

A		Savings and Loan Association	L
Deposits with Banks +2,000	(1)	Savings and Loan share accounts +2,000	(1)
Deposits at Banks −2,000	(2)		
Loans +2,000	(2)		

With this increase in loanable funds, the savings and loan association makes a mortgage loan of $2,000 to a builder who deposits the check in the banking system for payment purposes. The loan assets of the savings and loan association increases by $2,000. This is offset by a decrease of its deposit assets of the same amount. With regard to deposits in the banking system, there is a transfer of deposits from the account of the savings and loan association to the account of the borrower. All this is shown by transactions (2) in the balance sheets. When the borrowers draw on their accounts to make payments, deposits will be transferred to other accounts. It is clear from our example that the operation of the savings and loan association does not change the supply of money. The volume of deposit money in the banking system remains unchanged. There is an increase in the velocity of circulation of deposit money, however; it has passed from X's account to that of the savings and loan association; it has passed from that of the association to the borrower's account, and so on. All this has happened because the existence of liquid claims created by the savings and loan association has enabled Mr. X to reduce his idle balance in return for a savings and loan share account.

In periods of declining business activity, increased total expenditure resulting from the lending operations of financial intermediaries indeed produce desirable effects as it generates higher levels of real income and employment. But during periods of economic boom, when the economy is operating at high level of employment, increases in total spending generated by the lending operations of financial intermediaries would result in inflationary pressures. Since these institutions, unlike commercial banks, are not subject to the direct regulation of monetary authorities, their lending policies may weaken the effectiveness of monetary control. For example, in times of rising prices, while the monetary authorities attempt to reduce or curtail inflationary demand by controlling the volume of commercial bank credit, financial intermediaries may go on expanding their credit operations. They may attract funds from holders of idle balances by offering higher rates of interest on their liquid claims or selling part of the securities which they hold. Funds so obtained are then made available to borrowers whose spending would inflate the expenditure flow, putting more pressure on prices. As we have seen, while the operations of financial intermediaries may not change the supply of money, they increase the velocity of monetary circulation as a result of the activation of idle balances.[3] While the monetary

[3]It should be noted that the operations of nonbank financial intermediaries may at times result in an increase in the supply of money, (as conventionally defined), which reflects the transfer of savings deposits to demand balances in commercial banks. Assume that Mr. Y has a savings account of $2,000 in the banking system. Attracted by the higher rates of interest paid by savings and loan association, he withdraws $1,000 from his savings account and buys a share of $1,000 from a savings and loan association which deposits the proceeds in its account with the banking system. The change in the balance sheet of the banking system and the association is as follows:

A — Banking System	L	A — Savings and Loan Association	L
	Demand balances of savings & loan association +1,000 Savings deposits of *Y* −1,000	Deposits in banking system +1,000	Savings and loan share +1,000

Since savings deposits are not included in the money stock, the purchase of a share in the savings and loan association results in an immediate increase in the supply of money of $1,000 (increase in deposit money). Suppose that the saving and loan association, instead of depositing $1,000 in currency which it received from Y in its demand account with the banking system, keeps this amount in cash for lending, the increase in the money supply reflects the increase in currency in circulation. The balance sheet change of the banking system and of the savings and loan association in this case is:

A — Banking System	L	A — Savings and Loan Association	L
Cash reserves −1,000	Savings deposits −1,000	Cash assets +1,000	Savings and Loan Share +1,000

Although there is an immediate increase in the supply of money resulting from these transactions, their "secondary" effect on the money supply would depend upon the reserve position of the banking system at the time when these transactions took place.

authorities have some direct control on the money supply, they have no direct influence on the velocity of circulation. Yet an increase in the velocity of circulation of money can affect the level of aggregate spending just like an increase in the stock of money. It follows that the effort of central bank authorities to reduce the supply of money to relieve inflationary pressures may be partly thwarted by the increase in the velocity of circulation resulting from the lending activities of financial intermediaries.

Since the lending operations of financial intermediaries may weaken monetary control, the question is raised as to whether it is desirable to bring these institutions under some sort of control of the monetary authorities. We shall discuss this question and the various ways by which the central bank authorities can affect the lending policies of these institutions in Part V on stabilization policy. Aside from private financial intermediaries, we might add that the lending operations of governmental credit institutions may at times produce destabilizing pressures. For example, during periods of inflation, when restrictive monetary policy is called for, these public credit institutions may continue to expand credit to small businesses and farmers' organizations if the pursuit of their objectives calls for liberal lending; otherwise, they would defeat the purposes for which they were established.

SUMMARY

In addition to commercial banks, there are other credit institutions. They differ from commercial banks in that they do not create money as a result of their lending and investing operations. Savings institutions such as mutual savings banks and savings and loan associations receive savings from the public and pass them on to borrowers. Although they do not create money, these institutions do create claims which are almost as liquid as money. Other institutions such as finance companies, investment companies, investment banks, and mortgage banks do not accept savings from the public. They borrow from the public or other financial institutions either to lend or to provide brokerage services to both lenders and borrowers. While the credit operations of commercial banks are highly diversified, the operation of these institutions are somewhat specialized. Thus while savings and loan associations and mutual savings banks invest their funds mostly in mortgages, life insurance companies are specialized in mortgage and corporate lending and credit unions and finance companies devote themselves to consumer lending.

During the past few decades financial institutions were growing very rapidly. Savings and loan associations showed the highest rate of growth. Their share of total assets and total savings was rising sharply, whereas that of commercial banks and mutual savings banks was declining. Until recently the relatively high rates of interest paid by savings and loan associations on their share accounts, as compared with those paid by commercial banks and savings banks on savings and time deposits, appeared to be one of the important determinants of that trend.

Although the credit needs of some sectors of the economy were met by these private lending institutions, other sectors such as farmers and small businesses have limited access to these private sources of credit. To help meet their needs, several credit institutions have been established by the federal government. Some of these institutions lend directly to borrowers. Some others were designed to encourage the flow of credit from private financial institutions. The important governmental credit institutions include the Federal Home Loan Bank System, the Federal National Mortgage Association, the Federal Housing Administration, the Banks for Cooperatives, the Federal Intermediate Credit Bank, and the Small Business Administration.

In providing a mechanism for the translation of savings into investment, nonbank financial institutions play an important role in the process of capital formation, in determining the aggregate level of economic activity. The increase in the velocity of circulation of money as a result of their lending operations, however, may add to inflationary pressures during periods of economic boom. Inasmuch as they are not subject to the control of the monetary authorities, the effectiveness of monetary control may be weakened by their lending policies.

PROBLEMS

1. What are mutual savings banks? How are their operations compared with those of savings and loan associations? Explain some of the differences between these savings intermediaries and borrowing intermediaries.
2. What are investment banks? What is the role played by these institutions in the capital market?
3. Why was it necessary for the government to establish public credit institutions? Explain briefly the operations of some major governmental institutions.
4. Explain in some detail the role played by financial intermediaries in the savings-investment process.
5. Explain why the credit operations of financial intermediaries tend to increase the velocity of monetary circulation: use examples to illustrate your discussion.
6. Assume that Mr. X uses \$1,000 in currency which he has kept in his wall safe to purchase a \$1,000 share account in a savings and loan association. The association uses these new funds for a loan of \$1,000 to Mr. Y, who uses them in payment to Mr. Z. The latter banks with Bank A. (a) Show the balance-sheet changes of Bank A and the savings and loan associations. (b) Is there any change in the supply of money? Why or why not? (c) What is the effect of this activation of idle balances on the expenditure flow?
7. Mr. Y draws a check for \$500 on his checking account with bank B (he considers this portion of his account idle) for a \$500 savings account in a mutual savings bank which is also a customer of commercial bank B. (a) Show the balance-sheet changes of commercial bank B and the savings bank. (b) Is there any change in the supply of money? (c) Is there any change in the volume of liquid claims created by these institutions?

part III

CENTRAL BANKING

chapter **12**

American Central Banking: The Federal Reserve

A central bank is a bankers' bank, and a bank for the government. Central banks differ from commercial banks and other financial institutions in their objectives and functions. While commercial banks and other financial institutions are largely motivated by the profit motive, central banks are primarily motivated by the public interest, and by the need for monetary and credit control to promote the stability and growth of the national economy.

The general objectives and functions of central banks in various parts of the world are essentially the same. They differ from each other, however, in their structure and organization. Although central banks in most countries are governmentally owned and operated, central banking institutions in some countries are semipublic in nature. In this chapter and next, we shall describe the structure and organization of the Federal Reserve, its routine and service functions, the basic aggregates which it seeks to control, and the control instruments at its disposal.

BACKGROUND OF THE FEDERAL RESERVE

Prior to the passage of the Federal Reserve Act in 1913, providing for the creation of the Federal Reserve System the supply of money and credit in the country was not sufficiently responsive to the monetary and credit requirements of the public.

The supply of currency, then made up of gold and silver coins, gold and silver certificates, United States notes, and national bank notes was rather inelastic. Gold and silver coins and certificates changed only in accordance with the production of gold and silver, and the variation in the country's balance of payments which resulted in either inflow or outflow of gold. The amount of United States notes issued by the Treasury was limited by law. The volume of national bank notes was governed by the amount of government bonds at the disposal of national banks. As we have mentioned, after 1900 national banks were permitted to issue national bank notes equal to 100 percent of the value of the government bonds which they deposited with the Treasury as collateral for their note issue. Changes in the volume of bank notes thus primarily reflected the changes in the volume of bonds issued by the government, not the changing monetary requirements of trade and industry. It expanded when new bonds were issued by the Treasury and held by national banks, and contracted when bonds were retired and not reissued. The trouble was that the retirement of bonds, and consequently the contraction of national bank notes, sometimes took place when an expansion of bank notes was called for. For example, during periods of economic expansion when the government had surplus, it used the surplus to retire bonds, which resulted in a contraction in the volume of national bank notes when they were most needed. It follows that under the national banking system, the supply of currency was not responsive to the cyclical changes in the demand for currency. Nor was it responsive to the seasonal changes in currency demand. The demand for currency tended to reach its peak in the fall as farmers needed money to pay farm workers, and merchants, to pay for farm products, and fell off sharply during the early months in the year. The volume of national bank notes, limited in the short-run by the existing quantity of government bonds, was sometimes insufficient to meet unusually heavy seasonal currency demand. This caused difficulties to banks, especially those which were more or less loaned up, when confronted with heavy currency withdrawals.

The pressure on bank reserves generated by a heavy demand for currency tended to be magnified and widespread under the reserve arrangements of the National Banking System. We can recall that under the National Banking System country banks were permitted to hold three-fifths of their required reserves in the form of deposit balances with reserve city and other banks; the reserve city banks in turn could hold one half of their required reserves in demand balances with central reserve city banks in New York, Chicago, and St. Louis. The latter were required to keep their reserves in vault cash.

This system of pyramiding reserves tended to overstretch the reserve capability of the system. The funds deposited by country banks with reserve city banks were considered their cash reserves. These funds, when deposited by reserve city banks with central reserve city banks, were again counted as their cash reserves. Actual reserves, however, were practically the cash reserves of central reserve city banks which supported the whole system. Under this arrangement, in times when business was unusually active and larger amounts of cash were needed by the public for hand-to-hand circulation, country banks would call on their reserve city correspondents for additional cash. The latter, in turn, would call on central reserve city banks for additional funds. Reserve stringencies generated by heavy currency demand thus ultimately converged to central reserve city banks. Inasmuch as they were then not allowed to reduce their required reserves below the minimum levels (these reserves were intended by law not to be used even in emergencies), and there was no central institution (with power to issue currency) to which they could turn for additional cash reserves to meet the demand for funds from their customer-banks, they were forced to call loans from brokers, and liquidate their securities. These methods of increasing reserves would not work when there was a general pressure on bank reserves. The attempts of brokers to liquidate their assets to obtain funds to repay their loans to commercial banks, and the attempts of banks to sell their securities for cash would result mainly in declining securities prices. Banks which were unable to obtain additional cash would have to suspend payments to other banks and the public. Banks which were not able to obtain reserves from reserve city and central reserve city banks also would have to close their doors. The failures of a few banks would undermine the confidence of depositors in the ability of banks in general to pay them currency. This led to runs on banks and to general banking and financial crises. Such crises were very frequent under the pre-1914 national banking system, e.g., those taking place in 1873, 1884, 1893, and 1907.

Following the particularly severe crisis of 1907, the National Monetary Commission was appointed by Congress to investigate the monetary and banking problems of the country and to propose measures for reform. The Commission recommended the creation of a central institution with authority to supervise, and control the operations of commercial banks in order to avoid excessive expansion of bank credit, to make additional reserves available to banks in times of financial strains, and to provide the country with an elastic currency supply. In 1913 Congress passed the Federal Reserve Act, establishing the Federal Reserve System composed of twelve Federal Reserve Banks, supervised and coordinated by the Board of Governors in Washington. The System was aimed at correcting the above major defects of the national banking system. This was implicit in the original purposes of the Reserve Act which were to give the country an elastic currency, to provide facilities for discounting commercial paper, and to improve the supervision of banking, among other things. The objectives of the Federal Reserve and the scope of its operations have been broadened over the years in response to the changing economic and financial developments of the country.

Unlike foreign countries which have single central banks, e.g., the Bank of England in England, and the Bank of France in France, the twelve Federal Reserve banks in the United States are technically twelve separate central banks, each acting as a central bank in its own district. The establishment of this regional system of twelve Reserve banks was motivated by the desire for representation of the diverse economic and financial interests in the various regions of the country, as well as the fear of the financial domination of the eastern seaboard among other things. In practice, however, owing to the unifying influence of, and the centralization of powers in, the Board of Governors, the twelve Federal Reserve banks, in several respects, can be considered as twelve branches of a central bank with the Board of Governors as the central body. In addition, unlike the Bank of England and the Bank of France, which are government-owned institutions, the Federal Reserve banks are technically owned by private member banks. They are, however, semipublic institutions motivated solely by the public interest. This is embodied in the system's structure and organization.

STRUCTURE AND ORGANIZATION

The major divisions of the American Central banking system are the Board of Governors, the twelve Federal Reserve Banks, the Federal Open Market Committee, and the Federal Advisory Council. Member commercial banks constitute the foundation on which the system operates.

The Board of Governors

The Board of Governors is the highest administrative and policy-making body of the system. It consists of seven members appointed by the President of the United States (and confirmed by the Senate) "with due regard to fair representation of the financial, industrial, agricultural, and commercial interests, and geographic divisions of the country." They are appointed for terms of fourteen years, and their terms are so arranged that one expires every two years. Two members of the board are appointed by the President as chairman and vice-chairman of the board for four-year terms. The chairman is the chief executive officer, and he is the spokesman of the Board of Governors.

The Board of Governors has a broad range of powers over monetary matters and the operations of the Federal Reserve banks and member banks. Thus, the board reviews and determines the rates of discount charged by the Federal Reserve banks on discounts for and advances to member banks, and determines the character of paper eligible for rediscounting. It determines the margin requirements regarding loans used in the purchase and carrying of securities. It determines the maximum rates of interest payable by member banks on savings and time deposits. Together with officers of the Federal Reserve banks, the Board of Governors formulates policies regarding the sales and purchases of securities in the open market. It regulates and supervises the issue and retirement of Federal Reserve notes. It is empowered to fix the minimum legal reserve requirements against member banks' deposit liabilities and the like.

With respect to its powers over the Federal Reserve banks and member banks, the Board of Governors has the authority to appoint three of the nine directors of each Federal Reserve bank's board of directors, to suspend or remove any officer or director of a Federal Reserve Bank, and any officer or director of a member bank for repeated violation of banking rules and regulations. The Board authorizes the opening or closing of branches of the Federal Reserve banks and of member banks. It is in charge of supervising and examining the Federal Reserve banks to determine their financial condition and to assure compliance of their management with rules and regulations governing their operations. It is also charged with supervising and examining member banks to maintain high banking standards. Membership in the system is granted by the board to qualified state chartered banks.

Several proposals have recently been advanced to change the size of the Board of Governors. One such proposal would reduce the size of the Board to five members or less. It is argued that fewer members of the board would increase its prestige and would make its membership attractive to more able people. The board would be in a position to make decisions more promptly and more timely. One of the arguments against such a change is that it would lessen the advantages and probably the wisdom of collective deliberation and judgment. Also, there has been a proposal to increase the number of members of the Board to twelve, including the Secretary of the Treasury as Chairman of the Board. The proposal is objected to on the grounds that it would slow down the process of making monetary policy decisions. Furthermore, the presence of the Secretary of the Treasury, the officer in charge of government spending, would exert undue pressure on the board for more money to finance government expenditure.

The Federal Reserve Banks

The twelve Federal Reserve banks are located in twelve Federal Reserve Districts whose boundaries are initially determined by the Organization Committee of the system. The boundaries of the Reserve Districts do not always follow state lines.

Each Federal Reserve bank is administered by a Board of Directors composed of nine members. The directors are divided into three groups: A directors, B directors, and C directors. The A and B directors are elected by member banks. In the election of A and B directors, member banks are divided into three groups: small banks, medium-sized banks, and large banks. Each group elects one A and one B director. The A directors are to be selected from the banking profession, and the B directors from nonbanking pursuits, such as agriculture, commerce and industry. The law requires that the B directors must not be officers, directors, employees, or stockholders of any bank. The C directors, on the other hand, are appointed by the Board of Governors. They also must not be officers, directors, employees, or stockholders of any bank. One of the C directors is designated by the Board of Governors as chairman of the Board of Directors of the Federal Reserve bank, and another one, as vice-chairman. The Chairman of the Board of Directors also serves as Federal Reserve Agent, official representative of the Board of Governors with a Federal Reserve bank.

While the Board of Directors is in charge of the general functioning and policy of each Federal Reserve bank, the president, vice-presidents, and other executive officers appointed by the Board of Directors are charged with the bank's daily operations. The appointment of the president and first vice-president of the Federal Reserve bank by the Board of Directors is subject to the approval of the Board of Governors.

Each of the twelve Federal Reserve banks is a corporation whose capital is subscribed by member banks. The law requires that a member bank has to subscribe to the capital stock of the Federal Reserve bank of its district equal to 6 percent of its own capital and surplus, one half of which has to be paid-in, and the remainder is subject to call by the Board of Governors. The probability that member banks would be called upon to pay the remainder, however, appears remote. In return for its capital subscriptions, a member bank is entitled to a cumulative dividend of 6 percent of the par value of its paid-in stock in the Federal Reserve bank. Despite this apparent private ownership, the Federal Reserve banks are, in nature, semipublic institutions. To be sure, they do make a profit, but profit is not the motive of their operations. The semipublic nature of the Federal Reserve banks is reflected not only by the fact that all important policy decisions regarding their operations are made by government-appointed officials but also in the way in which their earnings are distributed. Most of the earnings of the Federal Reserve banks are derived mostly from their loans and discounts for member banks and their holdings of government securities. After payment of the 6 percent statutory dividend to members, a portion of their net earnings is added to their surplus account, and the remaining is paid to the United States Treasury. The portion of earnings going to the Treasury always represents the bulk of the Reserve banks' net income. During the 1914-68 period, about 89 percent of the net earnings of the Reserve bansk went to the U.S. Treasury. Member banks, as stockholders of the Federal Reserve banks, thus do not have the rights and privileges which customarily belong to owners of private corporations.

The Federal Open Market Committee

The Federal Open Market Committee is in charge of determining the system's policies regarding the sales and purchases of securities in the open market and of foreign exchange. The Committee consists of 12 members: seven members of the Board of Governors and five presidents of the Federal Reserve banks. The President of the Federal Reserve Bank of New York is a permanent member of the Committee and the remaining four are chosen from the presidents of the other eleven Reserve banks on a rotation basis. The Committee meets every two or three weeks in Washington, D.C., with the attendance of all the presidents of the Federal Reserve banks. The seven presidents who are not members of the Committee at the time have no vote on matters requiring vote. Although the committee is concerned mainly with policy decisions regarding open-market operations, it has become a forum where problems concerning the policy determination of the system are discussed.

With regard to open-market operations, the policy directives of the Committee are executed by a vice-president of the Federal Reserve Bank of New York, who serves as manager of the "System Securities Account" through which the sales and purchases of securities are made. (He also attends all the meetings of the committee.) Within the framework of the general instructions given by the committee and the limits which it prescribes, the manager of the System Account buys or sells securities as required by prevailing monetary and financial conditions. In carrying out the directives of the Committee between meetings, should the manager of the account face particularly troublesome problems, he could request a telephone conference of the full committee for further instructions. All the Federal Reserve banks are required to participate in the open market operations initiated by the Committee and the securities bought and sold by the manager are to be apportioned to each Federal Reserve Bank in accordance with its share of the combined securities of the system.[1]

The Federal Open Market Committee was initially not an integral part of the Federal Reserve. During the early years of the system, securities were bought and sold by the Federal Reserve banks for their own account as additional earning assets, particularly during periods when member banks had ample reserves and had no need for borrowing from the Federal Reserve banks. In the early 1920's it was recognized that the sales and purchases of securities in the open market by the individual Reserve banks affected not only conditions in the government securities market but also the general credit conditions as well. A System Open Market Committee, composed of the Presidents of five Federal Reserve banks, was then set up to coordinate the open-market purchases and sales of securities of the Federal Reserve banks to avoid the disturbances caused by operations carried out separately by the individual Reserve banks. The need for an Open Market Committee was recognized by the Banking Act of 1933 which provided for the creation of a Committee composed of twelve members selected annually by the Board of Directors of the twelve Federal Reserve banks. The present status and composition of the Open Market Committee was established by the Banking Act of 1935, and open-market operations have become the system's dominant instrument of monetary and credit control.

Several proposals have been made to change the existing structure of the Federal Open Market Committee. One such proposal has been advanced by the Commission on Money and Credit to vest the authority over open-market policy solely in the Board of Governors. There are several arguments in favor of such a change. In the first place, it is argued that in the interest of a single national credit and monetary policy, the power over open-market policy, just as the determination of the discount rates and changes in reserve requirements, should be vested in the same agency of the government, the Board of Governors of the Federal Reserve. Inasmuch as these powers are complementary, it is only logical that they should be governed by the same people in the same forum. Second, since policy decisions on open market operations, just like other policy decisions, are exercises of public regulatory authority, the responsibility for such decisions should belong exclusively to public officials. Third, the Board of Gov-

[1] It should be noted that all Federal Reserve banks are required by the committee to transfer all their securities to the Federal Reserve System account.

ernors, in making decisions on open market operations, still benefit from the advices and experiences of the Reserve Bank Presidents.

The existing arrangement is defended on the following ground. First, this arrangement is consistent with the basic concept of a regional Federal Reserve System. The Committee provides a forum where the participation of the Presidents of the Reserve banks, with their banking experiences and their broad contracts with current business and credit developments, both regional and national, would help promote a broader understanding of the monetary and credit problems of the country and closer relations between the Presidents and the Board in the determination of the policies of the system. Second, the open-market policies of the Committee and the general credit policies of the Board have been coordinated, and the existing arrangement has worked satisfactorily.[2]

The Federal Advisory Council

The council is an advisory body made up of twelve members appointed annually by the Boards of Directors of the twelve Federal Reserve banks. Council members are usually prominent bankers from the respective Reserve Bank districts. The council meets at least four times a year. It confers with the Board of Governors and presents advisory recommendations regarding matters within the board's jurisdiction.

In addition to the Federal Advisory Council, it should be noted that there are two other advisory bodies: the Conference of Presidents and the Conference of Chairmen. The Conference of Presidents is held about four times a year between the presidents of the Federal Reserve banks, to discuss problems of mutual interest and to be informed of banking and financial developments in other reserve districts. This body also renders advice to the Board of Governors. The Chairment of the Boards of Directors of the Federal Reserve banks also hold conferences several times a year to discuss problems of their concern and to make recommendations to the Board of Governors.

Member Banks

Member banks are the foundation of the system. As we have mentioned, nationally chartered banks are required to become members of the Federal Reserve. Qualified state chartered banks may apply for membership in the System. Application for membership is considered mostly on the basis of the soundness of the applicant state bank, its earning record and potential, the adequacy of its capital, and the competence of its management, among other things.

Membership in the system entails several privileges, as well as obligations. Thus member banks are obligated to hold minimum reserve requirements in the

[2] See David D. Eastburn, *The Federal Reserve on Record,* Federal Reserve Bank of Philadelphia, 1965, pp. 183-185. This book contains a number of comments by Chairman Martin on proposals for change in the structure and organization of the system.

form of vault cash and deposit balances with the Federal Reserve Bank of their district. They have to remit at par for all checks drawn against them and presented to them for collection. They have to strictly observe the rules and regulations regarding their lending and investment operations, the closing and opening of branches, and their relations with bank holding companies and their affiliates. They have to submit to the periodic examination by the Federal Reserve banks (the case of state chartered banks) or the Comptroller of the Currency (the case of national banks). They are required to subscribe to the capital stock of their district Federal Reserve Bank and satisfy the minimum capital requirements of their own.

In return for these obligations, membership bestows many privileges. When they need additional reserves, member banks can resort to the advance or rediscounting facilities of the Federal Reserve banks. They are provided with facilities for the clearing and collection of checks and for the transfer of funds. They are entitled to a 6 percent statutory dividend on the par value of their paid-in stock of the Federal Reserve banks. They have the right to vote for six of the nine members of the Board of Directors of the Federal Reserve Bank of their district. They can request cash shipment from the Federal Reserve banks whenever they need it.

In terms of number, member banks represent no more than 45 percent of all commercial banks. They hold, however, about 85 percent of the deposits of the banking system. There are several reasons for which state banks are reluctant to join the Federal Reserve. In the first place, the minimum legal reserve requirements for member banks are much higher than those imposed on nonmember state banks by the banking authorities in most individual states. In some states, state banks are even permitted to count their holdings of government securities as part of their legal reserves. The par clearance requirement is another deterrent to membership in the system. State banks, especially those located in rural areas, are reluctant to give up the "exchange charge," which is a sizable component of their income, by joining the system. Nonmember state banks in a large number of states moreover, are subject to less restrictions regarding their lending and investment practices than member banks. The fact that nonmember banks can have an indirect access to most of the facilities provided by the Federal Reserve banks to member banks is another incentive for state banks to remain outside the system. For example, a nonmember bank can use the clearing and collection facilities of the system either indirectly by depositing checks with a correspondent member bank, or directly by maintaining clearing balances with a Federal Reserve bank and complying with the system's clearing regulations. It can also borrow indirectly from a Federal Reserve bank by borrowing from a correspondent member bank against securities which the latter can use as collateral to secure advances from the Federal Reserve bank. Because of the "negative" nature of some of these privileges, membership in the system is usually thought of mainly as a matter of prestige.

SERVICE FUNCTIONS

The functions of the Federal Reserve banks fall into two major divisions: control functions and service functions. In contrast to their control functions (to be discussed in the next chapter) which require major policy decisions, the service functions of the Reserve banks are performed with no major policy actions involved. They are rather routine in nature, yet they are of great importance to member banks, to the government, and to the public. The service functions of the Federal Reserve banks are concerned chiefly with handling the reserve accounts of member banks, furnishing currency for circulation, facilitating the clearing and collection of checks, and acting as bankers and fiscal agents of the government.

Currency Issuing

The bulk of currency in circulation in the country is issued by the Federal Reserve banks. As of late February 1969, the amount of currency in circulation outside the Treasury and the Federal Reserve banks was $49 billion, of which $43 billion, or 87 percent, was in Federal Reserve notes. The remaining $6 billion was Treasury currency which consisted mostly of fractional coin.

Treasury currency issued by the Treasury is also distributed by the Federal Reserve banks which pay for it by crediting the Treasury account for the amount received.

The volume of Federal Reserve notes in circulation changes in accordance with the public's changing demand for currency. An increase in the currency demand of the public would result in greater withdrawals of cash from commercial banks. Member banks, in turn, replenish their currency holdings by requesting additional cash from the Federal Reserve banks and have it charged to their reserve accounts. Nonmember banks generally get their supplies of currency from member banks. When the currency needs of the public decline, excess currency will flow back to commercial banks. Member banks will redeposit the excess with the Federal Reserve banks and receive credit in their reserve accounts.

The Federal Reserve banks were required to hold gold certificates reserves equal to at least 25 percent of their note liabilities. For each dollar in gold certificates, the Federal Reserve banks could issue a maximum of four dollars in Federal Reserve notes. The ability of the Reserve banks to increase their note issue depended upon the volume of "free" gold certificates available—that is, the difference between total gold certificates reserves and required certificates reserves. For example, as of April 30, 1966, the total gold certificates reserves of the Federal Reserve banks was $13.19 billion and their required gold certificates reserves were $9.116 billion (25 percent of their note liability of $36.464 billion). The amount of "free" gold certificates was then $4.074 billion, which could support a total increase in Federal Reserve notes of more than $16 billion.

The Federal Reserve had operated with a substantial margin of free gold certificates and the expansion of reserve bank credit and currency had not been hampered by the statutory gold-reserve limitation. Moreover, the law regarding this requirement was rather flexible. Should the required reserve ratio (the ratio of gold certificates reserves to note liabilities) fall below the statutory minimum, the Board of Governors would have the authority to suspend temporarily the gold-reserve requirement. While this was a leeway for the Federal Reserve to continue unhampered desirable expansion of Reserve bank credit and currency, it was sometimes deemed necessary by Congress in the past to change the legal reserve ratio. For instance, the expansion of notes and deposit liabilities of the Federal Reserve banks during World War II reduced the free gold certificates margin to such a level that in 1945 it was deemed desirable by Congress to reduce the reserve ratios from 40 percent for the Federal Reserve banks' note liabilities and 35 percent for their deposits to 25 percent for their combined notes and deposits. Likewise, there was another change in 1965. During the early 1960's the margin of free gold certificates was declining steadily. This reflected the expansion of notes and deposits of the Federal Reserve banks (which required a larger amount of required certificates reserves) necessitated by economic expansion and growing income and population, on the one hand, and the steady decrease in the U.S. gold stock, hence the decline in total gold certificates, resulting from the continuing deficits in the U.S. balance of international payments, on the other. In early 1965 the amount of free gold certificates decreased to about \$1.0 billion. This could not only hamper the ability of the Federal Reserve Banks to expand Federal Reserve notes but also make it difficult for the United States to honor a large demand for gold by foreign central banks holding large dollar balances. Consequently, in March 1965 Congress abolished the gold certificates reserve requirements against the Reserve banks' deposit liabilities. The measure increased the amount of free gold certificates to \$5.6 billion, which gave more room to the Federal Reserve for currency expansion and for the Treasury to make gold payments to foreign countries. But the notes liabilities of the Federal Reserve banks remained subject to the 25 per cent gold required reserves. The gold reserve requirements for Federal Reserve notes were finally eliminated by Congress in March 1968 as a measure to boost foreign confidence in the United States dollar (and the ability of the United States to honor its official international obligations in gold) following the dollar and gold crisis in early 1968 that cost the Treasury more than \$1 billion of gold.

The Clearing and Collection of Checks

This is another important service function of the Federal Reserve banks. Prior to the establishment of the system, the collection of checks was costly, cumbersome and inefficient. Banks frequently did not remit at par for checks presented to them for payment. Paying banks usually charged collecting banks a fee, referred to as an exchange charge, which is the difference between the amount remitted and the face value of the check. The charge was justified on the ground that since the checks were not presented by the payee at paying banks' windows for cash, remittances to out-of-town collecting banks required the holding of correspondent balances with city banks on which paying banks could draw checks in payment. The exchange charge, it was argued, was necessary for paying banks to compensate for the costs involved in maintaining correspondent balances. This appears to be a rather weak argument. After all, country banks had to keep correspondent balances with city banks for the collection of checks drawn on out-of-town banks and deposited by customers. The main reason for the "exchange charge" was that it was a substantial source of income for nonpar banks. They did not pay the full value of checks to collecting banks, yet they charged the full value of these checks to the accounts of the drawers.

To avoid the charge, banks usually collected checks drawn on out-of-town banks not by mailing them directly to drawee banks but by "routing" them through their correspondents, who rendered collection services to them without charge in return for deposit balances which they received from them. A consequence of this routing practice was that checks sometimes traveled hundreds of miles through circuitous routes before they reached drawee banks which might be no more than a hundred miles away.

The establishment of the Federal Reserve System has greatly facilitated the process of clearing and collecting checks drawn on banks located in distant places. We have discussed in detail the collection of out-of-town checks through the Federal Reserve banks and the Inter-District Settlement Fund. Suffice it to mention here again that when the depositing banks and drawee banks are located in the same Federal Reserve District, checks are collected through the District Federal Reserve Bank, which credits the reserve accounts of collecting banks and debits the reserve accounts of paying banks. When the depositing banks and paying banks are located in different Federal Reserve Districts, the depositing banks collect from their District Federal Reserve Bank, which credits their reserve accounts while the reserve accounts of paying banks are debited by the Federal Reserve Bank of their own district. The net balances between the Federal Reserve banks are settled by the transfer of funds between their accounts with the Inter-District Settlement Fund in Washington.

In addition to the clearing and collection of checks, the Federal Reserve banks also offer to banks and others the service of their wire transfer facilities. Through their wire transfer system, the Federal Reserve banks can effect the transfer of funds or government securities from one part of the country to another in a matter of minutes. Thus, a bank in Chicago selling government securities to a dealer in New York can take the securities to the Federal Reserve Bank of Chicago. The latter invalidates the securities and wires the Federal Reserve of New York, telling it to issue and deliver to the New York securities dealer government securities of the same issue and amount.

Mr. X in San Francisco, who wishes to transfer by wire $10,000 to Mr. Y, a customer of the Philadelphia National in Philadelphia, can give a check to his San Francisco Bank. The later debits the checking account of X and asks the Federal Reserve Bank of San Francisco to transfer by wire that amount of funds to Mr. Y at the Philadelphia National through the Philadelphis Reserve Bank. The San Francisco Reserve Bank deducts the amount from the reserve account of the San Francisco bank and wires the Federal Reserve Bank of Philadelphia to transfer the funds to Mr. Y at the Philadelphia National Bank. The Reserve Bank of Philadelphia credits the reserve account of the Philadelphia National Bank, which in turn credits the checking account of Y and informs him of the transfer. The Reserve Bank of Philadelphia is reimbursed by the Federal Reserve Bank of San Francisco through the transfer of funds in their reserve accounts with the Inter-District Settlement Fund.

The Dallas Third National Bank, which sells $10 million of Federal funds at 3.6 percent for one day to the Fourth Chicago National, tells the Federal Reserve Bank of Dallas to make a wire transfer of $10 million to the Fourth Chicago National through the Federal Reserve Bank of Chicago which immediately credits the reserve account of the Fourth Chicago National. The following day, the Fourth Chicago National tells the Federal Reserve Bank of Chicago to make a wire transfer of $10,0001,000 ($1000 interest for one day) to the Dallas Third National through the Dallas Federal Reserve Bank.

The Federal Reserve leased wire system, coupled with the wire systems of banks, helps immensely speed up money market transactions and promotes the smooth flow of funds between the various money centers of the country as the temporary excesses of short-term funds in some centers are made immediately available in centers where there are temporary shortages. With this wire network, the money centers in the country are closely knitted into one integrated whole with New York City serving as the center.

The Reserve Banks as Bankers of Member Banks

Unlike some central banks in foreign countries, the Federal Reserve banks do not deal directly with the public. Their customers are member banks and the government. The services provided by the Federal Reserve banks to member banks are similar to those provided by member banks to their customers. The Reserve banks hold the reserve accounts of member banks and handle all receipts and payments relative to these accounts. When a member bank deposits currency with a Federal Reserve bank, its reserve account increases. When additional currency is requested, its reserve balance decreases. Funds are transferred between the accounts of member banks (and nonmember clearing banks) for the settlement of clearing balances between them.

Just as an individual, who needs additional funds, can borrow from his commercial bank, a member bank in need of additional reserves can borrow from the Federal Reserve bank of its district either in the form of rediscounting eligible paper or advances against its promissory note secured by government securities, or other obligations acceptable as collateral. Where a commercial bank can refuse the loan demand of a customer, the Federal Reserve bank can in principle deny the loan request of a member bank. For member banks, borrowing from the Federal Reserve banks is rather a privilege, not a right. Just as a customer can obtain currency from his bank by converting demand deposits into currency, a member bank can obtain currency from its Federal Reserve bank by drawing on its reserve balance.

Apart from being bankers for member banks, the Reserve banks are also supervisors of state member banks. The Federal Reserve banks, together with the respective state banking authorities, as we have mentioned, supervise state member banks to maintain high banking standards, to see to it that rules and regulations are observed, and to warn off unsound banking practices, among other things.

The Reserve Banks as Bankers and Fiscal Agents of the Government

The federal government, which receives and spends money in all parts of the country, is an important customer of the Federal Reserve banks. The latter carry the demand accounts of the Treasury and handle all receipts and disbursements in relation to these accounts. Treasury payments are mostly made by checks drawn on its accounts with the Federal Reserve banks. The Treasury can replenish these accounts by transferring funds from its "tax and loan" accounts with selected commercial banks where tax receipts and proceeds from the sales of government securities are deposited. The purpose of this arrangement is to avoid the disturbing effect on the general monetary and credit situation of heavy losses of bank reserves resulting from the immediate depositing of tax revenues and proceeds from the sales of government securities with the Federal Reserve banks. Indeed, at times of peak tax collections, the depositing of all tax receipts with the Federal Reserve banks would result in a drastic contraction in bank reserves and the supply of money, causing unwarranted monetary and credit stringencies. This can be illustrated by the following example regarding the (check) payment of $1,000 of tax by an individual to the Treasury. The Treasury, which receives the check for $1,000, deposits it with a Federal Reserve bank. The latter credits the account of the Treasury and charges it to the reserve account of the member bank on which the check was drawn. The balance sheet changes of the Federal Reserve bank and the member would be as follows:

A	Federal Reserve Bank L	A	Member Bank L
	Treasury account +1,000 Receive balance of the member bank −1,000	Reserve balance at FRB −1,000	Demand deposits −1,000

The member bank lost $1,000 of reserves. This could cause a multiple contraction in deposit money. To avoid this kind of disturbance, the Treasury simply records the amount received and redeposits the check, via the Federal Reserve bank, with the bank on which it was drawn. In this case the bank would not experience any immediate loss of reserves. Its total deposits remain the same. There is only a transfer of funds from the account of the taxpayer to the tax and loan account of the Treasury, as shown in the following sheet:

A	Member Bank	L
		Deposits of taxpayer -1,000 Tax and loan account +1,000

The Treasury then gradually transfers these funds to its accounts with the Federal Reserve banks for payment purposes. Banks are given notice by the Federal Reserve banks as to when and what percentages of these accounts which they will be called upon to pay. These gradual withdrawals of funds from tax and loan accounts are expected to be more or less offset by the payments made by the Treasury (which increase bank reserves), thereby minimizing any disturbing changes in the reserve position of the banking system as a whole.

The Treasury maintains tax and loan accounts in thousands of commercial banks all over the country. The major requirement for this privilege is that a bank has to pledge with the Federal Reserve bank of its district adequate government securities and other acceptable collateral to secure fully the balance of the account. These tax and loan accounts are administered by the Federal Reserve banks, acting as fiscal agents of the government.

The Federal Reserve banks assist in the flotation and retirement of government securities, and service the public debt. When the Treasury offers a new issue of government securities, the Federal Reserve banks distribute Treasury notices of new offerings to potential buyers—banks, securities dealers, and others, receive their applications, make allotments of securities among subscribers according to instructions from the Treasury, deliver the securities to the purchasers, receive payment for them, and credit the amounts received to the accounts of the Treasury. Most of these payments, however, are initially made into tax and loan accounts with commercial banks, and are gradually transferred to the Federal Reserve banks. The Reserve banks retire government securities as they mature, and pay interests to securities holders. In addition to the Treasury, the Federal Reserve banks act as depositories and fiscal agents for a number of government agencies, such as the Federal Farm Credit Association, the Housing and Home Finance Agency, the National Aeronautics and Space Administration, and the Atomic Energy Commission. The Federal Reserve Bank of New York, located in the major financial center of the country, also acts as agent for the Treasury in the purchases and sales of gold and foreign exchange, as depository for such international organizations as the World Bank and the International Monetary Fund and for foreign central banks and governments.

THE RESERVE BANKS' BALANCE SHEET

The balance sheet of the Federal Reserve banks is an accounting summary of the various phases of their operations on any given day. The Reserve bank functions which we have discussed, and the nature of reserve banking operations, among other things, are reflected in the balance sheet of the Federal Reserve banks. Table 12-1 shows the consolidated balance sheet of the Federal Reserve

TABLE 12-1
Consolidated Balance Sheet of All Federal Reserve Banks
March 31, 1969 (millions of dollars)

Assets			Liabilities		
Cash assets		$10,244	Federal Reserve Notes		$43,324
Gold certificates reserves	10,025		Deposits		23,044
Other cash	219		Member banks	21,588	
Discounts and advances		1,148	U.S. Treasury	783	
Acceptances		94	Foreign	164	
U.S. goverment securities		52,405	Other	509	
Cash items in process of collection		7,974	Deferred availability cash items		$ 6,472
Other assets		2,931	Other liabilities		433
			Total liabilities		50,229
			Capital accounts		
			Paid-in capital		643
			Surplus		630
			Other capital accounts		250
Total assets		$74,796	Total liabilities and capital		$74,796

Addendum	
Federal Reserve notes outstanding (issued to banks)	46,480
Collateral held against notes outstanding	
Gold certificates account	3,522
Eligible paper	...
U.S. government securities	44,970
Total collateral	48,492

banks on March 31, 1969. As can be readily seen by referring to this consolidated statement, almost all the assets held by the Reserve banks are claims on member banks (discounts and advances) and on the government (government securities, gold certificates, and Treasury currency). These assets are largely paid for by the Federal Reserve banks issuing claims against themselves—Federal Reserve notes and deposits, which are central bank money. The volume of central bank money thus increases when the Federal Reserve banks increase their assets, and decreases when their assets decrease. Although the objective of reserve banking operation is different from that of commercial banking operations, the nature of their operations is similar to that of the operations of commercial banks. The Reserve banks are basically dealers in debts, trading their monetary debts (notes and deposits which are central bank money) for the debts of member banks and the federal government.

Asset Accounts

Cash Assets. These constitute the second most important component of the assets of the Federal Reserve banks. They include gold certificates reserves and other cash items. Gold certificates reserves consist of gold certificates issued by the U.S. Treasury (against its gold stock) to the Federal Reserve banks and credits on the book of Treasury payable in gold certificates. Other cash items consist of subsidiary coins issued by the Treasury. When the Treasury buys gold, it issues gold certificates to the Reserve banks. When gold is sold to domestic users, or is released for export, gold certificates are retired. The Federal Reserve banks pay for gold certificates and coins from the Treasury by crediting the amounts to the Treasury accounts.

Discounts and Advances. Discounts and advances, together with acceptances and government securities are the earning assets of the Federal Reserve banks. This account represents mostly reserve bank credit granted to member banks in the form of advances secured by government securities or rediscounting of eligible paper. Changes in this account reflect the changes in the reserve position of banks and the loose or tight conditions in the money and financial markets.

Acceptances. These are prime bankers' acceptances purchased by the Federal Reserve banks in the open market. Such purchases are sometimes made under repurchase agreement, whereby the seller agrees to repurchase them within 15 days or less. For example, of the total acceptances of $94 million held by the Federal Reserve banks on March 31, 1969, $47 million were bought outright and $47 were held under repurchase agreements.

U.S. Government Securities. U.S. government securities are the major asset component of the Federal Reserve banks. They are composed of Treasury bills, Treasury notes and Treasury bonds. They provide the ammunition of the Federal Reserve's weapon of open market operations.

Large amounts of government securities were bought by the Federal Reserve banks during World War II to provide banks with reserves to meet the wartime monetary and credit demand, and during the postwar period to support the price of government securities. Government securities sometimes are bought by the Federal Reserve banks under repurchase agreements with nonbank securities dealers during periods of temporary credit stringency to make funds available to securities dealers with unusually large inventories of government securities and to help meet market needs for reserve funds. (Inasmuch as most of the earnings of the Reserve banks are derived from their holdings of U.S. government securities and most of their earnings are paid to the Treasury, the interest costs to the Treasury on securities held by the Reserve banks are substantially reduced.)

Cash Items in Process of Collection. These are mostly checks deposited by member banks and nonmember clearing banks and are in process of collection on the date of the statement of condition. When checks are received from depositing banks, they become "deferred availability cash items," appearing on the liability side of the balance sheet of the Reserve banks, since sending banks do not immediately receive credit for the checks deposited. Such credit is deferred according to a schedule which represents approximately the time which it would take the Federal Reserve banks to present checks to the drawee banks for payment. The maximum period for credit to be deferred currently is two business days. After that, the depositing banks receive full credit in their reserve accounts (funds are transferred from the deferred availability cash items to the accounts of sending banks). Inasmuch as it usually takes the Reserve banks longer than the time allowed by the schedule to collect from drawee banks, member banks frequently receive full credit for checks which have not yet been collected and charged to the reserve accounts of the banks on which they were drawn. The difference between the "cash items in process of collection" and the "deferred availability cash items," known as Federal Reserve "float," thus represents the amount of credit made available to depositing banks as a result of the national check collection process. As shown in Table 12-1, the cash items in process of collection on March 31, 1969, were $7.974 billion, and the deferred availability cash items were $6.472 billion; the "float" was then $1.502 million.

Other Assets. These assets include, in addition to bank premises, accrued interest, premiums on securities, foreign exchange, and gold deposited by the International Monetary Fund to mitigate the impact on the U.S. gold stock of purchases by foreign countries for gold subscription on increased quotas of the Fund.

Liability and Capital Accounts

Federal Reserve Notes. As indicated in the consolidated statement of the Federal Reserve banks, Federal Reserve notes represent the major component of the total liabilities of the Reserve banks. These notes are issued and retired in accordance with the variation in the demand for currency of the public and the vault cash holdings of commercial banks.

Deposits. The deposit liabilities of the Federal Reserve banks consist mostly of the reserve accounts of member banks, deposits of the Treasury, and deposits of foreign central banks and governments. Their deposit liabilities increase when the Federal Reserve banks receive gold certificates and currency from the Treasury, grant advances to member banks, purchase government securities and other obligations in the open market, and receive in deposit currency from member banks.

The reserve balances of member banks constitute the bulk of Federal Reserve deposits. The operations of the Reserve banks, designed to influence the volume of commercial bank loans and investments, are directly reflected by changes in the reserve accounts of member banks.

The deposit balance of the Treasury with the Federal Reserve banks is relatively small in relation to Treasury deposits held in tax and loan accounts with commercial banks. Current payments of the Treasury, however, are made by checks drawn on its deposit accounts with the Federal Reserve banks. As they are depleted, they are replenished with funds transferred from Treasury accounts with commercial banks according to the schedule of Treasury payments.

The Federal Reserve banks also hold deposit balances for foreign central banks and governments, either for international payments or for monetary reserve purposes. Other deposits include clearing balances held by nonmember clearing banks for the clearing and collection of checks and the gold deposit of the International Monetary Fund.

Other Liabilities. These include accrued dividends between the semiannual dividend payment dates, and miscellaneous accounts payable. Deferred availability cash items have been explained in conjunction with the "cash items in process of collection" account.

Capital Accounts. These are composed of paid-in capital, surplus and other capital accounts. The paid-in capital comes from member banks which are required to pay for the capital stock of the Federal Reserve bank of their district an amount equal to 3 percent of their own capital and surplus. Member banks return a statutory dividend of six percent of the par value of the paid-in stock. The surplus account represents the portion of the net earnings of the Federal Reserve banks retained after payment of the statutory dividends to member banks and the transfer of earnings to the Treasury. The law provides that in the event of dissolution of the Federal Reserve banks, the surplus is to go to the U.S. Government. Other capital accounts consist of unallocated net earnings to the date of the statement of condition.

SUMMARY

The American Central Banking System was inaugurated in 1914, following the passage of the Federal Reserve Act of 1913. The original purpose of the act was to correct the major defects of the National Banking System. The role and goals of the system have ever since been broadened in response to the changing economic and financial environment of the nation. The major divisions of the system are the Board of Governors, the twelve Federal Reserve banks, and the Federal Open Market Committee. They are responsible for major policy decisions of the system. Member banks represent the foundation on which the system operates. Although the Federal Reserve banks are technically privately owned, they are public institutions operating solely in the public interest. The Reserve banks perform several important service functions for the government, member banks, and the public. These include handling the reserve accounts of member banks, furnishing currency for circulation, facilitating the clearing and collection of checks, and serving as bankers and fiscal agents of the government.

PROBLEMS

1. Discuss the major factors which led to the creation of the Federal Reserve System. What prompted the establishment of twelve separate Federal Reserve banks instead of one single central banking institution?

2. Discuss some of the major powers of the Board of Governors of the Federal Reserve. What are the arguments for and against the proposal for reducing the number of members of the Board?

3. What is the Federal Open Market Committee for? Was it initially an integral part of the Federal Reserve? What are the arguments for and against the proposal which would vest the authority over open-market policy solely in the hands of the Board of Governors?

4. What are the obligations and privileges of membership of the Federal Reserve System? Are some of these privileges available to nonmember banks, either directly or indirectly? Is it partly because of this that a large number of state banks do not join the system?

5. Suppose that the public withdraws \$10 million in currency from member banks, which replenish their cash holdings by drawing on their reserve balances with the Federal Reserve banks. The latter ship to member banks (i) the whole amount in Federal Reserve notes, and (ii) half the amount in Federal Reserve notes and half in Treasury currency. (a) Show the balance sheet changes of the Federal Reserve banks and member banks. (b) Is there any immediate change in the supply of money and bank reserves?

6. Assume that the Treasury transfers \$10 million from its tax and loan accounts with member banks to its deposit accounts with the Federal Reserve banks. (a) Show the balance-sheet changes of the Treasury, the Federal Reserve, and member banks. (b) Is there any immediate change in the supply of money and bank reserves?

7. Mr. Y, a customer of the Dallas National Bank (in Dallas) makes a wire transfer of $1,000,000 to Mr. Z, a customer of Chicago National Bank in Chicago, through the Federal Reserve leased wire system. Show the balance-sheet changes of all parties involved after the transfer is completed.

chapter 13

The Federal Reserve: Control Functions

The various operations of the Federal Reserve which have been discussed in the preceding chapter are important indeed, but they do not constitute the essence of Federal Reserve banking. The essential function of the Federal Reserve, like that of other modern central banks, is to regulate the flow of money and credit in the public interest. For control purposes, the Federal Reserve has at its disposal a variety of monetary and credit control instruments which are either general or selective in nature. The general instruments tend to affect the availability and cost of bank credit without regard to its directional distribution. Selective or qualitative instruments, on the other hand, tend to affect the volume and the allocation of particular kinds of credit. We shall describe the various determinants of bank reserves, a variable that is directly amenable to Federal Reserve control, and the Federal Reserve's various technical tools of monetary management.

BANK RESERVES

Determinants

Here we shall deal with member bank reserves only, since unlike the reserve composition of nonmember state banks that varies from state to state, the composition of member bank reserves is uniform. Member bank reserves (R) are composed of vault cash (V) and reserve balances at the Federal Reserve banks (B). Inasmuch as the Treasury and the Federal Reserve banks are institutions that issue the kind of money used by member banks as reserves, an equation showing the determinants of member bank reserves can be derived from the consolidated balance sheet of these institutions. Let

a = volume of Federal Reserve credit outstanding
b = Treasury gold stock
c = Treasury currency outstanding
d = currency in circulation
e = Treasury cash holdings

f = Treasury and foreign deposits at the Reserve Banks
g = other accounts (net)

Then we have the following expression showing the determinants of member bank reserves: or

$$R = V + B = (a + b + c) - (d + e + f + g) \qquad \text{(I)}$$

Member bank reserves vary directly with *a, b,* and *c* (which may be termed expanding determinants), and inversely with *d, e, f,* and *g* (which may be termed contracting determinants). Other things being equal, an increase in either *a, b,* or *c* will cause member bank reserves to increase; and an increase in either *d, e, f,* or *g* will cause member bank reserves to decrease. Of these determinants, Federal Reserve credit outstanding and currency in circulation are the most important, as indicated in Table 13-1. Following is a brief discussion of how changes of these two determinants affect member bank reserves.

TABLE 13-1
Member Bank Reserves and Related Items, March 1969 (millions of dollars)

Expanding determinants		
Federal Reserve credit outstanding		55,439*
U.S. Government securities	52,122	
Discounts and advances	918	
Float	2,329	
Gold stock		10,367
Treasury currency outstanding		6,819
Total		72,625
Contracting determinants		
Currency in circulation		49,436
Treasury cash holdings		729
Treasury and foreign deposits at Reserve Banks		688
Other accounts (net)†		−4,982
Total		45,871
Member bank reserves = 72,625 − 45,871 = 26,754		
Vault cash . . . 4,507		
Deposits at Reserve banks . . . 22,247		

Source: Federal Reserve Bulletin, 1969.

*These include industrial loans and acceptances (the industrial loan program was discontinued on August 21, 1959).

†These include Treasury currency held by nonmember banks, deposit balances of nonmember clearing banks, Federal Reserve notes held by nonmember banks, and the net value of miscellaneous assets, liabilities, and capital accounts of the Federal Reserve Banks not accounted for elsewhere.

Federal Reserve Credit Outstanding. This consists mostly of U.S. Government securities held by the Reserve banks, Federal Reserve float, and discounts and advances granted to member banks. Suppose that the Federal Reserve banks grant an advance of $10 million to member banks. This increases member bank reserves (B component of R) as shown in the following balance-sheet changes of the Federal Reserve and member banks.

A	Federal Reserve L	A	Member Banks L
Discounts and advances +10 million	Deposits of member banks +10 million	Deposits at Reserve banks +10 million	Borrowings at the Federal Reserve +10 million

The effect of an increase in Federal Reserve holdings of securities and "float" on member bank reserves is the same as an increase in direct advances or rediscounting for member banks. There is a difference, however. While increases in reserves resulting from borrowings from the Reserve banks do incur the obligation of member banks to repay, increases in reserves resulting from Federal Reserve purchases of securities do not give rise to any repayment obligations.

Currency in Circulation. An increase (decrease) in currency in circulation decreases (increases) member bank reserves. The volume of currency in circulation changes with the changing demand for currency of the public. This varies greatly from season to season. When the public wishes to hold more currency, it withdraws currency from commercial banks which causes their reserves to decrease either in the form of vault cash or reserve balances with the Federal Reserve banks. Suppose that the public withdraws $20 million of cash from member banks to satisfy its seasonal demand for currency. Member banks replenish their cash holdings by requesting additional currency from the Federal Reserve banks. In terms of balance-sheet entries, the effect of such withdrawals on member bank reserves is as follows:

A	Federal Reserve L	A	Member Banks L
	Deposits of member banks -20 million Federal Reserve notes +20 million	Deposits at Reserve banks -20 million	Demand deposits -20 million

In slack seasons, on the other hand, when the public redeposits its excess currency with member banks, member bank reserves increase.

Among the determinants of member bank reserves, only the holdings of securities of the Federal Reserve banks are under their direct control, that is, they can change them at their own initiative. With regard to advances and discounts for member banks, the Reserve banks primarily react to the initiative of member banks. Federal Reserve credit in the form of float is determined mostly by the time which it would take the Reserve banks to collect checks and the time schedule according to which member banks automatically receive credit for checks deposited. Changes in the gold stock depend largely on the nation's international payment position and gold production. Changes in Treasury deposits are determined mostly by the schedule of Treasury payments, while changes in foreign deposits are initiated by foreign central banks and governments. The fluctuations in the volume of currency in circulation reflects primarily the shifting currency demand of the public. While the Federal Reserve has no direct control over the variations of these variables, the effects of their changes on bank reserves, however, can be offset by Federal Reserve actions such as changes in its holdings of U.S. Government securities.

Stock and Flow of Reserves

Bank reserves, as shown in equation (I) is a cumulative stock determined by the stock determinants in the equation. The flow of reserves, on the other hand, refers to their changes over time. From equation (I) we have

$$\Delta R = \Delta V + \Delta B = (\Delta a + \Delta b + \Delta c) - (\Delta d + \Delta e + \Delta f + \Delta g) \qquad \text{(II)}$$

which shows the increment of bank reserves as the sum of the increments of their various determinants. Divide both sides of (II) by Δt which represents a given increment of time

$$\frac{\Delta R}{\Delta t} = \frac{\Delta V}{\Delta t} + \frac{\Delta B}{\Delta t} = \frac{1}{\Delta t}(\Delta a + \Delta b + \Delta c) - \frac{1}{\Delta t}(\Delta d + \Delta e + \Delta f + \Delta g)$$

This equation shows the average rate of change (or the amount of flow) of bank reserves with respect to time.[1] Actions of the Federal Reserve affect the rates of change of bank reserves, hence the rates of change of the supply of money and credit. The important responsibility of the central bank authority is to control changes of bank reserves and the supply of money and credit such that full employment of human and material resources and high rates of economic growth may be promoted without undue pressures on the price level.

We now turn to the instruments with which the Federal Reserve controls bank reserves and the supply of money and credit.

[1]This is a discrete flow, as it is measured over finite time periods. The continuous flow of R or its rate of change at a moment in time is

$$\lim_{\Delta t \to 0} \frac{\Delta R}{\Delta t} = \lim_{\Delta t \to 0} \left[\frac{\Delta V}{\Delta t} + \frac{\Delta B}{\Delta t}\right] = \frac{dR}{dt} = \frac{dV}{dt} + \frac{dB}{dt}$$

CONTROL INSTRUMENTS

Open-market operations, variable reserve requirements, and the discount mechanism are the major general instruments of monetary management at the disposal of the Federal Reserve. In addition to these general or quantitative control instruments, the Federal Reserve has at times been invested with powers to impose selective or qualitative control devices, such as margin requirements, consumer credit control, and real estate credit control. With the exception of margin requirements regarding credit granted for the purchase and carrying of securities, the authority of the Federal Reserve to use consumer and real estate credit controls has been withdrawn by Congress.

Open-Market Operations

Open-market operations consist of the sales and purchases of securities and foreign exchange in the open market by the Federal Reserve. Decisions on open-market operations, as noted earlier, are made by the Federal Open Market Committee and executed by the Manager of the System Account in the Federal Reserve Bank of New York. Open-market operations are taken at the initiative of the Federal Reserve authority.

The sales of securities by the Federal Reserve reduce bank reserves and the supply of money. Conversely, the purchases of securities increase the money supply and bank reserves. Suppose that the Federal Reserve sells $10 million of securities to the public—for example, a nonbank securities dealer who pays for them by drawing a check on his account with a commercial bank in New York. The Federal Reserve Bank of New York receives the check from the seller, sends it to the drawee bank, and debits the amount of the check to the bank's reserve account. The balance-sheet change of the Federal Reserve and the banking system is

A	Federal Reserve	L
Securities -10 million		Member bank deposits -10 million

A	Banking System	L
Reserve balances at FRB -10 million		Demand deposits -10 million

The transaction causes bank reserves and the supply of money to decrease by $10 million. If this transaction takes place at a time when banks are more or less fully loaned and invested, the resulting loss of reserves would cause a multiple contraction in bank credit and deposit money. The effect of the sales of securities on bank reserves is the same when securities are sold not to the nonbank public but directly to commercial banks. This is shown in the following balance-sheet changes:

A	Federal Reserve	L	A	Banking System	L
Securities −10 million		Member bank deposits −10 million	Reserve balances at FRB −10 million		
			Securities +10 million		

There is no immediate change in the supply of money in this case, however.

Open-market purchases of securities, on the other hand, increase bank reserves and the supply of money. When securities are purchased by the Federal Reserve from the nonbank public, both bank reserves and the money supply increase. When they are bought directly from commercial banks, bank reserves increase, but the supply of money does not change immediately. The signs of balance-sheet entries with respect to these transactions are the opposite of the entries in the above balance sheets. To the extent that profitable lending and investment opportunities are available, the increases in bank reserves resulting from open-market purchases of securities by the Federal Reserve will likely lead to a multiple expansion of bank credit and deposit money.

In addition to their quantity effect, which is reflected by the change in the volume of reserves available to banks for credit and deposit expansion, open-market operations also affect the rate of interest or the cost of credit. The rate of interest increases when securities are sold and decreases when they are purchased by the Federal Reserve. The interest effect of open-market operations is illustrated by Fig. 13-1. *OX* represents the stock of a certain type of securities (subject to open-market operations) available on any given day, and D_1D_1, the

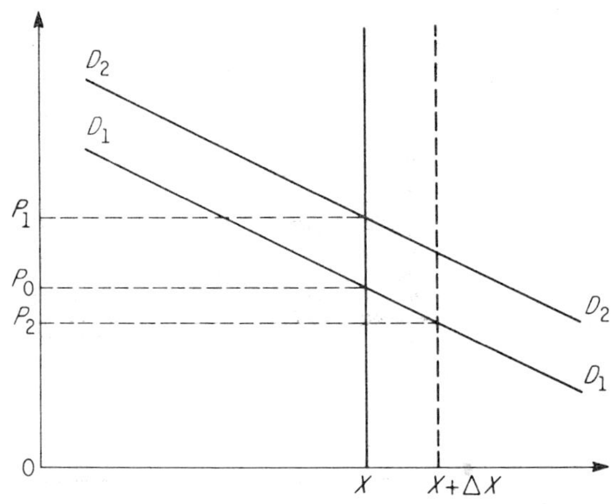

Fig. 13-1. Price (interest) effects of open-market operations.

total demand for this stock. Given OX and D_1D_1, the equilibrium price of this type of securities is OP_0.

Let i_0 be the market yield corresponding to the market price OP_0 of the security. Now suppose that the Federal Reserve decides to purchase a given amount of this security. The added demand of the Federal Reserve, which shifts the demand curve to D_2D_2, causes the price of the security to increase to OP_1, or its market yield or rate of interest to decrease to, say, i_1 $(i_1 < i_0)$.

Given the free movement of the funds within and between the short and long ends of the financial market, the decline in the rate of interest of this security would cause both short- and long-term rates of interest to decrease as a result of arbitrage. If we refer to "the market rate of interest" as an index of all market rates, we may say that the open-market purchases of securities by the Federal Reserve cause the rate of interest to decrease. Conversely, when securities are sold by the Federal Reserve in the open market, the rate of interest will rise. In reference to Fig. 13-1, the sales of security increase the total supply from X to $X + \Delta X$. Given the total demand curve D_1D_1, the price of the security falls from OP_0 to OP_2, or its market yield rises to, say, i_2 $(i_2 > i_0)$.

To the extent that the demand for credit is sensitive to interest changes, open-market sales of securities which cause interest rates to rise would reduce the demand for credit, thereby reducing inflationary pressures in times of inflation. But even if the demand for credit is not sufficiently responsive to interest changes, open market sales of securities still exert a restrictive influence on aggregate spending through their effects on the volume of reserve available to banks for lending purposes. On the other hand, the increase in bank reserves and the decline of interest rates brought about by open-market purchases of securities in times of recession or depression may not be sufficient to stimulate investment demand, due to pessimistic business outlooks on investment opportunities. This leads many an economist to suspect that the use of instruments of monetary management is relatively more potent in combating inflationary expansion than in stimulating economic recovery.

Effective open-market operations require the existence of two conditions: (a) a developed securities market, and (b) adequate holdings of securities by the central bank for operating purposes. Open-market operations are out of the question in the absence of a securities market. This is the case of most underdeveloped countries where central bank authorities have to rely on other control instruments than open-market operations simply because in these countries, securities markets either do not exist or are too underdeveloped for open-market operations. In addition to a well-developed securities market, the central bank also has to possess a large quantity of the types of securities which are the subject of open-market operations. Should the amount of securities held by the central bank be insufficient, it could run out of ammunition before open-market sales could make any significant dent in the reserve position of the banking system. But this can rarely happen. When the absorption of a large amount of excess reserves is called for, open-market operations can be effected in conjunction with other control instruments, such as reserve requirements and selective control devices.

Open-market operations can serve two purposes. They can be used either to regulate the flow of money and credit or to support the prices of government securities. These two objectives are mutually exclusive. If open-market purchases and sales of securities are purported to absorb or release bank reserves, their prices are left to determination of free-market forces. If such operations are designed to support the prices of government securities, then the potency of open-market operations as a credit control device is lost, since the central bank authority stands ready to purchase securities both short- and long-term at practically fixed prices. This was the experience of the Federal Reserve during World War II and the postwar period up to the early 1950's. Open-market operations were then committed to "maintain the present general level of prices and yields of government securities," to "assure that an ample supply of funds is available at all times for financing the war effort . . . "and to "avoid inflicting heavy losses on holders of government securities who had been urged to buy Treasury obligations in order to help finance the war." Used to support the prices of government securities, open-market operations then could not be used as an anti-inflationary device. Banks which needed additional reserves for credit expansion could sell government securities (which they held in large quantities) to the Federal Reserve, which was under obligation to purchase them at "pegged" prices. This practice continued until the Federal Reserve-Treasury Accord of 1951. After that, open-market operations regained their potency as a credit control instrument.

Open-market operations can be used either dynamically or defensively. Dynamic operations are designed to change the overall reserve position of the banking system to bring about a certain degree of ease or tightness in the credit market, as called for by the objective of general monetary and economic policy. Defensive open-market operations, on the other hand, are undertaken to avoid unwarranted stringency or ease in the credit market caused by seasonal variations in the demand for currency by the public, gold movements, unusually heavy receipts, or payments by the U.S. Treasury, and other seasonal disturbances. Dynamic and defensive open-market operations can be taken simultaneously. Suppose that the banking system experiences a loss of reserves of $200 million as a result of heavy currency withdrawals by the public, and this takes place at a time when a greater degree of ease in the credit market is deemed desirable by the Federal Reserve. The Reserve authority thus may have to purchase a larger amount of securities in the open market, say, $400 million, in order to make up for the reserve loss of the banking system but also to further ease conditions in the financial markets.

In terms of the provisions of the Federal Reserve Act, the Federal Reserve authority is permitted to buy and sell a variety of securities, such as Treasury obligations, bankers' acceptances, tax anticipation obligations of state and local governments maturing in six months or less. But open-market operations have been confined mostly to U.S. Government securities, especially short-term Treasury obligations, and to some extent, bankers' acceptances. Securities are usually bought and sold outright by the Federal Reserve. But on occasion, they are purchased from securities dealers under repurchase agreements whereby dealers promise to buy them back within a stipulated period of time, usually 15 days. Repurchase agreements may be used to help securities dealers carry inventories of securities when they could not secure credit from other sources at reasonable rates, and to make funds available to the market which experiences temporary credit stringency.

In addition to the sales and purchases of government securities and bankers' acceptances, the Federal Reserve also buys and sells foreign exchange. Although operations in the exchange market affect bank reserves and the supply of money, just as operations in the government securities and acceptances markets, the sales and purchases of foreign exchange by the Federal Reserve have been undertaken not to influence the reserve position of the banking system but mostly for the stabilization of the exchange rates between the U.S. dollar and foreign currencies. For instance, when the demand for foreign exchange, say, the French franc, on the New York foreign exchange market is strong relative to its supply, the dollar price of the franc tends to increase. To stabilize the dollar-franc exchange rate, the Federal Reserve can enter the market as a seller of francs. This will increase the supply of the franc and prevent the dollar-price of the franc from rising. Conversely, when the demand for the French franc is weak in relation to its supply, the Federal Reserve can enter the market as a buyer of foreign exchange, thereby preventing the dollar price of the franc from falling.

Open-market operations are probably the most flexible weapon of credit policy in the arsenal of the Federal Reserves. The sales and purchases of securities can be effected in very small as well as large amounts, depending upon the degree of credit ease or tightness which the Federal Reserve wishes to achieve. They are also completely reversible. Securities may be purchased this week and sold next week, for example, if such action is needed to smooth out undesirable disturbances in the credit market.

Variable Reserve Requirements

Like open-market operations, changes in reserve requirements are initiated by the Federal Reserve authorities. But unlike open-market operations which affect the total reserves of the banking system, changes in reserve requirements do not affect total reserves. They affect only the level of excess reserves—that is, the difference between legal reserves and required reserves. This is illustrated by the following example. Assume that the legal reserve ratio against member banks' demand deposits is 15 percent, and the condition of member banks on a given day is shown in this hypothetical balance sheet:

A Member Banks	L
Required reserves: 15 billion	Demand deposits 100 billion
Excess reserves: 7 billion	
Loans and investments 78 billion	

The total reserves of member banks is $22 billion, of which $15 billion is required reserve and $7 billion is excess reserve. Suppose that the legal reserve ratio is raised to 20 percent. Required reserves, as a consequence, increase to $20 billion, and excess reserves are reduced to $2 billion, but total legal reserves remain unchanged—at $22 billion.

If instead of raising the legal reserve ratio to 20 percent the Federal Reserve elects to sell $5 billion of securities, total bank reserves will decrease to $17 billion, required reserves to $14.25 billion, and excess reserves to $2.75 billion, if the securities are sold to the nonbank public. If the securities are sold directly to member banks, then required reserves will remain at $15 billion and excess reserves will decrease to $2 billion. These transactions are shown in the following two balance sheets:

A Member Banks (Securities Sold to Public)	L
Required reserves 14.25 billion	Demand deposits 95 billion
Excess reserves 2.75 billion	
Loans and investments 78 billion	

A Member Banks (Securities Sold to Banks)	L
Required reserves 15 billion	Demand deposits 100 billion
Excess reserves 2 billion	
Investments 83 billion	

As can be seen from this example, variable reserve requirements are potentially a more powerful weapon than open-market operations, as they reduce the extent of the expansion of bank credit and deposit money more than does open-market policy. When the legal reserve ratio is raised from 15 to 20 percent, the excess reserves of member banks are reduced to $2 billion, but now that the legal reserve ratio is higher, 20 percent, the theoretical limit of the expansion of bank credit and money is only $10 billion, as compared with $13.333 billion (net) when $5 billion of securities are sold by the Federal Reserve.

Unlike in a number of foreign countries where reserve requirements are uniform for all classes of deposits, in the United States, legal reserve requirements are not only different for different classes of deposits but also for different classes of banks. We have already mentioned that in regard to members of the Federal Reserve system, the legal reserve ratios against demand deposits are from 10 to 22 percent for reserve city banks and 7 to 14 percent for country banks, and the legal reserve ratio against time deposits is from 3 to 10 percent for both reserve city and country banks. The foundation of this reserve arrangement appears to be the old-fashioned notion that legally required reserves protect the liquidity of banks; since time deposits are less volatile than demand deposits, they should be subject to lower legal reserve ratios. As the modern objective of required reserves is to control the flow of money and credit, uniform legal reserve ratios for all classes of deposits appear desirable. Such an arrangement is not only less cumbersone, but it has the merit of preventing the tendency of banks to encourage customers to shift from demand to time deposits, which are subject to lower legal reserve ratios to obtain greater excess reserves for loan and investment expansion during periods of tight money. For example, given the legal reserve ratios of 20 percent for demand balances and 5 percent for time liabilities, a shift of $1,000 from demand to time balances would enable the banking system to increase its loans and investments by $750.

Variable reserve requirements, although a potentially powerful instrument of control, have not been used frequently by the Federal Reserve. During the 1919-66 period, reserve requirements were changed only fifteen times by the Federal Reserve, and mostly in the downward direction. Increases in reserve requirements raise several objections. First, since interest is not paid on the reserve balances held by member banks with the Federal Reserve banks, increases in reserve requirements which reduce the funds available to member banks for loans and investments reduce bank earnings. To compensate for the loss of earnings, member banks would be forced to charge higher interest on their loans to customers. The effect of variable reserve requirements, it is argued, is just like some sort of tax imposed on the borrowers. But if the purpose of this and other monetary control instruments is to curtail the level of aggregate spending by reducing the availability of funds of the lenders, and raising the interest cost to the borrowers, in times of inflation, then, the increase in interest cost consequent upon an increase in reserve requirements in hope of reducing credit demand is only the objective which the monetary authorities seek to achieve in the first place.

Second, it is argued that an increase in reserve requirements affects all member banks immediately and directly, regardless of the liquidity position of the individual bank. Banks which are tight in reserves are hard hit, whereas relatively liquid banks may not be seriously affected by the measure. But, after all, banks that are in a tight reserve position are usually those that are expanding credit more rapidly than others, it is only logical that they should feel the pinch of restrictive monetary control in periods of inflationary pressures.

Third, unlike open-market operations which can be conducted in either small or large amounts, increases in reserve requirements which represent percentages of very large sums, usually result in heavy losses of reserves to member banks. Those banks which are deficient in required reserves may have to sell U.S. Government securities and other obligations to meet the minimum reserve requirements. This could cause substantial fluctuations in securities prices as potential buyers might defer their bids following the announcement regarding increases in reserve requirements. To avoid disorderly conditions in the securities market, the Federal Reserve may have to purchase securities in the open market, thereby partly defeating the purpose of changes in reserve requirements. Frequent and small fractional changes in the legal reserve ratios, of course, can be effected, but this would cause difficult problems of adjustment for member banks.

Fourth, inasmuch as nonmember state banks are subject to lower reserve requirements than are members of the Federal Reserve, increases in member banks' reserve requirements would put them in a less favorable position vis-à-vis nonmembers, and may cause wholesale defection from system membership. To avoid this possibility, and to give the Federal Reserve a broader control base, among other things, proposals have been advanced to subject nonmember banks to the same reserve requirements as member banks. Nonmember banks are likely to object to these proposals, as they prefer the less restrictive reserve requirements of state laws. These proposals are also objected to on the grounds that they represent an encroachment of federal rights on state rights; state authorities should have the right to regulate banks which they themseleves have chartered.

Owing to some of the problems associated with reserve requirement changes, they have been used mostly in unusual situations in which uses of other instruments are inadequate to mop up excess reserves or in which immediate reserve relief is needed. For example, when there is a heavy inflow of gold, an increase in reserve requirements may be necessary, since open market sales of securitites may not be sufficient. On the other hand, immediate relief needed to make up for heavy losses of reserves resulting from, say, heavy currency drains, can best be met by lowering reserve requirements. Open market purchases of securities, in this case, may not achieve the desirable result, as it would take some time for the effects of open-market operations to be transmitted throughout the banking system.

The Discount Mechanism

Borrowing from the Federal Reserve is one of the privileges of membership in the system. Member-bank-borrowing may take the form of rediscounting of commercial, agricultural, and industrial paper, bankers' acceptances, and other eligible paper, or advances against member banks' promissory notes secured by U.S. Government securities, or any other collateral acceptable to the Federal Reserve banks. Reserve bank lending, however, has been chiefly in the form of advances secured by government securities.

The use of the discount mechanism as an instrument of credit policy consists in changing the discount rates (interest rates charged by the Federal Reserve banks on their loans to member banks) and the conditions attached to paper eligible for advance or rediscounting purposes. Lowering the rate of discount and liberalizing the eligibility rules would induce member banks to borrow. Conversely, raising the discount rate and tightening the eligibility rules would make Reserve bank credit more expensive and difficult for member banks to obtain. Unlike open-market operations and changes in reserve requirements which are taken at the initiative of the Federal Reserve, in the case of discount policy, the Federal Reserve reacts mostly to the initiative of member banks which decide whether to borrow or not.

The effectiveness of the use of the discount mechanism requires the fulfillment of three basic conditions: (a) a highly developed money market, (b) sufficient quantities of paper eligible for advance or rediscounting, and (c) regular reliance of member banks on the Federal Reserve banks for credit facilities. Of these conditions, the last one does not appear to be satisfied. There is a longstanding tradition among member banks against being frequently indebted to the Federal Reserve banks. They resort to Federal Reserve credit primarily to meet unusual situations. In fact, many member banks never borrow from the Federal Reserve banks. They prefer to make reserve adjustments either by buying federal funds, selling government securities, or borrowing from other commercial banks, even though the cost of securing such credit may be comparatively higher than that of borrowing from the Federal Reserve. This tradition, however, is reinforced by the attitude of the Federal Reserve banks with regard to member banks' borrowing. Member banks which resort to Reserve bank credit for extended periods of time are frowned upon by the Federal Reserve authorities.

Discount policy in the United States is quantitatively a relatively weak instrument of monetary control as compared with open-market operations and other control devices. The effectiveness of its use has been on and off. During the early years of the Federal Reserve, it was used very actively, reflected by heavy borrowing by member banks. But from the early 1930's to the early 1950's, discount policy was little used, as banks had no need for borrowing from the Federal Reserve banks. They either had ample reserves or other convenient means to secure additional reserves when needed. During the depression, banks were flooded with excess reserves. During World War II and the postwar period, as a consequence of the policy of the Federal Reserve to support the prices of government securities, member banks generally found it advantageous to replenish their reserves by selling U.S. government securities to the Federal Reserve banks rather than borrowing from them. After the Accord of early 1951 between the Federal Reserve and the Treasury, which marked the end of the support policy, and open-market operations were again used as a monetary and credit control instrument, discount policy was "rediscovered." Member banks again resorted to borrowing from the Federal Reserve banks, especially during the years of economic expansion when their reserve positions were under heavy pressures following restrictive open market operations on the one hand, and the strong demand for credit by the public, on the other. The increased use of Reserve bank credit facilitites by member banks was reflected by the change in member banks' borrowings, which increased from $142 million in December 1950, to $839 million in December 1955, $906 million at the end of 1959 and $1,407 million in June 1969.

Under the influence of restrictive open-market operations and other policy measures which lead to frequent reserve deficiencies, member banks are forced to replenish their reserves by either selling Treasury bills and liquid assets or borrowing from the Reserve banks. Which of these alternative methods of reserve adjustment would be used by member banks would depend in part upon their relative costs. If the rates on short-term securities are lower than the discount rate, banks may prefer selling short-term securities for additional reserves rather than borrowing from the Reserve banks. This, however, would increase the market supply of short-term securities and tend to lower their prices or raise their market yields. As these rates rise above the discount rate, there will be some shift in the preference of member banks in favor of borrowing from the Federal Reserve. The Reserve authority then can raise the discount rate. To the extent that member bank borrowing is sensitive to changes in the discount rate, raising the rate of discount would restrict member banks' borrowings, and hence their credit and deposit expansion. As a consequence of the liquidation of short-term securities at low prices, or borrowing from the Reserve banks at higher rates of discount, member banks would raise the rates which they charge for short-term credits. Experience shows that there is a positive correlation between the Federal Reserve's discount rate, the rates on short-term bank credit, and money market rates. Given some degree of mobility of funds between the short and long ends of the credit market, changes in short-term money rates following changes in the rate of discount, if they prevail for a certain length of time, would cause long-term money rates to change as well. Whether the increase (or decrease) in long-term money rates would lead to a contraction (or expansion) of aggregate spending would depend to a large extent upon the sensitivity of the investment demand of businesses with respect to changes in long-term rates. Inasmuch as interest is only one of the several variables determining investment demand, there are cases in which a rise in long-term money rates does not discourage, nor a decrease promote, investments.

Usually, an increase in the discount rate leads to some contraction in the volume of bank credit. This reflects in part the increase in the cost of credit, and in part the psychological reaction of banks in relation to a boost in the discount rate. A change in the rate of discount is an indication of a shift in the direction or intensity of monetary policy. An increase in the rate of discount is a signal of restrictive monetary and credit policy. Banks, accordingly, are expected to be more cautious and selective in their lending policies. The expectational effect of bank rate changes, however, is unpredictable, and may at times be adverse, especially on the part of the borrowers. An increase in the discount rate may be interpreted as an indication of further rising prices, profits and interest in the future. They may decide to borrow more now in order to avoid higher future interest costs. Adverse expectations may also arise from misinterpretation of the intended use of bank rate changes. Suppose that an increase in the discount rate is made by the Federal Reserve as a technical adjustment designed to keep it in line with money market rates, to maintain the existing degree of credit restraint. But banks may react to such a move by reducing bank credit, thereby causing a higher degree of credit restraint than that considered desirable.

In order to eliminate possible adverse expectations associated with either defensive or dynamic changes in the discount rate, it has been suggested that the discount mechanism be abolished altogether, or that the discount rate be automatically tied to and maintained at a constant differential above a market rate, such as the Treasury bill rate. An objection to the proposal for the complete abolition of the discount mechanism is that it does away with a device which serves as a useful safety valve allowing commercial banks to adjust their reserve positions when other restrictive monetary instruments are used, and the Federal Reserve to assist the banking system in times of liquidity crises. The automatic tying of the discount rate to money-market rate would preserve the discount mechanism as a safety valve, and at the same time would eliminate adverse expectations associated with discretionary changes in the discount rate. This policy was, in fact, used by the Bank of Canada during the 1956-62 period which adjusted the bank rate so as to keep it at one-fourth to one percent above the latest average auction rate for Treasury bills. This practice, however, was abandoned by the Bank of Canada in mid-1962 when she raised the discount rate to 6 percent, in view of defending the exchange value of the Canadian dollar. She has ever since returned to the discretionary use of discount policy.

Margin Requirements

Unlike open-market operations, variable reserve requirements and discount policy, which affect credit in general, margin requirements and consumer and real estate credit controls (to be discussed in the next section) are selective control devices which influence the allocation of particular kinds of credit. The use of selective instruments is desirable when excessive expansion of credit prevails only in particular sectors of the economy. The application of general monetary weapons in these situations may cause unwarranted credit restriction and deflationary tendencies in other sectors.[2]

[2] Admittedly, the application of selective control instruments also influences the general credit situation, The effects of credit stringency or ease generated in a particular sector of credit markets by the use of selective control devices would eventually be propagated to other market sectors as well, where credit markets are highly developed. It is just like throwing a pebble in a pond–no matter where it is thrown, the ripples if unobstructed would eventually reach all corners.

Margin requirements are concerned with the amount of credit granted by banks (Regulation U), brokers, dealers, and others (Regulation T) for the purchasing or carrying of securities. The main purpose of this control instrument is to avoid excessive use of credit in the stock market, which could lead to excessive stock market speculation. The authority of the Board of Governors to impose margin requirements was provided by the Securities Exchange Act of 1934, following the collapse of the stock market in 1929, which resulted from overspeculation fostered by excessive "trading on the margin." Depending upon the margin fixed by the Federal Reserve authority, a purchaser of securities will have to pay certain portions of the purchase price in cash and the remainder can be borrowed from either dealers or commercial banks. Suppose that the margin requirement is 10 percent. This means that a buyer of securities will have to pay 10 percent of the price in cash. An individual with $1,000 may thus purchase 100 stocks at the price of $100 each. In addition to $1,000 in cash, he can borrow $9,000 to conclude the transaction. If the margin requirement is raised to 100 percent, he can purchase only 10 shares. By raising the margin requirements, the Federal Reserve can therefore restrict the volume of loans available for stock market speculation.

Margin requirements have been changed several time by the Federal Reserve. For instance, during the 1945-46 period, margin requirements were changed three times, from 40 to 50 percent of market value in February to 75 percent in July 1945, and then to 100 percent in January 1946, remaining at that level until February 1947, owing to the then not so healthy continued upward trend of stock prices, volume of trading, and stock market credit. From 1947 to 1966, the limits of margin requirements varied between 50 and 90 percent, the common range being between 50 and 70 percent. It would appear reasonable to believe that the authority of the Board of Governors to use margin requirements for stock market credit is an important factor contributing to the moderation of stock market speculation, which otherwise could be excessive, especially in the 1960's, a period which witnessed continuous economic prosperity and expansion. But it would be rash to assume that the use of margin requirements would eliminate stock market booms and busts. After all, the scope of margin requirements is limited. Thus, subject to Regulation U are only stocks listed on the national exchanges, such as the New York Stock Exchange and the American Stock Exchange. Moreover, the requirements are applicable to credit extended for the purpose of purchasing or carrying securities, not to loans for other purposes. Yet, it is difficult to control the end uses of loans allegedly extended for "other purposes." The use of margin requirements, nevertheless, renders improbable the recurrence of a stock market collapse of the magnitude comparable to the one which took place in the late 1920's.

Consumer and Real Estate Credit Controls

The Board of Governors no longer has the power to regulate directly the volume of consumer and real estate credit. It is nevertheless of interest to discuss briefly the operation of these control devices. The authority to regulate consumer credit was first granted to the Board by the Presidential Executive order of 1941, and later by the Defense Production Act of 1950, which was withdrawn in 1952. The measures were purported mainly to curtail consumer credit demand that would add to inflationary pressures during World War II, to release resources for defense production, and to restrict inflationary consumer spending again during the Korean conflict. Consumer credit control was concerned with the prescription of minimum down payments and maximum repayment periods for installment sales contracts. The restriction of the demand for consumer goods was achieved by raising the minimum down payment and shortening the maturity terms of sales contracts. The power of the Board to regulate consumer credit was later extended to cover charge accounts and noninstallment consumer loans as well.

The authority of the Board to control real estate credit was also granted by the Defense Production Act of 1950, following unprecedented expansion of real estate credit, and was withdrawn in 1953. This control mechanism is similar to consumer credit control. It was chiefly concerned with the minimum down payments and maturity terms of conventional real estate mortgage loan contracts. The regulations on FHA-insured and VA-guaranteed real estate loans were administered by the Housing and Home Finance Agency.

The experience with real estate credit control was rather brief. Its effectiveness was hampered by the delay involved in securing authorization which permitted builders and contractors to obtain large loan commitments before controls were actually introduced, and resistance from builders, real estate lending institutions, and veterans. With regard to consumer credit control, the evidence of its effectiveness was not very conclusive. The amount of consumer credit did decrease during World War II, but this could have been at least in part a result of the unavailability of consumer durables, resources then being diverted mostly to the production of war materials.

The application of consumer and real estate credit controls encountered numerous administrative problems. The most difficult one was probably the enforcement of regulations. We can imagine the difficulty involved in "policing" a large number of institutions and business establishments lending to consumers and the regulations of a great variety of consumer goods. Congress, however, has considered at various times the question of again giving the Board of Governors stand-by authority to impose consumer credit controls should this become necessary. Except for the case of heavy inflationary pressures, such action would meet with formidable opposition from consumer lending institutions such as banks, sales finance companies, consumer finance companies, as well as individuals with limited means who depend on installment loans for the acquisition of consumer durables, and legislators who still abhor the use of direct control devices which would tamper with the operation of "free-market" forces.

COMBINATIONAL USES OF CONTROL INSTRUMENTS

The Federal Reserve can use the various instruments of credit policy at its disposal either separately, all at the same time, or in combination of two or three at a time, at its own discretion. They are, however, usually used in combination. Among the different possible combinations of control instruments which can be selected by the Federal Reserve, there is always one which, under given circumstances, is optimal in the sense that its contribution to the achievement of a given set of policy objectives is maximum.[3] The selection of an appropriate control instrument or combination of instruments to deal with particular monetary and credit developments is an essential responsibility of the control authority.

The Federal Reserve can so combine its various control weapons as to strengthen the effects of its dynamic operations, to mitigate the dynamic effects of the uses of some other instruments, or to exercise differential dynamic and defensive effects in different sectors of the economy. For example, during periods of heavy inflationary pressures, the Federal Reserve can use open-market operations, reserve requirements, and other control devices all at once for the maximum dynamic effects of monetary control. In times of heavy gold inflows, which tend to cause bank reserves to rise to higher levels, the use of open-market operations alone may not be adequate to mop up undesirable excess reserves. They may have to be supplemented by reserve requirements and other control instruments. Likewise, at times of heavy gold outflows or serious currency drains, open-market operations may be combined with lowering reserve requirements to bring about rapid relief to banks adversely affected by such developments.

Monetary instruments can also be combined so that the use of one may dampen excessive dynamic effects of the use of others. For example, disorderly conditions in the financial market generated by substantial increases in the legal reserve ratio may be, to some extent, corrected by the defensive use of open-market purchases of securities. Thus in 1948 when the Federal Reserve raised the legal reserve ratios on demand and time deposits as a means to absorb excessive reserves resulting from gold inflows, it also purchased $2 billion in government securities to maintain orderly conditions in the government securities market, and to assist member banks in adjusting their reserve positions to increased reserve requirements. Again, in early 1951, a 2 percent increase in the legal reserve ratio on demand deposits and a 1 percent increase in the reserve ratio on time deposits was coupled with Federal Reserve purchases of $800 million of government securities.

[3] With a set of four control instruments, there are $2^4 = 16$ possible combinations that the Federal Reserve may use, including, of course, the no-action set $\binom{4}{0}$, which is the case in which no action is taken on open market operations, the discount mechanism, the legal reserve requirements, and margin requirements.

Discount policy can be combined with open-market operations. The former serves as a leeway to alleviate the restrictive effects of open-market operations. Banks which are deficient in required reserves, as a result of open-market sales of securities, can borrow from the Federal Reserve banks to make up for such deficiencies. On the other hand, open-market puchases would enable banks to obtain additional reserves to repay their debts. The Federal Reserve banks may raise the discount rate and sell short-term securities to keep short-term money rates at levels comparable to those prevailing in other international money centers, such as London and Paris, in order to avoid heavy outflows to short-term capital that would aggravate further the nation's balance-of-payments deficits. At the same time, it can purchase long-term securities to keep long-term interest rates at relatively low levels in order to promote private domestic investments, higher levels of income and employment. This is in fact the kind of combination that has been used at various times by the Federal Reserve in the 1960's to promote external equilibrium on the one hand, and domestic employment and growth, on the other.

Differential effects on the various sectors of the economy may also be achieved by various combinations of instruments. For instance, it may so happen that there is an undesirable expansion of credit in the stock market and contraction of credit in other sectors of the economy. In such a situation, it is possible for the Federal Reserve to raise margin requirements and at the same time to increase its holdings of securities or to reduce reserve requirements or both. But this seldom happens. Decisions regarding restraint or relaxation with respect to stock market credit usually parallel similar decisions with other instruments of credit policy.

Not only is the selection of the proper instruments or combinations of instruments important, but their timely application is also a matter of great importance. The application of control instruments at the wrong time would not only minimize the effectiveness of monetary control but would also produce at times adverse consequences. Thus, in times of inflationary developments, if actions are deferred until there are unmistakable signs of inflation, then this deferment of action may result in more drastic anti-inflationary measures than those which would otherwise be required when they are applied at the early stage of the inflationary process. On the other hand, the application of restrictive measures at a time when a downturn in economic activity is brewing may speed up recessionary developments.

SUMMARY

Discretionary regulation of money and credit is the essence of Federal Reserve banking. Bank reserves are a variable directly amenable to the control power of the Federal Reserve. They are determined by the following expanding and contracting determinants:

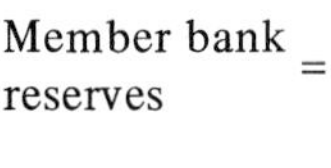

Member bank reserves =	Federal Reserve credit outstanding + Gold stock + Treasury currency outstanding	Currency in circulation + Treasury cash holdings + Treasury and foreign deposits + Other accounts (net)

To exercise its control power, the Federal Reserve has at its disposal several control instruments. These include open-market operations, variable reserve requirements, discount policy, and margin requirements. Open market operations consist of the sales and purchases of securities by the Federal Reserve in the open market. The purchases of securities tend to increase, and sales to reduce bank reserves and the supply of money. This is the most important and most frequently used Federal Reserve control instrument. Unlike open-market operations, which affect total bank reserves, changes in reserve requirements affect only excess reserves. An increase in the legal reserve ratio absorbs, and a decrease in the ratio releases excess reserves. While potentially the most powerful weapon in the arsenal of the Federal Reserve, changes in reserve requirements, owing to problems involved in their use, have been resorted to only to meet unusual situations, such as heavy gold inflows, heavy inflationary pressure or unusual reserve drains. Federal Reserve's discount policy consists in changing the terms and conditions attached to Federal Reserve credit granted to member banks. Discount policy is a relatively weak instrument of monetary control. But it serves as a useful safety valve whereby member banks may adjust their reserve deficiencies caused by restrictive open-market operations or changes in reserve requirements.

While open market operations, reserve requirements, and discount policy are general control instruments which affect credit in general without regard to its distribution in particular directions, margin requirements (and consumer and real estate credit controls) are selective control instruments which affect the allocation of particular kinds of credit. Raising the margin requirements tends to restrict, and lowering the margin requirements tends to increase the volume of credit available for the purchase and carrying of securities. The authority of the Federal Reserve to impose consumer and real estate credit controls is no longer available. But in the event of heavy inflationary developments, such authority may be restored by Congress.

While the control instruments of the Federal Reserve can be used separately, they are usually used in combination. The effectiveness of Federal Reserve control operations depends to a large extent upon the selection of the proper combinations of instruments and their timely application.

PROBLEMS

1. What are the major purposes of open-market operations? Are they mutually exclusive or complementary? What are necessary conditions for effective open-market operations? What do you understand by dynamic and defensive open-market operations? Explain in some detail the quantity and interest effects of open-market operations?

2. What are various forms in which discount policy can be carried out? Why is it that discount policy is quantitatively a weak instrument of monetary and credit control in the United States? What are psychological effects which the use of discount policy might generate? Are these psychological effects always in the favorable direction?

3. What are proposals for reform of the discount mechanism? What are the arguments for and against these proposals? Discuss in some detail.

4. Is the purpose of variable reserve requirements to protect the liquidity of banks? If not, what are they for?

5. Why is it that variable reserve requirements have been seldom used? What are the major objections to changing reserve requirements? In order to avoid some of the inequities involved in the use of variable reserve requirements, would you favor the application of differential legal reserve ratios for banks with different liquidity positions? What problems would you expect to arise from such a measure?

6. Explain the major differences between general and selective instruments of monetary and credit control? Which selective control devices are no longer at the disposal of the Federal Reserve? Why is it that the Board of Governors as well as Congress have been reluctant in using selective control devices? What are problems involved in the uses of these weapons?

7. By means of balance-sheet entries, show the immediate effects of the following transactions on bank reserves and the supply of money:

(a) The Federal Reserve sells $10 million of securities to the nonbank public.

(b) The Treasury purchases $10 million of gold from a domestic gold producer.

(c) The Treasury sells $50 million of gold to the Bank of France, which pays for it by drawing on its accounts with the Federal Reserve Bank of New York.

(d) The Treasury transfers $10 million from its tax and loan accounts with member banks to its account with the Federal Reserve banks.

(e) The Federal Reserve lends $50 million to member banks.

(f) The public withdraws $10 million of currency from member banks.

(g) Member banks purchase $5 million of stocks from the Federal Reserve banks.

(h) The public increases its savings deposits by $10 million by drawing on its demand balances.

(i) A foreign firm draws a check for $100,000 on its account with the San Francisco Third National Bank in payment to the XUZ company, which is a customer of the Fourth National Bank of Los Angeles.

chapter 14

Central Banking Development

Central banks, like other financial institutions, have undergone evolutionary changes before reaching the present stage of their development. This evolutionary development is reflected by the steady broadening of the functions and goals of central banks. This evolution is likely to continue. Central banking functions are likely to be further broadened, and new central banking techniques will be developed in view of the rapid pace of economic changes of modern time.

THE RISE OF CENTRAL BANKING

The development of central banking is fairly recent as compared with the development of commercial banking. The concept of central banking did not take shape until late in the nineteenth century. Banks which were to emerge as central banks, such as the Bank of England, the Riksbank of Sweden, and the Bank of France, were similar at the time when they were founded, to other commercial banks. Their operations were solely motivated by the objective of long-run profit maximization. They competed directly with other commercial banks. They nevertheless had special privileges and assumed functions and duties not performed by ordinary commercial banks. They were granted the quasi-monopoly of note issue. They were the sole bankers and fiscal agents of their governments, handling all public receipts and payments. They served as custodians of reserves of other commercial banks, and acted as "lender of last resort," providing other banks with additional reserves in times of a liquidity crisis. These banks, however, did not come to assume these special functions all at once but rather gradually over the years as a consequence of their dominant position in the banking business. Their special privileges and duties vis-à-vis their governments and other commercial banks gradually led to their recognition as central banks. Inasmuch as their functions and goals as central banks were incompatible with the pursuit of ordinary commercial banking in direct competition with other commercial banks, they gradually ceased to conduct any substantial amount of commercial banking and concentrated more and more on dealing only with the government and commercial banks. The profit motive gradually gave place to the public interest which finally becomes the predominant criterion of their action.

The emergence of central banking thus represents an evolutionary transformation of some privileged commercial banks into central banks. This evolutionary transformation was exemplified by the Bank of England, the first bank to be recognized as a central bank. This pattern was later followed by other banks in continental Europe—the Riksbank of Sweden (1856), the Bank of France (1800), the Bank of The Netherlands (1814), the Bank of Norway (1817), and the National Bank of Austria (1817). The establishment of the Federal Reserve System in 1914 drew to some extent on the experiences of the Bank of England and other European central banks. The system, in turn, heavily influenced the establishment of central banks in various parts of the world, especially in Latin America and Asia.

During the period between the two world wars, several central banks were established in many countries in Europe, Asia, and the Americas. These included, for example, the National Bank of Hungary (1924), the Bank of Canada (1935), and the Reserve Bank of India (1935). The post-World War II period and the 1960's witnessed the creation of many central banks in various parts of the world, particularly in newly independent countries of Africa and Asia. These included the Bank of Korea (1950), the Union Bank of Burma (1952), the Reserve Bank of Malawi (1964), and the Central Bank of Kenya (1966).[1]

There are at present central banks in almost all independent countries of the world, with the exception of a few countries, such as Haiti and Panama.

THE DEVELOPMENT OF THE BANK OF ENGLAND

The development of modern central banking principles and techniques owes a great deal to the Bank of England. The latter, which served as model for the establishment of central banks in many countries, came into being in 1694 when the British government, hard-pressed by financial requirements of the war with France, granted a group of City of London merchants a bank incorporation charter in return for a loan of £1.2 million. The Bank of England thus started with no specie capital but with a portfolio of government securities against which she could, however, issue an equal amount of bank notes.

After a rather shaky start, which witnessed the bank being forced to suspend specie payments in 1696, its position was gradually strengthened by subsequent monetary and banking legislation (the acts of 1697, 1708, and 1742)

[1] It should be noted that in these countries prior to the establishment of central banks, certain central banking functions were performed by commercial banks, foreign central banks, or currency boards. For instance, in Burma, before the creation of the Union Bank of Burma, central banking in Burma was assumed by the Rangoon branch of the Reserve Bank of India. In Korea prior to the establishment of the Bank of Korea, central banking functions were carried on by the Bank of Chosen, itself a commercial bank. The central banks of Kenya, Tanzania, Uganda, and Guyana grew out of currency boards which issued currency and conducted foreign-exchange operations.

which granted the bank the quasi-monopoly of note issue by prohibiting banking institutions with more than six partners from issuing demand notes, and made it the exclusive banker and fiscal agent for the government. In addition, organized as a joint-stock company with limited responsibility of the owners, the bank was able to mobilize large capital resources by selling shares to a large number of shareholders. This could not be done by other commercial banks since, until the passage of the act of 1836, they could not be organized on a joint-stock basis. The close relations between the bank and the government—its special privileges and great resources—gradually enabled it to acquire the dominant position in the British banking system.

The notes issued by the Bank of England, which were fully convertible into specie, commanded widespread confidence and nationwide circulation. They were gradually accepted by other commercial banks as substitutes for specie reserves. London bankers then found it convenient to hold reserves with the Bank of England for interbank payment purposes. Country banks, in turn, held correspondent balances with London banks for remittances to London and for securing reserves when needed. The Bank of England thus gradually became the custodian of reserves of the British banking system which was already closely knitted in the second half of the nineteenth century, following the consolidation of small, weak country banks with large London joint-stock banks as a consequence of periodic banking crisis. In addition to serving as custodian of reserves of the banking system, the bank also acted as a lender of last resort, providing banks with additional reserves in times of crises.

The role of the Bank of England as a central bank was legalized by the Bank Charter Act of 1844. The Bank was granted the exclusive right to issue notes in England. It was divided into two departments: The Issue Department and the Banking Department. The responsibility of the Issue Department was to issue bank notes. The amount of notes issued by the Bank in excess of £14 million was to be covered by 100 percent gold reserves. The Banking Department was in charge of banking operations, accepting deposits, and making loans.

The prestige of the Bank of England and its successful operations constituted a stimulus to the development of central banking in continental Europe and other parts of the world as well. With its increasing responsibility as a central bank, the Bank of England, by the end of the nineteenth century, reduced substantially its commercial banking business. To date, the bank still conducts some commercial banking as part of her tradition, but this is not important in magnitude. The bank no longer opens new accounts for the public. Its commercial business is concerned with the handling of the accounts of some old, established business houses, which dated from the period in which the bank still competed with private banks for banking business.

The Bank of England was nationalized in 1946 by the Labor government, but the internal structure of her organization has remained practically the same since the Act of 1844. The Bank is managed by a governor, a deputy governor, and sixteen directors appointed by the Queen. The Bank's Issue Department has the exclusive right to issue notes in England.[2] The volume of notes which it can issue is under the control of the Treasury, by provisions of the Currency and Bank Notes Act of 1928. The Treasury can authorize the Bank to increase or reduce the volume of notes within certain limits without parliamentary approval. Following the abandonment of the gold standard by England in 1931, the obligation of the Bank to redeem its notes in gold has been removed, and its note issue has become an entirely fiduciary one. Nevertheless the pound sterling is still defined in terms of gold, and sterling balances held by foreigners (non-British residents) are exchangeable for any other currency. But these foreign-held sterling balances, unlike official foreign-held dollar balances, are not convertible into gold. Since the Bank of England is under no obligation to sell or buy gold against currency, it does not hold gold reserves. England's gold reserves are held by the Exchange Equalization Account (managed by the bank) whose major function is to maintain orderly conditions in foreign exchange markets.

The Bank of England, through its Banking Department, serves as bankers' bank and as the government's bank and fiscal agent. The bank keeps accounts for commercial banks (Bankers' Deposits) which are used for the settlement of clearing balances, among other things, and provides them with additional currency whenever this is needed. The bank handles all the receipts and payments relative to the accounts of the government (Public Deposits), pays interest on the national debt, and raises and repays loans of the government. The bank is the regulator of the British monetary and banking system. To carry out this function, the bank has relied mainly on the bank-rate changes, open-market operations, moral suasion, and occasionally, on direct controls, particularly controls on installment sale contracts.[3] In terms of the Act of 1946, the bank may also, if so authorized by the Treasury, issue directives to commercial banks, when

[2] The Treasury is in charge of issuing coins. During World War I, the Treasury also issued notes, which were withdrawn in 1928. It should be noted that certain banks in Scotland and Ireland still issue notes, but these banks are required to hold in their vaults Bank of England notes equal to the volume of notes which they issue. The volume of notes of these banks is relatively small.

[3] It should be noted that in England, the Bank of England does not lend directly to commercial banks, as in the case in the United States and other countries, but only to discount houses which specialize in discounting bills of exchange. These discount houses normally borrow "at call or short notice" from commercial banks to finance their portfolios. When commercial banks are less willing to lend (as, in times of tight money) discount houses are forced to borrow more often from the Bank of England. To put pressure on the market, should this be considered desirable, the bank can then raise the bank rate. As they pay higher rates on borrowed funds from the Bank of England, the discount houses also would raise the rates on bills which they buy to retain their profit margin. Increases in bill rates will, through arbitrage, cause other money rates to rise as well. It should also be noted that when the Bank of England sell securities (in England, the sales and purchases of Treasury bills by the Bank of England are conducted through a brokerage firm known as the "special buyer" which receives buying and selling instructions from the bank), the reserves of commercial banks decrease. To replenish their reserves, banks would call in some of their loans to discount houses, thereby forcing the latter "into the bank" for accommodation. Open-market operations thus strengthen the effectiveness of bank-rate policy.

such action is deemed desirable. This power, however, has seldom been used. Commercial banks usually cooperate voluntarily with the Bank of England, knowing too well that should that fail, the Bank can always enforce its will through bank-rate policy and open-market operations, and its statutory power to issue directions to banks.

EARLY DEVELOPMENT OF CENTRAL BANKING POLICY

Before the outbreak of World War I, the scope of central banking operations was relatively limited. The important goals of modern central banking–such as full employment and a maximum sustainable rate of economic growth–were not thought of. Such central banking techniques as variable reserve requirements, margin requirements, and selective control devices were not yet developed. The use of open-market operations was almost nonexistent. Under the pre-1914 international gold standard, the predominant objective of central banking policy was to maintain the covertibility of national currency into gold at the legal parity. Since convertibility required the holding of gold reserve, the major policy criterion was then the central bank reserve ratio (that is, the ratio of gold and foreign exchange to central bank notes and deposit liabilities) which changed in accordance with the movements of gold and foreign exchange, and with changes in the demand liabilities of the central bank. The major instrument for the protection of gold reserve was the manipulation of the discount rate. When the reserve ratio decreased to levels which were considered by central bank authorities as critical in regard to currency convertibility, an increase in discount rates was called for as a corrective measure which was at times substituted or supplemented by the use of other policy instruments. Conversely, increases in the reserve ratio, which resulted in substantial excess reserves, usually led to a lowering of the discount rates, if for no other reason than to keep the discount rates in line with money market rates.

Effective bank rate changes–that is, bank rate changes accompanied by changes in market rates–if not offset by increases in money rates brought about by defensive discount rate changes in foreign money centers, tended to restore equilibrium in the reserve position of the central bank through their influence on international capital movements, and on the balance of trade via domestic price and income changes.

The effectiveness of the use of discount policy as a measure to correct reserve disturbances, however, varied from country to country. It was most effective and most frequently used by the Bank of England as London was then the international financial center with a free gold market and a well-developed discount market; bills drawn in any part of the world were mostly accepted and discounted in the London discount market. Increases in the bank rate initiated by the Bank of England, when faced with reserve drains, once reflected by corresponding changes in money market rates, tended to induce net inflows of capital by discouraging the withdrawal of foreign balances or the remittance of bills to London for discount, delaying the flotation of foreign securities in London, slowing down the transfers abroad of the proceeds of foreign bonds which had already been issued, and attracting liquid foreign balances to London in view of relatively high London money rates.

While international capital movements were sensitive to changes in money rates in London, the effect of high money rates following discount rate increases on the reserve position of the Bank of England, and for that matter, of other central banks, through their influence on the balance of trade was believed to be slow and uncertain. Given the flexibility of prices and wages and the sensitivity of the demand for credit with respect to changes of money rates, an increase in money rates following an increase in the rate of discount would tend to reduce the level of effective demand, income, and prices through its influence not only on the cost of borrowing but also on the availability of bank credit and the expectations of the business and financial community. Declining domestic prices and income would tend to encourage exports and discourage imports. The resulting trade surplus would cause gold to flow in, thereby contributing to strengthening the reserve position of the central bank. On the other hand, if wages and prices were inflexible downwardly and the demand for credit, not sensitive to interest changes, then increases in money rates brought about by central bank action would not substantially help improve the balance of trade.

At any rate, regardless of whether discount policy affected the reserve position of the central bank through its influence on both international movements of capital and the balance of trade or only through the former channel, it proved a potent instrument to check reserve drains, especially in the case of the Bank of England, and to a lesser extent, the Reichbank of Germany, the Bank of the Netherlands, and the Riksbank of Sweden. In point of fact, the effectiveness of bank rate policy was an important factor accounting for the successful operations of the Bank of England, although its gold reserve was comparatively small relative to the tremendous volume of business and financial transactions conducted through London.

With regard to some other European central banks, especially the Bank of France, the scope of discount policy was limited. Since the Bank of France then had relatively ample excess reserves which could sustain mild and temporary reserve strains, raising the discount rate was used mostly when there was substantial drain on its gold reserve. As a result, the rate of discount was changed less frequently by the Bank of France and the range of changes was relatively narrow. For example during the 1844-1914 period, the rate of discount was reported to have been changed 121 times by the Bank of France, as compared with 466 times by the Bank of England. The relative stability of the discount rate maintained by the Bank of France and some other central banks appeared to be motivated by the desire to avoid adverse influences of substantial money rate changes on domestic business conditions, among other things.

Inasmuch as it was the increase in market rates which affected international capital movements and the demand for credit, the effectiveness of an increase in the rate of discount by the central bank as a measure to check reserve drains would depend upon the responsiveness of market rates to bank rate changes. Raising the discount rate would be helpless if it were not followed by a corresponding increase in money-market rates. In London and other large money centers, money rates were highly responsive to bank-rate changes. But at times when banks had ample excess reserves which precluded any need for central bank credit facilities, the Bank of England could "borrow in the market," that is, from discount houses and bill brokers using government securities as collateral, thereby taking money off the market and forcing money rates to any desirable level. The same effect was also achieved by the Bank of England at times through "borrowing on consols," a technique by which the Bank sold consols spot and bought them back at a later date to withdraw funds temporarily from the market and drive up money rates.

In view of avoiding undesirable effects on the domestic economy caused by discount rate changes, central banks of the day sometimes used other methods to protect their gold reserves. For instance, the Bank of France, instead of raising the rate of discount to stop reserve drains, adopted what was referred to as a "gold premium policy" whereby a premium was charged by the bank on gold sold to the public in times of gold exports. The increase in the selling price of gold raised the gold export points which would, to some extent, discourage gold dealers from purchasing gold from the central bank for sale abroad. On the other hand, as a measure to induce gold imports, a number of central banks, including the Bank of England and the Reichbank of Germany, at times raised slightly the buying price for gold. To the extent that this is not offset by defensive increase in the selling price for gold abroad, gold dealers would be willing to purchase foreign balances at the prevailing exchange rate and use the proceeds to acquire gold abroad and repatriate it for resale to the central bank. It should be noted, however, that the range within which the central bank could raise the selling and buying prices for gold was narrow. In addition to operations in gold, a number of central banks, when faced with serious losses of reserve, occasionally resorted to borrowings from their governments which had floated securities in foreign markets, and borrowed from foreign governments and commercial banks, and foreign central banks as well.[4] This was the experience, at one time or another, of the Bank of England, the Riksbank of Sweden, and some other central banks.

While in practice discount policy was used by the Bank of England and other central banks as the major instrument to protect gold reserves, the desirability of raising the discount rate as a corrective measure was questioned by a

[4]This kind of international cooperation is quite familiar in present-day central banking. For example, the Bank of England, in order to defend the pound had resorted to massive borrowings from the Federal Reserve System, the IMF, and European central banks.

number of writers. According to them, the outflow of gold was a temporary matter. The decrease in the price level caused by the contraction of bank credit and the supply of money as a consequence of reserve losses would encourage exports and discourage imports and would eventually reverse the gold movements. There would be no need for raising the discount rate, which would adversely affect domestic business. What was necessary was for the central bank to carry larger gold and foreign-exchange reserves which would help sustain substantial gold losses before price and income changes could reverse the gold flows. But this was believed to be slow in taking effect. In addition, it was argued that as the rate of discount was raised promptly when the outflow of gold began, this would quickly stop the outflow of gold and induce inflows of capital which would help relieve pressures on credit markets generated by higher discount rates. These appear to be alternative measures. The holding of ample reserves by the central bank would not require frequent changes in the rate of discount. On the other hand, effective uses of discount policy would preclude the need for ample reserves.

Although currency convertibility was then the major objective of central banking policy, central bankers were perfectly aware of other goals as well, and sometimes their actions were directed toward achieving these objectives when such actions did not directly interfere with the primary goal of convertibility. Thus bank-rate changes and other instruments were at times deliberately used by a number of central banks, including the Bank of England and the Reichbank of Germany, to avoid overexpansion of bank credit and excessive speculation which would eventually result in financial panics. For instance, before 1914 the Reichbank of Germany had on occasion used open-market operations in the form of the sale of foreign bills and Treasury bills in the open market in view of curtailing credit expansion by commercial banks.

CENTRAL BANKING FUNCTIONS IN THE UNITED STATES PRIOR TO THE FEDERAL RESERVE

Before the Federal Reserve System was established in 1914, certain central banking functions were performed by the First Bank of the United States (1791-1811) and then the Second Bank of the United States (1816-36). Following the disolution of the second bank, these functions were occasionally exercised by the Independent Treasury System (1846-1920) which was legally set up only to serve the fiscal needs of the government. The Suffolk Bank of Boston, during the 1824-58 period, also initiated an arrangement whereby it acted as a regulator of notes issued by banks in New England.

The Banks of the United States

The First and Second Banks of the United States, as we have already mentioned, were basically commercial banks engaged primarily in the private commercial banking business. But, like the Bank of England, owing to their special relations with the government their dominant position in the banking system—a result of their substantial capital resources which were partly subscribed by the federal government itself, and other privileges—assumed certain functions and duties not performed by ordinary commercial banks of the day. They served as bankers and fiscal agents for the government, receiving in deposit government funds, collecting and transferring government bonds from one part of the country to another, and granting advances to the government in anticipation of tax collections. They were suppliers of bank notes which were legal tender for all payments to the Government of the United States. They acted as regulators of the note issues of state chartered banks, especially the Second Bank under Nicholas Biddle, by varying their holdings of state bank notes. They held notes of state banks and used them for payment purposes when credit expansion was deemed desirable. Conversely, when credit restraint was needed, they presented bank notes to issuing state banks for specie redemption. The resulting losses of specie reserves would tend to restrict bank credit and note issues. Inasmuch as these notes could be presented by the banks of the United States for specie payments on demand, state banks had to be always prepared for such specie withdrawals by holding adequate reserves in relation to notes emitted, since a bank which failed to redeem its notes in specie would have to close its doors. This practice, which constituted a deterrent to the overissuance of state bank notes, was a subject of discontent of state banks and was one of the factors contributing to the early demise of the First Bank in 1811 and the Second Bank in 1836. Had the second bank been rechartered, it could have developed into a full-fledged central bank, like the Bank of England and other European commercial banks which turned into central banks.

The Suffolk System

In the early 1820's the Suffolk Bank of Boston used the same tactics as had been used by the Banks of the United States to force New England's weaker country banks to maintain par redemption of their notes. Since the notes of these banks were in circulation at a discount in Boston, they remained in circulation, whereas notes of the strong Boston banks were either hoarded or taken to these banks for par redemption. To correct the situation, the Suffolk Bank of Boston, in 1824, initiated a plan whereby it accumulated large amounts of notes of country banks and presented to them for specie payments, unless they agreed to maintain sufficient deposit balances at the Suffolk Bank which agreed to redeem the notes of any New England banks participating in the plan. In 1825 almost all banks in New England joined the system. The arrangement had provided New England's banks with clearing facilities and had exerted a healthy restraining influence on the volume of bank notes of other state banks, as they could be easily redeemed through the Suffolk Bank. The plan had given New England a sound currency system. It was, however, terminated in the late 1850's following the establishment of the Bank of Mutual Redemption, a clearing house, by banks in New England.

The Independent Treasury

The tremendous growth of state banks following the dissolution of the Second Bank of the United States led to overexpansion of state banks. This resulted in substantial losses to the government which had deposited funds in a number of state banks.[5] To handle its own funds, the government in 1846 established the Independent Treasury System, made up of a number of Treasury offices located in large cities, serving as agents collecting taxes and making payments.[6]

In terms of the act of 1846, under the system fiscal operations were divorced from the commercial banks, and the government became its own banker. Government receipts and disbursements were effected mostly in specie. When taxes were paid to the government, the specie reserves of the banking system decreased, causing the volume of bank notes and bank credit to decrease. Conversely, when payments were made by the Treasury, specie reserves of commercial banks were replenished, and bank credit could be expanded. By varying its specie balances, the Treasury thus could temporarily ease or tighten conditions in the money market. This, however, could be used as a policy instrument by the Treasury only when Treasury receipts substantially exceeded Treasury spending. Yet until the mid-1860's the Treasury was preoccupied with covering its deficits by issuing interest-bearing Treasury notes which were used by the public as currency since they were made receivable in all payments to the United States government. It was only under Secretary James Guthrie (1853-56) that specie balances accumulated in the Treasury were deliberately manipulated to influence the money market, and to avoid both undesirable credit expansion or contraction. When the money market was unduly tight, the Treasury used its balances to retire part of the public debt, increasing currency in circulation and injecting more reserves into the banking system which would allow the expansion of bank credit. On the other hand, when there was indication of excessive expansion of bank credit and overtrading, the Treasury allowed its specie balances to accumulate and hence caused a contraction in bank reserves and credit. This policy was reflected in the following statement of Secretary Guthrie: "The Independent Treasury, when overtrading takes place, gradually fills its vaults, withdraws the deposits, and, pressing the banks, the merchants and the dealers, exercise that temperate and timely control which serves to secure the fortunes of individuals and preserve the general prosperity."[7]

[5]We may recall that as early as 1834, President Andrew Jackson, who opposed the rechartering of the Second Bank of the United States, had ordered government funds withdrawn from the Second Bank and deposited in state banks.

[6]It should be noted that such a system had already been tried in 1840 under the Independent Treasury Act of that year.

[7]U.S. Treasury Department, *Report of the Secretary,* 1856, p. 31.

During the Civil War period the Treasury was preoccupied with financing the war efforts by issuing United States notes or greenbacks as authorized by the act of February 25, 1862, which, unlike the Treasury notes of the preceding period, were legal tender. In the post-Civil War period, the policy of the Treasury was mainly oriented toward an orderly return to specie redemption of greenbacks which had been suspended during the war. As budget receipts substantially exceeded spending, United States notes that returned to the Treasury following the payment of taxes were not reissued. At the same time, the Treasury accumulated specie balances through specie payments of taxes and the flotation of government bonds in the New York money market. These measures, which resulted in a net absorption of specie into Treasury balances, caused bank reserves, bank deposits, and the supply of money to decline. This, coupled with the expansion of output at the time, caused prices to decline gradually. After 1876, the value of green backs in terms of gold approached parity and redemption was resumed in 1879. After a period of disturbance in the 1890's, which witnessed heavy gold drains on the Treasury following the wholesale conversion of silver certificates authorized by the Sherman Silver Purchase Act of 1890, the gold position of the Treasury was improved consequent upon the repeal in 1893, of the act of 1890, the enactment of the Gold Standard Act of 1900, and the discovery of gold in various parts of the world, especially in South Africa.

The Treasury, under Secretary Leslie Shaw, again used its specie holdings and deposit balances with national banks as a policy instrument to eliminate seasonal disturbances in the money market. Thus, to help the banks meet currency demands which usually reached a peak in the fall, the Treasury increased its deposit balances with national banks and reduced its holdings of specie or used part of its specie balances to retire some public debt to put more coins into circulation. Maturing Treasury bonds which could have been retired out of current budget surplus were reissued in order to avoid a contraction in the volume of national bank notes (we can recall that national banks could issue notes up to 100 percent of the value of government bonds that were pledged with the Treasury as collateral for note issues). In addition, to enable national banks to increase bank notes, the Treasury at times allowed them to substitute nongovernment, high-grade securities as collateral for Treasury deposit balances, thereby freeing government bonds which could be used to support more national bank notes. On the other hand, during seasons where the demand for currency declined, the Treasury accumulated its specie balances by drawing down its deposits with national banks to absorb excess funds in the money market.

It should be noted, however, that while Treasury operations were deliberately used by some Treasury secretaries as an instrument to influence conditions in the money market, others strictly observed the provisions of the laws which established the Independent Treasury System, and Treasury operations were carried on with little regard to their general monetary and banking implications. There was therefore no continuity in Treasury "central banking" operations. Moreover, discretionary Treasury monetary operations were then strongly opposed by economists, financial writers, and others, who firmly believed that the supply of money and credit would regulate itself under the operation of market forces. It increased or decreased in accordance with the needs of business and there would be no need for discretionary monetary regulations by any institution. This line of thought in fact remained influential in the establishment of the Federal Reserve System, which was supposed to operate automatically within the framework of the gold standard and the commercial-loan theory. The international movements of gold would regulate the volume of central bank reserves and the rediscounting of commercial bills by the Reserve Banks would limit the volume of money and credit to the needs of trade.

CENTRAL BANKING: AUTOMACITY VERSUS DISCRETIONARY CONTROL

The existence of central banks is nowadays taken for granted by most economists. It is widely recognized that central banks are necessary for the discretionary control of the monetary system. But the desirability of discretionary monetary management is still questioned by a number of writers who prefer a set of permanent rules or automatic formulas for monetary operations to the discretionary judgment of central bankers.

The opposition to discretionary management of the monetary system in fact dates back several centuries. Advocates of the real-bills doctrine firmly believed that the monetary mechanism would be self-regulating and its functioning should not be tampered with by the artificial intervention of central bankers. In lending against bills representing real commercial transactions, the volume of money in circulation would change strictly in accordance with the monetary requirements of business. An expansion of business would give rise to greater borrowings–hence more bank credit and money. Conversely, a business contraction would result in less borrowings; debts would be repaid and money would flow back to the banking system. The issuance or retirement of money would be automatically regulated by business conditions, and banks could not force their notes into circulation.

Disciples of the currency school, while differing from the real-bills doctrinists in several respects, especially the manner in which bank notes should be issued and the nature of deposit money, among other things, also strongly opposed the discretionary management of the currency in any form. To this school of thought, whose writings heavily influenced the passage of the English Bank Charter Act of 1844, the circulation of paper currency should be strictly limited to the amount of gold reserve held by the issuing banks. Within this framework, currency would vary precisely as would a purely specie circulation, and there was no room for discretionary action by the Bank of England which would serve mainly as a "warehouse" issuing notes against gold deposits. The volume of notes issued would be automatically controlled by the movements of gold in accordance with the country's external payment position. An inflow of gold as a result of an international payment surplus would lead to an expansion of money and credit. On the other hand, an outflow of gold following upon an external payment deficit would result in a contraction in the volume of bank reserves, and hence, a contraction in the supply of money. There was no need for central bank control.

It has been argued elsewhere that discounting and rediscounting of commercial bills by commercial banks and central banks would not result in a "proper" volume of money and bank credit. The mechanism contains an inherent inflationary as well as a deflationary bias. Rising prices, following an increase in total spending, would lead to higher values of inventories and "real-bills," and hence, to further expansion of bank credit and money, and heavier inflationary pressures. Conversely, declining prices caused by a contraction in aggregate demand would lead to lower values of inventories and commercial bills, and then to further contraction in money and bank credit, and more deflationary pressures.

The functioning of the monetary system under the gold standard was substantially automatic. Within the framework of the gold system, regardless of whether it is a system in which pure specie was in circulation or a system in which the circulating media bore some fixed relationship to gold reserves, the supply of money would vary pretty much in accordance with gold flows. Such an automatic system, however, was subject to inflationary and deflationary pressures and other vicissitudes caused by gold movements, the accidental discovery of gold, and gold hoardings. Therefore, even in the heyday of the international gold standard, it was not uncommon for central banks to sterilize gold movements in order to avoid undesirable implications on domestic business conditions. Indeed, the British gold standard system was definitely managed by the Bank of England. So were the gold systems in other countries.[8] Sterilization of gold was also frequently practiced by the Federal Reserve in the 1920's and 1930's consequent upon heavy inflows of gold. With the world-wide abandonment of the gold standard in the 1930's, elements of automacity under gold disappeared and money has come to be managed entirely by discretionary central bank action.

[8]This was attested by the findings of Professor Arthur Bloomfield in his study on Monetary Policy under the International Gold Standard: "It is often argued that monetary policy before 1914, except perhaps in the case of the Bank of England, was essentially "automatic," involving more or less mechanical responses to gold movements and a minimum of "discretionary" action and judgment. This is a misconception. Not only did central banking authorities, so far as can be inferred from their actions, not consistently follow any simple rule or criterion of policy, or focus exclusively on considerations of convertibility, but they were constantly called upon to exercise, and did exercise, their judgment on such matters as whether or not to act in any given situation and, if so, at what point of time to act, the kind and extent of action to take, and the instrument or instruments of policy to use. . . . " Arthur I. Bloomfield, *Monetary Policy Under the International Gold Standard: 1880-1914* (Federal Reserve Bank of New York, 1959), p. 25.

Even under present-day economic conditions, there are advocates of the abandonment of discretionary management of money, however. Although they do believe, as did Bagehot hundreds of years ago, that "money will not manage itself," they prefer a set of permanent rules or automatic formulas to regulate the functioning of the monetary mechanism to any form of discretionary central bank control. The foundation of such preference appears to be the fear that errors of human judgment would tend to amplify business fluctuations, and hence, to undermine the value of the monetary unit. Since a substantial amount of time would be required for discretionary monetary measures to take effect, and since these time lags could not be predicted with any degree of accuracy, there is a possibility of untimely application of monetary measures which would, as a consequence, magnify cyclical fluctuations. Hence, instead of discretionary central bank action, various simple, mechanical rules of monetary policy have been suggested. One such suggestion is to allow the supply of money to grow at a fixed percentage per year.

The trouble is that the supply of money is a rather arbitrary concept. It is subject to changes in the light of the constantly changing operations of those institutions which directly affect money. What is not considered money today may be so a decade from now. There is also the question of determining the rate of change in the supply of money. In addition, the rule presupposes the constancy of the velocity of monetary circulation. But experience suggests that the rate of turnover of money is not constant and its movement is rather pro-cyclical in that it tends to rise in times of prosperity and declines in periods of recession. Given the fixed rate of change of the quantity of money, the changes in its rate of turnover do affect aggregate spending and therefore are capable of causing substantial price changes.

It is true that discretionary decisions, when in error, could amplify cyclical variations in prices, income, and employment. But to say that these decisions are in error most of the time is an exaggeration. In most instances, policy decisions of central bankers did contribute to dampening the ups and downs in business and economic activity. After all, the determination of a set of rules or formulas is itself a discretionary action, whether made by central banks or other institutions and organizations. There is no reason for us to believe that such an action is an all-wise action. And if it is not all-wise because of changing conditions, then it would hardly be thinkable that it could be applied permanently. But to modify the rules to meet changing economic conditions, then there is not much sense talking about automatic monetary control.

The objectives that modern central banks seek to achieve are numerous, and the achievement of an objective or a set of objectives may require different combinations of measures under different monetary and financial conditions. Inasmuch as these goals are sometimes in conflict with one another, we can hardly expect that a fixed rule could be used to achieve goals which may be to some extent mutually exclusive. The responsibility of the central bank is to select a course of action such that, in order to achieve certain policy objectives, its social benefits would be maximized, given the expected social hardships, or given the expected social benefits, its social hardships would be minimized. Most economists would agree that definite automatic rules would be preferable to "managed money," provided such rules can be found and can be applied to all circumstances and at all times. But in the light of constant economic and financial changes, such all-wise rules do not exist, and since they do not exist, we need central banks to exercise discretionary monetary management.[9]

SUMMARY

Central banking is largely a development of the twentieth century. A good number of central banks in Europe were "privileged" commercial banks which, as a consequence of their special privileges and responsibilities, gradually developed into central banks. This evolutionary transformation was exemplified by the Bank of England which served as model for the establishment of central banks in various parts of the world, and was largely responsible for the development of modern central banking principles and techniques.

Prior to 1914 the scope of central banking operations was rather limited. The objective of central banking policy was then primarily the maintenance of the convertibility of national currency into gold. The major guide of monetary policy was the gold-reserve ratio, and the main policy instrument was manipulation of the discount rate. Central bankers, at the time, however, were perfectly aware of other objectives of monetary policy as well. At times when currency convertibility was of no immediate concern, central banks used bank-rate changes and other instruments to tighten conditions in the credit markets to avoid overexpansion of bank credit and excessive speculation. In addition, in order to avoid adverse effects of bank-rate changes on domestic economic conditions, central banks also used devices other than discount policy to protect their gold reserves.

Before the establishment of the Federal Reserve System, central banking functions in the United States were performed by the Banks of the United States and the Independent Treasury System. The First and Second Banks of the United States, in addition to serving as bankers and fiscal agents of the Federal Government, controlled the volume of notes issued by state banks by presenting them at intervals to these banks for specie payments. This tended to exert a restrictive influence on the volume of notes that could be issued by state banks. The Treasury, under some secretaries, also attempted to correct seasonal disturbances in the credit markets by varying its holdings of specie balances, and retiring or reissuing maturing bonds, thus allowing the volume of national bank

[9]See R. S. Sayers, "The Theoretical Basis of Central Banking," *Central Banking After* Bagehot (New York: Oxford U.P., 1958).

notes to increase or decrease in accordance with seasonal currency requirements. But there was no continuity in this kind of Treasury monetary policy. This was rather the effort of some individual Treasury authorities who were aware of implications of Treasury activities on the monetary welfare of the country.

It is widely recognized today that central banks are needed for the discretionary regulation of the flow of money and credit for the achievement of specific goals of economic policy. But this is questioned by a number of writers who prefer to substitute automatic monetary control in terms of fixed rules and formulas for discretionary monetary management. While it is agreed by many that permanent automatic rules that could be used in all circumstances at all times are preferable to discretionary monetary control, but inasmuch as such permanent rules do not exist in view of constant economic changes, we need discretionary central bank control.

PROBLEMS

1. What was the major objective of central banking policy under the pre-1914 international gold standard? What was then the main criterion of central banking policy? Explain.

2. Explain in some detail how Bank rate changes were used by central banks before 1914 as a major instrument to protect their gold reserves. How was it supposed to operate? Why is it that the use of bank rate changes was particularly effective in England? What were other methods used by certain central banks in Europe to prevent drains on their reserves?

3. Explain some of the important central banking functions performed by the First and Second Banks of the United States and the Suffolk System. How did the operations of the Independent Treasury System affect money market conditions? How were these operations manipulated by certain Treasury secretaries to influence the supply of money and credit? Why did economists and financial writers of the time object to such operations? Explain.

4. What are the arguments for and against discretionary monetary management?

5. "In the beginning, most central banks, being first among equals and merely endowed with certain special priviliges and duties, were hardly distinguishable from a commercial bank." Explain in the light of the development of the Bank of England.

chapter **15**

Central Banking in Underdeveloped Countries

We have discussed the control functions of the Federal Reserve. These are fairly representative of the control operations of central banks in most industrially advanced countries which operate within a monetary and financial institutional setting not too different from that of the United States. It is true that the money and capital markets in these countries are not as developed as those existing in the United States, but they are far more developed than those in underdeveloped regions. There are of course differences in regard to the legal framework and the emphasis placed by these central banks on the combinational uses of monetary weapons, but like the Federal Reserve they rely for control purposes primarily on the traditional quantitative control instruments, namely bank rate changes, open-market operations, and variable reserve requirements.

Here, we are concerned only with central banking in underdeveloped countries, which differs from central banking in industrially advanced nations, not only in the legal framework in which central banks of underdeveloped countries operate, but, more important, in the monetary and financial institutional environment in which they function.

Most of the central banks in underdeveloped countries were established either during the interwar period (namely central banks in Latin America) after World War II (central banks in South and East Asia), or in the 1960's (mostly central banks in newly independent countries in Africa). These central banks were largely founded on the experiences of older central banks. In point of fact, central banking legislation in most of these countries was drawn up mainly with the assistance of experts from the Federal Reserve and the Bank of England. The establishment of these central banks was generally aimed at promoting price and exchange stability, full employment, economic development and growth, and the development of the banking structure. Like older central banks, they perform the same routine and service functions, such as issuing currency, acting as banker for commercial banks, as banker and fiscal agent for the government,[1] administering foreign exchange controls, and serving as intermediary between the gov-

[1] In Brazil, however, the Bank of Brazil continues to serve as fiscal agent of the government instead of the Central Bank of the Republic, which was established in 1965.

ernment and international financial organizations. They differ from central banks in industrially advanced nations in their control operations, however. Unlike advanced central banks which rely mainly on general control instruments for the purpose of controlling money and credit, central banks in underdeveloped countries, circumscribed by the narrow scope of the financial mechanism, not only have to adapt traditional central banking instruments and practices to their own needs and circumstances but also have to develop new techniques to meet the special problems of underdevelopment. We shall describe the scope of central bank control in underdeveloped economies, the uses of various control instruments at the disposal of the central banks, some aspects of their administrative structure and organization, and the problem of commercial banking by central banks that is not uncommon in underdeveloped areas.

THE SCOPE OF CENTRAL BANK CONTROL

The scope of central banking in economically backward countries, as well as in developed nations, is governed mainly by such institutional and structural factors as the use of money and credit, the development of the money and capital markets, the development of the banking habit of the public, and the general banking structure and development. In underdeveloped economies, the use of money and credit is limited, the banking habit and banking system is undeveloped, the money market is not well organized, and the capital market is either in its infancy or nonexistent. Yet the classic role of the central bank as a regulator of the flow of money and credit depends largely upon the degree of development of these institutional and structural factors.

In most underdeveloped countries, the use of money is chiefly confined to urban and semiurban areas. In rural areas, where the majority of the people live, transactions outside the market places are usually conducted on a barter basis. Where money is used, it is predominantly in the form of currency, not bank deposits. While in developed economies, such as the United States and the United Kingdom, the bulk of the supply of money is made up of demand deposits held by the public; in underdeveloped countries, demand deposits represent a relatively small percentage of the money supply, as shown in Table 15-1. This suggests the low development of the banking habit in these countries, which is partly a result of the inadequacy of banking facilities and the fact that the majority of the people fail to realize the safety and usefulness of bank deposits. This pattern of currency composition obviously tends to limit the activities of the central bank authority as to its power to control money and credit through its control over bank reserves, bank credit, and deposit money.

The scope of central bank control in underdeveloped economies is also limited by the state of undevelopment of the money market. In these countries, side by side with the "organized" money market as dominated by commercial banks, operate a great variety of unorganized moneylenders with entirely differ-

TABLE 15–1
Ratios of Demand Deposits to Money Supply in Some Selected Countries (February 1966)

Canada	75	Burma	25
France	63	Ethiopia	26
Italy	73	India	33
Japan	79	Korea	45
United Kingdom	80	Pakistan	40
United States	80	United Arab Republic	32
Australia	80	VietNam	30

Source: International Financial Statistics, 1966.

ent business practices. The organized money market is loose and undeveloped, characterized by inadequate banking development and the limited availability of credit instruments used for short-term borrowing and lending, such as commercial bills of exchange, short-term government securities, and bankers' acceptances. There are no discount markets in the true sense of the term. With undeveloped discount markets, the central banks have only a loose contact with commercial banks. If the central banks have some direct influence on the organized money markets through its control over banking operations, the activities of moneylenders are completely out of the fold of central bank control. Yet, moneylenders, in most underdeveloped countries, cover a large portion of the rural and small-trade sectors and the low-income section of the urban population. There is no connection whatsoever between the organized money markets, represented by commercial banks and other financial institutions, and the activities of the moneylenders. They usually operate with their own funds and seldom resort to the credit facilities of commercial banks. They are free and independent in their policies and methods of business. In the absence of a link between the organized money markets and the unorganized moneylenders, there is a wide gap between money rates prevailing in the money market and those charged by moneylenders. While rates charged by commercial banks are relatively low, as they are influenced by central banking operations, rates charged by unorganized moneylenders may go up to hundreds of percent per year. In a number of countries, even in the organized money markets, the central banks have little influence over money rates, since commercial banks in these countries are more or less self-sufficient and therefore have little need for advance or rediscounting facilities from the central banks. This is particularly true in countries where the banking system is dominated by the branch offices of foreign banks which, in periods of tight credit, can call on their head offices in foreign money centers to obtain additional reserves for credit expansion instead of relying on local central banks for accommodation.

Capital markets in underdeveloped countries are either nonexistent or undeveloped. The propensity to save in these economies is rather low, as a consequence of the low level of national income. The overwhelming majority of low-income earners hardly have the capacity to save. The inequality of income distribution, however, makes it possible for a small segment of the population to save. But, in view of the small size of the upper-income group—which is the case of most underdeveloped countries—total savings are not large. Where savings are available, they are not available for investments in shares and bonds, owing to the high liquidity premium attached to gold and precious stones, the habit of hoarding, the desire to invest in immovable properties, and the extravagant consumption propensity by some of the large-income earners. In lieu of savings accounts, savings certificates, corporate bonds and shares, gold and real estate are traditional means in which savings are held in underdeveloped economies. These traditional habits, coupled with political unrest and social disturbances and the lack of confidence in corporate enterprises which prevail in some underdeveloped countries, give birth to a hostile attitude on the part of savers toward investment in bonds and shares. These factors, together with the inadequacy of institutional facilities for the mobilization of savings resources, have prevented the development of capital markets in some of these underdeveloped regions. The absence of capital markets tends to limit still further the scope of central bank control. The central banks are in no position to influence long-term money rates and thus the volume of long-term investments, income, and employment.

WHY CENTRAL BANKS?

Since the banking and credit structure is primitive in most underdeveloped countries, why was it necessary for these countries to establish central banks at all? There are several reasons which account for the establishment of central banks in these various countries. In the first place, although they are circumscribed in their control operations by the undevelopment of the money markets and the absence or quasi-absence of capital markets, these central banks can contribute significantly to maintaining stability through the development and use of new central banking techniques and the adaptation of traditional control instruments to their specific problems.

In the second place, they can help finance government spending by making loans and advances to the government and development institutions (to the extent that this does not seriously interfere with their responsibility for promoting domestic price stability), and assisting in offering government obligations to banks, financial institutions, and the public at large.

In the third place, they can help promote the development and growth of the banking and credit structure. While this is not a concern of central banks in industrially advanced countries where the money and capital markets are highly developed, it is one of the major responsibilities of central banks in underdeveloped countries. Without developed money and capital markets, the effectiveness of central bank control is limited and savings resources cannot be efficiently mobilized for productive operations. These central banks can contribute to the development of the banking and financial structure by encouraging and assisting private commercial banks in opening branch offices in urban as well as provincial areas, by assisting in the establishment of state commercial banks to expand credit facilities in areas where private banking is inadequate or unavailable, and by establishing institutes for the training of banking specialists to meet the need of expanding banking facilities. They can assist in widening the scope of the money market by making rediscounting facilities available to private commercial banks and other financial institutions against securities whose market they wish to develop, such as Treasury bills, other government securities, and commercial paper. They can also assist in laying the foundation for the establishment of capital markets by preparing to act as intermediaries between buyers and sellers of corporate bonds and shares.

Last but not least, national prestige was also a basic factor accounting for the establishment of central banks in these various countries, especially in former colonies and protectorates where all monetary and economic policy decisions were made by foreign authorities. It was an assertion of their monetary independence.

INSTRUMENTS OF CENTRAL BANK CONTROLS

Central banks in underdeveloped areas are vested with broad statutory control powers. Apart from the traditional instruments of monetary control, such as open market operations, discount policy, and variable reserve requirements, a large number of these central banks are also empowered to impose liquidity ratios or securities reserve requirements against bank deposits, to fix ceilings on interest rates on, and the volume of, commercial bank loans, and to use other direct control devices. These instruments are frequently used selectively. This reflects in part the desire of underdeveloped countries to divert credit to fields preferred for development purposes, and in part, the undeveloped structure of financial markets.

Discount Policy

Discount policy is governed by two basic functions of the central bank: the obligation to act as a "lender of last resort" and the duty to regulate the volume of bank credit. The central bank, through its discount window, provides commercial banks with additional means for the conversion of certain of their liquid assets into cash when their cash reserves are adversely affected and fall below the minimum requirements, or when they need additional reserves for other liquidity purposes. The discount policy of the central bank can be exercised under two forms: the central bank can either change the discount rate, or vary the terms and conditions attaching to its various discounts and advances, or a combination of both.

The efficient functioning of the discount mechanism as a quantitative control instrument, we can recall, requires (a) the dependence of the commercial banks upon the central bank for advances and rediscounting, (b) the holding on the part of commercial banks of adequate amounts of those credit instruments which are eligible for rediscounting or for use as collateral against central bank advances, and (c) a well-developed money market. In view of these criteria, the use of the discount mechanism as a general instrument of monetary and credit control is not effective in most underdeveloped economies, as none of the above requirements is fulfilled, perhaps with the exception of India and a few countries in Latin America where the money market is fairly well developed and commercial banks operate on narrow margins of reserves and rely heavily on the central bank for accommodation.

Discount policy, instead, is used in these various countries mostly as a selective device either to restrain the expansion of particular types of credit or to encourage the flow of credit to channels considered as essential from the standpoint of economic development. The selective use of the discount mechanism is in the form of differential discount rates, with preferential rates applicable to certain types of credit, and penalty rates to some other kinds of loans. Differential discount rates have been used by several countries in Asia and Latin America, such as Argentina, Chile, Colombia, Costa Rica, Guatemala, India, Korea, Peru, and Venezuela. The criteria for differential discount rates vary from country to country. They are either based on different classes of borrowers, various forms of loans, or the end uses of credit. For instance, in the 1950's, in Columbia, preferential discount rates were set for paper representing medium-term loans for industry, cattle raising, irrigation, and low-cost housing. In Peru, preferential rates were in effect for agricultural, industrial and mining paper, and for advances to the government. In Guatemala, preferential rates were granted to the rediscounting of paper arising from agricultural, stock raising, and industrial operations; penalty rates were applied to loans arising from import operations. The Bank of Korea charged rates slightly lower than the basic rate for the rediscounting of paper arising from agricultural production and for import and export financing. Rates charged by the Reserve Bank of India for paper on loans to cooperative associations were two percent below the bank rate. In Chile, multiple discount rates were applied to various borrowing institutions, such as the state bank and other governmental credit institutions, public agencies, the railroad industry, agricultural and commercial cooperatives, commercial banks, and municipal governments.

In view of restraining banks and other financial institutions from taking advantage of the liberal access to central bank credit facilities which could lead to undesirable expansion of bank credit, a number of central banks fix maximum ceilings on the amount of advances and rediscounting which they would be willing to grant to banks. In some countries, such as Uruguay and Venezuela, rediscounting ceilings have been determined by law. In some other countries, such as Bolivia, Chile, the Dominican Republic, Guatemala, Korea, Peru, Vietnam, maximum advance and rediscount ceilings have been determined by the central bank, in accordance with the rate of credit expansion and prevailing general economic and financial conditions. By raising or lowering rediscount ceilings, the central bank can increase or reduce its accommodation to commercial banks and other lending institutions. In periods of heavy inflationary pressures, lowering rediscount ceilings, coupled with increases in the bank rate, has been resorted to by various central banks as a means to restrain the expansion of bank credit.

Restriction or liberalization of the rules regarding the conditions of paper eligible for rediscounting or as collateral against advances has also been used by a number of central banks in addition to changing discount rates and rediscount ceilings. For instance, in 1951-52, the Bank of Korea was authorized by the Monetary Board to make advances to banking institutions against promissory notes, bills of exchange, and other credit documents arising from various industrial operations, building construction, and operations of public institutions and enterprises specified by the government, among other things. The list of paper eligible as collateral against central bank advances was reduced substantially by the Monetary Board in late 1957.[2]

It should be noted that central banks in underdeveloped economies, like those in developed nations, are authorized to make loans and advances to their government. This is in fact one of the *raisons d'être* of central banks in underdeveloped countries. But to guard against the possibility that the government of these countries, in their drive for rapid economic development, may unduly resort to central bank credit to finance overambitious development programs that would generate heavy inflationary pressures, there are provisions in the central bank legislation of these various countries to limit the amount of credit that the central bank could grant to the government. In Burma, for example, in terms of the Union Bank of Burma Act of 1952 (Art. 61), the amount of direct advances which can be made by the Union Bank to the government cannot exceed 15 percent of the estimated budgetary revenues for the fiscal year in which the advances are made. The purchase of Treasury bills by the Union Bank during any given fiscal year is subject to a fixed ceiling. Ceilings are also to be fixed annually for the purchases of government-guaranteed debentures issued by such government agencies as the Industrial Development Corporation, and the Electricity Supply Board.[3]

In Argentina, in the late 1950's, the ceiling on central bank loans and advances to the government was fixed at 15 percent of the average of the preceding three years' revenue. In Nicaragua, the ceiling was 10 percent of the assets of the central bank. In Sierra Leone, central bank advances are limited to 5 percent of current government budget revenues.[4] These statutory limitations appear to

[2] S. Gethyn Davies (ed.), *Central Banking in South and East Asia* (Hong Kong: Hong Kong U. P., 1960), p. 98.

[3] *Central Banking in South and East Asia, op. cit.*, p. 7.

[4] Brazil is an exception. The National Monetary Council is required to authorize the central bank to cover, by direct purchase of Treasury bills, any portion of the government deficit not financed through other means.

offer only paper protection. The central bank, as advisor to the government, is legally obligated to advise the government on the monetary implications of fiscal policy. But that is all. In the final analysis it can hardly refuse credit to the government which needs it to meet its obligations.

Open-Market Policy

Central banks in underdeveloped countries are all explicitly or implicitly empowered to engage in open-market operations as a means to influence bank reserves and the supply of money. But to a large number of these central banks, open-market operations still remain a dream, owing to the absence of securities markets in which securities operations can be conducted. In some other countries, where securities markets are still undeveloped, the scope of the use of open-market operations as a control instrument remains very limited.

As a consequence of the absence or undevelopment of markets for securities, open-market policy in underdeveloped economies has been directed by central banks toward assisting the financing of government spending by promoting the maximum sale of government securities, and toward stimulating the development of securities markets. In their efforts to develop markets for securities, a number of central banks have pegged the prices of government securities to avoid unduly large price fluctuations which would discourage institutional as well as individual investors from holding securities. The effort of some central banks in this direction, however, has been hampered by the desire of the government to avoid high costs of the public debt by setting unrealistically high prices for its obligations. Since rates on government securities in these various countries have been comparatively low in relation to rates on other loans and investment opportunities, financial institutions, as well as the public, have been reluctant to invest in government securities. Consequently, securities offered by the governments of these countries have mostly ended up in the vault of the central bank.

While open-market policy has been used by various central banks in underdeveloped areas primarily as a means to facilitate the financing of government spending and to promote the development of securities markets, it has been used for monetary management purposes by several central banks at times of heavy inflationary pressures. But unlike the Federal Reserve and central banks of some industrially advanced countries which conduct open-market operations mainly in government securities, open-market policy undertaken by these central banks involves not only government securities but also a variety of other public and private obligations. This reflects, in part, the desire of some of these central banks to avoid selling large quantities of government securities which could upset the government securities market which they undertake to develop, and in part, their insufficient holdings of government securities for the purpose of open-market operations.

Thus in addition to operations in government securities, a number of central banks at one time or another have engaged in open-market operations involving their own obligations. The sale of these central bank obligations, just like the sale of government securities, tends to reduce bank reserves (and the supply of money). The central banks which have been authorized to sell their own obligations for control purposes include the central banks of Argentina, Ceylon, Chile, Costa Rica, El Salvador, Ecuador, the Dominican Republic, Korea, Paraguay, and the Philippines. The conditions of issue of these obligations differ in different countries, and they bear different names, but their purpose is the same; they provide the central bank with a means to reduce excessive liquidity in the money market. For instance, the obligations which may be issued by the central banks of Korea, Costa Rica, Guatemala, Ecuador, and Nicaragua are referred to as stabilization bonds. Those which may be issued by the central bank of Honduras are called "absorption certificates." These are all general obligations of the central bank in that they are not tied to any particular central bank assets. The obligations issued by the central bank of Argentina and Honduras have been participating certificates which are specific obligations supported by specific central bank assets. To make their obligations more attractive to potential investors, some central banks add special features to their obligations. For instance, obligations issued by the central bank of El Salvador could be made receivable in payment of taxes and customs duties.

In addition to operations in their own obligations, a number of central banks in Latin America, such as the central banks of Colombia, Chile, Ecuador, Guatemala, Mexico, the Dominican Republic, and Venezuela, have engaged in operations in mortgage obligations of government-owned mortgage banks and other public institutions. These central banks, especially the Bank of Mexico, the Bank of the Republic of Colombia, and the Central Bank of Chile, hold sizable amounts of mortgage obligations as a means to provide these mortgage institutions with long-term funds. These central banks have also engaged in operations involving medium- and long-term general obligations issued by both public and private agricultural and industrial enterprises.[5]

While foreign-exchange operations have been carried on by most central banks primarily for international payment purposes, some central banks in Latin America and Asia have at times sold foreign exchange in the exchange market as a means to reduce inflationary pressures. The sale of foreign exchange, coupled with the liberalization of import controls, would help absorb a segment of money income from the spending stream and increase the volume of imports and the supply of goods. This would contribute to relieving inflationary pressures. The effectiveness of foreign-exchange open-market operations, of course, would depend upon the amount of exchange reserves held by the central bank. Some central banks have refrained from this type of operation either because of inadequate holdings of foreign exchange or because of fear of exhaustion of exchange reserves which would make it difficult for them to meet large future payment deficits. It should, however, be noted that under a system of multiple

[5] Frank Tamagna, *Central Banking in Latin America*, C.E.M.L.A., 1965, pp. 137-140.

exchange rates which prevails in a large number of underdeveloped countries, there is greater room for open market operations in foreign exchange, since under such a system, the sale of foreign exchange for control purposes would not cause as heavy a burden on the volume of exchange reserves of the central bank as under a unitary fixed exchange rate arrangement.

Cash Reserve Requirements

In underdeveloped countries where open-market operations are either non-existent or limited in scope, and discount policy, in general, has limited influence, variable cash reserve requirements have been used frequently in some countries and have proved to be the most powerful instrument of credit control. Unlike the use of the discount mechanism whose effect is uncertain, lowering or raising the legal reserve ratios immediately relieves or immobilizes commercial banks' excess reserves.

The composition of legal reserves varies from country to country. While in Bolivia, Cambodia, Ceylon, Costa Rica, Ecuador, Guatemala, India, Pakistan, among others, legal reserves have represented deposit balances held by commercial banks with the central bank; in Colombia, Korea, Peru, Venezuela, Honduras, Nicaragua, Thailand, and other countries, legal reserves were composed of both vault cash and deposits with the central bank. In some of the latter countries, however, the amount of vault cash which could be included in legal reserves was subject to certain upper limits (for example, no more than 25 percent in Korea, 15 percent in Peru).

In most countries, different legal reserve ratios have been fixed for different classes of deposits, with higher ratios for demand deposits and lower ratios for time liabilities. In some other countries, such as Thailand, however, the legal reserve ratios have been uniform for all classes of deposits. In many countries, the range within which the central bank may vary the legal reserve ratios is bound by certain upper and lower limits which are fixed by law. For instance, in Chile, the range has been 5 to 10 percent for demand deposits, and 2 to 8 percent for time deposits. In India, the reserve requirements for scheduled banks vary from 5 to 20 percent for demand liabilities, and 2 to 8 percent for time liabilities. In some countries, the range of variation has one open end, no upper limits, or no lower limits. In Bolivia, for example there have been no lower limits fixed for the legal reserve ratios, but the upper limits have been 40 and 20 percent for demand and time deposits respectively. Likewise, in Kenya, Tanzania, Uganda, and Guyana, the central banks may fix the legal reserve ratio up to a maximum of 20 percent. In Pakistan, Venezuela, and Trinidad-Tobago no maximum limits have been specified. In Zambia and Malawi, neither a ceiling nor a floor has been established in the statutes.

In a number of countries, while the range within which reserve requirements may be varied is limited, the central bank, in periods of pronounced inflation, is empowered to impose supplementary cash reserve requirements against increases in deposits after a specified date, and the requirements may be set as high as 100 percent. The central banks of Colombia, Chile, Costa Rica, Ecuador, the Dominican Republic, Guatemala, Korea, Mexico, the Philippines, among others, are vested with such powers. This power has been used only occasionally in some of these countries. In some others, it has remained a standby authority which could be resorted to by the central bank in times of excessive expansion of bank credit. One of the merits of the use of supplementary cash reserve requirements is that it would eliminate the problem involved in an across-the-board increase in the legal reserve ratio, which tends to affect adversely banks which have low margins of excess reserves at the time when the ratio is raised.

Variable cash-reserve requirements have been relied upon as a major weapon of monetary and credit control by central banks in most underdeveloped countries. They have proved effective in several countries. But in some other countries, such as Ceylon and Viet Nam, the effectiveness of this instrument appeared to have been limited mostly because of the limited range of variation of the legal reserve ratios relative to the liquidity position of commercial banks. To be sure, raising the legal reserve ratios to sufficiently high levels would dry up banks' excess reserves. But such action would tend to penalize severely relatively young and small domestic banks, while foreign banks can increase their reserves by calling on their head offices in foreign countries.

While variable cash reserve requirements have been used generally as an instrument of control, in some countries they have been used at times selectively as a means to promote the flow of bank credit to preferred fields. For instance, in Colombia, the Dominican Republic, Mexico, and Nicaragua, for development purposes, certain kinds of loans extended by commercial banks to key sectors of the economy have been allowed to be included in the computation of legally required reserves.

Securities Reserve Requirements

Securities reserve requirements or liquidity ratios which were first introduced by a number of European countries are currently adopted by many central banks in underdeveloped countries. Under this arrangement, commercial banks are required to hold minimum required reserves against their deposit liabilities in the form of specified liquid assets, such as cash and government securities.

Securities reserve requirements can be used either as a general instrument of credit policy or as a means to channel bank funds into financing governmental budgetary requirements and to promote the development of government securities markets. In countries where securities markets are fairly well developed, securities reserve requirements have been introduced primarily to restrain the expansion of bank credit, reinforcing other general instruments of credit control. For example, Belgium and France resorted to securities reserve requirements after World War II, as a means to limit the expansion of credit by commercial banks to the private sector by preventing them from liquidating their holdings of government securities which had increased sharply during the war and postwar periods to obtain additional reserves to support loan and investment expansion.[6]

In underdeveloped economies, on the other hand, liquidity ratios have been used mainly as a means to channel bank resources into the financing of government spending. This source of financing helps to reduce the needs for central bank advances. Thus while the instrument is a convenient means of raising funds for the government, it does exert a stabilizing influence in the sense that it precludes the need of otherwise greater amounts of central bank credit to cover budget deficits. In addition, the requirements would help to develop the habit of holding government securities on the part of the commercial banks, a first step toward the development of government securities markets.

A large number of central banks have the statutory authority to impose liquidity ratios (Argentina, Cambodia, Chile, The Dominican Republic, Ecuador, Guyana, Honduras, Indonesia, Iraq, Jordan, Malawi, Mexico, Nicaragua, Philippines, Turkey, Vietnam, and Zambia). The characteristics of securities reserve requirements vary widely from country to country, especially in regard to their composition and the types of bank liabilities against which they are required. For instance, in Chile, the Dominican Republic, Honduras, Mexico, Nicaragua, and the Philippines, demand and time deposits are subject to separate liquidity ratios, with higher ratios for demand deposits and lower ratios for time liabilities. In the Republic of Vietnam, Turkey, like in the Netherlands, uniform liquidity ratios can be set for total deposits. In Indonesia, and Iraq, like in France and Canada, liquidity ratios were required against demand liabilities alone. The securities eligible for liquidity ratios consist mostly of government securities (Vietnam, Chile, Peru, Honduras, Uruguay, and the Dominican Republic, among others). In some countries, aside from government securities, certain nongovernment securities may also be allowed in the computation of liquidity ratios. For instance, in the Philippines, negotiable paper eligible for rediscounting at the central bank can be included. In Ecuador, commercial banks can hold part of securities reserves in obligations approved by the National Securities Commission. In Argentina, special series of bonds issued by the government have been eligible. In Cambodia, bank liquid assets are acceptable.

In many countries, such as the Philippines, Chile, Indonesia, Nicaragua, and Uruguay, cash reserves may be included in the computation of securities reserve requirements. In some other countries, cash reserves are to be excluded. The ranges within which liquidity ratios may be varied by the central banks of these various countries are fixed by law, with both upper and lower limits. In addition to these general limits, the central banks of a few countries, such as the Philippines, Honduras, and the Dominican Republic, are also empowered to impose supplementary liquidity ratios against increases in bank deposits, which could be as high as 100 percent.

[6] Peter G. Fousek, *Foreign Central Banking: The Instruments of Monetary Policy* (Federal Reserve Bank of New York, 1957), p. 58.

Although many central banks in underdeveloped areas have the authority to impose securities reserve requirements, the instrument has been used mainly by a number of countries in Latin America. In some other countries, such as Cambodia, the Philippines, and Vietnam, it has not been used. Where liquidity ratios have been used, they have proved to be a useful device assuring a convenient source of financing for the government. Their effectiveness as an instrument of monetary and credit control remains to be seen, as they are yet to be used for this purpose. But we can safely say that like variable cash reserve requirements, liquidity ratios are potentially a powerful control device. As their liquid assets are locked in as a consequence of securities reserve requirements, commercial banks, in order to obtain additional reserves for lending operations, would have to liquidate other less liquid assets; but in view of the limited marketability of securities in underdeveloped countries, owing to the undeveloped state of financial markets, the capital losses involved in such attempts would be substantial. Banks, of course, can rely on the discount window of the central bank for accommodation, but there they would have to face higher discount rates and more restrictive rediscount ceilings. The use of liquidity ratios thus would not only help restrain the expansion of bank credit but also to improve the effectiveness of other instruments of central bank control.

Direct Credit Regulation

In addition to the above instruments of monetary management, several central banks are granted the power to use direct control devices. The forms of these devices vary widely from country to country, in accordance with their special conditions and problems, and in the same country, these devices vary over time.

Interest Rate Ceilings. Central banks in many underdeveloped economies, such as Chile, Colombia, Costa Rica, Korea, Vietnam, Uganda, and Guyana, are given statutory authority not only to determine maximum rates of interest payable by commercial banks to their customers on their various classes of deposits but also to fix maximum rates of interest which commercial banks may charge for their loans. While the power of central banks to fix ceilings on interest rates which may be paid by banks on deposits is aimed mainly at avoiding unsound banking competition and practices, the purpose of the authority to fix maximum rates for bank loans is either to lower money market rates and to maintain an orderly, consistent structure of rates, or to assure that credit is available for productive operations at relatively low cost.

The financial institutions for which the central bank may fix maximum interest rates vary in different countries. In Colombia, Korea, Mexico, and Vietnam, among others, this power is to apply only to banking institutions, while in Ecuador, Guatemala, and the Dominican Republic, it covers all private, semipublic, as well as public, credit institutions. In Korea, Kenya, Tanzania, Uganda, Zambia, and Guyana, the central banks may also issue instructions specifying the purposes and conditions under which loans, advances, or investments may be made.

Loan Ceilings. Several central banks in Asia, Latin America, and Africa (Bolivia, Chile, Colombia, Costa Rica, Mexico, South Korea, Vietnam, Kenya, Tanzania, Uganda, Zambia, and Guyana) have the authority to fix ceilings on the aggregate volume of loans, advances, and investments of commercial banks or to place limits on the increase in the total of such assets.[7] This device, however, has been used only occasionally by a few central banks. For instance, in Korea, in 1958, new loans and investments made by banking institutions were not to exceed private time deposits received, proceeds from repayments of old loans, and some other sources. In 1959 the increase in bank credit was limited to the growth of time and savings deposits. In Bolivia in 1953 new loans made by commercial banks were limited only to the proceeds from repayments of old loans.

This is potentially a powerful device of credit control. The central bank can check the expansion of bank credit simply by fixing low ceilings for bank loans and investments regardless of their liquidity position. Where the device has been used, however, it has contributed insignificantly to reducing inflationary pressures, since loan ceilings were believed to have been so high that they left plenty of room for banks to expand loans and investments.

The applications of the loan-ceiling device, just like variable cash reserve requirements and variable liquidity ratios, presents inequities and difficulties. If uniform ceilings are applied to all banks, they are likely to cause some difficulty to those banks that may have expanded loans at slower rates than their competitors. "By penalizing the slow and steady banks and favoring those who did the very thing that is now being sought to control, it may create the same bad feeling which arose in the mind of the son who stayed with his father against his prodigal brother."[8] This could be avoided by allowing higher ceilings for banks which have expanded credit less rapidly than others. This, however, would tend to defeat the objective for which the device is used, namely to hold down inflationary pressures. While some banks are prohibited from increasing loans and investments, other banks are allowed to go on expanding credit, which would add more to inflation. Owing to some of these problems, the device should be used only in periods of grave inflationary pressures when other measures prove inadequate to prevent a rapid expansion of bank credit.

While the loan ceiling device is designed primarily as a general anti-inflationary instrument, the monetary legislation in some countries (Korea and Vietnam) also provides room for its selective use in the form of differential ceilings (or differential limits on rates of increase in bank loans) for different categories of bank loans and investments. Thus to promote development high ceilings may be set for agricultural and industrial loans and low ceilings for loans which are

[7] *Foreign Central Banking, op. cit.*, p. 80.

[8] S. N. Sen, *Central Banking in Underdeveloped Money Markets* (Calcutta, 1952), p. 167.

nonessential from the development standpoint. The device can also be used selectively to restrain the overexpansion of certain kinds of loans and investments which, if left unchecked, could lead to general inflation. The selective use of this device was attempted by the Bank of Korea in early 1952, but it was discontinued late that year because of the difficult problem of enforcement.

Import-Predeposit Requirements. Under a system of import-predeposit requirements, either commercial banks are required to deposit in a special account with the central bank funds equal to some prescribed percentages of the value of import letters of credit they have issued in favor of importers, or the latter are required to deposit with the central bank specified amounts of funds necessary for import transactions. Such advance deposit requirements tend to reduce bank reserves (and the supply of money). The magnitude of bank reserves so reduced depends upon the size of the deposit requirements. If the requirements are more than 100 percent of the value of imports, they not only reduce in advance bank reserves (and the supply of money), which would otherwise take place only when foreign exchange is released, but also would immobilize for certain periods of time bank reserves or importers' cash assets, since the amount of deposits in excess of the value of imports will not be released until the import transaction is liquidated.

In several countries in Asia and Latin America, namely Argentina, Chile, Colombia, Ecuador, the Philippines, Peru, and Vietnam, import-predeposit requirements have been used at one time or another as a measure of credit control. While the ratios of advance import deposits to the value of imports may be uniform for all classes of imports, in countries where these requirements have been used, different ratios have been applied to different categories of imports. In the Philippines, for instance, the amount of cash deposits required against the import of "nonessentials" were as high as 200 percent. In Chile, lower ratios have been fixed for imports that were high on the priority list, such as fuels and food products, and very high ratios for luxury products. For instance, in 1960, the maximum ratios in Chile were up to 3,500 percent.[9] In Vietnam, on the other hand, in 1955, the required ratios varied from 25 to 100 percent of the value of import letters of credit.

ADMINISTRATIVE STRUCTURE AND ORGANIZATION

Most central banks in underdeveloped countries are government-owned institutions (Burma, Ceylon, Costa Rica, Honduras, Korea, Nicaragua, Paraguay, the Philippines, Vietnam, Bolivia, Guatemala, El Salvador, Peru). There are also several semipublic central banks, such as the central banks of Pakistan, Mexico, Ecuador, Chile, and Venezuela. The Bank of the Republic of Colombia is a privately owned institution.

These central banks operate under the general direction of a board of direc-

[9] *Central Banking in Latin America, op. cit.*, p. 187.

tors, which in various countries is referred to as the Monetary Board or Administrative Council. The number of directors, the way by which they are selected, and the various groups from which they are selected vary from country to country. In regard to state-owned central banks, most of the directors are appointed by the government. They may be selected from officers of official banks, representatives of banking, commercial, industrial, and other economic interests, and from among citizens who have had experience in economic, monetary, and banking problems. In addition, in many countries, several high-ranking government officials also serve as ex officio members of the central bank board. In the Philippines, for instance, the central bank is administered by a seven-member Monetary Board, which includes the Minister of Finance, the Governor of the central bank, the president of the state-owned National Bank, the Chairman of the Board of the Development Bank (they are all ex officio members), and three members selected from the public. The central bank of the Republic of Argentina is under the direction of a twelve-member board composed of the president and vice-president of the bank, five members from official banks, and five representatives of various banking, financial, and economic interests. The seven-member Monetary Board of the Bank of Korea includes the Minister of Finance, the governor of the bank, and five members selected from candidates submitted to the President of the Republic by the Reconstruction Board, the Ministry of Agriculture and Industry, and the Korean Chamber of Commerce. The six-member Board of the Central Bank of Reserve of El Salvador consists of the Ministers of Agriculture, Economy, and Finance, and three members selected from banking, agricultural, and industrial organizations.

In regard to central banks of mixed ownership the number of directors appointed by the government bears little or no relation to the proportion of its ownership. The government of Venezuela holds 50 percent of the total shares of the central bank but appoints four members of the seven-member board of directors, including the Minister of Finance serving as an ex officio member; the remaining three are elected by business associations, private commercial banks, and the general assembly of stockholders, respectively. The government of Pakistan, which holds 51 percent of the capital of the state bank, appoints six of the nine members of the Central Board of Directors of the bank. The other members are elected by shareholders. The Monetary Board of the Bank of the Republic of Colombia, a private central bank, is composed of the Minister of Finance, the Ministers of Agriculture and Development, the Director of the Planning and Technical Services Department, and the Manager of the Bank.

In many countries, the Minister of Finance plays an influential role in the overall management of the central bank. In Argentina, Bolivia, Chile, Costa Rica, Peru, Paraguay, Uruguay, and Venezuela, among others, the Minister of Finance advises the President of the government and proposes to him the appointment of directors and/or central bank executives. In Colombia, Ecuador, El Salvador, the Dominican Republic, Guatemala, Honduras, etc., the Minister of Finance not only advises the President of the government on the appointment of directors but also serves as an ex officio member of the central bank board.

While the overall administration of the central bank is in the hands of the Monetary Board or Administrative Council, it is the President (or Director General, or Governor) who, as the chief executive of the central bank, is in charge of the daily operations of the central bank, carrying out the decisions of the monetary board. In a number of countries such as Bolivia, El Salvador, the Dominican Republic, Korea, Pakistan, and the Philippines, the President or Governor of the central bank is appointed by the President of the government. On the other hand, in some other countries—including Chile, Mexico, and Peru—the President or Governor is elected by the central board of directors.

In most countries decisions regarding the routine service, as well as control operations of the central bank, are made by the board of directors which, as we have seen, are dominated by government officials and government-appointed directors. In some countries (Brazil, Bolivia, Uruguay, Chile, and Peru), however, all or certain policy decisions are shared by the central bank and other government agencies. In Brazil, for example, while the service operations are carried out by the Central Bank of the Republic (and to a lesser extent, by the Bank of Brazil), policy decisions are made by the National Monetary Council, whose basic responsibility is to regulate money, credit, foreign exchange, and the operations of both public and private financial institutions. The council is composed of nine members, of whom the Minister of Finance acts as chairman, the President of the Bank of Brazil, and the President of the National Economic Development Bank are ex officio members; the remaining six members are appointed by the President of the Republic. Four of the last six members serve as directors, with one acting as president, of the central bank. Policy decisions made by the council are executed by the Central Bank of the Republic. In Bolivia, decisions regarding reserve requirements, interest ceilings, and direct controls, among other things, are made by the President of the government and the National Council for Monetary Stabilization, upon recommendation of the central bank.

The appointment of central bank executives, and of most or all directors by the government, the participation of nondirector government officials in monetary-policy decisions, and the unique position of the Minister of Finance—the highest government official responsible for the financial affairs of the state—reflect the controlling influence of the government in the formulation of monetary policy. After all, monetary policy is an integral part of a country's general economic and financial policy, the formulation of which is the responsibility of the government; it should be formulated in the light of the government's overall economic policy. In some countries, the Minister of Finance (or other government officials) is granted broad authority regarding central banking matters. In Mexico, for example, the Minister of Finance has the power to suspend or veto measures taken by the Director General and the Board of Directors of the Bank of Mexico. In Colombia, policy decisions of the Bank of the Republic require the affirmative vote of the Minister of Finance.[10] In Tanzania, a Treasury representative, who is a voting member of the central bank's board of governors, may postpone any of the decisions made by the board. In Kenya, he may suspend a vote of the board and refer the matter to the Minister of Finance, whose decision is binding. In Trinidad-Tobago, and Zambia, the Minister of Finance, or his representative, after consultation with the central bank's governor, may issue general directives that bind the central bank to implement the policies of the government.

But central banks in underdeveloped countries are far from being completely subordinated to the government, serving at its pleasure. There are provisions in the central banking legislation of a number of countries which are designed to give the central bank a substantial degree of autonomy within the structure of the government. It is recognized that unless the central bank is granted a more or less independent position, and some measure of freedom of action, it would not be in a position to develop objective viewpoints in its capacity as advisor to the government on general economic and financial matters. Thus, in some countries, the President and Vice-President (or Governor and Deputy-Governor) of the central bank are appointed by the government for fixed periods. With the exception of violations specified by law, they cannot be removed from office, and the terms and conditions of their services cannot be altered by the government during the tenure of their office. They can also make their influence felt through their presence in government policy-making agencies and committees of which they are members. For example, in Argentina, Honduras, and Paraguay, among other countries, the executives of the central bank, together with cabinet members and other government officials, are members of various committees in charge of planning and coordinating the general economic and financial policy of the government. The officials of the central bank may represent the minority in these policy decision-making committees or agencies, but, owing to the prestige of their bank, their expert knowledge in the field of economics and finance, they may have an influential voice in the deliberations of these policy-formulating and policy-coordinating committees. Finally, they can also make their influence felt in their informal contacts with other government officials.

COMMERCIAL BANKING BY CENTRAL BANKS

Most commercial banks in underdeveloped countries are not authorized to conduct commercial banking operations. But in a number of countries, such as Bolivia, Cambodia, Laos, and Uruguay, the central bank is also engaged in commercial banking.

The mixing of central banking with commercial banking by the central bank has been a subject of much discussion. One of the arguments against commercial

[10] *Central Banking in Latin America,, op. cit.*, p. 94.

banking operations by the central bank is that by engaging in the commercial banking business, the central bank would place itself in the paradoxical position of being both a regulator and a competitor of private commercial banks. Inasmuch as the cooperation of commercial banks with the central bank is necessary for successful central banking operations, this kind of competition has to be avoided as it would antagonize commercial banks and cause them to be more reluctant in cooperating with the central bank. In addition, in the conduct of commercial business, the central bank may be unduly inclined to engage in profitable lending operations which could lead to too liberal expansion of credit. This is inconsistent with the responsibility of the central bank for supervising and controlling the monetary and credit system.

Those who favor the establishment of a commercial banking department within the central bank, on the other hand, contend that commercial operations would give a central bank opportunities to be in touch with the market, and to bring needed credit facilities to areas where credit extended by private banks is inadequate or unavailable. While the proper attitude of central banks in industrially advanced countries is to concentrate on central banking operations alone, what is proper for these central banks may not be so for central banks in underdeveloped areas, as they operate in different monetary and financial environements. In an underdeveloped country, because of lack of regular discounting by commercial banks because of the undevelopment of the money market, it may be necessary for the central bank to conduct certain amounts of business directly with the public, to establish regular, daily contacts with the money market, to influence money rates and financial policies of commercial banks. This would involve some competition with private banks, but competing with banks to keep in touch with and control the market, not to make a profit, does not appear to be undesirable at all. In a country where the banking system is undeveloped, where banks are mostly branch offices of foreign banks (whose activities are predominantly directed toward foreign trade and foreign exchange transactions), and where bank credit to the domestic sector is inadequate, the central bank may not only help to alleviate the problem of credit shortage but also to contribute to the development of the banking habit and broadening the monetary and credit base of the economy by engaging in commercial banking. This is an important function of the central bank in an underdeveloped economy. After all, what is there for the central bank to control if it does not make efforts to develop the banking system which is the foundation of its control operations? To minimize the antagonism generated by its commercial business, the central bank may gradually withdraw its banking operations from areas where private commercial banks are ready to establish their own facilities. This is in fact the pattern which was more or less followed by come central banks in Latin America which were engaged in commercial banking during their early years. With the expansion of commercial banking facilities, they withdrew gradually from dealing with the public, and the banking department was separated from the issue department to become an independent commercial bank.

At any rate, in underdeveloped countries where central banks are not authorized to engage in commercial banking operations, they have, nevertheless, contributed to the developement of the monetary, credit, and banking system by assisting in the development of state commercial banks, development banks, and other public credit institutions to make credit facilities available in those sectors of the economy where private credit facilities are inadequate. In Vietnam, for instance, the National Bank played an important role in the establishment of the Commercial Credit Bank (a state bank), which has provided short, medium, and long-term credit to both commercial and industrial enterprises. In Burma the Union Bank helped to set up the State Commercial Bank, a bank that has filled an important gap in the country's financial system by making credit for working capital available to local industries. In Ceylon the central bank took the initiative in the establishment of the Development Finance Corporation with broader powers to finance private industrial projects. In the Philippines the central bank has contributed to the development of an impressive system of rural banks.

SUMMARY

Central banks in underdeveloped countries have broad powers to control money and credit, ranging from the traditional instruments of discount policy, variable cash reserve requirements, and open-market operations to liquidity ratios and such direct control devices as interest ceilings, loan ceilings, and import-predeposit requirements. The instruments which are usually used by central banks in economically developed countries for general credit control purposes have been used selectively in several underdeveloped countries. This reflects partly the narrow scope of financial markets which prevents the propagation of impulses generated by central bank operations, and partly the desire to encourage the flow of credit to sectors of the economy considered as essential for the promotion of economic development. The effectiveness of the selective uses of the various instruments of monetary management, for development purposes, in general, appears to have been very limited. Their uses for quantitative credit controls in many countries, however, have contributed significantly to holding down inflationary pressures in times of inflation.

In most underdeveloped countries, the government has a controlling influence on the formulation of monetary policy. This is reflected by the fact that the overall management of the central bank is in the hands of the government officials and government-appointed directors and executives. This is necessary for the integration of monetary policy with general economic and financial policy, the formulation of which is the responsibility of the government. The central banks in these various countries, however, are not completely subordinated to the government. There are provisions in their central banking laws which grant the central banks some degree of autonomy within the government structure. In addition to these legal provisions, central bank officials can influence the formulation of monetary and economic policies through their membership in various policy-planning and coordinating committees and through their informal contacts with government officials in charge of the economic and financial affairs of the state.

Most central banks in underdeveloped countries are prohibited from doing business directly with the public. But there are several central banks which are engaged in commercial banking operations. While it is generally recognized that the proper attitude of a central bank is to concentrate on central banking operations only, it is, nevertheless, not unjustifiable for a central bank in an underdeveloped economy to engage in commercial business to keep in touch with and control the market, to assist in the development of the monetary and credit structure, and to offer needed credit facilities to the public where private banking facilities are inadequate or not available.

PROBLEMS

1. What are the major factors which tend to limit the scope of central bank control in underdeveloped countries? If the structure of their banking and credit system is undeveloped, why is it necessary for underdeveloped countries to establish central banks? Explain.

2. While the promotion of the development of the banking and credit structure is not a concern of central banking in industrially advanced countries, it could well be the major *raison d'être* of central banking in underdeveloped countries. Do you agree? Why or why not? Explain.

3. Why is it that, unlike most central banks in developed countries which rely primarily on general instruments of monetary mangement for control purposes, central banks in underdeveloped countries use them mostly on a selective basis? Describe various ways by which these instruments are used selectively.

4. What are securities reserves requirements? What are the purposes of these requirements in underdeveloped countries? Would the uses of variable securities reserve requirements involve the same problems as variable cash reserve requirements? If so, could these problems be eliminated by supplementary securities reserves requirements? Explain.

5. What are the various forms of open-market operations which have been undertaken in some underdeveloped countries? What are the objectives of these operations? Why is it that under the multiple exchange rates system, open-market operations in foreign exchange would not cause as heavy a burden on central bank reserves as under the unitary fixed exchange rate system? Explain.

6. What are differences, in forms and objectives, of the uses of discount policy in developed and underdeveloped economies?

7. What are arguments for and against commercial banking by central banks?

8. Describe some of the direct control devices at the disposal of central banks in underdeveloped areas. What are problems which you would expect to arise from the uses of these devices?

part IV

MONEY AND INCOME THEORY

chapter 16

The Value of Money: Concept and Measurement

We have discussed in Parts I, II, and III the nature and functions of money, the evolution of money, various monetary systems, the instruments for the transfer of money and credit, the markets for dealings in these instruments, and the operations of institutions which create and control money and credit. Part IV deals with monetary theory, which is the analysis of the influence of money on the economic process, namely, the relationships between money and the behavior of such economic variables as the general price level, the aggregate levels of output and employment, and the rate of economic growth. Monetary theory is thus macroeconomic theory as it deals with the relationships between aggregative economic variables in contrast with microeconomic theory, which is concerned with the analysis of the behavior of individual economic units, such as the behavior of individual firms, their output and costs, the behavior of individual consumers, the pricing of commodities, and the determination of wages. An understanding of the relationships between money and the above economic aggregates not only gives us insights into the effects of money on the functioning of the economic system but also serves as a guide to policy decisions which are actions designed to control these variables.

THE GENERAL PRICE LEVEL

When we speak of the value of money, we mean its exchange value or general purchasing power that is represented by the amount of "goods and services in general" that can be purchased by the unit of money. Since the amount of goods and services which can be obtained with a monetary unit depends upon their prices, it is apparent that the value of money depends upon prices. High prices of goods and services mean low exchange value of money. Conversely, low prices of goods and services mean high purchasing power of money. The value of money, therefore, varies inversely with the general price level, which is an average of individual prices. Inasmuch as prices are not equally important, the general price level would have to be a weighted average of some sort, so that the relative importance of the contribution of each individual price in the movement of the whole structure of prices may be accounted for. Assume that $p_1, p_2, \ldots, p_n$ are the prices of the n goods and services, and $w_1, w_2, \ldots, w_n$ represent their relative importance; then, the sum of the weighted prices is the general price level—that is,

$$w_1 p_1 + w_2 p_2 + \cdots + w_n p_n = P$$

The reciprocal of P represents the value of money or its general purchasing power, $V_m = 1/P$. An increase (decrease) in P is a decrease (increase) in V_m. Since changes in the general price level mean changes in the value of money, the study of factors which cause the value of money to change is the study of factors which cause the general price level to change.

The general price level, being an average, can change only when prices, in general, either move upward or downward. This change in the absolute level of prices, which is our main concern here, has to be differentiated with changes in the price of a good in relation to the prices of other goods, or relative prices. Relative prices change as production cost and technology (supply) and consumers' preferences (demand) change. It is conceivable that while the structure of relative prices changes, the general price level remains unchanged, as increases in some prices are offset by decreases in other prices. In a free-market economy, these changes in relative prices serve as guides to the allocation of economic resources; productive efforts would go to the production of the variety of goods which are most preferred by the consumers. It is true that, as a consequence of relative price changes, the composition of output and employment changes; but, the aggregate levels of income and employment will not change substantially. Resources simply move from the production of goods less favored by the consumers to the production of goods more favored by them. It is true that changes in relative prices enable some groups of individuals to gain (for example, producers of goods, the demand for which increases) and causes losses to some others (producers of goods, the demand for which decreases), but society as a whole would be in no way adversely affected by these changes. In point of fact, the welfare of society as a whole is enhanced as resources are allocated to their most efficient uses in accordance with consumers' preferences. On the other hand, changes in the general price level or the purchasing power of money generated by monetary forces, as will be seen, not only cause a redistribution of income and wealth between various groups of individuals in society, but are also a source of economic instability, causing substantial changes in the levels of real income and employment. It is for these reasons that the analysis of factors which cause the value of money or the general price level to change is important from both the theoretical and practical standpoints.

PRICE INDEXES

Nature

Changes in the value of money over time are measured by the use of price indexes. An index number is a device by which changes in the magnitude of a group of related variables can be combined into one single number that reflects the movements of these variables as a whole. The index-number technique consists in relating the magnitude of a set of variables at a period of time as a percentage of the magnitude of the same variables at another period of time taken as a base. The base magnitude of these variables is customarily given the number 100, which implies that it is one hundred percent of the value of the variables in the base year; as an example, suppose we have the following series of prices of a number of commodities for 1950 and 1952:

Commodities	Prices/lb	
	1950	1952
A	$0.25	$0.28
B	0.22	0.20
C	0.30	0.35
D	0.32	0.28
E	0.25	0.30

We can compile an index number to express the average change of these prices between 1950 and 1952, using 1950 as a base year. We first convert the prices in each series as percentages of the base year. These percentages are referred to as price relatives. By taking the average of these price relatives, we have an index number for prices in 1952 relative to the base year, that is, 1950 = 100 and 1942 = 105 (last line). This means that on the average, the prices of these commodities have risen by 5 percent during the 1950-52 period.

Commodities	Price Relatives	
	1950	1952
A	100	112
B	100	91
C	100	117
D	100	87
E	100	120
Total	500	527
Index (percent of 1950)	100	105

In this example, the index is the simple arithmetic mean of price relatives. If we assume that all of these prices are of equal importance, then this index can be used. If they are not equally important, then the index is misleading, since the prices of commodities which exert the most influence on the index could be the least important ones; we can allow for the difference in the importance of prices by weighting these prices with the values of these commodities in the base year (quantities time prices). We multiply the price relatives of each year by the base-year values, sum these products year by year, and divide the total for each year by the sum of the weights, and obtain the weighted arithmetic means of the price relatives. The weighted index indicates that prices, on the average, have declined by 3 percent between 1950 and 1952! This reflects the fact that the prices of the two most important commodities (B and D) have declined during the period.

The price index, being a statistical average, is an oversimplified measurement. It is possible that none of the individual prices supposed to be represented by the index may behave like the average. For instance, when the index for wholesale prices was 100 for 1960 and 110 for 1965, we say that on the

Commodities	Base-Year Value	Base-Year Value × Price Relatives 1950	1952
A	$400	400	448
B	600	600	546
C	200	200	234
D	800	800	696
E	100	100	120
Total		2100	2044
Index (percent of 1950)		100	97

average wholesale prices have increased by 10 percent during the 1960-65 period. Yet no single wholesale price may have displayed this behavior. Some prices may have risen by more than 10 percent, some other prices, by less than 10 percent, some prices may have remained unchanged, and still some prices may have fallen. The dispersion of the component prices from which price indexes are computed could be such that the average is deprived of much of its meaning. In practice, however, prices, in general, tend to move in the same direction since they are subject to a variety of common economic pressures, and it is because of this sympathetic movement that the use of price indexes to express changes in groups of related prices is justified. Admittedly, price indexes are not accurate (nor do the people who compile them claim them to be), but they are simple and useful devices which show the general direction of price changes.

Some Index-Number Problems

There are several problems involved in index numbers.

Purpose. In constructing an index number, first we would have to know the purpose for the use of such an index. For example, to measure the value of money in terms of "things in general," we would have to construct an index which is representative of the prices of all goods and services. To measure the value of money in terms of some groups of commodities such as consumer goods, we would have to construct an index for consumer prices. In regard to price indexes, there has been a change of emphasis from the general price level or the general purchasing power of money to the value of money in particular uses, reflected by indexes of groups of prices which are of particular interest to different groups of individuals in society. For example, retailers are interested in wholesale price indexes relative to retail price indexes. Wage earners are interested in the index of labor prices (wages) in relation to the consumer price index. Residential construction firms are interested in the measurement of construction costs and the prices of houses. And farmers are interested in the price index for manufactured products and the index of prices of farm products.

Inclusion and Exclusion. When the purpose of price index is defined, we have to decide which prices are to be included and which prices are to be excluded from the computation of the price index. Suppose we want to construct an index for retail prices. It is practically impossible to include all retail prices. There are millions of retail prices. A retail commodity bears different brands, and a brand bears different prices in different places. In fact, the prices of the same brand vary in stores no more than half a mile apart. An effort to include all these prices is too costly and too time-consuming. We thus have to take a sample (a subset) of retail prices in such a way that it is representative of the set of retail prices, that is to say, it behaves like the set of prices from which the sample is drawn. The United States Bureau of Labor Statistics, for instance, compiles the consumer price index from a sample of a few hundred prices of goods and services which constitute a market basket representative of the goods and services purchased by moderate-income families in urban areas; the wholesale price index is compiled from a sample of a couple of thousand prices of commodities in wholesale trade. In a finite set of prices, the larger the proportion of the prices included in the sample, the more reliable is the mean of the sample as an estimate of the mean of the population of prices. But the larger the sample the greater the computation cost. On the other hand, the smaller the sample the less cost, but the less reliable its mean. Our choice then is that given the computation cost, we take the sample which gives us the most information, or alternatively, given the information we want, we take the sample that minimizes cost.

Data. The selection of the sources of data that are the raw materials for price indexes is an important and difficult problem. Unreliable data will lead to misleading indexes. Data have to be obtained where the basic information is available. For instance, wholesale prices may be obtained from regularly published quotations, from manufacturers, wholesalers, importers, exporters, etc. Retail prices may be obtained from department stores, supermarkets, drugstores, independent stores, and other retail outlets. Consideration would have to be given to discounts since list prices may be substantially different from prices actually paid by the consumers.

Weighting. A price index is an average of many prices. Since prices are not equally important, as we have mentioned, we must deliberately use some system of weighting to allow for their relative importance; otherwise, there will be concealed weighting which results in unsatisfactory indexes. In the computation of the consumer price index, for example, a 5 percent increase in the price of some jewel is certainly not as important as a 5 percent increase in the price of bread; a 10 percent increase in bus fare is not as important as a 10 percent increase in rent. The choice of weights, however, is not unique. And, in principle, the use of different sets of weights would give rise to different numerical assertions on the extent of price changes over a specified period of time. But in practice, indexes computed with different systems of weighting generally do agree with one another. Once a system of weighting is selected we must adhere to it for some time, so that price indexes reflect largely price changes. Otherwise, changes in weights would affect the index, just as price changes and the resulting index will measure not price changes alone but some kind of value-product mix. Nevertheless, as time goes by, the consumption pattern of people tends to change; they may spend relatively more on some goods and relatively less on some others. These changes can be accounted for by changing weights. It goes without saying that indexes compiled on the basis of new weights are not comparable with those constructed on the basis of old weights.

The Selection of Base. In the construction of an index number, it is customary to select some period of time as a base expressed as 100 percent, with which to compare other indexes. Any year may be selected as the base. To be a good basis for comparison, the year selected should be a year in which economic conditions are "normal." Should a "depression" year be selected, a false impression of continuing prosperity would be implied in the indexes of subsequent years. Since any given year can hardly be considered as normal, an average of several years is usually used. For instance, the 1957-59 period was once used as a base by the United States Bureau of Labor Statistics for price indexes.

The base period should not be too far distant into the past, since the variation of price relatives could become so great that the average is not meaningful; and, changes in the quality of goods, which are nominally the same, may be such that they are not comparable. Yet to measure price changes, prices quoted must apply to identical products. As an example, take a 1935 Chrysler and a 1967 Chrysler. It is true that a car is a car. But the 1967 car is hardly comparable with the 1935 car in quality. It gives much greater riding comfort. It is safer and lasts longer. Suppose that the price of the 1935 car was $1,000 and the price of the 1967 car was $4,000. Shall we say that the price of the car was increased by four times? Or, is the 1967 Chrysler simply four times as much car? Or, is this a combination of both price increase and quality improvement? If so, how much is due to quality improvement and how much is due to price change? The question can be answered only when we can measure quality improvement, but such an index is yet to be developed. To account for quality changes, the base has to be shifted to a more recent period. This is a costly and time-consuming process, but, unless this is done, we cannot keep indexes "up-to-date."

Index Construction

We can construct a price index either by computing aggregate values or by averaging price relatives. We have already mentioned the simple average of price relatives and weighted average of price relatives in the examples in the section on the nature of price indexes. Here, we shall describe the aggregative index method. The aggregative index can be a simple aggregate or weighted aggregate.

The simple aggregative index is compiled by adding together the price of each commodity in any given year and expressing this total as a percentage of the total of some year used as base, which is set equal to 100. The following example is a simple aggregative index. The total of the base year (1960) is \$78 and that of 1965 is \$82. The index for 1965, as a percentage of the base year, is then 82/78 × 100 = 105.

The general expression of the simple aggregative index is then:

$$P = \frac{\Sigma p_n}{\Sigma p_0}$$

where

Σp_n = sum of prices of a given period

Σp_0 = sum of prices in the base period

Commodities	Prices	
	1960	1965
X (pound)	\$15	\$16
Y (gallon)	10	9
Z (ounce)	45	50
S (box)	8	7
Total	78	82
Index numbers (percent of 1960)	100	105

The simple aggregate index which looks in appearance "unweighted," in fact conceals weighting. The influence of the price of each commodity on the index depends on the unit of quotation. In the example, the price of *Z* has a dominant influence on the index. If the price of *S* were quoted in terms of, say, 10 boxes instead, then the index for 1965 would have been 145/150 × 100 = 97, which shows a decline in prices on the average for the 1960-65 period. The index also fails to account for the relative importance of prices. An index which changes as the units of quotation change, and fails to allow for the importance of individual prices, is clearly unsatisfactory.

This can be avoided by using a weighted aggregative index. There are several methods by which aggregates can be weighted. A simple method which is customarily used in the computation of weighted aggregative price indexes is to multiply the price of each commodity by its quantity in the base year. For instance, in the above example, suppose that the quantities of *X, Y, Z,* and *S* produced in 1960 were 100 lb, 1,000 gallons, 20 oz, and 500 boxes respectively; then the aggregate for 1960 was \$16,400 and that for 1965 was \$15,100, and the weighted aggregative index for 1965 relative to 1960 would be 151/164 x 100 = 92. Prices in general have declined by 8 percent during 1960-65 because the prices of the two most important commodities (*X* and *S*) have fallen.

The general expression for the aggregative index, using base-year quantities as weights, is:

$$P = \frac{\Sigma p_n q_o}{\Sigma p_o q_o}$$

where q_o = base period quantity of each commodity

p_o = base-period price

p_n = given-period price

This expression is usually referred to as the Laspeyres' index.[1] It is clear from the expression that the aggregative index of prices measures the changing value of a fixed market basket of goods and services. In the example, the cost of the market basket containing *X, Y, Z,* and *S* was \$16,400 in 1960 and the cost of the same aggregate was \$15,100. The change in value must be due to price changes or changes in the value of money.

The aggregative price index, using base-period quantities as weights, has several shortcomings. The index fails to take full account for the improvements in the quality of goods and services, particularly when the given period and base-period are too far apart. It does not take into account the introduction of new products that become more and more important. Nor does it account for the fact that as prices change, individuals may be able to maintain the same level of "well-being" by substituting commodities whose prices have declined for goods whose prices have risen. Indeed, they may even maintain the same level of "well-being" with smaller total outlays. These problems indicate that the aggregative index weighted by base-period quantities has an upward bias; it tends to overstate the extent of real price changes.

In lieu of the base-period quantities, we can use the given-period quantities, that is, the quantities of the year to be compared with the base year, as weights. The expression for this aggregative index is

$$P = \frac{\Sigma p_n q_n}{\Sigma p_0 q_n}$$

where q_n = given-period quantity

p_n = given-period price

p_0 = base-period price

This index, known as the Paasche's index, runs into several problems. First, the use of this index requires the selection of a new set of weights each year. This is simply too costly, both in terms of money and time. Second, as the weights are changed every year, the index would reflect both price and weight changes. Third, since people tend to increase their purchases of goods and services that

[1]It should be noted that this index is the same as the weighted average of price relatives, which is:

$$P = \frac{\sum \frac{p_n}{p_0} p_0 q_0}{\Sigma p_0 q_0} = \frac{\Sigma p_n q_0}{\Sigma p_0 q_0}$$

have declined in prices (especially industrial products that have a relatively high elasticity of demand), this index tends to give undue weight to these goods. A downward bias is thus inherent in this index.

To eliminate both the upward bias of the Laspeyres' index and the downward bias of the Paasche's index, an average of these two indexes has been suggested. Since the indexes are concerned with percentage changes, the average proposed is the geometric mean of these indexes, that is:

$$P = \left[\frac{\Sigma p_n q_n}{\Sigma p_0 q_n} \times \frac{\Sigma p_n q_0}{\Sigma p_0 q_0}\right]^{1/2}$$

This index is referred to as "Fisher's Ideal Index," since it meets certain mathematical tests. The trouble with this index is that it not only poses a more formidable computation problem but also does not tell us precisely what it measures. Although in principle the use of base-period weights and given-period weights may give rise to indexes of different magnitude but in practice indexes computed on the basis of these systems of weighting closely agree with each other.

SOME IMPORTANT PRICE INDEXES

The Consumer Price Index and the Wholesale Price Index are two most important of price indexes. In the United States, these indexes are compiled by the U.S. Bureau of Labor Statistics.

The Consumer Price Index (C.P.I.)

The Consumer Price Index is an index used to measure price changes of a market basket of goods and services representative of the goods and services purchased by moderate-income families living in urban areas. The Bureau studies family spending patterns in a given period and selects a sample of some 400 items from which price information is collected at regular intervals in 50 cities. From this information, the monthly index of consumer prices is compiled. The sample includes such commodities as meats, dairy products, vegetables, and apparel, and such services as rent, transportation, and medical care. The index is essentially a weighted aggregative index using base-year weights, each item being weighted in terms of its relative importance in family spending (e.g., the weight of the food group was 29.6 percent; housing, 32.5 percent; transportation, 11.3 percent; and apparel, 3.2 percent; and so on).

The U.S. Consumper Price Index, although among the best in the world, has its limitations. Like the Laspeyres' index, it does not allow for changes in the composition of consumer spending. Nor does it take full account of quality improvement. Thus, during the 1958-66 period, the C.P.I. has advanced by 9 percent, an average annual increase of 1.2 percent. But if the annual increase in quality improvement were from 1 to 1.5 percent, as believed by most experts, if such quality index could be developed, then there were no real price changes. The C.P.I. is not intended to measure all consumer prices, but to measure "prices of goods and services purchased by City wage-earner and Clerical-worker families."[2] It does not include goods and services purchased by very high or very low-income families. Nor is it applicable to families living in small towns and rural areas. The C.P.I. erroneously knows as "the cost-of-living" index is certainly not an index of the cost of living. An increase in the price of meat is reflected in the C.P.I., but it would in no way affect my cost of living if I were a vegetarian! My cost of living would not be affected by rising automobile prices if I ride a bicycle to work. Nor is it affected by rising rents if I own my home. Moreover, even if I do rent my home, my cost of living would not be adversely affected if I live in Albuquerque and rents are rising in Chicago.

In spite of these limitations, the C.P.I. is a reasonably satisfactory indicator of the direction of changes in consumer prices. It has served as a guide to policies designed to stabilize the purchasing power of money. It has been widely used as a criterion in various labor contracts with "escalator clauses," allowing for automatic increases in wages in accordance with rising consumer prices. This would help to prevent the costly and time-consuming process of contract renegotiations when there are substantial increases in consumer prices which adversely affect the real income of workers.

The Wholesale Price Index

This index measures the average changes of wholesale prices from a list of some 2,200 most important goods in wholesale trade. These goods are classified into 15 major groups, 88 subgroups, and 200 product classes. The major groups include farm products, processed foods, machinery, textile products and apparel, tobacco products and bottled beverages. Index numbers are published monthly for "all commodities" as well as major groups, subgroups, and product classes.

The wholesale price index is also a weighted aggregative index, with base-year quantities as weights. It is subject to some of the same limitations as the consumer price index. The wholesale and consumer price indexes in general move in the same directions. But, sometimes, while the wholesale price index may remain practically unchanged, the consumer price index rises moderately (for example, the 1958-64 period).

There are several reasons for such behavior. The Consumer Price Index includes the prices of services (excluded from the Wholesale Price Index) which, on the average, rise relatively faster than the prices of commodities. Moreover, as a result of constant improvement in technology which increases labor productivity, manufacturers have been able to hold down manufacturing costs in spite

[2]Hence, the name "Index of Changes in Prices of Goods and Services Purchased by City Wage-earner and Clerical-worker families to maintain their level of living."

of rising wage costs; on the other hand, as a consequence of the limited extent of technical improvements in the distributive system, distributive costs cannot be held down in the face of rising wages. In addition, the movement of goods from producers to consumers requires a much vaster distributive network which is more prone to the development of bottlenecks that would result in higher retail prices.

CONSEQUENCES OF PRICE-LEVEL CHANGES

Changes in the level of prices would not cause any harmful effects if all prices vary in the same proportion. By all prices, we mean not only prices of goods but also prices of financial claims, wages, salaries, interest, rents, and so on. Suppose all prices are doubled (my wage included). I would not be in any way adversely affected by such price changes. With my money income doubled, I can still purchase the same amount of goods and services as before the doubling of prices. The trouble is that in the real world, prices do not change at the same rate as a consequence of contractual arrangements, among other things. If I sign a contract to work for a business corporation for five years at $15,000 each year, then I am bound to that contractual obligation regardless of the variation in prices unless my contract contains some kind of escalator clause allowing for the adjustment of price changes. When the prices of things which I purchase fall, my real income increases, and when they increase, my real income declines. It is because of the fact that prices do not vary at precisely the same rate that fluctuations in the price level affect not only the distribution of income and wealth between different groups of individuals in society but also the level of output and the volume of employment.

Creditors and Debtors

Rising prices tend to favor those who borrow money at the expense of those who lend. Borrowers receive money of high real value and repay money of low purchasing power. Suppose that A loaned $100 to B for one year at five percent interest. After one year, B repaid A $105 in principal plus interest. Assume that during the period, the price level has risen by 20 percent. Then the real value of $105 which B received from A in repayment would be equal to the real value of $87.5 at the time he made the loan to A. Therefore, although B loaned money to A at a nominal interest rate of 5 percent, the real rate of interest was in fact a negative rate, at −12.5 percent. B loaned money to A and paid him interest!

Conversely, when prices fall, the creditors gain and debtors suffer. They lend money of relatively low real value and receive in repayment money of high purchasing power. In the above example, if the price level were to fall by 20 percent instead, then the real value of $105 which B received from A in repayment would be approximately equal to the purchasing power of $131 at the time when the loan was made. The nominal rate of interest was 5 percent, but the real rate was substantially higher. Thus, as the price level changes, the fortune swings between debtors and creditors. In times of sharply rising prices, especially hyperinflation, creditors would have to accept in repayment money which has lost most of its value. They may have to run away from debtors! In times of serious depression, on the other hand, the ones who have to go into hiding are debtors!

Fixed and Variable-Income Earners

Price increases hurt people whose income is fixed or does not move in step with rising prices and bestow favors on people whose income increases with increases in prices, such as businessmen and entrepreneurs. Workers whose wages and salaries do not rise as fast as consumer prices will find their real wages and the levels of their well-being substantially reduced. The only workers who are insulated from the effects of rising prices are those who hold contracts with provisions for automatic adjustment to price increases. People with fixed income, such as pensioners, rentiers holding long-term lease contracts on their properties, and owners of fixed-interest financial claims, will find the real value of their fixed income gradually eaten away by rising prices. The incomes of businessmen and entrepreneurs, on the other hand, rise as prices rise. As wages and other costs lag behind rising prices, business income, a residual income, will other costs lag behind rising prices, business income, a residual income, will increase faster than prices. This simply means that the income of the business class increases both in money and real terms. Until wages and other costs catch up with rising prices, the business group continues to receive increasing real income. The reverse, however, holds when prices decline. As wages and costs lag behind falling prices, business profits are squeezed. Wage earners enjoy rising real wages. The income of rentiers substantially increase in real value. It follows that if the distribution of income is in favor of the business class at the expense of wage earners and the rentier class when prices rise, then declining prices benefit the rentier class and wage-earners at the expense of the business group.

Holders of Real Assets and Financial Claims

A large portion of the wealth of individuals is held in the form of fixed-value, fixed-interest-yielding claims such as corporate bonds and government securities. Since the face values of these securities are fixed, their real value decreases as prices increase. For example, if I hold a note promising to pay $1,000 at maturity (for example, two years from now), and if at maturity the price level is doubled, then the real value of my note will have been reduced in half. If rising prices are serious, the holders of financial assets may find their wealth disappearing into thin air in no time. It is true that the face values or nominal values of these assets are fixed, but these values can be secured only at maturity. Should holders of these claims decide to sell them before maturity, they may sustain substantial capital losses. And this is what happens in periods of rising prices. Since, as prices rise the price of money or the rate of interest also rises, which means declining market values of securities. Holders of real assets (land, houses, and commodities) and corporate stocks (certificates of corporate ownership), on the other hand, benefit from rising prices as the value of these assets increases with price increases. Thus, if holders of long-term lease contracts on real properties may find the real value of their rent income reduced, but this may be more than offset by the rising value of their properties. Holders of corporate stocks benefit not only from higher dividends in periods of rising prices as a consequence of rising business profits, but also from the appreciated value of their shares. Inasmuch as holders of corporate stocks and real properties are mostly rich people, the distribution of wealth in times of rising prices is in favor of the rich at the expense of the middle-and low-income groups whose wealth is largely held in the form of financial claims. This pattern of wealth distribution is reversed when prices fall. While the value of real assets decreases, holders of financial assets enjoy the rising real value of their claims.

Losses and Gains to Society

We have seen that in times of rising or declining prices, some groups of individuals in society gain and others suffer, but the gains realized by some groups are not necessarily offset by the losses experienced by others. For instance, in periods of rising prices, we know that debtors and variable-income groups gain and creditors and fixed-income people lose. But, as far as society as a whole is concerned, there may be no net loss in terms of real income and employment. In point of fact, it is believed by many that price increases, if they are moderate, stand to benefit society as a whole. Gently rising prices mean rising business profits and increased business profits are a strong stimulant to business expansion, which will result in higher levels of output and employment. Of course, in the case of rising prices which reach the "galloping" proportion, then the course of economic activity would eventually reverse itself from maximum output and employment to monetary breakdown and economic collapse when money becomes worthless, since at that point nobody would want to produce, work, and sell for money which has no value.

In the case of falling prices, if they are serious, then almost everybody stands to lose. It is true that when prices fall, creditors gain and debtors lose. But if the extent of declining prices is such that borrowers are not able to pay off their debts, then creditors stand to lose as well. They may have to scale down their credit or may be forced to sell assets taken over from debtors at depressed prices. Wage earners may gain in real wages as wages lag behind falling prices, but this is true only for those workers who have jobs. Labor, as a group, would lose, as a larger proportion of the labor force may not be able to find employment. The result is a smaller total wage bill. It follows that in the case of deflation, society as a whole stands to lose, and loss is reflected by declining output and rising unemployment. It is to be noted that our discussion does not necessarily imply that rising prices are "good" and declining prices are "bad." We have seen that both rising prices and declining prices, if they are serious enough, carry in their wake undesirable economic consequences. If we are forced to make a choice between price increases and price decreases, then the former may appear to be the lesser of the two evils. An important problem of economic policy is to stabilize the price level so that the hardships generated by the redistribution of income and wealth between different groups of individuals in society as a result of price changes would be minimized and at the same time it does not hamper efforts to promote maximum output and full employment. This is easier said than done!

EARLY THEORETICAL FORMULATIONS ON THE VALUE OF MONEY

Theoretical attempts to provide an answer to such questions as what gives money its value and what causes the value of money (or the price level) to change are numerous. The commodity theory and the state theory are among the oldest theoretical formulations on the value of money. These theories are essentially concerned with the source of the value of money.

The Commodity Theory

In essence, the commodity theory holds that the value of money is only a reflection of the value of the commodity used as money, and the value of the money commodity, just like the value of any other commodity, is determined by the commodity supply and demand—that is, production cost and the preference of the buyers for it as a commodity. The theory can be illustrated by the following example. Suppose there are three commodities x, y, and z, with the following exchange relations:

$$10x \text{ (pound)} = 2y \text{ (pound)} = 1z \text{ (ounce)}$$

Assume that a given weight of commodity z (say, gold) is used as a standard unit in terms of which the values of other commodities are expressed. The standard unit is called the dollar, for example, and is defined as equal to 1/10 of an ounce of z. This means that the monetary value of one ounce of z is fixed at \$10. Once the monetary unit is defined, the money prices of the above commodities are:

$$Px = \$1$$
$$Py = \$5$$
$$Pz = \$10$$

Suppose that for some reason there is an increase in the commodity demand for z. As a consequence, the value of z relative to x and y increase, as indicated by the following hypothetical relation:

$$20x = 4y = 1z$$

Since the monetary unit is defined in terms of a given weight of z, and the value of z increases relative to x and y, the value of the monetary unit in terms of x and y also increases or the money prices of x and y fall: that is,

$$Px = \$0.50$$
$$Py = \$2.5$$

The money price of z, of course, remains unchanged, at $1z = \$10$ (since money is defined in terms of z).

Conversely, a decrease in the commodity demand for z would reduce its value in terms of x and y, and hence their money prices rise (the value of money in terms of x and y falls). Suppose that we have the following new relation between x, y, and z:

$$5x = 1y = 1z$$

Then

$$Px = \$2$$
$$Py = \$10$$

From these examples, it is not too difficult to arrive at the conclusion that the value of money is the commodity value of the money commodity relative to other commodities.

The theory is no sheer intellectual exercise attempting to explain the value of money. In fact, it once served as a guide to economic policy. The theory was indeed the theoretical foundation behind the monetary policy of the United States in the early 1930's. We know that the country was then deep in the Depression. Prices declined, output fell, and unemployment soared. The prescription for economic recovery was then to raise prices. But how to bring this about? To advocates of the commodity theory, the answer was simple: raise the dollar price of gold—that is, devalue the monetary unit in terms of gold. The logic of this proposal can be seen by referring to one of the above relations:

$$10x = 2y = 1z = \$10$$
$$Px = \$1$$
$$Py = \$5$$
$$Pz = \$10$$

The dollar is defined in terms of 1/10 ounce of gold (z). Now, suppose we want to double the prices of x and y. According to the theory, this could be accomplished by raising the dollar price of gold from \$10 = 1 ounce to \$20 = 1 ounce (the dollar is redefined as equal to 1/20 of one ounce of gold). The relation between x, y, z, and the monetary unit now becomes

$$10x = 2y = 1z = \$20$$

or

$$Px = \$2$$
$$Py = \$10$$
$$Pz = \$20$$

The prices of x and y are doubled! This line of argument in fact did influence the decision of the Roosevelt administration to raise the dollar price of gold from about \$21 = 1 ounce (the Gold Standard Act of 1900) to \$35 = 1 ounce (the Gold Reserve Act of 1934) (the gold definition of the dollar was changed from 23.22 grains of pure gold to 13.7 grains of pure gold). If the commodity theory were to work, then the postdevaluation prices in the United States would have to increase by approximately 70 percent (35/21 x 100 = 170) above the predevaluation prices. This, as we know, did not come about. Prices in fact did inch upward after 1932–that is, prior to the devaluation, and continued to rise at a very slow rate. Not until in the early 1940's did the price level reach the average of 1926.

What, then, is wrong with the commodity theory of the value of money? The fallacy lies in the fact that the theory fails to consider the influence of the monetary demand for the commodity on its value. The fact that gold is used as money results in greater demand for it: demand for gold as a commodity and demand for gold either for gold coinage or as a monetary reserve to insure the convertibility of circulating currency into gold. An increase in the monetary demand for gold would cause its value to rise, even though there may be no change in the cost of the production of gold and the commodity demand for gold. Since the monetary demand is the largest component of the total demand for gold, the value of gold, unlike the value of other metals, largely depends on its use as monetary reserve. Indeed, should there be a world-wide agreement regarding the abolition of the use of gold as an international reserve, it would be doubtful that the value of gold would be as high as it is at present.

In a monetary system in which money is a commodity or is freely convertible into a commodity, it is easy to arrive at the fallacious conclusion that the value of money is the value of the commodity used as money, independent of its monetary role. Such a conclusion, of course, would be absurd when money is inconvertible paper money. We can hardly say that the value of a paper dollar bill is the value of its commodity paper. Nevertheless, the idea that money retains its value only when it is tied to or backed by some commodity remains popular. This does not imply that the value of the commodity used as "backing" would give money its value, but rather that when money is tied to a commodity, the supply of which changes only slowly over time, there would be no room for excessive monetary expansion which would result in sharply rising prices or declining value of money.

The State Theory

While the commodity theory attributes the source of the value of money to the commodity value of the "thing" used as money, the state theory holds that the source of the value of money is the monetary law of the state, and the material substance of money has nothing to do with its value. G. F. Knapp, in his "The State Theory of Money" stated that "money is the creature of the law. . . ," and that "the soul of currency is not in the material of the pieces but in the legal ordinances which regulate their use."[3]

This is a false proposition. The state, of course, can issue money in any desirable quantities. It may enhance the acceptability of money by granting to it legal tender power–that is, making it the legally enforceable means for the settlement of debts; and by accepting it in payment of taxes and other public payments. But all this is neither a necessary nor a sufficient condition for the money issued by the state to be generally accepted as such by the public. The acceptability of something as money ultimately rests with the public. And the latter cannot be forced by the state to accept money which it does not want to accept. In the monetary history of nations, there were periods in which the money issued by the state was rejected outright by the public. The continental currency, issued by the Continental Congress, was rejected, as it rapidly depreciated with regard to silver and gold. In Germany, during the hyperinflation of the early 1920's, the mark was not accepted as money, as we have already noted.

Nor is money necessarily a creature of the state. Again, in the early 1920's, in Germany, people used as money not state money but foreign currencies and certificates issued by private institutions. The failure of legal bimetallism intended by the acts of 1792 and 1834 in the United States was another example of the fact that when monetary laws were inconsistent with the operations of market forces, the latter would prevail over the monetary laws of the state. To be sure, the state can influence the value of money through its power to change and control the quantity of money, but it surely is not the source of the value of money.

DEVELOPMENT OF THE QUANTITY THEORY OF MONEY

Unlike the commodity theory and state theory which are concerned mainly with the source of the value of money, the quantity theory is concerned with changes in the level of the value of money. According to the quantity theory, changes in the level of prices or the value of money are caused by changes in the quantity of money–hence the expression "quantity theory." The linking of price level changes to the changes in the quantity of money dated back to as early as the sixteenth century. Jean Bodin (1530-96), believed to be the originator of the quantity theory, in his "Reply to the Paradox of Malestroit Regarding the Dearness of All Things and the Remedy Therefor," argued that rising prices in France in the sixteenth century were accounted for mainly by increases in the quantity of gold and silver which were then used as money. "I find that the high prices we see today are due to four or five causes. The principal and almost the

[3]G. F. Knapp, *The State Theory of Money* (New York: St. Martin's Press, 1924).

only one is the abundance of gold and silver, which is today much greater in the kingdom than it was four hundred years ago. . . "[4] The increase in the quantity of gold and silver in France (and in Europe in general) arose from the import of large quantities of these metals from the New World.

The quantity theory, as proposed by Jean Bodin, was embraced in the seventeenth and eighteenth centuries by such writers as John Locke (1612-1704), founder of British empirical philosophy, Richard Cantillon (1680-1734), French banker and economist, and David Hume (1711-76), British empirical philosopher. Richard Cantillon went far beyond his predecessors in his analysis of the influence of money on prices. He undertook to explain why changes in the quantity of money cause the level of prices to change. He was the first to relate rising prices to increased effective demand generated by increases in the quantity of money. According to him, an increase in the quantity of money "whether lent or spent, will enter into circulation and will not fail to raise the prices of products and merchandise in all channels of circulation which it enters. Increased money will bring about increased expenditure, and this will cause an increase of market prices in the highest years of exchange and gradually in the lowest."[5] And, he further states, "I consider in general that an increase in actual money causes in a State a corresponding increase of consumption which gradually brings about increased prices."[6]

Adherents to the quantity theory in the seventeenth and eighteenth centuries, aware of the fact that increases in the quantity of money could lead to both increases in prices and output (when there were unutilized resources) and the unknown extent of changes in the "rapidity in the circulation of money (which would affect price changes just as changes in the quantity of money) resulting from monetary changes, did not draw any definite conclusion on the extent of price changes arising from changes in the quantity of money." On this point, Richard Cantillon stated: " . . . I conclude that by doubling the quantity of money in a State, the prices of products and merchandise are not always doubled. A river which runs and winds about its bed will not flow with double the speed when the amount of its water is doubled."[7] And, he goes on, "the dearness caused by an increase in the quantity of money does not affect equally all kinds of products and merchandise proportionably to the quantity of money, unless what is added continues in the same circulation as the money before. . . . I conceive that when a large surplus of money is brought into a State, the new money gives a new turn to consumption and even a new speed to circulation; but it is not possible to say exactly to what extent."[8]

[4]Arthur E. Monroe (ed.), *Early Economic Thought* (Cambridge, Mass.: Harvard U. P., 1924), p. 107.

[5]Richard Cantillon, *Essai Sur la Nature du Commerce en Général* (Paris: Institut National D'Etudes Démographiques, 1952), pp. 89–90.

[6]*Ibid.*, p. 91.

[7]*Ibid.*, pp. 98–99.

[8]*Ibid.*, p. 100.

Writers of the nineteenth century, including David Ricardo and John Stuart Mill, went a step further in their discussion on the relations between money and prices. Proceeding on the assumption that full employment is a normal state of the economy and that the velocity of circulation is constant, they arrived at what we today refer to as the "crude quantity theory of money" which, in essence, held that changes in the quantity of money result in proportionate changes in the level of prices.

This version of the quantity theory remained the center of monetary analysis in the early decades of the twentieth century. Remarkable achievements in the quantity-theory analysis, however, were accomplished, reflected by the development of a new analytical framework—the famous equation of exchange, and by the attempts of quantity theorists to verify their theory by the systematic use of statistical methods.

SUMMARY

The value of money is its exchange value represented by the amount of "goods and services in general" which can be purchased by a unit of money. It is the reciprocal of the general price level which is an average of prices. An increase (decrease) in the general price level means a decrease (increase) in the value of money. Changes in the value of money are measured by price indexes. A price index is a (weighted) average showing the average movement of prices between periods of time. Price indexes may be computed by several methods, the most popular one being the aggregative index using base-period weights. The construction of a price index poses several difficult problems, such as weighting, sampling, collecting data, selecting base, the introduction of new products, changes in the composition of spending, and quality improvement. In spite of problems and limitations, a carefully compiled price index is a useful indicator of the general direction of price changes. The two most important price indexes are the Consumer Price Index and the Wholesale Price Index. In the United States, they are compiled at frequent intervals by the Bureau of Labor Statistics. The former is a measure of changes in the cost of a market basket purchased by average-income families living in urban areas. The latter is an average of wholesale prices.

Inasmuch as prices do not change at the same rate over time, some groups of individuals within the national economy fare well, and others suffer, in the face of price-level changes. Rising prices, in general, tend to favor debtors, variable-income earners, and holders of real assets, and hurt creditors, wage earners, and holders of financial claims. When prices fall, the redistribution of income and wealth is the other way around. In regard to society as a whole, the economic gains and losses resulting from price changes are not equalized. With moderate price increases, society may stand to gain in terms of higher levels of output and employment. In deflation, on the other hand, society as a whole may suffer a net loss as a result of declining output and rising unemployment.

There are several theories on the value of money. The commodity theory and the state theory are among the early theoretical formulations on the value of money. According to the commodity theory, the value of money is the value of the commodity used as money, independently of its monetary usage. The state theory holds that the source of the value of money is the law of the state. It is true that the state can influence the value of money through its power to control and change the quantity of money, but it cannot issue a decree to make money have value. The quantity theory, unlike the commodity theory and the state theory, is concerned with changes in the value of money. According to this theory, price-level changes are caused by changes in the quantity of money.

PROBLEMS

1. What is the value of money? How are changes in the value of money measured? Is the measurement of changes in the value of money an accurate measurement?

2. What is a price index? What are the various methods which can be used for the construction of price indexes? What are problems involved in the construction of price indexes?

3. What are the effects of price changes on creditors and debtors? On wage earners and entrepreneurs? Holders of real assets and financial claims? Are the losses of some groups of individuals exactly offset by the gains of others as a consequence of price changes?

4. What is the Consumer Price Index, as compiled by the U.S. Bureau of Labor Statistics? What does it measure? Is it a cost-of-living index? Why is it important?

5. You have the following price and quantity series:

Goods	1960's Quantity, pounds	Price per Pound	
		1960	1961
Orange	10,000	$0.20	$0.22
Pineapple	12,000	0.10	0.12
Lemons	6,000	0.30	0.28
Grapefruit	10,000	0.15	0.16
Apricots	2,000	0.25	0.24
Apple	15,000	0.22	0.25

Compile:

(a) simple average of price relatives,
(b) weighted average of price relatives, and
(c) weighted aggregative index.

6. Following is the information on prices and quantities of certain products produced and sold in 1950 and 1955:

Products	Quantities, (box)		Price (per Box)	
	1950	1955	1950	1955
x	20,000	22,000	$2.0	$2.5
y	15,000	12,000	3.0	3.5
z	16,000	14,000	1.5	1.0
s	30,000	32,000	2.0	3.0
t	25,000	22,000	2.5	2.0

Compile:

(a) the Laspeyres' Index,
(b) the Paasche's Index, and
(c) the Fisher's Ideal Index.

chapter 17

The Value of Money: The Quantity Theory

Monetary theory during the nineteenth century and up to the 1930's centered largely on the quantity theory. However, following the appearance of J. M. Keynes' *General Theory*—the foundation of modern monetary analysis—which integrated monetary theory with the general theory of output and employment determination, the scope of monetary theory was broadened and the quantity theory declined in popularity. Interest in the quantity theory, however, has been revived, and the theory restated. But the restated version of the theory is in fact much closer to the modern theory of income determination than to the classical quantity theory. In this and the next few chapters, we shall discuss the quantity theory in its traditional form, and the shift from the theory of the value of money to the analysis of the influences of monetary expenditure on output, employment, as well as the general price level.

THE SCOPE OF MONETARY THEORY IN THE CLASSICAL FRAMEWORK

To classical economists, as we have mentioned, money is a technical device used to facilitate exchanges. Goods and services are exchanged for money which in turn is exchangeable for goods and services. And that is all. Aside from this technical function, money does not exert any real influence on the economic process, which behaves in the same way as it would without money. Money is only a "veil" that tends to obscure the relationships between things which really matter. The analysis and description of the fundamental aspects of economic life thus would have to be in real terms—that is, with the money veil discarded. Once the veil is removed then goods are essentially exchanged for goods and their values are represented by their barter rates of exchange (exchange ratios) which are determined by the "real" forces of supply and demand. Saving is essentially the surrendering of resources from the production of consumption goods, and investment is the conversion of these "unconsumed" resources into capital goods such as buildings, machinery and equipment for further production of capital and consumption goods in the future; lending and borrowing is the transfer of the use of goods between lenders and borrowers. Inasmuch as the relationships between fundamental variables of economic life can be described and analyzed in terms of goods and services, and money has no influence on the behavior of these real variables, the only role played by money is in the determination of the absolute level of prices. This is the province of classical monetary theory. The theory of money, in the classical tradition, was thus relegated to the background of the theory of "value" and "distribution," which is concerned with the determination of the relative prices of goods and services, the outputs of individual firms, and the compensation of productive factors: real wages, interest, rents, and profits.

THE EQUATION OF EXCHANGE

There are three ways to look at the total value of transactions: (a) the expenditures or payments of the buyers, (b) the receipts of the sellers; or (c) the value of goods and services transacted. They are three ways of describing exactly the same thing. Let $T_1, T_2, \cdots, T_n$ be the numbers of units of transactions in the n goods, services, financial claims and other assets transacted, and $p_1, p_2, \cdots, p_n$, their unit prices, then the total value of transactions is the following sum:

$$p_1 T_1 + p_2 T_2 + \cdots + p_n T_n = \Sigma\, p_i T_i = PT$$

where T is the total physical volume of trade and P is the weighted average of all the prices.

The value of all the goods transacted is equal to the total expenditure on these goods. The latter can be expressed as the product of the quantity of money M and its average rate of turnover V–that is, MV. It follows by definition that

$$MV = PT$$

which is the equation of exchange.[1] This can be illustrated by the following example. Suppose that you had a \$2 bill and spent it on a book. The bookseller received your \$2 bill and in turn spent it on a haircut; the barber in turn spent the \$2 bill on an old pair of shoes. All these transactions took place during a given time period. It follows from the example that during that period of time, the quantity of money (M = \$2) changed hands three times ($V = 3$), from you to the bookseller, from the bookseller to the barber, and from the barber to the shoemaker. The payment total was the MV = (\$2)(3) = \$6. But this is obviously

[1]$MV = PT$ is in fact more than an equation. In an accounting sense, $MV = PT$ is an identity. MV and PT represent exactly the same thing. An equation, we may recall, is a statement that is true only for allowable values of the variable, whereas an identity is a statement which is true for all values of the variable. For example, $2y = y + y$ is an identity since it is true for all values of y, whereas $x + 3 = 4$ is an equation which is defined only for the value of $x = 1$ or $x^2 + 2 = 18$ is defined only for $x = +4$ and $x = -4$.

equal to the value of the goods and services transacted, i.e. $PT = (\$2)(3) = \$6$. At the aggregate level the M term in the equation is the sum of currency and demand deposits held by the public and foreign demand balances at the Federal Reserve banks. The quantity of money M is influenced by a host of factors such as the willingness of banks to lend and invest and the desire of individuals and business corporations and others to borrow; and all this is in turn influenced by the level of business activity, expectations on the future course of interest, prices, and profits. The central bank authorities, of course, can change the supply of money by using the monetary instruments at their disposal.

V is the average number of times the quantity of money turns over (the velocity of circulation) a specified period of time, for example, a year. The behavior of V is determined by many factors, such as the development of banking and credit institutions, the community's methods of income payments, the fiscal policy of the government, the monetary and credit policy of the central bank; the expectations of people on future incomes and prices, among other things. For instance, if prices are expected to rise in the future, they would tend to buy now to avoid future rising prices and the induced increases in spending would cause V to increase. V is higher when wages and salaries are paid weekly instead of monthly. In a sense, V is a residual element in the equation. It is derived from PT and M. The quantity of money is a stock existing at a given moment in time. PT, on the other hand, is a flow; it is the total value of the flow of transactions over a given period of time. M thus cannot be directly compared with PT. V is an adjustment coefficient which makes M, a stock, comparable with PT, a flow, by telling how often M turns over to meet the transactions flow PT over a specified period of time.

The total volume of trade T represents all goods, services, securities and other assets transacted. Thus the same unit of output which is bought and sold 10 times would represent 10 units of transactions included in T. T is largely determined by the natural and human resources of the economy, their quantity, quality, accessibility and the level of their utilization, the state of technology, the degree of labor specialization, and the structure of business organization, to mention a few. The ways business corporations are organized also affect the total volume of transactions. In a system in which business firms are organized along vertical lines, the volume of trade is smaller than in a system in which various stages of production are performed by independent firms. For example, if automobile manufacturers purchase steel, glass, tires, engines, and so on from independent supply firms, then the volume of transactions will be greater than in the case in which they mine their own ores, make their own steel, produce their own glass, tires, and engines and sell automobiles as final products. The several stages of production which would otherwise be undertaken by a number of independent firms are performed by one single firm and the product remains with the firm through all stages of production, from the raw-material stage to the finished-product stage.

The general price level P is influenced by the interactions between V, M and T. Changes in P may, in turn, influence the behavior of V, T and M as well.

As it is, the equation of exchange $MV = PT$ is not a theory since it does not imply any casual relations between M, V, P and T. A change in M, for example, may be accompanied by a change in V, P, and T. From the equation, we only know that should, say M change, then either V, P or T or any combinations between V, P and T would have to change. An increase in M which is offset by a decrease in V may leave P and T unchanged. Similarly, an increase in M which is accompanied by a change in T may leave P unchanged. In an accounting sense, $MV = PT$ is true under any circumstances: the value of money spending is necessarily equal to the value of goods and services on which money is spent. The equation is a truism. But it is not to be discarded as useless. It is a useful accounting device which reduces the complex of receipts and payments to some simple, comprehensive aggregates such as MV and PT. Since the equation shows the interrelations between M, V, P, and T, it can be used as a frame of reference from which some theorizing may be made on the variables determining the behavior of the general price level or the value of money.

The Transactions-Velocity Formulation

The equation $MV = PT$, as we have seen, is not a theory but it can be developed into a theory of the value of money by making certain assertions regarding the behavior of P, T, V, and M. The theoretical conclusion drawn from these assumptions, however, may not be valid because M, V, P, and T may not behave the way they are assumed to behave, although $MV = PT$ is always true. Irving Fisher, the American economist and mathematician, made use of the equation of exchange to derive a theory explaining the behavior of the general price level. Fisher proceeded with the following assumptions:

The general level of price, P, the variable to be explained, is made the dependent variable to be determined by the other elements of the equation, M, V, and T, that is: $P = f(M, V, T) = MV/T$. M, V, and T determine P but are in no way influenced by P. In other words, P is a completely passive variable.

The velocity of circulation V is assumed to be institutionally constant, on the ground that factors which determine the behavior of V such as payment habits, and the development of banking and credit institutions change only very slowly.

The physical volume of trade T is also considered to be approximately constant as its determinants such as population growth, the development of technology, the availability and accessibility of resources also do not change over short periods of time. This reflects the assumption of classical analysis that full employment is the "normal state of affairs" of the economy.

With V and T assumed to be approximately constant, that leaves M to be the only variable determining P. From $P = \frac{MV}{T} = \frac{V}{T}M$, let $\frac{V}{T} = k$, we have $P =$

$k \cdot M$. It follows that the price level changes proportionately with the quantity of money. The general conclusion of the theory developed by Irving Fisher and his followers during the early decades of the twentieth century was thus not different from that of earlier writers but such a conclusion was arrived at after explicit assumptions were made on the behavior of the variables involved in the analysis.

The Income-Velocity Formulation

The equation $MV = PT$ is the transactions velocity equation and the theoretical formulation derived from it is referred to as the transactions–velocity formulation. We may recall that PT is the total value of all monetary transactions which include goods, services, financial claims, and other assets. If we include in the equation only the value of final products and services (intermediate goods, and securities are all excluded), we have another variant of the equation of exchange which may be referred to as the income-flow equation of exchange:

$$MV_y = P_y Y_r$$

where Y_r is the quantity of final products and services produced over a year; P_y is the average level of prices of final products and V_y is the average rate at which the quantity of money M turns over to meet the income flow $P_y Y_r$ (the income velocity of circulation).

$P_y Y_r$ is gross national product—that is, the money value of the flow of final goods and services produced; and MV_y is the flow of expenditure on gross national product. By definition, Y_r is much smaller than T (since it includes only final output) and the income-velocity $V_y = \dfrac{P_y Y_r}{M}$ is smaller than the transactions-velocity $V = \dfrac{PT}{M}$. Suppose that M = \$200 billion, PT = \$1,800 billion and $P_y Y_r$ = \$600 billion, then $V = 9$ and $V_y = 3$. The transactions velocity is three times the income velocity. This means that on the average it takes three dollars of transactions to generate one dollar of income.

Like the transactions variant of the quantity theory, the strict income version also assumes that V_y and Y_r to be approximately constant, hence the same conclusion that changes in the quantity of money cause proportional changes in the general price level. The income version, however, lends itself to relatively more accurate statistical estimation. With data on M and $P_y Y_r$ readily available, the income velocity V_y can be readily computed. For example, in 1966, gross national product in the United States was \$648 billion and the average quantity of money was \$170 billion, the income velocity was then 3.8. On the other hand, the transactions velocity is rather difficult to estimate because of problems involved in estimating the total value of transactions.

Limitations of the Velocity Formulation

Whether the velocity theory is valid depends largely on the validity of the assumptions regarding the behavior of M, V, P, and T (or V_y, P_y, and Y_r). The assumption that V is institutionally constant appears unrealistic. There is evidence that V is affected by the cyclical changes in the level of business activity. In periods of prosperity when interest rates are high, income and prices rise, and people are more disposed to spend, V tends to rise. Thus when interest rates are high or prices of financial assets are low, there is greater incentive on the part of investors to hold financial assets instead of money. The cost of holding money—the interest income to be forsaken—in such times is high. The increase in the demand for financial assets or the decrease in the demand for money would result in an increase in the velocity of circulation. Conversely, in times of declining business activity, when interest rates are low, income and prices decline, and people are less disposed to spend, the velocity of circulation decreases. It follows that in the short run, the velocity of circulation is affected by, among other things, changes in interest rates, changes in expectations on future incomes and prices, which in turn affect consumption and investment outlays of individuals and businesses, hence the total volume of transactions. But changes in interest rates are influenced by changes in the quantity of money. There is, therefore, interdependence between M, V, and T. The assumption of independence between M, V, and T is unrealistic.

It is also not realistic to assume that P is a completely passive variable having no influence on M, V, and T. The quantity of money is largely determined by the level of economic activity, and this in turn is influenced by the general price level. P is far from being determined by M. It influences M through its effects on the level of business activity.

The theory deviates from the general theory of value. We know that prices are determined by supply and demand. Yet the quantity theory shows that the general price level is determined by the quantity of money. Thus, if there is any relationship between M and P the relationship has to be indirect. The general price-level increases only when there is an excess of total demand over total supply. To show that whenever there is an increase in the quantity of money there is a corresponding increase in the general price level, we must show that (a) an increase in M leads to an increase in total demand D and (b) an increase in D results in an increase in P. But neither (a) nor (b) necessarily holds. For the moment, let us assume that (a) is satisfied—that is, when M changes D also changes. This does not necessarily mean that an increase in D would lead to an increase in P. Whether P will change or not depends upon the price elasticity of supply. Assume that OP_0 and OQ_0 in Fig. 17-1(a) is the initial equilibrium price-output combination with SS representing the total supply curve, DD the total demand curve and OQ_F, the full employment level of output. The extent of the unutili-

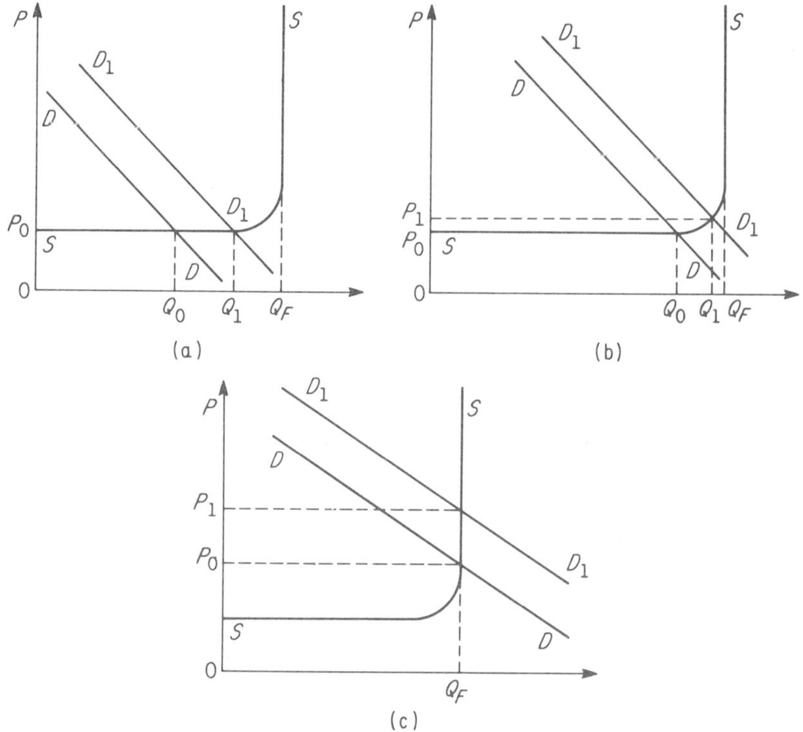

Fig. 17-1. Changes in effective demand and price changes.

zation of resources is such that an increase in total demand from *DD* to D_1D_1 generated by an increase in *M* results in an increase in real output from OQ_0 to OQ_1 without any change in the general price level (the new demand curve still intersects the supply curve at the latter's perfectly elastic portion). If the initial price-output equilibrium is as indicated by Fig. 17-1(b), then an increase in total demand would result in both price and output increases because as the full employment level of output is approached, production costs rise as a result of the development of bottlenecks in various sectors of the economy (shortage of labor, materials, and so on) and the bidding up of prices of productive factors by competitive firms. Only in the case of full employment does an increase in total demand bring about changes in the general price level alone. In Fig. 17-1(c), since the total demand curve *DD* already intersects the supply curve at its perfectly inelastic portion, an increase in total demand from *DD* to D_1D_1 causes *P* to rise from OP_0 to OP_1 with output unchanged. The general conclusion of the quantity theory therefore represents a limiting case applicable only when full employment prevails, since only in full employment is the assumption of given

Y_r (or T) valid. If Y_r and T are not constant in the short run as instability generated by the changing behavior of the public in regard to consumption, savings, and investment, causes fluctuations in employment and output, neither are they constant in the long run. As the economy grows with growing population, with technological changes, among other things, Y_r and T are likely to rise overtime.

We have assumed that a change in M would cause D to change. But this may not always be the case. It is conceivable that we may have a change in M without any significant change in total demand. This may happen when the rate of interest, which is a link between M and D according to modern analysis and is ignored by the quantity theory, may already be so low that any increases in M are held as idle balances by the public.

These are some of the limitations of the velocity formulation of the quantity theory of money. It is a very oversimplified explanation of the mechanism of price change. The quantity of money is but one of the several variables which could influence the behavior of the general price level. The influence of M on P is not direct but rather through its influence on interest rates which in turn affect total demand and the level of prices. Yet the rate of interest is completely ignored by the theory. It is true that M and P tend to move historically in somewhat the same direction over time, but the point to be stressed is that the relationship between M and P is not a one-way relation as postulated by the quantity theory; M may influence P and P in turn may influence M.

In the case of hyperinflation, however, price changes are largely attributable to changes in the quantity of money. The experiences of "galloping" inflation in Germany in the early 1920's and in other countries were largely the consequence of astronomical increases in the quantity of money freely printed by the government. In addition, the quantity of money is still the basic aggregate which central banking authorities seek to control in promoting general economic stability, including the stabilization of the level of prices. Open market operations, variable reserve requirements and discount policy, among other things, are used by central banks to influence the volume of bank reserves, the supply of money, and the structure of interest rates, and, hopefully, aggregate demand and the level of real income and employment.

The Cash-Balances Formulation

The cash-balances formulation of the quantity theory was developed and popularized by Cambridge economists, namely Marshall, Pigou, Robertson, and Keynes. While the income-velocity formulation is concerned with the average number of times which the quantity of money turns over to meet the income flow, the cash-balances formulation is concerned with the volume of money balances which the public desires to have on hand for a certain length of time in anticipation of expenditure on goods and services. Money balances are needed by the public to bridge the gap between receipts and payments which are not synchronized. Suppose that the community as a whole desires to have on hand cash balances sufficient to purchase goods and services for two months, the real value of desired cash balances is then equal to 1/6 of the annual flow of goods and services. Given the real value of money balances as a fraction of real income which the public desires to hold (the demand for real balances), the demand for nominal or money balances depends upon the general price level, which can be expressed as kP_yY_r, where P_yY_r is gross national product and k is that fraction of GNP which the public wants to hold in the form of money balances. Given the supply of money M, the community's demand for, and supply of, money are in equilibrium only when

$$M = kP_yY_r$$

which is the cash-balances equation. It is a condition for monetary equilibrium. So long as this condition is not satisfied, then there will be changes in the various elements of the equation until the demand for money by the public is exactly equal to the quantity of money available for holding. But which variables are to change to restore equilibrium between supply and demand? Of M, k, P_y, and Y_r, the Cambridge theorists, like adherents of the velocity formulation, assume that the factor k and the level of real output Y_r are approximately constant. Given M, then the price level P_y would have to change, once equilibrium is disturbed, until equilibrium is once again restored.

Let us start from an equilibrium position with M_0 = \$100 billion, $k = 1/6$ and $P_y{}^0\,Y_r{}^0$ = \$600 billion. Assume that as a result of central banking operations, the quantity of money is doubled, M = \$200 billion. At the existing price level $P_y{}^0$, there is an excess of supply over the demand for money. Since the quantity of money existing at any moment in time has to be held by individuals and others in the community (it does not just float around without being held by somebody), with M_1 = \$200 billion, what the public has on hand is more than what it desires to hold at $P_y{}^0$. Individuals of course can reduce their money balances by spending. But if all the individuals in the community attempt to do the same thing, the result is increases in total money spending. Given the level of output Y_r, increased demand would cause the general price level to rise. When P_y is doubled (and money income P_yY_r is doubled), equilibrium is restored, since with P_yY_r = \$1,200 billion, the supply of money of \$200 billion is exactly equal to the demand for money by the public:

$$M = kP_yY_r = (1/6)(1{,}200) = \$200 \text{ billion}$$

The movement of Py is reversed when M decreases. Assume that the quantity of money decreases from \$100 billion to \$50 billion. At the price level $P_y{}^0$, there is an excess of demand over the supply of money. The only way by which the community can build up money balances is to reduce spending. Decreased total spending would then cause P_y to decline. When it is reduced by one-half, monetary equilibrium is reestablished:

$$M = kP_yY_r = (1/6)(\$300) = \$50 \text{ billion}$$

With k and Y_r assumed to be constant, the strict interpretation of the cash-balances formulation is the same as the velocity formulation: changes in M cause proportional changes in P_y. In point of fact, the two formulations are two alternative ways of describing the same point. One can be readily converted into the other and vice verse. From the income-flow equation $MV_y = P_y Y_r$, we have $V_y = \frac{P_y Y_r}{M}$: From the cash-balances equation $M = k P_y Y_r$, we have $k = \frac{M}{P_y Y_r}$.

It follows immediately that $k = \frac{1}{V_y}$. Suppose that $V_y = 4$, then $k = 1/4$. This means that if the rate of turnover of M is 4 times a year, then money balances held by the public are $1/4$ of income, that is, they would be sufficient to purchase goods and services for three months. Since $V_y = 1/k$, whatever affects V_y affects k, although inversely. An increase in V_y means a decrease in k and vice versa. For example, an increase in the regularity of income payments (weekly instead of monthly) would cause V_y to rise. But as people are paid incomes more frequently than before, they would not need to hold as large cash balances as they otherwise would.

Although the two formulations are interchangeable, the cash-balances formulation, in many respects, is an advance on the velocity formulation. While the velocity formulation emphasizes the supply of money M, the cash-balances approach is concerned with both the demand for and supply of money. The theory thus lends itself to the general theory of value; the value of money is determined by the demand for money and supply of money. The characteristic of the demand curve for money of the cash-balances formulation is that it is a rectangular hyperbola—a curve having a unitary demand elasticity.[2] The *DD* curve in Fig. 17-2 is such a curve. Given the demand for real balances kY_r, the amount of money demanded increases or decreases in proportion with the general price level. With the demand curve for money *DD* and the supply of money M_0, the value of money $\frac{1}{P_0}$ (or the general price level P_0) is determined. When the quantity of money increases from M_0 to M_1, the general price level increases from P_0 to P_1 or the value of money decreases from $1/P_0$ to $1/P_1$.

The cash-balances formulation, in asking why people want to hold money balances, lends itself to the analysis of the motives and decisions of individuals in holding money. It is the extension of the analysis of the various motives of the public in holding money—a nonearning asset—and interest-yielding claims which leads to the development of the liquidity preference theory of interest which is a link between money, effective demand, and the level of business activity. The

[2]From $M = kY$, (where $Y = P_y Y_r$), it follows that

$$E_m = \frac{dM}{dY}\frac{Y}{M} = k\frac{Y}{kY} = 1$$

where E_m is the elasticity of the demand for money.

velocity concept, on the other hand, is somewhat mechanical. It is basically a residual element in the equation of exchange.

The cash-balances formulation, furthermore, lends itself to the analysis of the effects of changes in the demand for money (changes in k) on the general price level. Suppose that we have the following equilibrium position $M = kP_yY_r = (1/8)(800) = \$100$ billion. Assume that for some reason or others (for example, increase in the regularity of income payments), the public desires to hold only 1/16 of income in money balances. Given $M = \$100$ billion, the only way which individuals can reduce desired balances is to spend. The increase in total demand as a consequence of the attempt of the community to reduce cash balances would drive up the price level. When P_y is doubled, the demand for money balances is again brought into balance with the supply of money:

$$M = k\,P_yY_r = (1/16)\,(1{,}600) = \$100 \text{ billion}$$

In Fig. 17-2, given M_0, the decrease in the demand for money from DD to D_1D_1, causes the price level to increase from P_0 to P_2. Of course, if the central

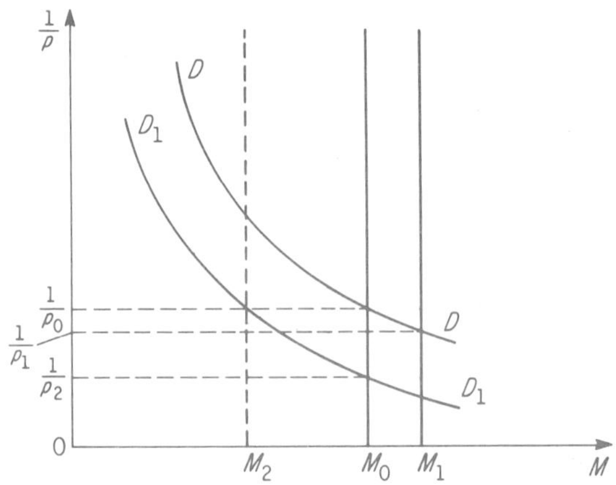

Fig. 17-2. The value of money.

bank authorities take action to reduce the supply of money from M_0 to M_2, then the price level would remain unchanged at P_0, inasmuch as the decrease in the demand for money is coupled with an equivalent decrease in the supply of money. Similarly, if the fraction of income which the community desires to hold in the form of money increased from 1/8 to 1/4, then, given M, the attempt of the community to build up money balances by reducing spending would cause the general price level to decline until the quantity of money available is what the public desires to hold.

The cash-balances formulation, nevertheless, is subject to numerous limitations. It is not a satisfactory theory explaining the mechanism of price change. The theory considers only the demand for money for transaction purposes (money as a medium of exchange alone), hence, money balances over and above those needed for transaction purposes are assumed to be spent, which causes P_y to change. Although the formulation implies a theory of choice of individuals between holding money and consumption, it did not go far enough to include the choice between holding money as an asset and other financial claims. In ignoring the asset demand for money which is closely related to the rate of interest, the theory fails to recognize the possibility that at a low rate of interest, the public may elect to hold any increase in M in the form of idle balances, hence no change in total spending and the general price level.

THE QUANTITY-THEORY ANALYSIS EXTENDED

In the analysis of the effects of changes in the quantity of money on the price level, the quantity theory provides no explanation of the way by which a change in the quantity of money acts upon expenditure and the level of prices. The analysis is comparative-static which states that starting from an initial equilibrium position a change in the quantity of money, ceteris paribus, would cause a proportional change in the price level in the new equilibrium situation.

Other writers of the early twentieth century, who were essentially quantity theorists, went a step further in analyzing the manner in which monetary changes influence expenditure and the level of prices. Their analysis is dynamic in that it traces the path of monetary disturbance between two equilibrium situations. According to Knut Wicksell, the basic aggregate whose changes cause the price level to change is the expenditure flow $E(=MV)$. But what causes E to change and how changes in E cause the level of prices to change? To him, the rate of interest is the strategic variable. It is the source of changes in money, expenditure, prices, and economic fluctuations. He conceived of two rates of interest in a monetary economy: the natural rate of interest r and the market rate of interest i. The natural rate of interest is defined as the expected yield on an extra unit of capital asset (similar to what we refer to as the marginal efficiency of capital), or the rate at which the demand for loan capital is equal to the supply of savings, or the rate at which the general price level has no tendency to change. The market rate of interest is the rate charged by commercial banks. So long as the natural rate of interest and the market rate of interest equal, there is monetary equilibrium with no change in the price level. When r is not equal to i, then economic forces are set in motion causing either a cumulative price inflation or deflation until another equilibrium is reached in which r and i are again brought into balance with each other. Suppose that as a consequence of an increase in the quantity of money, i falls below r $(i < r)$, there will be an increase in investment demand inasmuch as the cost of borrowed funds is lower than the expected rate of return on capital assets. The increase in the demand for capital goods would lead to an increase in E which, in a full employment economy, would cause the price level to rise. This cumulative price inflation is however not a never-ending process. It is self-correcting. At higher levels of prices and money income, people would need more circulating currency (coins and notes) for transaction purposes by drawing on commercial banks. Such currency withdrawals would cause bank reserves to fall. The losses of reserves would prompt banks to restrict lending, thereby causing the market rate of interest to rise until it is equal to the natural rate of interest.

On the other hand, when the market rate of interest rises above the natural rate brought about by losses of reserves as a result of, say, restrictive central bank actions, a cumulative price deflation would take place. The higher cost of borrowed funds would cause a contraction in investment (and consumption) outlays. As a result, prices would fall. At lower levels of prices and money income, currency balances held by the public would be more than balances desired for transactions. Part of these balances would return to the banking system making it possible for banks to reduce the money rates. The cumulative price deflation would end when i is again in equilibrium with r.

It follows from the Wicksellian analysis that a change in the quantity of money (and bank reserves) leads to discrepancy between the natural rate and market rate of interest which in turn causes monetary expenditure to change. In a full employment economy this results in price-level changes. If the Wicksellian analysis were valid, then the task of price stabilization policy is to keep the market rate of interest equal to the natural rate. According to him, "The only possibility of a rational control of the price level must lie in the proper regulation of the interest policy of banks."[3] The guide to monetary policy, according to Wicksell and his followers, is the price level itself. If M and i can be so manipulated that the price level is stable, then there is no discrepancy between i and r. The discrepancy between i and r however, may be generated either by monetary changes which cause i to change or technological changes which cause r to change. Assume that r rises above i because of a technological advance which increases the productivity of capital and lowers production costs and prices. To keep the market rate equal to the natural rate, the central bank in this case would have to raise the rate of interest by reducing bank reserves and the supply of money. But this would lead to further decline in prices. On the other hand, to keep the price level stable, the central bank would have to increase bank reserves and the supply of money. But this would cause i to fall, bringing about further discrepancy between r and i. The price-level criterion is therefore consistent only with the case in which the discrepancy between i and r is caused by changes in i generated by monetary changes. Yet, according to Wicksell, "the difference between the actual loan and normal rates . . . arises less frequently because the

[3] K. Wicksell, *Lectures on Political Economy*, p. 216.

loan rate changes spontaneously whilst the normal or real rate remains unchanged but on the contrary because the normal rate rises or falls whilts the loan rate remains unchanged or only tardily follows it."[4]

Wicksell, like other quantity theorists, based his analysis on the assumption of complete flexibility of prices and wages upward as well as downward and of a full-employment economy. Therefore changes in expenditures only cause price changes, not output changes. He thus failed as did others to recognize the possibility that if prices and wages were not flexible downward, then in the face of declining demand business corporations could reduce output and lay off workers—hence a less than full-employment equilibrium economy. The contributions made by Wicksell to monetary economics were nevertheless important. His analysis was concerned not only with the long-run equilibrium of money, interest, and prices but also the path of short-run disequilibrium disturbances generated by monetary changes. His analysis brought into focus the rate of interest as the strategic link between monetary changes and price level changes. His theory left its marks in the writings of economists in the 1920's and 1930's including Hawtrey, Hayek, Mises, and Keynes. The theory of cyclical fluctuations developed by Hayek and Mises and others largely rested on the Wicksellian interest theory.

Prior to the appearance of the *Treatise on Money*, Keynes was a quantity theorist in the cash-balances tradition. But in the *Treatise* he attempted to improve upon the classical quantity theory and link the rate of interest and cash balances to the determination of the level of prices. He started with a set of definitional equations. Income Y–(the product of the price level P_y and the volume of output O, that is, P_yO) was defined as the sum of payments to factors of production E (which includes wages, salaries, interest, rents, and normal profits) and windfall profits Q (profits over and above normal). Savings S is defined as that unspent portion of income paid out to production factors ($S = E - C$); and investment I, the difference between income (Y) and consumption (C) ($I = Y - C$). It follows that

$$Y = E + Q = C + S + Q$$
$$Y = C + I$$

Hence

$$Q = I - S$$

and we have

$$Y = P_yO = E + Q = E + (I - S)$$

and

$$P_y = \frac{E + (I - S)}{O}$$

[4]*Ibid.*, p. 205.

This equation is Keynes' framework for the analysis of the mechanism of price change. Assume that there is an increase in the quantity of money which leads to an increase in bank reserves. With greater ability to lend, banks will be willing to lower the rate of interest. The lower cost of borrowed money means more profitable investment opportunities. The increase in investment demand (and probably the decrease in savings as a result of low rate of interest) causes a discrepancy between I and S and windfall profits appear. As a result, prices rise. In a full-employment economy, increases in I would generate greater monetary income payments which cause P_y to rise further. As P_y rises, the public, to increase currency holdings for transactions, withdraws currency from banks, causing bank reserves to deplete. Banks would be forced to restrain lending and raise the loan rate. As the rate of interest rises, savings would be stimulated and investment slowed down. The rate of interest would continue to change until $S = I$. At this point, windfall profits disappear and equilibrium is restored. The process is reversed when the quantity of money decreases.

This analysis is an extension of the quantity theory analysis to include the Wicksellian interest theory. The discrepancy between I and S which is considered as the strategic variable determining the behavior of P_y is generated by the discrepancy between the natural rate of interest and market rate of interest. When $r > i$, then $I > S$, and P_y rises. When $r < i, I < S$, and P_y falls. In equilibrium, $r = i$ which means $I = S$. The equation $P_y = \dfrac{E + (I - S)}{O}$ is basically a modified form of the income equation of exchange. The price level P_y is the sum of cost (including normal profit) per unit of output (E/O) and abnormal profit per unit of output ($Q/O = I - S/O$). But in equilibrium, $I - S = Q = 0$; hence, $P_y = E/O$ or $P_yO = E = MV_y$, the familiar income-flow equation of exchange. Keynes in the *Treatise*, like Wicksell and other quantity theorists, also based his analysis on the assumption of a given level of output. Therefore an increase in M would eventually result in a corresponding change in P_y; "In equilibrium . . . there is a unique relationship between the quantity of money and the price levels of consumption goods and of output as a whole, of such a character that if the quantity of money were double the price levels would be double also."[5]

SUMMARY

According to classical analysis, all phenomena of economic life can be described and analyzed in terms of goods and services. The economic role of money is to serve as a technical device to facilitate exchanges. It does not exert any real influence on the economic process which functions as it would without money. Money is thus a veil and its influence is only on the absolute level of

[5] J. M. Keynes, *A Treatise on Money*, Vol. 1, p. 16.

prices. To explain the influence of money on the general price level, economists in the past used the transactions equation of exchange, $MV = PT$, or its income variant, $MV_y = P_y Y_r$ as an analytical framework. The equation itself is not a theory. But it was developed into a theory of the value of money or price-level determination by economists when they assumed that $P = f(M, V, T)$ (or $Py = f(M, V_y, Y_r)$ and that V and T (or V_y and Y_r) are approximately constant. The general conclusion drawn from these assumptions was that the price level changes proportionately with changes in the quantity of money. Such a strict conclusion, however, is not valid because the assumptions on the behavior of P, M, V, and T are not valid. V and T do change over the short as well as long run. The price level P, instead of being a completely passive variable, may influence the behavior of V, T, and M as well.

While the velocity formulation of the quantity theory is concerned with money moving, the cash-balances formulation is concerned with money holding. By dividing both sides of the income equation of exchange $MV_y = P_y Y_r$ by V_y, we have $M = \left(\frac{1}{V_y}\right) P_y Y_r = kP_y Y_r$, where $\left(k = \frac{1}{V_y}\right)$. This is a condition for monetary equilibrium when the right-hand side represents the demand for money —that fraction of income which the public desires to hold in the form of money in anticipation of expenditure on goods and services; and M is the supply of money. In equilibrium P_y is such that the quantity of money available is just what the public desires to hold. With $k = \frac{1}{V_y}$ and Y_r assumed to be approximately constant, the conclusion of the strict interpretation of the cash-balances formulation is the same as the velocity formulation, that is, changes in M cause proportional changes in P_y.

Although these formulations are alternative ways of describing the same thing, the cash-balances formulation, in many respects, is superior to the velocity formulation. It explains the value of money in terms of the general theory of value: the value of money is determined by the demand for, and supply of, money. While the V concept is somewhat artifical, the k concept lends itself to the analysis of the motives of the public in holding money balances. The theory, however, remains inadequate. It still considers money only as an exchange medium. Hence money balances over and above balances desired for transactions are spent, which leads to rising prices. The theory ignores the rate of interest. It is concerned only with the general price level and passes over the effects of price changes on the level of output and employment.

The quantity theory analysis was broadened by such writers as Wicksell, Keynes, and others in the 1920's and 1930's. Their analysis was not only concerned with the long-run equilibrium of money and prices but also with short-run monetary disturbances, and the manner in which monetary changes affect the expenditure flow and the price level. The rate of interest was established as a strategic variable linking monetary changes with changes in expenditure and the level of prices. It is the discrepancy between the natural rate of interest and the market rate of interest which causes investment (and consumption) outlays to change which brings about either a cumulative price inflation or deflation. Their analysis, however, still rested on the assumption of a full-employment economy. Thus the consequence of monetary changes is only price changes.

PROBLEMS

1. Why is the theory of money relegated to the background of the theory of value and distribution in the framework of classical analysis?

2. What is the equation of exchange? What are basic determinants of the various elements of the equation? In what sense is the equation an identity? Is it a theory of the general price level? Explain the difference between the transaction equation of exchange and the income equation of exchange.

3. Explain the transactions-velocity and income-velocity formulations of the quantity theory. What are their limitations? Are they useless in explaining price-level changes?

4. What is the cash-balances formulation of the quantity theory? What are its shortcomings? Is it true that the cash-balances formulation and the velocity formulation are alternative approaches to the same problem? Why is the cash-balances approach, in many respects, superior to the velocity formulation?

5. In what way was the quantity theory analysis extended by such writers as Wicksell and Keynes (in his Treatise on Money)? What is the relationship between Keynes' fundamental equation and the income-flow equation of exchange? In equilibrium, is his analysis of the mechanism of price change any different from the strict version of the quantity theory?

6. Assume that the quantity of money M = \$100 billion; that $k = 1/4$ and Y_r = 200 billion units (k and Y_r are constant), and the price level is P = \$1.00. (a) What is the demand for money balances at that price level? (b) Is there equilibrium between the demand for and supply of money at that price level? (c) What would be the equilibrium price level and how would this be brought about in terms of the cash-balance formulation?

chapter 18

National Income: Accounting and Composition

Classical economists did recognize the independent influences of money on the levels of output and employment when the monetary mechanism is out of order, but these were considered as temporary deviations from the full-employment equilibrium path, which tended to be self-correcting. Such a conclusion was arrived at on the basis of classical assumptions in regard to the behavior of savings, investment, wages, and prices. Investment was assumed to rise, and savings, to fall, as the rate of interest falls. Therefore, an increase in savings would cause the rate of interest to fall. And a fall in the rate of interest would cause investment to rise. Changes in savings and investments would be sufficient to restore equilibrium between them at full employment. Wages and prices were assumed to be completely flexible in either direction. Decreases in consumption would cause prices and wages to decline. Declining prices and wages would lead to greater demand for goods and labor. All this would work toward restoring full-employment equilibrium.

These assumptions, which did not appear to be contradicted by economic conditions of the nineteenth-century world, were inconsistent with developments of the 1930's. The Great Depression was anything but temporary. It lasted almost a decade. Attention of theorists was then shifted from the long-run determination of the price level to the analysis of the influences of short-run changes in money spending on the levels of employment and output and to policy measures for promoting economic recovery. The theoretical search for the answers to the economic problems of the 1930's culminated in the development of a new theoretical body, the income-expenditure theory, which substantially parted with, and reexamined the basic assumptions and premises of, classical analysis. The theory emphasizes the influences of money spending on the level of economic activity. The development of the theory which reflected largely the work of J.M. Keynes has been refined and broadened by modern theorists. The theory is referred to as the "income-expenditure" theory having as its analytical framework the income-expenditure equation. The center of focus of the theory is the level of income, how income is formed, and factors which cause the level of income to change. In this chapter we shall describe the accounting and composition of the various income magnitudes, such as gross national product, net national product and national income. The process of income formation will be described in the next chapter.

GROSS NATIONAL PRODUCT (GNP) AND ALTERNATIVE MEASURES

GNP is the market value of all final goods and services produced by an economy over a specified period of time, usually a year. Let $q_1, q_2, \ldots, q_n$ be the quantities of goods 1, 2, . . . , n produced, and $p_1\ p_2, \ldots, p_n$ their unit prices respectively; then GNP is the sum of the pq's.

$$\text{GNP} = p_1q_1 + p_2q_2 + \cdots + p_nq_n = \sum p_iq_i = PQ$$

The value of goods produced is necessarily equal to (a) the expenditure on these products. and (b) the income and profits generated by the production of these goods. They all, in fact, represent exactly the same thing looked at from different view points:

Expenditures on final outputs = Value of final products = Income (costs) and profits earned

It follows that we can measure GNP either by the sum of the expenditures of the various sectors of the economy on goods and services or the sum of income and profits earned by those who contribute to their production. To arrive at the expenditure total on final products, we subtract from total sales the sales of intermediate goods and raw materials used in the production of final outputs; otherwise, double counting would be involved. For example, the retail price of a wool suit of \$100 embodies the value of (e.g.) \$15 of wool material. If we include the retail value of the suit and the \$15 worth of material used, then the value of the material is counted twice. To subtract the sales of intermediate goods and raw materials from gross sales is equivalent to taking the sum of the "value-added" in the production of goods, through all stages of production, from the raw material stage to the finished product stage. The value-added by a firm at a given stage of production is equal to the receipts from the sales of its products less payments made to other firms for raw materials and other supplies. The equality between the market value of a final product and the sum of value-added is illustrated by the following example regarding the production and sale of corn flakes (Table 18-1). It is assumed that the corn producer does not purchase intermediate goods. Hence all payments which he made including his profits constitute value-added which is \$30. The producer of corn flakes purchased corns from the corn producer, processed it and sold corn flakes to the retailer at the wholesale price of \$45. This sale receipt included \$30 as payment to the corn producer for corn used as material and the processing cost and profit

TABLE 18-1

Final Price And Value Added

Stage of Production	Intermediate Goods	Other Costs and Profits	Sales Receipts	Value Added
Producer of corn				
Rent		5		
Labor and other cost . . .		20		
Profits		5		
Corn	0		30	30
Producer of corn flakes				
Corn purchased	30			
Labor and other cost . . .		10		
Profits		5		
Corn flakes (wholesale) . . .			45	15
Retailer				
Corn flakes Purchased (wholesale)	45			
Retail cost		5		
Profits		5		
Corn flakes (retail)			55	10
Total	75	55	130	55

of $15. The value-added contributed by the producer of corn flakes was thus $15. The retailer in turn purchased corn flakes wholesale and sold them to consumers at $55. The retail price included $45 as intermediate purchases and $10 as retail cost and profit. The value added by the retailer was thus $10. The sum of value-added through different stages of production was $55 which is equal to the retail price. This is of course equal to the difference between total sale receipts and the costs of intermediate goods ($130 – $75 = $55).

Gross National Product or Expenditure

To estimate gross national product as expenditures on outputs, we divide the economy into four sectors: the business, household, government, and foreign sectors, and take the sum of the expenditures of these sectors on goods and services. GNP is thus the sum of personal consumption expenditures (C), gross private domestic investment (I), government expenditures on goods and services (G), and net exports ($X - M$). Table 18-2 shows GNP of the United States in 1968 as the sum of sectoral expenditures.

TABLE 18-2
GNP or Expenditures on Outputs of the United States in 1968 (in billions of dollars)

Personal Consumption Expenditures (*C*)			536.6
Durable goods		83.3	
Non-durable goods		230.6	
Services		222.8	
Gross Private Domestic Investment (*I*)			126.3
Non-residential structures		29.3	
Producers' durable equipment		59.5	
Residential structures		30.2	
Changes in business inventories		7.3	
Government Purchases of Goods and Services (*G*)			200.3
Federal		99.5	
National defense	78.0		
Other	21.5		
State and Local		100.7	
Net Exports of Goods and Services ($X - M$)			2.5
Exports (*X*)		50.6	
Imports (*M*)		48.1	
Gross National Product (Y) $= C + I + G + (X - M) =$			865.7*

Source: *Federal Reserve Bulletin*, August 1969.
*Items may not add up to total due to rounding.

Personal Consumption Expenditures

These represent the expenditures of households on consumption goods—both durable and nondurable—such as automobiles, refrigerators, other household appliances, and food products and services, such as rents and medical expenses. As indicated in Table 18-2, the purchases of consumer nondurables constitute the largest component of total consumption. The expenditures on consumer durables are relatively small compared to the other components of personal expenditures.

Gross Private Domestic Investment

These represent newly produced capital assets purchased by business corporations and individuals. These include machines and equipment acquired by firms and new houses purchased by individuals. Just as consumers are final users of consumer durables and consumer nondurables, business corporations are final users of capital goods. Change in business inventories is another component of gross domestic investment. This represents the amount of goods which businesses "sell" to themselves. Changes in inventories, of course, may be intended or unintended. They may pile up simply because consumer demand is inadequate to absorb all the goods produced by businesses. Increases in business inventories, whether planned or not, are treated as an expenditure on capital goods, while depletion in inventories is considered as disinvestment or negative investment. This component of total expenditures is referred to as "gross" investment because it represents expenditure on capital goods both for the replacement of capital equipment consumed in production (that is, capital consumption allowances or depreciation) and net additions to the capital stock.

Government Expenditures on Goods and Services

These are purchases of goods and services by government at all levels: federal, state, and local. Newly produced goods sold by businesses to the government range from office supplies to aircraft, battleships, guns, and tanks. Wages and salaries are paid to government employees for their services which are passed on to the public in the form of police protection, education, and the administration of justice, and so on. Inasmuch as the services rendered by the government are mostly not priced, they are valued at what they cost the government to render such services.

Net Exports or Net Foreign Investment

The value of goods which we purchase from abroad is our imports. The value of goods which we sell to foreigners is our exports. Our expenditures on imported products are a component of total expenditure. Yet such expenditures generate income–not for us, but for the foreign producers selling the goods to us. On the other hand, the goods and services which we sell to foreign countries are part of the volume of goods and services which we produce. They generate incomes to those engaged in their production. But since they are sold abroad, there are no domestic sales which correspond to this source of income. To allow for the expenditures on foreign products and the sales of domestically produced goods to foreign countries, the national income statisticians subtract import expenditures from total expenditure on goods and services and add the value of exports. The difference between exports and imports is referred to as net exports or net foreign investment, which of course may be zero, positive, or negative, depending upon the value of exports and imports. Net foreign investment is relatively an unimportant component of GNP of the United States, substantially less than 1 percent of GNP in 1968. But this does not mean that foreign trade is not an important component of overall economic activity. It is, as reflected by the fact that during the same year the United States sold $50.6 billion of goods and services to foreigners and bought $48.1 billion from them.

Gross National Product or Income

The expenditures on final goods and services are receipts of businesses and individuals engaged in their production. These receipts would be allocated to wages and salaries of workers, interest to owners of money capital, rents to owners of land, profits to entrepreneurs, and capital consumption allowances. GNP is thus also the sum of income and profits earned. Table 18-3 shows GNP

TABLE 18-3
GNP or Income of the United States in 1968
(in billions of dollars)

Compensation of Employees			513.6
Wages and Salaries		465.0	
Private	369.0		
Military	18.0		
Government civilian	78.0		
Supplements to wages and salaries		48.6	
Employer contributions for social insurance	24.4		
Other labor income	24.2		
Proprietors' Income			63.8
Business and professional		49.2	
Farm		14.6	
Rental Income of Persons			21.2
Corporate Profits and Inventory Valuation Adjustment			87.9
Profits before tax		91.1	
Profits tax liability	41.3		
Profits after tax	49.8		
Dividends	23.1		
Undistributed profits	26.7		
Inventory valuation adjustment		-3.2	
Net Interest			28.0
National Income at Factor Cost			714.4
Plus: Indirect business tax and non-tax liability			77.9
Business transfer payments			3.4
Capital consumption allowances			73.3
Statistical discrepancy			-2.5
Surplus of government enterprises less government subsidies			-0.8
Charges against Gross National Product =			865.7

Source: Federal Reserve Bulletin, August 1969

of the United States in 1968 as the sum of income and profits. Most of the items in the table are self-explanatory. Some items, however, require further explanation. Inventory valuation adjustment represents the change in the value of business inventories arising not from changes in volume but from changes in the market value of goods making up inventories. Profits realized from rising prices of inventories are part of business profits. Conversely, the loss in the value of inventories resulting from declining prices is subtracted from business earnings. Net interest is total interest payments less interest paid by the government on the public debt, which is somewhat arbitrarily excluded from GNP. We have defined GNP as the market value of final goods and services—that is, the sum of the quantities of goods and services times their market prices. But the market prices of products include both factor as well as nonfactor payments. Therefore, in estimating GNP as the sum of incomes and profits, we have to add to factor payments—wages and salaries, interest, rents and profits—such nonfactor payments as indirect business taxes and business transfer payments that are nevertheless component parts of market prices. Surpluses of governmental enterprises, which are a kind of indirect taxes, are also to be added. On the other hand, subsidies paid by the government to subsidized firms which are in essence negative taxes have to be subtracted; they do not constitute a component part of the market prices of products sold by these subsidized firms.

Table 18-3 shows the measurement of GNP as the sum of income and profits of productive factors. GNP can also be measured in terms of the sum of the disposable incomes of households, governments, and businesses—that is, the income available to these sectors for the purchases of capital goods, consumption goods, and services. The disposable income of the household sector Y_d is the difference between total personal income and personal taxes. Personal income is the sum of wages and salaries received by individuals, interest, rents, and dividends paid by businesses, government transfer payments, business transfer payments, and interest paid by government. After deduction of personal taxes and other nontax liabilities, what is left is personal disposable income. That portion of disposable income which is not spent on consumption C is personal savings S_p. The disposable income of businesses S_b is the sum of corporate profits plus inventory valuation adjustment and depreciation reserves less the sum of corporate profit tax liability and dividends paid to shareholders.

TABLE 18–4
GNP of the United States in 1968 as the Sum of Sectoral Disposable Income (in billions of dollars)

Personal Disposable Income (Y_d)		575.0
Personal Consumption Expenditures (C)	536.6	
Personal Savings (S_p)	38.4	
Business Disposable Income (or Savings) (S_b)		96.8
Corporate profits plus inventory valuation adjustment	87.9	
Capital Consumption allowances	73.3	
Less:		
Profits tax liability	41.3	
Dividends	23.1	
Government Disposable Income (T)		195.6
Indirect business tax and non-tax liability	77.9	
Profits tax liability	41.3	
Personal tax and non-tax liability	97.9	
Contributions for social insurance	47.0	
Less:		
Government transfer payments	55.8	
Interest payments	11.9	
Subsidies less government surplus	0.8	
Statistical Discrepancy		-1.7
Gross National Product = $Y_d + S_b + T$ =		865.7

Source: Federal Reserve Bulletin, August 1969

The disposable income of the government *T* is what remains of government tax revenues (and surplus of governmental enterprises) after deduction of government transfer payments, interest on the public debt, and subsidies to business enterprises. This represents the amount of income available to the government for payments of wages and salaries to government employees, and purchases of goods from businesses. Gross national product as the sum of sectoral disposable incomes is shown in Table 18-4.

NET NATIONAL PRODUCT AND NATIONAL INCOME

GNP does not measure the value of current production inasmuch as it includes the estimated value of capital assets for the replacement of those consumed in production (depreciation allowances). In order to arrive at the value of net national output or net national product, we must subtract from GNP the amount of capital consumption. Thus NNP = GNP - Depreciation. Depreciation, however, is extremely difficult to estimate. There are several methods of depreciation valuation, and the use of each method would lead to a different figure for capital consumption allowances—hence, a different figure for NNP. Estimates of capital depreciation are nevertheless given by the U.S. Department of Commerce, the main source of national income statistics. For instance, for 1968 capital consumption allowances were $73.3 billion; therefore NNP for the year was $865.7 - 73.3 = $792.4 billion.

Both GNP and NNP are estimated at market prices. But we have mentioned that certain components of market prices in fact do not represent payments to productive factors. If we wish to arrive at the income which represents factor payments alone, then we have to subtract from NNP those nonfactor payments such as indirect business taxes, business transfer payments, surpluses of governmental enterprises, and then add government subsidies. When all nonfactor payments are subtracted from NNP and subsidies are added, the result is National Income (at factor cost). Table 18-5 indicates National Income (at factor cost) of the United States in 1968.

TABLE 18-5
National Income of the United States in 1968
(in billions of dollars)

Net National Product		792.4
Less: Indirect business tax and non-tax liability	77.9	
Business transfer payments	3.4	
Statistical discrepancy	-2.5	
Plus: Subsidies less surplus of government enterprises	0.8	
National Income		714.4

Source: Federal Reserve Bulletin, August 1969

Gross national product, net national product, and national income are important income magnitudes. Changes in these income magnitudes over time are approximate indicators of an economy's performance. Each of these income concepts is useful for the investigation of specific economic problems. For instance, gross national product is the most useful aggregate in the study of the short-run level of employment; it is the gross volume of output that determines the short-run level of employment. Net national product which is the value of current production, on the other hand, is particularly useful in the study of the long-run growth of output of an economy. It shows changes in the capital stock which is a basic variable determining the potential growth of a country in the long run. National income, as the sum of factor payments, is particularly useful in the study of the distribution of income between production factors: labor, land, capital, and entrepreneurship. The study of the changes in the relative shares of these income groups would give us insights into the forces that bring about such changes, affecting not only the total welfare of society as a whole but also the welfare of the various groups of individuals in society.

LIMITATIONS OF NATIONAL INCOME STATISTICS

National income statistics are not accurate, nor do the people who compile them claim them to be. They are rough estimates not only because some of the data used may be inadequate and untrustworthy but also because of somewhat arbitrary decisions of national income statisticians on what to be included in and excluded from the estimates of various income magnitudes. We have seen that GNP is the market value of all final goods and services produced, but what about goods and services which are not for sale–goods and services produced and consumed directly by producers? Inasmuch as these goods and services are part of the actual volume of goods and services produced, national income statisticians include them in their estimate of GNP by assigning an imputed cash value for these goods and services. For instance, farm products produced and directly consumed by farmers receive an imputed cash value. So do the services from houses occupied by owners. Just like rents on rented dwellings which are part of GNP, estimates on the value of housing services enjoyed by homeowners are included in GNP. Homeowners are regarded as landlords renting their houses to themselves. It goes without saying that the estimates of these imputed values may be subject to wide margins of error. Furthermore, there are services which are not included in GNP simply because there is no realistic way of estimating their value. We know that millions of housewives are rendering services to their own families, but value of these services is not included in GNP. But when housewives, instead of doing their own household services, get them done by housemaids and pay for these services, then GNP increases; yet there is actually no change in the volume of goods and services produced. By the same token, services rendered by members of families for themselves, say in mowing lawns, are not included in GNP. But if the same services are performed by gardeners who are paid for the same services, then GNP increases.

In addition, incomes earned from certain services are counted as part of GNP where they are legal and not as part of GNP where they are ruled illegal. For instance, in Reno and Las Vegas where gambling is legalized, income earned from gambling business is of course part of GNP, but in states where gambling is illegal, the income earned from that source is not part of GNP. By the same token, income earned from such illegal sources as black market operations and sales of prohibited goods is not counted as part of GNP. There is simply no realistic basis to assign a value to these goods and services. But even if there were a realistic basis to estimate the value of these goods and services, there are people who would argue against such inclusion on the ground of "immorality"or "social undesirability."!

Then there is the question of how to treat interest on the public debt. Should it be included in, or excluded from, GNP? Interest paid by business corporations is part of GNP, since it represents payment for services rendered. But interest on the public debt is excluded from GNP by the National Income Division of the Department of Commerce. Such exclusion is justified on grounds that the major portion of the government debt was incurred to finance wars and current expenditures instead of income-producing assets, as in the case of business borrowings.

INCOME AND PERFORMANCE

We have mentioned that GNP is an index of economic performance. Changes in GNP, however, do not always represent corresponding changes in the economic performance of a society. Inasmuch as GNP is the money value of goods and services produced, changes in GNP may reflect either increases in the actual volume of output, increases in prices, or both. If increases in GNP are accounted for largely by rising prices, then such changes do not represent any real changes in the level of economic performance. Therefore, to use GNP as an indicator of economic performance we have to convert GNP in current dollars into GNP in constant dollars–that is, GNP in terms of the purchasing power of the dollar of a certain year used as base year so that they can be compared with each other. GNP in current dollars is converted into GNP in constant dollars by the use of price indexes. The conversion is made by dividing GNP in current dollars by the index of current prices times the base-year index. As an example, suppose that 1959 is used as a base-year and GNP for the year was $480 billion. The price index of 1959 is then 100. Assume that GNP in current dollars for 1960 was $600 billion and the index of prices in 1960 was 120. Because the price level has risen between 1959 and 1960, the change in GNP was partly a result of price increases. To measure GNP in 1960 in terms of the purchasing power of the dollar of 1959, we simplv divide 600 by 120 and multiply by 100, we have GNP for 1960 in dollars of 1959 purchasing power—that is, 600/120 × 100 = $500 billion. It follows that while GNP in current dollars for 1960 was $600 billion, "real" GNP for the year was only $500 billion. The difference between GNP in current dollars and GNP in constant dollars of course depends upon the extent of price changes. Table 18-6 shows GNP of the United States in current dollars and in constant (1958) dollars during 1929-68. But it should be noted that changes in GNP in constant dollars sometimes may be fictitious rather than "real" in that there is no actual change in the volume of goods and services produced. We have seen that household services performed by housewives are not included in GNP. Gross national product can increase merely because housewives, instead of doing the family laundry, take it to cleaning services. The increase in GNP in this case is clearly nominal. Services which were not included in GNP now enter into GNP statistics. Furthermore, when we consider the change in the amount of goods and services per capita as an indicator of the change in the average level of living of a society, then an actual increase in its GNP would not mean an increase in the average standard of living should population increase to the same extent. If a 3 percent increase in the volume of goods and services is matched by a 3 percent increase in population, then there is no change in the average standard of living of the people. The latter would be improved if the rate of population growth were less than 3 percent and deteriorated if the population were to increase by more than 3 percent.

Given these qualifications and others, gross national product estimate never-

TABLE 18–6
GNP in Current and Constant (1958) Dollars of the United States in 1929–1968
(in billions of dollars)

Year	GNP in Current Dollars	GNP in Constant Dollars
1929	103.1	203.6
1933	55.6	141.5
1941	124.5	263.7
1950	284.8	355.3
1961	520.1	497.3
1962	560.3	529.8
1963	590.5	551.0
1964	631.7	580.0
1965	681.2	614.4
1966	739.6	647.8
1967	784.7	673.1
1968	860.6	706.7

Source: Federal Reserve Bulletin, June 1969.

theless remains the most comprehensive aggregate indicating the performance of a society. The real GNP of a country, which is growing at a relatively high rate over time, indicates in general that it is making economic progress, that it has an increasing capacity to produce goods and services, and that its citizens are enjoying higher and higher levels of living.

THE CIRCULAR FLOW OF INCOME

Income is a flow. When we say that gross national product of the United States in 1968 was $865.7 billion, we refer to the value of the flow of outputs produced during the year of 1968, not the value of outputs at a particular moment in time. The income flow is a circular flow. Household families sell productive services to business and the government and receive income payments in wages and salaries. These incomes are used for the payment of taxes to the government, for expenditures on goods produced by businesses, and for savings. The business sector which sells goods to household and government receives income which is partly paid out in wages and salaries, interest, rents, and dividends to the household sector, and taxes to the government; what is left is retained earnings which can be plowed back as investment in new machines and equipment. The government which receives tax revenues from households and businesses uses portions of them for transfer payments, and the remaining is spent on goods and services produced by businesses and households. A simplified picture of the circular flow of income is shown in Fig. 18-1.

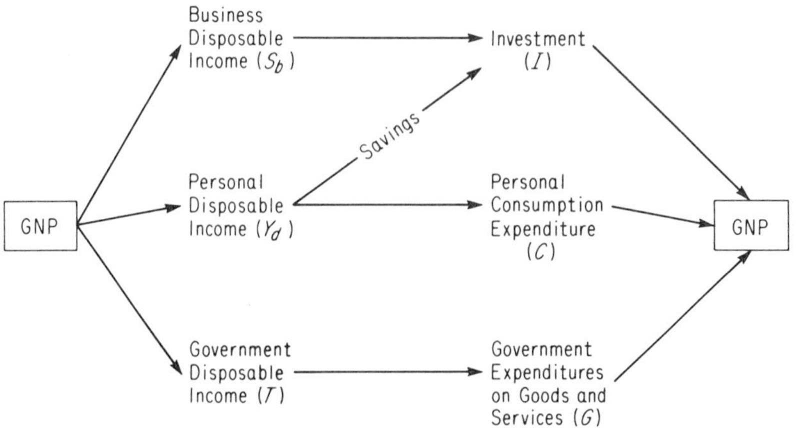

Fig. 18-1. The circular flow of income.

The circuit flow of income, however, is not a closed circuit. In the income flow, savings is an outlet, and investment is an inlet. Savings, which is the withholding of income from expenditure on goods and services, causes the income flow to decrease. Suppose household families save by reducing their consumption on certain products. This would cause the income of people who sell these products to decline. But that is not all. The decrease in the income of these people which would lead to a decrease in their expenditures in turn would cause the income of people who depend on their expenditures to decline, and so on. By the same token, when the government saves—that is, spends on goods and services less that its tax income ($T - G > 0$)—then the income of businesses and individuals depending on the government for the sales of goods and services would decrease. Similarly, when the business sector fails to use all of its income (S_b) in the purchase of new capital assets, then the income of producers of capital goods and their employees would decline.

While savings causes the income flow to contract, investment has a reverse effect. An increase in investment causes the income flow to expand. Suppose that business firms, either through retained earnings or borrowed funds from financial institutions, increase their purchases of new inventories, and new machines and equipment; this increase in business investment expenditures will cause the flow of income to increase (the income of producers of capital goods and others). The effects of savings and investments on the level of income are thus similar to those of the water inlet and outlet on the level of water in a water tank. So long as the inflow of investment is equal to the outflow of savings, then the level of income will remain unchanged—just as the water level in the tank when the water inflow is equal to the water outflow. When the inflow of investment exceeds the outflow of savings, the level of income will rise. On the other hand, when the outflow of savings exceeds the inflow of investment, then the level of income decreases.

MEASURED OR EX POST SAVINGS AND INVESTMENT

We have mentioned saving and investment here and there, we shall now further explain what we mean by saving and investment in the context of income analysis. By saving, we mean not spending. Savings is that portion of income which is not spent on consumption. By investment, we mean the expenditure on goods other than consumption goods—for example, newly produced capital goods and inventories. It follows that the acquisition of corporate bonds and government securities by commercial banks, which we have referred to as "bank investments," is not investment in the context of income analysis. These bonds and securities are earning assets of the banks but they are obligations of the issuing corporations and the government. They are financial investments and are all canceled out in the consolidated statement of the economy as a whole. Of course, the proceeds from the sale of newly issued bonds could be used by a business corporation for the purchase of new machines and equipment, but it is the acquisition of these new capital goods which constitutes investment, not the purchase of corporate securities. Nor is investment the purchase by a firm of an old piece of machinery from another firm. As far as the community as a whole is concerned, there is no change in its stock of capital goods. The transaction is merely a transfer of an existing asset between two firms: it is "investment" for the buying firm and "disinvestment" for the selling firm.

It is true that saving and investment are sometimes undertaken by the same unit as in the case of a business corporation which purchases new capital goods out of retained earnings and deprection reserves, but in general, saving and investment decisions are made by different groups of people and are determined by different determinants (discussed in the next chapter). Yet measured or ex post savings is always equal to measured or ex post investment. They are two sides of the same coin. Indeed, from Tables 18-2 and 18-4, which show gross national product as the sum of sectoral expenditures or the sum of sectoral disposable income, we have:

$$Y = C + I + G + (X - M)$$
$$Y = C + S_b + S_p + T$$

It follows that

$$I + G + (X - M) = S_b + S_p + T$$

Transposing G to the right-hand side, we have

$$I + (X - M) = S_b + S_p + (T - G)$$

which shows that total investment—gross private domestic investment I and net foreign investment $X - M$—is equal to total savings (the sum of personal savings S_p, business savings S_b, and government savings $T = G$). This equality is inescapable by definition. Saving represents the portion of income which is not spent on consumption, and investment represents the expenditure on things other than consumption goods. Hence, savings ex post is equal to investment ex post.[1] The equality between realized savings and investment in the United States in 1968 is shown in Table 18-7. As a further explanation of the equality between realized savings and investment, just consider GNP as the volume of goods and services produced. The portion of output which is not consumed is by definition savings. But the accumulation of unconsumed output is, by definition, investment. We know that savings of individuals and business may take several forms. They may hold part of their savings as idle-money balances, use them in the acquisition of financial assets such as bonds and securities, or in the acquisition of real assets other than consumption goods. But as we have mentioned, for the community as a whole, financial claims including money are canceled out in the consolidated statement (e.g., the net financial investment of the community is zero), the savings of the community is thus the accumulation of newly produced assets, other than consumption goods, but this is what we mean by investment.

[1] If we assume away, G, T and $X - M$, then $Y = C + I$ and $Y = C + S$ (where S is the sum of personal savings and business savings). It follows that $C + I = C + S$ and $I = S$.

TABLE 18-7
Savings and Investment in the United States in 1968
(in billions of dollars)

Gross Investment		128.8
Private domestic investment (I)	126.3	
Net foreign investment ($X - M$)	2.5	
Less: Capital consumption allowances	73.3	
Net Investment		55.5
Gross Savings		128.8
Personal savings (S_p)	38.4	
Business savings (S_b)	96.8	
Government savings ($T - G$)	−4.7	
Statistical Discrepancy	−1.7	
Less: Capital consumption allowances	73.3	
Net Savings		55.5

Source: Federal Reserve Bulletin, August 1969

The equality between measured savings and measured investment does not mean that there is also equality between planned savings (or ex ante savings) and planned investment (or ex ante investment), that is, what some groups of individuals wish to save and other groups of individuals wish to invest. As will be seen, while ex post savings is always equal to ex post investment at any level of income, there is one and only one level of income at which planned savings is equal to planned investment—the equilibrium level of income. So long as planned saving is not equal to planned investment, the level of income will change until an equilibrium position is reached at which planned savings is equal to planned investment.

INCOME FLOWS VERSUS FINANCIAL FLOWS

National income and product accounts show that aggregate ex post savings is always equal to aggregate ex post investment. This equality holds regardless of the fact that the savings and investment of the individual sectors of the economy (or for that matter, individual savings and investment) are hardly equal. As a matter of fact, such equality would be quite a coincidence. The sector which saves more than it invests realizes a surplus. On the other hand, the sector which invests more than it saves undergoes a deficit. Since in the aggregate realized savings is equal to realized investment, the excesses of savings over investment of some sectors are necessarily balanced by the excesses of investment over savings of some other sectors. The deficit sectors would have to borrow either directly from the surplus sectors or from financial institutions to cover their deficits. The surplus sectors, on the other hand, may use their surpluses to build up cash balances, or to acquire financial assets such as corporate bonds or government securities. National income and product accounts, however, do not show the financial transactions between sectors, the methods used by deficit sectors to finance their deficits, and the ways surplus sectors use their savings. Such information is obtained from flow-of-funds accounts.

Flow-of-funds accounting is concerned not only with income transactions but also financial transactions, that is, the lending and borrowing between sectors. Flow-of-funds analysis starts with sectoral transactions statements which show the sources and uses of funds by each sector. The sources of funds represent current receipts and changes in liabilities, and uses of funds, current expenses and changes in financial assets. Sources and uses of funds of each sector are thus both financial and nonfinancial in nature. For instance, for the business sector, nonfinancial sources of funds arise largely from the sales of goodsto household and government, and financial sources, from borrowing. Nonfinancial uses of funds represent payments of wages and salaries to household and taxes to government, and financial uses, the purchase of financial assets or the building

TABLE 18-8
Sectoral Transactions Statements

Household		Business	
Sources		Sources	
Wages paid by business	150	Goods sold to household	140
Wages paid by government	60	Goods sold to government	60
		New equipment and Inventories .	30
Total	210	Total	230
Uses		Uses	
Goods purchased from business .	140	Wages paid to household	150
Taxes paid to government	40	Taxes paid to government	30
Government securities	20	Equipment and Inventories	30
Demand deposits	10	Demand deposits	20
Total	210	Total	230
Government		**Banks**	
Sources		Sources	
Personal taxes	40	Demand deposits of household . .	10
Business taxes	30	Demand deposits of business . . .	20
Securities issued	20	Total	30
Bank borrowings	30		
Total	120		
Uses		Uses	
Goods purchased from business .	60	Loans to government	30
Wages paid to household	60		
Total	120		

up of money balances. From these sectoral transactions statements, a flow-of-funds table can be constructed which systematically shows sectoral savings and investment, and the financial flows between sectors. Table 18-8 shows the simplified transactions statements of the household, business, government, and banking sectors of a hypothetical economy. It can be seen from the table that the source of funds of one sector is the use of funds of some other sectors. For instance, the sources of funds of the household sector are made up of wages paid by business and government which constitute the uses of funds of business and government respectively. Thc portion of household income which is paid out for consumption goods and taxes on the other hand represents the sources of funds for business and government. Similarly, the amount of loans which commercial banks extend to the government is their use of funds and the government's source of funds. From these transactions statements, the adjacent flow-of-funds table is constructed (Table 18–9, in which *S* means source of funds, and *U*, use of funds).

The first half of the table indicates that for all the sectors, total nonfinancial sources of funds (510) are equal to total nonfinancial uses of funds (510), but sectorally, for the household and business sectors, their nonfinancial sources of funds exceed their nonfinancial uses while the government uses more funds than could be supported by its nonfinancial sources. The household sector saves 30, and the business sector, 50. But since the government sector dissaves by 50, aggregate savings is 30 which is equal to investment (new equipment and inventories).[2]

The second half of the table shows how the household and business sectors which save use their savings, and how the government covers its deficit. The household sector, with a savings of 30, allocates 20 to purchase securities directly from the government and 10 to build up money balances with the banking sector. The business sector which saves 50 plows back 30 into new equipment and inventory and uses 20 to build up demand balances with the banks. The government, on the other hand, covers its deficit by borrowing 20 directly from household (sale of securities) and 30 from the banking sector. The latter receives in deposit 30 from household and business and makes a loan of 30 to the government. Inasmuch as financial assets acquired by some sectors are financial liabilities of some other sectors, the net financial investment of all sectors is necessarily equal to zero (shown in the table), as we have mentioned in the explanation of the equality between ex post savings and investment.

The development of flow-of-funds accounting was largely the work of Morris Copeland, which has been refined by the Federal Reserve from which

[2]It should be noted that unlike national income and product accounts, flow-of-funds accounts include expenditures on consumer durables as an investment component. Thus while savings and investment, measured ex post, are equal in flow-of-funds accounts just like in national income and product accounts, the figures for savings and investment in flow-of-funds accounts exceed those in income and product accounts by the consumer durables component. Consumer durables, however, are not represented in our example.

TABLE 18-9
Flow of Funds

Transactions	Household		Business		Government		Banks		Total	
	Uses	Sources	Uses	Sources	Uses	Sources	Uses	Sources	Uses	Sources
Non financial										
Personal income		210	150		60				210	210
Personal consumption expenditure . . .	140			140					140	140
Personal taxes .	40					40			40	40
Business taxes .			30			30			30	30
Government purchases of goods and services				60	60				60	60
Equipment and inventories . .			30	30					30	30
Total	180	210	210	230	120	70			510	510
Deficit or surplus	30		20		-50				0	0
Savings		30		50		-50				30
Investment . . .			30						30	
Financial										
Net financial investment . .	30		20		-50				0	0
Net change in financial assets	30		20		0		50		100	
Net change in financial liability		0		0		50		50		100
Government securities . . .	20					20			20	20
Demand deposits	10		20					30	30	30
Bank loans . . .						30	30		30	30

statistics on flows of funds are now made available.[3] It is undoubtedly a very useful accounting system which shows among other things, the magnitude of savings and the ways savings is used, which would not only influence the aggregate level of output but also the composition of output. A theoretical body based on flow-of-funds accounting for the explanation of economic behavior and relationships, however, is yet to be developed.

[3] Morris Copeland, *A Study of Money Flows in the United States* (New York, 1952).

SUMMARY

Gross national product is the market value of all final goods and services produced by an economy in one year. GNP can be measured either by the sum of expenditures on output (personal consumption expenditure, gross private domestic investment, net foreign investment, and government purchase of goods and services) or the sum of income and profits generated in the production of output (wages, salaries, interest, rents and profits etc.). Net national product which is the measure of the value of current production is GNP less capital consumption allowances. National Income at factor cost is the sum of factor payments.

Income estimates are rough estimates, due not only to inaccurate data but also arbitrary inclusion and exclusion of certain income components. As GNP is the money value of goods and services produced, changes in GNP may be due to price changes, changes in physical output, or both. To arrive at GNP in constant dollars that indicate the real performance of an economy, we divide GNP in current dollars by price indexes relative to the index of a base year.

The income flow is a circular flow. The expenditure of a sector becomes the income of another sector which is spent and becomes the income of still other sectors. The portion of income which is not spent on consumption is savings and the expenditure on things other than consumption goods is investment. It follows that statistical savings and investment are always equal. They refer to exactly the same thing.

National income statistics show the flow of goods and services produced by various sectors but they do not show the lending and borrowing between these sectors. The flow-of-funds analysis, on the other hand, shows both income and financial transactions, the way surplus sectors use their savings and deficit sectors finance their deficits.

PROBLEMS

1. Define GNP. What are the alternative measures of GNP? What is the difference between GNP and NNP? What is the difference between GNP and National Income at factor cost? Explain the reasons for the adjustments to be made in order to arrive at National Income at factor cost.

2. What is the difference between GNP in current dollars and GNP in constant dollars? How is GNP in current dollars converted into GNP in constant dollars? Does a change in real GNP always show a corresponding change in the level of welfare of society?

3. What are the limitations of National income statistics? Is morality a rational ground for the exclusion of certain goods and services from GNP? Would you consider interest on the public debt a component of GNP? Give your reasons.

4. Why is the income flow a circular flow? Show why realized savings and

realized investment are identical? Does the equality between realized saving and realized investment necessarily mean that there is always equality between planned savings and planned investment?

5. Compute GNP, using the data in the transactions statements in Table 18-8 as (a) The sum of expenditures on outputs, (b) The sum of income and profits, and (c) The sum of sectoral value added.

6. You are given the following information:

Household		Business	
Receipts		**Receipts**	
Wages paid by business	190	Goods sold to household	200
Wages paid by government	70	Goods sold to government	100
Dividends	20	New equipment and inventory	50
Rents and other income	30	Bonds issued	10
Bank loans	10	Bank loans	30
Allocations		**Allocations**	
Goods purchased from business	200	Wages to household	190
Personal taxes	80	Indirect business taxes	30
Government securities	20	Corporate profit taxes	50
Corporate bonds	10	Dividends	20
Demand deposits	10	Rents and other payments to household	30
		Equipment and inventory	50
		Demand deposits	20

Government		Banks	
Receipts		**Receipts**	
Indirect business taxes	30	Demand deposits of business	20
Corporate profit taxes	50	Demand deposits of household	10
Personal taxes	80	Demand deposits of government	20
Securities issued	20		
Bank loans	10		
Allocations		**Allocations**	
Goods purchased from business	100	Loans to business	30
Wages paid to household	70	Loans to household	10
Demand deposits	20	Loans to government	10

(a) Compute GNP as (1) the sum of expenditures, (2) the sum of value added.

(b) Show savings, investment, sectoral deficits and surpluses, the ways savings are used and deficits are financed.

chapter 19

The Theory of Income Determination

In the preceding chapter, we look at income as a statistical record, that is, the realized level of income for an accounting period. We look at this record either as the sum of sectoral disposable income, $Y = Y_d + S_b + T$, or the sum of sectoral expenditures, $Y = C + I + G + X - M$. We refer to the last equation as the income-expenditure equation. It is an accounting equation just like $MV_y = PY_r$. It is not a theory explaining how the level of income is determined, as it does not tell us anything about the behavior of consumption, investment, and government purchases of goods and services.

But like $MV_y = P_y Y_r$ which serves as an analytical framework for the study of the mechanism of price change, the income-expenditure equation also serves as a framework for the study of the mechanism of income determination by studying the factors which determine the various components of the expenditure flow. In this chapter we shall discuss the various determinants of consumption, saving, and investment, and shall present models of income determination with the oversimplified abstraction of the government and foreign sectors. The influence of the economic activity of the government on the level of income will be discussed in the next chapter. The effects of international trade on income will be discussed in Chapter 28, on income, trade, and the balance of payments.

CONSUMPTION AND SAVING

Propensity to Consume and to Save

The consumption plans of individual family households are largely determined by their income. We can say that in general the consumption spending of family households increases as income increases, but not to the same extent as the increase in income. Human wants, though insatiable, are not equally urgent. As income increases, which permits the satisfaction of wants of higher orders of priority, individuals would be in a position to save more out of increases in income as they move down the priority scale of their consumption needs. Indeed, people with very large incomes cannot help but save a large proportion of their income. The relation between various levels of consumption of individual households associated with alternative levels of income which they may receive is referred to as the individual household consumption function. From these individual consumption functions, we can derive the aggregate consumption function or the aggregate propensity to consume for the whole economy, which is the aggregation of all individual household consumption functions. It is expressed symbolically as $C = C(Y)$ where C is total consumption and Y is income.[1] It is difficult to assert the precise form of this consumption-income relation. For simplicity, we shall assume that consumption is linearly related to income by: $C = C(Y) = a + bY$ (where a and b are positive constants and $0 < b < 1$). Such an assumption is not overly unrealistic in the light of historical records, as shown by Fig. 19-1. The coordinates of each point on the

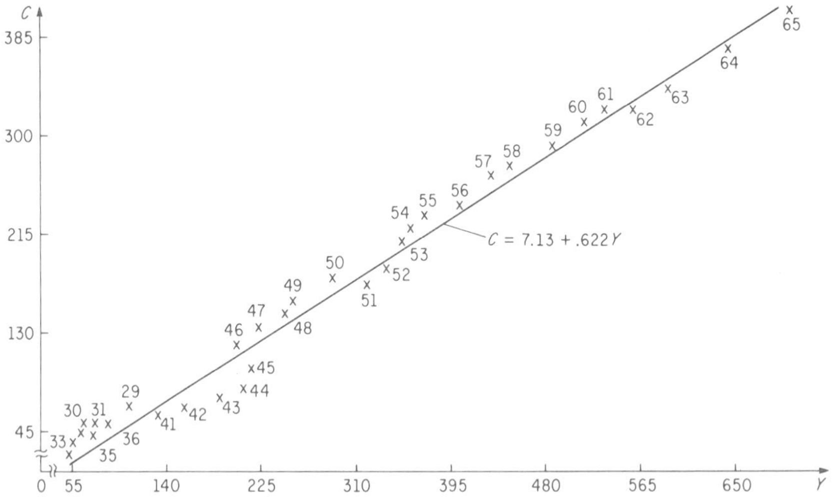

Fig. 19-1. Estimated consumption-income relation.

scattered diagram represent observed consumption and income for a given year, and the straight line $C = 7.13 + 0.622\,Y$ represents the statistical estimate of the consumption-income relation. While the general form of the linear consumption-income relation is $C = a + bY$, a specific form may be something like:

$$C = 80 + 3/5\ Y$$

It is obvious that from this relation we know the level of consumption only when the level of income is known. For instance, given a level of income of $300 billion, the corresponding level of consumption is $260 billion.

The curve in Fig. 19-2 is the propensity-to-consume curve representing the consumption function $C = 80 + 3/5\ Y$. The straight line bisecting the right angle COY is referred to as the 45-degree line. Every point on this line is equidistant

[1] Hereafter by income we shall mean gross national product. When other income concepts are used, they will be explicitly stated.

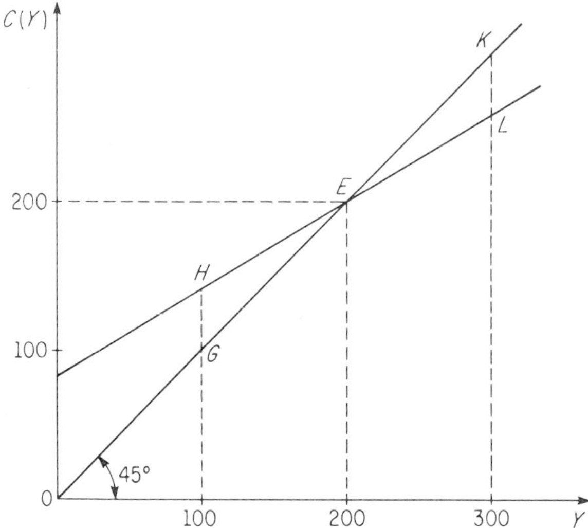

Fig. 19-2. The propensity to consume.

from the consumption and income axes, which means that when we move along this line, consumption is equal to income. The point E, which is the intersection between the consumption line and the 45° line, thus shows that at the level of income of \$200 billion, the whole amount of income is devoted to consumption. To the left of E consumption exceeds income and the consumption curve lies above the 45° line.

Since savings is equal to the difference between income and consumption ($S = Y - C$), it is represented by the vertical distance between the consumption curve and the 45° line. For instance, when income is equal to \$300 billion, consumption is \$260 billion, and hence, savings is \$40 billion, which is equal to KL. When income is \$100 billion, consumption is \$140 billion, savings is therefore negative at −\$40 billion, and so on. It is clear that once we know consumption at various levels of income, we automatically know savings at these income levels. Given $C = 80 + 3/5\,Y$, it follows immediately that $S = Y - C = -80 + 2/5\,Y$. This savings function is presented geometrically in Fig. 19-3, together with the propensity to consume. At the "break-even" level of income $Y = 200$, savings is zero, and the savings curve meets the income axis. For an income level smaller than 200, savings is negative, that is, the savings curve lies below the income axis as consumption exceeds income. For an income level higher than 200, income exceeds consumption and savings is positive—that is, the savings curve is above the income axis. The vertical distance between the savings curve and the income axis at a given level of income is of course equal to the vertical distance between the consumption curve and the 45° line since they depict the same thing, savings (e.g., $KL = MN$ = \$40 billion at Y = \$300).

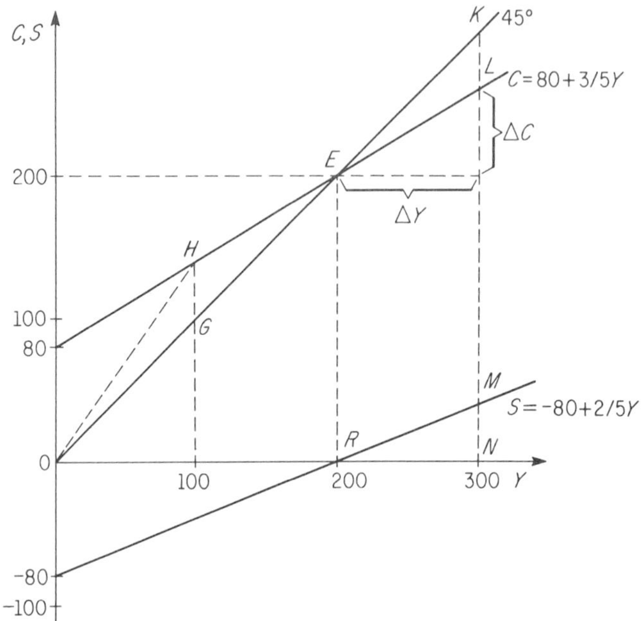

Fig. 19-3. The propensity to consume and to save.

The Average and Marginal Propensity To Consume and To Save

The slope of a straight line from the origin to a given point on the consumption curve (e.g., *OH*) is the average propensity to consume. It is the ratio of consumption to income ($APC = C/Y$), showing the proportion of income spent on consumption. For example, when income is 100 billion, consumption is equal to 140, and the average propensity to consume is $140/100 = 1.4$. It is clear from the consumption line that as income increases, the average propensity to consume decreases.

The average propensity to save is simply the ratio of savings to income ($APS = S/Y$). It shows the proportion of income withheld from consumption. The average propensity to consume (and the average propensity to save) is a rather important concept in terms of short-run fluctuations of income and long-run growth of output. In the short run, given other components of the expenditure flow, frequent or unfrequent changes in the proportion of income devoted to consumption (or the proportion of income being saved) would mean frequent or unfrequent changes in total demand and the level of income and employment. On the other hand, a relatively low average propensity to consume means that a relatively larger proportion of resources is available for capital formation, a basic determinant of the long-run growth of output.

Even of more importance than the average propensity to consume and the average propensity to save is the marginal propensity to consume *MPC*, and the marginal propensity to save, *MPS*. The *MPC* is defined as the change in consumption resulting from a unit change of income, $MPC = \Delta C/\Delta Y$. It shows the proportion of an increase in income being devoted to consumption. In Fig. 19-3, as income increases from 200 to 300 billion, consumption correspondingly increases from 200 to 260. The change in income is therefore $\Delta Y = 100$, and the change in consumption, $\Delta C = 60$. Hence, $MPC = 3/5$. It follows that the marginal propensity to consume is the slope of the consumption curve. Since our consumption function is linear, it has a constant slope or marginal propensity to consume.

The marginal propensity to save is the change in savings resulting from a unit change of income, $MPS = \Delta S/\Delta Y$, which is the slope of the savings curve. It indicates the proportion of an increase in income being saved. Since income is either spent and/or saved, the sum of the marginal propensity to consume and the marginal propensity to save is necessarily equal to one. We know that

$$Y = C + S$$

Hence

$$\Delta Y = \Delta C + \Delta S$$

Dividing both sides by ΔY, we have

$$\frac{\Delta Y}{\Delta Y} = \frac{\Delta C}{\Delta Y} + \frac{\Delta S}{\Delta Y}$$

or

$$MPC + MPS = 1$$

The marginal propensity to consume (and the marginal propensity to save) is a very important concept. As will be seen later on, it indicates the extent of the secondary changes in consumption resulting from a given change in investment expenditure or a change in the propensity to consume, and therefore the extent of changes in the level of income.

Other Determinants

Up to this point we have considered income as if it is the only determinant of consumption (and savings), but things are not that simple. In addition to income, which is the predominant determinant of consumption, there are other factors which tend to affect consumption behavior, such as the level of prices, the rate of interest, and the distribution of income, among other things. Given the level of money income, price increases (decreases) mean decreases (increases) in real income. As a consequence of decreases in real income, some people may reduce savings in order to maintain the same level of real consumption. Other people, however, may reduce consumption in order to maintain the same level of "real" savings. The effects of moderate price changes on aggregate consumption therefore depends upon the relative force of the consumption motive and the savings desire.[2] If consumption motives dominate, price increases would lead to greater monetary consumption. But if the savings motive prevails, price increase may lead to smaller consumption. It follows that moderate price changes, while affecting the consumption behavior of individual family households, may not very significantly affect the aggregate propensity to consume if the forces of the consumption and savings motives which pull in opposite directions tend to neutralize each other.

The rate of interest may also influence consumption demand. A low rate of interest, which means low cost of borrowing, may induce consumers to borrow more for the purchase of consumer durables. In addition, low interest rates, low down payments, and longer payment periods could also induce consumers to more spending. Past consumption patterns also influence current consumption. A family accustomed to high consumption standards sustained by a high income, say, $20,000 a year, would probably maintain a higher level of consumption should its income decrease to $15,000 than a family whose income has just increased to $15,000. The way income changes are expected can also influence consumption. Increases in income which are expected to be more or less permanent would probably lead to greater consumption spending than if increases in income are expected to be temporary. Changes in the way increases in income are distributed also influence aggregate consumption behavior. We have mentioned that the aggregate consumption function is the aggregation of the consumption functions of individual households. As such, it reflects the relative consumption patterns of individual households. Therefore, if there is a change in the distribution of income as income increases, aggregate consumption is likely to change. If the increase in income is distributed largely in favor of the low-income people, aggregate consumption is probably higher than in the case in which the increase in income is distributed in favor of the upper-income class.

Savings is, of course, an important determinant of consumption. Given the level of income, to save more means to consume less, and vice versa. In addition to the level of income, savings is determined by the interest income which could be earned by putting savings in income-yielding claims, by the desire of individuals to accumulate wealth for dependents, and for unexpected consumption requirements, and the importance which they attach to future needs relative to present needs. The direction of the influence of the rate of interest on aggregate savings is difficult to ascertain. Some people may save more as the rate of interest rises. But other people who wish to receive a fixed interest income in the future may save less as the rate of interest increases, since at a higher rate of interest, they will not have to save as much as they did before to attain fixed savings targets. The prevalence of both the positive and negative effects of inter-

[2] It goes without saying that in the case of "galloping" price increases, people would tend to move as quickly as possible from money to goods to avoid practically instant losses in purchasing power of their money income.

est changes on the savings behavior of different groups of individuals has led to the general suspicion that interest changes do not exert any substantial influences on the level of aggregate savings. As for the desire of individuals to save for future generations and the importance which they give to future consumption in relation to current consumption, they are largely psychological in nature. The rate of savings is probably higher in a community in which the spirit of thriftiness is promoted than in a community of prodigal individuals.

The foregoing discussion shows that consumption and savings is a function of several variables. Only when we assume that these other determinants are given can we say that consumption is a function of income alone. As these determinants change, the consumption function also changes. For the linear consumption function $C = a + bY$, the change may be reflected by changes in the a term (the intercept), the b term (the slope), or both, which means changes either in the average propensity to consume, the marginal propensity to consume, or both. Whether or not the consumption-income relation is stable or not depends upon the susceptibility of these other determinants to sudden and frequent changes. It is stable if they do not change frequently, otherwise not. Many believe that the consumption income relation is fairly stable, since such factors as the distribution of income and consumption habits are not likely to change rapidly. Even expectations of individual households regarding future prices and income, in normal times, are not likely to change suddenly. Moreover, the aggregate consumption-income relation would remain stable even in the face of changes in these determinants provided these individual changes are such that they are more or less canceled. The stability or instability of the consumption function or the savings function are important, particularly in regard to stabilization policy which is action designed to stabilize the level of income, and employment. An unstable consumption function would render more difficult the task of stabilization policy.

INVESTMENT

Investment is a relatively small but very unstable component of total spending, as it depends upon elements which can change suddenly and frequently.

Investment Determinants

The investment behavior of business firms is influenced by different motives, but profit is probably the predominant one. So long as profit is the predominant motive for investment, business firms would purchase new capital assets only if the expected receipts derived from these assets are at least adequate to cover costs.

The purchase of a capital asset is profitable when the expected revenue from the use of the asset is greater than its cost. The expected stream of revenue derived from the use of the asset depends largely on the expectations of the entrepreneur in regard to the demand for the output to be produced by the asset and output price thoughout the life of the asset, which may last for many decades. Investment is thus a long-term decision, and once it is made, it can hardly be abandoned. It is a "guess" by the entrepreneur about future profitability. The guess is largely based on records of past and current performance and the probability that the expected demand, prices, and profits would be realized, among other things. The right guess would lead to profits and successes, and the wrong guess could result in ruin and bankruptcy. The investment decision of the entrepreneur may be falsified by a large number of factors, such as changes in the preference of the buyers for the ouput of his firm, the development of new technology which renders obsolete overnight what was considered the most modern equipment by the time it was acquired, changes in the policy of the government with regard to taxes and spending, changes in the competitive position of the firm in the industry, changes in the pattern and rate of population growth, and changes in the cost and availability by other cooperating inputs, such as labor and materials. Changes in these factors which increase the uncertainty of business outlook may lead to drastic revision of business expectations concerning new investment. And changes in business expectations are contagious; optimism gives rise to more optimism and leads to sharp investment expansion; pessimism, on the other hand, begets pessimism, and could lead to drastic contraction in investment demand.

The costs of a capital asset consist of its purchase price or supply price and interest on the funds borrowed for the acquisition of the asset. The interest cost has to be considered in the case in which a business corporation uses its own funds, such as retained earnings in the purchase of the capital asset, inasmuch as if the funds are not locked up in the equipment, the firm would be able to earn interest income by buying securities, etc. The loss of interest income which would otherwise be obtained is obviously part of the cost of acquiring the capital equipment. While the purchase price of a capital asset is not likely to change very rapidly, at least in the short run, the interest cost is capable of sudden and frequent changes. Given the stream of expected revenue derived from a capital asset and its supply price, changes in interest cost may influence the decision of the entrepreneur to buy or not to buy the asset. A sharp increase in the rate of interest may cause the postponement of an investment project which would otherwise be undertaken if the interest rate did not increase.

As an example to illustrate the foregoing discussion, assume that an entrepreneur contemplates the purchase of a new machine with the purchase price of $10,000 and a life expectancy of 20 years. Our entrepreneur expects an average annual net return from the use of the machine, after deduction of all operating costs and depreciation allowances, of $1,000 a year, or an average rate of return of 10 percent over cost. Suppose that the interest on borrowed funds is 6 percent; then our entrepreneur would earn a net profit of 4 percent. If the rate of interest is 10 percent, then the expected net profit is just enough to cover interest cost. The purchase of the machine would not be an economic proposition should the rate of interest be higher than 10 percent. Given the rate of interest of 6 percent, the purchase of the machine can also become unprofitable if there is an increase in the supply price of the machine or a downward revision in the expected annual net return of the machine from \$1,000 to, say, \$550.

Marginal Efficiency of Capital

The marginal efficiency of capital (MEC) is the rate of net return over cost of the last unit of newly invested capital. In the above example, the marginal efficiency of capital is 10 percent. It is an internally determined rate which reflects the expected profitability and risk of investment as contrasted with the market rate of interest that is determined by the supply of and demand for funds. So long as the marginal efficiency of capital is greater than the rate of interest, it is profitable for entrepreneurs to increase their investment. The cutoff point for investment is the level of investment at which the marginal efficiency of capital is equal to the market rate of interest. No rational entrepreneur, motivated by the profit motive, would carry investment beyond that level.

The above investment criterion can be stated in another form, using Keynes' definition of the MEC. Keynes defined the MEC as the rate of discount which makes the discounted value of the series of expected net returns from a unit of capital asset equal to its cost or supply price. More formally, let n be the life expectancy of a capital asset in years; C, its supply price; and R_i, the expected average annual net revenue for the ith year; and r, the marginal efficiency of capital. We have:

$$C = R_1 (1+r)^{-1} + R_2 (1+r)^{-2} + \cdots + R_n (1+r)^{-n} \qquad \text{(I)}$$

Given the supply price of the capital asset C, the marginal efficiency of capital is determined by the average expected return R. It is a subjective rate of discount which reflects, among other things, the risk of investment. The higher this rate of discount, the greater the allowance for investment risk. A comparison between the supply price of a capital asset and the present or capitalized value of the stream of expected return at the prevailing market rate of interest will show whether the proposed investment is profitable or not. Let P be the present value of the series of expected returns; and i, the current market rate of interest. We have the following expression for P:

$$P = R_1 (1+i)^{-1} + R_2 (1+i)^{-2} + \cdots + R_n (1+i)^{-n} \qquad \text{(II)}$$

The proposed investment project is profitable when the present value of expected returns is greater than its supply price ($P > C$). It is not when $P < C$. From expressions (I) and (II), it follows immediately that $P > C$ when the marginal efficiency of capital r is greater than the rate of interest i. P is smaller than C

when $r < i$; when $r = i$ then $P = C$, the case in which net expected revenue is equal to interest cost.

The marginal efficiency of capital is not a constant. It varies inversely with the level of investment. In making investment plans, entrepreneurs assign various rates of return to various levels of investment. As investment increases, the MEC is expected to decrease. The schedule which relates the MEC to alternative levels of investment of an individual firm is referred to as the firm's marginal efficiency of capital schedule. The sum of all these individual MEC schedules gives us the aggregate MEC schedule.

Table 19-1 shows a hypothetical MEC schedule:

TABLE 19–1
The Marginal Efficiency of Capital Schedule

Investment (in billions)	MEC
5	15
10	14
15	13
20	12
25	11
30	10
35	9
40	8
45	7
50	6
55	5

As investment increases from $5 billion to $10 billion, the marginal efficiency of capital decreases from 15 to 14 percent, and so on. The MEC curve in Fig. 19-4 presents the same information diagramatically (which can be drawn when changes in investment and MEC are small enough). This is referred to as the MEC curve. The inverse relation between investment and the marginal efficiency of capital can be accounted for by a number of reasons. These may be the rising marginal cost in the capital goods industry, the increase in operating costs reflecting high material and other costs, price decreases following increased production and sales, or the decrease in the marginal physical products of capital, which may take place when other inputs fail to increase in the same proportion as capital.

The marginal efficiency of capital schedule changes as technology changes and business expectations change. A highly optimistic attitude of business leaders regarding the expected returns of capital investments generated by, say, rising demand and prices, or by technological improvements which increase the productivity of capital assets and reduce their cost, would cause the MEC schedule to shift upward. Such a shift is depicted by the MEC_1 curve in

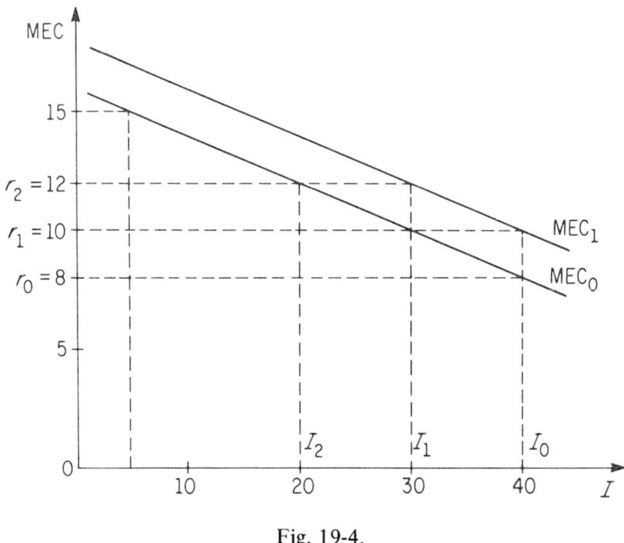

Fig. 19-4.

Fig. 19-4. With the prevalence of business optimism, the expected rate of return for a given level of investment (e.g., I_1) is higher for MEC_1 than for MEC_0 (r_2 as compared to r_1) or for a given rate of return (e.g., r_1), the level of investment is greater for MEC_1 than for MEC_0 (at r_1, the level of investment is I_1 for MEC_0 and I_0 for MEC_1). Conversely, when business pessimism prevails, and expectations are gloomy, the MEC schedule is likely to shift downward.

The Investment Function

The marginal efficiency of capital schedule is not the same as the investment demand schedule. The former relates expected rates of returns to alternative levels of investment. But we have seen that so long as the marginal efficiency of capital is higher than the rate of interest, it is profitable for businesses to increase investments spending until the cutoff point at which the expected rate of return is equal to the rate of interest. It follows that given the MEC schedule, the level of investment demand is determined by the rate of interest. This can be seen from Table 19-1 and Fig. 19-5. When the market rate of interest is equal to 8 percent ($i_0 = r_0$), investment is equal to \$40 billion (I_0). When the rate of interest increases to 10 percent ($i_1 = r_1$), investment decreases to \$30 billion (I_1). At 12 percent interest ($i_2 = r_2$), investment declines to \$20 billion, and so on. Fig. 19-5 shows the investment demand curve relating investment to alternative levels of interest, $I = I(i)$.

The investment demand schedule changes for the same reasons which cause the MEC to change. When the MEC schedule shifts from MEC_0 to MEC_1, the investment demand schedule also shifts from II to I_1I_1. Before the shift in the MEC schedule, the level of investment corresponding to the rate of interest of,

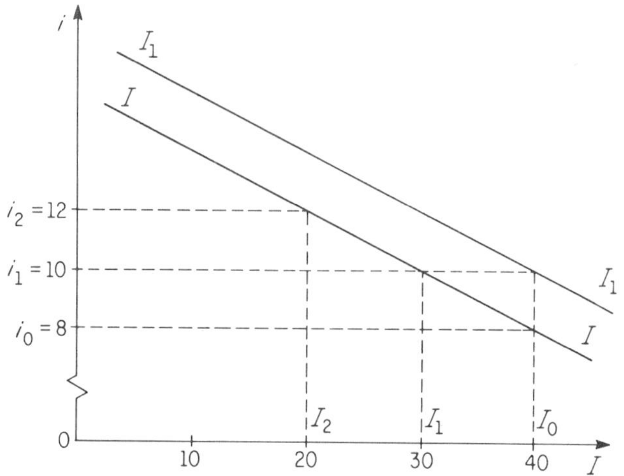

Fig. 19-5. The investment schedule.

say, $i_1 = 10$ percent, is $I_1 = \$30$ billion. But, as the MEC schedule shifts upward, the expected rate of return ($r_2 = 12$) is higher than the market rate of interest ($i_1 = 10$) at that level of investment. Consequently, investment increases to \$40 billion, causing the expected rate of return to decrease to 10 percent, which is equal to the rate of interest.

Investment has been so far related to the rate of interest. This is particularly the case for investment, in new residential constructions, and in business building plants and other fixed assets. As expressed by equation (II) above, a small change in the market rate of interest would cause substantial changes in the present value of the expected returns on these long durable assets. It follows that given an increase (decrease) in the rate of interest, the decrease (increase) in the present value of expected returns may be so large that it tends to discourage (encourage) these long-term investments.[3] In addition to new residential dwellings and business machines and equipment, business inventory is also a component of total investment. Inventory investment is largely determined by the volume of sales; the greater the volume of sales, the greater is expected to be the level of inventory investment. Inasmuch as the volume of sales is positively related to the level of income, inventory investment is positively related to income. Even business investment in machines and equipment also bears a positive relation to income. The existing productive equipment of businesses can sustain only certain maximum levels of output demand. An increase in the demand for output generated by an increase in income beyond

[3]Investment in business assets of shorter durability (say three or four years), however, may not be so responsive to interest changes, since the present value of the expected returns of these assets would not change very substantially as interest changes owing to their short durability.

that level would require an increase in investment. Total investment then is an increasing function of income. With income added, investment now becomes a function of two variables, interest and income.

$$I = I(i, Y)$$

Given Y, I becomes a function of i alone; or given i, I becomes a function of income. Figure 19-6 shows an investment curve representing the following linear

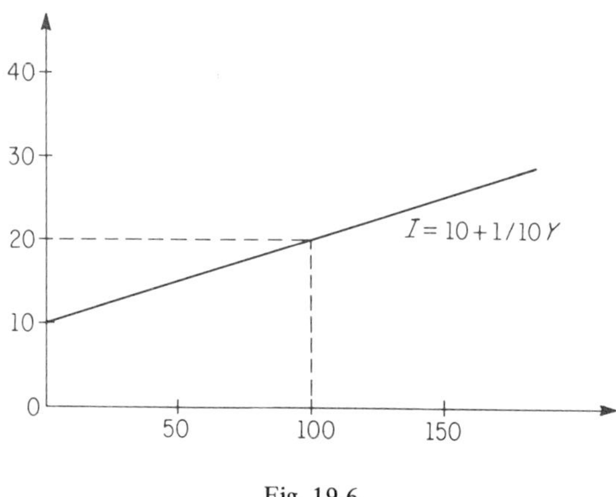

Fig. 19-6.

relation between investment and income:

$$I = g + eY = 10 + 1/10Y$$

The constant term $g = 10$ reflects the influence of interest and other factors than income, which are assumed to be given. The slope of the curve (which is equal to 1/10) is referred to as the marginal propensity to invest; it is the change in investment resulting from a unit change of income ($dI/dY = 1/10$); (an increase in income by one unit would induce an increase in investment by 1/10). We shall make use of this important concept later on.

MODELS OF INCOME DETERMINATION

We have briefly discussed the various determinants of consumption and investment. We shall now put them together in a theory of income determination. Before doing so, however, we shall state some of the important assumptions underlying the theory of income determination to be examined in the next few sections. First, the theory is based on the assumption of a constant capital stock. The theory is, therefore, a short-run theory. The assumption of a constant capital stock implies that the short-run level of investment is so small relative to the capital stock that its influence is only on the level of income. Such an assumption is not overly unrealistic, since the short-run level of investment is indeed a small fraction of the total stock of capital. Second, it is assumed that the price level is constant. It follows that income in our models means "real" income. The assumption of a constant price level may be somewhat unrealistic, especially when the economy is approaching the full-employment level of ouput, but if we allow the price level to change as income changes, the analysis becomes unnecessarily complicated for our purpose. We shall be concerned with the analysis of rising prices in Chapter 23 on the theory of inflation. We shall first consider a very simple model of income determination with investment, assumed to be positive and constant. Later, we shall consider income models with investment as a function of income and the rate of interest.

A Model With Autonomous Investment

The Spending Approach. Assume that investment is given at $20 billion:

$$I = 20 \tag{1}$$

and the relation between consumption and income is given by

$$C = 80 + 4/5\, Y \tag{2}$$

With this information on the propensity to consume and investment, what is the equilibrium level of income? We know from our discussion of national income accounting that for a given accounting period, income is equal to consumption plus investment, that is,

$$Y = C + I \tag{3}$$

From the set of relations (1), (2), and (3), we can assert the equilibrium level of income, that is, the level of income that simultaneously satisfies the planned consumption of households as expressed by the consumption function (2) and the planned investment spending of businesses (which is assumed to be constant at $20 billion). This is derived by solving the set of simultaneous equations (1), (2), and (3). Substituting $I = 20$ and $C = 80 + 4/5Y$ in (3),

$$Y = 80 + 4/5Y + 20$$

and solving for Y we have

$$Y = 500$$

This is the equilibrium level of income, since this is the only level of income which is consistent with the planned consumption of households of 480 (at that level of income), and the planned investment of firms. At that level of income, total demand, which is consumption plus investment ($C + I = 480 + 20$) is equal to total supply, that is, the value of the flow of final goods and services produced.

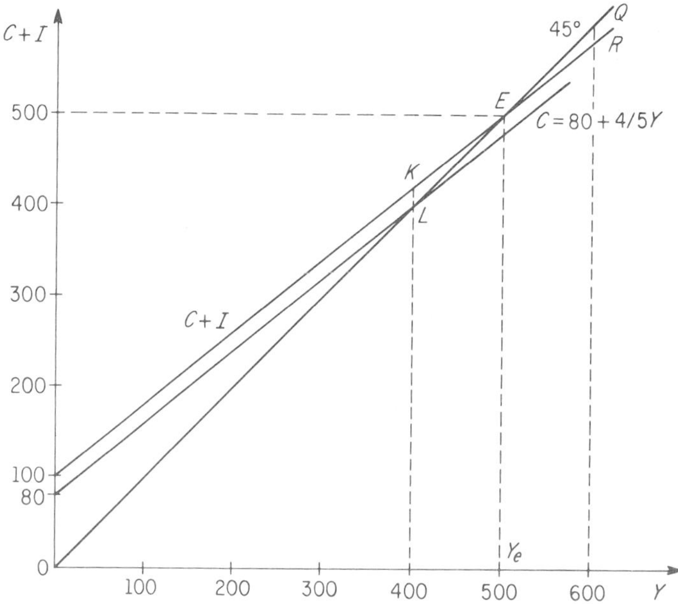

Fig. 19-7. The equilibrium level of income.

The same result is presented geometrically in Fig. 19-7. The vertical axis represents total spending $(C + I)$, and the horizontal axis, income. The CC curve represents the linear consumption function $C = 80 + 4/5Y$. Inasmuch as investment is constant, we can draw the total spending curve by adding to the CC curve a vertical distance equal to investment. The $C + I$ curve is the total spending curve. Since every point on the 45° line is equidistant from the axes, which means equality between income and total spending (we shall refer to this line as the equilibrium line), the point of intersection E between the total spending curve and the equilibrium line determines the equilibrium level of income $Y_e = 500$.

Given the propensity to consume $C = 80 + 4/5Y$ and investment $I = 20$, there is one and only one equilibrium level of income. Any level of income other than Y_e is not the equilibrium level of income. Suppose that the ex ante level of income were \$400 billion. At that level of income, consumption would be 400 billion, according to the consumption function, and total demand would be 420. It follows that at that level of income, total demand exceeds total supply by 20 billion (equal to the KL segment in Fig. 19-7). Consequently, income would tend to rise. On the other hand, for an income level higher than Y_e, for example, \$600 billion, total supply would exceed total demand $(600 - 580 = 20)$ and income would tend to contract. Only at an annual rate of $Y_e = 500$ does the level of income have no tendency to change.

In general, given the propensity to consume $C = C(Y)$, and investment demand I, the equilibrium condition for income is:

$$Y = C(Y) + I \tag{4}$$

It follows that in an ex post sense, the income-expenditure equation is an identity, but in an ex ante or expected sense it represents an equilibrium condition for income: income is in equilibrium when it is consistent with the planned consumption of households and planned investment of firms, or, alternatively, when total supply is equal to total demand.

The Savings-Investment Approach. In the preceding sections, we approach the determination of income from the standpoint of total spending. We can obtain the same result by using another approach: the S-I approach. We have shown that income is in equilibrium when

$$Y = C(Y) + I$$

Subtract $C(Y)$ from both sides of the equation, we have

$$Y - C(Y) = I$$

Since the difference between Y and C is savings, we have:

$$S(Y) = I \tag{5}$$

This is an alternative equation showing the equilibrium condition of income: income is in equilibrium when and only when planned savings is equal to planned investment. In our example, since $C = 80 + 4/5\ Y$, then $S = -80 + 1/5\ Y$. Set savings equal to investment and solve for Y:

$$-80 + 1/5\ Y = 20$$

We have

$$Y = 500$$

which is the equilibrium level of income. At this, and only this level of income, intended savings ($S = 20$) is equal to intended investment; the addition to the income flow by investment at an annual rate of \$20 billion is exactly offset by the leakage from the flow of income by savings at an annual rate of \$20 billion. Fig. 19-8 presents the same result diagrammatically.

The vertical axis measures $S(Y)$ and I, and the horizontal axis, income. Since investment is an assumed constant, it is represented by a straight line parallel to the income axis: regardless of the level of income, investment remains the same. The savings curve, on the other hand, is positively sloped: S increases as Y rises. The intersection between the savings curve and investment curve (point G) determines the equilibrium level of income. Only at that level of income is planned savings equal to intended investment. This condition is not satisfied for any other levels of income. To the left of Y, intended investment exceeds planned savings and income tends to rise. To the right of G, on the other hand, intended savings exceeds planned investment, and income would tend to contract.

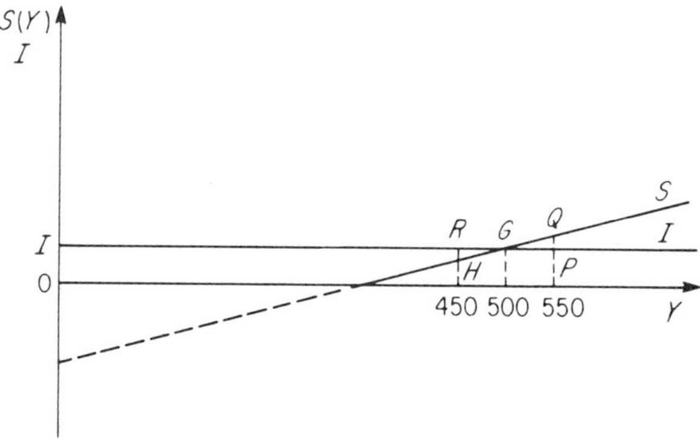

Fig. 19-8. Savings-investment.

Now while planned savings is equal to planned investment only at the equilibrium level of income, savings and investment, measured ex post, as we have already discussed, are always equal for any level of income. The latter always holds because ex post savings and investment included both intended and unintended investment and savings. To illustrate, suppose that the ex ante level of income was \$450 billion. At that level of income, intended investment exceeded savings (equal to \$10 billion, according to the propensity to save) by \$10 billion, which means that consumption of households was greater than was anticipated by firms. According to the consumption function, consumption was \$440 billion (when income was \$450 billion), but consumption expected by firms was only \$430 billion, an excess of \$10 billion. (Firms were surprised, as they missed the mark by \$10 billion.) This would result in an unintended depletion of business inventory (or unintended disinvestment) of the same amount (equal to segment *RH*). Actual investment, therefore, was only \$10 billion, which was equal to actual savings at that level of income. The replenishment of unintended depletion of inventory would cause income to rise until it reaches the equilibrium level Y_e. Conversely, suppose that the ex ante level of income was \$550 billion. Actual consumption at that level of income would be \$520 billion, which was smaller than consumption expected by firms of \$530 billion, a deficiency in consumption demand of \$10 billion. The result would be an unintended increase in inventory (or unintended investment of \$10 billion) (equal to the the segment *QP* in Fig. 19-8, which shows the excess of savings over investment). The sum of intended and unintended investment (\$30 billion) was equal to actual savings at that level of income. The reduction of unintended accumulation of inventory by businesses would lead to the contraction of income.

The level of income is thus the equilibrating mechanism for planned savings and planned investment just as the price level is the equilibrating mechanism for supply and demand. We know that the amount of a commodity actually bought is always equal to the amount actually sold at any price. But the amount which the buyer is willing to buy is equal to the amount which the seller is willing to sell, only at the equilibrium price. If price is not in equilibrium, then either excess demand or excess supply would cause price to change until it reaches an equilibrium position at which what the buyer wishes to buy is equal to what the seller wants to sell. By the same token, although actual savings is always equal to actual investment, but so long as intended savings is not in equilibrium with planned investment, then the level of income will continue to change until it attains an equilibrium position in which planned saving is equal to intended investment.

An Income Model with Investment As a Function of Income

Investment, up to this point, has been assumed to be autonomous—that is, determined independently of the level of income. Now, we remove that assumption and consider investment as a function of income. Suppose that a unit increase in income induces an increase in investment by 1/30, that is, the marginal propensity to invest is 1/30. By adding this induced investment term to our previous autonomous investment of $20 billion, we have the following investment function:

$$I = 20 + 1/30Y$$

Total investment (I) is now made up of two components: autonomous investment (20) and induced investment ($1/30Y$). Given the consumption equation $C = 80 + 4/5\ Y$, what is the equilibrium level of income? To find the equilibrium level of income, we simply substitute I and C in the expression for the equilibrium level of income—that is,

$$Y = C(Y) + I(Y)$$

or using the savings function, $S(Y) = I(Y)$, and solve for Y,

$$Y = 80 + 4/5\ Y + 20 + 1/30\ Y$$

We then have

$$Y = 600$$

which is the equilibrium level of income. At this level of income, consumption is equal to 560 and investment is equal to $40 billion. The planned investment of $40 billion is equal to planned savings at that level of income. Fig. 19-9 presents the same result geometrically. The intersection between the total spending curve $[C(Y) + I(Y)]$ and the equilibrium line determines the equilibrium level of income.

Note that the total spending curve is not parallel to the consumption curve, as in Fig. 19-7, since investment, in this case, includes not only autonomous investment but also induced investment, which rises as income rises. The difference between the dotted curve and the consumption curve represents the autonomous portion of total investment.

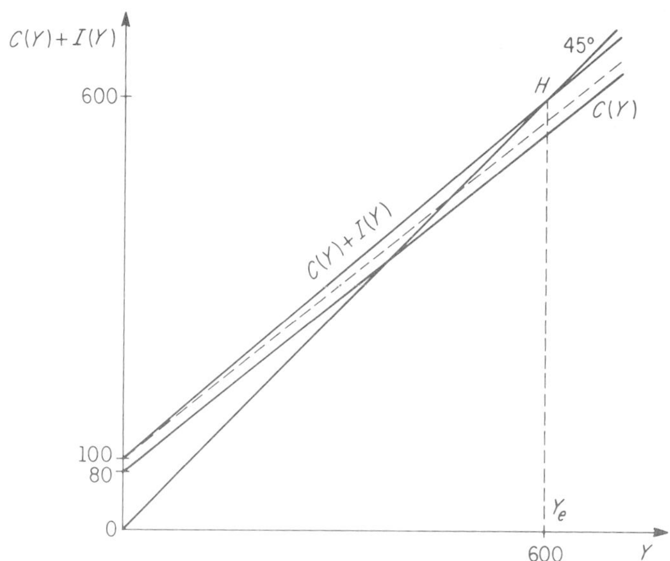

Fig. 19-9. The equilibrium level of income.

The Stability of Equilibrium

We have shown how the equilibrium level of income is determined under different assumptions regarding the behavior of investment. Is the equilibrium level of income a stable one? What is the condition for it to be stable? An equilibrium level of income is stable only if we start with a level of income different from the equilibrium one, a process of income changes will be generated which would lead back to the equilibrium level of income. Otherwise, the equilibrium position is not stable.[4]

Given the propensity to consume $C = 80 + 4/5\ Y$ and autonomous investment $I = 20$, in our example, there is a unique equilibrium level of income $Y_e = 500$. This equilibrium position is stable, since starting with a level of income other than $500 billion, income will change, which will eventually converge to the equilibrium position. In Fig. 19-10, which is the same as Fig. 19-7, if we start with an initial level of income of $Y_0 = 300$, then the excess of total demand over total supply would cause income to increase to $Y_1 = 340$ in the next period, then to $Y_2 = 372$ in the following period, and so on. The process of income changes will continue until the equilibrium level of income is reached. The path PQRST represents the path of convergence toward equilibrium.

Inspection of Figs. 19-9 and 19-10 would lead to the conclusion that the equilibrium level of income is stable when the marginal propensity to consume is

[4]The analysis of the stability of income equilibrium is thus dynamic, as it involves the time dimension.

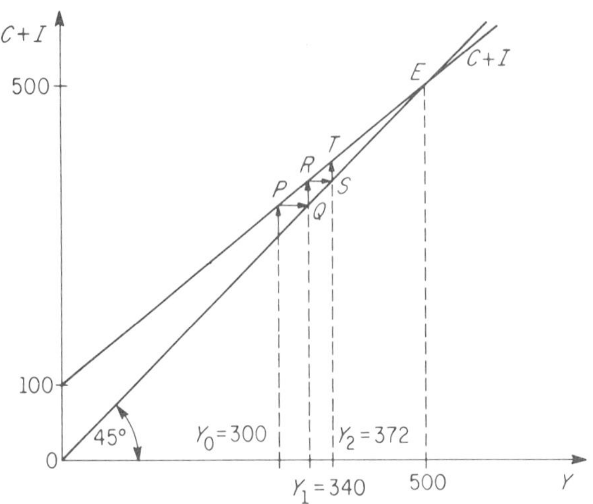

Fig. 19-10. Income movement toward equilibrium.

smaller than one in the neighborhood of the equilibrium position (when $I = \text{const.}$), or the sum of the marginal propensity to consume and the marginal propensity to invest is smaller than one–the slope of the total spending curve $C(Y) + I(Y)$–when $I = I(Y)$, since only under these conditions does the total spending curve cross the equilibrium line for a unique equilibrium level of income.[5]

[5]Following is a somewhat more rigorous discussion of the stability condition for equilibrium. Let current consumption (C_t) (where t is a time subscript, $t = 0, 1, 2, \ldots, n$) be linearly related to income of the preceding period (Y_{t-1}) as follows:

$$C_t = a + bY_{t-1}$$

(where b is the MPC), and investment, a constant (I), then:

$$Y_t = C_t + I = a + bY_{t-1} + I \tag{1}$$

Equation (1) is a difference equation. It links current income to income of the preceding period. The solution of this equation is

$$Y_t = Y_0 b^t + (a + I)\left(\frac{1}{1-b}\right) - (a + I)\left(\frac{b^t}{1-b}\right) \tag{2}$$

where Y_0 is a given initial level of income (income at time $t = 0$). It follows from (2) that as $t \longrightarrow \infty$, Y_t will converge to $(a + I)\left(\frac{1}{1-b}\right)$, the equilibrium level of income, if and only if $0 < b < 1$. In our example, $a = 80$, $I = 20$, and $b = 4/5$; hence, $Y_e = (a + I)\left(\frac{1}{1-b}\right) = 100 \times 5 = 500$. Suppose that we start with the initial level of income $Y_0 = 300$, then from (2), income in the next period ($t = 1$) will be $Y_1 = 340$; in the following period, ($t = 2$), income will be $Y_2 = 372$, and so on. Fig. 19-9 is, in fact, a graphic presentation of this

Income Changes: The Multiplier

It has been shown that given the propensity to consume and the propensity to invest, a unique equilibrium level of income is determined. It follows that when there is a change either in the propensity to consume or the propensity to invest, or both, the equilibrium level of income is bound to change. But how much will be the change in income, given a change in investment or consumption?

We know that the income flow is a circular flow. Somebody's income is always somebody else's expenditure. An increase in the investment expenditure by businesses on newly produced capital assets means more income of those who participate in their production—wages and salaries of workers in the capital goods industry, and so on. Part of these incomes will in turn be spent on the outputs of others. The latter will in their turn spend part of their new incomes, and this will go on ad infinitum in principle. The change in income is thus made up of the initial change in investment expenditure and the "secondary" expansion of consumption generated by new incomes. The magnitude of the income change depends upon the size of the initial change in investment and the marginal propensity to consume, which determines the size of the secondary expansion of consumption and income. More formally, assume that investment increases permanently by ΔI, what is the final change in the equilibrium level of income? In the first period, income will change by the same amount, $\Delta Y_1 = \Delta I$. Given the MPC $= b$, income in the second period will increase by another $\Delta I \cdot b$ (part of the increase in income in the first period will go to consumption), that is $\Delta Y_2 = \Delta I + \Delta I \cdot b$; in the third period, income will increase by another $\Delta I \cdot b^2$; hence, $\Delta Y_3 = \Delta I + \Delta I \cdot b + \Delta I \cdot b^2$, and so on. Following is the sequence of

---

sequence of income changes toward equilibrium. In the case in which $I = I(Y)$, assume that $I_t = g + eY_{t-1}$ (current investment is linearly related to income of the preceding period, where e is the MPI), we have:

$$Y_t = C_t + I_t = a + bY_{t-1} + g + eY_{t-1}$$

$$Y_t = (a + g) + (b + e)Y_{t-1} \qquad (3)$$

The solution of (3) is:

$$Y_t = Y_0 (b + e)^t + (a + g)\left[\frac{1}{1 - (b + e)}\right] - (a + g)\left[\frac{(b + e)^t}{1 - (b + e)}\right] \qquad (4)$$

It is clear from (4) that Y_t will converge to the equilibrium level of income $Y_e = (a + g)\left[\frac{1}{1 - (b + e)}\right]$ if and only if $0 < (b + e) < 1$. In our example, $(b + e) = \frac{25}{30}$ ($b = 4/5$ and $e = 1/30$); hence:

$$Y_e = (a + g)\left[\frac{1}{1 - (b + e)}\right] = 100 \times 6 = 600$$

which is the equilibrium level of income.

income changes:

$$\begin{aligned}
\Delta Y_1 &= \Delta I \\
\Delta Y_2 &= \Delta I + \Delta I \cdot b \\
\Delta Y_3 &= \Delta I + \Delta I \cdot b + \Delta I \cdot b^2 \\
&\cdots\cdots\cdots\cdots\cdots\cdots \\
\Delta Y_n &= \Delta I + \Delta I \cdot b + \Delta I \cdot b^2 + \cdots + \Delta I \cdot b^{n-1} \\
&= \Delta I (1 + b + b^2 + \cdots + b^{n-1})
\end{aligned}$$

It can be seen that income increases with diminishing forces as part of the increase in income leaks through increased savings. The last line shows the change in income in the nth period. As $n \longrightarrow \infty$, the final change[6] in the equilibrium level of income ΔY is:

$$\Delta Y = \lim_{n \to \infty} (\Delta Y)_n = \Delta I \left(\frac{1}{1 - b} \right) \tag{6}$$

The change in the equilibrium level of income is equal to the product of the initial change in investment and the multiplication factor $\left(\frac{1}{1 - b} \right)$. This factor is conventionally referred to as the multiplier $\left(k = \frac{\Delta Y}{\Delta I} = \frac{1}{1 - b} \right)$. It shows the extent of the change in income, given the initial change in investment. It is obvious from (6) that the greater the value of the MPC (or the smaller the value of the MPS), the greater the size of the multiplier; and the greater the size of the multiplier, the larger the change in the level of income, given the change in investment. Expression (6) can also be derived as follows:[7] Given $C = a + bY$

[6]It should be noted that the expression applies only for a permanent increase in investment. If the increase in investment is temporary—it increases in period 1 and goes back to the old level afterward, then the change in the level of income will taper off to zero as time goes by. Following is such a sequence of income changes:

$$\begin{aligned}
\Delta Y_1 &= \Delta I \\
\Delta Y_2 &= \Delta I \cdot b \\
\Delta Y_3 &= \Delta I \cdot b^2 \\
&\cdots\cdots\cdots \\
\Delta Y_n &= \Delta I \cdot b^{n-1}
\end{aligned}$$

Thus as $n \longrightarrow \infty$, $\Delta Y_n \longrightarrow 0$.

[7]Following is a more rigorous derivation of the formula for the multiplier. We know that $Y = C(Y) + I$. To find the change in income resulting from a unit change in I (dY/dI = the multiplier), we differentiate both sides of the equation with respect to I. We have:

$$\frac{dY}{dI} = \frac{dC}{dY} \cdot \frac{dY}{dI} + 1$$

Hence:

$$\frac{dY}{dI} = \frac{1}{1 - \dfrac{dC}{dY}}$$

where dC/dY is the marginal propensity to consume, $\dfrac{dC}{dY} = \lim_{\Delta Y \longrightarrow 0} \dfrac{\Delta C}{\Delta Y}$

and I = constant, we have:

$$Y = a + bY + I$$

Hence

$$Y = a\left(\frac{1}{1-b}\right) + I\left(\frac{1}{1-b}\right) \tag{7}$$

Let I change by ΔI; the new equilibrium level of income will be:

$$Y + \Delta Y = a\left(\frac{1}{1-b}\right) + (I + \Delta I)\left(\frac{1}{1-b}\right) \tag{8}$$

Subtracting (7) from (8), we have:

$$\Delta Y = \Delta I\left(\frac{1}{1-b}\right) = \Delta I\left(\frac{1}{s}\right)$$

where $s = 1 - b$, the marginal propensity to save.

Figure 19-11 shows the multiplier effect geometrically:

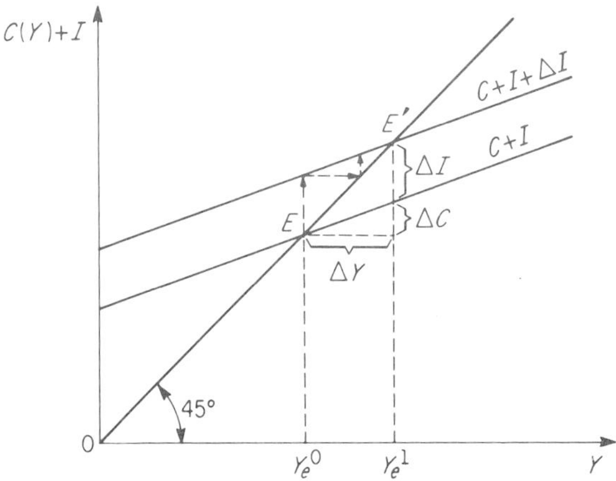

Fig. 19-11. The multiplier effect.

As investment increases by ΔI, the equilibrium level of income increases by ΔY (from Y_e^0 to Y_e^1). ΔY is equal to the sum of the initial increase in investment (ΔI) and the secondary increases in consumption $\Delta C = \Delta I\left(\frac{b}{1-b}\right)$ (the sum of the last $n - 1$ terms in the above expression for ΔY_n), that is $\Delta Y = \Delta I + \Delta I\left(\frac{b}{1-b}\right) = \Delta I\left(\frac{1}{1-b}\right)$. The zigzag path in Fig. 19-11 shows the movement of income changes toward the new equilibrium position through the multiplier process.

For a numerical illustration of the multiplier effect, assume that investment in the above example increases by \$2 billion (from \$20 to \$22 billion), given the propensity to consume $C = 80 + 4/5Y$, the change in the equilibrium level of income will be:

$$\Delta Y = \Delta I \left(\frac{1}{1 - b} \right) = 2 \times 5 = 10$$

As the increases in income reach \$10 billion, planned savings increases by \$2 billion ($S = -80 + 1/5\ Y$), which is equal to the increase in intended investment. There income stops increasing.

We have been concerned with the multiplier effect of a change in investment. But would the same multiplier effect apply to a change in the propensity to consume? The answer is yes. In our example, instead of allowing investment to increase by \$2 billion, we allow the propensity to consume to shift vertically upward by \$2 billion (in lieu of $C = 80 + 4/5\ Y$, we now have $C = 82 + 4/5\ Y$), the increase in the equilibrium level of income will be the same as that generated by an equal increase in investment. This can easily be shown by going back to Equation (7). Instead of a change in investment, we allow the intercept of the consumption function to increase by Δa (a vertical shift); the increase in the level of income will be:

$$\Delta Y = \Delta a \left(\frac{1}{1 - b} \right)$$

The multiplier effect, of course, works both ways, upward as well as downward. If an increase in the propensity to consume or in investment causes the equilibrium level of income to increase by the extent of the multiplier, a decrease in the consumption function or investment, will cause the level of income to decrease by the extent of the multiplier effect. It follows that if investment increases and, for some reason, the consumption function decreases (or the savings function increases), then there might be no change in the equilibrium level of income.

So much for the multiplier effect for the case in which investment is a constant parameter. But what about the case in which investment is a function of income? For this case, the multiplier is slightly different. We have to take into consideration not only the marginal propensity to consume but also the marginal propensity to invest. Again, assume that:

$$C = a + bY$$

$$I = g + eY$$

Then

$$Y = (a + g) + (b + e)Y$$

Solving for Y, we have

$$Y = a\left[\frac{1}{1-(b+e)}\right] + g\left[\frac{1}{1-(b+e)}\right] \tag{9}$$

From (9), it follows that:

$$dY = \left[\frac{1}{1-(b+e)}\right] da$$

and

$$dY = \left[\frac{1}{1-(b+e)}\right] dg$$

where dY/da is the change in the equilibrium level of income resulting from a small change in the propensity to consume, which is of course the same as dY/dg, the change in income resulting from a small change in the propensity to invest. It is called the total expenditure multiplier.[8] In the example in which $C = 80 + 4/5\,Y$ and $I = 20 + 1/30\,Y$, assume that the consumption function shifts vertically upward by \$4 billion ($\Delta a = 4$), the change in the equilibrium level of income will be \$24 billion (the expenditure multiplier is 6), which is the same as the change in income generated by a vertical shift in the propensity to invest ($\Delta g = 4$), other things being equal.

Interest and Income Determination

We shall consider a model of income determination with investment as a function of the rate of interest. This is rather important. Since the rate of

[8] In general, since both C and I are a function of income, we can express the related total spending function $C(Y) + I(Y)$ as $\phi(\lambda, Y)$ where λ is the position of the function. We want to find out the change in the equilibrium level of income resulting from a displacement in the position of the total spending function, that is, a change in λ, which may be brought about by either a change in the propensity to consume or the propensity to invest, or both. Differentiate Y with respect to λ, and we have:

$$\frac{dY}{d\lambda} = \frac{\partial\phi}{\partial Y}\cdot\frac{dY}{d\lambda} + \frac{\partial\phi}{\partial\lambda}$$

Hence

$$\frac{dY}{d\lambda} - \frac{\partial\phi}{\partial Y}\cdot\frac{dY}{d\lambda} = \frac{\partial\phi}{\partial\lambda}$$

and

$$\frac{dY}{d\lambda} = \frac{\partial\phi}{\partial\lambda} \Big/ 1 - \frac{\partial\phi}{\partial Y}$$

which shows the multiplier effect of a small change in the position of the total spending function $\phi(\lambda, Y)$.. In our discussion, since both C and I are assumed to be linearly related to income, $\phi(\lambda, Y)$ takes the form $\lambda + kY$. Hence

$$\frac{dY}{d\lambda} = \frac{1}{1-k}$$

where k is the marginal propensity to spend, which is the sum of the MPC and MPS ($k = b + e$) or the slope of the total spending curve.

interest is influenced by monetary forces (and nonmonetary factors as well, as will be seen), it serves as a channel through which monetary factors affect the level of income and employment through their influence on the rate of interest and investment demand.

When investment is taken as a function of the rate of interest, $I = I(i)$, the equilibrium condition for income is:

$$Y = C(Y) + I(i) \tag{10}$$

or, using the savings function,

$$S(Y) = I(i) \tag{11}$$

Equation (10) or (11) contains two unknowns, the level of income and the rate of interest. Thus, we cannot solve either (10) or (11) for the equilibrium level of income unless the rate of interest is given. For each assumed value of i, a corresponding equilibrium level of income is determined.[9] Figures 19-12(a) and 19-12(b) show geometrically the determination of income when I is a function of i. The propensity to invest is depicted in Fig. 19-12(a), and the propensity to save is shown by Fig. 19-12(b). Suppose that the rate of interest is i_0, which is

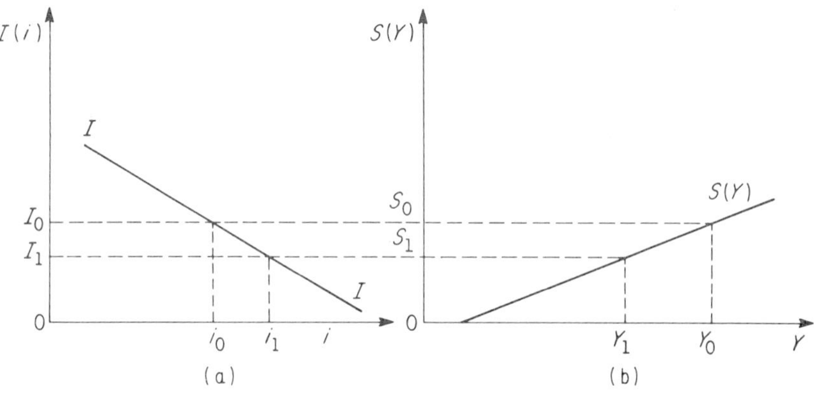

Fig. 19-12. Income equilibrium.

determined by central banking actions. At that rate of interest, investment is I_0, according to the investment function. The equilibrium level of income corresponding to that level of investment is Y_0, since, at that level of income, planned savings is equal to S_0 (according to the propensity to save), which is equal to planned investment at the rate of interest i_0.

Now, assume that the rate of interest increases to i_1 (for example, as a result of tight monetary policy), investment demand, as shown by the investment demand curve, decreases to I_1. Planned savings is equal to planned investment

[9]The theory of interest determination will be presented in Chapter 21.

when the level of income decreases to Y_1, which reduces savings to $S_1 = I_1$. Given the propensity to save (or the propensity to consume), and the investment demand function $I = I(i)$, the equilibrium level of income changes inversely with the rate of interest; the higher the rate of interest, the lower the equilibrium level of income. The extent of the change in the level of income resulting from a given change in the rate of interest, as can be seen from Fig. 19-12, depends upon the degree of responsiveness of investment demand to interest changes (the interest elasticity of investment), and the responsiveness of savings relative to income changes (the income elasticity of savings).[10] The smaller the income elasticity of savings, and the greater the interest elasticity of investment, the greater the extent of income change resulting from a given change in the rate of interest.[11] On the other hand, if investment is not at all responsive to interest changes (the investment curve is parallel to the interest axis), then interest changes would have no influence on the level of income. The interest elasticity of investment demand has an important implication on monetary policy. As will be seen, the effectiveness of monetary policy depends substantially on this elasticity. If investment demand is very responsive to interest changes, then monetary policy will be effective in influencing investment, and hence, income and employment; if it is not, then monetary policy would have little effect.

SUMMARY

The propensity to consume and the propensity to invest determine the equilibrium level of income, that is, the level of income which is consistent with planned consumption of households and planned investment of businesses. The propensity to consume, or consumption function, relates consumption to in-

[10] Note that the steeper the slope of the investment curve relative to the investment axis, the less is investment responsive to the rate of interest. The steeper the slope of the savings curve to the income axis, the more responsive is savings to income changes.

[11] This can be shown algebraically as follows. Let $C = a + bY$ (the propensity to consume) and $I = h - mi$ (the propensity to invest). Then:

$$Y = a + bY + h - mi$$

or

$$Y = (a + h)\left(\frac{1}{1-b}\right) - m\left(\frac{1}{1-b}\right)i$$

It follows that:

$$\frac{dY}{di} = -m\left(\frac{1}{1-b}\right) = -m\left(\frac{1}{s}\right)$$

(where m is the slope of the investment function; b, the MPC; and s, the MPS). It is clear that the smaller the value of s (or the greater the value of b), and the greater the value of m, the greater the extent of income change resulting from a given change in the rate of interest. The minus sign indicates the inverse relation between interest and income changes. When investment demand is not responsive to interest changes (the case in which $m = 0$), $dY/di = 0$, which means that interest changes have no effect on the level of income, that is, the interest effect on income is zero).

come, and the propensity to invest relates investment to income and the rate of interest. Assume that investment is a function of income alone; then the equilibrium condition of income is:

$$Y = C(Y) + I(Y) \tag{I}$$

or, using the savings function,

$$S(Y) = I(Y) \tag{II}$$

Income is in equilibrium when total supply is equal to total demand (Equation I), or when planned savings is equal to planned investment (Equation II)—that is, the addition to the income flow by investment expenditure is equal to the leakage from the flow of income resulting from savings. The equilibrium level of income is stable when the marginal propensity to consume is smaller than one (the case in which I = constant) or the sum of the marginal propensity to consume and the marginal propensity to invest is smaller than 1 (the case when investment is a function of income). As the equilibrium level of income is determined by the propensity to consume and the propensity to invest, a change in either the consumption function or the investment function, or both, would cause the equilibrium level of income to change. The extent of the change in the level of income resulting from a shift in the propensity to consume and/or the propensity to invest depends upon the size of the multiplier which is determined by the MPC or the sum of the MPC and MPI. The expression for the multiplier is

$$k = \frac{1}{1 - MPC} = \frac{1}{MPS} \qquad (I = \text{const.})$$

or

$$k_y = \frac{1}{1 - (MPC + MPI)} = \frac{1}{MPS - MPI} \qquad [I = I(Y)]$$

When we consider investment as a function of the rate of interest, the equilibrium condition of income is

$$Y = C(Y) + I(i)$$

or

$$S(Y) = I(i)$$

For each assumed rate of interest, an equilibrium level of income is determined. The extent of the influence of interest changes on the level of income depends upon the interest-elasticity of investment and the income elasticity of savings. The greater the former, and the smaller the latter, the greater the change will be in the level of income, given the change in the interest rate.

chapter 20

The Government Sector and Income Determination

We have, up to this point, assumed away the economic activity of the government. Such an assumption would not be unrealistic before the outbreak of the first World War, as the economic activity of the government was then not a very important component of aggregate economic activity. But in the present-day world, the economic activity of the government is too important a determinant of income to be ignored. We shall now bring the government into the picture and consider the effects of government spending and taxing on the level of income.[1]

GOVERNMENT RECEIPTS AND EXENDITURES

The purchases of goods and services by the government represent the major portion of its expenditures. These consist largely of wages and salaries paid to government employees for their services in the administration of justice, police and fire protection, public education, and national defense, and the acquisition of government office buildings and equipment and defense goods, such as battleships, tanks, and missiles. Another relatively important component of government expenditures is transfer payments–pensions, unemployment compensation, and other welfare disbursements. Unlike private consumption, which is largely determined by the level of income, governmental expenditures reflect primarily political decisions by national and state legislatures and local governing bodies, international political conditions and relations, the philosophy of the government in regard to its economic role, the size, growth, and age distribution of the population, and so on. Thus, except for such transfer payments as unemployment compensation, which tends to decrease as the level of income and employment rises, we can say that the level of income is not a direct determinant of government expenditures. Of course, the government can plan its expenditures so as to promote full employment income and output, but this does not mean that government spending is a function of income.

[1] Here, by government, we refer to governments at all levels–federal, state, and local.

Whereas, an individual family normally budgets its expenditures in terms of its income, the government usually determines its expenditures in terms of what is necessary for the "public interest," and then raises revenue either by taxing or borrowing, or both, to finance its expenditures. Taxes are the major source of revenue of the government. Given the tax rates and tax bases which are determined by national and state legislative bodies and local governments, taxes are mostly a function of income. Corporation income taxes and personal income taxes that are progressive (they represent the lion's share of total tax revenue) increase as income rises. State income taxes, progressive in some states, also change as income changes. In addition to these direct taxes, indirect taxes are also related to the level of income. For example, sales taxes are related to the level of consumption which is, as we have mentioned, determined by income. It follows that, in general, government tax revenue is a function of income. If we assume away government nontax receipts—such as the sales of goods and services, and the acquisition of new loans and the repayment of loans—then total government expenditures are made up of purchases of goods and services G, and transfer payments Tr, and government revenue, of gross taxes T_G. The government budget is balanced when expenditures are equal to revenue:

$$G + Tr = T_G$$

If we subtract transfer payments, which are in fact negative taxes, from gross taxes, we have net taxes ($T = T_G - Tr$), which are what is available to the government for the purchases of goods and services, or government disposable income.

In what follows we shall be concerned mainly with the effects of government expenditures on goods and services G and net taxes T and their changes, on the level of income and income changes. We shall mention only very briefly the effects of transfer payments that are inversely similar to those of net taxes. An increase in net taxes, *ceteris paribus,* causes the level of income to decline as a result of the consequent decrease in the disposable income and consumption of the private sector; on the other hand, an increase in transfer payments causes the level of income to rise, as it increases the disposable income and consumption of the private sector.

AN INCOME MODEL WITH *G* AND CONSTANT *T*

Government expenditures on goods and services G (which we assume to be constant) acts on the level of income in much the same way as investment. They add to the income flow. The wage and salary incomes received by government employees are the expenditures of the government. The spending of these incomes by government employees in turn creates incomes for others, and so on. With government expenditures on goods and services added, the equilibrium condition of income, using the total spending approach, is

$$Y = C + I + G, \tag{1}$$

Income is in equilibrium when total demand $(C + I + G)$ is equal to total supply Y. When aggregate demand exceeds aggregate supply $(C + I + G > Y)$, the level of income will rise. Conversely, when aggregate demand is not sufficient to absorb all the goods and services currently produced $(C + I + G < Y)$, then income tends to contract. Given the propensity to consume, investment, and government expenditures on goods and services, there is one and only one equilibrium level of income. Equation (1) is presented geometrically in Fig. 20-1.

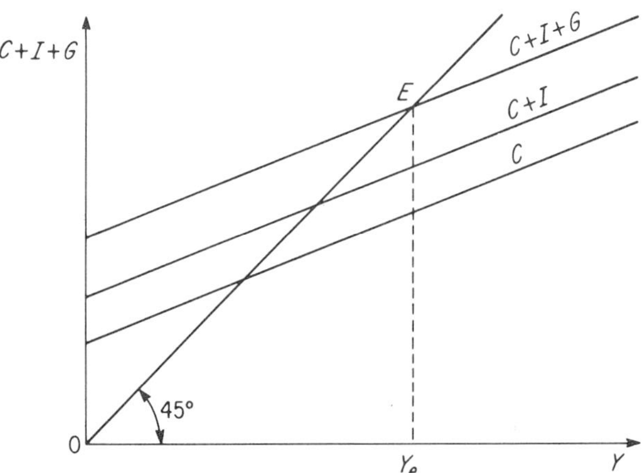

Fig. 20-1. The equilibrium level of income.

To the linear consumption curve we add investment (here assumed to be constant, for simplicity) and government purchases of goods and services. We have the total spending curve, $C + I + G$. The point of intersection between the total spending curve and the equilibrium 45° line determines the equilibrium level of income, *Ye*.

Inasmuch as income is also equal to the sum of consumption C, private savings S and net taxes T, that is:[2]

$$Y = C + S + T \tag{2}$$

It follows from (1) and (2) that

$$I + G = S + T \tag{3}$$

[2]Private savings S is the sum of personal savings *Sp* and business savings *Sb*. For simplicity, we assume away business savings, and, hence, there is no difference between private savings and personal savings; private disposable income is the same as personal disposable income.

Equation (3) is an alternative definition of the equilibrium level of income; income is in equilibrium when the sum of planned investment and government expenditures on goods and services is equal to the sum of planned savings and net taxes. While I and G add to the flow of income, S and T cause the income flow to leak. Therefore, when the inflow of $I + G$ is equal to the outflow of $S + T$, the level of income has no tendency to change; it is in equilibrium. This alternative approach is presented diagrammatically in Fig. 20-2.

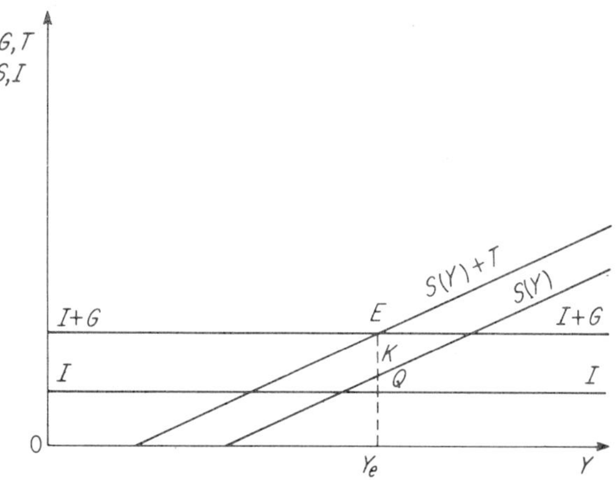

Fig. 20-2. The equilibrium level of income

Since I and G are assumed constants, $I + G$ is represented by a straight line parallel to the income axis. As tax is assumed to be constant, we derive the $S + T$ curve by adding to the linear savings function the constant amount of taxes. The intersection between the $I + G$ curve and the $S + T$ curve determines the equilibrium level of income. It should be noted from Eqution (3) and Fig. 20-2 that when we add G and T, it is no longer necessary for planned investment to be equal to planned savings for the level of income to be in equilibrium. The level of income will remain in equilibrium so long as the excess of planned investment over planned savings (or vice versa) is exactly offset by the excess of net taxes over government purchases of goods and services (or vice versa). This is clear in Fig. 20-2. At the equilibrium level of income Ye, planned savings exceeds planned investment by QK, but this is exactly offset by the excess of government spending on goods and services over net taxes, which is also equal to QK.

Now since we have added G and T to our model of income determination, we have to consider private consumption as a function of private disposable income (Y_d) instead of Y, inasmuch as family households would have to make their consumption plans on the basis of what is available to them for spending—their disposable income. However, since $Y_d = Y - T$ (disposable income is the difference between income and taxes), we can express the consumption function as follows:

$$C = C(Y_d) = C(Y - T)$$

The consumption curve in Fig. 20-1 indeed represents the consumption function of this form (and the savings curve in Fig. 20-2 also represents savings as a function of $Y_d = Y - T$). The imposition of taxes causes the propensity to consume to shift downward. This can be seen from the following assumed linear relation between consumption and disposable income $C = a + bY_d = a + b(Y - T)$: the downward shift in the consumption function is equal to the amount of taxes times the marginal propensity to consume (that is, $-bT$). Given the above consumption function, the general algebraic expression of the equilibrium level of income is

$$Y = C(Y_d) + I + G = (a + I + G)\left(\frac{1}{1 - b}\right) - b\left(\frac{1}{1 - b}\right)T \qquad (4)$$

As an example, assume that consumption is related to disposable income by $C = 40 + 3/4\ Y_d$; net taxes are \$10 billion, government purchases of goods and services are also \$10 billion (the case of a balanced budget), and investment expenditure is \$20 billion, then, the equilibrium level of income is

$$Y = 40 + 3/4(Y - 10) + 20 + 10$$

Hence

$$Y = \$250 \text{ billion}$$

or, alternatively, using Eqution (3), we have:

$$-40 + 1/4\,(Y - 10) + 10 = 30$$

and again

$$Y = \$250$$

CHANGES IN *G*, *T*, AND INCOME CHANGES

We have seen that both G and T are determinants of income (as shown in Equations (1) and (2). Changes in either G or T, or both, therefore, will cause the level of income to change. We shall first consider the effects of isolated changes in G and T on the level of income; then the effects of simultaneous changes in both T and G will be considered.

The Effect of Changes in *G*

An increase (decrease) in government purchases of goods and services, other things being equal, will cause the level of income to increase (decrease). The question is: given a change in government expenditures on goods and services, how much would be the change in the equilibrium level of income? This can be answered by referring to Equation (4), showing the equilibrium level of income, given the propensity to consume, investment demand, and government purchases of goods and services.

Now, allow G to change by ΔG; the new equilibrium level of income will be

$$Y + \Delta Y = (a + I)\left(\frac{1}{1 - b}\right) - b\left(\frac{1}{1 - b}\right)T + (G + \Delta G)\left(\frac{1}{1 - b}\right) \tag{5}$$

Subtracting (4) from (5), we have

$$\Delta Y = \Delta G \left(\frac{1}{1 - b}\right) \tag{6}$$

The change in the equilibrium level of income is equal to the product of the change in G and the multiplier which is the same multiplier for a change in investment spending or a change in the propensity to consume $\left(\frac{dY}{dG} = \frac{dY}{dI} = \frac{dY}{da} = \frac{1}{1 - b}\right)$. In the above example, suppose that G increases by $\Delta G = 5$, the increase in the level of income will be \$20 billion, and the new equilibrium level of income will be \$270 billion. Conversely, if G decreases by \$5 billion, the decrease in income will be $\Delta Y = -\$20$.

The Effect of Changes in T

The effect of taxes on the level of income is in the opposite direction with the effect of government expenditures on goods and services. While government spending adds to the income flow, like investment, taxes reduce the flow of income, like savings. An increase in taxes, other things being equal, results in a decrease in private disposable income which leads to decreases in consumption and income. The extent of the change in the level of income resulting from a given change in taxes follows immediately from Eq. (4) above:

$$\Delta Y = \left(\frac{-b}{1 - b}\right) \Delta T \tag{7}$$

It is equal to the product of the change in taxes and the taxation multiplier $\left(\frac{-b}{1 - b}\right)$. It is clear that, given the change in taxes, the magnitude of income change depends upon the marginal propensity to consume which determines the size of the taxation multiplier; in the above example, suppose that taxes increase by \$4 billion, the level of income will decrease by $-\$12$ billion.

From expressions (6) and (7), we can see that the absolute value of the government expenditure multiplier is greater than that of the taxation multiplier:

$$\frac{1}{1-b} > \left| -\frac{b}{1-b} \right|$$

This reflects the fact that while a change in government purchases of goods and services will cause income to change by the same amount in the first period and then by the secondary changes in consumption in the following periods, a change in taxes will not cause income to change in the first period. Only in the second and following periods does income change as a result of secondary changes in consumption.

We should mention in passing here that the analysis of the effects of changes in net taxes applies equally to the case of changes in transfer payments, although inversely. Inasmuch as an increase in transfer payments Tr is a decrease in net taxes, an increase in Tr would cause the level of income to increase precisely the same way as a decrease in net taxes. With the existence of transfer payments, disposable income becomes

$$Y_d = Y - T + Tr$$

Given $C = a + b\,Y_d$, we have

$$Y = (a + I + G)\left(\frac{1}{1-b}\right) - b\left(\frac{1}{1-b}\right)T + b\left(\frac{1}{1-b}\right)Tr \qquad (8)$$

It follows from (8) that

$$\frac{dY}{dTr} = \frac{b}{1-b}$$

The multiplier effect of transfer payments differs from the taxation multiplier only by the algebraic sign:

$$\frac{dY}{dT} = -\frac{b}{1-b}$$

Effects of Simultaneous Changes in *G* and *T*

We have considered the effects on the level of income of an isolated change in G and T. Now we allow G and T to change simultaneously and see what happens to the equilibrium level of income. We have seen that, given a change in G, *ceteris paribus*, the consequent change in the equilibrium level of income is equal to $\Delta G\left(\frac{1}{1-b}\right)$. On the other hand, given a change in T, *ceteris paribus*, the change in income is equal to $\Delta T, \left(-\frac{b}{1-b}\right)$. It follows that the change in the equilibrium level of income resulting from a simultaneous change in G and T is

$$\Delta Y = \Delta G\left(\frac{1}{1-b}\right) + \Delta T\left(-\frac{b}{1-b}\right) \qquad (9)$$

In the above example, assume that $\Delta G = 5$ and $\Delta T = 4$, the change in the level of income will be \$8 billion. Now, suppose that the change in government spending on goods and services is matched by an equal change in taxes (i.e., $\Delta G = \Delta T$, a balanced budget) what would be the corresponding change in the equilibrium level of income? Would it decrease, increase, or remain unchanged? Since $\Delta G = \Delta T$, expression (9) becomes

$$\Delta Y = \Delta G \left(\frac{1-b}{1-b}\right) = \Delta T \left(\frac{1-b}{1-b}\right)$$

or

$$\Delta Y = \Delta G = \Delta T$$

It follows that an increase (decrease) in G, matched by an equal increase (decrease) in taxes, will cause the equilibrium level of income to increase (decrease) by the same amount. We say that the multiplier effect of a balanced budget[3] is equal to one, $\frac{\Delta Y}{\Delta G}\left(=\frac{\Delta Y}{\Delta T}\right) = 1$. This is diagrammed in Fig. 20-3. The dotted curve represents the downward shift in the original total spending curve as a result of the downward shift in the consumption curve following the increase in taxes. To this shifted total spending curve, we add the increase in government purchases of goods and services to obtain the new spending curve $(C + I + G + \Delta G)$. The increase in income is equal to the increase in G, that is, $\Delta Y/\Delta G = 1$.

This appears to be proof against the old fallacy that the effect of a governmental balanced budget is neutral—that an increase in government expenditures on goods and services financed by an equal increases in taxes would leave the level of income unchanged. According to Equation (9), for the level of income to remain unchanged (i.e., $\Delta Y = 0$), the increase in net taxes would have to be

[3]It should be noted that the multiplier effect of a balanced budget is 1 only when the MPC is the same for all. If the MPC of taxpayers is smaller than the MPC of all others, then the change in the level of income will be greater than the change in G. On the other hand, if the MPC of taxpayers is greater than that of all others, then ΔY would be smaller than $\Delta G(=\Delta T)$. Let b_1 be the MPC of taxpayers, and b_2 the MPC of all others; then Equation (9) becomes:

$$\Delta Y = \Delta G \left(\frac{1}{1-b_2}\right) + \Delta T \left(-\frac{b_1}{1-b_2}\right)$$

or

$$\Delta Y = \Delta G \left(\frac{1-b_1}{1-b_2}\right)$$

Thus, when $b_1 < b_2, \Delta Y > \Delta G$
when $b_1 > b_2, \Delta Y < \Delta G$

Assume that $b_1 = 0.6$ and $b_2 = 0.8$. Then, given $\Delta G = \Delta T = 5$, ΔY is equal to 10, which is greater than the change in G and T. On the other hand, if $b_1 = .8$ and $b_2 = .6$, then $\Delta Y = 2.5$ only. (See Erich Schneider, *Money, Income and Employment*. New York: MacMillan, 1962, pp. 207-208.)

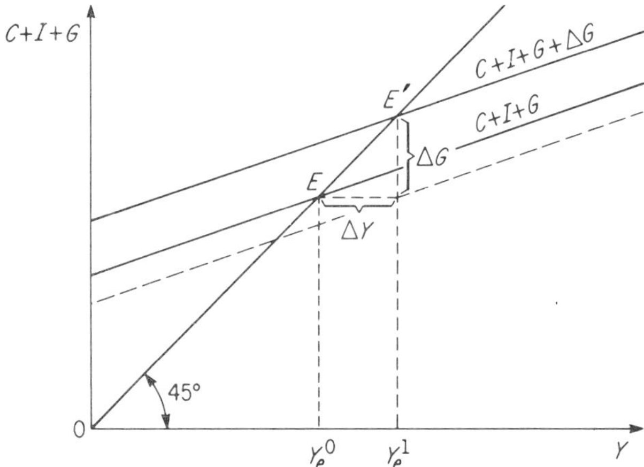

Fig. 20-3. The balanced-budget multiplier.

greater than the increase in G or a budget surplus is required. From Equation (9), we can see that the increase in taxes necessary to keep $\Delta Y = 0$ is

$$\Delta T = \Delta G \left(\frac{1}{b}\right)$$

In the numerical example which we have presented above, to keep the equilibrium level of income unchanged following an increase in government expenditures on goods and services of \$5 billion, the increase in taxes would have to be $\Delta T =$ \$6.67 billion. A budget surplus of \$1.67 is needed.

AN INCOME MODEL WITH TAXES AS A FUNCTION OF INCOME $T = T(Y)$

We have considered a model of income determination with taxes assumed to be constant. This assumption is now removed. We know that taxes are positively related to the level of income. As income increases, taxes increase. Assume that taxes are proportionally related to income by:

$$T = T(Y) = t\,Y$$

where $0 < t < 1$ is the marginal tax rate—that is, the change in taxes resulting from a unit change in income $dT/dY = t$, which is in this case the same as the average tax rate, $T/Y = t$. Private disposable income is therefore equal to $Y_d = (1 - t)Y$. Assume that private consumption is linearly related to disposable income by:

$$C = a + b'\,Y_d$$

Where b' is the marginal propensity to consume with respect to disposable income. Since $Y_d = (1 - t)Y$, consumption can be expressed in terms of Y as:

$$C = a + b'(1 - t)Y$$

It is obvious that in the case of variable taxes, the marginal propensity to consume with respect to disposable income is greater than the marginal propensity to consume with respect to Y, which is, in this case,[4] equal to $(b' - b't)$. The equilibrium level of income, when T is a function of income, is:

$$Y = C[(1 - t)Y] + I + G = a + b'(1 - t)Y + I + G$$

Hence

$$Y = (a + I + G)\left[\frac{1}{1 - b' + b't}\right] \tag{10}$$

Figure 20-4 shows the same equilibrium level of income, using the alternative approach: $S[(1 - t)Y] + T(Y) = I + G$. The difference between Figs. 20-4 and 20-2 is that in Fig. 20-4, the $S + T$ curve is no longer parallel to the savings curve, since taxes rise as income increases.

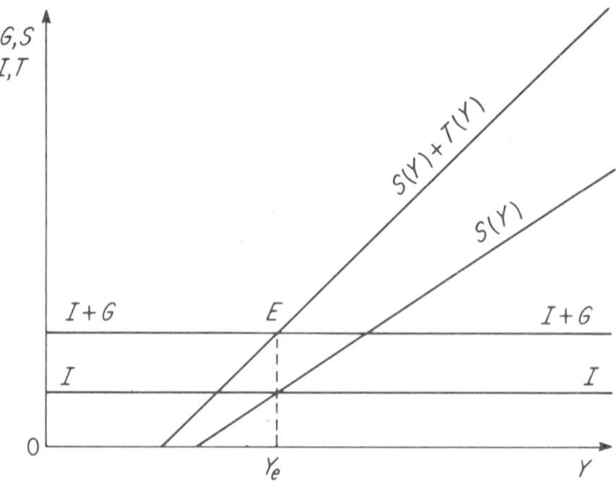

Fig. 20-4. Income equilibrium when $T = T(Y)$.

For a numerical example, suppose that $C = 40 + 5/6\ Y_d$; $T = 1/10Y$; $I = 20$; and $G = 25$, then the equilibrium level of income is

$$Y = 40 + 5/6\,(Y - 1/10\ Y) + 20 + 25$$

Hence

$$Y = \$340$$

[4]Note that when T is constant, $t = 0$, and $b't = 0$; hence, the MPC with respect to disposable income is the same as the MPC with respect to Y.

At this level of income, $T = 34$; disposable income $Y_d = 306\ (340 - 34)$. Consumption $C = 295$; and private savings $S = 11$; and $S + T = I + G = 45$. From Equation (10) above, we can see that in the case of variable taxes, given a change in the propensity to consume Δa, or investment ΔI, or government expenditures on goods and services ΔG, the extent of the corresponding change in the level of income is

$$\frac{\Delta Y}{\Delta a} = \frac{\Delta Y}{\Delta I} = \frac{\Delta Y}{\Delta G} = \frac{1}{1 - b' + b't}$$

The multiplier effect of changes in G, I, or C is thus smaller when taxes vary with the level of income than when T is fixed:

$$\frac{1}{1 - b' + b't} < \frac{1}{1 - b'}$$

This is understandable. When T is an increasing function of income, the increases in taxes induced by increases in income generated by an increase in, say, government spending on goods and services constitute a leak from increases in the income flow in addition to induced increases in savings. But in the case in which taxes are fixed, the source of leakage from increases in the flow of income is induced increases in savings alone. In the example above, if G were to increase by \$5 billion, from 25 to 30, then the change in the equilibrium level of income, after the multiplier process works itself out, would be $\Delta Y = 20$. But if T were constant ($t = 0$ and $b't = 0$), the corresponding change in the equilibrium level of income would be \$30 billion. Conversely, if G were to decrease by \$5 billion, the decrease in the level of income would be −\$20 billion where T is an increasing function of income, and −\$30 when T is fixed. It follows that variable taxes tend to slow down the increase in the level of income generated by an increase in G (or I or C) and slow down the decrease in the income level brought about by a decrease in G (or I or C). It is therefore an automatic or built-in stabilizer which helps insulate to some extent the level of income from fluctuations generated by outside disturbances.

POLICY IMPLICATIONS

The analysis of the effects of the economic activities of the government on the level of income suggests that the government, by changing its policy in regard to spending and taxing, can directly affect the level of income and employment. For instance, to promote economic expansion, higher levels of employment and output, the government can increase its expenditures, reduce taxes, or use a combination of increases in expenditures and tax cuts. Conversely, in times when the economy shows evidence of overheating with rising prices, the government can dampen excessive economic expansion by reducing expenditures, raising taxes, or both. The manipulation of spending and taxing is thus a powerful instrument in the hands of the government to promote prosperity and stability. Contrary to the old line of thinking on fiscal matters which equates fiscal responsibility with the balanced budget, modern fiscal analysis considers the balanced budget desirable only at full employment. So long as there is a high rate of unemployment of human and material resources, properly planned budgetary deficits are a means to reduce unemployment and raise the level of income and output. On the other hand, budgetary surpluses realized in times of inflation would put a brake on inflationary developments. We shall discuss in more detail the effects of discretionary fiscal measures and automatic stabilizers in Chapter 25 on monetary policy, fiscal policy, and economic stabilization. As will be seen, such automatic stabilizers as variable taxes and others, while serving as buffers against recession, may substantially hinder policy measures aimed at achieving certain income and output targets in promoting maximum economic growth and full employment on account of their "slowing down" or "dragging" effects on the level of income.

SUMMARY

Government expenditures on goods and services G, like investment spending, adds to the income flow; taxes T, just like savings, are a leakage from the flow of income. With G and T, the equilibrium condition of income is

$$Y = C\,(Y - T) + I + G$$

Again, income is in equilibrium when aggregate supply is equal to aggregate demand. Using the savings and tax function, an alternative equilibrium condition of income is

$$S(Y - T) + T = I + G$$

Income is in equilibrium when the additions to the flow of income by investment and government spending on goods and services is equal to the leakage from the income flow by savings and net taxes. A change in G will cause the level of income to change. The extent of the change in the level of income resulting from a given change in G depends upon the size of the multiplier which is the same for investment and consumption changes $\left(k = \dfrac{1}{1 - b}\right)$. An increase in net taxes, on the other hand, will cause income to decrease. The extent of the change in income as a consequence of a given change in taxes (ΔT) depends upon the taxation multiplier, which is a negative number $\left(-\dfrac{b}{1 - b}\right)$. When a change in G is matched by an equal change in T (the case of a balanced budget), the level of income would increase by the same amount: $\Delta Y = \Delta G = \Delta T$. We say that the multiplier effect of a balanced budget is equal to one ($\Delta Y/\Delta G = 1$). The multiplier effect of a change in G, I, or C, in the case in which T is an increasing function of income, is slightly more complicated. It is equal to $\frac{1}{1 - b' + b't}$, where b' is the MPC with respect to disposable income and t is the marginal tax rate.

PROBLEMS

1. You are given the following information (in billions of dollars). Consumption C is related to income Y by $C = 40 + 4/5\ Y$; Investment I is constant, at \$20.

(a) What is the equilibrium level of income? What would be the new equilibrium level of income if the consumption function were to shift vertically upward by \$5 billion? What is the multiplier? Would the change in the equilibrium level of income be the same if, instead of a shift in the consumption function by \$5 billion, investment were to increase by the same amount?

(b) Now, suppose that investment, instead of being an assumed constant, is linearly related to income by $I = 10 + 2/35\ Y$. Given $C = 40 + 4/5\ Y$, what is the equilibrium level of income? If the investment function were to shift downward by \$4 billion, what would be the new equilibrium level of income? What is the multiplier?

(c) We expand the model a little further and consider investment as a function of both the level of income and the rate of interest ($I = I(Y,i)$). Suppose that $I = I(Y,i) = 10 + 2/35\ Y + 0.8/i$. Given $C = 40 + 4/5\ Y$, what is the equilibrium, level of income?

2. (a) Assume

$$C = 40 + 4/5\ Yd$$
$$I = 30$$
$$G = 20$$
$$T = 15$$

(i) Find the equilibrium level of income, disposable income, consumption, and savings.

(ii) If G were to increase by \$2 billion, what would be the change in income?

(iii) What would be ΔY if T were to increase by \$5 billion?

(iv) In part (ii) above, what would the necessary increase in T be to keep the equilibrium level of income unchanged?

(b) Suppose that T, instead of being a constant is related to income as follows:

$$T = 1/6\ Y$$

(i) What are the equilibrium levels of income, tax, disposable income, consumption, and savings?

(ii) What would be the change in the equilibrium level of income if G were to increase by \$5 billion?

3. On the basis of what you have learned on the theory of income determination, write a brief essay on how you would use taxes and government expenditures on goods and services to reduce fluctuations in income and employment.

4. Discuss some of the important determinants of consumption. What is the marginal propensity to consume? What role does the MPC play in the theory of income determination? Would policy designed to stabilize income and employment be less or more difficult if the consumption function is very unstable? Explain.

5. Why is investment considered to be the most unstable component of total spending? If investment and savings are undertaken in general by different groups of people and are determined by different factors, why is measured savings always equal to measured investment? Illustrate your discussion with numerical examples.

chapter 21

Interest Determination

The rate of interest plays an important role in the theory of income determination. As we have seen, the rate of interest is a determinant of investment demand which, together with the propensity to consume, determines the level of income. We shall now deal with theories of the determination of the rate of interest, a channel through which changes of monetary factors influence the level of economic activity. We shall discuss the classical theory, the neoclassical or loanable-funds theory, and the Keynesian liquidity-preference theory. We shall also discuss briefly some recent refinements on the theory of the demand for money, the structure of rates, and theories explaining the term structure of interest rates.

NATURE AND MEANING OF INTEREST

The rate of interest is the price paid for money on loan. Money commands a price because it is useful and scarce. The consumer pays a price to use somebody else's money as it enables him to acquire goods and services which he would otherwise not be in a position to obtain unless he has accumulated adequate savings. The entrepreneur pays interest for the service of money which makes it possible for him to acquire capital goods expected to yield profits more than adequate to cover the interest. The price of money or interest embodies a reward to the lender for parting with liquidity and the risk premium involved in lending. The longer the period in which the lender is expected to part with money liquidity, and the greater the risk that he might not be able to recover his funds, the higher is the rate of interest which he expects the borrower to pay.

"The rate of interest" may mean a number of different rates. We may refer to the rate of interest as the contractual rate or coupon rate which is the rate specified in the lending contract. For instance, a corporate bond promising to pay 5 percent interest of the face value carries a coupon rate of 5 percent. We may refer to the rate of interest as the current yield to the bondholder, which is the interest income expressed as a percentage of the purchase price of the security. For example, an investor who purchases for $950 a $1,000 bond paying 5 percent interest earns a running or current yield of 5.3 percent. We may also refer to the rate of interest as the computed rate of discount which makes the present value of the series of interest income and redeemed value equal to the purchase price of the security. The rate of interest is usually referred to as this computed rate of discount or market yield.

But by "the" rate of interest, do we mean a single rate or an average rate of some kind? For simplicity, we shall assume that there is only one rate of interest or one type of interest-yielding claim available to lenders. We may of course refer to "the" rate of interest as an index of the movement of the whole structure of money rates just like the general price level which is an index of the movement of prices. Such use is justifiable, inasmuch as interest rates or security prices, like commodity prices, do move sympathetically over time as they are subject to a variety of common pressures.

THE CLASSICAL THEORY OF INTEREST

To classical economists, the rate of interest is determined by the demand for, and the supply of, savings. The demand for savings, or investment, is assumed to be inversely related to the rate of interest. As the rate of interest rises, investment demand declines. Savings, on the other hand, is assumed to be positively related to the rate of interest; savings increases as the rate of interest rises. The rate of interest is in equilibrium when the supply of savings is equal to the demand for investment—that is,

$$I(i) = S(i) \tag{1}$$

Equation (1) is the classical equilibrium condition of the rate of interest. It is represented geometrically in Fig. 21-1. The coordinates of the point of intersection between the savings curve and the investment curve represent the equilibrium rate of interest, savings, and investment. Should the rate of interest be

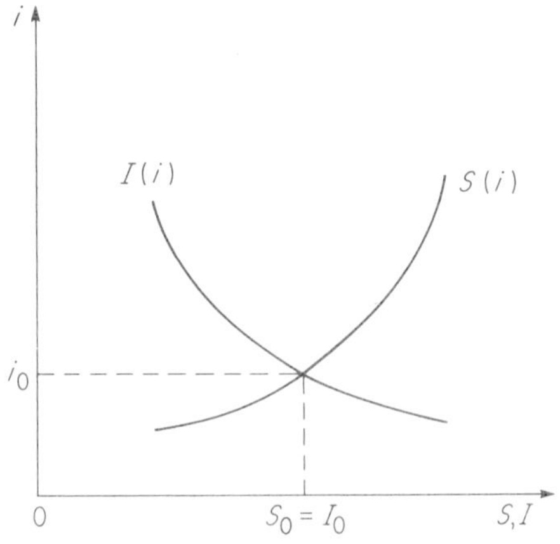

Fig. 21-1. Savings-investment theory of interest.

above the equilibrium rate, the excess of the supply of savings over the demand for investment would cause the rate of interest to go down. On the other hand, should the rate of interest be lower than the equilibrium rate, the excess of investment over savings would drive up the rate of interest. Only at the equilibrium rate of interest is the flow of savings onto the capital market per unit of time matched by the flow off the market through investment demand.

Thus, unlike the Keynesian saving-investment theory, which is a theory of income determination, the classical savings-investment theory is a theory of interest determination; saving and investment are brought into equilibrium by the rate of interest, and the level of income has nothing to do with this equilibrating mechanism. Income is in fact assumed to be a full-employment constant. Since they failed to recognize the asset function of money, classical economists assumed that savers would always use their savings in acquiring income-yielding claims instead of holding idle-money balances. Savings, therefore, would always be made available to businesses for investment purposes. Inasmuch as the level of income is assumed to be constant, the effect of the interaction between saving and investment, according to classical analysis, is not on the aggregate level of output but rather on the composition of output. An increase in savings (or a decrease in consumption) would mean lower interest and smaller demand for consumption goods. But lower interest would lead to higher investment demand and greater production of investment goods. The total level of output would remain unchanged.

Now if we consider savings to be closely related to the level of income rather than to the rate of interest, then an increase in savings (a decrease in consumption) would cause the level of income to decline and the decrease in the level of income may cause investment demand to decrease even at relatively lower interest brought about by the increase in savings. The demand for investment goods is, after all, derived from the demand for consumption goods which can be produced by these capital goods. If the decrease in the demand for consumption goods (an increase in savings) is such that there is an excess in existing productive facilities, there is no point in adding more capital goods to a stock which already proves excessive. It follows that a decrease in the demand for consumption goods may lead to a smaller demand for investment goods, hence a lower level of income and employment. Saving and investment thus do influence the level of income and employment, but such an influence was not considered in the classical theory as it proceeded on the assumption of a full employment level of output.

THE NEOCLASSICAL OR LOANABLE-FUNDS THEORY

The loanable-funds theory of interest is an extension of the classical version. According to this theory, the rate of interest is determined by the total demand for, and total supply of, loanable funds. Supply and demand are made up of several sources.

On the demand side, there is first the demand for loanable funds for investment. This consists of the demand for funds by business firms for capital equipment (*Ib*) and the demand for funds by family households for new residential dwellings (*Ic*). This investment component of total demand is assumed to be negatively related to the rate of interest. Not all the funds needed for the financing of investment expenditures, however, constitute demand for loanable funds. Thus funds needed for investment purposes which are met out of savings do not enter the loanable-funds market as they represent a subtraction from the demand for, and supply of, funds, which are cancelled when demand is equated with supply. A firm which uses internal funds (retained earnings) does not enter the loanable-funds market as a demander of funds, since it acts as its own supplier of funds.

Family households also borrow for consumption purposes (*Cb*) such as the purchases of consumer durables–automobiles, household appliances, and others. This component of total demand is assumed to be inversely related to the rate of interest. Consumers would probably borrow less at higher rates of interest (though, admittedly, few consumers are aware of the real interest cost of consumer credit which is much higher than the nominal rate quoted by consumer credit institutions).

The government also borrows to cover budgetary deficits which are the excesses of government purchases of goods and services over net tax revenue. This component of the demand for loanable funds bears some relation to the rate of interest, especially borrowings by state and local governments.

In addition to the demand for funds for investment and consumption purposes, there is the demand for money for hoarding (*H*). This depends largely upon the interest income which would otherwise be obtained by acquiring income-yielding claims. The lower the rate of interest (that is, the cost of holding money balances) the greater the demand for money for hoarding. But while some people hold idle balances or hoard, other people dishoard–offer to lend or invest their idle funds (*DH*). If we subtract from hoarding the amount being dishoarded, we have net hoarding ($\Delta H = H - DH$) which of course may be positive or negative. Positive hoarding is an addition to the demand for loanable funds and negative hoarding, a subtraction from the demand for or an addition to the supply of loanable funds.

On the side of the supply of loanable funds, we also have several sources. In the first place, we have savings which consists of personal savings, business savings, and government savings–the difference between net taxes and government purchases of goods and services. Government savings enters the loanable-funds market as a supply component when it is used in retiring outstanding debts. It is not a supply component if it is used by the government to build up cash balances. Business savings or retained earnings (we add depreciation allowances when we refer to gross business savings) normally does not enter the loanable funds market as a supply component as they are mostly plowed back in new capital equipment. The portion of business savings which enters the loan market in search for income-yielding claims is rather unimportant. Personal savings constititues a major source of supply of loanable funds. Not all personal savings would enter the loan market, however. Since that portion of savings which is used by savers to build up cash balances does not enter the loanable funds market (it is a subtraction from both the supply of and demand for funds), only the part of personal savings which is offered on the loan market for interest-bearing claims does enter the market for loanable funds as a source of supply. But while some people save out of current income, others may dissave (reduce their holdings of claims) to cover excesses of current expenditures over current incomes. It is obvious that if savings is a source of supply of loanable funds, then dissavings, (DS), constitute a source of demand for funds. To derive the net flow of savings (S_n) into the loanable funds market, we may subtract dissavings and consumers' borrowings (Cb) from savings (it does not in fact matter if instead of subtracting dissavings from savings, we add dissavings, consumers' borrowings, to the demand for funds).

Apart from net savings, another component of the supply of loanable funds is the change in the money stock (ΔM) which is largely a consequence of the actions of the monetary authorities. An expansionary monetary policy would result in an increase in the money stock, whereas a tight monetary policy would cause the supply of money to decrease. ΔM thus may be positive or negative, depending upon the direction of changes in the supply of money.

Assume that government purchases of goods and services are equal to net taxes, the total supply of loanable funds is then made up of net savings and the change in the stock of money $(Sn + \Delta M)$, and the total demand for loanable funds consists of investment demand $(I = Ib + Ic)$ and the net demand for funds for hoarding ΔH, i.e., $(I + \Delta H)$. Aside from the change in the money stock which is exogenously determined, savings, investment, and hoarding are assumed to be related to the rate of interest, the first positively and the last two negatively. The rate of interest is in equilibrium when the demand for loanable funds is equal to the supply of loanable funds:

$$I(i) + \Delta H(i) = S(i) + \Delta M$$

This is shown diagrammatically in Fig. 21-2. The point of intersection between the total supply and demand curves of loanable funds determines the equilibrium rate of interest i_0. At that rate of interest, savings exceeds investment by the amount KL but this is offset by the excess of the demand for funds for hoarding over the change in the money stock by exactly the same amount $(KL = PQ)$. As can be seen from Fig. 21-2, an increase in savings or in the supply of money, other things being equal, will cause the rate of interest to decline. An increase in the demand for funds for investment or hoarding, *ceteris paribus*, will cause the rate of interest to go up.

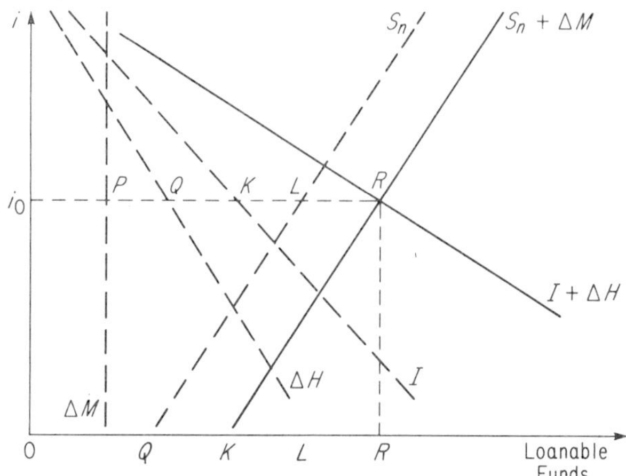

Fig. 21-2. The loanable-funds theory of interest.

The loanable-funds theory of interest is an improvement over the classical version in recognizing the fact that the flow of funds onto the loanable-funds market is more than savings, and the flow of funds off the market is more than the demand for funds to finance investment expenditures. It considers the asset function of money and the influence of the asset demand for money (demand for money for hoarding) and of changes in the supply of money on the rate of interest. An increase in the preference of economic units for money balances (e.g.; by reducing their holdings of interest-bearing claims) would put as much pressure on the rate of interest as does an increase in the demand for funds for investment spending. An increase in the supply of money, on the other hand, would relieve pressure on the rate of interest as does an increase in the supply of savings.

The loanable-funds theory of interest, however, contains a number of shortcomings. Fig. 21-2 shows that, for a certain specified unit of time, the flow of funds onto the market of loanable funds is matched by the flow of funds off the market at the equilibrium rate of interest i_0. The flow of funds off the market at that rate of interest consists of $0Q$ for hoarding and $0K$ for investment. This implies that given the total supply and demand schedules, the public would keep adding, per unit of time, a constant amount of funds equal to $0Q$ to its money balances, which does not appear to be sensible.

The loanable-funds theory, like the classical theory, presumes that savings is rather responsive to interest changes. But savings may not be as responsive to interest changes as assumed by these theories. It is true that some people will save more as the rate of interest increases since higher rates of interest mean greater rewards for their efforts to forgo current consumption. But as we have already mentioned while some people save more as the rate of interest rises, some others may save less at higher interest rates especially those who save in order to receive a fixed amount of income in the future. If these opposite effects of interest on savings are equally strong, then there would be no substantial changes in savings as a result of interest changes. If we assume that savings is largely a function of income, rising as income increases, then a disequilibrium between savings and investment will cause not only the rate of interest to change but also the level of income which in turn brings about changes in savings, investment, the rate of interest, and the level of income. A general theory of interest determination thus would have to be concerned with the simultaneous determination of the level of income and the rate of interest. The loanable-funds theory, which is based on the assumption of a given level of income, is therefore like the classical savings-investment theory—a partial equilibrium theory valid only within the market for loanable funds.

THE LIQUIDITY-PREFERENCE THEORY OF INTEREST

The classical theory that the rate of interest is the equilibrating mechanism between savings and investment was attacked by Keynes. To him, it is not the rate of interest but the level of income that is the mechanism bringing savings into balance with investment. Then what determines the rate of interest? According to Keynes, the rate of interest is the price which equilibrates the desire of the public to hold wealth in the form of money and the quantity of money available. The influence of the desire to hold money balances on the rate of interest, as we have mentioned, was recognized by the loanable-funds theory but it was Keynes who fully clarified the influence of the asset demand for money on the rate of interest.

If at any moment in time, we look at the wealth accumulated by individual economic units, we shall find that it is composed of certain amount of money, certain amount of nonmonetary financial claims (bonds) and real assets. The question is: Why would people want to hold part of their wealth in the form of money instead of converting it into financial claims which yield income, or real assets which yield services and pleasure? There are several reasons for which people want to hold part of their wealth in the form of money. In the first place, they want to have money balances on hand to meet current transactions, to tie up the gap between payments and receipts. Household families need money for payments of goods and services within the interval between income receipts, wages and salaries, which may be made either on a weekly or monthly basis. Business corporations need money balances for the payments of wages and salaries to workers, for raw materials, supplies, and the like, which do not coincide with the sales receipts of goods produced. The size of money balances required for current transactions depends upon the size of receipts and expenditures, the time pattern of expenditures, the intervals between receipts, and the price level. Given the level of prices, the time pattern of expenditures and the size of receipts and payments, then the greater the interval between income receipts, the greater the money balances required for transactions.

As an example, suppose that Mr. X and Y receive the same amount of income per month, say, \$400; they plan to spend the whole amount of income, and the same amount every day. But while Mr. X receives his income on a monthly basis, Mr. Y receives his income on a weekly basis. At the beginning of each month Mr. X has on hand \$400. At the end of the month, the amount is exhausted. To meet current transactions throughout the month, it is obvious that Mr. X needs an average money balance of \$200. In the case of Mr. Y, at the beginning of the week, he has \$100. At the end of the week no money is left. He needs an average money balance of \$50 for transactions purposes. It can be seen that since Mr. Y receives his income at a shorter interval, the average money balance needed for transactions is much smaller. Since the time pattern of expenditures and the interval between receipts do not change at least in the short run, because of institutional habits among other things, then, given the level of prices, the demand for money for transactions is related to the size of receipts and expenditures. Inasmuch as the latter depends upon the level of income, we can say that the demand for transactions balance L_T is an increasing function of the level of income $L_T = L_T(Y)$; the higher the level of income, the greater the money balances required for transactions. Fig. 21-3 shows the demand for transactions balances proportional to the level of income.

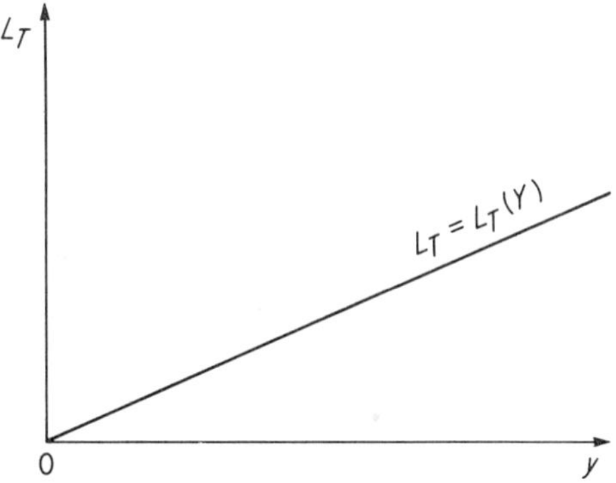

Fig. 21-3. The demand for transaction balances.

In addition to the demand for money for transactions purposes, people also want to hold money balances for unanticipated expenditures such as those involved in accidents, unexpected business liabilities, and other emergencies requiring immediate cash outlays. This is conventionally referred to as the demand for money for precautionary purposes. This demand for money, like the demand for transactions balances, is for expenditures, the difference being that while the former is for unexpected expenditures, the latter is for anticipated transactions. The precautionary demand for money may be considered as positively related to the level of income. The higher the level of income, the greater the ability of people to put aside cash balances for emergency spending. It can also be considered as related to the rate of interest. People may be induced to reduce the size of precautionary balances for interest-bearing assets if interest rates are high. They, however, may be deterred by the possibility that they may be forced to dispose of these assets at unreasonably low prices to meet emergency spending. We shall consider the precautionary demand for money as a function of income alone and include it in the L_T component of total demand.

A third reason for which people want to hold money balances is that because under certain conditions, it is most advantageous to hold wealth in the form of money instead of interest-bearing claims. This asset demand for money varies inversely with the rate of interest. To see the relationship between the rate of interest and the choice of assets, we shall assume for simplicity that in addition to money the public can hold its wealth in a certain kind of perpetual bond. Holding idle money balances thus means forgoing the interest which could be earned from holding bonds. On the other hand, holding bonds would earn interest, but the bondholder would have to assume the risk of losses which may result from rising interest or declining price. Inasmuch as the rate of interest represents the cost of holding idle balances, holding bonds appears to be more attractive than holding money when the rate of interest is high as a high rate of interest means greater reward for assuming the risk involved in holding bonds (the high cost of holding money). It follows that at a high rate of interest there is greater incentive for holding bonds instead of money. On the other hand, when the rate of interest is low, holding money appears to be more attractive than holding bonds as the reward for the risk of holding bonds is small or it is not too costly to hold idle balances. Another factor that accounts for the inverse relationship between the rate of interest and the asset demand for money is the expectations of people in regard to what the future rate will be. There is a certain rate of interest which is considered as "normal" by asset holders. When the current rate of interest deviates from the "normal" rate, it is expected to return to the "normal" level. Suppose that the current rate of interest is above the "normal" rate. Then holding bonds is more attractive than holding money, as holders of bonds would benefit from the currently high rate of interest and probable capital gains in the future when the rate of interest is expected to decline. On the other hand, when the current rate is below the "normal" rate, then holding money is more attractive than holding bonds, since the latter alternative would involve the risk of capital losses resulting from the increase in the rate of interest expected to prevail in the future. A third factor that accounts for the inverse relationship between the asset demand for money and the rate of interest is that when the rate of interest declines, the value of bonds rises. This means that there is an increase in the wealth of bondholders. To the extent that there is a positive relation between wealth and the asset demand for money, an increase in wealth would lead to some increase in the demand for money.

Figure 21-4 shows the inverse relationship between the speculative demand for money *Ls* and the rate of interest. The curve flattens out at low rates of

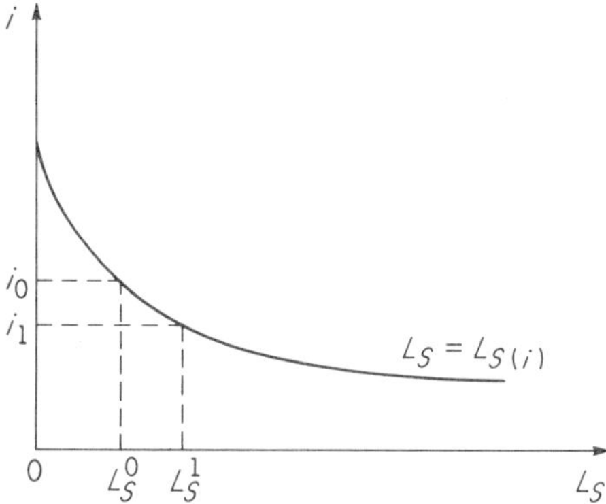

Fig. 21-4. The speculative demand for money.

interest. This is drawn on the belief that at a very low rate of interest, the probability that it would rise is so strong that few people would be interested in holding bonds. The demand for money becomes perfectly elastic with respect to the rate of interest.

The total demand for money—the sum of L_T and L_S—is thus related to both the level of income and the rate of interest:

$$L = L_T(Y) + L_S(i) = L(Y, i)$$

It is positively related to the level of income and negatively related to the rate of interest. Given the level of income and the supply of money M the rate of interest is in equilibrium when the demand for money, at the given level of income, is equal to the supply of money—that is,

$$M = L(Y, i)$$

This is presented geometrically in Fig. 21-5. The demand curve for money LL, referred to as the liquidity-preference curve, is drawn at an assumed level of income Y_0. Since the supply of money is fixed at any moment in time, it is represented by a straight line parallel to the interest axis. The point of intersection between the liquidity-preference curve and the supply curve determines the equilibrium rate of interest. Given the level of income Y_0, the public is willing to hold the quantity of money available only at the equilibrium rate of interest i_0. It can be seen from Fig. 21-5 that an increase in liquidity preference (an upward shift of the liquidity-preference curve) would cause the rate of interest to rise. On the other hand, given the liquidity function, an increase in the quantity of money would cause the rate of interest to decline. An increase in liquidity preference accompanied by an increase in the quantity of money therefore may not result in any changes in the equilibrium rate of interest.

There is a point that needs clarification. We know that the quantity of money available at a given moment has to be held by "somebody" in the

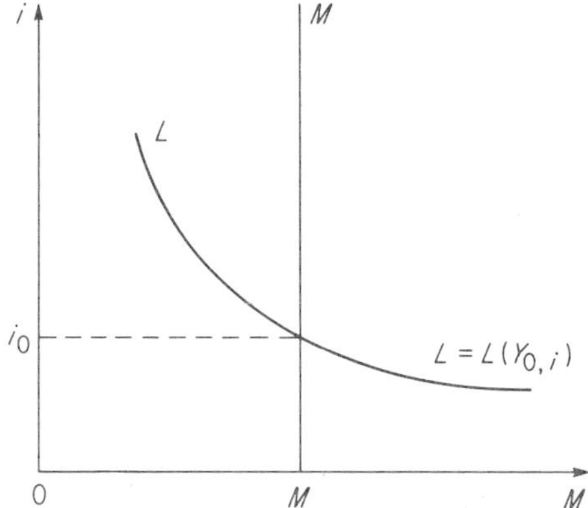

Fig. 21-5. The equilibrium rate of interest.

economy. It does not just float around. But the public is willing to hold the quantity of money available only at the equilibrium rate of interest. If the prevailing rate of interest is higher than the equilibrium rate, then the quantity of money available is more than what the public desires to hold. The way by which people can reduce excessive idle balances is to purchase securities. The resulting buying pressures would cause the price of bonds to go up or the rate of interest to go down, which will continue until it reaches the equilibrium level. On the other hand, if the prevailing rate of interest is lower than the equilibrium rate, then the quantity of money available is less than what people wish to hold. Their attempt to build up idle balances by selling securities would cause the price of bonds to go down or the rate of interest to go up until the equilibrium rate.

It should also be noted that unlike the classical savings-investment theory of interest which is a purely flow theory, the Keynesian liquidity-preference theory is a purely stock theory; it shows the equilibrium rate of interest at which the public is willing to hold the existing stock of money. The liquidity-preference theory of interest is also a partial equilibrium theory which is valid only when it is confined to the money market, since it is based on the assumption of a given level of income. A general theory of interest determination thus has to deal with the simultaneous determination of income and the rate of interest. This will be discussed in detail in Chapter 22 on the integration of money, interest, and income.

RECENT REFINEMENTS ON THE DEMAND FOR MONEY

The Keynesian theory of the demand for money has been refined and broadened, and numerous empirical studies have been conducted to establish the degrees of responsiveness of the demand for money with respect to income, the rate of interest, and other variables.

To a number of economists, it is an oversimplification to consider the demand for transactions balances as a function of income alone. They argue that the demand for money for transactions purposes is positively related to income and inversely related to the rate of interest.[1] Given a linear time pattern of expenditure in the receipts-payments interval, then the longer this interval the greater the average transactions balances required by spending units. Holders of sizable transactions balances may find it profitable to invest part of these balances in securities of different maturities for income and convert them gradually into cash to meet transactions requirements as they arise. Whether this is profitable or not depends upon the interest rates on these securities on the one hand and the costs of securities transactions on the other. Given the costs of securities transactions, the greater the interest income which can be earned on these securities, the greater the incentive on the part of asset holders to economize on transactions balances.

The classification of the demand for money into "transactions demand" and "speculative demand," however, has been considered by a number of investigators as somewhat artificial. They, instead, attempt to explain the total demand for money. But using different definitions of the money stock, empirical studies along this approach yield divergent results. Studies based on the conventional definition of the money stock (that is, the sum of currency held by the public and adjusted demand deposits in commercial banks) suggests that the demand for money is responsive to both income and the rate of interest.[2] Professor Friedman, on the other hand, uses a different definition of the stock of money; defining the money stock to include time deposits in commercial banks, his study suggests a high income elasticity, and practically no interest elasticity, of the demand for money.[3] This led to his conclusion that money is a "luxury" good the demand for which increases in greater proportion than the increase in income. The absence of any significant response of the demand for money to interest changes in his study, however, may be attributable among other things to the inclusion of time deposits in the money stock which tends to obscure the movement between demand and time deposits as a result of interest changes.

Apart from income and rate of interest, wealth, and other variables have been introduced into the demand-for-money function. But while it is generally

[1] William J. Baumol, "The Transactions Demand for Cash: An Inventory Theoretic Approach," *Quarterly Journal of Economics* (November 1952); James Tobin, "The Interest Elasticity of Transactions Demand for Cash," *Review of Economics and Statistics* (August 1956).

[2] See, for example, Henry A. Latane "Income Veleocity and Interest Rates: A Pragmatic Approach," *Quarterly Journal of Economics* (November 1960).

[3] Milton Friedman, "The Demand for Money: Some Theoretical and Empirical Results," *Journal of Political Economy* (August 1959).

agreed that national wealth bears some relation to the demand for money, it is statistically difficult to assert the independent effects of wealth and income on the demand for money as income and wealth are highly correlated.[4] It has also been argued that the liquidity function is irreversible in that its downward trail after an increase in the supply of money may be different from its upward path after a corresponding decrease in the money supply. This reflects changes in the composition of assets and assets value as the rate of interest changes. As an example, assume that the public, in addition to money, holds perpetual bonds paying a fixed annual interest of $50 a piece. The price of bonds then would be $1,000 a piece at the rate of interest of 5 percent. Suppose that the central bank, to increase the money supply by $1.25 billion, purchases 1 million bonds at the price of $1,250 or the rate of interest of 4 percent. Should the central bank wish to reduce the supply of money to the original level and restore the rate of interest back to 5 percent, it would have to sell 1,250,000 bonds to the public. The latter would have 250,000 bonds more than before. To the extent that this has some positive influence on the public's demand for money, there would be some pressure on the demand for money that would cause the rate of interest to rise above 5 percent. It follows that to restore the rate of interest back to 5 percent, the reduction of the supply of money would be less than the increment needed to reduce it from 5 to 4 percent. The monetary policy implication of this is that "in the case of open-market operations, the twist of the money screw required to reestablish a former higher interest level needs to be shorter than the earlier turn of money injection undertaken to induce a given degree of ease, as reflected in interest rates. . ."[5]

The earlier Keynesian theory of the demand for money is a theory of choice between money and long-term bonds of the same maturity and risk. This does not represent an accurate picture of the real world with a multitude of securities carrying a wide range of maturities and varying degrees of risk. Some of these securities such as savings deposits in commercial banks and savings banks, savings and loan shares in savings and loan associations, and Treasury bills are almost as liquid and safe as money. When we take into consideration these liquid assets, the choice of asset holders is no longer a simple choice between money and homogenous long-term bonds, but rather between money, liquid, low-risk and low-yield claims, and illiquid, high-yield, and risky assets. Changes in the decisions of asset holders in regard to holding money, liquid assets, and long-term claims as a result of changes in their liquidity and income preference therefore affect the relative prices of securities or the structure of interest rates. The analysis of the structure of interest rates, especially the term structure of rates, has received increasing attention in recent years.

[4]In the terminology of econometrics, the problem involved is known as the problem of *multicollinearity* among the variables.

[5]Sidney Weintraub, *An Approach to the Theory of Income Distribution,* (Philadelphia: Chilton Company, 1958), p. 161.

THE STRUCTURE OF INTEREST RATES

We have seen that the determination of "the" rate of interest is an oversimplification. We know that in actual financial markets, there is a multitude of interest rates, each reflects the risk, maturity and other features associated with a particular kind of security. All these rates together form the structure of interest rates.

A Static Equilibrium Structure of Rates

In our discussion of the money and capital markets we have mentioned that security prices are determined by the supply of, and demand for, securities, just like commodity prices are determined by the supply of and demand for commodities. The demand for securities reflects largely the liquidity and income preferences of investors, and the supply of securities, the liquidity and credit requirements of borrowers. The determination of security prices in turn determines the levels and structure of interest rates. With information on the demand and supply functions of securities, we can find a set of prices or market rates of interest which clear the market.

It is generally agreed that there is a substantial degree of substitutability among securities within a maturity range. For instance, holders of Treasury bills may switch to such short-term commercial paper as bankers' acceptances and notes of business corporations of very high credit standing if the yields on Treasury bills are relatively low as compared with the yields on these short-term securities. Likewise, holders of long-term securities may switch from one type of long-term instrument to another if there are substantial yield differentials between them. While there is a high degree of substitutability among short-term securities and long-term securities, the substitutability between short and long-term securities may not be substantial because of habits and institutional restrictions on the part of institutions operating in these markets. Investors as well as borrowers, however, may find it to their advantage to switch between the two ends of the securities market if the difference in relative yields to the investor (or the relative cost of borrowing to the borrower) is such that such a switch is justified. Given some degree of substitutability among securities throughout the maturity spectrum, we can consider the demand for each kind of security as a function not only of its market yield alone (or market price) but also of the yields of all other securities, and other variables such as the quantity of money M and wealth W. Suppose that we have n types of securities in the market, we then have n demand functions of securities:

$$D_1 = D_1\ (i_1, i_2, \ldots, i_n, M, W)$$
$$D_2 = D_2\ (i_1, i_2, \ldots, i_n, M, W)$$
$$D_n = D_n\ (i_1, i_2, \ldots, i_n, M, W)$$

where D_r is the demand for rth security and i_r is its market yield or rate of interest ($r = 1, 2, \ldots, n$).

Since the supply of securities at a moment of time is fixed, we have n supply quantities of securities $S_1, S_2, \ldots, S_n$, where S_r being the stock of the rth security at a given moment.

The structure of interest rates is in equilibrium when there is equality between the supply of, and demand for, each and every type of security—that is,

$$\begin{aligned} D_1 (i_1, i_2, \ldots, i_n, M, W) &= S_1 \\ D_2 (i_1, i_2, \ldots, i_n, M, W) &= S_2 \\ D_n (i_1, i_2, \ldots, i_n, M, W) &= S_n \end{aligned} \tag{1}$$

Given M and W, we have a set of n simultaneous equations in n unknowns, the unknowns being the market rates of interest $i_1, i_2, \ldots, i_n$. The solution of the system of Equations (1) assuming that it is determinate, represents the equilibrium structure of interest, that is, the set of interest rates at which investors are willing to hold the existing stocks of securities; there is no desire on their part to switch from one kind of security to another kind. It is clear from the system of Equations (1) that changes in the demand for, and supply of, various types of securities would bring about adjustments in the structure of rates through the operations of market forces until another equilibrium structure is reached in which the supply of, and demand for, each and every type of securities are again brought into balance. In actual markets the adjustment process, however, is continuous as the income and liquidity preferences of lenders and the liquidity and credit requirements of borrowers change constantly.

The Term Structure of Interest Rates

The structure of interest rates as expressed by the system of Equations (1) represents all the features associated with securities, including risk of default, maturity, callability, convertibility and so on. The term structure of interest rates, on the other hand, refers only to the relationship between yields and maturities. To consider the relationship between maturities and yields it is obvious that we have to select securities which are homogenous in all respects except for maturities, otherwise the differences in the market yields of different securities may not reflect differences in maturities alone but also in risk and other aspects as well. The obligations of the U. S. Government are very close to such homogenous securities. These securities are practically free of the risk of default. If we plot the market yields of government securities of different maturities at a given moment and draw a curve to fit the scattered points plotted, we have what is referred to as yield curve representing the term structure of rates. The curve *AA* in Fig. 21-6 is a yield curve. The two yield curves in Fig. 21-6 represent rather extreme forms of yield curves. The *AA* curve indicates that yields rise sharply as maturity lengthens. The *BB* curve—an inverted yield curve—is downward-sloping, showing declining yields as maturity increases. Between these two extremes, yield curves may take a multitude of shapes. They may slope gently upward: yields rise slowly with maturities. They may be "humped": yields rise with maturities up to a point then decline beyond that maturity range.

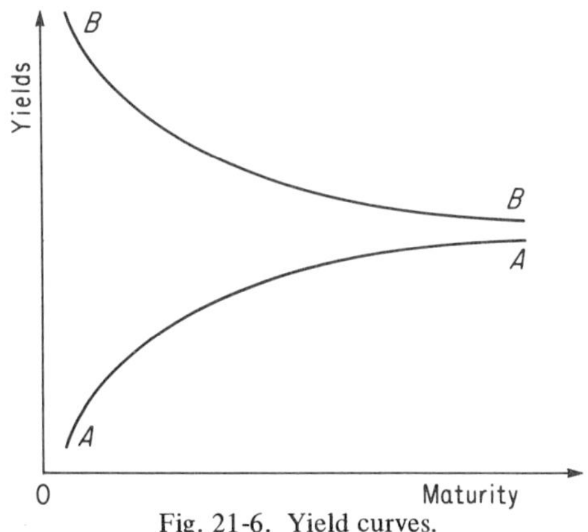

Fig. 21-6. Yield curves.

THEORIES EXPLAINING THE TERM STRUCTURE OF RATES

What are factors which determine the term structure of rates? There are three theories proposed to explain the relationship between yields and maturities: The expectations theory, the liquidity preference theory, and the market segmentation theory.

The Expectations Theory

According to this theory, the yield curve is what it is because of expectations of investors and borrowers of what future rates will be. It is held that investors and borrowers have in their mind certain levels of interest rates which they consider as "normal" rates. When the rates of interest are below the "normal" rates, the probability is that they would go up. Conversely, when interest rates are above what is considered as "normal," chances are that they would go down. When interest rates are expected to rise (or security prices to decline), investors would tend to move out of long-term securities and into short-term securities in order to avoid capital losses resulting from expected higher rates in the future. The resulting increase in the supply of long-term securities would cause their prices to go down or their market yields to go up. The market yields of short-term securities, on the other hand, would go down as a consequence of the increase in demand. This movement of short and long-term rates tends to be reinforced by the reaction of borrowers which is in the opposite direction. Borrowers would tend to move to the long-term market in view of avoiding higher interest costs expected to prevail in the future. The increase in the supply of long-term securities by borrowers for long-term funds would cause long-term yields to increase further. At the same time, the decrease in the demand for short-term funds (that is, decrease in the supply of short-term securities) would cause short-term interest rates to decline. It follows that when interest rates are expected to rise, the yield curve is positively sloped.

The reverse holds when interest rates are expected to decline. The switch of investors from the short end to the long end of the market for expected capital gains and the postponement of long-term borrowing by borrowers who want to take advantage of lower long-term rates in the future, would cause the long-term rates of interest to be lower relative to short-term rates. Thus when interest rates are expected to go down, the yield curve is downward-sloping.

The strict interpretation of the expectations theory implies that default-free securities of different maturities are perfect substitutes; the effective yields (calculated with the inclusion of capital losses or gains) would therefore be the same for holding either short-term securities or long-term securities for identical periods. For instance, the yield from holding a three-year security is expected to be the same as holding a sequence of three one-year securities successively. Since if holding the three-year security is expected to yield more than holding a sequence of three one-year securities, then investors would tend to switch from one-year securities to three-year securities and this would cause the price of three-year securities to go up or its market yield to decline until it is equal to the expected yield from holding one-year securities for the same period. Thus, suppose that the current one-year rate is 1 percent and the market expects with confidence that the one-year rate one year hence would be 3 percent. No investor would be willing to purchase two-year securities for a market rate less than 2 percent if he can purchase one-year securities now for 1 percent interest and then one-year securities one year hence with an expected yield of 3 percent. Nor would any borrower be willing to pay more than 2 percent for two-year money if he can borrow one-year money now for one percent and one-year money one year hence for 3 percent. It follows that according to the expectations theory, the long-term rates of interest are an average of expected short-term rates.

The Liquidity-Preference Theory

This theory asserts that since the risk of capital loss is positively related to term to maturity, the longer the maturity of a security, the higher its yield; the difference between the return on a long-term security and that on a short-term security represents the greater risk of capital loss.

The Market-Segmentation Theory

Unlike the expectations theory, the market-segmentation theory holds that securities of different maturities are poor substitutes. In regard to borrowers, the maturity terms of securities offered reflect the specific purposes for which borrowed funds are needed. Short-term funds are needed largely for such short-term credit requirements as the financing of inventory, the processing of unfinished products, and other working capital requirements. Intermediate-term funds are needed by businesses for the acquisition of business assets of medium durability, and long-term funds are required for new plants, buildings, equipment, and other assets of long durability. Because of institutional habits, among other things, borrowers would not be ready to move freely between the two ends of the market. Institutional lenders likewise are more or less specialized in operating within certain maturity ranges. While commercial banks are mostly lenders of short-term funds, such institutions as savings banks, savings and loan associations, and insurance companies are largely providers of long-term funds. Banks may be ready to change the composition of their short-term portfolios, they may be more reluctant to switch between short-term and long-term securites if for no other reason than institutional restrictions and habits. Financial markets, according to this theory, are therefore imperfect markets. They are segmented, and each segment reflects the lending and borrowing of funds within certain maturity ranges. It follows that the movement of yields within certain maturity ranges bears little relationship to yield movements in other maturity ranges.

Empirical Evidence

The empirical evidence relevant to these theories is not conclusive. While the liquidity-preference theory is consistent with the upward-sloping yield curve, it is inconsistent with the inverted yield curve (yields decline as maturity rises) and the "humped" yield curve (yields decline beyond certain maturity ranges). The massive shift out of short-term into long-term government securities during World War II following the policy of the Federal Reserve to stabilize interest rates on U.S. Government securities as a consequence of the downward revision of the prestabilization long-term rates then believed to be too high was consistent with the expectations theory (and the liquidity preference theory) and inconsistent with the market segmentation theory.[6] If, as postulated by this theory, short-term and long-term securities were poor substitutes, there would not be such a tremendous shift between the two ends of the government securities market. David Meiselman research also led to the acceptance of the expectations theory.[7] J. M. Culbertson, on the other hand, rejected the expectations theory as he found that yields to investors, including capital gains and losses, on default-free securities of different maturities were not identical for the same holding periods. There were significant differences between their yields.[8]

It appears that none of the three theories presented is alone adequate to explain the term structure of rates, but it can be explained by a combination of these theories. Reuben A. Kessel, for instance, has explained the term structure of interest with a combination of the expectations theory and the liquidity

[6] Charles E. Walker, "Federal Reserve Policy and the Structure of Interest Rates on Government Securities," *Quarterly Journal of Economics* (February 1954).

[7] David Meiselman, *The Term Structure of Interest Rates* (Englewood Cliffs, N.J.: Prentice Hall, 1962).

[8] J. M. Culbertson, "The Term Structure of Interest Rates," *Quarterly Journal of Economics* (November 1957).

preference theory. The expectations of investors and borrowers regarding future rates influence the current term structure of rates and the difference in yields reflects the liquidity premium for risk of capital loss.[9]

Policy Implications

We have mentioned that the rate of interest is a channel through which monetary policy influences the level of income and employment. Monetary changes brought about by actions of the monetary authority would cause the rate of interest to change. Interest changes in turn cause investment demand and hence, the level of income, to change. But which rate of interest would affect investment spending? Is it the short-term rate of interest or the long-term rate of interest? It is generally agreed that it is the long-term rate of interest which influences long-term investment. Since measures taken by the monetary authority to change interest rates are largely the sales or purchases of securities in the open market, the question is, what kinds of securities are to be bought and sold? Should they be short-term securities, long-term securities, or both? The answer depends substantially on the relationship between the yield movements of short-term and long-term securities. If securities of different maturities were perfect substitutes, which implies that impulses of yield changes brought about by monetary actions in one end of the market would be transmitted to the other end of the market with little or no time lag, then it would not make any difference as to whether short-term securities or long-term securities should be bought and sold, inasmuch as increases (decreases) in short-term money rates brought about the sales (purchases) of short-term securities by the central bank would in no time cause the long-term rates to rise as well, and vice versa.

On the other hand, if there were substantial time lags in the propagation of interest changes between the two ends of the securities market, then, in order to bring about direct changes in the long-term rates of interest either to promote or deter the expansion of long-term investments, direct open-market purchases or sales of long-term securities are necessary. Operations in the short end of the market alone may not bring about desired changes in the long-term interest rates. While short-term and long-term money rates in general tend to move in the same direction such movement involves time lags. At times they may indeed move in opposite directions. Flexible open-market policy therefore should be conducted in securities of all maturity ranges. The departure from the "bills-only" policy (which had confined open-market operations only to the short end of the market) by the Federal Reserve in the early 1960's to conduct open-market operations in both ends of the market was a case in point. This policy shift was designed primarily to keep down the long-term rates of interest to promote domestic investment and economic expansion, and raise the short-

[9] *The Cyclical Behavior of the Term Structure of Interest Rates* (New York: National Bureau of Economic Research, 1965).

term rates of interest to discourage the short-term capital outflows which would aggravate the U.S. balance-of-payments deficits.[10]

SUMMARY

The classical savings-investment theory, the loanable-funds theory, and the Keynesian liquidity-preference theory are major developments in the theory of interest. The classical theory holds that the rate of interest is determined by savings and investment. The neoclassical or loanable-funds theory adds changes in the stock of money to savings, and the demand for funds for hoarding to investment demand, as determinants of the rate of interest. According to this version, the rate of interest is the equilibrating mechanism between the total demand for loanable funds (the sum of investment demand and net hoarding) and the total supply of loanable funds (the sum of net savings and changes in the supply of money). In terms of the Keynesian liquidity-preference theory, the rate of interest is determined by the demand for money balances and the quantity of money available. Money is held as a store of value by the public not only because it is needed to meet current transactions and unexpected expenditures, but also because under certain conditions, it is the best alternative means to store wealth.

The analysis of the determination of "the" rate of interest is an oversimplification. In actual financial markets there is a multitude of interest rates associated with a multitude of different securities. These rates altogether form the structure of rates. It is determined simultaneously by the demand for, and supply of, each and every type of securities in the market. The term structure of interest rates refers to the relationship between yields and maturities of securities which are homogenous in all other respects. There are three theories proposed to explain the term structure of rates. The expectations theory holds that expectations in regard to future rates influence the current term structure of rates. The liquidity-preference theory contends that the longer the maturity of a security, the greater the risk of capital loss, and the higher its yield. The market-segmentation theory believes that financial markets are imperfect and the yield movements in each market segment bear little relationship to yield movements in other market segments.

The relationship between the short and long-term rates of interest has important policy implications. If the movement between short and long-term rates is sympathetic and if changes in short-term rates immediately affect long-term rates, and vice versa, then it would not matter if open-market operations are conducted either in the short or long-term securities market. But if the movement between long and short-term rates involves substantial time lags, then it would appear desirable for the monetary authority to conduct open-market

[10] More details on this will be given in Chapter 26 on Monetary and Fiscal Policy of the United States since 1951.

operations in both ends of the securities market to bring about direct changes in either short or long-term rates as required by circumstances.

PROBLEMS

1. Explain briefly the difference between the classical savings-investment theory and the Keynesian savings-investment theory. What are some of the assumptions underlying the classical savings-investment theory? Is it a flow or stock theory?

2. Explain some of the major sources of supply of, and demand for, loanable funds. In what way would you consider the loanable-funds theory of interest an improvement over the classical theory? Are there any common grounds between the loanable funds theory and the liquidity-preference theory of interest?

3. What are basic reasons for which people want to hold money balances? What are factors which account for the inverse relationship between the speculative demand for money and the rate of interest?

4. The liquidity-preference theory of interest is a partial equilibrium theory. Do you agree? Why or why not? Is it a stock or flow theory? Explain.

5. What do you understand by term structure of interest rates? What are theories proposed to explain term structure of rates? What are policy implications of the relationship between the short and long-term rates of interest?

6. Assume that the supply of money is fixed at $M = 50$ and the total demand for money is $L(Y, i) = 1/20Y + 0.8/i$ where Y is the level of income, and i the rate of interest. Find the equilibrium rates of interest when the level of income is $Y_0 = 200$ and $Y_1 = 300$.

7. Assume that the demand for money is related to income and the rate of interest by $L(Y, i) = 1/5Y - 200i$. Given the quantity of money $M = 30$, find the equilibrium rate of interest when the level of income is $Y_0 = 200$ and $Y_1 = 250$.

chapter 22

Money, Interest, and Income: An Integration

We have treated the determination of the rate of interest and the formation of income as if they were independent. We have seen that, given the level of income, the rate of interest is determined in the monetary sector by the demand for, and supply of, money. On the other hand, given the rate of interest, the level of income is determined in the "real" sector by savings and investment. The monetary sector and real sector are, however, interdependent. Changes in the demand for, and supply of, money causes the rate of interest to change. Interest changes affect investment demand (and probably savings) and the level of income. Income changes, in turn, affect the demand for money and the rate of interest. It follows that the demand for money, the supply of money, interest, income, savings, and investment are elements of an interdependent system and a general macroequilibrium analysis has to deal with the simultaneous determination of these variables.

MONEY, INTEREST, AND INCOME: AN INTEGRATED MODEL

The liquidity-preference theory of interest, as already noted, is a partial equilibrium theory. It shows the equilibrium rate of interest only at a given level of income, as indicated by the money equilibrium equation:

$$M = L(Y, i) \tag{1}$$

Given the supply of money M, the equilibrium rate of interest i is determined only when the level of income Y is given. As income changes, the equilibrium rate of interest also changes as a consequence of changes in the demand for money generated by income changes. In Equation (1), assume that the equilibrium rate of interest corresponding to the given level of income Y_0 is i_0. Now suppose that income increases from Y_0 to Y_1. Given the speculative demand for money, the total demand for money will increase as a result of the increase in the transactions demand for money generated by the higher level of income. The increase in the demand for money will cause the rate of interest to rise. A general theory of interest and income determination, therefore, requires that the rate of interest and the level of income be determined simultaneously. For the simultaneous determination of income and interest, we simply add to the money equilibrium Equation (1) the equilibrium equation for income:

$$S(Y) = I(i) \tag{2}$$

The system of Equations (1) and (2) contains three unknowns: M, Y, and i. Given the supply of money, M, we can solve (1) and (2) simultaneously for the equilibrium rate of interest and the equilibrium level of income. It is clear from Equations (1) and (2) that, given the supply of money, the liquidity-preference function, the propensity to save, and the propensity to invest, interest and income are simultaneously in equilibrium when they reach the levels at which savings is equal to investment, and the demand for money is equal to the supply of money.

For an algebraic illustration of the simultaneous determination of the rate of interest and the level of income, assume that we have the following functions regarding the demand for money, savings, investment, and the supply of money:

$$L(Y,i) = mY - ni$$
$$M = M_0$$
$$S(Y) = -a + s \cdot Y$$
$$I(i) = g - ei$$

Setting the demand for money equal to the supply of money and savings equal to investment, and solving for i in terms of Y and M, we have:

$$M = mY - ni \tag{3}$$
$$-a + sY = g - ei \tag{4}$$

and

$$i = -\left(\frac{1}{n}\right) M + \left(\frac{m}{n}\right) Y \tag{3a}$$

$$= \frac{1}{e}(a + g) - \left(\frac{s}{e}\right) Y \tag{4a}$$

It follows from Equations (3a) and (4a) that the equilibrium level of income is:

$$Y = \frac{1}{\frac{me}{n} + s}(a + g) + \frac{1}{m + \frac{ns}{e}} \cdot M \tag{5}$$

Given the stock of money M, the equilibrium level of income can be ascertained. Substitute the equilibrium level of income in either Equation (3a) or (4a), we can find the equilibrium rate of interest.

This integrated model of income and interest is presented geometrically in Figs. 22-1, 22-2, and 22-3.

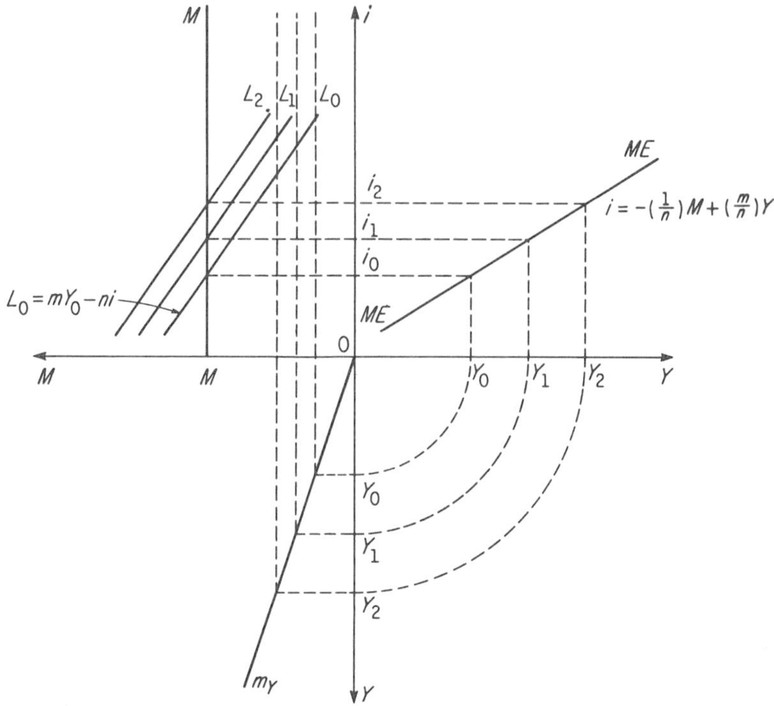

Fig. 22-1. Money equilibrium.

Figure 22-1 shows the relation in Equation (3) or (3a). The straight line in the third quadrant shows the relationship between the demand for transactions balances at alternative levels of income. In the second quadrant, given the speculative demand for money, we have a family of liquidity-preference curves (each corresponds to a given level of income) which, together with the quantity of money M, determines various equilibrium rates of interest at various assumed levels of income. When the level of income is Y_0, for example, the liquidity-preference curve corresponding to that level of income is L_0 and the equilibrium rate of interest is i_0, and so on. The *ME* curve in the first quadrant is the money equilibrium curve. It is reproduced in Fig. 22-3. The curve shows the equilibrium rates of interest at alternative levels of income.

Figure 22-2 shows the relations in Equation (4) or (4a). The second quadrant shows the investment function, and the third quadrant shows the propensity to save. Given these functions, an equilibrium level of income is determined for each assumed rate of interest. For instance, when the rate of interest is given at i_3 the equilibrium level of income is Y_3. When the rate of interest increases to i_4, the equilibrium level of income decreases to Y_4, and so

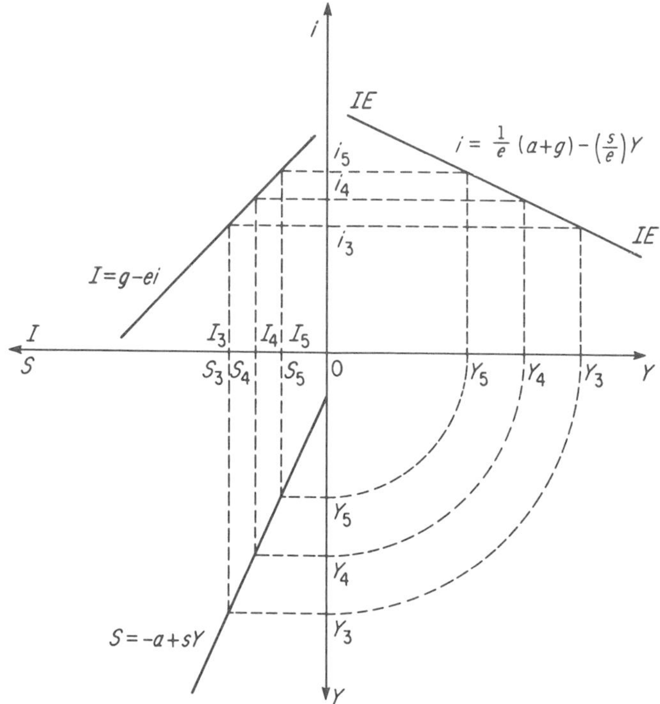

Fig. 22-2. Income equilibrium.

forth. The *IE* curve in the first quadrant is the income equilibrium curve. It is also reproduced in Fig. 22-3. The curve shows the equilibrium levels of income at alternative rates of interest.

Inasmuch as every point on the *ME* curve satisfies Equation (1) and every point on the *IE* curve satisfies Equation (2), the point of intersection *G* between the *ME* and *IE* curve in Fig. 22-3 (which is common to both) satisfies Equations (1) and (2) simultaneously. The coordinates of *G* therefore represent the equilibrium rate of interest (i_e) and the equilibrium level of income (Ye).

For a specific numerical example, assume that investment is related to the rate of interest by $I = g - ei = 30 - 100i$, savings, to income by $S = -a + sY = -20 + 1/5Y$, and the demand for money, to income and the rate of interest by $L = mY - ni = 1/5Y - 100i$; the money supply is given at $M = 25$. To find the equilibrium rate of interest and the equilibrium level of income, we set $S = I$ and $L = M$:

$$1/5Y - 100i = 25$$
$$30 - 100i = -20 + 1/5Y$$

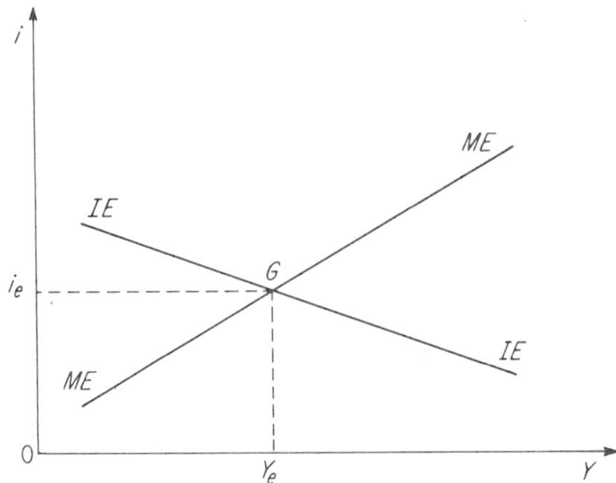

Fig. 22-3. Interest and income equilibrium.

Solving simultaneously for i and Y, we have

$$Y = 187.5$$
$$i = 12.5\%$$

At this level of income and interest, savings is of course equal to investment and the demand for money is equal to the supply of money ($S = I = 17.5$ and $L = M = 25$). It should be noted that the above integrated model is a stock-flow model, since it contains both elements of the liquidity preference theory which is a stock theory, and the savings-investment theory which is a flow theory. Interest and income are influenced by the stock of money and the demand for this stock as well as by the flows of savings and investment.

Effects of Changes in the Supply of Money

We have seen that, given the supply of money, the equilibrium rate of interest and the equilibrium level of income are determined simultaneously by Equations (1) and (2). It follows that when the supply of money changes, the rate of interest and the level of income are bound to change. An increase (decrease) in the supply of money will cause the money-equilibrium curve *ME* to shift downward (upward) and the rate of interest to decline (to rise). The decrease in the rate of interest will cause investment demand and the level of income to rise. The extent of the change in the level of income resulting from a given change in the supply of money can be ascertained from Equation (5)—that is,

$$dY = \left(\frac{1}{m + \frac{ns}{e}} \right) dM$$

The magnitude of income changes is the product of the given change in the supply of money, and the multiplication factor $\left(\frac{1}{m + \frac{ns}{e}}\right)$, which may be referred to as the money-supply multiplier. The latter in turn depends upon the extent of the response of the demand for money to income and interest (m and n), the marginal propensity to save (s), and the marginal propensity to invest (e). With the change in the level of income known, we may find the corresponding change in the equilibrium rate of interest from Equation (4a) or (3a):

$$di = -\left(\frac{s}{e}\right) dY = -\left(\frac{1}{\frac{me}{s} + n}\right) dM$$

It can be seen from the above expressions that changes in the supply of money cause direct changes in the level of income and inverse changes in the rate of interest. As a numerical example, assume that through open-market purchases of securities by the central bank, the supply of money in the example in the preceding section increases by 5 (from 25 to 30). The corresponding change in the level of income is then

$$dY = \frac{1}{m + \frac{ns}{e}} dM = \left(\frac{1}{0.4}\right)(5) = 12.5$$

and the change in the rate of interest is

$$di = -\left(\frac{s}{e}\right) dY = -\left(\frac{0.2}{100}\right)(12.5) = -\ 2.5 \text{ percent}$$

Changes in related variables are presented in the following table:

Variables	Equilibrium Values When $M_0 = 25$	Equilibrium Values When $M_1 = 30$	Changes
Income (Y)	187.5	200	+12.5
Interest (i)	12.5%	10%	- 2.5%
Savings (S)	17.5	20	+ 2.5
Investment (I)	17.5	20	+ 2.5
Demand for Money $L(Y,i)$	25	30	+ 5

It is to be noted that since, in our integrated model, the level of income changes as the supply of money changes, the extent of the change in the equilibrium rate of interest is smaller than in the case in which the level of income is assumed to remain unchanged (the case of the simple liquidity preference theory) because of the fact that the increase in the level of income causes the demand for money to increase (increase in the demand for transactions balances), and this induced increase in the demand for money tends to offset to some extent the downward pressure exerted on the rate of interest by the increase in the supply of money. This can be seen very clearly from Equation (3a). When the level of income changes as the supply of money changes, the corresponding change in the rate of interest is

$$di = -\left(\frac{1}{n}\right) dM + \left(\frac{m}{n}\right) dY$$

If the level of income were to remain unchanged as the money supply changes (i.e., $dY = 0$), then the change in the rate of interest would be $di = -(1/n)\,dM$. In the above example, if the level of income were to remain at 187.5 when the supply of money increases by 5, the rate of interest would decrease by -5 percent (instead of -2.5 percent). This would be the result of the liquidity preference model which, as we have already mentioned, is based on the assumption of a given level of income.

Effects of Changes in the Demand for Money

The effects of changes in the demand for money on the level of income and the rate of interest are in opposite direction of the effects of changes in the supply of money. While an increase in the money supply causes the rate of interest to decline and the level of income to rise, an increase in the demand for money causes interest to rise and income to decline. To see the effects of changes in the demand for money, let us add a constant term (q) to the demand-for-money function: $L(Y,i) = q + mY - ni$. This term may be said to reflect the influences on the demand for money of variables other than income and interest, such as the general price level, the expected rate of change of goods prices, expectations regarding future income and interest, which are assumed to remain unchanged. Changes in these variables will change the position of the demand-for-money function. With the constant term (q) added, Equation (3a) becomes:

$$i = -\left(\frac{1}{n}\right) M + \left(\frac{1}{n}\right) q + \left(\frac{m}{n}\right) Y$$

and the equilibrium level of income is

$$Y = \frac{1}{\frac{me}{n} + s}(a + g) + \left(\frac{1}{m + \frac{ns}{e}}\right) M - \left(\frac{1}{m + \frac{ns}{e}}\right) q$$

It can be seen from this equation that an increase (decrease) in the demand for money (that is, increase in q) will cause the level of income to decrease (increase) by:

$$dY = -\left(\frac{1}{m + \frac{ns}{e}}\right) dq$$

The expression for the effects of changes in the demand for money on the level of income differs from that for the effects of changes in the supply of money only in the algebraic sign; the former is negative and the latter is positive. An increase in the demand for money accompanied by an equivalent increase in the money supply therefore will leave the level of income and interest unchanged. (There is no change in the position of the *ME* curve, since the upward shift caused by an increase in the demand for money is exactly offset by the downward shift caused by an equal increase in the supply of money.) From the above equation, it can be seen that

$$dY = \left(\frac{1}{m + \frac{ns}{e}}\right) dM - \left(\frac{1}{m + \frac{ns}{e}}\right) dq = 0$$

since $dM = dq$. Hence

$$di = -\left(\frac{1}{n}\right) dM + \left(\frac{1}{n}\right) dq + \left(\frac{m}{n}\right) dY = 0$$

Effects of Changes in the Propensity to Consume (or to Save) and the Propensity to Invest

In the investment function $I = g - ei$, and the savings function $S = -a + sY$, the terms g and $-a$ represent their position (or intercept). Since $C = Y - S$, the term a represents the position of the consumption function $C = a + (1 - s)Y$, where $1 - s = b$ is the marginal propensity to consume. Changes in g reflect the changes in the propensity to invest. An increase (decrease) in the propensity to invest will cause the income-equilibrium curve *IE* to shift upward (downward), thereby causing the level of income and the rate of interest to rise. The extent of the change in the level of income and the rate of interest as a result of a given change in the propensity to invest can be ascertained from Equations (5) and (4a), respectively:

$$dY = \left(\frac{1}{\frac{me}{n} + s}\right) dg = \left[\frac{1}{\frac{me}{n} + (1 - b)}\right] dg$$

and

$$di = \left(\frac{1}{e}\right) dg - \left(\frac{s}{e}\right) dY = \left(\frac{1}{e + \frac{ns}{m}}\right) dg$$

As an illustration, assume that in the numerical example presented earlier, there is a decrease in the propensity to invest by 10 (that is, $dg = -10$). The equilibrium level of income will decrease by $dY = -25$, and the equilibrium rate of interest, by $di = -5$ percent.

It can be seen from Equations (4a) and (5) that the effect of changes in the propensity to consume on income and interest is the same as that of the propensity to invest. An increase in the propensity to consume (or what is the same thing, a decrease in the propensity to save) causes the *IE* curve to shift upward and the rate of interest and the level of income to rise,

$$dY = \frac{1}{\frac{me}{n} + s} da$$

and

$$di = \frac{1}{e} da - \frac{s}{e} dY = \left(\frac{1}{e + \frac{ns}{m}} \right) da$$

A given increase in the propensity to invest, accompanied by an equivalent increase in the propensity to save (or an equivalent decrease in the propensity to consume) therefore will leave income and interest unchanged:

$$dY = \frac{1}{\frac{me}{n} + s} dg + \frac{1}{\frac{me}{n} + s} da = 0$$

and

$$di = \frac{1}{e} dg + \frac{1}{e} da = 0$$ [1]

[1] Note that in our discussion of the effects on the level of income and the rate of interest of changes in the demand for, and supply of, money, and in the propensity to consume (to save) and the propensity to invest, we leave out government spending G and taxes T to avoid further complication. This, however, can be easily integrated into our model. With government expenditures on goods and services and taxes, the equilibrium level of income, as shown by Equation (5), becomes

$$Y = \frac{1}{\frac{me}{n} + s} (a + g + G) + \frac{1}{m + \frac{ns}{e}} M - \frac{(1 - s)}{\frac{me}{n} + s} T$$

It can be seen from this expression that the effects of changes in government spending on goods and services on the level of income are the same as those of changes in the propensity to consume and the propensity to invest:

$$dY = \frac{1}{\frac{me}{n} + s} dG$$

Income Equilibrium and Full Employment

The simultaneous determination of income and the rate of interest by the system of Equations (1) and (2) does not imply full employment. In fact, the demand-for-money function, the propensity to save, and the propensity to invest could be such that we may have a stable equilibrium level of income with substantial unemployment of human and material resources. But the analysis is based on the assumption of constant prices and wages. Now, if prices and wages were perfectly flexible upward as well as downward, would a less-than-full-employment equilibrium level of income be impossible? According to older concepts, the answer to this question is in the affirmative. This affirmation is based largely on certain assumptions regarding the behavior of savings and investment with respect to the rate of interest and the assumed perfect flexibility of wages and prices.

Starting from a full-employment position, assume that an increase in the propensity to save causes voluntary savings to exceed voluntary investment and

---

Also from the above equation we have the following expression for income changes as a result of changes in taxes:

$$dY = -\frac{(1-s)}{\dfrac{me}{n} + s} dT = -\frac{b}{\dfrac{me}{n} + (1-b)} dT$$

For the case of variable taxes, let us assume that taxes are proportional to income by $T = tY$. The equilibrium level of income in this case is

$$Y = \frac{1}{\dfrac{me}{n} + (1 - b' + b't)} (a + g + G) + \frac{1}{m + \dfrac{n(1 - b' + b't)}{e}} M$$

where $b' = 1 - s'$ is the marginal propensity to consume with respect to disposable income. The effect of a given change in government spending on the level of income (which is the same as that of changes in the propensity to consume and the propensity to invest; that is, changes in the a and g terms) is given by

$$dY = \frac{1}{\dfrac{me}{n} + (1 - b' + b't)} dG$$

and the effect of a given change in the supply of money on income is

$$dY = \frac{1}{m + \dfrac{n(1 - b' + b't)}{e}} dM$$

The extent of changes in the rate of interest as a result of changes in government spending is

$$di = \left(\frac{1}{e}\right) dG - \left[\frac{1 - b' + b't}{e}\right] dY$$

Since the expression for the rate of interest for the case of variable taxes is

$$i = \frac{1}{e}(a + g + G) - \left(\frac{1 - b' + b't}{e}\right) Y$$

brings about a downward deviation of income from the full-employment level. Such a downward deviation, according to older concepts, would be automatically corrected through savings, investment, and interest changes. The increase in savings would cause the rate of interest to decline. The decrease in the rate of interest, in turn, causes investment to rise (and savings to fall again). Rising investment and declining savings would restore equilibrium between them at full employment. In this respect, Keynesian theory differs from older theories in that it does not recognize interest changes as an automatic mechanism which brings savings and investment into balance at full employment. According to Keynesian analysis, savings is essentially a function of income, not the rate of interest. Moreover, investment demand may not be as responsive to interest changes as presumed by older concepts. Savings and interest changes thus may not stimulate investment demand sufficiently to restore full employment. An excess of voluntary savings over voluntary investment at full employment will result mainly in declining income, and declining income will cause savings to fall until it is again brought into balance with investment. Savings-investment equilibrium is therefore perfectly consistent with less than full employment.

Savings, investment, and interest changes, however, constitute only one of the several avenues which would operate to restore full employment. Wages and prices, if they were perfectly flexible upward as well as downward, would also work to restore full employment should there be any downward deviation from that situation, according to older theories. As a result of unemployment, competition among workers would cause money wages to fall relative to prices–that is, a fall in real wages. A fall in real wages means an increase in business profits. This would lead to a greater demand for labor and would eventually remove unemployment. What is ignored in this argument, however, is that if wages are a component of production costs to business firms, they are incomes of workers. Decreases in the real incomes of workers could well cause the aggregate demand for output and the total demand for labor to decline. Given the stock of money, decreases in wages would lead to decreases in the total demand for money as a result of decreases in the demand for transactions balances. This would cause the rate of interest to go down. The decrease in the rate of interest may cause investment to rise sufficiently to restore full employment. But whether decreases in money and real wages would operate to remove unemployment or not, through the interest channel, depends largely on the interest elasticity of investment and of the demand for money. If investment is highly elastic with respect to interest changes, and the demand for money is relatively inelastic, then decreases in wages would probably work toward restoring full employment. On the other hand, they would not work to that effect if the demand for money is perfectly elastic, or investment, completely inelastic, with respect to the rate of interest. Thus when the demand for money is perfectly elastic at a low rate of interest, money, released from transactions balances as a result of declining wages, will be held as idle balances, and the rate of interest will remain unchanged. Hence there will be no change in investment, the level of income, and employment.

But what about changes of goods prices? Would declining prices operate to remove unemployment when it takes place? The answer is also in the affirmative, according to older theories. Decreases in the general level of prices caused by an increase in savings (or a decrease in consumption) would work to restore full employment through the propensity to consume, the propensity to invest, the demand for money, and the rate of interest. We can recall that our discussion of the simultaneous determination of income and the rate of interest through the system of Equations (1) and (2) is based on the assumption of a constant level of prices. Now, if we allow the general price level to change, then the demand for money also will change as the price level changes. An increase (decrease) in the general price level will cause the demand for money to increase (decrease) as a result of the increase (decrease) in the demand for transactions balances.

In Fig. 22-4 we see that the intersection between the ME_0 and IE_0 curves determines the level of income Y_0 and the rate of interest i_0. The price level

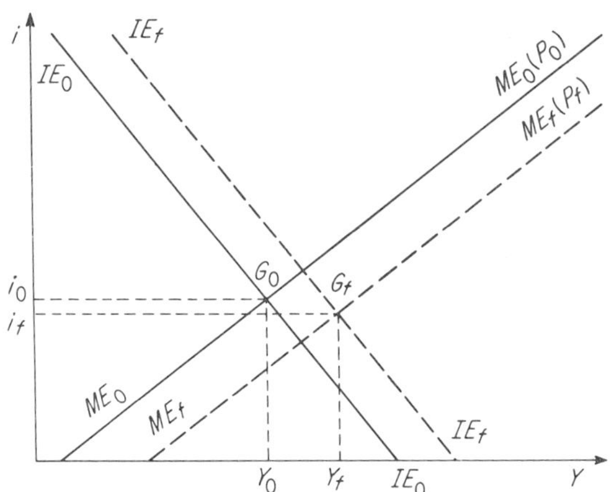

Fig. 22-4. Interest and income equilibrium.

adjusted to that level of income is P_0. Y_f is assumed to represent the full employment level of income. Suppose that a decrease in the propensity to consume causes income to deviate from the full employment level to Y_0. This will cause the level of prices to decline. The decrease in the price level will result in a decrease in the demand for money for transactions purposes. Given the asset demand for money, this will cause the money equilibrium curve ME_0 to shift downward, thereby causing the rate of interest to decrease. The decrease in the rate of interest will cause investment, income, and employment to rise until the full employment equilibrium is restored.

This is not all, however. The decrease in the level of prices also means an increase in the real value of cash balances. Holders of these assets, now that they are wealthier, tend to consume more.[2] The increase in the propensity to consume reflected by an upward shift in the income equilibrium curve IE_0 will cause the level of income to rise. The downward shift in the ME_0 curve and the upward shift in the IE_0 curve, as a result of declining prices would eventually lead the level of income back to the full-employment position. *Pf* in Fig. 22-4 is the level of prices adjusted to the full employment level of income.

Price decreases, however, may not work to restore full employment, as presumed by older theories. In the first place, whether the increase in the real value of cash balances as a result of price decreases will cause the rate of interest to decline, and investment and income to rise again, depends much on the interest elasticity of the demand-for-money function and the investment function. If the demand for money is completely elastic with respect to the rate of interest, then the release of cash from transactions demand will be absorbed into idle balances, and there will be no change in the rate of interest. On the other hand, even if the demand for money is inelastic vis-à-vis interest changes, but if investment demand is completely interest-inelastic, then any changes in the rate of interest caused by changes in the demand for money will not cause any changes in investment and income. Likewise, increases in the real value of cash balances may or may not lead to increases in consumption or demand. If as a result of sharp price decreases, the consumers expect prices to continue their downward course in the future, they may reduce spending in order to take advantage of further decreases in prices. These adverse expectations may indeed accelerate decreases in prices, wages, income, and employment. Thus according to modern theory there are no automatic market forces which operate to remove unemployment quickly; the propensity to consume, the propensity to invest, and the demand-for-money function may be such that a downward deviation from full employment may persist for a prolonged period of time. This is believed to hold even in a perfectly competitive system with perfect flexibility of wages and prices. In the real world which is characterized by imperfection of competition and downward rigidity of wages and prices, to promote full employment of human and material resources requires deliberate economic and financial actions of the government designed to affect directly and indirectly the determinants of the level of income and employment.

Note on the Restated Quantity Theory of Money

We have seen that, according to the traditional quantity theory of money, the effects of monetary changes are only on the price level. The theory, based on the assumption of a full-employment level of output, asserts that changes in the quantity of money cause proportional changes in the price level and money income. Modern monetary theory, on the other hand, is concerned with the analysis of the effects of monetary changes on the level of economic activity, on

[2]The effect of price decreases on consumption through increases in the real value of cash balances is popularly referred to as the *Pigou effect.*

the level of employment and output, as well as the price level. It is concerned with decisions that affect the flow of money spending—that is, decisions on monetary outlays for consumption and investment, both private and public, as determinants of the level of income and employment.

The quantity theory of money, however, has been reformulated, and the reformulated version, in some respects, is not too different from Keynesian (and post-Keynesian) theory. Professor Milton Friedman of the University of Chicago, a leading figure among modern adherents of the quantity theory of money, stated that

> The quantity theory is in the first instance a theory of the demand for money. It is not a theory of output, or of money income, or of the price level. Any statement about these variables requires combining the quantity theory with some specifications about the conditions of supply of money and perhaps about other variables as well.[3]

The demand for money is considered as a function of real income, interest rates, the level of prices, and other relevant economic variables. The restated quantity theory, like Keynesian theory, emphasizes the effects of monetary changes on the short-run changes in the level of economic activity. According to Professor Friedman, the new approach to the quantity theory

> . . . insisted that money does matter—that any interpretation of short-term movements in economic activity is likely to be seriously at fault if it neglects monetary changes and repercussions and if it leaves unexplained why people are willing to hold the particular nominal quantity of money in existence.[4]

But while the restated quantity theory operates with a demand-for-money function not too different from that of post-Keynesian theory, it differs from the latter in several respects, namely in its views on the relationship between the quantity of money and income. According to the new quantity theory, the income velocity of money (an alternative form in which the demand for money can be expressed) is highly stable over the long run (over periods of 10 to 20 years), and hence, the long-run changes in money income mirror changes in the nominal quantity of money. This differs from the traditional quantity theory in that while the latter asserts that changes in money income are proportional to changes in the quantity of money, the former does not make any definite assertion regarding the extent of changes in money income relative to changes in the stock of money; it only stresses the positive relationship between the quantity of money and money income. Whether changes in the quantity of money would bring about changes in real income and prices cannot be answered without additional information about the state of employment. If the information is that the economy is operating at full employ-

[3]Milton Friedman, "The Quantity Theory of Money: A Restatement," *Studies in the Quantity Theory of Money* (Chicago: U. of Chicago Press, 1956), p. 4.

[4]*Ibid.*, p. 3.

ment, then the conclusion of the new quantity theory is the same as that of the traditional version: changes in the quantity will cause proportional changes in money income and the price level. On the other hand, increases in the quantity of money at times of substantial unemployment may cause both real income and the price level to increase. The new quantity theory of money thus considers the quantity of money as a strategic determinant of the level of monetary expenditures. Critics of the new theory consider this as an oversimplification. The money stock is undoubtedly important, but it is only one of the important variables which influence spending decisions and the level of income.

SUMMARY

Since the demand for money, the supply of money, savings, investment, interest, and income are elements of an interdependent system, a general macroequilibrium analysis has to be concerned with the simultaneous determination of these variables. This can be accomplished through the system of equations

$$M = L(Y,i) \tag{1}$$

$$S(Y,i) = I(Y,i) \tag{2}$$

where Equation (1) shows the equilibrium between the supply of and demand for money, and Equation (2), the equilibrium between savings and investment. Given the quantity of money, the simultaneous solution of this system of equations gives us the equilibrium rate of interest and the equilibrium level of income. The rate of interest and the level of income will change as the quantity of money, the demand for money, savings, and investment change.

With prices and wages assumed to remain constant, the model does not imply full employment. If prices and wages were to change freely upward as well as downward, then, according to older concepts, a less-than-full-employment equilibrium level of income would be impossible. Changes in the demand for money, the rate of interest, and investment demand would work to remove any downward deviation of income from the full employment level. According to Keynesian theory, on the other hand, there are no automatic market forces which would operate to restore full employment. The demand for money, the propensity to save (or to consume) and the propensity to invest could be such that a less-than-full-employment equilibrium level of income may persist for a prolonged period of time.

PROBLEMS

1. If the liquidity-preference theory of interest is a partial equilibrium theory, how would you modify it to make it valid in a general macroequilibrium framework? Explain what your modified model suggests.

2. Using the *ME-IE* curves, show the effect of an increase in the supply of money on the rate of interest and the level of income. Why is it that the extent of interest changes as a result of changes in the supply of money is smaller when the level of income changes than when it is assumed to remain unchanged? Explain.

3. Is a less-than-full-employment equilibrium level of income possible? Discuss some of the arguments of older theories and modern theories on this point.

4. In what respects does the restated quantity theory of money resemble Keynesian and post-Keynesian theory? In what respects does it differ from the latter?

5. You are given the following information: Investment I is related to the rate of interest i by $I = 20 - 200\,i$. Savings S is related to income Y by $S = -10 + 1/5Y$. The demand for money L is related to income and interest by $L = 1/4Y - 100\,i$. The quantity of money M is given at 20.

(a) Find the equilibrium rate of interest and the equilibrium level of income.

(b) Assume that the supply of money increases by 2 from 20 to 22, what is the corresponding change in the level of income and the rate of interest? What would be the change in the rate of interest if the level of income were to remain unchanged?

(c) Show the effect of an upward shift of 4 in the investment function on Y and i.

chapter 23

Inflation

Inflation can hardly be said to be an unfamiliar phenomenon. Men in the street are aware of it when the real value of their pay checks gradually dwindles. Housewives are aware of it when they get less and less groceries for the same amount of money. It is an opportunity for certain groups of individuals to make greater profits and a source of distress and discontent for other people, especially those living on fixed incomes. Inflation is a symptom of economic illness the diagnosis of which is still explored by theoretical economists, and methods recommended to prevent and control it remain a subject of controversy.

WHAT IS INFLATION?

The word inflation is not always used by economists to refer to the same thing. It is sometimes applied to refer to a situation in which the supply of money and credit increases, profits increase, or the value of domestic currency in terms of foreign currency decreases. But inflation is commonly defined as a situation in which the general price level increases or the general purchasing power of money decreases. However, we run into some problems with this definition of inflation. Should we consider inflation a one-shot increase in the general price level—for example, increase in the price level as a result of increases in import prices following a currency devaluation? Or should we consider inflation a situation in which the price level increases at certain rate and for certain duration? And if so, what should be the rate of price increase and what duration? The answers to these questions are necessarily arbitrary. We shall refer to inflation as price increases which continue for some extended period of time. According to the rate of price increase and the duration of price increase, different adjectives are used together with the term inflation to differentiate various inflationary developments. Thus we have mild inflation, serious inflation, galloping inflation, creeping inflation, cyclical inflation, convergent inflation, and self-generating inflation.

Now, since we refer to inflation as a continuous upward movement in the price level, we must decide whether to consider inflationary a situation in which there are all the ingredients that would cause the price level to rise but where the latter is prevented from rising, or from rising as fast as it otherwise would, because of the imposition of price controls and rationing by the public authority (for example, price controls and rationing in the United States during World War II). This situation is usually referred to as "repressed" inflation or "suppressed" inflation, in contrast with "open" inflation in which the price level is allowed to rise through the somewhat free play between supply and demand forces. Repressed inflation may or may not lead to open inflation. Much depends on the duration of control and rationing and the ability of an economy to increase the supply of goods which individuals and firms were not able to acquire during the period of control and rationing. If price controls and rationing are lifted while the supply of consumer goods and capital goods remains acutely short, then the attempt of consumers to unload savings (accumulated during the controlled period) on consumer goods, and business firms, on capital goods to replace old capital equipment, would result in sharply rising prices. Repressed inflation then becomes open inflation. On the other hand, if control and rationing are extended so that the supply of goods can be increased to the extent that it gradually reduces the steam of bottled-up demand, then the abandonment of price controls and rationing would not result in sharp price increases. An artificial equilibrium in prices and production achieved through controls and rationing thus may be changed into "normal" equilibrium without incurring sharp open inflationary pressures.

Price changes, as we have seen, are measured in terms of price indexes. But which index should be used? The Consumer Price Index? The Wholesale Price Index? Although these indexes in general tend to move together but sometimes an index may remain relatively stable (for example, the W.P.I.) and other indexes (the C.P.I.) rise. The use of the wholesale price index or the consumer price index as an indicator of inflationary tendencies could lead to different assertions regarding the extent of price increase and inflationary developments. Moreover, price indexes are biased. As noted earlier, these indexes fail to take into consideration the improvement in the quality of products, the changes in the composition of expenditure etc. It follows that when the price level (as shown by the Consumer Price Index) increased on the average by 3 percent for certain time period, we may say that we had inflation; but the extent of inflationary pressures could have been overstated if during the same period the improvement in the quality of products was on the average 2 percent a year. This was ignored, however, because there is no index which could be used to show the improvement in the quality of products.

It is also to be noted that "inflation" and "deflation" are not always used to refer to the opposite states of affairs. If inflation refers to the continuous upward movement in the general price level, deflation, in contemporary usage usually refers to rising unemployment and declining income. Moreover, the return of the general price level back to its normal trend after an economic recession or depression is not referred to as "inflation" but "reflation."

A HISTORICAL RECORD

Figure 23-1 is a record of the movement of consumer prices and wholesale prices in the United States from the early 1910's to the late 1960's. As can be

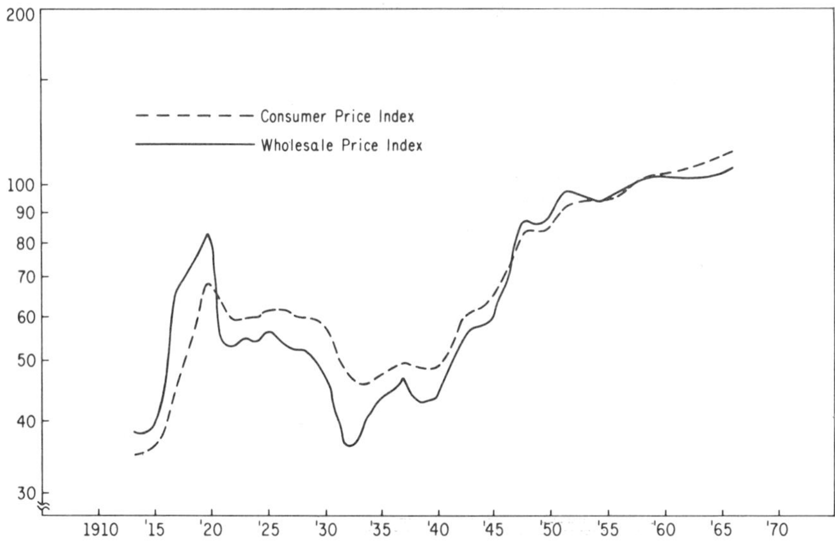

Source: Statistical Abstract of the United States, 1960–67

Fig. 23-1. Price indexes, 1910–67 (1957–59 = 100).

seen, rising prices are largely associated with wartime periods. The pressure of demand generated by rising income brought about by increases in wartime economic activities coupled with the limited availability of consumer goods as resources were largely diverted to defense and defense-oriented production, caused the level of prices to rise sharply. Thus during World War I the Consumer Price Index and the Wholesale Price Index were doubled. During World War II prices did not rise sharply as a consequence of price controls and rationing. But after 1946, as price controls and rationing were removed, prices rose sharply as consumers and business firms rushed to spend on goods and equipment which they were not able to obtain during the war. The Korean War also witnessed price inflation despite price and wage controls. After periods of remarkable price stability in the late 1950's and early 1960's, prices again rose substantially after 1965 following increases in expenditures necessitated by the intensification of the war in Vietnam.

Figure 23-1 reveals no definite long-term trend in the movement of prices. When we consider the period between the 1920's and the 1940's, the trend line is practically parallel to the time axis. The price index in 1922 was about the same as it was in 1942. On the other hand, since the early 1940's the movement of consumer prices follows an upward trend. The index of consumer prices in 1967 was about twice the index of 1940. This upward trend was largely accounted for by World War II, the Korean War, and the Vietnam War. While prior to World War II, consumer prices did decline during the postwar periods and during periods of recession, after the 1940's, prices continued to rise moderately in periods of declining economic activity and rising unemployment. The pressure of strong trade unions for higher wages, and the great concentration of economic power in the hands of oligopolistic firms which means greater ability to "administer" prices, the high level of defense and defense-related spending required by cold war tensions, and the commitment of public policy toward promoting maximum economic growth and full employment of human and material resources through expansionary economic and financial measures, apparently have had a great deal to do with that upward trend of prices. Whether this trend will continue or not is difficult to tell. But prices would probably continue to move upward, reaching higher and higher plateaus over time even in the event of a complete relaxation in cold war tensions (which would greatly reduce defense spending), mainly because of concentration of economic power, strong labor unions, and the commitment of the government to a full-employment policy.

We have seen the historical record of price increases in the United States. During recent years the degree of price inflation in the United States, however, was rather moderate as compared with inflationary developments in some other countries. Thus during the 1958-66 period, consumer prices in the United States rose from 100 to 109.7 as compared with 100-126 in the United Kingdom, 100-144.2 in Japan, 100-123.3 in France, 100-129.9 in Italy, and 100-118.8 in Germany. What then causes inflation? There are several theories advanced to explain this phenomenon.

DEMAND INFLATION

The price level is determined by the interplay between total demand and total supply. Whether an increase in aggregate demand will cause the price level to rise or not depends upon total supply conditions. When the supply of output can be increased with unchanged marginal cost—that is, the supply curve is still perfectly elastic with respect to price, increases in total demand will cause the level of output, not the price level, to rise (The *SA* segment of the total supply curve in Fig. 23-2). But when the supply of output can be increased only with rising marginal cost (the *AB* segment of the *SS* curve) or supply can no longer be increased (the case of full employment), increases in total demand will cause the price level to rise. Price inflation generated by increases in aggregate demand is referred to as *demand inflation.* It is the pressure of demand which pulls up the price level.

The quantity theory of money and the income-expenditure theory approach inflation in terms of excess demand. According to the quantity theory, price

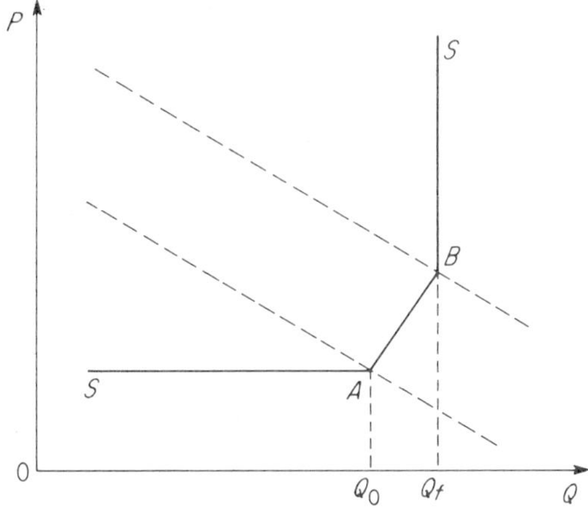

Fig. 23-2.

increases are generated by increases in the quantity of money. With full employment assumed to be the normal state of affairs, increases in the quantity of money which increase expenditures cause the level of prices to increase. The theory, however, does not explain how increases in the quantity of money cause the level of money spending to increase which in turn causes the price level to rise. It does not explain why the quantity of money changes. According to the income-expenditure approach, the addition to the income flow (as a result of increases in expenditures), which is not completely offset by increased leakage from the flow of income through savings and taxes, creates, at the full-employment level of output and existing level of prices, an "inflationary gap"—an excess of expenditure over the supply of output at the prevailing price level. The pressure of excess demand then causes the price level to rise. The increase in the expenditure flow may be generated by (a) increases in the expenditure of the government on goods and services, (b) increases in the propensity to consume and the propensity to invest motivated by, say, expectations of higher income, prices, and profits in the future, and (c) increases in the supply of money which cause total demand to increase through their effects on the rate of interest (lower interest) and investment demand (greater investment demand).

COST-PUSH INFLATION

Excess demand alone, however, is not adequate to explain inflation. We may have inflation when there appears to be no evidence of excess demand. Take, for instance, the 1950-64 period in the United States. While the Consumer Price Index continued its upward course, the rate of unemployment was at times as high as 7 percent (for example, in 1958, 4.7 million of the civilian work force of 64 million were unemployed) (see Fig. 23-3), and the rate of utilization (output

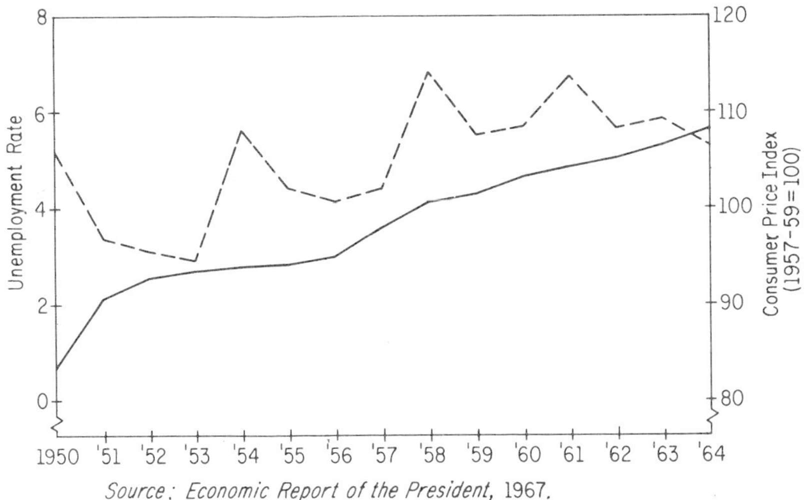

Source: Economic Report of the President, 1967.

Fig. 23-3. Unemployment rate and consumer price index, 1950–64.

as per cent of manufacturing capacity) was at times as low as 74 percent. Then what causes inflation amid unemployment and high rates of unutilization of resources? An alternative approach to inflation runs in terms of cost: the cost-push theory. According to this theory, a general rise in the price level is generated by a rise in cost reflecting increases in either overhead unit cost, or variable unit cost or both. Speaking of cost, we think of wage cost which represents in most cases the major component of total cost. Increases in wage cost may be forced upon unionized industries by strong labor unions. Increases in wage cost, however, do not necessarily result in higher output prices so long as wage increases are not in excess of productivity gains. Thus, if wages increase by 4 percent and at the same time labor productivity also increases by 4 percent, then there is no change in unit wage cost. It follows that the cost-push theory implies, among other things, that wage increases gained by labor unions are in excess of productivity gains so that unit cost increases. Increases in unit cost then push up the level of price. For the price level to continue its upward course, increases in wage cost would have to be continuously in excess of productivity gains. But would labor unions be able to continue to push up wage cost in excess of productivity gains? This is difficult to know. For one thing, given aggregate demand, increases in prices would cause the level of output to decrease and unemployment to rise. This can be seen in Fig. 23-4. The *SS* curve is the total supply curve and Q_f is the full-employment level of output. Given the total demand curve *DD*, the price level consistent with the full-employment level of output is OP_0. Increases in unit wage cost (forced upon industries by trade unions) would push the total supply curve up to $S'S$. As a consequence, the price level rises to OP_1 and output decreases to OQ_0. This would give rise to unem-

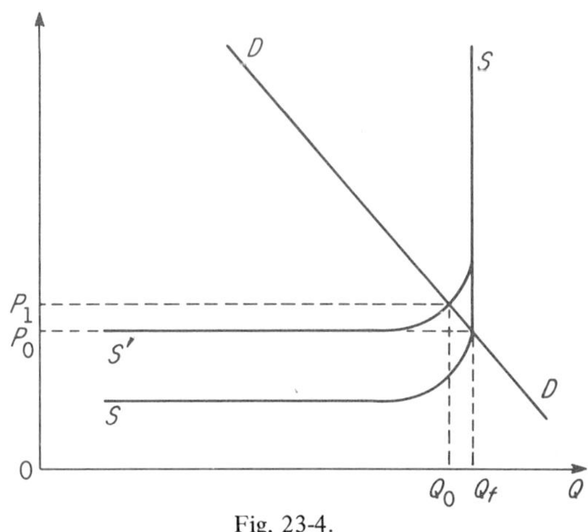

Fig. 23-4.

ployment. (The extent of the unemployment and output gap depends of course upon the shape of the total demand curve.)

Would unemployment serve as a buffer against union pressures for further wage increases? It may or may not, depending upon the attitude of unions regarding unemployment. If unions are concerned with unemployment, then the existence of an unemployment gap would probably serve as a cushion moderating unions' wage demands.

Increases in wage cost in excess of productivity gains, however, do not necessarily result in higher output prices if increases in wage cost are absorbed by management in the form of lower profit margins. The cost-push theory thus also implies that management is able to pass the higher unit cost on to the consumers. In oligopolistic industries, firms would probably be able to raise prices high enough to cover increases in unit wage cost. Regardless of whether contracts are negotiated on an industry-wide basis or with individual oligopolistic firms, increases in wage cost would result in higher prices for the whole industry. When an individual firm gives in to the wage demand of labor unions and raises prices, other firms would likely follow suit, as they are perfectly aware that they are next on the list for strike and that unions would demand settlement with terms comparable to those granted by other oligopolistic firms. In regard to more competitive industries, their ability to raise prices sufficiently to cover increases in cost is limited. But limited ability to raise prices means greater resistance of management to union wage pressures. In the face of union demands for higher wages, the choices opened to firms in competitive industries are either to raise prices to cover increases in cost and run the risk of losing part of their businesses to other industries (not subject to union wage pressure), to give in to the wages demand of unions and absorb most of the increases in cost, or to resist and let unions go on strike. It is largely a matter of deciding which alternative is potentially the least costly.

Now what induces labor unions to press for higher wages? This may be motivated by rising output prices which result in declining real wages (rising prices generated by the pressure of consumer demand) or by the conviction on the part of unions that at existing prices the demand is such that business firms are making "excessive" profits which they wish to share with management by pressing for higher wages. On the other hand, business firms raise prices to absorb higher costs only when they expect the state of demand to be such that they will be able to sell their outputs at higher prices. It follows that cost-push on prices already implies the pull of demand on prices and cost. A rise in the general price level pushed up by increases in cost would probably not continue unless demand continues to rise. This leads many to believing that cost cannot continue to push up prices without increases in demand. Increases in demand, of course, may be generated by the public sector which is committed to a full employment policy through expansionary economic measures; or they may be generated by increases in the expenditures of workers in anticipation of higher wages if they are confident that they will get most of what they want in terms of wage increases.

SECTORAL INFLATION

Inflation has been explained in terms of the pull of demand and the push of cost. But we may have inflation when there seems to be no excess demand pull nor excessive cost push. How to account for such inflationary development? A theory has been suggested to explain this type of inflation. The theory runs in terms of changes in the composition of demand and the downward rigidity of wages and prices. Assume that for some reasons or other there is a shift in sectoral demand which results in decreases in demand in some sectors of the economy and increases in demand in some other sectors (aggregate demand may remain unchanged). If prices and wages are inflexible downward, then prices and wages do not decline in the sectors with decreases in demand. (The decrease in demand would probably result in some unemployment in these sectors). On the other hand, in sectors with increases in demand, if this occurs at a time when they are operating at or near capacity, then excess demand would cause prices in these sectors to rise. (Of course, if this takes place at a time when there is substantial unutilization in these sectors, then increases in demand would probably lead to the expansion of output without price increases at least initially). Since prices do not decline in sectors with demand deficiency and rise in sectors with demand excess generated by changes in sectoral demand, the general price level tends to rise. To meet demand excesses, these sectors would attempt to acquire additional materials and labor by offering higher prices and wages. Rising prices of materials mean rising material costs to other sectors which experience no demand excesses. Higher wages in the excess-demand sectors also induce higher wages in other sectors. Rising material costs and wage costs thus would result in higher prices of the products of these sectors. It follows that price increases initiated by changes in sectoral demand and the downward inflexibility of wages and prices may cause further price increases in other sectors as a consequence of induced higher wages and material costs.

THE TIME PATH OF INFLATION

The inflationary process, once initiated by whatever forces, may be convergent or self-sustained.

Convergent Inflation

An inflationary process in which the rate of price increase decreases over time and converges to some limit may be termed convergent inflation. Figure 23-5 shows a simplified case of convergent inflation. In Fig. 23-5(a), Y_f is the full-employment level of income. Until Y_f is reached, the price level is assumed to remain constant at P_0. The propensity-to-consume curve C_rC_r shows the relation between real consumption and real income which is the same as the monetary consumption-income relation (up to Y_f, the marginal propensity to consume with respect to real income is the same as the marginal propensity to consume with respect to money income). Beyond the full-employment level of income Y_f, the consumption curve is kinked since, to maintain real consumption, households would have to increase monetary consumption in the same proportion with increases in prices and money income (that is, beyond Y_f, the marginal propensity to consume with respect to money income is equal to the average real propensity to consume).[1]

Given real consumption $CrCr$ and investment demand I, the full-employment level of income Y_f is determined. $Y_f = P_0 Q_f$ where Q_f is the full-employment level of output and P_0 is the "full-employment" price level. Now suppose

[1] We know that $C = P \cdot C_r(Y_r)$ where C is money consumption, P the price level, C_r real consumption and Y_r real income. The marginal propensity to consume with respect to money income Y is dC/dY. From the above expression, we have

$$\frac{dC}{dY} = \frac{dCr}{dYr} \cdot \frac{dYr}{dY} \cdot P + C_r \frac{dP}{dY} \qquad (1)$$

Since P is assumed to remain constant up to the full-employment level of income, then until that level of income is reached, the price level does not change, hence from (1),

$$\frac{dC}{dY} = \frac{dCr}{dYr}$$

That is, the marginal propensity to consume with respect to money income is the same as the marginal propensity to consume with respect to real income, up to the full-employment level of income. On the other hand, beyond the full-employment level of income, price and money income change but real income does not change, hence

$$\frac{dC}{dY} = C_r \frac{dP}{dY} = \frac{Cr}{Yr} \left[\frac{dP}{dY} \cdot \frac{Y}{P} \right]$$

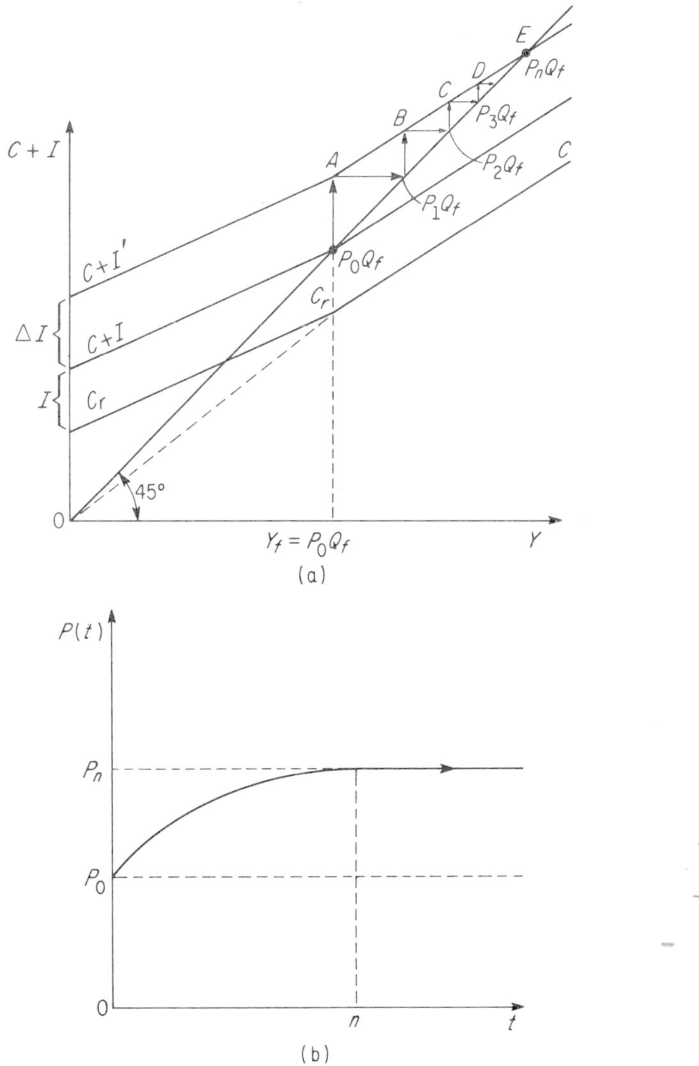

Fig. 23-5. Convergent price increase.

Since beyond Y_f, price and money income change by the same proportion—that is, $\frac{dP}{dY} \cdot \frac{Y}{P} = 1$, therefore

$$\frac{dC}{dY} = \frac{Cr}{Yr}$$

In other words, beyond Y_f, the marginal propensity to consume with respect to money income is equal to the real average propensity to consume—hence the kink in the consumption curve at Y_f.

that there is an increase in investment demand from I to I'. Then, at the existing price level P_0, there is an inflationary gap—that is, aggregate demand exceeds aggregate supply at that level of prices. The excess demand gap is represented by the segment P_0A. Excess demand causes the price level to rise to P_1 and the value of total output (money income) to increase to P_2Q_f. At that level of prices and money income, the real consumption plan of households is disturbed. To maintain real consumption, the household sector, assumed to plan current consumption on the basis of prices and income in the preceding period, increases monetary expenditure in the second period by P_1B. This, however, causes the price level to rise to P_2 and money income to increase to P_2Q_f. Another adjustment is then made in the third period which causes the price level to rise to P_3 and money income, to P_3Q_f. The adjustment process represented by the zig-zag path in Fig. 23-5(a), shows that the change in money income and the price level becomes smaller and smaller as time goes by. The adjustment is ended when the new equilibrium E is reached at which real investment is reduced to the full employment level and planned consumption of households is again consistent with the prevailing price level and money income. Figure 23-5(b) shows the path of change in the price level toward the new equilibrium level P_n. Although real investment is reduced to the full employment level in the new equilibrium position, it does increase temporarily during the adjustment period, which is made possible by unplanned decreases in real consumption or increases in unplanned savings.[2]

[2]Following is an example that illustrates the above process of convergent inflation. Let Q_f be the full employment level of output. Assume that current money consumption (C_t) is proportional to money income of the preceding period ($P_{t-1}Q_f$) by $C_t = bP_{t-1}Q_f$, and monetary investment is fixed at I. From $Y_t = C_t + I$, we have

$$P_t = b\,P_{t-1} + \frac{I}{Q_f} \tag{1}$$

The solution of (1) is

$$P_t = P_0 \cdot b^t + \left[\frac{I}{Q_f}\right]\left[\frac{1-b^t}{1-b}\right]$$

Since $b < 1$, P_t approaches $\frac{I}{Q_f}\left[\frac{1}{1-b}\right]$ as the equilibrium price level as $t \to \infty$.

It follows that if I increases by ΔI, the price level will rise and eventually converge to a new equilibrium level

$$P_n = \left[\frac{I+\Delta I}{Q_f}\right]\left[\frac{1}{1-b}\right]$$

Suppose that $Q_f = 200$ units, $P_0 = \$2.50$ per unit, and $I = \$100$ and $C_t = 0.8P_{t-1}Q_f$. At this price level, the full-employment level of income is $Y_f = P_0Q_f = \$500$. It is consistent with planned investment of \$100 and planned consumption of \$400. Assume, now, that investment increases by \$100 ($\Delta I = \$100$). This will cause the price level to increase to $P_1 = \$3$ in the first period. The adjustment of consumption by households in period 2 as a result of the increase in the price level and money income in period 1 will cause the price level to rise to

The model is of course a very simplified model. Wages and salaries are assumed to remain constant. Thus households maintain real consumption by borrowing and running down accumulated savings. On the other hand, if workers, through unions, press for higher money wages in the face of rising prices and consequently declining real wages and succeed in their wage demand, and managements in turn raise prices to cover increased costs, then inflation may become self-sustained. Moreover, business investment in the model is assumed to be fixed in money terms. Consequently, real investment decreases as the price level rises. But if the business sector attempts to maintain real investment, it would then raise prices and monetary investment and this would speed up the rate of price increase. Certain groups of individuals in society, however, may not be able to borrow or dissave to maintain real consumption as is assumed in the above model. If these individuals (for example, pensioners) reduce real consumption in the face of price increase generated by, say, an autonomous increase in monetary investment, then in the new equilibrium position, real investment will increase, which is made possible by the release of resources from the decrease in the real consumption expenditure of these individuals.

Self-Sustained Inflation

We have discussed an example of convergent inflation. But inflation, once iniatiated, may become self-sustained following the reactions of spending units frustrated by actual price and income changes and expected changes in prices and income, among other things.

The Wage–Price Spiral. The wage-price spiral is an inflationary process sustained by the wage reactions of labor organizations and the price reactions of business firms. Suppose that the price level rises as a consequence of excess demand. A rise in the price level means a decline in real wages. To maintain real wages, unions would press for higher money wages. If unions succeed in forcing wage increases on management such that the profit margins of firms are reduced, then they would raise prices. Price increases in turn cause real wages to decline. Unions would then press for further increases in money wages. We thus have a situation in which wage and price chase each other in an upward spiral. The time

---

P_2 = \$3.40. The adjustment will continue until the new equilibrium price level is reached P_n = \$5. At this price level, money income is doubled, P_nQ_f = \$1,000, real investment is reduced to the full-employment level

$$I_r = \frac{\$200}{\$5.} = \frac{\$100}{\$2.50} = 40 \text{ units}$$

and real consumption is restored, and

$$C_r = \frac{\$800}{\$5.00} = \frac{\$400}{\$2.50} = 160 \text{ units.}$$

But during the adjustment period, real investment was higher. For instance, in period 1, real investment was 67 units; in period 2, it was 56 units, and so on, before it was reduced back to 40 units at equilibrium.

path of price increases depends upon the reaction function between wage and price. It may converge or diverge. Which is the likely path is difficult to say.[3] If the monetary and fiscal policies of the government are not committed to maintain full employment, then the time path of price increases would probably be convergent. Wage increases cause the transactions demand for money to increase. Given the supply of money, firms can meet the increases in their demand for transactions balances by selling securities. This would cause the rate of interest to rise and increases in the rate of interest would cause investment demand to decline. Decreases in investment demand would result in a greater output and unemployment gap. Declining output and rising unemployment would tend to moderate unions' pressure for further wage increases and generate greater resistance of management to the wage demand of unions. On the other hand, if the government is committed to eliminate the output and unemployment gap through expansionary fiscal and monetary policies, then the wage-price spiral would become self-sustained. This can be seen from Fig. 23-6. Given the total supply curve S_0S and the total demand curve D_0D_0, the full-employment level of output Q_f is achieved and the price level is determined at OP_0. Suppose that wage increases forced by unions on management cause unit cost to increase and the supply curve to rise to S_1S. Given the demand curve D_0D_0, this will cause the price level to rise to OP_1 and the level of output, to decline to OQ_0. Unemployment, as a consequence, appears. To eliminate the unemployment gap, the government then can resort to expansionary measures (for example, increases in government spending) to raise total demand to D_1D_1. This in turn will cause the price level to rise to OP_2. At this level of prices, real wages decline. Unions would then press for higher money wages and so on. It follows that the wage-price mechanism of inflation would operate when the economic policy of the government is committed to full employment. Without such commitment,

[3] Following is a simplified example illustrating the conditions for this type of inflation to converge or diverge. Assume that the current price level (P_t) is related to the wage level in the preceding period (W_{t-1}) by

$$P_t = a + r \cdot W_{t-1} \qquad (1)$$

and the current wage level is related to the current price level by

$$W_t = n + h \cdot P_t \qquad (2)$$

Then we have the following expression for the time path of the price level

$$P_t = (a + rn) + rh \cdot P_{t-1}$$

The solution of this equation is

$$P_t = P_0(rh)^t + (a + rn)\left[\frac{1 - (rh)^t}{1 - rh}\right]$$

It follows that, given an initial increase in the price level (that is, an increase in a), the price level would increase and converge to a limit if the product of the slopes of equations (1) and (2) is less than one ($rh < 1$) and diverge if it is greater than one ($rh > 1$).

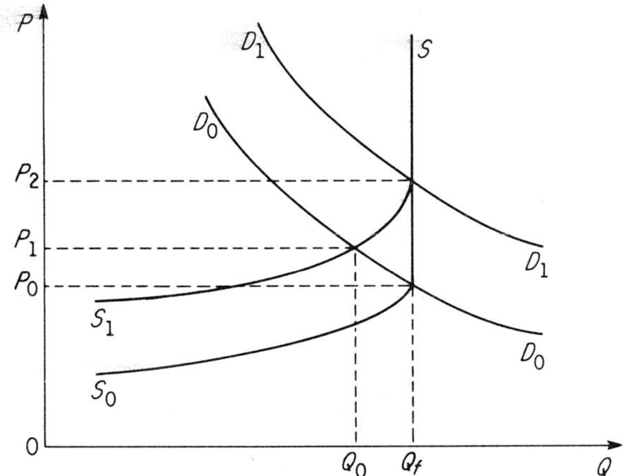

Fig. 23-6. The wage–price spiral.

the wage-price spiral probably could not be sustained due to mounting pressures on unions generated by rising unemployment. It would appear that the choice of economic policy in this framework is some combination of two of three objectives: price stability, full employment, and free collective bargaining. A combination of free collective bargaining and full employment would allow some degree of inflation. A combination of price stability and free collective bargaining would result in some degree of unemployment. On the other hand, a combination of full employment and price stability would call for some measure of wage and price controls. The task of public policy is to select a combination of objectives of which the social costs are minimized or the social benefits are maximized under given circumstances.

Hyperinflation. The terms "runaway inflation," "galloping inflation," or "hyperinflation" all refer to an inflationary process in which the price level increases at ever-increasing rates which eventually reaches astronomical magnitudes and results in monetary reform as the existing monetary system breaks down. Hyperinflation is generated by ever-widening excess demand gaps brought about by abnormal increases in the quantity of money and abnormal increases in the velocity of circulation caused by abnormal changes in the expectations of people regarding future prices. Rising prices, if they continue for an extended period of time, would lead to expectations of further future price increases. To avoid losses in the buying power of their monetary assets, people then rush from monetary assets to goods not only for current needs but for future needs as well. Producers and sellers, on the other hand, would tend to build up their stocks by holding goods off the market, expecting to make greater profits in the future as prices are expected to rise further. The excessive demand generated by the attempt of people to convert monetary assets into goods and the limited supply of output causes the level of prices to rise sharply. Prices increasing lead to expectations of further price increases. Rising prices lead to wage increases. Price and wage increases, however, mean increased costs to the government. If the extent of price and wage increases is such that the government is not able to raise additional revenue to finance rising costs (the government may not be able to raise taxes fast enough; moreover, there are limits to the ability of the government to raise taxes beyond which further tax increases are not possible), it may resort to the printing press for more money to sustain its financial requirements. But increases in the volume of money printed by the government mean increases in bank reserves and the supply of money. With added reserves, banks will be able to lend more to merchants and others who are eager to borrow to build up stocks. This causes the supply of money to rise further. Increases in the flow of money spending sustained by increases in the quantity of money will cause the price level to rise to higher levels. Higher prices, however, require the printing of more money by the government to meet still greater financial needs. Increases in the quantity of money and increases in the velocity of circulation caused by continuous upward revision of expected price increases are thus interwoven in an ever-rising spiral. This will continue until a stage is reached at which money becomes practically worthless and is rejected by the public as such. The existing monetary system then breaks down and monetary reform is introduced. The hyperinflation in Germany in the early 1920's and that of China during the 1937-47 period, among other countries, all ended in this fashion.

Hyperinflation is a phenomenon which is largely associated with wars and political upheavals, events which drastically undermine the confidence of the public in the ability of the public authority to maintain the value of money. In wars, for example, the government is forced to print enormous quantities of money to acquire goods and services as tax revenues and borrowings from the public are not adequate to finance continuous increases in wartime spending requirements. The pressure of demand generated by wartime increases in income, coupled with the limited supply of basic products as a large proportion of available resources is devoted to defense production (not to speak of decreases in the supply of output where productive facilities are subject to war destruction) causes the level of prices to rise to "runaway" proportions.

Hyperinflation is an abnormal situation characterized by abnormal increases in the quantity of money. If the velocity of circulation can rise only to some limit—presumably when idle balances are all activated—then hyperinflation cannot be sustained without large increases in the quantity of money. Of course, before the velocity of circulation reaches that limit, the extent of price increase may already be very substantial, particularly when idle balances represent a large proportion of the existing money stock. But it would take an extreme shock to cause sharp increases in the velocity of circulation. It follows that the kind of moderate inflation—2 or 3 percent per year which prevails in the United States and other industrialized societies—can hardly degenerate into runaway inflation because of many reasons. In the first place, this kind of price increase is not likely to cause drastic changes in the expectations of people about future prices. Second, the control of the central bank over bank reserves and the supply of money will not allow the quantity of money to increase to proportions required to sustain runaway inflation. Third, so long as the international movement of goods is free, increases in imports induced by domestic inflation would help increase the supply of goods (and at the same time reduce domestic income and demand) and slow down the rate of price increase.

INFLATION THEORIES AND POLICY IMPLICATIONS

We have seen that inflation may be initiated by the pull of excess demand, the push of cost, or by changes in sectoral demand. Since the onset of inflation may be generated by a variety of factors, the monetary authority would have to use combinations of antiinflationary monetary weapons which are most appropriate for a given set of inflation-generating factors. Thus when inflation is generated by an aggregate excess demand gap, it would appear appropriate to use general control weapons to slow down this type of inflationary development. On the other hand, when inflation is initiated by changes in the composition of demand, it would appear appropriate to use selective control instruments to reduce sectoral excess demand.

The use of general control instruments, which affect all sectors of the economy, in the case of sectoral inflation, may cause adverse repercussions on sectors which experience no demand excess. They may depress demand in these sectors, causing unemployment and decreases in output. At any rate, in the case of inflation generated by general excess demand and changes in sectoral demand, the monetary authority does not face any serious dilemma. It is largely a matter of selecting proper combinations of control measures at its disposal. In the case of inflation generated by the push of cost, the monetary authority faces a real dilemma. If price increase is pushed up by increase in wage cost, then the application of restrictive monetary control measures to stabilize prices would cause unemployment to rise. To stabilize the level of prices without causing substantial rise in unemployment requires some policy over wages. But what would be the form of wage policy? Should it be in the form of some guideline for wage increase set up by the government to be observed voluntarily by unions and management? Or should it be in the form of legislation limiting wage increase to certain rate? The fixing of wage guideline to be observed voluntarily by unions and management may not be an effective means to prevent excessive wage increases, as indicated by the experience of the United States in the late 1960's when the guidepost of 3.2 percent was ignored in most cases by management and unions. Voluntary guidelines at best would exert some restraining influence on unions and management the consequence of which is probably a slower rate of wage increase than otherwise. At any rate, whether wage increase is subject to some voluntary limit or legal limit, the limit would have to be expressed in terms of some measure of productivity gains, say, the average rate of productivity gains of the economy as a whole.

If, in the cost-push inflationary process, wage cost is the dynamic element which pushes up prices (that is, price increase is a passive reaction to increase in unit wage cost), then wage control alone is adequate. This however is not the case. Price increase may be a passive reaction to increase in unit cost at one point in time and active at another point in time. Oligopolistic firms not only may raise prices as a reaction to increases in wage cost to keep their profit margins, but they may also mark up prices or raise prices even though there is no significant increase in wage cost simply to increase profits. If prices may be raised by firms in less competitive industries with or without increases in unit cost, then the stabilization of the price level requires both wage and price controls. Wage and price controls, however, involve several problems. It is very difficult to enforce these controls. In addition, it has been argued that price and wage controls prevent the efficient functioning of the price mechanism which results in inefficient allocation of resources and welfare losses.[4] Controls over wages also may lead to increases in unit wage cost as a consequence of deliberate slowdown, carelessness and excessive absenteeism, particularly in industries where workers consider controlled wages to be substantially below what they should receive! If firms in these industries were not allowed to raise prices sufficient to maintain profits, they may elect to lay off workers. The stabilization of prices thus may give rise to unemployment with or without control over wages. If the cost-push mechanism is generated by the economic power of labor unions and oligopolistic firms, then the best means of preventing it is to promote greater competition in labor markets and output markets. This, however, is easier said than done. Oligopolistic firms and labor unions, with their tremendous political power—a product of their economic power—will resist any attempt at breaking down their power structure. What could be done by the monetary authority in this case is to follow some optimum trade-off path between price stability and full employment. For instance, a commitment to full employment which causes the price level to rise beyond certain critical level would call for restrictive measures to stop price increase. When the rate of unemployment rises to some critical limit caused by restrictive measures, then a switch to an easier monetary policy is called for. The monetary authority may help keep price increase and the rate of unemployment within some "acceptable" limits.

SUMMARY

By inflation we refer to a situation in which the price level continues to rise for some period of time. Inflation may be initiated by the pull of demand—that

[4]The argument is undoubtedly valid in a competitive system. But in a system dominated by monopolistic and oligopolistic elements, the price mechanism is prevented from functioning efficiently any way. In this case, the imposition of price and wage controls could help alleviate the added burden of wage-price inflation.

is, at the existing price level, aggregate demand exceeds aggregate supply and the pressure of demand causes the price level to rise. Inflation may also be initiated by increase in unit cost resulting from wage increases in excess of productivity gains. Inflation may also be initiated by changes in sectoral demand. As a consequence of the downward inflexibility of wages and prices, wages and prices do not decline in sectors with demand deficiency and rise in sectors with demand excess. This causes the general price level to rise.

Inflation may be convergent or self-sustained. It is convergent when price increase tapers off and converges to some higher level. It may become self-sustained when price increase tends to feed further price increase. This may be a consequence of the wage-price reactions of labor unions and oligopolistic firms, facilitated by governmental policy committed to full employment, or abnormal increases in the quantity of money and the continuous upward revision of the expectations of people regarding future price increases.

While in the case of excess demand inflation and sectoral inflation, the problem of monetary policy is largely the selection of optimum combinations of monetary control instruments, in the case of cost-push inflation, monetary policy faces a dilemma: The use of restrictive monetary measures would result in unemployment. Price stabilization in this case necessitates, in addition to monetary policy, some form of wage-price policy as well.

PROBLEMS

1. Discuss some of the major factors which you believe account for the continuous upward trend in the Consumer Price Index in the United States since the 1940's? Would you believe that that trend will continue in the future even with the relaxation of cold war tension? If so, why? Explain.

2. What do you understand by demand inflation? Is it correct to say that the traditional quantity theory and the income-expenditure theory explain inflation in terms of excess demand?

3. What is cost-push inflation? What is sectoral inflation? What are monetary policy implications of demand pull inflation, cost-push inflation, and sectoral inflation?

4. What is the wage-price spiral? Could the wage-price spiral be sustained without the commitment of the government to a full-employment policy? Why or why not? Give your reasons.

5. What are the characteristics of hyperinflation? Can the kind of inflation which prevailed in the United States in the 1950's and 1960's degenerate into hyperinflation? Why or why not? Explain.

part V

ECONOMIC STABILIZATION

chapter **24**

Objectives of Stabilization Policy

Up to this point we have been concerned with the operations of institutions that create and control money, and with the relationships between money and other economic variables. We shall now discuss how policy decisions are formulated in the light of these theoretical relationships, the various objectives of stabilization policy, the tools of monetary and fiscal policies, their effectiveness and limitations, and the monetary and fiscal policies of the United States in recent decades.

THEORY AND POLICY

Theory and policy are not the same but they are closely connected. Theory is a form of intellectual activity which, through logical reasoning, aims at establishing a body of principles in terms of which observable economic phenomena can be described, classified, and related. Theoretical analysis not only helps better our understanding of various phenomena of economic life but also assists in deriving solutions to practical economic problems. Policy, on the other hand, is action designed to bring about desired changes in the values of economic variables under consideration (for example, the level of prices or the level of employment). For an economic illness, theory provides the tools for diagnosis and policy is prescription for its cure. We can hardly expect to be able to take appropriate measures to check price inflation, to prevent rising unemployment and declining income, for instance, without some knowledge of the mechanism of price change and the basic determinants of the level of income and employment. Thus policy action formulated on the basis of a broadly and realistically conceived theory has a better chance of success. A policy maker not guided by a good theory is not different from a traveler traveling without a road map. Correct policy decisions may indeed be made without a realistic theoretical interpretation of the problem in question. But this is largely a matter of luck. The policy action prescribed on the basis of inadequate theoretical diagnosis turns out to be applicable for the problem involved.

Different policy conclusions of course may be derived from a given theoretical model under different conditions. Consider, for example, the Keynesian theory of income determination. We have seen that according to this theory the level of income and output is determined in the short run by the level of aggregate demand. But aggregate demand may at times be too much and at times too little. And policy decisions under conditions of too little aggregate demand are different from those required under conditions of too much demand. When demand is excessive in that it generates largely price increases without any significant increase in real income and output, then contractionary policy measures are called for to check price inflation. On the other hand, when demand is deficient and the level of income and employment as a consequence, declines, then expansionary policy actions are in order. It would therefore appear misleading to term Keynesian theory "depression" or "expansion" theory; it is neither the one nor the other. It is rather neutral in that it may be used as a guide to policy measures designed to stimulate economic expansion as well as to combat inflation as the case may be.

OBJECTIVES OF MODERN STABILIZATION POLICY

The level of economic activity in a free-market economy is subject to frequent fluctuations. Periods of economic boom and recession alternate. In periods of boom, income and employment rise. Excessive boom, however, generates price inflation. In periods of recession, on the other hand, income and employment decline. The primary task of stabilization policy is to reduce the amplitude of fluctuations in these variables. Inasmuch as rapidly rising prices can lead to economic distortions and topple an economy from boom to recession, can erode a country's competitive position in international markets and undermine the well-being of people living on fixed incomes—whereas rising unemployment means unrecoverable economic losses in terms of waste of manpower and resources—stabilization policy then must aim at maintaining "full employment" and reasonable price-level stability. But since full employment can be sustained only by a high and steady rate of growth of income and output, full employment thus implies the objective of a high rate of economic growth. In addition to price-level stability, full employment, and a high rate of economic growth, balance of payments equilibrium is another important objective of modern stabilization policy. Persistent deficits in the balance of payments of the United States would cause steady depletion of its gold reserves, erode the confidence of foreign countries in the dollar as an international reserve currency, and impair its value in international transactions.

It is generally agreed that these are important goals of modern stabilization policy. They do not always receive equal emphasis, however. The emphasis on these goals shifts as economic conditions change. Nor are they always mutually consistent. As will be seen, the achievement of some of these goals may interfere with the achievement of some other goals. Maintaining full employment and a high rate of economic growth, may render maintaining price-level stability more difficult, since measures required to promote full employment and economic growth might generate inflationary pressures. Moreover, these objectives, as stated, appear somewhat vague. What do we mean by "full" employment, a high rate of economic growth, and price-level stability? As practical guides to policy formulation, they would have to be expressed in some definite quantitative terms. We shall discuss in some detail the meaning of these goals.

FULL EMPLOYMENT

Full employment became a concern of economic policy (and theoretical economics) following the depression of the 1930's during which the rate of unemployment at times soared as high as 25 percent. Unemployment remained high in the early 1940's, 15 percent in 1940 and 10 percent in 1941. It was not surprising that after World War II, Congress, fearing that unemployment would again rise as wartime spending was reduced, formally declared the achievement of full or "maximum" employment (among other things) a responsibility of the federal government in the Employment Act of 1946 which states that "it is the continuing policy and responsibility of the federal government to use all practicable means to foster and promote free competitive enterprise and the general welfare, conditions under which there will be afforded useful employment opportunities for those able, willing, and seeking to work, and to promote maximum employment, production, and purchasing power."

It is not difficult to see why full employment is an important national goal. Unemployment is economic waste in terms of manpower and resources. It is a main root of poverty with all its economic and social deprivations. Poverty begets poverty. It is a source of crime and social unrest. Poor parents hardly have the means to educate their children and in a world in which well-paid employment requires certain amount of skills which can be acquired only through education, uneducated children will grow up to join the rank of the "persistently unemployed" or "partially unemployed." Poverty is "a world apart, whose inhabitants are isolated from the mainstream of American life and alienated from its values. It is a world where Americans are literally concerned with day-to-day survival. . . . It is a world where a minor illness is a major tragedy, where pride and privacy must be sacrificed to get help, where honesty can become a luxury and ambition a myth. Worst of all, the poverty of the fathers is visited upon the children."[1] High-level employment is a remedy, of primary importance to poverty. It provides earned incomes to the unemployed who are able and willing to work. "The maintenance of high employment—a labor market in which the demand for workers is strong relative to the supply—is a powerful force for the reduction of poverty."[2]

What then is full employment? By full employment we do not mean that everybody has a job. In a dynamic, growing economy, some unemployment is

[1] *Economic Report of the President*, 1964, p. 55.
[2] *Ibid*, p. 73.

bound to occur. In the first place, we have what is commonly referred to as "frictional" unemployment. It would take workers just entering the work force some time to look for jobs. It would take workers transferring between jobs some time to effect such transfers. Changes in the seasonal labor requirements of some sectors of the economy, particularly in agriculture and the construction industries, would give rise to seasonal unemployment. It would take the seasonally unemployed some time to find jobs during the off seasons. In some industry, workers in certain plants may be temporarily laid-off because of strikes of workers in related plants. The complete elimination of "frictional" unemployment is neither possible nor desirable. The ability of workers to leave low-productivity employment for high-productivity jobs promotes greater efficiency in the allocation of resources. Then there is what is loosely referred to as "structural" unemployment. There are people who are unemployed even when employment opportunities are available either because of lack of skills, or because of social prejudices, poor work habits, poor health, emotional instability, and lack of motivation and discipline. In addition, while the introduction of new products and new production methods create new job opportunities, they also destroy jobs, particularly jobs requiring no particular skills. Last but not least, we have what is sometimes termed "cyclical" unemployment, the type of unemployment largely generated by inadequate demand for goods and services. This type of unemployment is most amenable to policy controls. It can be reduced through the expansion of demand for goods and services which would induce greater demand for labor to produce them. The expansion of aggregate demand also can reduce frictional unemployment to some extent in that the greater availability of employment opportunities generated by demand expansion would reduce the amount of time it would take new workers to look for jobs and make it easier for seasonal workers to find employment in the off seasons. But for frictional unemployment, expansion of demand alone is not sufficient since it is accounted for partly by inadequate information about the availability of jobs and artificial barriers against entrance in some labor markets, among other things. For the "structurally" unemployed, the expansion of demand for goods and services obviously is not the answer. To expand demand to create jobs which cannot be filled because of the unavailability of qualified labor would inevitably lead to upward price and wage pressures. To make employment opportunities available to the structurally unemployed through demand expansion requires in the first place programs designed to train or retrain them for productive contribution.[3]

Inasmuch as some minimum unemployment always exists in a dynamic, growing society, full employment is defined by economists in terms of some

[3]It should be noted that in view of lowering overall unemployment by reducing structural unemployment, efforts have been made by the government to train and retrain the structurally unemployed. These include the Manpower Development and Training Act, Job Corps, Neighborhood Youth Corps, Work Experience, Adult Work Program, the Office of Economic Opportunity, and so on.

unemployment rate. But what rate of unemployment to be used as a practical target for policy formulation? There is disagreement in this regard. According to Neil H. Jacob, "... the United States economy has full employment in a practical sense when 96 percent of the work force has jobs and 4 percent are in process of changing jobs."[4] Arthur Goldberg, former secretary of labor, suggested an unemployment rate of 3 percent as a feasible target. Some economists believe that the reduction of unemployment to less than 5 percent would lead to serious labor bottlenecks. The Council of Economic Advisors consider the unemployment rate of 4 percent to correspond with full employment which could be achieved with price level stability. The expansion of demand to reduce unemployment below that level would only lead to minimum increases in employment and major increases in prices. Consequently, the gains in employment would be more than offset by the losses generated by distortions resulting from inflation. There is, of course, nothing sacred about the 4 percent rate of unemployment. In point of fact, if structural unemployment and frictional unemployment can be reduced through effective job-training programs and better information on jobs availability, then an unemployment rate of, say, 3 percent may then become a more realistic target than 4 percent. At any rate, the unemployment rate of 4 percent appears to be the most reasonable "full employment" target under labor market conditions of the 1960's.

Now what does the rate of unemployment of four percent represent? It represents the unemployed as a percentage of the civilian labor force which includes civilians of the noninstitutional population age 14 or older who are working or are looking for work.[5] The civilian labor force is the total labor force exclusive of members of the armed forces. Thus in 1966, for example, the total labor force was 80.1 million and the armed forces numbered 3.1 million, hence the civilian labor force was 77 million of which 74 million were employed (4 million were employed in agriculture and 70 million, in nonagricultural activities) and 3 million were unemployed, hence an unemployment rate of 3.9 percent.

The unemployment rate is an aggregate. As such, it does not show the unemployment rates of the various subgroups of the labor force in terms of, say, age groups and ethnic groups, which information, however, is important for policy formulation. The overall unemployment rate may be, say, 5 percent, yet this may correspond to full employment because of increases in "structural" unemployment in some subgroups of the labor force, for example. Attempts to

[4] *Harvard Business Review* (May-June 1957), p. 26.

[5] The noninstitutional population represents all persons 14 years of age or older exclusive of persons in institutions. The total labor force is that portion of the noninstitutional population, including the armed forces, who are working or looking for jobs. The voluntarily unemployed, that is, people who do not wish to work, housewives, and students who are not working while attending school constitute the difference between the noninstitutional population and the total labor force. For instance, in 1966, the total population of the United States was 196.8 million, of which 138.4 million were included in the noninstitutional population. Of this, 80.1 million were included in the total labor force.

raise employment through the expansion of demand in such a situation would result in serious labor shortages and undesirable upward pressures on wages and prices. The unemployment rate is estimated from sampling process. Therefore it may be affected by changes in sample size, among other things.[6] In addition, it may be changed simply because of changes in the definition of the "employed" and "unemployed" which involves some arbitrary decisions. According to the Bureau of Census, employed persons include those who did any work for pay or for profit during the (census) week, worked without pay for 15 hours or more in a family enterprise (farm or business), or did not work or looked for work but had a job or business from which they were temporarily absent during the week. Unemployed persons include those who did not work at all during the week but were looking for work or were on layoff from jobs. But the inclusion or exclusion of, say, workers laid off with instructions to return to work in the computation of employment for instance, would affect the employment figures. Thus as of January 1957, persons on layoff with definite instructions to return to work within 30 days of layoff and persons waiting to start new wage and salary jobs within the following 30 days, have been classified as unemployed. They had previously been considered as employed. Likewise, students waiting to start new jobs who had previously been classified as employed have been excluded from the labor force. Although the methods used by the Department of Labor to measure employment and unemployment are not free of flaws because of problems of definition and other complexities, unemployment estimates of the Bureau of Census in general have been considered by many as reliable guides to policy formulation.

ECONOMIC GROWTH

The problem of economic growth has for centuries been a concern of economists. But economic growth became an objective of economic policy only recently partly as a consequence of the sluggish rate of growth of the United States economy in the 1950's as compared with high growth rates in most Western European countries, Japan, the Soviet Union and other countries in Eastern Europe. Economic growth was considered a national economic goal in the Report of the President's Commission on National Goals (1959) and in the Study of Employment, Growth, and Price Levels (1959) by the Joint Economic Committee of Congress. It was a major issue in the Presidential campaign of 1960. Considerable time and effort have been devoted by professional econo-

[6] For instance, civilian labor force data beginning with January 1963 were based on a 357-area sample; for January 1960-December 1962, on a 333-area sample; for May 1950-December 1959, on a 330-area sample. When the sample increased from 68-area sample (for 1946-53) to 230 area sample (for 1954-56) the new larger sample showed that unemployment was about 31 percent higher than the former smaller sample.

mists, private organizations, and public agencies to the study of economic growth and to devise ways and means to promote growth.

What then is economic growth? How is it measured? What is the optimum rate of growth? Growth is a rate of change. Economic growth usually refers to the rate of change of real income or output over time. But which income and output? Some economists prefer to measure economic growth in terms of the rate of change of per capita real income, others in terms of the rate of change in output per man-hour. The most common measure of economic growth, however, is the rate of change of real gross national product (GNP in constant dollars). While it is generally agreed that economic growth is a major goal of economic policy, there is difference of opinion in regard to the specific rate of growth to be used as target for policy formulation. President Kennedy in his 1962 Economic Report to Congress stated that, "Our postwar economic growth—though a step ahead of our record for the last half-century—has been slowing down. We have not in recent years maintained the 4 to 4 1/2 percent rate of growth which characterized the early postwar period. We should not settle for less than the achievement of a long-term growth rate matching the early postwar record. Increasing our growth rate to 4 1/2 percent a year lies within the range of our capabilities during the 1960's. It will lay the groundwork for meeting both our domestic needs and our world responsibilities."[7] According to Professor Samuelson, 4 percent per year is the target to aim at.[8] The Rockefeller Report considered 5 percent as a feasible rate.[9] The target rate for the 1960-70 decade established in 1961 collectively for the member countries of the Organization for Economic Cooperation and Development (OECD) was 50 percent (4.1 percent per year).

The growth rate target is an average to be achieved over a specified time period. We may have different targets depending upon the time period considered. A 4 percent rate of growth may be the proper target for a long period of time—say, 25 years. Yet a higher rate of growth of, say, 5 percent may be realistic for a shorter period (say five years) particularly when there are readily available idle resources which may be put into productive uses, and a substantial rate of unutilization of the economy's stock of capital and so on. Since economic growth is not an end in itself, but rather a means to other goals, a proper rate of growth may be considered as the rate required to attain some of these goals. The target rate of economic growth is thus related by the Council of Economic Advisors to the concept of growth of potential GNP which is defined as the level of GNP required to sustain full employment with reasonable price level stability. The proper rate of growth is the rate required to attain the growth potential of

[7]*Economic Report of the President*, 1962, p. 9.

[8]Paul A. Samuelson, "Fiscal and Financial Policies for Growth," *Proceedings of A Symposium on Economic Growth* (The American Bankers Association, 1963).

[9]Rockefeller Report, *The Challenge to America: Its Economic and Social Aspects* (Garden City, New York: Doubleday 1958).

GNP.[10] The difference between actual GNP and potential GNP is the "gap" which represents the amount of output which could be produced to sustain full employment. The presence of a positive gap indicates that the growth of actual GNP is inadequate to achieve full employment. The relationship between the GNP gap and unemployment is shown in Fig. 24-1. For the 1958-65 period, as

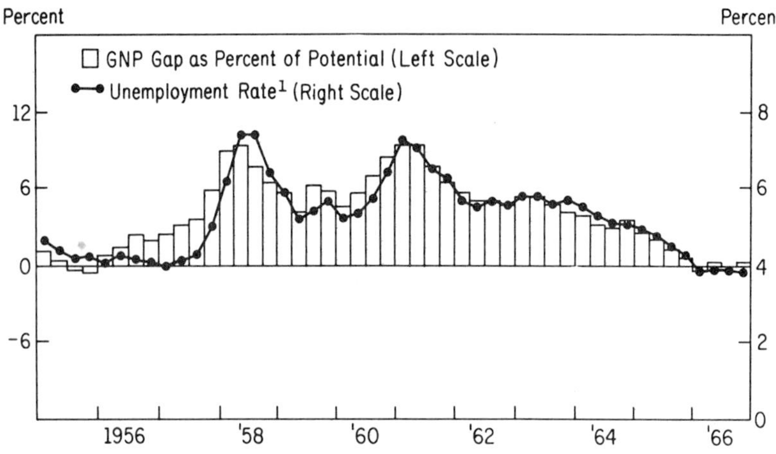

Fig. 24-1. GNP gap and unemployment rate.

the economy failed to achieve potential GNP (the cumulative gap for the period was $260 billion), the unemployment rates were substantially higher than the full-employment rate of 4 percent. In 1966, the gap was closed; potential GNP and full employment were attained.

The potential GNP trend line in Fig. 24-2 was obtained through the growth-rate extrapolation method. The GNP of mid-1955 was selected by the Council of Economic Advisors as the base as it was assumed to have been identical with potential GNP (the rate of unemployment was then close to 4 percent). The constant dollar potential GNP series for the 1956-62 period was extrapolated by applying a constant real rate of growth of 3 1/2 percent to the GNP of mid-1955. The real rate of growth of 3 1/2 percent was used by the Council because "the trend rate of growth of GNP . . . has averaged about 3 1/2 percent in the post-Korean period. Thus the path of potential GNP can be represented

[10]The growth of potential GNP is determined by two major determinants: (a) the growth of total man-hours worked which reflect both the rise in the labor force and changes in annual average hours worked per man, and (b) the growth of average output per man-hour–that is, growth of productivity. Thus, assuming that the growth of total man-hours worked was 1 1/2 percent and the growth of average output per man-hour 2 1/2 percent, potential output would grow at 4 percent.

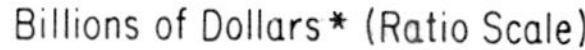

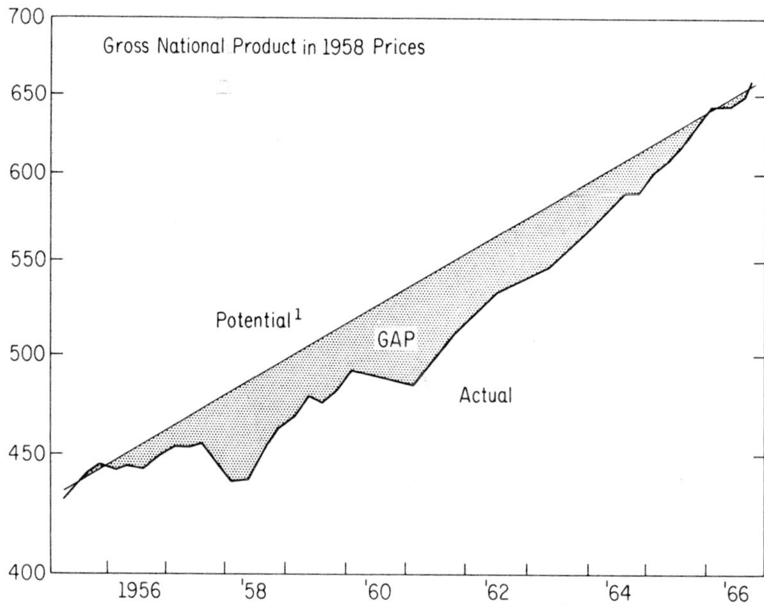

Source: Economic Report of the President, January 1967.

* Seasonally adjusted annual rates.

[1] Trend line of $3\frac{1}{2}$% through middle of 1955 to 1962 IV, $3\frac{3}{4}$% from 1962 IV to 1965 IV, and 4% from 1965 IV to 1966 IV.

Fig. 24-2. Gross national product, actual and potential.

by a 3 1/2 percent trend from actual GNP in mid-1955."[11] It can be seen that the estimate of real potential GNP on the basis of the extrapolation method depends upon the base period selected and the trend rate of growth of potential GNP used. The use of alternative base periods and different rates of potential growth would yield different estimates of potential GNP. The trend rate of growth of potential GNP is not constant as assumed by the growth rate extrapolation method, but changes in accordance with the sample period selected. For instance, real growth averaged 4.5 percent from 1960 to 1965, as compared with the 2.4 percent annual rise from 1953 to 1960, 3.8 percent from 1948 to 1957, 2.5 percent from 1929 to 1948, or 5.4 percent from 1961 to 1966. Should we apply a trend rate of growth of 4 percent, instead of 3 1/2 percent, we would have different estimates for potential GNP. In fact, the Council of Economic Advisors has changed the trend rate of growth from 3 1/2 percent to 3 3/4 percent for the period after 1962 since "for recent years, a real growth rate of actual GNP somewhat greater than 3 1/2 percent has been required to

[11] *Economic Report of the President*, 1962, p. 51.

hold the unemployment rate constant. Hence, the Council . . . raised its estimated rate of growth of potential GNP to 3 3/4 percent beginning in 1963."[12] In addition, given the trend rate of growth used, the use of different base periods (such as GNP of mid-1966 when the rate of unemployment was 4 percent) would also result in different estimated "gaps" between potential GNP and actual GNP series for the same period. The extrapolation method is thus not free from weaknesses. But used with care, it would yield fairly reliable estimates of potential GNP targets for the formulation of economic policy.

Why is economic growth important? There are several reasons why economic growth is given high priority. In the first place, the average level of living can be maintained only when GNP grows at the same rate as population. For individuals to enjoy a rising standard of living, GNP has to grow at a faster rate than does population. Second, economic growth provides growing employment opportunities for growing population. As already noted, unemployment is closely related to the GNP gap. The wider the GNP gap, the higher the unemployment rate (see Fig. 24-1). Third, economic growth means growth in our capability to assist the less developed countries in their development efforts. To these countries, a high rate of economic growth of the United States is a demonstration of the ability of a free enterprise system to grow and prosper. Fourth, so long as the cold war tension and limited open armed conflicts continue, economic growth assures its ability to maintain military security at home and carry out its military commitments abroad. Last, but not least, as the economy grows, greater resources are available for the expansion and reconstruction of transportation facilities, for the expansion of health care facilities, for better conservation of natural resources, for the expansion and improvement of education at all levels, for the expansion and improvement of research and development facilities, and for the establishment of programs for training and retraining the "disadvantaged," and so on. All this in turn will contribute to accelerating the rate of economic growth and improving further living conditions of future generations.

PRICE-LEVEL STABILITY

Price-level stability has long been an important goal of economic policy. Public authorities, throughout history, have had to deal with the problems of inflation. But price stability is at times overshadowed by other economic goals. When prices begin to rise substantially, either under the pressures of demand generated by expansionary policy to promote growth and employment or by rising spending requirements of wars, or under the excessive push of costs, price stabilization is then given prior consideration. During the 1961-65, for instance, the preoccupation of public policy was largely to reduce unemployment and accelerate the growth rate, but after 1965, as prices began to rise substantially as

[12] *Economic Report of the President*, 1966, p. 40.

a result of increased expenditures for the war in Vietnam, among other things, restoring price stability became the primary objective of economic policy.

Price-level stability, as an objective of economic policy, however, has not been explicitly stated in any legislation. The provision ". . . to promote maximum employment, production, and purchasing power" of the Employment Act of 1946 does not appear to refer to price level stability but rather to income, which case it implies an inflationary bias. Policy action aimed at generating maximum income and output could lead to inflationary developments. Since the Act is not clear in regard to the goal of price-level stability, the Commission on Money and Credit proposes an amendment to the Act to include price-level stability as a goal of national economic policy; the responsibility of the government would be" . . . to formulate the goals of a low level of unemployment, an adequate rate of economic growth, and reasonable price stability as applicable to all federal agencies administering economic programs."[13]

Price stability refers to the stability of the general price level or the general purchasing power of money. In a dynamic society, relative prices (price of a good relative to the price of other goods) of course change as consumer preferences and relative costs change. But so long as the increases in some prices are offset by decreases in some other prices, the general price level would not change substantially. The object of price-level stabilization is not to keep the structure of relative prices from changing (which is neither possible nor desirable as the efficient use of resources requires the movement of resources to their best alternative uses guided by relative price changes) but to keep all or most prices from changing in the same direction which would result in changes in the general price level.

To see why price-level stability is an important goal, we can look at some of the adverse economic consequences of rapid price-level changes. Rapidly rising prices, in the first place, inflict hardships to people living on fixed incomes (pensioners), people whose incomes do not usually increase as fast as price increases (school teachers, government employees), and holders of fixed-value financial claims (savings accounts, government securities). They can lead to disruptive speculations and distortions which can eventually reverse the course of economic activity from boom to recession. As prices rise rapidly, business planning is rendered more difficult because of greater uncertainty involved in cost and revenue estimates. Expectations of price increases generated by rapidly rising prices would cause diversion of resources from productive to speculative operations. The holding of goods and materials off markets in order to make greater profits from expected higher prices could lead to serious bottlenecks and disruption of production and cause prices to rise further. Rapidly rising prices can also weaken quickly the U.S. competitive position in world markets, causing loss of reserve assets, and undermining the position of the dollar as an interna-

[13] Report of the Commission on Money and Credit, *Money and Credit, Their Influence on Jobs, Prices, and Growth* Englewood Cliffs, N.J.: (Prentice-Hall, 1961).

tional reserve. Rapidly declining prices, on the other hand, are equally if not more disastrous. A consequence of sharp price decreases which squeeze business profits as wages and other costs usually lag behind falling prices, is depressed production and rising unemployment. Debtors and creditors both suffer. Lenders may not be able to recover what they lent if debtors were forced out of business as a result of declining prices and profits. Price stability removes these distortions and inequities. It creates an environment in which consumption and investment planning can be undertaken with confidence; and this is considered as essential to the promotion of balanced growth and full employment at home and maintaining the value of the dollar in international transactions.

While rapidly changing prices, either upward or downward, are considered as undesirable, there are advocates for a mild rate of price increase and those who favor a small rate of price decrease instead of a stable level of prices. According to proponents of a small decline in prices overtime, the level of prices should decline as productivity rises. This would allow businessmen, wage earners, and holders of financial claims to share the fruit of productivity gains. This, however, does not appear to be practical. As a consequence of declining price level, those businesses which hold large inventories may be subject to serious losses. The attempt to minimize inventory losses by reducing inventory holdings would exert depressive influence on the level of output and employment. The expectation of future lower prices may also induce consumers as well as businessmen to defer the purchases of goods and equipment to take advantage of expected lower prices. In addition, in an institutional framework in which strong labor organizations are inclined to press for money wages in excess of productivity gains, price decreases would result in lower output and employment. Advocates of a mild rate of price increase in the order of one to 2 percent per year, on the other hand, hold that this would increase business profits, improve business outlook, hence, stimulate investment, production, and employment. Long-term business planning would not be unduly disrupted so long as price increase is confined to some predictable narrow limits. Small price increases, nevertheless, still erode the well-being of fixed-income people. A rate of price increase of 2 percent per year would reduce the value of money in half in less than four decades. It is also difficult to maintain mild inflation as the mechanism of price increase contains a bias toward further price increases. When price increases leaves the public to expect greater price increases, their attempt to "beat" inflation by buying now would inevitably result in higher price rise. A "little" inflation may indeed lead to a "little and little more" inflation. While arguing that a stable price level is most desirable and aware of the pitfalls involved, some economists remain in favor of some "mild" inflation as a matter of practical policy. In an environment dominated by labor unions with power to push up wage costs and concentrated industries with power to "administer" prices, maintaining a stable price level would result in unacceptable high levels of unemployment and intolerable economic wastes. Furthermore, small price increases of 1 to 2 percent per year probably would not generate the kind of price expectations which result in disruptive speculative operations and distortions. The use of the term "reasonably stable price level" in the economic reports of the President and the Council of Economic Advisors and the Report of the Commission on Money and Credit appears to imply an allowance for some small price increase.

INTERNATIONAL PAYMENTS EQUILIBRIUM

The U.S. economy is part of the world economy. The economic relationships of the United States with other countries are manifested by the complex of international business and financial transactions which give rise to receipts and payments between the United States and the rest of the world. Receipts arise from such "current" transactions as U.S. exports of goods, foreigners' expenditures for travel in the United States, interest and dividends received by U.S. residents from foreign firms, the repatriation of income from investments of U.S. firms abroad, and such "capital" transactions as foreign investments in the United States. Similarly, payments arise from such current transactions as U.S. imports of goods, remittances of U.S. residents to relatives abroad, U.S. travel expenditure abroad, and such capital transactions as U.S. purchases of foreign securities, U.S. direct investments and bank loans in foreign countries. The excess deficiency of payments over receipts on current transactions accounts and nonliquid capital transactions such as long-term loans and investments represents one measure of our balance of payments deficit (surplus). The settlement of U.S. payments deficits would result in either a loss of gold reserves, an increase in foreign liquid claims on the United States, or a decrease in U.S. liquid claims on foreigners or any combination of these. A payments surplus, on the other hand, adds to U.S. gold reserves, U.S. liquid claims on foreigners or reduces foreign liquid claims on the United States.

During the interwar period and up to the early 1950's, the United States, then practically the buying market for the rest of the world, had accumulated a huge gold reserve. After the early 1950's, the payments position of the United States was reversed which was partly accounted for by the economic recovery and rising competition of Europe and partly by the rising expenditures required to sustain U.S. economic and military commitments abroad. The deficits which have persisted since the 1950's have resulted in a steady depletion of U.S. gold stock. The gold loss was initially not a subject of concern. In fact it was considered as a desirable redistribution of gold reserve essential to the healthy expansion of international trade and payments. The deficit, however, became a problem of economic policy in late 1950's following heavy losses of gold. The deficit of course cannot be sustained indefinitely without eroding foreign confidence in the dollar as international money. Restoring equilibrium between international receipts and payments therefore became imperative if foreign confidence in the safety and stability of the dollar was to be maintained. Thus

President Kennedy, in his Economic Report of 1962, stated: "Persistent international payments deficits and gold outflows have made the balance of payments a critical problem of economic policy. We must attain a balance in our international transactions which permits us to meet heavy obligations abroad for the security and development of the free world, without continued depletion of our gold reserves or excessive accumulation of short-term dollar liabilities to foreigners."[14] Likewise, President Johnson stated in his Economic Report of 1967 that: "Our goal in the coming year is to continue to move toward balance of payments equilibrium. . . .[15]

OTHER IMPORTANT GOALS

The goals of full employment, economic growth, price stability, and international payments equilibrium are by no means the only important goals of economic policy. But the achievement of these goals is believed to be most amenable to policy controls. There are, of course, other goals which, at least to some groups of individuals, are equally if not more important. These include a more equitable distribution of income, promotion of competition, better conservation of natural resources, and extension of equality of opportunity, and so on. Establishing economic goals is establishing priorities. And determining priorities involves judgment on social values. Since people have different attitudes regarding social values, some goals may be judged important and desirable by some people and not by others. For instance, while a high rate of economic growth is considered by many to be an important goal of economic policy, to some it is not even considered as a goal; policy measures to promote growth may interfere with the freedom of individuals and businesses in their economic pursuits—to which they give high priority. According to Professor Milton Friedman: "The strivings of countless individuals for a better world will produce some rate of change in the statistical aggregate we call national income or output, but there is no way in a free society to say in advance that one or another numerical rate of change is needed or desirable, or that a higher rate of change is better than a lower. . . . Whatever rate of change in the statistical aggregate results from the efforts of free men to promote their own aspirations is the right rate."[16]

CONFLICTS OF GOALS

Of the goals of economic policy which we have discussed, some are mutually consistent while some others may under certain conditions be mutually incompatible—that is, policy action required to achieve some goals may interfere

[14] *Economic Report of the President*, 1962, p. 10.

[15] *Economic Report of the President*, 1967, p. 14.

[16] Statement in *Employment, Growth, and Price Levels*, Hearings, Joint Economic Committee, 86th Cong., (1959), Part 9A, pp. 3019-3020.

with action needed to promote other goals. The goals of full employment and economic growth appear to be mutually consistent. The level of output depends on the utilization of resources. The greater the degree of utilization of resources, the higher the level of output. It is true that the level of output can be raised by the use of more productive machines and equipment and at the same time unemployment rises as some workers may be displaced by new machines, but if the level of demand is such that employment opportunities are available to these displaced workers, then their employment would further increase total output. In other words, the employment of the unemployed always results in higher levels of output. While there appears to be no conflict between full employment and economic growth, the same cannot be said for full employment and price-level stability. As mentioned in the preceding chapter, price stability and full employment may be mutually incompatible, this incompatibility arising largely from institutional factors underlying the structure of the American Economy such as strong labor organizations, the concentration of economic power in the hands of oligopolistic firms, the downward rigidity of wages and prices, and so on.

Increases in wages in excess of productivity increases forced on management by unions would raise cost per unit of output. The stabilization of prices in such a situation would only result in rising unemployment as business profits are squeezed. The incompatibility between price stability and high employment under this institutional setting, however, may prevail only after unemployment is reduced to some critical range which may be termed the incompatibility range. When the rate of unemployment is substantially higher than this range where unions tend to be more concerned with unemployment than with excessive wage increases, and employers are more reluctant to give in to unions' wages demand, then the expansion of demand can reduce unemployment substantially without any significant increases in unit wage cost and level of prices.

But once unemployment is reduced to within the critical range (which is believed to be inacceptably high), to expand demand to reduce unemployment would generate inflationary pressures, as there is greater room for unions to force high wage increases and employers are less resistant to wages demand. A guaranteed policy of high employment by the government tends to accentuate the degree of incompatibility between price stability and high employment, since it constitutes an impetus for labor unions to push up wages more than they otherwise would and for concentrated industries to raise prices as the demand for their output is more or less assured by the government.

The inflationary bias inherent in existing institutional arrangements leads Professor Gordon to state that: "If we do succeed in keeping aggregate demand high enough to permit something close to full employment and a reasonably rapid rate of growth, then the institutional arrangements which today impinge on the price-making process are virtually certain to impart a significant upward tilt to the trend in the price level. In short, under today's conditions, high level employment and rapid growth are not consistent with a secularly unchanging price level."[17] It should be noted that while price stability and high employment may be incompatible under conditions of cost-push inflation, they are consistent under conditions of excess-demand inflation and "overfull" employment. Policy action required to stabilize the level of prices in this case would not reduce employment but rather the excess demand for labor—that is, bringing the demand for labor into balance with the supply of labor.

Economic growth and high employment may also at times be incompatible with international payments equilibrium. A case in hand is the existence of a payments deficit side by side with a sluggish rate of economic growth and a high unemployment rate. Policy action to correct the payments deficit may hinder action to promote employment and growth. Thus to expand aggregate demand to reduce unemployment and stimulate growth would generate price increase and widen the deficit. On the other hand, restrictive policy measures to raise interest rates, to reduce demand and price increase in order to narrow or remove the payments gap would cause unemployment to rise and impede economic growth. When payments imbalance is in the form of a payments surplus, then it is consistent with the promotion of growth and employment, since the expansion of demand to spur growth and employment would reduce the payments surplus as increases in income and employment would tend to induce increases in imports and slow down exports. The influences of international trade and payments on income and employment are somewhat complicated. They are treated in more detail in Part VI. Much depends on international monetary organizations and exchange rate policies. The impacts of international transactions on income and employment under a fixed exchange-rate system are not the same as under a freely fluctuating exchange rate system.

In as much as the various goals of economic policy which we have discussed, under certain conditions, cannot be achieved simultaneously, the problem faced by policy makers is the determination of an optimum trade-off course of action between these conflicting objectives. It would appear that this would have to be made in the light of the economic and social gains from the achievement of some objectives and the economic and social losses resulting from some degree of sacrifice of some other goals. Take, for instance, high-level employment and price stability. Granted their incompatibility, then the economic and social gains from reducing unemployment by a given percentage would have to be weighed against the social and economic hardships which would result from some degree of price increase generated by action to reduce the unemployment rate. It goes without saying that the approximation of these gains and losses is a formidable if not impossible task for policy makers.

SUMMARY

Economic theory and economic policy are closely related. Theory provides the tools for diagnosis and policy is action for correction. Theory serves as guide

[17] *Employment, Growth, and Price Levels, op cit.*, p. 2958.

to policy formulation. The goals of economic policy change as economic conditions change. It is generally agreed that the important goals of modern economic policy consist of full employment, a high rate of economic growth, price-level stability, and international payments equilibrium. As a practical target for policy formulation, full employment is defined as a situation in which the unemployment rate is reduced to 4 percent or less. A high rate of economic growth represents the rate of growth of GNP to sustain full employment, it is the growth rate of real potential GNP. International payments equilibrium refers to the balance between international receipts and payments arising from "current account" transactions such as imports and exports of goods and nonliquid capital transactions such as long-term loans and investments. In regard to price-level stability, some economists refer to a stable price level while some would allow for some small rate of increase and some others, a small rate of decrease, in the level of prices. These objectives are by no means the only important goals of economic policy. Nor are they mutually consistent. Some of these goals may be incompatible with other goals in that the achievement of some of these goals may interfere with efforts to achieve other goals. Price stability and full employment represent such a case. Inflationary pressures can be generated by policy to promote unemployment and growth. Likewise, policy to promote growth and employment may increase international payments deficits. Given the incompatibility between some of these goals, policy makers would have to weigh the economic and social gains from the achievement of some goals against the economic and social hardships resulting from some degree of sacrifice of other goals.

PROBLEMS

1. Why is full employment defined in terms of some unemployment rate? What rate of unemployment would you consider consistent with full employment? Discuss some of the problems involved in the estimation of the unemployment rate.

2. Explain some of the reasons why you would give high priority to high level employment as a goal of national economic policy.

3. What is economic growth? How would you measure economic growth? Would you consider economic growth an important goal of economic policy? Why or why not? Give your reasons.

4. What is the meaning of the GNP gap? How is the gap measured? What are some of the shortcomings of the method used for estimating the GNP gap? What does the gap serve in terms of policy formulation? Explain.

5. In regard to price-level stability, would you prefer a stable level of prices, a small rate of price increase, or a small rate of price decrease? Give your reasons.

6. Are the objectives of economic policy always mutually consistent? If not, give some examples of incompatibility between some of these objectives. How would you reconcile these objectives? What criteria would you use in reconciling them?

7. What are relationships between economic theory and economic policy? Is it possible for different policy recommendations to be made on the basis of a given theoretical analysis? Why or why not?

chapter 25

Monetary Policy, Fiscal Policy, and Economic Stabilization

We have discussed the goals of stabilization policy in the preceding chapter. But what are the means available for the achievement of these goals? They are monetary policy and fiscal policy. As instruments of economic policy, monetary policy is much older than fiscal policy; but fiscal policy is believed by many to be potentially more powerful. Monetary policy and fiscal policy are complementary. They tend to reinforce each other in their influence on the level of economic activity when they are used in close coordination. But conflicts between monetary policy and fiscal policy may (and did) arise, as there is no agency with power to coordinate and integrate fiscal and monetary policies. When conflicts arise, the effects of monetary policy may be weakened or neutralized by fiscal policy and vice versa.

THE MEANING OF FISCAL POLICY

Government activities which give rise to receipts and payments can be classified into three groups: (a) buying and selling, (b) giving and taking, and (c) lending or repaying and borrowing.

Buying adds to total demand and the flow of income and output. Selling reduces income by reducing the demand for private goods. Giving promotes private demand by raising disposable income. Taxing reduces private disposable income and demand. Lending increases the supply of credit in the private sector. Borrowing from the nonbank public raises interest rates and reduces the availability of credit to private borrowers and spenders. Repaying loans held by the public increases the supply of its spending funds.

Buying, giving, lending, and repaying loans constitute government expenditures. Selling, taxing, and borrowing give rise to receipts. Fiscal policy, in a broad sense, refers to actions of the government covering all these three groups of activity. Under prevailing usage, however, fiscal policy refers to actions of the government which affect the first two groups of activity, that is, buying and selling, giving and taxing. Policy of the government regarding lending, repaying, and borrowing is referred to as debt management. A basis for the differentiation between fiscal policy and debt management is the difference in the ways borrowing and lending on the one hand, and buying, selling, giving, and taxing, on the other hand, affect total demand and level of economic activity. Buying and selling, and giving and taxing affect directly and indirectly the income flow through direct injection or withdrawal of purchasing power from the spending stream or through changes in private disposable income which is the major determinant of private demand and the expenditure flow. On the other hand, making loans, repaying loans, and borrowing affect demand and the level of economic activity largely through their influence on bank reserves, the supply of money, asset prices, asset holdings, and the liquidity position of the private sector.

THE ADMINISTRATION OF FISCAL POLICY

The administration of fiscal policy is the responsibility of Congress and the Executive branch of the government. For each fiscal year,[1] the President submits the budget to Congress, requesting funds to support his fiscal program. The budget document is a summary of the revenue and expenditure programs for the fiscal year. The budget is developed by the Bureau of the Budget on the basis of estimates anticipated expenditures of various governmental departments and agencies and estimates of anticipated revenues submitted by the Treasury. The budget document is considered and revised by various committees in the House and the Senate. There are two separate stages involved in Congressional action on the budget: authorization and appropriation. Congressional authorization expresses Congressional intent to authorize particular expenditure programs, but not to provide funds to support them. Congressional appropriation grants "obligational authority" to governmental agencies and departments—that is, permission or authority to obligate the U.S. Government for expenditures. Appropriation bills traditionally begin with the House of Representatives. Senate appropriation follows that of the House. When appropriation bills pass both the House and the Senate, they go to the President for approval. Once approved, obligational authority is apportioned by the Bureau of the Budget to departments and agencies of the government, which then incur obligations for expenditures.

EARLY AND MODERN VIEWS ON FISCAL POLICY

The primary rule of fiscal policy, according to early thinking, is that the budget should be annually balanced. The balanced-budget concept of classical analysis rests on the classical assumption that full employment is the normal state of affairs. Given the full-employment level of output, deficit financing

[1]In the United States the fiscal year begins on July 1 of each year and ends on June 30 of the following year. The fiscal year is dated for the year in which it ends.

would cause upward pressures on the level of prices, since given the total supply of output, a budget deficit means an excess of total demand over supply at the prevailing level of prices. It follows that government expenditures should be financed out of taxes. In this fashion, resources are either transferred from the private sector to the public sector (when expenditures and taxes are raised) or from the public sector to the private sector (decreases in government expenditures and taxes).[2] The choice is thus either more public goods and less private goods, or more private goods and less public goods but more of both is not possible given the full employment level of output.

The full-employment assumption of classical theory was shattered by the experience of the Great Depression, as we have mentioned. With high rates of unemployment and unutilization of resources, it was obvious that both public goods and private goods, and the level of income and employment, could be raised. Attention was then directed to the discussion of the possibility of using the taxing and spending powers of the government to stabilize the economy at full-employment income and output. The concept regarding the manipulation of the federal budget to stimulate economic activity in periods of recession or depression and to check private demand in periods of excessive expansion is referred to as "functional finance." The foundation of the theory of functional finance is the keynesian theory of income determination. We have seen that, in the short run, the level of income and output is determined by total spending which is made up of spending of consumers, businesses, and the government. Income and output are therefore affected by government expenditures and taxes. Government spending adds to total demand and the income flow, while taxation reduces disposable income, hence private demand and the flow of income.

Depending upon the level of employment and the rate of utilization of resources, an increase in government spending on goods and services or a cut in

[2]It should be noted that the balanced budget concept implies that a balanced budget is neutral in its influence on total demand and income; it is neither expansionary nor contractionary. This, however, is not the case. We have seen in Chapter 20 that an increase in government expenditures on goods and services financed by an equal increase in taxes would cause demand and income to rise. Therefore, given the supply of output, an increase in government spending accompanied by an equivalent increase in taxes would result in excess demand and cause an upward pressure on the level of prices. As an example, assume that current consumption (C_t) is related to disposable income of the preceding period (Yd_{t-1}) as follows:

$$C_t = b\,Yd_{t-1} = b(Y_{t-1} - T)$$

where T is taxes and $Y_{t-1} = P_{t-1}\,Q_f$ (Q_f is the full-employment level of output and P is the level of prices); that investment is constant at $I = 30$ and government spending is equal to taxes, $G = T = 50$. Given $Q_f = 200$ and $b = 0.8$, then the equilibrium level of prices is \$1 per unit of output and equilibrium income is \$200. Now suppose that the government increases its expenditures by \$10 financed by an equal increase in taxes, the new equilibrium level of prices would rise to \$1.05, and equilibrium money income, to \$210, an increase of \$10, which is equal to the increase in government spending. It follows that with the above assumption, an increase in government spending coupled with an equivalent increase in taxes (the budget is balanced) causes money income and the level of prices to rise.

taxes raises the level of income and employment and/or prices, while a decrease in government spending or an increase in taxes reduces income and employment and or slows down price increases. The use of the federal budget as a stabilization device thus calls for increases in government spending or a reduction in taxes or a combination of both in periods of recession, and increases in taxes or decreases in government spending or both in periods of excessive expansion and inflation. A simplified illustration of the use of the budget as a stabilization device is shown in Fig. 25-1. Y_f is the full-employment level of income and Y_0 is

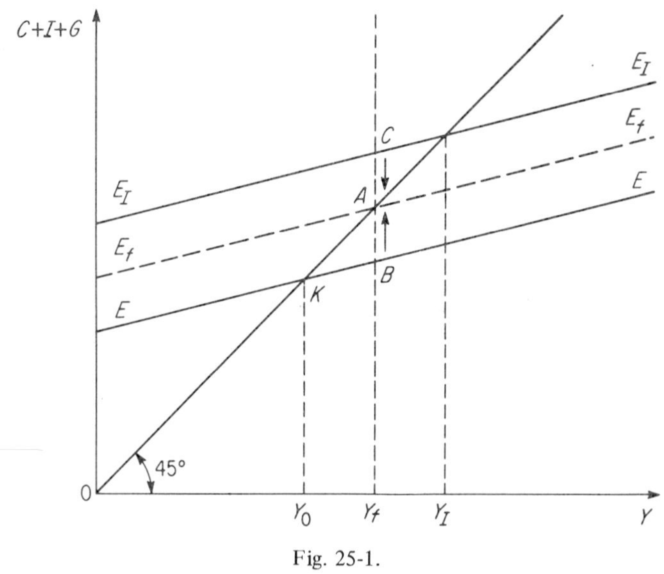

Fig. 25-1.

the actual level of income. The economy fails to achieve full-employment output because aggregate demand falls short of the full-employment supply by the amount *AB*–the deflationary gap.

To remove this demand-deficiency gap, the government can increase spending and reduce taxes. This would cause the total spending curve *EE* to shift upward until it is at E_fE_f, at which full-employment income is realized. Conversely, if the actual level of income is Y_I, the economy is subject to inflationary pressures since at that level of income total demand exceeds total supply by *AC*–the inflationary gap. To remove excess demand, the government can raise taxes and reduce spending. This would cause the total spending curve E_IE_I to shift downward until excess demand is removed.

The concept of functional finance has generally been accepted by professional economists after the publication of the general theory but it was not until in the early 1960's that it received broad support from politicians. Opposition to the use of the federal budget as a stabilization device, however, remains strong among politicians (and the public) either because of the fear that deficit financing would result in inflation and would lead to big government which would stifle private free enterprise and individual freedom or simply because of their failure to distinguish between individual and family finances and government finances.

The concept of functional finance is obviously inconsistent with the annually balanced budget concept. Functional finance implies budget deficits in periods of declining economic activity (as taxes are reduced and/or government spending is raised) and budget surpluses in periods of prosperity. Maintaining the annually balanced budget would tend to aggravate the amplitude of income fluctuations. In periods of economic expansion, as the level of income rises, tax revenue also rises. To keep the budget balanced, the government would have to raise government spending or reduce tax rates and this would add to inflationary pressures. On the other hand, tax revenue goes down in periods of recession or depression as income and profit decline. The reduction of government spending to balance the budget would further depress the depression. Under functional finance, the guiding criterion is the promotion of full employment income and output, economic growth, and relatively stable prices. The position of the budget—whether surplus or deficit—is not a guide but rather the consequence of tax and expenditure programs designed to achieve the above objectives of economic policy. But this does not mean that functional finance would result in persistent budget deficits. The budget may still be balanced but over a different time unit. Instead of an annually balanced budget, under functional finance, the budget may be balanced over a longer time span—say over the length of the cycle as budget surpluses generated in years of boom may offset deficits generated in years of recession.

There are two channels through which fiscal policy affects the level of economic activity: one is automatic, the other is discretionary; one works automatically to dampen economic fluctuations and the other works through discretionary actions of fiscal authority.

Discretionary Fiscal Policy

By discretionary fiscal policy we mean discretionary changes in government expenditures and taxes in view of promoting economic growth, full employment, and other objectives of economic policy. Whether changes in tax rates, changes in expenditures, or both are used depends largely upon prevailing economic (and political) conditions and the relative strength and weaknesses of these alternatives. Changes in government expenditures on goods and services are generally regarded as more powerful than tax changes in their influences on total demand and the level of income and employment. An increase (decrease) in government spending on goods and services generates a greater multiplier effect on the level of income than does a decrease in taxes, for it not only generates a direct impact on aggregate demand but also induces increase in private demand.

A decrease (increase) in taxes, on the other hand, raises (reduces) the level of income only through the increase (decrease) in private demand induced by the increase (decrease) in income after taxes.

Government expenditures may be directed to specific targets. Thus in periods of recession increases in government spending may be directed to those industries hard hit by declining business activity. Direct payments to low-income families, the needy, and the unemployed, may be raised to sustain private demand. Cutting taxes on the other hand may be least beneficial to those who need assistance the most. The unemployed do not have earned incomes to benefit directly from a tax reduction. They benefit indirectly from tax cuts only to the extent that the increase in private demand resulting from increases in income after taxes would generate greater employment opportunities for them. In regard to government expenditures, however, while some spending categories are amenable to countercyclical uses, others are not as they are motivated largely by noneconomic considerations. National defense spending is an example. Defense spending does exert great impacts on income and employment but it can hardly be used for stabilization purposes. It is hardly conceivable that the government would be willing to reduce defense spending to slow down economic expansion at a time when national security and international tension call for greater defense outlays. Expenditures on public works (highways, streets, parks, power stations, dams, and public buildings) are most amenable to stabilization uses. But even these categories of spending have limitations. Public work projects may take years to complete; once started, they cannot be discontinued half way but have to be carried through to completion. Therefore they may exert perversive influences on the economy as completion may have to be carried through periods of inflationary pressures. Tax changes, on the other hand, appear to be more flexible. They can be reduced during periods of recession and raised in times when private demand is "excessive." Government expenditures in the form of transfer payments, which are negative taxes, are also more flexible as they can be raised or reduced to stimulate or slow down private demand as the case may be.

Changes in government expenditures and taxes are of course effected in the environment of politics and the political environment may at times not be conducive to such changes even though such changes are sound from the economic standpoint. Raising government spending may meet with political difficulty particularly when the level of government expenditures is already high. The deficit generated by increasing government expenditures may be too large to be acceptable to legislators. Likewise, reducing government spending may run into difficulty with legislators particularly when the categories of spending to be reduced directly affect the economic interest of their constituents. Raising taxes may also be difficult when tax rates are already high. On the other hand, while reducing taxes may not be as serious a problem, a tax cut may not exert any significant expansionary influences on the economy when tax rates are already too low. In addition, when taxes are reduced, it would be difficult to raise them again in times of excessive economic expansion.

Then there is the problem of forecasting. The use of discretionary fiscal actions for stabilization purposes requires the forecasting of the future course of economic activity. The timing of discretionary fiscal action rests on the forecasting of future economic conditions. But economic forecasting is a developing "art." It may be subject to wide margins of error. Forecasting errors could lead to mistiming and mistiming of fiscal action would result in destabilizing impacts. For example, if a slowdown in the level of business activity is interpreted to be a signal of a reverse in the course of economic activity from expansion to recession, but if this is in fact only a short break in business activity before it continues its expansionary course, a large dose of injection of government spending to avert recession could result in heavy inflationary pressures.

Then there is the problem of time lags involved in discretionary fiscal action. It takes Congress some time to consider and approve proposed changes in government expenditures and taxes. When decisions on these fiscal actions are made, it will also take some time to put them into effect. With regard to tax changes such as income taxes and excise taxes, they may be put into effect without any substantial delay. But the implementation of public work projects may involve considerable delay—delay involved in drawing up contracts, in planning and specifying work details, in competitive bidding, and so on. The speed with which discretionary fiscal actions influence demand, income, and employment depends largely upon the reaction of the private sector to the impact of fiscal actions. While government spending on goods and services affects directly aggregate demand and the income flow, the impact of tax changes depends pretty much on the reaction of individuals and businesses in regard to changes in their disposable income. And this in turn depends upon the extent of tax changes and the various income groups affected by tax changes. A reduction in income taxes for the low-income groups which generally have a high marginal propensity to consume would probably generate an immediate and substantial increase in demand. On the other hand, when the cut in income taxes favors largely the high-income groups which generally have a relatively low marginal propensity to consume, then most of the increase in disposable income would probably be saved and invested in financial claims. This type of tax cut would affect demand largely through its effect on asset prices (higher asset prices or lower interest rates) and the supply (increase) of spendable funds in the private sector. A substantial cut in corporate income taxes which improves corporate profits would probably induce substantial increase in corporate investments.

The use of discretionary fiscal measures for stabilization purposes, in the light of the foregoing discussion, therefore, does not seem to be as strong as it appears at first glance. It has limitations and weaknesses. But some of these limitations could be removed or alleviated. The reliability of economic forecasting would be improved in the future with the improvement of existing forecasting techniques and the development of new forecasting methods. Advance planning on expenditure programs would help eliminate delays involved in putting proposed programs into operation. The action lag could also substantially be reduced or eliminated by granting the President the authority to change taxes and government expenditures within some definite limits. It would, however, be difficult for the President to secure such an authority. It would appear unlikely that Congress would be willing to give up part of its prerogatives on public expenditures and taxes.[3]

Fiscal Automatic Stabilizers

Discretionary fiscal action is by no means the only channel available to promote stabilization. In our fiscal structure, there exist built-in devices that work automatically to dampen the amplitude of cyclical changes in income and employment. These are commonly referred to as fiscal automatic (or built-in) stabilizers. Our personal income tax system is progressive, that is, personal income taxes increase at a faster rate than personal incomes. Thus in periods of economic prosperity, as personal incomes rise, more and more of the income increases are absorbed by the government through income taxes, which means less and less of the increases in income are available to earners to spend. This tends to moderate increases in private demand. On the other hand, in periods of economic recession, as personal income declines, personal taxes decline at a faster rate. This would help moderate decreases in private disposable income and private demand. On the expenditure side, there are certain items which also act as automatic stabilizers as they automatically increase when the level of economic activity declines and decreases when the level of economic activity rises. Unemployment compensation payments are an example. In periods of depression, as employment declines, unemployment compensation payments rise. This would help hold up disposable income and demand. Conversely, in times of prosperity, payments to the Unemployment Compensation Fund increase, and payments by the Fund decrease as unemployment goes down. In addition to unemployment benefits, there are other federal payments which have the characteristics of automatic stabilizers. These include social security benefits and welfare reliefs.

The operation of fiscal automatic stabilizers tends to generate either a budget surplus or deficit, depending upon the level of economic activity. Given the level of government spending on goods and services, the decline in tax revenue coupled with the increase in aggregate government spending (increases in unemployment-compensation payments and welfare payments) at a low level of economic activity would generate a budget deficit. At a high level of economic activity, the increase in tax revenue coupled with the decrease in total govern-

[3]President Kennedy in 1962 did ask for stand-by authority to reduce individual income tax rates temporarily to avert recession and to initiate up to $2 billion of public work programs when the rate of unemployment rises. This request was, however, denied.

ment spending (decrease in unemployment benefits) would bring about a budget surplus. The budget deficit generated in times of declining income and employment serves as a cushion against severe recession. The budget surplus realized in periods of economic boom, on the other hand, serves as a shield against excessive expansion. But while the operations of fiscal automatic stabilizers moderate the impacts of both economic recession and expansion, they may at times impede efforts to promote economic growth and full employment. Indeed, a fiscal structure may be so restrictive that it can generate a budget surplus at a level of activity substantially below the level consistent with full-employment income and output. The contractionary effects of the budget surplus would render difficult the achievement of full employment. This "drag" effect of automatic stabilizers, however, can be alleviated by discretionary fiscal action (and monetary policy) through raising government spending and reducing taxes.

The Full-Employment Budget Surplus

We have seen that the position of the budget—a surplus or deficit—affects the level of economic activity. But the level of economic activity in turn affects the position of the budget. That is, for a given budget program a budget surplus or deficit may be realized, depending on the level of economic activity. It follows that the actual budget surplus or deficit is an inadequate indicator of the impact of a given budget program on the level of economic activity. A budget program that actually yields a deficit does not necessarily mean that it is an expansionary program. Nor is it restrictive when it actually yields a budget surplus. In the words of Michael E. Levy, "a budget deficit which appears to be very expansionary may, in fact, be merely the end result of a highly restrictive budget structure which depresses both economic activity and government revenue."[4] To analyze and compare alternative budget programs in their impacts on economic activity, therefore, the deficit or surplus of each alternative budget program has to be estimated on the basis of a given level of economic activity. This level of activity is, by convention, the full employment level. The full-employment budget "surplus" is the surplus which would be realized at full employment. Figure 25-2 shows the positions of a given budget structure at various levels of economic activity and the full-employment surplus. The vertical axis represents the surplus or deficit as a percentage of potential GNP, and the horizontal axis, the level of economic activity represented by actual GNP as a percentage of potential GNP. Given the budget structure *A* (that is, given both tax rates and spending programs) the position of the budget moves from a deficit to a surplus as actual GNP approaches potential or full-employment GNP. For instance, when actual GNP is 92 percent of full-employment GNP, the budget structure generates a deficit equal to 1 percent of potential GNP. The budget is

[4] "Supplementary statement by Michael E. Levy," in *The Federal Budget as an Economic Document*, U.S. Congress, Hearings before the Subcommittee on Economic Statistics of the Joint Economic Committee, 88th Cong., 1st Sess., 1963, p. 230.

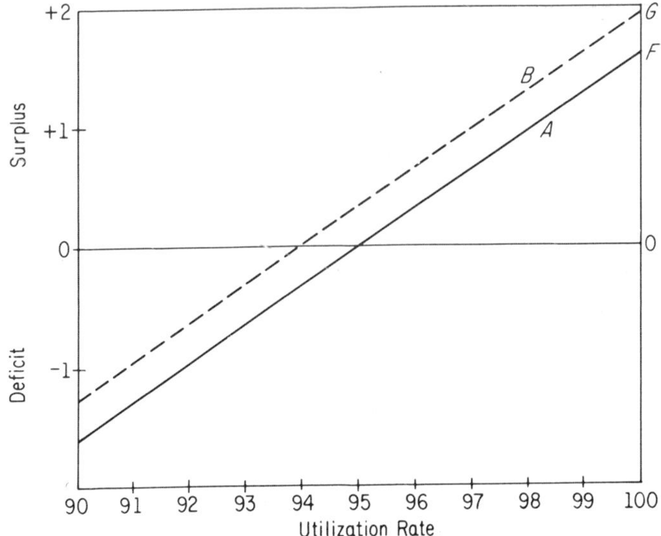

Fig. 25-2. The full-employment budget surplus.

balanced when actual GNP is 95 percent of potential GNP. When the economy is operating at its full-employment potential, the full employment surplus of 1.5 percent (*OF*) of potential GNP is realized. The deficits or surpluses generated by the movement along the line *A* at various levels of economic activity reflect the operation of fiscal automatic stabilizers since as we move along that line, the budget structure is fixed. Discretionary fiscal action—changes in government expenditures and tax rates changes—depending upon the direction of the changes, would cause the budget line to shift either upward or downward. Reducing tax rates and raising government expenditures or both would be reflected by a downward shift in the line, which means that the size of the budget deficit or surplus at each level of economic activity is smaller.[5]

The estimated full-employment budget "surplus" of various budget structures is a measure of their relative expansiveness or restrictiveness. A budget structure with a smaller full-employment budget surplus may be said to be less restrictive than a budget program that yields a greater full-employment surplus. Thus in Fig. 25-2 the budget structure represented by the dotted line *B* is more restrictive than program *A* as it yields a larger full-employment surplus (*OG*). The restrictiveness or expansiveness of a given budget program would have to be considered in the light of private demand, since fiscal policy is after all aimed primarily at supplementing or reducing private demand to promote economic growth and full employment with relatively stable prices. An appropriate budget

[5]It should be noted that since potential GNP grows over time, it would cause the budget line of a fixed budget structure to shift vertically upward. Maintaining a constant full-employment surplus over time thus implies discretionary fiscal actions.

program would yield a full employment surplus (deficit) that would roughly offset the excess (deficiency) of private investment over private savings at full employment ($T - G = I - S$). A budget program may be considered as expansive when it yields a surplus which is small relative to the gap between private investment and private savings at full employment. Total demand then exceeds total supply and the result is inflationary pressure. Price stabilization calls for increases in tax rates, decreases in government expenditures, and restrictive monetary policy to reduce demand. Conversely, a budget program may be considered as restrictive when the estimated full-employment surplus is large relative to the excess of private investment over private savings. The withdrawal of purchasing power by the government from the spending stream through taxes would more than offset the net injection into the spending flow through private investment expenditure. Consequently, economic activity would be depressed. The realized budget surplus would fall short of the full-employment surplus, and actual output, would fall short of the potential level. This reflects the "drag" effect of automatic stabilizers which we have mentioned in the preceding section. Stabilization policy would call for tax cuts, increases in government expenditures, and easy monetary policy to stimulate demand. Inasmuch as private demand changes over time, a budget program which is appropriate in some time period may prove too restrictive or expansive in another period. The adjustments then can be made through discretionary fiscal action and monetary policy.

MONETARY POLICY: EFFECTIVENESS AND LIMITATIONS

Monetary policy is an alternative instrument of stabilization policy. But unlike fiscal policy which directly affects the flow of income and output, monetary policy, as the term implies, affects demand and economic activity largely through its influences on monetary variables.

The Interest Effect

According to the traditional view, monetary policy influences the level of economic activity mainly through its influence on the rate of interest or the cost of credit which in turn is supposed to influence investment spending. Monetary actions taken by the central bank either in the form of open-market operations, changes in required reserves and the discount rate or any combination of these instruments cause interest rates to change. Interest-rate changes influence the willingness of businesses to borrow for investment expenditures. An increase (decrease) in interest rates is supposed to lead to a reduction (increase) in investment spending; businesses are expected to be less willing to borrow for investment due to the higher cost of credit. The effect of monetary policy on demand through the interest or cost of credit channel thus depends mainly on (a) the responsiveness of the demand for money of the public to the rate of interest (the interest elasticity of the demand for money) and (b) the sensitivity of investment demand to the rate of interest (the interest elasticity of investment demand.) The smaller the degree of responsiveness of the demand for money to the rate of interest, and the greater the degree of sensitivity of investment demand to the rate of interest, the greater the effect of monetary changes on investment spending and the level of economic activity. On the other hand, if the demand for money is highly sensitive to the rate of interest, and investment demand, insensitive to the interest rate, then monetary changes would not exert any substantial influence on demand and the level of income and output. This is shown in Fig. 25-3(a) and (b).

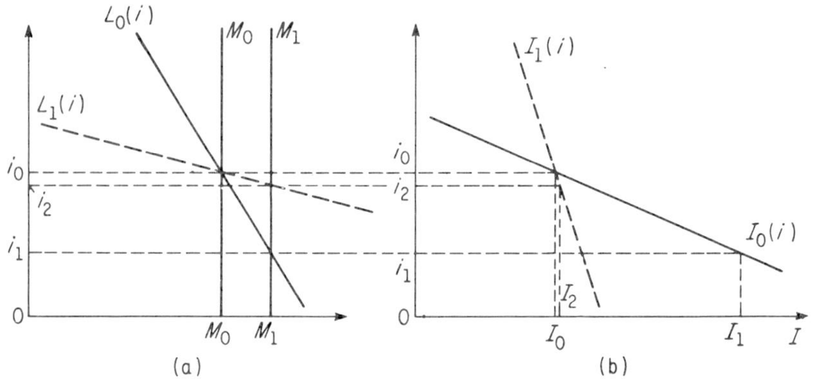

Fig. 25-3. Interest effect of monetary policy.

With the demand-for-money function $L_0(i)$ (relatively insensitive to the rate of interest) and the investment demand function $I_0(i)$ (relatively elastic with respect to the rate of interest), an increase in the supply of money from M_0 to M_1 causes the rate of interest to decline substantially from i_0 to i_1 and investment demand to increase substantially from I_0 to I_1. On the other hand, with the demand-for-money function $L_1(i)$, which is highly interest elastic, and the investment-demand function $I_1(i)$, which is relatively insensitive to the rate of interest, then the change in the supply of money does not cause any significant change in the interest rate (from i_0 to i_2) and investment demand (from I_0 to I_2). For an investment function like $I_1(i)$, the cost of credit serves neither as a stimulus nor a deterrent to borrowing for investment spending.

Empirical evidence on the interest elasticities of the demand-for-money and investment demand, however, has not been very conclusive. As we have mentioned, studies on the relationship between the demand for money and the interest rate have yielded divergent results. Some studies suggest that the demand for money is relatively responsive to interest-rate changes. Other studies show that while the demand for money is highly elastic with respect to income, it is insensitive to the rate of interest. There is also no general agreement on the degree of sensitivity of investment to the interest rate. According to the Radcliffe Report, the cost of credit does not seem to exert any significant influence on decisions of business corporations concerning investment in inventory and plant and equipment.[6] A survey of a thousand largest manufacturing companies in the United States conducted by the National Industrial Conference Board shortly after the decision of the Federal Reserve to raise the rate of discount in late 1965 also suggested that expected increases in the cost of borrowing do not have any significant immediate effects on their decisions on capital authorizations or expenditures.[7] But some recent econometric studies indicate that the cost of borrowing is a significant determinant of manufacturing firms' fixed investment expenditures.[8] Expenditure on new residential construction, an important component of total investment spending, is likewise found by empirical investigation to be significantly related (negatively) to the cost of credit.[9]

In terms of the traditional view on monetary policy, changes in the cost of credit are supposed to affect the level of economic activity only through their influence on investment demand. Consumption spending is assumed to be insensitive to interest-rate changes. This, however, may not be the case. An increase (decrease) in interest costs may deter (encourage) consumers to borrow for consumption expenditures, particularly expenditures on consumer durables. Indeed, a number of studies have shown that the interest cost is a significant determinant of the demand for consumer durables such as automobiles and other durable goods.[10] In addition, an increase in the rate of interest means an increase in the reward for savings. Therefore, people may be induced to reduce current consumption to save more at high interest rates for greater consumption capability in the future.

Taking all these above factors into consideration, we may safely say that changes in interest costs generated by monetary policy would have at least some marginal influence on spending decisions.

The Availability Effect

The availability concept is of recent origin. It was developed following World War II as an answer to the traditional view on monetary policy. According to this concept, the effect of monetary policy on demand and the level of

[6] *Committee on the Working of the Monetary System Report* (London: Her Majesty's Stationery Office, 1963).

[7] Testimony of Martin R. Gainsbrugh, National Industrial Conference Board, in *Recent Federal Reserve Action and Economic Policy Coordination*, Hearings, Joint Economic Committee, 89th Cong., first session, Part 2, 1965.

[8] See, for example, F. deLeeuw, "The Demand for Capital Goods by manufacturers: A Study of Quarterly Time Series," *Econometrica* (July 1962); T. C. Liu, "An Exploratory Quarterly Econometric Model of Effective Demand in the Postwar U.S. Economy," *Econometrica* (July 1963).

[9] See, for example, R. F. Muth, "The Demand for Nonfarm Housing," in A berger (ed.), *The Demand for Durable Goods* (Chicago: University of Chicago Pr

[10] See M. J. Hamburger, "Interest Rates and the Demand for C Goods," *American Economic Review* (December 1967); F. deLeeuw Household Saving and Investment," Progress Report, Board of Reserve System, June 1966.

economic activity is not so much through its influence on the willingness of spenders to borrow as through its influence on the availability of credit—the ability and willingness of lenders to lend. Restrictive monetary measures (open-market sales of securities and higher required reserves) would reduce the volume of reserves available to commercial banks for loan and deposit expansion. Borrowers may be willing to borrow at higher costs, but they may not be able to simply because banks do not have funds available for lending. To obtain funds to meet loan demands, banks may of course sell securities. But the sales of securities by banks coupled with the sales of securities by the central bank would further depress securities prices or raise interest rates. As securities prices decline, banks may become more reluctant to sell, especially when capital losses involved in securities sales are heavy. Consequently they become more restrictive in lending, refusing or reducing loans to new borrowers and tightening credit terms. Depressed securities prices as a result of tight monetary policy thus reduce the willingness of banks to lend by "locking-in" their securities.

The effect of tight money on the willingness of banks to lend because of declining securities prices does not appear to be very significant, however. This is indicated by the fact that during periods of economic expansion and strong credit demand, commercial banks do dispose of government securities for making loans. This "locked-in" aspect of the availability concept rests among other things on the assumption of market imperfections which prevent a rapid transmission of price and yield changes in the government securities market to the market for other financial claims. Consequently, the prices and yields of these securities would not change sufficiently to induce banks to dispose of government securities. On the other hand, if the price and yield changes in the government securities market are rapidly transmitted to other financial claims and cause the prices and yields of these claims to change quickly, then banks would be willing to sell government securities for other securities if changes in the prices and yields of these securities are such that such a conversion proves profitable. It follows that if the transmission of price and yield changes between financial markets does not involve substantial lags, then the lock-in effect, if any, is at most temporary. It will taper off as soon as prices and yields of other earning assets are fully adjusted to changes in prices and yields of government securities.

Money Supply or "Liquidity"?

We have seen that monetary policy affects demand through its influence on the supply of money, and the cost and availability of credit. To a number of onomists the control of the supply of money, however, is not adequate, since believed that it is not the supply of money but the supply of "spendable" which is the primary determinant of total spending. Since commercial esent only one source of supply of spendable funds, monetary control should be extended beyond commercial banks to cover other sources of supply of spending funds as well.

In periods of economic expansion and rising credit demand, for instance, while the credit expansion of commercial banks is subject to the direct control of the Federal Reserve, other nonbank financial institutions such as savings banks, savings and loan associations, and insurance companies can go on expanding credit. Yet they are not directly under the fold of monetary control. To be sure these nonbank intermediaries, unlike commercial banks, do not have the ability to create deposit money, but they can create claims which are for all practical purposes as liquid as money. Savings deposits in mutual savings banks, and savings and loan share accounts in savings and loan associations are practically withdrawable on demand. By offering these liquid claims to holders of idle money balances, these institutions can obtain funds for lending. Their operations tend to increase the liquidity position of the economy, the velocity of monetary circulation, and the expenditure flow. To holders of money balances, there is practically no change in their liquidity positions when money balances are converted into liquid claims on these institutions. The latter, with new cash receipts, are in a position to provide ultimate borrowers with spending funds which otherwise might not be available.

The credit operations of these nonbank financial intermediaries, which grow very rapidly, thus may interfere with effective monetary control. It is then not surprising that a number of economists propose to bring the operations of these institutions under the control of the Federal Reserve. This has been a subject of much discussion. There are economists who believe that although the Federal Reserve does not have a direct control over these institutions, monetary policy does affect them indirectly, and this indirect effect is strong enough to preclude any form of direct monetary control over them. Federal Reserve control operations affect the lending activities of these institutions in several ways. It is true that these institutions rely on savings receipts as the primary source of lending funds but they also borrow from commercial banks for lending purposes, especially when the inflow of savings is not adequate for them to meet strong loan demand. But under the pressure of tight money, banking institutions may not be able to accommodate these intermediaries. The pinch of monetary control which is felt by commercial banks therefore is also felt by nonbank intermediaries. Inasmuch as claims on these institutions are payable in currency practically on demand, they have to hold cash reserves to meet not only required reserves but also cash withdrawals. Thus heavy losses of reserves as a result of currency withdrawals by savings depositors or holders of savings and loan share accounts which take place at times when their cash reserves are at minimum operational levels would force them to cut back loans to maintain their liquidity position. Cash withdrawals may arise from the conversion by holders of savings deposits and share accounts in savings and loan associations to other securities made more attractive by tight monetary policy (lower prices or higher yields), the rates paid by these institutions being somewhat "sticky," as they are subject to maximum legal ceilings. These institutions, of course, may obtain additional lending funds by selling government securities, but they may be less willing to do so because of capital losses. Insurance companies and savings and loan associations may borrow from the Federal Home Loan Banks, but the lending resources of these institutions are limited.

Granted the indirect influences of Federal Reserve's controls on nonbank financial intermediaries, the question is how long would it take for the impacts of monetary controls to be felt by these institutions. If there is no substantial time lag for the impacts of Federal Reserve's policies to be transmitted to nonbank intermediaries, then direct control of the Federal Reserve over the operations of these institutions does not appear to be necessary. On the other hand, if the time lag is considerable, then direct control by the Federal Reserve may have to be extended to cover nonbank financial institutions as well, otherwise figuratively the house may be burned to ashes long before the arrival of the fire department! The lags, if any, involved in the transmission of the effects of monetary controls to nonbank intermediaries, however, remain a subject for empirical investigation.

It should also be noted that another reason why the control of the supply of money alone may be inadequate is the development of new payment techniques. With the widespread use of bank credit cards tending to reduce the use of currency and deposit money, new control devices would have to be developed to cope with these new developments.

MONETARY POLICY VERSUS FISCAL POLICY

Having discussed monetary policy and fiscal policy as instruments of economic policy, we shall now compare these instruments on their virtues and weaknesses, some of which we have already mentioned. Monetary policy, like fiscal policy, faces the problem of timing and forecasting. Forecasting errors would result in mistiming of monetary actions, and this would tend to inflate inflationary pressures or further deflate deflation. Various time lags such as action lags and impact lags are also involved in monetary policy just as in fiscal policy. But in the case of fiscal policy, the action lag appears to be substantially greater than for monetary policy. Changes in tax rates and tax bases and increases in government expenditures require Congressional approval and authorization. And legislative action on these matters is rather time-consuming. It would take months for Congress to act on proposed tax and expenditure changes. The action lag appears to be minimum in the case of monetary policy. Monetary measures such as open-market operations and discount rate changes can be taken rather quickly by the Federal Reserve. It is true that legislative action is required for the Federal Reserve authority to lower the legal reserve ratios below the legally prescribed minimum, or raise them above the legal maximum, but so long as changes in required reserves are within the legal limits it is a matter of complete discretion of the Federal Reserve authority. Monetary policy is much more flexible than fiscal policy, not only in the sense that monetary actions can be taken quickly but also in that they are completely reversible. The Federal Reserve can sell securities in the open market to mop up liquidity of banks. But if the extent of securities sales is such that their restrictive effects on the money market are more than deemed desirable then the Federal Reserve can reverse its action by purchasing securities instead of selling. By the same token, the direction of changes in the rate of discount and legally required reserves can be easily reversed. In regard to fiscal measures such as long-term public work projects, they are hardly reversible, as noted earlier. Once underway, these projects have to be carried to completion; they cannot be turned off halfway. Consequently, projects initiated to mitigate a recession may have to be carried through the expansion for completion and this may contribute to overheating the expansion.

Fiscal policy, on the other hand, is believed to be relatively more powerful than monetary policy in terms of impact on total demand and the level of income and employment. Monetary policy tends to influence demand only indirectly through its effect on bank reserves, the supply of money, and the cost and availability of credit. As the effects of monetary actions on the economy are transmitted through many intermediate stages, the potency of these effects tends to be diffused along the chain of transmission and the final impact diminished. Fiscal policy, in contrast, affects both directly and indirectly total demand and the flow of income. Increases in government expenditures on goods and services add directly to the flow of income and output and decreases in government spending reduce output and the income flow. Tax increases reduce disposable income and private spending, while tax cuts increase disposable income and stimulate private demand. Fiscal policy is thus powerful in either direction—upward as well as downward. It is as powerful in restraining inflationary pressures as in stimulating recovery and economic expansion. The same cannot be said for monetary policy. It is believed by many to be asymmetrical. While it is generally considered as an effective weapon to curb excessive demand and inflation, it is regarded as a relatively weak device to stimulate economic activity. In periods of severe recession or depression, easy monetary policy may result largely in piling up excess reserves in commercial banks if profit prospects are so depressed that business firms in general are not disposed to borrow for investment.[11]

[11]These are primarily the views of "fiscalists." "Monetarists," through empirical investigation, have challenged these views. One study that has recently stirred up interest among professional economists was the study by Leonall C. Anderson and Jerry L. Jordan, "Monetary and Fiscal Actions: A Test of Their Relative Importance in Economic Stabilization," *Review*, Federal Reserve Bank of St. Louis, November 1968. The results of their regression of current changes in gross national product (GNP) on current and lagged changes in the supply of money and in fiscal variables (high-employment budget surplus and high-

Monetary policy and fiscal policy have different influences on the composition of output and the long-run growth potential of an economy. Monetary policy is thought to influence largely the investment component of total spending, hence, capital formation and long-run growth. Whether monetary policy would promote or hinder economic growth depends upon its direction. Easy (tight) monetary policy tends to promote (deter) long-term investment and capital formation. In regard to fiscal policy, its effects on the composition of output depends largely on the types of government expenditures and the kinds of taxes. Government expenditures on capital projects such as highways, dams, research and development, and education promote both visible and "invisible" capital formation and long-run growth. Conversely, if a large proportion of government expenditures consists of noncapital expenditures, then consumption goods are promoted, not investment goods and capital formation. With respect to taxes, changes in personal income taxes would tend to promote (tax cuts) or discourage (tax increases) the production of consumption goods, while changes in corporation income taxes which change corporate profits would tend to stimulate (tax reduction) or deter (tax hike) long-term investment and capital formation. If the objective of economic policy is primarily economic growth, then the optimum mix between monetary policy and fiscal policy at high-level employment would be tight fiscal policy and easy monetary policy. Easy monetary policy would allow the flow of money and credit to rise to meet the monetary and credit requirements of growth, and tight budget policy would release resources for long-term investment and capital formation.

---

employment expenditures and receipts) suggested that the response of economic activity to monetary actions is (a) larger, (b) more predictable, and (c) faster than the response of economic activity to fiscal actions, all in contrast with the results of the Federal Reserve-MIT econometric model (*Federal Reserve Bulletin*, January 1968) that confirmed the fiscalist views. According to the Anderson-Jordan study, a once-and-for-all increase in the supply of money of $1 billion in a given quarter would cause GNP to increase by $1.6 billion in the same quarter, and after 4 quarters, GNP would increase by a total of $6.59 billion, while in terms of the Federal Reserve-MIT model, the same increase in the supply of money would have practically no effect on GNP in the given quarter and the next, and after 4 quarters, GNP would increase by about $400 million. In regard to fiscal actions, the Anderson-Jordan study suggested that "an increase in government expenditures is mildly stimulative in the quarter in which spending is increased and in the following quarter. However, in the subsequent two quarters this increase in expenditures causes offsetting negative influences. The overall effect of a change in expenditures distributed over 4 quarters . . . is relatively small and not statistically significant." This as compared with the results of the Board-MIT model which suggested that an increase in government expenditures in a given quarter would generate a multiplier of about 3.4 after 4 quarters.

The results of the Anderson-Jordan study would have important implications for the conduct of economic stabilization policy–namely, greater reliance on monetary actions than on fiscal actions for stabilization purposes. Some questions, however, have been raised in regard to these statistical results, especially the question of "bias" of the coefficients of the various equations in the study. In addition, if they were good for the sample period under study (1952-1968), they did not appear to stand well for other sample periods. For some comments on this study, see Richard G. Davis, "How Much Does Money Matter? A Look at Some Recent Evidence," *Monthly Review*, Federal Reserve Bank of New York, June 1969.

DEBT MANAGEMENT

The management of the public debt, according to professor Warren Smith, "covers all measures which affect the composition of the publicly held debt."[12] Debt management is one aspect of fiscal policy in the broad sense of the term. It is the Treasury which decides on the types and maturities of government securities to be issued either for refunding maturing securities or financing new budget deficits, thereby affecting the composition of the federal debt. But Federal Reserve operations also influence debt management. The Federal Reserve System, through open-market purchases and sales of securities, influences the size and the composition of federal securities in the hands of the public. Debt management may therefore be said to belong to both fiscal policy and monetary policy.

The Financing of Deficits and the Use of Surpluses

Transfer payments and taxes, purchases and sales of goods by the government—each of these fiscal actions exerts its own influence on the economy, but their influence taken together on the level of economic activity depends on the position of the budget: a budget deficit tends to expand demand and income and a budget surplus reduces demand and the flow of income. But given a budget deficit (surplus), the extent of its expansionary (contractionary) influence on economic activity depends largely on how it is financed (used). A budget deficit financed through borrowing from the Federal Reserve has maximum expansionary effects on the economy, since in this case commercial banks' reserves increase by the amount of the deficit which would permit a multiple expansion of credit and deposit money. If the deficit is financed through borrowing from the public, bank reserves and the supply of money remain unchanged. Funds are transferred from the account of the public to the Treasury's account when securities are purchased, and retransferred to the public when these funds are disposed of by the Treasury. Direct borrowing from the public is thus considered as neutral as the purchases of government securities reduce the availability of spendable funds to private borrowers and spenders. If the deficit is financed through borrowing from commercial banks, bank reserves remain unchanged but the supply of money increases following Treasury's expenditure payments to the public. Borrowing from commercial banks therefore tends to increase total spending, but the extent of the expansionary effect of bank borrowing depends on the reserve position of commercial banks. If their reserve position is tight so that they are forced to reduce credit to the private sector when they purchase government securities, then the reduction of bank loans to private borrowers would tend to cancel to some extent the expansionary effect of bank lending to the government.

[12]Warren L. Smith, "Debt Management in the United States," Study Paper No. 19, in *Study of Employment, Growth, and Price Levels,* Joint Economic Committee of Congress, Washington D.C., 1960, p. 27.

Similarly, the effect of a budget surplus on the economy depends on how it is used. If the surplus is used by the government to retire its debts held by the Federal Reserve, it would exert the most contractionary effect on economic activity. Bank reserves in this case decrease by the amount of the surplus, and this could result in a multiple contraction of bank credit and deposits. If the surplus is used by the government to retire its obligations held by commercial banks, then bank reserves remain unchanged but excess reserves increase as a consequence of decreases in their demand liabilities.

Increases in excess reserves would allow banks to expand loans, and this would partly offset the contractionary influence of the budget surplus. If the surplus is used to retire debts held by the public, then its contractionary influence on the economy, if any, may be limited, since nonbank sellers of securities to the Treasury would probably use the receipts to purchase securities from private borrowers and spenders.

The Volume of Debt

The volume of public debt held by the "public" at the end of 1966 was $216.8 billion, of which $75.6 billion were owned by individuals, $57.1 billion, by commercial banks, $14.3 billion, by mutual savings banks and insurance companies, $14.9 billion by other corporations, and $23.8 billion, by state and local governments.[13] The average maturity of marketable, interest-bearing government securities declined from an average of 8 years and 2 months at the end of 1950 to an average of 4 years and 11 months at the end of 1966. This reflected largely the sharp increase in the issue of securities maturing within one year (from $42.3 billion to $89.1 billion), and within one to five years (from $51.3 billion to $60.9 billion), and the decrease in the issue of securities maturing within 10 to 20 years (from $28.0 billion to $8.4 billion) and 20 years and over ($25.9 billion to $17 billion).

Changes in the size and maturity distribution of the public debt have important influences on the economy. A debt structure dominated by short-term securities adds to the liquidity and spendability of the private sector, and this could exert unhealthy influence on the economy in times of overheated expansion as individuals and institutions holding these liquid assets could easily and quickly dispose of them for funds for lending and spending.

The maturity structure of securities issued either to finance deficits or to refund maturing obligations is governed largely by the specific goals of debt management. If the goal of debt management is economic stability then in periods of excessive demand and inflation, maturing obligations would be refunded with long-term obligations. This would raise long-term interest rates and reduce the liquidity of the private sector and private demand. High interest rates which the government may have to offer to make its obligations competitive

[13]The total public debt at the end of 1966 was $329.8 billion of which $68.8 billion were held by U.S. Government investment accounts, and $44.3 billion were held by the Federal Reserve banks.

with other private long-term securities, of course, constitute a price to pay for economic stabilization. On the other hand, if the objective of debt management is to minimize borrowing cost, then it would have destabilizing influences on the economy, as this would call for the sales of short-term securities in periods of expansion and long-term securities in periods of recession.

Such an effect appears to be the objective of debt management in recent years. But while the Treasury has offered short-term securities in periods of expansion, it has also offered short-term obligations in periods of depressed economic activity in order to avoid competing with the private sector for long-term funds. Such a policy has resulted in the substantial shortening of the maturity structure of the national debt as above mentioned. The shortening of the maturity distribution of the debt stands in the way of effective monetary control. As noted above, in times of inflationary developments, when restrictive monetary measures are taken to reduce the flow of money and credit, holders of these short-term claims can sell them for funds for spending or lending. With a short-term structure of debt, the Treasury has to go to the market at frequent intervals for refunding maturing debts. Consequently, the Federal Reserve is under frequent pressure to assist the Treasury in refinancing its debt by keeping market conditions on an "even keel," thereby refraining from dynamic actions which may be needed to bring about some desirable degree of tightness in the money market. For example, during the period of Treasury's refunding operations, the liquidity position of the banking system may be such that substantial sales of government securities by the Federal Reserve are deemed desirable, but the Federal Reserve may have to refrain from such action as these operations may upset the government securities market and hinder Treasury's financial operations.

POLICY COORDINATION

Monetary policy and fiscal policy are complementary instruments of economic policy. They should therefore be closely coordinated for the achievement of the common goals of economic policy. It would indeed be difficult to achieve these goals if monetary policy and fiscal policy pull in opposite directions. Coordination between monetary policy and fiscal policy, unfortunately, does not always prevail. Sometimes there is conflict between fiscal policy and monetary policy—conflict not in terms of goals of public policy but largely in terms of means and the timing of these means. A case in hand was the decision of the Federal Reserve authority to raise the rate of discount from 4 to 4.5 percent late in 1965 without the advice and against the wishes of the President, which resulted in a series of Congressional hearings on the pros and cons of some degree of "independence" of the Federal Reserve System within the government.

Inadequate coordination between monetary policy and fiscal policy is largely a result of the absence of a coordinating body with powers to coordinate and integrate fiscal policy and monetary policy into an overall plan of action.[14] The administration of fiscal policy is the responsibility of the Executive and the Congress. It is the President who formulates and submits fiscal programs to Congress for Congressional authorizations and appropriations. In regard to monetary policy, the Federal Reserve System is a creation of Congress, and members of the Board of Governors are appointed by the President; yet major monetary policy decisions (open-market operations in principle and other policy decisions in practice) are made by members of the Board jointly with the Presidents of the Federal Reserve banks (the Federal Open Market Committee), officials appointed mainly by people elected by private commercial banks (member banks). Although monetary powers are ultimately in the hands of Congress, monetary decisions are in practice made by the Federal Reserve authority "independently" from both the President and Congress. It is then not surprising that monetary actions at times negate fiscal actions and vice versa.

To promote closer policy coordination, a number of alternatives have been suggested. According to the alternative suggested by the Commission on Money and Credit, members of the Board of Governors of the Federal Reserve would be reduced from 7 to 5. The President would designate the Chairman and vice-Chairman of the Board for four-year terms to coincide with the terms of the Presidency, and the terms of members would be so arranged that the President would be in a position to appoint a new number shortly after coming to office. In this framework, the President would be able to promote closer coordination between monetary policy and fiscal policy, while leaving the Federal Reserve with some measure of "independence." A stronger alternative for policy coordination is to make the Federal Reserve a department of the government with the chairman of the Board to be appointed by the President as a cabinet member serving at his "pleasure."

There are many who object to these alternatives mainly on the ground that they would result in policy decisions being unduly influenced by politics and political pressures of special-interest groups. They propose, instead, either the creation of a commission to be responsible to Congress for policy coordination or granting the Board of Governors of the Federal Reserve the authority to coordinate monetary and fiscal policies. But policy decisions made either by a Commission or by the Board of Governors are not free from political influences and influences of private pressures. In point of fact, policy decisions made by a body not directly elected by the people are more amenable to the influences of private special-interest groups than decisions made by a democratically elected authority.

Since Congress—the ultimate source of economic and monetary powers—is a

[14]Attempts at policy coordination have been made mainly through informal meetings between the Chairman of the Board of Governors of the Federal Reserve, the Secretary of the Treasury, the Director of the Bureau of the Budget, and the Chairman of the Council of Economic Advisors, and their staffs.

lawmaking body and is hardly in a position to coordinate and manage monetary-fiscal programs with all their technical complexities, it would appear that the Presidency with its command over a vast network of government agencies and departments is the proper place for policy coordination. It is the President who formulates and submits to Congress the overall fiscal program, and it is only logical to extend this responsibility to cover monetary policy and the coordination of monetary-fiscal policies. After all, the President (with Congress) ultimately has to answer to the people about the failure of public economic policy. Monetary policy is an integral part of overall economic policy and it should not be allowed to be "independent" to the extent that it could seriously interfere with the performance of the government's economic policy. At any rate, regardless of the formal framework in which the coordination of monetary-fiscal policies is to be effected, there is need for effective coordination which is essential for the achievement of the objectives of stabilization policy.

SUMMARY

Fiscal policy is action of the government regarding the purchases and sales of goods and services, transfer payments and taxes. The purchases of goods inject purchasing power into, and the sales of goods withdraw purchasing power from, the spending stream. Transfer payments increase, and taxes reduce, private disposable income and demand.

The primary rule of early thinking on fiscal policy is the annually balanced budget while "functional finance" is the modern view on fiscal policy. In terms of functional finance, the federal budget is a tool of economic stabilization. To stimulate economic activity in a recession, the government can reduce taxes and increase expenditures. Conversely, to curb inflationary demand the government can raise taxes and reduce expenditures to withdraw steam from an overheated economy.

Fiscal policy influences the level of economic activity through two channels, one automatic, the other discretionary. Discretionary fiscal policy is action of the government in changing tax rates and expenditures programs for stabilization purposes. But the use of discretionary fiscal actions may at times have destabilizing influences, and these perverse effects reflect largely the mistiming of action due to forecasting errors, delay involved in taking action, and the inflexibility of certain spending programs. There are inherent in the fiscal structure, built-in devices (such as progressive personal income taxes and unemployment compensation payments) which work automatically to moderate demand and income changes. As the level of economic activity rises, income taxes rise and transfer payments decline, thereby moderating increases in disposable income and private demand. Conversely, as economic activity declines, transfer payments rise and income taxes decline, thus moderating decreases in disposable income and demand. But with a restrictive budget structure, the operation of built-in stabilizers could hinder the achievement of high rates of economic growth and full employment. This "drag" of automatic stabilizers, however, may be mitigated by expansive discretionary fiscal action and easy monetary policy.

Monetary policy is action of the Federal Reserve authority designed to influence the flow of money and credit and economic activity. Unlike fiscal policy which has both direct and indirect impacts on the flow of income and output, monetary policy affects demand and economic activity only indirectly through its influence on the cost and availability of credit. Tight monetary policy raises the rate of interest or the cost of credit and reduces the availability of "lendable" funds, thereby reducing the willingness of borrowers to borrow and the ability and willingness of lenders to lend. While the effect of monetary policy on demand through each of these separate channels is believed to be marginal but its influence through all these channels taken together is generally regarded to be important particularly in restraining excessive demand and inflation.

Debt management refers to actions of the government that affect the composition of the public debt. Debt is incurred mainly to cover budget deficits. Given a budget deficit, the extent of its expansionary influence depends on the way it is financed. It has the most expansionary effect when it is financed through borrowing from the Federal Reserve. Debt is reduced when a surplus is realized and is used to retire outstanding debts. Given a budget surplus, the extent of its contractionary effect on the economy depends on how it is used. The use of the surplus to retire debt held by the Federal Reserve Banks has maximum contractionary influences. Given the volume of the publicly held debt, changes in its maturity distribution has important effects on the economy. Lengthening the maturity structure of the debt raises long-term interest rates and reduces the liquidity of the private sector. Conversely, shortening the maturity distribution of the debt tends to increase the liquidity and "spendability" of the private sector. A short-term structure of debt tends to weaken the effectiveness of monetary policy, since holders of short-term assets can dispose of them for funds for spending or lending in periods of tight money. In addition, the frequent trips which the Treasury has to go to the market for refunding short-term debts would make it difficult for the monetary authority to take dynamic monetary actions for control purposes as it has to assist the Treasury in its funding operations.

Monetary policy and fiscal policy are complementary instruments of public policy. They should be closely coordinated. But coordination does not always prevail. This reflects mainly the absence of an institution with power to coordinate and integrate monetary-fiscal policies. There is need therefore for a formal framework for policy coordination which is essential for economic stabilization.

PROBLEMS

1. What is "functional finance"? How does it differ from the early view on fiscal policy? What is the theoretical foundation behind the concept of functional finance? Explain.

2. What is discretionary fiscal policy? What are major limitations of discretionary fiscal policy? What are fiscal automatic stabilizers? What concept would you use to differentiate the effects of discretionary fiscal policy and built-in fiscal stabilizers?

3. Explain in some details how you would use fiscal actions in periods of recession and in periods of boom.

4. "The effectiveness of monetary policy depends on the interest elasticity of the demand for money and the interest elasticity of investment demand." Do you agree? Why or why not? What are other channels through which monetary policy affects spending decisions? Explain.

5. Would you be in favor of or against the extension of the control of the Federal Reserve to cover nonbank financial intermediaries? Give your own reasons.

6. In what ways does a short-term structure of the national debt tend to weaken the effectiveness of monetary policy? How would you change the maturity distribution of the national debt for stabilization purposes?

7. Give your own arguments for or against the "independence" of the Federal Reserve. In your opinion, what should be done to promote closer coordination of monetary-fiscal policies?

8. Using T-accounts, show the effects on bank reserves and the supply of money of the Treasury using $1 billion of budget surplus to retire its debts held by (a) the Federal Reserve banks, (b) commercial banks, and (c) the public.

9. Using T-accounts, show the effects on bank reserves and the supply of money of the Treasury covering a $2 billion budget deficit by borrowing from (a) the public, (b) commercial banks, and (c) the Federal Reserve.

chapter **26**

Monetary and Fiscal Policy Since 1951

This period witnessed important developments in economic policy: the return to flexibility of monetary policy, the more positive use of fiscal policy as a tool of economic stabilization, and the introduction of policy innovations to deal with problems which render more delicate the task of stabilization policy: rising prices amid slow rates of growth of output, high unemployment rates, and persistent balance of international payments deficits. We shall divide this period into subperiods and analyze monetary and fiscal policy developments in each subperiod. This period included four recessions and a record expansion which started in the early 1960's.

THE KOREAN BOOM EXPANSION (1951-53)

The recovery from the 1948-49 recession began in early 1950 when the outbreak of the Korean War triggered a new boom which continued until the Spring of 1953. Real GNP during the period increased by 17 percent. The unemployment rate fell from 5.3 to 2.9 percent of the labor force. The expansion was, however, riddled with heavy inflationary pressures particularly during the early months as the public hurried to purchase goods for hoarding in anticipation of shortages. The consumer price index, for instance, increased from 101.8 in June 1950 to 110 in February 1951, and the wholesale price index from 100.2 to 116.5 during the same period (1947-49 = 100). But after early 1951, price increases were halted or slowed down following the imposition of price, wage, and credit controls, and higher taxes.

Monetary Policy

The Accord of 1951 and the Return to Flexibility. To facilitate Treasury financing, the Federal Reserve, during World War II as well as the postwar period, was committed to support government bonds prices by purchasing at face value all bonds offered in the open market in view of maintaining the prevailing interest rate on government bonds at 2½ percent, thereby minimizing the cost of servicing the large national debt.[1] Such a policy clearly rendered

[1] It may be of interest to note that from June 30, 1940—the beginning of the defense program—to the end of 1945 the government raised $228 billion by borrowing. Of this total, $95 billion or 40 percent was derived from selling government securities to commercial banks.

impotent the ability of the Federal Reserve to use existing instruments to combat inflationary pressures unleashed after the war as pent-up demand supported by high levels of income and enormous liquid assets accumulated during the war found its way to the market for both consumer and capital goods. Commercial banks could easily obtain additional reserves for loan and deposit expansion by offering part of their portfolios of intermediate and long-term Treasury bonds to the Federal Reserve, which was committed to purchase them at face value. But if the policy of "pegging" bond prices was an "engine of inflation," it was also a handicap in dealing with recession. As business activity and the demand for credit declined, banks would invest excess reserves in government securities. This would cause government securities prices to rise or yields to decline. To maintain the existing pattern of rates on government securities would call for the sales of government securities. But this would absorb reserves and reduce the supply of money, which was inconsistent with antirecession monetary policy.

Following the difficulty faced by the Federal Reserve in dealing with the 1948-49 recession, it was then considered by the Federal Reserve authority essential to either modify or abandon the policy of maintaining a rigid rate structure to allow for more flexible monetary policy. Support of the departure of the "support policy," however, met with objection from the Treasury. The development of heavy inflationary pressures generated by sharp increases in defense spending following the outbreak of the Korean War in mid-1950 added fuel to the dispute between the Federal Reserve and the Treasury regarding the direction for monetary policy. The Treasury insisted that the Federal Reserve continued the support policy on the grounds that departure from this policy would unduly upset the government securities market, impair confidence in government credit, and make more difficult Treasury financing of rising government expenditures. The Federal Reserve, on the other hand, held that confidence in the credit of the government and the willingness of the public to hold government securities would be maintained by preserving the purchasing power of the dollar; and the Federal Reserve could contribute to promoting price-level stability only through a return to monetary flexibility which would permit more effective control over bank reserves and the supply of money.

The conflict was finally resolved by the Agreement of March 4, 1951, referred to as the Federal Reserve-Treasury Accord, which was aimed at the twofold objective of reducing to a minimum the creation of bank reserves through monetization of the public debt and assuring the successful financing of the government's requirements.[2] On March 8, deciding to let the government securities market stand on its own, the Open Market Committee instructed the Federal Reserve of New York to engage in open-market operations "as may be necessary in the light of current and prospective economic conditions and the general

[2]To this effect, the Federal Reserve agreed to maintain an orderly market for government securities without commitment in respect to par on any issue. The Treasury, to remove long-term restricted issues from the market, decided to issue a new series of long-term, nonmarketable bonds at 2.75 percent interest in exchange for $19 billion worth of 2.5 percent marketable bonds then outstanding.

credit situation of the country, with a view of exercising restraint upon inflationary developments, to maintain orderly conditions in the government securities market, to relating the supply of funds in the market to the needs of commerce and business."[3] . . . The Accord thus marked the end of Federal Reserve "bondage." But the Federal Reserve did not enjoy fully its newly acquired freedom until the early 1960's.

A New Open-Market Policy. Following the Accord, a new open-market policy was gradually developed and was finally adopted by the Federal Open Market Committee toward the end of 1953. The new policy was commonly referred to as the "bills only" policy. It marked a shift from one extreme to another extreme: from intervention in the market as needed to maintain the prices of government securities to fostering free market through minimum market intervention. In terms of this policy, open-market operations were confined to the short end of the market, preferably bills, and such operations were conducted not to impose any particular pattern of prices or yields but solely to achieve the objectives of monetary and credit policy.

The arguments in favor of the policy were that confining open-market operations to the short end of the market would minimize dealer uncertainty about the impact of open-market transactions on prices of longer-term issues, thereby promoting the development of a government securities market with greater "depth, breadth and resiliency," essential to effective uses of open-market operations as an instrument of monetary policy; and that through arbitrage, the effects of operations in the short end of the market would be quickly transmitted to the long end of the market. These arguments, however, were subject to question. If the impact of open-market transactions in the short end of the market were quickly transmitted to the long end of the market, then it would appear that such operations would hardly minimize dealer uncertainty regarding their effects on the prices of longer maturities; and it would not matter whether open-market operations were conducted in the short end, long end or both ends of the market. On the other hand, if, at times there are considerable time lags involved in the transmission of impacts of open-market transactions between the two ends of the market, it may be desirable for the system to operate directly in the long end of the market to exert a direct influence on medium and long-term money rates either to stimulate or deter investment spending as the case may be. At any rate, the policy was abandoned by the Federal Reserve in the early 1960's in the pursuit of two seemingly conflicting objectives: promoting economic expansion and reducing balance-of-payments deficits. To supply the economy with ample credit and keep a downward pressure on long-term money rates to stimulate investment expansion and economic recovery and at the same time avoid a direct downward pressure on short-term rates of interest which would induce short-term capital outflows and aggravate balance of payments

[3]Clay J. Anderson, *A Half Century of Federal Reserve Policy Making, 1914-64* (Federal Reserve Bank of Philadelphia, 1965), p. 109. The discussion in this section is mostly drawn from this source.

deficits, the Federal Reserve was engaged in purchasing securities of longer maturities which were partly offset by the sales of short-term obligations.[4]

Monetary Restraint. The policy of the Federal Reserve during the Korean boom expansion was that of moderate restraint, using both selective as well as general control instruments. Under the authority of the Defense Production Act of 1950, consumer credit control and real estate credit control were imposed to curtail the inflationary expansion of consumer credit and real estate credit. Consumer credit control, however, was relaxed in July, and real estate credit control in September 1951.[5] To prevent excessive stock-market speculation, the Federal Reserve raised the margin requirements on stock exchange securities loans from 50 to 75 percent of market value in January 1951. Reserve requirements against both demand and time deposits were raised to the maximum limits (2 percent increase on demand deposits and 1 percent increase on time deposits) for all classes of banks except for central reserve city banks. The rate of discount which was raised from 1½ to 1¾ percent in late 1950 was again raised to 2 percent in January 1953. But this was largely a defensive action to bring the discount rate into closer alignment with higher money market rates generated by strong credit demands and tight credit markets. Open-market operations during most of the period were used by the Federal Reserve primarily to maintain orderly conditions in the government securities market and assist Treasury refunding operations, as well as to alleviate too restrictive effects on bank reserves caused by higher reserve requirements.

Fiscal Policy

In late 1950, government expenditures rose appreciably following the commitment of the government to a large-scale rearmament program. To mitigate inflationary pressures generated by rising government spending ($75.2 billion in 1953 as compared to $41.4 billion in 1950), the Administration requested higher taxes to keep the mobilization on a "pay-as-you-go" basis. Higher taxes were enacted accordingly by Congress. The Revenue Act of 1950 raised the individual and corporate income tax rates and imposed excess profit taxes. The Act of 1951 again raised individual income tax rates by about 11 percent, and the maximum corporate income tax rates to 52 percent and the excess profit tax base was expanded. Excise tax rates on a number of goods were also increased. With higher taxes, increases in government spending in 1951 did not appear to have added to inflationary pressures. In fact, as a consequence of higher tax rates and rising income, the increase in tax receipts in 1951 were in excess of increases in government expenditures, thereby producing a National Income Account (NIA) budget surplus of some $6.2 billion for calendar 1951. But the failure of

[4] More on this later in this chapter.

[5] The authority to impose consumer credit control was repealed in June 1952. Real estate credit control was suspended by the Federal Reserve in September 1952. This authority expired in April 1953.

Congress to act to provide additional revenues to meet the increases in government expenditures for fiscal 1952 and 1953 resulted in a NIA budget deficit of $1.0 billion and $6.5 billion during these two fiscal years respectively. This certainly was a source of inflationary pressures in the economy.

THE 1953-54 RECESSION

The Korean boom expansion reversed its course in the spring of 1953 as the government began to reduce defense spending, business reduced inventory holdings, and consumer expenditures slowed down. The recession was, however, mild, lasting from July 1953 to August 1954. GNP declined by about 4 percent and unemployment, at its peak, was less than 6 percent of the labor force.

The Federal Reserve which had moderately restrained credit conditions in 1952 and early 1953 acted to ease conditions in credit markets in mid-1953 through open-market operations, but the recession was already under way. Consequently, further easing actions were taken by the Federal Reserve. In July 1953, reserve requirements on demand deposits were reduced by 2 percent at central reserve city banks and 1 percent at reserve city banks and country banks. In mid-1954 reserve requirements on demand deposits were again reduced by 2 percent for central reserve city banks and 1 percent for other classes of banks. Reserve requirements on time deposits were likewise reduced by 1 percent for other classes of banks. The discount rate was reduced from 2 to 1¾ percent in early 1954 and then to 1½ percent in May of the same year.

As a consequence of these actions, credit market conditions were substantially eased. Banks were able to repay their debts to the Federal Reserve banks and improve their reserve positions. Member bank reserves in December, 1954 were $457 million as compared with $252 million in December 1953 and $870 million in December 1952. The greater availability of credit combined with relatively weak credit demands led to substantial decreases in interest rates. The 4-6 month commercial paper rate, for example, went down from 2.52 in 1953 to 1.58 percent in 1954; and the corporate bonds rate (Moody's Aaa) from 3.20 to 2.90 percent. The policy of active ease of the Federal Reserve during this recession undoubtedly played a significant part in its speedy recovery in late 1954.

In regard to fiscal policy, no significant antirecession measures were taken as the Administration viewed the recession of the time as a "minor readjustment" and economic expansion would soon resume its course. The government continued to reduce expenditures hoping to move toward a balanced budget. But as a result of the automatic lapse of excess profit taxes and increases in individual income tax rates (enacted in 1951), the reduction of certain excise taxes in 1954, and declining income and employment, government receipts decreased by a greater amount than the reduction in government spending, thereby producing a NIA budget deficit of some $6 billion for calendar 1954. This could have acted to reinforce easy monetary policy in mitigating the recessionary developments of the period.[6]

THE 1955-57 BOOM

The recovery from the 1953-54 recession which began in late 1954 accelerated and reached a peak in 1955 following record increases in automobile output and sales and expansion of business investment in plant and equipment. In 1956, although the demand for automobiles slacked off largely as a consequence of overbuying in 1955 and housing construction declined as a result of credit constraints and higher interest rates, increases in consumer expenditures for nondurable goods, increases in state and local government spending, and increases in defense expenditures following the Suez Canal crisis, together with increases in exports, maintained economic activity at high levels until mid-1957. The economic gains during this boom were indicated by a 15 percent increase in industrial production, a 25 percent increase in GNP, and the decrease in the unemployment rate from 5.6 percent of the labor force in 1954 to an average of slightly more than 4 percent for the 1955-57 period. The expansion, however, did not fail to generate strong inflationary pressures. The wholesale price index rose from 110 in late 1954 to 118 in late 1957 (1947-49 = 100), and the consumer price index from 130 to 135 for the same period.

To cope with inflationary developments, the Federal Reserve shifted its policy from active ease to active restraint using both open market operations and discount rate changes. For the 1955-57 period the Federal Reserve reduced its holdings of government securities by more than $1 billion. The discount rate was raised at successive stages from 1½ percent to 3½ percent during the same period. Monetary restraint, coupled with the strong demand for credit, caused bank liquidity to decline and interest rates to rise appreciably. Member bank free reserves declined from $457 million in December 1954 to -$245 million in De-

[6] It should be noted that a budget deficit generated by a given decrease in government expenditures and a greater decrease in tax receipts does not necessarily have an expansionary effect on economic activity. Whether it would have this effect or not depends upon the ratio of the decrease in government spending to the decrease in tax receipts (i.e., $\Delta G/\Delta T$) relative to the marginal propensity to consume (i.e., b). When $\Delta G/\Delta T > b$, the deficit reduces income; when $\Delta G/\Delta T < b$, the deficit is expansionary; and when $\Delta G/\Delta T = b$, the deficit is neutral. As an example, assume that the marginal propensity to consume is $b = 0.8$; $\Delta G = -8$, and $\Delta T = -10$. Then the change in income will be

$$\Delta Y = \Delta G\left(\frac{1}{1-b}\right) + \Delta T\left(-\frac{b}{1-b}\right) = -8\,(5) + [-10\,(-4)] = 0$$

since $\Delta G/\Delta T = b = 0.8$. On the other hand, if $\Delta G = -6$ and $\Delta T = -10$, then $\Delta Y = -6\,(5) - 10(-4) = +10$, since $\Delta G/\Delta T < b = 0.8$; the effect of the deficit is expansionary. But if $\Delta G = -9$ and $\Delta T = -10$, then $\Delta Y = -5$ as $\Delta G/\Delta T > b = 0.8$. The deficit reduces income by 5.

cember 1955 and −$133 million in December 1957. The three-month Treasury bill rate, for instance, increased from 0.95 percent in 1954 to 3.267 percent in 1957.

The policy of restraint of the Federal Reserve, while undoubtedly contributing to reducing the inflationary potential at the time, was believed to be insufficient in the light of prevailing inflationary pressures. Monetary restraint was achieved primarily through the uses of general control instruments: open market operations and discount rate changes. Except for the increase in margin requirements on stock exchange securities transactions from 50 to 60 and subsequently to 70 percent in 1955, the public authority failed to enact and impose selective credit controls as suggested by the President in his 1956 Economic Report that "in view of the increasing importance of the consumer durable-goods industries in our economy and their marked tendency to fluctuate, consideration should be given to restoring the government's power to regulate the terms of consumer installment credit." And this was somewhat unfortunate, since a major source of inflationary pressures during the period was the sharp increases in consumer expenditures on consumer durables sustained by the excessive expansion of consumer credit.

In the area of fiscal policy, no positive fiscal measure was taken except for the extension of corporate income tax and excise tax increases (enacted in 1951 and scheduled to expire in early 1955) to sustain increases in federal outlays required by national security. But with the increases in income and economic activity, the increases in tax revenue were more than sufficient to cover federal outlays, thereby leaving a NIA budget surplus of $5.7 billion for calendar 1956 and $2.1 billion for calendar 1957. The contribution of fiscal policy to economic stabilization during this period, just as during the previous period, was thus achieved mainly through stabilizers built in the fiscal structure.

RECESSION, HALF RECOVERY, AND RECESSION, 1957-61

The 1957-58 Recession

The 1955-57 expansion ran out of steam in early 1957. During the first half of the year, economic activity leveled off and then plunged sharply downward in the second half. This was generated largely by the decline in business investment in plant and equipment which was a delayed reaction to the decline in production in early 1956 as a consequence of overbuying of consumer durables in 1955, decreases in defense spending (after the Suez crisis was over) and the decline in exports. The recession lasted from August 1957 to April 1958. It was the shortest recession but also the sharpest. The production of consumer durable goods declined by 28 percent, and total industrial production, by 13 percent. Unemployment jumped from 2.5 million in October to 5.2 million or about 7.2 percent of the labor force in April 1958.

But while economic activity declined, the level of prices continued to rise. The consumer price index increased from 121 in August to 124 in June, and the wholesale price index from 118 to 119 for the same period. This rendered more delicate the operation of monetary control. Actions taken to ease credit conditions to alleviate recessionary pressures on income and employment could cause the level of prices to rise further. But to stabilize prices through monetary restraint would further depress employment and output. This appeared to have accounted for the somewhat belated shift in Federal Reserve policy to credit ease in November with a reduction of the discount rate from 3½ to 3 percent, which was subsequently reduced at successive stages to reach 1¾ percent in mid-1958. Reserve requirements were reduced successively in February, March, and April of 1958, freeing an estimated $1.5 billion of reserves to member banks.

These measures, combined with expansionary open-market operations, led to marked improvement in the liquidity position of banks and a rapid growth in the supply of money. Member banks' free reserves changed from -$293 million in November 1957 to $382 million in August 1958. The supply of money increased at a rate of 8 percent between January and July of 1958. The increase in the supply of loanable funds and the relatively weak demand for credit resulted in substantial decreases in interest rates. The three-month Treasury bill rate, for instance, fell from 3.50 percent in November 1957 to 1.52 in August 1958; the 4-6-month commercial paper, from 4.07 to 1.96 percent, and the yield on corporate bonds (Moody's Aaa), from 4.08 to 3.85 percent. The availability of credit at lower cost played an important part in stimulating greater outlays for consumption, investment, and housing construction—major factors generating the recovery toward the end of 1958.

The 1957-58 recession was regarded by the Eisenhower administration as nothing more than a "mild rolling adjustment" that would soon come to an end and there was no need for strong fiscal intervention. Alarmed by the unemployment of more than 5 million in early 1958, liberal members of Congress demanded tax cuts and proposed spending programs to stimulate economic recovery. But most of these programs were considered by the administration as "pump-priming schemes" which would result in "the wholesale distribution of the people's money in dubious activities under federal direction." With the exception of the repeal of the excise tax on transportation of freights and a small tax relief granted to small business, increases in corporate income taxes, and certain excise taxes acted on in 1951 were extended. The decline in tax receipts as a result of declining income and employment and the increases in government spending, particularly defense spending, following the spectacular missile and space achievements of the USSR in 1958, resulted in a NIA budget deficit of some $10.2 billion for calendar 1958. This served as a cushion against recessionary developments.

Half Recovery, 1958-60

Toward the end of 1958, the recession began to recover. Industrial production took a sharp upward turn following an upsurge in consumption outlays in defense orders, and a rapid advance in residential construction induced by easier and cheaper credit and the relaxation of mortgage terms. Except for a setback in mid-1959 as a consequence of the 112-day steel strike, the expansion of economic activity continued at relatively high levels until early 1960. From the second quarter of 1958 to the first quarter of 1960, GNP increased by more than 16 percent. The consumer price index which remained stable in the first half of 1959 inched upward in the second half. Unemployment declined from the 1958 peak but remained more than 5 percent throughout the period showing that even during the expansion, the economy was operating substantially below its potential.

The Federal Reserve, fearing a repeat of the 1955 experience, moved quickly to tighten monetary conditions at the beginning of the recovery. The rate of discount was raised several times in 1959. By September, the discount rate for all Reserve banks was 4 percent as compared with 1¾ percent in late 1958. To deter excessive stock market speculation, the Federal Reserve raised the margin requirements to 90 percent in October 1958. Open market operations were undertaken largely to moderate the effects on bank reserves and the supply of money of gold outflows generated by the worsening in the U.S. balance-of-payments deficits beginning with 1958 and to correct disorderly market conditions caused by the shift from bonds and notes to stocks by investors in anticipation of inflationary development.

To meet strong customer loan demands, banks had to increase borrowings from the Federal Reserve banks and liquidate part of their investment portfolios. Interest rates, consequently, rose appreciably. The three-month Treasury bill rate increased from 0.83 percent in June 1958 to 4.5 in January 1960, and the yields on corporate bonds (Moody's Aaa), from 3.57 to 4.91 percent.

Fiscal policy did not reinforce the policy of restraint of the Federal Reserve. Except for the extension of corporate income taxes and certain excise taxes and an increase in gas tax to meet rising highway construction costs, no important fiscal measure was taken. The increases in government expenditures for fiscal 1959 ($80.342 billion for 1959 as compared to $71.369 billion for fiscal 1958) and the slight drop in net receipts ($67.915 billion for 1959 versus $68.550 billion for 1958) resulted in an administrative budget deficit of some $12 billion. The Treasury, facing the statutory limit of 4.5 percent on interest rates payable on Treasury bonds of five or more years' maturity, found itself in stiff competition with other borrowers of long-term funds as market yields on other long-term securities were above 4.25 percent. It was then forced to raise money to finance the deficit and to refinance maturing debts through short-term issues and this contributed to the sharp increases in Treasury bill rates. The NIA budget deficits which ran at a rate of $915 billion in the first two quarters of 1958 and about 9.4 billion in the third and fourth quarters was a major force in stimulating the recovery. But the decrease in the size of the budget deficit as income and employment rose in 1958 and 1959 (the NIA budget deficit decreased from $10.2 billion for calendar 1958 to $1.2 billion for calendar 1959)–that is, the decrease in the rate of injection of purchasing power into the spending stream by the government while the economy was still operating substantially below potential–was a major factor contributing to the early end of the recovery as it acted as a brake on recovery forces.

Recession Again, 1960-61

Toward mid-1960, most indications pointed toward the fourth postwar economic recession. Business investment in inventory and in plant and equipment declined. So did consumption expenditures and outlays for residential construction. Tight credit and higher interest rates as a consequence of restrictive monetary policy and the restraining effects of the federal budget which swung from a deficit in 1959 (NIA basis) to a surplus in 1960 ($8.1 billion in the first calendar quarter) were among contractionary forces generating the onset of the recession. The recession "bottomed" out in early 1961 when the economy slowly moved toward recovery under the stimulus of expansionary fiscal and monetary policy. During the recession, GNP declined from an annual rate (seasonally adjusted) of $518.3 billion in the second quarter of 1960 to $509 billion in the first quarter of 1961. Unemployment rose and reached 4.9 million or 6.9 percent of the labor force by December 1960. The sagging state of the economy during the period was undoubtedly a contributing factor to the election of the Kennedy administration which promised to "get the country moving again."

As evidence of a recession became clear in early 1960, the Federal Reserve acted to ease money and credit using open-market operations as well as variable reserve requirements and discount rate changes. To provide banks with reserves for credit and deposit expansion, the Federal Reserve, apart from open-market purchases of securities, authorized member banks to include vault cash as part of legal reserves to meet minimum reserve requirements and reduced reserve requirements in December 1960. These helped ease credit market conditions and improve the reserve position of banks. Member banks' free reserves changed from -$424 million in December 1959 to about $953 million in late January 1960.

No significant antirecession fiscal action was taken. High corporate income taxes and excise taxes continued to be extended. The stabilizing influence of the federal budget on the recession was largely achieved through built-in elements in the tax structure which operated to shift the budget position from a surplus in the first quarter of 1960 ($8.1 billion) to deficits of $6.3, $4.3, $3.3 and $1.3 billion in quarters I, II, III, and IV of 1961, respectively.

In retrospect, the burden of economic stabilization in mid and late 1950's was largely borne by monetary policy. But monetary policy reacted at times too prematurely or too late. The recession of 1957-58 was well under way in mid-1957, yet the Federal Reserve did not move to ease credit conditions until in November. On the other hand, the recovery from the 1957-58 recession had barely started when the Federal Reserve shifted from ease to credit restraint, which was a contributing factor to the early reversal of the economic expansion. Discretionary fiscal policy in general was not used as an instrument of economic stabilization. This appeared to reflect conservative thinking on fiscal policy at the time: annually balanced budget and debt reduction. The contribution of fiscal policy to economic stabilization was achieved primarily through built-in stabilizers. Yet the tax structure was rather restrictive, as it tended to generate budget surpluses at levels of economic activity far short of the potential full-employment level. The restrictive fiscal structure was a factor accounting for high unemployment rates which prevailed even during periods of economic recovery and expansion. Another important factor appeared to be the prevalence of price-level stability objective over full employment and high rates of economic growth. At a time when price increases were partly supply-induced, the attempts of the public authority to control price increases from the demand side would hold up unemployment and down the level of economic activity.

THE RECORD EXPANSION OF THE 1960's

By the end of December 1969 the current economic expansion which began in 1961 entered its 106th consecutive month, the longest expansion in history. The record-breaking boom, however, was not without strains. If from 1961 to 1965, the expansion was achieved with remarkable price-level stability; after 1965 it was riddled with heavy inflationary pressures.

STABLE EXPANSION, 1961-65

The recovery from the 1960-61 recession which began in early 1961 continued uninterrupted under the stimulus of expansionary monetary and fiscal policy. GNP from the first quarter of 1961 to the fourth quarter of 1965 increased from \$503.6 billion to \$704.4 billion, an average annual rate of growth of more than 7 percent. After adjustment for modest price increases, the average annual rate of growth of real GNP over the period was 5.5 percent. This exceeded the growth target established collectively by the member countries of the Organization for Economic Cooperation and Development of 4.1 percent for the 1960-70 decade. The unemployment rate which had been 7 percent in early 1961 declined to 4.1 percent by the end of 1965. Prices remained reasonably stable. While the consumer price index drifted slightly upward from 104.2 in 1961 to 110 in 1965 (1957-59 = 100) the wholesale price index remained practically unchanged, from 100.3 to 102.5 for the same period. Table 26-1 shows some major measures of the expansion.

The major motor generating the expansion was the concerted action of

TABLE 26-1
Measures of Expansion

Measures	1961	1962	1963	1964	1965
GNP (current prices), billions of dollars	520.1	560.3	590.5	631.7	681.0
Consumption expenditures	335.2	355.1	375.0	401.4	431.5
Gross investment	71.7	83.0	87.1	93.0	106.6
Government expenditures	107.6	117.1	122.5	128.9	136.2
Net exports	5.6	5.1	5.9	8.5	7.0
GNP (1958 prices)	497.2	529.8	551.0	580.0	614.4
Total industrial production (1957–59 = 100)	109.7	118.3	124.3	132.3	143.4
Wholesale prices (all commodities, 1957–59 = 100)	100.3	100.6	100.3	100.5	102.5
Consumer prices (all items, 1957–59 = 100)	104.2	105.4	106.7	108.1	109.9
Unemployment (all workers)	6.7	5.6	5.7	5.2	4.1*
Money supply (billions of dollars)†	145.5	147.5	153.1	159.7	167.2
Bank loans and investments, (billions of dollars)	209.6	227.9	246.2	267.2	294.4
Treasury bills rate (3-month)	2.378	2.778	3.157	3.549	3.954
Corporate bonds rates (Moody's Aaa)	4.35	4.33	4.26	4.40	4.49

Source: Economic Report of the President, 1967.
*Fourth quarter.
†December; sum of currency and adjusted demand deposits.

monetary and fiscal policy committed to (a) the achievement of full employment and sustained prosperity without inflation, (b) the acceleration of economic growth, and (c) the restoration of balance of payments equilibrium.

Fiscal Policy

Recovery from the 1960-61 recession was to be speeded up by a number of measures taken under the Kennedy administration in 1961-62 to increase aggregate demand by increasing in government spending and promoting private demand. These included increases in social security benefits, extension of unemployment compensation payments, increases in federal outlays to states and localities for area redevelopment, urban renewal, and public assistance. Increases in defense outlays for defense and space exploration, though motivated by considerations other than economic stabilization, also helped increase total demand. To promote private investment spending, which had been sluggish since 1957, the President in April 1961 proposed an investment tax credit as an incentive for the modernization and expansion of private plant and equipment. It was enacted in October 1962. The Act provided for a credit against income tax liabilities of as much as 7 percent of outlays for new investment in machinery and equipment. More liberal guidelines for determining depreciation schedules for tax purposes were issued by the Treasury in July 1962, resulting in increases in the rate at which business firms can write off plant and equipment, thereby reducing corporate profits tax liabilities. These and other measures played a part in the advance in economic activity in 1961 and 1962. Industrial production increased by 13 percent between February and December 1961, and GNP rose from an annual rate of $503.6 billion in the first quarter to $542 billion in the fourth quarter. For 1962, GNP rose by 7 percent to $556 billion, and industrial production by 8 percent.

But despite these substantial gains in income and production, unemployment remained relatively high–6.1 percent at the end of 1961 and 5.6 percent in December 1962. The lagging performance of the economy, according to the Council of Economic Advisors (CEA) and other administration economists, was traceable to the restraining effects of the federal tax structure on the economy. It tends to come into balance at excessively high rates of unemployment, and to produce too large a surplus even at moderately full employment; under the prevailing tax structure, tax receipts tend to grow more rapidly than GNP, thereby acting as a "brake" on the nation's rate of economic growth.

President Kennedy in his January budget message made it clear that ". . . unless we release the tax brake which is holding back our economy, it is likely to continue to operate below its potential, federal receipts are likely to remain disappointingly low, and budget deficits are likely to persist." The President accordingly asked for a permanent cut in both individual and corporate income tax rates as a means to promote private demand and attain full employment. This met with opposition in Congress as tax cuts coupled with projected higher expenditures would result in greater deficits in the federal budget. But under the Johnson Administration, a revenue act which contained essentially the tax legislation proposed by President Kennedy was enacted by Congress early in 1964, providing for reductions in individual and corporate income taxes. Individual tax liabilities were cut in two stages, one in 1964 and the other in 1965. Rate reductions and reforms combined were expected to cut tax liabilities an average of 19.4 percent in 1965. Corporate income taxes were also reduced in two stages in 1964 and 1965, and the cuts represented a 7.7 percent reduction when fully effective. The passage of the Revenue Act of 1964 showed the rally of Congress to the concept of using fiscal policy as a tool to promote economic growth and full employment, since the budget remained in deficit of more than $5 billion, although President Johnson in his budget message had announced some cutback in federal spending.

Subsequent economic changes were considered by many to be the anticipated effects of the tax cuts. In 1964, business fixed investment rose by 9 percent, and consumption outlays by 8.5 percent. GNP rose by nearly $40 billion as compared with a gain of about $29 billion in 1963. Unemployment declined to 5 percent of the labor force but this was still short of the 4 percent target. As the second stage of the tax cut of the Revenue Act of 1964 was considered to be insufficient to assure sustained reduction in unemployment, a general revision of excise taxes was proposed early in 1965 to give additional stimulus to private demand. In July 1965 Congress passed the Excise Tax Reduction Act providing for the repeal of excise taxes on such consumer durables as radios, television sets, and appliances, and reductions in rates on automobiles, telephones, and other communication services. The cuts would total \$4.7 billion between 1965 and 1969. In the first stage, effective June 1965, the cut would amount to about \$1.8 billion; the second stage, of \$1.6 billion, was to be effective in July 1966.

The economy appeared to have responded to the excise tax cuts and income tax cuts, moving close to its full employment potential as reflected by the increase in GNP of almost \$50 billion in 1965 and the drop in the unemployment rate of 4.1 percent toward the end of the year.

Monetary Policy

Unlike in previous periods in which it changed its policy from ease to restraint as economic activity swung from recession to recovery, the Federal Reserve continued to maintain a policy of credit ease (until late 1965) to provide for the growth in money and credit needed to promote economic growth and high level employment.

Federal Reserve policy, however, was constrained by a serious balance-of-payments situation. The persistent international payments deficits which deteriorated after 1958 threatened to undermine the value of the dollar in international markets and the confidence of foreigners in the dollar as an international currency. Policy measures to encourage bank credit and monetary expansion which would exert downward pressure on short-term interest rates would aggravate balance of payments deficits because of short-term capital outflows attracted by higher interest rates abroad. The conversion of part of the newly acquired dollar reserves by foreign monetary authorities into gold would reduce U.S. gold reserves.

To support domestic expansion without stimulating outflows of short-term funds, the Federal Reserve (and the Treasury) introduced a new open market technique—referred to as operation "twist," aimed at raising short-term interest rates to discourage short-term capital outflows while keeping long-term interest rates down to stimulate private investment expenditures. The operation consisted of purchasing securities with maturities of over one year (particularly in the 3 to 6 years range) which were partly offset by the sales of short-term securities. The operation was initiated in February 1961 when the Open Market Committee gave the Manager of the Open Market Account authority to buy up to \$500 million of government securities with maturities up to 10 years and to sell short-term maturities. This marked the end of the "bills only" policy which had been adopted since the early 1950's and the return to full flexibility of open market operations.

Federal Reserve purchases of securities provided banks with steady increases of reserves. The reduction of reserve requirements against savings and time deposits in late 1962 likewise helped increase banks' loanable funds. All this enabled a steady growth of bank credit and the supply of money; the latter increased by some $20 billion from December 1962 to December 1965.

Furthermore, to enable domestic banks to compete effectively not only with foreign banks but also with domestic nonbank financial institutions for savings funds, the Federal Reserve raised the maximum interest rates payable by member banks on savings and time deposits successively in January 1962, July 1963, and again in December 1965. This served the double purpose of moderating the pressure on the balance of payments and channelling private savings and business liquidity into savings and time deposits. Since a large part of these funds would flow to long-term loans and investments, it would reinforce "operation twist" in maintaining downward pressures on long-term rates of interest.

The effect of the operations of the Federal Reserve on the structure of rates can be seen by the stability of long-term interest rates as short-term rates rose, as indicated in Table 26-1. The long-term rates of interest were well protected despite measures used to raise the short-term money rates for balance-of-payments purposes; these included, in addition to the sales of short-term securities, the increase in the rate of discount from 3 to 3½ percent mid-1963, and to 4 percent in September 1964 to counter the effect on short-term capital flows following the rise in the official and market rates in London. But the effect of the policy on short-term capital movements was not clear. The policy assumed that short-term capital flows were interest-elastic, but the degree of interest-sensitivity of short-term capital flows is difficult to estimate.

INFLATIONARY EXPANSION, 1966-19____

The beginning of 1966 marked the end of five years of economic prosperity without significant inflation and the beginning of a period of expansion laden with heavy inflationary pressures. Consumer prices increased at an average annual rate of 3.3 percent in 1966, 3 percent in 1967, more than 4 percent in 1968, and more than 5 percent in the first three quarters of 1969 as compared with an average annual rate of increase of about 1.4 percent during the 1961-65 period. The upsurge of inflationary pressures was generated by sharp increases in defense spending following the escalation of the Vietnam War, coupled with continued strong consumer spending, business outlays for plant and equipment, and expenditures of state and local governments at a time when the economy was approaching its full employment potential.

Defense spending which remained at approximately $50 billion during the 1963-65 period increased to $60.6 billion in 1966, and $72.4 billion in 1967. Defense outlays, though slowing down in 1968, still reached an annual rate of $79 billion in the second quarter. GNP for 1966 increased by almost $63 billion or 9 percent over 1965. This, however, was accounted for partly by the large increase in prices. The increase in real GNP in 1966 was only 5.4 percent as compared with 5.9 percent in 1965. In 1967, because of major strikes in the auto and copper industries and some slowdown in consumer spending in the first half of the year, GNP increased by only $42 billion or 5.5 percent over 1966. But the real rate of growth was only 2.5 percent, the smallest gain since the early 1960's. Unemployment which was 4.1 percent of the labor force in December 1965, fell to 3.7 percent in December 1966, remained at 3.7 percent in December 1967 and dropped to 3.3 percent in late 1968 and early 1969 substantially below the target of 4 percent set by the CEA.

Unlike the preceding period in which fiscal policy assumed the major share of stimulating economic expansion, during this period, it was monetary policy which assumed the major burden of restraining inflationary pressures.

Monetary Policy

Toward the end of 1965, as consumer prices began to inch upward under the influence of rapidly rising demand, the Federal Reserve shifted its policy to restraint. If in the preceding period the Federal Reserve was constrained in its effort to promote economic expansion because of balance-of-payments considerations, it was no longer hampered by such constraint after 1965 as its policy was aimed at combating inflation and reducing balance of payments deficits, two perfectly compatible objectives. The shift of Federal Reserve policy was signaled by the increase in the rate of discount from 4 to 4½ percent in December 1965 (a move which did raise objection from the President and stir up debates in Congress regarding the "independence" of the Federal Reserve, but in retrospect did not seem to be untimely).

As the Federal Reserve reduced the rate at which it supplied banks with reserves, banks, to meet the strong credit demand of well-established customers, had to increase borrowings from the Reserve Banks, reduce investment in securities, and raise interest rates paid on time deposits to obtain additional loanable funds. Banks were able to increase their business loans by 20 percent in the first half of 1966 as compared with the 18 percent increase in 1965. Yet funds needed by business firms both to meet accelerated tax payments and new capital outlays were far from being satisfied. Consequently they had to raise additional external funds by issuing large amounts of new securities. This, combined with new issues of securities of various federal agencies, caused interest rates to rise sharply. The advances of interest rates on both short- and long-term market instruments which induced increases in the direct flow of household and corporate savings to securities markets put heavy pressures on nonbank financial institutions, particularly such savings institutions as mutual savings banks and savings and loan associations. If commercial banks were able to hold their own and attract funds from individual and other investors by raising interest rates on certificates of time deposits (CD's) through the expanded use of savings certificates and other types of nonnegotiable CD's, these savings institutions were not able to prevent withdrawals of funds by interest-sensitive "depositors" for investment in higher-yielding securities and banks' CD's. With greatly reduced inflows of funds, these institutions had to reduce mortgage lending sharply in 1966. Net acquisition of residential mortgages decreased by 25 percent in the first two quarters of 1966 despite significant government aid through the purchases of almost $4.5 billion of mortgages by the Federal National Mortgage Association and funds provided by the Federal Home Loan Banks to savings and loan associations to offset deposit losses.

To alleviate inflationary pressures generated by rapid expansion of business loans and at the same time the differential impact of tight credit conditions on nonbank financial institutions—hence the mortgage markets—the Federal Reserve toward the second half of 1966 raised the reserve requirements against time deposits in excess of $5 million from 4 to 5 percent in mid-July, and then to 6 percent in mid-August. The maximum rate of interest payable on multiple-maturity time deposits was lowered to 5 percent (from 5½ percent) on deposits maturing in 90 days or more and to 4 percent on deposits maturing in less than 90 days. In late September, the maximum rate payable on time deposits of single maturity of less than $100,000 was reduced from 5½ to 5 percent. These rates, together with parallel rates established for mutual savings banks by the FDIC and for savings and loan associations by the Federal Home Loan Bank Board, helped forestall excessive interest rate competition among financial institutions.

Banks, facing more restrictive monetary policy, had to rely more heavily on borrowings from the Reserve Banks and reduce government securities holdings to meet strong loan demands. The pressure of strong credit demands in tight credit markets pushed interest rates up to record levels. The three-month Treasury Bill rate, for example, reached a peak of 5.59 percent in late September. Banks' negotiable CD's with interest rates limited to the maximum ceiling of 5½ percent were no longer competitive with other short-term money market instruments. Banks consequently were unable to roll over all maturing negotiable CD's after mid-August and found their outstanding CD's reduced by $2.7 billion from mid-August to the end of October. They therefore further restricted their lending policies.

Toward the end of 1966 the investment boom and consumer spending tapered off under the influence of tight credit and higher interest rates. The Federal Reserve then moved to ease money-market conditions somewhat. Member banks' reserves increased and interest rates declined. As the slow pace of economic expansion continued in early 1967 with the sluggish pace of business and consumer spending, the Federal Reserve shifted its policy to greater ease. In March the legal reserve ratio against regular savings deposits (and time deposits under $5 million) was lowered from 4 to 3 percent. In April, the rate of discount was reduced from 4.5 to 4 percent. These actions helped ease further money market conditions. Member banks' free reserves increased appreciably from −$165 million in December 1966 to $298 million in August 1967. The three-month Treasury Bill rate dropped from 4.96 percent in December 1966 to 3.53 percent in June.

Toward the end of the summer there was indication, however, that the economy was again overheated. The rapid increases in government spending to meet the rising requirements of the war in Vietnam while tax receipts slowed down threatened to generate a budget deficit of some $20 billion. Private borrowers, anticipating heavy borrowings by the government and tighter credit conditions, borrowed heavily to cover their expected credit needs. This drove the interest rates up to levels which prevailed early in the year while monetary policy remained relatively easy except for the increase in the discount rate from 4 to 4½ percent which was a reaction to the devaluation of the British pound in late 1967. With renewed inflationary pressures in the first half of 1968 sustained by rapid increases in both public and private spending coupled with the deterioration in the U.S. balance of trade, the Federal Reserve moved toward monetary restraint. The legal reserve was raised from 16½ to 17 percent for reserve city banks and from 12 to 12½ percent for country banks in January. The rate of discount was raised from 4½ to 5 percent in March and then to 5½ percent in April, largely a reaction to the dollar crisis and the consequent loss of gold reserves. The continued strong demand for credit combined with tight credit markets caused interest rates to rise sharply. The three-month Treasury Bill rate, for example, rose from 4.96 percent to a record level of 5.65 percent between December 1967 and May 1968, and the corporate bonds rate, from 5.51 percent in 1967 to 6.28 percent in June 1968.

The advance of market interest rates acted to limit the growth of commercial bank time deposits as the maximum rate payable on time deposits was limited to 5½ percent. Corporate and household savings, instead of going to bank CD's, were invested in other higher-yield market instruments. Consequently, the maximum rate payable on single-maturity time deposits of $100,000 or more was raised by the Federal Reserve to 6¼ percent in mid-April 1968. Banks accordingly raised the rates paid on time deposits. But the volume of CD's did not increase significantly. To meet customers' loan demands, banks then had to continue reducing their holdings of government securities, borrowing from the Federal Reserve Banks and from other sources. Member bank borrowings, for instance, increased from $237 million in January to $746 million in May. Following the enactment of fiscal-restraint legislation in June, the Federal Reserve was able to ease slightly monetary conditions. Interest rates on all maturities declined afterward. The three-month Treasury Bill rate dropped to 5.08 percent and the corporate bonds rate to 6.02 percent in August. The Federal Reserve's rate of discount was accordingly adjusted downward from 5½ to 5¼ percent.

Inflationary pressures, in the meantime, continued unabated. Consumer prices, as we have mentioned, increased at an average annual rate of more than a percent in the second half of 1968 and more than 5 percent during the first three quarters of 1969. The Federal Reserve again tightened the money screw. The rate of discount was raised to 5 ½ percent in December 1968, and to 6 percent in April 1969. The reserve requirements were raised to 17 1/2 percent for reserve city banks and 13 percent for country banks. These measures caused bank liquidity to decline and interest rates to rise sharply. Member banks' free reserves decreased from −$132 million in September 1968 to −$1,074 million in July 1969. The market yield on three-month Treasury bills increased from 5.94 percent in December 1968 to 7.08 percent in September 1969. The federal funds rate increased from 6.02 percent to 9.15 percent, and the corporate bonds rate (Aaa), from 6.45 percent to 7.14 percent for the same period. Toward the end of 1969 restrictive actions appeared to have led to some decrease in industrial production and some slow down in consumer spending, although business spending on plant and equipment remained strong. Prices, however, continued to rise. Then what would be the direction of monetary policy in this situation? To slow down the rate of increase in the level of prices would call for continued monetary restraints but this course of action would probably cause the onset of a recession. On the other hand, to ease the money brake to avert a recession would probably cause the level of prices to rise even at a faster rate. There were differences of opinions among economists in this regard. Some favored the latter course of action, while others, the former, even at the greater risk of a recession.

Fiscal Policy

The reformed tax structure appropriate under conditions that prevailed during the 1961-65 period was no longer so under the new economic environment. Continued increases in defense spending combined with the existing tax structures would tend to generate a "full employment" surplus which was more than offset by excess of private spending. This resulted in inflationary pressures. It follows that tax increases or cuts in government expenditures, or both, would be necessary to assist monetary policy in restraining excessive demand and inflation. To this effect a number of measures were taken. These included the acceleration of corporate payments to make collection of taxes on profits closer to a pay-as-you-earn basis and to provide for faster depositing of taxes withheld by businesses. (It was this acceleration of tax payments which was partly responsible for the strong corporate borrowings in 1966.) A graduated withholding tax was introduced to speed up still further collections of withheld personal income taxes. But these measures simply shifted the timing of cash payments of taxes rather than increasing their magnitude. In an effort to slow down the pace of business investment and at the same time permit some degree of ease in monetary policy and hence some relief in credit and housing markets, Congress in late 1966 acted to suspend for 15 months the investment tax credit, along with accelerated depreciation options as they applied to buildings. At the same time, moderate cuts in federal spending were made.

With the pace of economic expansion slowed down in early 1967, Congress acted on the recommendation of the administration to restore the 7 percent investment tax credit to stimulate the economy. A 6 percent surcharge on both corporate and individual income taxes proposed by the President in the Union message in January to help cover the rising cost of the war in Vietnam was not pursued with vigor until August because of the sluggish performance of the economy in the first half of the year. But with renewed inflationary pressures in the summer, the administration reiterated its request for the enactment of the surtax of 10 percent (instead of 6 percent as intitially proposed). This met with strong congressional opposition mainly on the ground that the appropriate way of easing inflationary pressures was not increasing taxes but reducing government expenditures. Action on the surtax was consequently deadlocked. But continued inflationary strains in early 1968, the deterioration in the U.S. balance of trade, the dollar crisis and the heavy loss of gold following the uncertainty generated by the devaluation of the pound sterling in late 1967, and heavy pressures in financial markets exerted by monetary restraint finally led the administration and the Congress to a compromise fiscal package involving both tax increases and spending cuts: the Revenue and Expenditure Act of 1968. The enactment of the Act in June provided for a temporary 10 percent surcharge on personal and corporate income taxes (the former retroactive to April 1, and the latter, to January 1) and a reduction of $6 billion in planned federal outlays. The measure was expected to reduce private spending and inflationary pressures, improve foreign confidence in the dollar, and allow some measure of ease of monetary policy. The measure appears to have helped boost foreign confidence in the dollar as the action was interpreted in foreign quarters as a positive action by the U.S. Government to restore its financial conditions and help improve the balance of payments position. But it does not appear to have had any significant restrictive effects on private spending as expected.

Fiscal restraint continued under the Republican Administration with the extension of the surtax, the trimming of the federal budget (by $7.5 billion), and reductions in government construction. A tax reform bill (pending in Congress in late December 1969) that was intended at the start to increase the tax shares of the rich also provided for tax reliefs (an increase in the exemption per dependent from $600 to $750) and a 15 percent increase in social security benefits. To mitigate the inflationary potential of such reliefs, however, they were made effective only gradually over a number of stages.

Now, in the face of rising prices and money incomes, would the monetary and fiscal authority continue restrictive actions to slow down price increases and at the same time run the greater risk of a recession? If not, then would some form of wage and price guideline or control be called for? A good number of economists and legislators appeared to be in favor of some control over wages and prices. But in late 1969 there was no indication that the Administration would resort to such measures.

Wage-Price Guidepost Policy

The introduction of guideposts for private wage and price decisions was an important policy innovation which merits a brief mention. The use of the guidepost policy was in recognition of the public interest in the content and consequences of certain private wage and price decisions which affect the progress of the whole economy as they involve large numbers of workers and large amounts of output, and have pattern-setting implications. The awareness of the public of the significance of major wage and price decisions, and of their compatibility with the national interest, would create an atmosphere in which private parties to such decisions would act with greater responsibility. The establishment of guideposts provides aids to public understanding as to whether a particular price or wage decision may be inflationary. The benchmark of the guideposts suggested by the CEA in the 1962 annual report for noninflationary price and wage behavior was the rate of increase of productivity. In the words of the CEA: "The general guide for noninflationary wage behavior is that the rate of increase in wage rates (including fringe benefits) in each industry be equal to the trend rate of overall productivity increase. General acceptance of this guide would maintain stability of labor cost per unit of output for the economy as a whole—though not, of course, for individual industries.

"The general guide for noninflationary price behavior calls for price reductions if the industry's rate of productivity increase exceeds the overall rate—for this would mean declining unit labor costs; it calls for an appropriate increase in price if the opposite relationship prevails; and it calls for stable prices if the two rates of productivity increase are equal."[7]

In the 1962 report as well as that of 1963, no figure for trend rate of productivity increase was specified by the CEA as gauge for noninflationary price and wage behavior. This appeared to reflect, among other things, the cautious approach of the Council in regard to the numerous conceptual difficulties involved in making an appropriate choice of a productivity measure, and the state of the economy which was operating substantially below its full employment potential. As the economy moved toward full employment which would give greater room to inflationary price and wage decisions, the CEA in the 1964 report gave indication that wage movements should be governed by a 3.2 percent trend of productivity increase. This was repeated in the 1965 report and specifically recommended in the 1966 report.

The guidepost policy appeared to have achieved some degree of success, at least until early in 1966, considering the attempts of labor and management, on numerous occasions, to justify their positions by referring to the guideposts, and union settlements which were at or close to the guideposts, including the key steel settlement in September 1965 and the rollback in aluminum prices in late 1965, although some of these were achieved largely because of government pressures and direct intervention. The policy however failed to survive the real test which came in 1966 when the economic atmosphere was conducive to either excessive wage demands or sharply increased prices. In manufacturing, mining,

[7]*Economic Report of the President*, 1962, p. 189.

construction, and transportation where strong labor unions are concentrated, wage settlements were far in excess of the permissible boundaries set by the guideposts. These included the wage increases of employees of the New York Transit Authority, and the five airlines involved in the July-August strike.

The CEA recognized in the 1967 report that "the recent rise in living costs makes it unlikely that collective bargaining settlements in 1967 will fully conform to the trend increase of productivity." The average wage increase in 1967 was 5.5 percent, indeed in excess of the trend increase of productivity of 3.6 of the first half of the 1960's, not to speak of the 3.2 percent figure which had been specified by the Council. In the light of continued increases in wages and prices, the Council, in the 1968 report, instead of specifying some higher standards for wage increases, set out a pattern of wage and price decisions required in 1968 to turn the trend of prices back toward stability. According to the Council, a decline in the rate of price increases could be achieved only if union wage increases were "appreciably lower than the 1967 average of 5.5 percent." At the same time, it was "patently unrealistic" to accept wage increases that would be wiped out in real terms by the 3 percent increase in 1967 consumer prices. Whether a return to specific price-wage guideposts would be attempted by the Republican Administration remains to be seen.

The existence of guideposts for private wage and price decisions and the pressure exerted by the CEA and the administration through persuasion and denunciation may well have had significant restraining influences on wage and price increases in recent years which could have otherwise been much more inflationary. The consultation of the Board Chairman of GMC with the CEA regarding the average increase in the price of its 1969 automobiles, which was subsequently declared to be reasonable, was a case in point.

CONCLUDING REMARKS

A number of observations can be drawn on the basis of policy performance of the past decade or so. The remarkably stable expansion during the 1961-65 period was a testimony to the positive use of fiscal and monetary policy as an instrument to promote economic expansion and growth. But could these policies which seemingly worked so successfully in promoting economic expansion be tailored to meet the challenge of inflation and excessive demand? The experience of the last few years suggested that it is more difficult, as expressed by Gardner Ackley, former Chairman of the Council of Economic Advisors: "It is easy to prescribe expansionary policies in periods of slack" but "managing high-level prosperity is a vastly more difficult business." And the difficulty appears to lie partly in the limited flexibility of the fiscal tools under existing institutional arrangements, apart from the problem of "lags" and irreversibility inherent in fiscal actions. The flexibility of fiscal policy certainly could be improved substantially by Congress through granting limited stand-by authority to the President to change taxes and expenditures within specified limits, just as the Federal Reserve is given authority to vary the legal reserve ratio within legally prescribed limits. The Congress can retain its prerogative on taxes and spending by reserving congressional veto. Armed with such stand-by authority, the President may change taxes promptly to counteract either inflationary or recessionary developments. Current inflationary pressures indeed could have been less heavy had the surtax been acted on promptly in the second half of 1967. By the time the surtax was enacted in mid-1968, the pressure of demand had reached such a level that the surtax was not strong enough to reduce to any substantial degree the steam of demand.

Monetary policy, although constrained by balance-of-payments considerations in the early 1960's, certainly had contributed its share in promoting economic expansion. The introduction of such a policy innovation as "operation twist" showed that objectives which are seemingly mutually inconsistent may be reconciled through the development and use of new policy techniques.

Since in large segments of the economy, business firms and labor unions may have considerable discretion on price and wage decisions, rising prices may exist side by side with high unemployment rates and low levels of resources utilization. The control of inflation through demand restriction in a "cost-push" environment could be achieved only at the high cost of frequent recessions, chronic unemployment, and idle capacity. Setting guideposts for noninflationary price and wage behavior appeared to have had some restraining influence on wage and price increases but it was not generally observed, particularly after 1965 when excess demand and tight labor market conditions prevailed. When pressure, persuasion, and appeal for voluntary cooperation from strong labor unions and oligopolistic firms to restrain price and wage increases fail, then price and wage controls in key industries having pattern-setting implications may be called for if full-employment growth were to be sustained with reasonably stable prices.

PROBLEMS

1. Discuss the circumstances which led to the Federal Reserve-Treasury Accord of March 1951.

2. What is the "bills only" policy? What are the arguments for and against the bills-only policy? What are the circumstances which led to its abandonment in 1961?

3. Was discretionary fiscal policy used as a tool of stabilization under the Eisenhower administration? If not, why?

4. Appraise the performance of monetary policy during the 1955-57 expansion, the 1957-58 recession, and the 1958-60 recovery.

5. Evaluate the performance of fiscal policy during the 1961-68 expansion.

6. Would you say that fiscal and monetary policy may be used to promote economic expansion as well as check excessive demand and inflation? In your

opinion, what would be some of the requirements to be fulfilled for fiscal policy to be a flexible policy instrument?

7. Explain and appraise the wage-price guidepost policy of the Kennedy-Johnson administration.

part VI

ELEMENTS OF INTERNATIONAL FINANCE

chapter 27

Foreign Exchange and the Balance of Payments

Our economy is an open, not a closed economy. U.S. nationals are engaged in trade and transactions with residents of countries of the rest of the world. Money, credit, and monetary institutions, which play an important role in facilitating internal trade and the formation of income, also play a major role in international trade and payments. International trade activity of the U.S. is relatively a significant component of overall economic activity, although not as important relative to countries which heavily depend on foreign trade as a source of livelihood. In 1968, for instance, U.S. nationals sold $50.594 billion of goods and services abroad and purchased $48.078 billion of goods and services from foreigners. This represented a net addition to the U.S. income flow at an annual rate of $2.516 billion.

Just as regional trade is motivated by the differences in relative regional efficiencies, international trade is motivated by the differences in the relative efficiencies between trading countries, which reflect the differences in their endowments of human and material resources. Just as regional trade permits regional specialization and division of labor, international trade allows international division of labor and specialization. Trade with other nations enables a country to concentrate mainly on the production of the goods and services for which it enjoys greater relative efficiencies and trades part of its goods for the goods produced by other countries for which they are relatively more efficient. Free trade between nations consequently is mutually beneficial to all participants.[1] But unlike internal trade and payments which involve the same monetary unit, international trade and payments involve a great variety of national currencies. Some national monetary units may have the same name, but they are different from each other. The Canadian dollar is not the same as the U.S. dollar and the U.S. dollar is different from the Australian dollar. The Swiss franc is

[1] Trade between nations, in real life, is not free, however. It is subject to a variety of restrictions such as quotas and tariffs on imports. The reasons for these restrictions are largely political and social rather than economic. Thus a country may protect an industry for which it is relatively inefficient by imposing quotas and tariffs on competitive imports on the ground that free international competition may force it out of business, thereby cutting off a source of strategic supply in the event of war.

certainly different from the Belgian franc and the Belgian franc is not the same as the French franc. Likewise, the Norwegian krone is not the same as the Danish krone.

In the course of international trade, many individuals and business firms in the United States receive foreign currencies in payment for the goods and services which they sell to foreigners, while many others have to make payments in foreign currencies for goods and services which they purchase from abroad. Thus an American considering a visit to Paris needs French francs for his travel expenditures in France. A U.S. importer purchasing British automobiles may need pound sterling for payment to the British exporter. A U.S. company may need Swiss francs for the expansion of its plants in Switzerland. A U.S. financial investor may need Canadian dollars for the purchase of Canadian treasury bills. Recipients of foreign currencies (e.g., exporters) obtain dollars by offering foreign currencies for sale. Users of foreign currencies, on the other hand, secure them for payments abroad by offering dollars in exchange. These sales and purchases of foreign currencies are effected through the medium of the foreign exchange market.

THE FOREIGN-EXCHANGE MARKET

The foreign-exchange market is a market for foreign currencies. New York is the market center for foreign exchange transactions in the United States. Although a variety of foreign currencies are traded in the New York foreign exchange market, only a few currencies are actively traded, namely the pound sterling, the Canadian dollar, and some continental currencies such as the German mark, the Swiss franc, the French franc, and the Belgian franc. Unlike the stock market or the commodity exchange market which has a definite locality in which transactions are made, the foreign exchange market has no single locality. It is rather a complex of arrangements through which buyers and sellers of foreign currencies are brought together, and trading is carried out largely by telephone, mail, and cable. Participants in the New York foreign exchange market include a number of agencies and branches of foreign banks, a few foreign exchange brokers, a couple of dozen commercial banks–mostly New York banks–and individuals and business firms which are the ultimate users and suppliers of foreign currencies.

The bulk of foreign exchange transactions is handled mostly by a number of New York banks and a few commercial banks in other money centers of the country, which hold deposit balances with commercial banks in foreign exchange centers abroad to facilitate foreign exchange dealings. It is through the correspondence with these banks that commercial banks throughout the country provide foreign exchange services to their customers.

The sales and purchases of foreign exchange are effected by the transfer of bank balances–for instance, from dollar balances into Swiss franc balances or

Swiss franc balances into dollar balances. The sales of foreign exchange reduce (and purchases increase) a bank's working balances with foreign commercial banks. In the normal course of events, the sales of foreign currencies are more or less offset by purchases. Banks therefore serve largely as intermediaries providing the facilities for clearing international transactions, matching customers' claims on foreigners with customers' liabilities to foreigners. Some banks, however, may find their working balances with foreign banks depleted as a result of the excess of foreign-exchange sales over purchases. They may replenish their foreign balances by purchasing foreign exchange from banks which have an excess of purchases over sales and consequently have more foreign exchange than they need for working purposes. These interbank exchange transactions are usually handled through foreign exchange brokers who serve as intermediaries between buying and selling banks as well as between banks and their commercial customers. Another alternative for banks to replenish their working balances is to purchase foreign currencies from foreign commercial banks which may need dollars to meet their customers' dollar requirements. They may offer dollars to their foreign correspondents for foreign currencies, borrow directly from them, or offer short-term notes in foreign money centers for foreign currencies and have the exchange proceeds credited to their accounts with foreign correspondents. Banks may also obtain foreign exchange from the Federal Reserve Bank of New York which operates in the foreign exchange market from time to time as seller or buyer of foreign exchange on behalf of the Federal Reserve System and the U.S. Treasury, and foreign central banks and governments.

The New York foreign exchange market, which is the center for foreign exchange transactions in the United States, is closely connected with major foreign exchange markets abroad such as London and Paris. They are parts of a world-wide exchange system which immensely facilitates transactions and payments across national boundaries.

Instruments of International Transfer

Most international payments, like domestic payments, involve the transfer of bank balances. But while the ordinary check is the popular means of transferring of bank balances in domestic transactions, international transactions involve specialized instruments. These include cable transfers, air mail transfer, bills of exchange, and travelers' checks.

Cable Transfer and Air Mail Transfer. Cable transfer is a major device used in foreign exchange transactions. A cable transfer is an order sent by cable to a foreign bank to debit the sender's account and credit the account of the payee, or the account of the person designated by the payee, with a specified amount. An importer in New York, for instance, may make a payment to an exporter in Paris in French francs by purchasing a cable transfer from his New York bank. He pays for the cable by drawing on his account with the bank and the amount is calculated on the basis of the going rate of exchange between the U.S. dollar and the French franc. The New York bank sends a cable to its correspondent in Paris with instructions to transfer the amount of francs from its account to the account of the exporter. Similarly, a person in Albuquerque, New Mexico, may send some amount of dollars payable in lira to his relative in Rome by cable order through his local commercial bank. Upon request from the customer, the local bank charges the customer's account of the dollar amount to be transferred (plus cable fee etc.) and sends a cable to its correspondent in New York requesting a cable transfer to Rome payable to the order of the customer's relative in Rome. The New York bank charges the account of the customer-bank in Albuquerque and directs its correspondent in Rome, by cable, to pay the payee the equivalent amount of lira. A U.S. exporter holding a Swiss franc balance with a Swiss bank in Zurich may sell it to a New York bank by instructing the Swiss bank by cable to transfer the amount from his account to the account of the New York bank which in turn pays the exporter the equivalent amount in dollars.

Cable transfer is convenient and fast. Payments abroad can be effected in a day or two. But the fee of cable transfer is higher than the fee of airmail transfer—another convenient and fast method of transfer, although not as fast as cable transfer. Airmail transfer is similar to cable transfer except that the transfer order is effected by airmail. In the above examples, the person transferring money to his relative in Rome may request his local bank to make the transfer by airmail. The exporter holding a balance in Swiss francs may direct, by airmail, the Swiss bank to transfer the amount from his account to the account of the New York bank. The importer in New York may pay the exporter in Paris by buying a bank check (or bank draft) from his New York bank, which is a check drawn by the New York bank on its account with its correspondent in Paris payable to the order of the exporter in Paris. The importer then mails the draft to the Paris exporter who in turn presents the check to the Paris bank for collection.

Bills of Exchange. Bills of exchange, also referred to as "drafts," are used in both domestic and international transactions. A bill of exchange is an order to pay drawn by the maker ordering the drawee to pay a specified sum of money either on sight (upon presentation) or at some fixed future date. When a bill is to be paid on sight, it is called a sight bill. It is referred to as a time bill when payment is to be made after some specified time period (say 60 days after sight). Bills of exchange used in international payments are usually documentary bills—that is, bills accompanied by other documents such as the bill of lading showing title to goods in transit, the sale of which gives rise to the bill of exchange. Thus a U.S. exporting firm selling goods to a Belgian importer in Brussels draws a bill on the importer for the amount of export. The bill is called a commercial bill, as it is drawn on the importer. The exporter can sell the bill with shipping documents to his New York bank for dollars. The New York Bank then sends the bill and documents attached to its correspondent in Brussels which presents the bill to the importer for payment if the bill is a sight bill, or for acceptance if it is a time bill. It is, however, customary for the exporter to draw a bill on the importer's bank (or its correspondent) instead of on the importer. In this case the bill is referred to as banker bill. The importer in Brussels can arrange with his bank (or the bank's correspondent) to issue a letter of credit in favor of the exporter. Under the letter of credit the exporter draws a bill on the bank. The letter of credit substitutes bank credit for the credit of the importer. It is an assurance that the bill will be paid by the bank on which it is drawn upon presentation if it is a sight bill, or will be accepted for payment if it is a time bill. The exporter can sell the banker's bill with other documents attached to his New York bank for dollars. The New York bank then sends the bill together with other documents to its correspondent in Brussels for payment or acceptance from the importer's bank. The importer obtains documents from his bank, receives the goods, sells it, and pays the bank.

Commercial bills usually sell for less than banker's bills since it is somewhat riskier to hold a commercial bill than a banker's bill. The former is supported by the credit of an individual while the latter is supported by the credit of a banking institution. Time bills sell for less than sight bills, since in the case of time bills interest has to be allowed for the buying banks, which pay the seller immediately in dollars yet are not able to use foreign currencies until the bills mature.

Travelers' Checks. Travelers' checks are instruments which can be used by tourists for their domestic and foreign travel expenditures. These checks are obligations of issuers (e.g., First National City Bank of New York, The American Express Company). Those who receive travelers' checks in payment can collect by presenting them to their banks which in turn collect from the issuers, if they are countersigned by proper owners.[2] A British tourist visiting New York thus can purchase travelers' checks issued by some London banks. He converts checks denominated in pound sterling into dollars in New York for his expenditures. Recipients of these checks can sell them to New York banks, which collect them from London issuers through their London correspondents. Similarly, a New Yorker traveling in Rome can purchase travelers' checks issued by the First National City Bank of New York and use these checks for his expenses in Rome. Those who receive these checks can sell them to local commercial banks for lira. These banks in turn collect from the First National City Bank through their New York correspondents. Tourists can also use travelers' letters of credit for their travel expenditures abroad. An American tourist visiting Toronto may purchase a travelers' letter of credit from a New York bank which permits him to draw on its accounts with its correspondents in Toronto up to a specified amount. The Toronto banks in turn receive payments from the New York bank.

[2]When a tourist buys travelers' checks, he has to sign these checks. When he presents these checks in payment, he has to countersign them. This is a means of verifying that the holder is the proper owner.

FOREIGN-EXCHANGE RATES

The rate of exchange for a foreign currency in the New York foreign exchange market is the rate of conversion between the dollar and a unit of that foreign currency. It is the dollar price of a foreign currency unit. For example, the average quotation (in cents) in October 1969 was 239.02 for the pound sterling, 23.229 for the Swiss franc, 92.762 for the Canadian dollar, 139.91 for the South African rand, and 17.907 for the French franc. The price of a foreign currency, just like any other prices, is determined in the foreign exchange market by the relative forces of supply and demand. The demand for foreign exchange arises from the import of goods, services, foreign securities, and gold, and the supply of foreign exchange, from the export of goods and services, securities, and gold.[3] The settlement of U.S. exports would result either in an increase in foreign exchange balances of U.S. banks with foreign correspondents or a decrease in dollar balances of foreign banks with U.S. banks—depending upon whether they are settled in foreign currencies or in dollars. When they are paid for in foreign currencies, the foreign exchange holdings of U.S. banks with foreign banks increase. On the other hand, when they are settled in dollars, dollar balances of foreign banks with U.S. banks decrease. The situation is reversed in the case of U.S. imports.

A New York exporter receiving pounds sterling from a London importer in payment will sell his sterling balance to a New York bank. This represents a supply of pounds sterling (and a demand for dollars) in New York. When he receives dollars in payment, there is a demand for dollars in London. (The British importer purchases, say, a cable transfer from his bank in London to pay the New York exporter. This results in a transfer of dollar deposits from the account of the London bank with the New York bank to the account of the New York exporter.) Since the New York and London markets are closely connected by "cable," the demand for dollars in London is almost immediately translated into a supply of pounds sterling in New York, as the London bank can offer pounds sterling received from the importer in London to a New York bank for dollars to replenish its balance with its New York correspondent. In either case, the increase in the supply of sterling (the demand for dollars) would tend to cause the dollar to appreciate vis-à-vis the pound sterling (that is, the dollar price of the pound declines). On the other hand, when a U.S. importer pays an exporter in London in dollars, the dollar balance of the London bank with its New York correspondent (as well as the supply of dollars in London) rises. When payment is to be made in pounds sterling, there is a demand for sterling in New York. This

[3]It is to be noted that certain international transactions constitute both supply of, and demand for, foreign exchange, and therefore do not enter the foreign exchange market as a supply component or demand component. For instance, a U.S. firm may finance its business expansion in Toronto through business earnings in Toronto. It is both a user and supplier of foreign exchange. An American tourist may cover his travel expenses in Rome with interest income and dividends he receives on his investments in Italy.

is translated into a supply of dollars in the London foreign exchange market, as the New York bank can offer dollars (received from the importer) to banks in London for sterling to replenish its sterling balance (depleted as a result of the settlement of imports) with its London correspondent. In either case, the increase in the demand for sterling (supply of dollars) would cause the dollar to depreciate in terms of the pound sterling.

The movement in the exchange rate of a foreign currency of course depends on the relative strength of supply and demand. When demand is strong relative to supply, the exchange rate tends to rise. Conversely, when supply is strong relative to demand, it tends to fall. Behind the demand for and supply of foreign exchange operate a host of economic and noneconomic factors, such as the level of income, prices, and interest rates in a country relative to income, prices and interest rates in other countries, expected changes in exchange rates, national and international political conditions. These affect a country's external payments position, hence, the supply of and demand for foreign exchange and exchange rates.

The foreign-exchange rates fluctuate as supply and demand conditions change, but these fluctuations tend to be limited as a consequence of exchange operations undertaken by central banks and monetary authorities for the purpose of stabilizing exchange rates. These limits represent some percentage deviations on either side of the par values of foreign currencies in terms of the U.S. dollar established under international agreements. The par value of the Canadian dollar, for instance, was established by the Canadian monetary authority in terms of $0.925 U.S., and the fluctuations in the exchange rate between the Canadian dollar and the U.S. dollar are limited to within 1 percent on either side of the par value (under the Articles of Agreements of the International Monetary Fund).[4] In other words, $0.934250 U.S. represents the upper limit and $0.915750 U.S. the lower limit of permitted fluctuations. When the exchange rate rises to the upper limit, the Bank of Canada would purchase U.S. dollars to prevent further rise. Conversely, when the exchange rate approaches the lower limit, the Bank of Canada would sell U.S. dollars for Canadian dollars to prevent further decline.

The exchange rates between currencies actively traded in various foreign exchange markets tend to be in line with one another. When they are "out of line," arbitrage operations of foreign exchange dealers would bring them back into line. Arbitrage operations consist of buying foreign exchange in one market and selling it in another market when the differences in the cross-rates of exchange between currencies make it profitable for exchange traders to engage in such operations. Assume that the pound sterling was bid at $2.409 U.S. in New York, and the Canadian dollar was offered in Toronto at $0.925 U.S. The implied cross-rate between the pound sterling and the Canadian dollar was then

[4]The operations and policies of the International Monetary Fund are discussed in Chapter 29.

2.604 Canadian dollars to the pound. But suppose that in London the pound sterling was offered for Canadian dollars at 2.602 Canadian dollars. A foreign exchange dealer in New York then can make a profit by purchasing Canadian dollars in Toronto, selling Canadian dollars for pound sterling in London, and selling sterling for dollars in New York. For instance, he can purchase 100,000 Canadian dollars for $92,500 U.S. With 100,000 Canadian dollars, he can purchase approximately 38,432 pound sterling in London. By selling this amount of sterling in New York, he would receive $92,583 U.S. and make a gross profit of roughly $83 U.S. And this can be accomplished in a matter of minutes. These arbitrage operations would tend to cause the Canadian dollar to appreciate vis-à-vis the U.S. dollar (the supply of U.S. dollars in Toronto increases) and to depreciate in terms of pound sterling (the supply of Canadian dollars in London increases), and the pound sterling to depreciate in terms of the U.S. dollar (the supply of sterling in New York increases). Consequently the cross-rates of exchange between these currencies would tend to move toward uniformity in all three exchange markets[5] (e.g. $2.408 U.S. = 1£; 2.603 Canadian dollars = 1£; and $0.9249 U.S. = 1 Canadian dollar).

FORWARD EXCHANGE

Exchange rate fluctuations, just like other price fluctuations, constitute a risk to those whose businesses involve foreign exchange. Those with obligations to pay foreign currencies at some future date (e.g., importers) run the risk that they may have to pay more in dollars for the same amount of foreign currency should the currency in question appreciate vis-à-vis the dollar. On the other hand, those expecting to receive foreign currency in payment in the future (exporters) run the risk that they would receive less in dollars for foreign currency should it depreciate in terms of the dollar. Expected users of foreign exchange may cover the risk of exchange appreciation by buying forward exchange in the forward-exchange market, which is an integral part of the foreign exchange market. Expected suppliers of foreign exchange, conversely, can cover the risk of exchange depreciation by selling exchange forward. A forward-exchange contract is a contract regarding the sale or purchase of a foreign currency for delivery in the future and the rate of exchange on such a contract is called the "forward" exchange rate, in contrast with the "spot" exchange rate which is the exchange rate on a contract for "immediate" delivery.

Following are some examples illustrating the process of covering exchange risk through the forward exchange market. Consider the case of a U.S. importer who purchases goods from an exporter in Frankfurt for 250,000 marks. Suppose that the spot rate for the mark is $0.2500 U.S. to the mark and the 2-month

[5] Because of the costs involved in arbitrage operations, there is some discrepancy between the cross-rates between currencies traded in foreign exchange markets. But arbitrage operations would take place so long as the earnings realized from such operations are more than adequate to cover their costs.

forward rate for the mark is quoted at $0.2502 U.S. (rate on marks to be delivered in two months). The importer is to pay the amount in, say, 60 days after he accepts the exporter's draft. It can be seen that the importer may have to pay more in dollars for 250,000 marks if at the time of payment the spot rate for the mark is higher than the two-month forward rate quoted at the time when the draft is accepted. To avoid the exchange risk, the importer can negotiate a forward exchange contract with a New York bank for 250,000 marks to be delivered in two months at the forward rate of $0.2502 to the mark. When the time of payment comes, the importer receives 250,000 marks from the bank and pays the bank $62,502 U.S. regardless of the spot rate of the mark then. If the spot rate of the mark happens to be $0.2508 U.S. to the mark, the importer has every reason to be happy. If it is, say, $0.2405 U.S. to the mark, it would be a cause for him to regret. It follows that if the currency with which the importer is to make payment tends to depreciate more frequently than to appreciate in terms of the dollar, the importer may find it to his advantage not to purchase forward exchange, since he may be able to pay less in dollars for his foreign exchange obligation. At any rate, the purchase of a forward contract to cover his future payment in foreign exchange would give him peace of mind!

An importer having accounts with commercial banks abroad may cover exchange risk by buying spot exchange and invest, through foreign banks, the foreign exchange proceeds in foreign securities of the same maturity as the time draft which he has accepted. When these securities mature he receives foreign currency with which to pay the exporter. The problem is that our importer may not have funds to purchase spot exchange not to speak of the costs and inconvenience involved in such an operation.

A U.S. exporter who sells goods to a British importer and expects to receive payment in pound sterling in, say, 90 days, may cover the risk of exchange depreciation by selling exchange forward. Similarly, a holder of dollar deposits may wish to purchase British treasury bills to take advantage of relatively higher British Treasury bills rates by buying spot sterling for the acquisition of British Treasury bills, and reconvert pounds sterling in dollars when the bills mature. Again, to avoid the risk of exchange depreciation, he may arrange to sell sterling forward at the time when he purchases British treasury bills.

In the forward-exchange market, banks sell forward exchange to importers and other users, and purchase forward exchange from exporters and holders of short-term foreign securities, etc. Should the sales and purchases of forward-exchange contracts involve roughly the same amounts and maturities, there would be no exchange risk on the part of banks. The future delivery of foreign exchange is matched by future receipts of foreign exchange. But they may not be able to make such arrangements. A bank selling a long-term forward exchange contract may not be able to obtain an offsetting purchase contract of the same maturity. To cover exchange risk, the bank can purchase foreign exchange in the spot market for future delivery. The spot market and the forward market, and consequently, the spot and forward exchange rates, are thus closely related as they are subject to a variety of common pressures. For instance, when a foreign currency is expected to appreciate vis-à-vis the U.S. dollar, those expected to use this foreign currency in the future would be anxious to purchase forward exchange. Those expected to receive it in payment in the future, on the other hand, would not be anxious to sell exchange forward as it would be to their advantage not to do so. As a consequence, in the forward-exchange market the demand for forward exchange increases relative to supply, and this would tend to cause the forward-exchange rate to rise. Banks would have to purchase foreign exchange in the spot market to cover forward sales, as they would not be able to offset forward-exchange sales by forward purchases. Consequently in the spot market the demand for spot exchange increases, and this would tend to cause the spot-exchange rate to rise as well. The movement is in the opposite direction when a foreign currency is expected to depreciate.

Although the spot- and forward-exchange rates tend to move in the same direction, there is spread between them, but its extent tends to be limited by the difference in the levels of interest rates in different money centers. According to the theory of forward exchange, given the free movement of funds between two money centers—say, London and New York—the forward sterling rate tends to fall to a discount from the spot sterling rate if the rate of interest in the London money market is higher than the interest rate in the New York market. Conversely, it tends to rise to a premium on the spot rate when the rate of interest in New York is higher than the interest rate in London. The spread between the spot and forward sterling rates tends to approach the interest differential between New York and London.

As an example, suppose that the spot sterling rate is $2.400 U.S. to the pound, that the rate of interest in New York is 4 percent per year (or 2 percent for six months) with the rate of interest in London 6 percent per year (or 3 percent for 6 months).[6] A New York bank that wishes to cover a six-month forward sale of £103,000 to a New York importer can purchase £100,000 spot for $240,000 and invest the amount of pounds in London. At 3 percent for 6 months, the bank would earn £3,000 interest. At maturity, the bank receives £103,000 for delivery to the importer. Had the bank not purchased £100,000, it could have invested $240,000 in New York at 2 percent for six months and earned $4,800 interest. It follows that the 6-month forward sterling rate would be somewhat near $2.3766 ($244,800/£103,000). Suppose that the 6-month forward sterling rate is quoted at $2.378 in New York. The bank selling forward exchange to the importer would receive $244,934 for £103,000, thereby making $134 more than what it would earn by investing $240,000 in New York at 2 percent for 6 months. This would help cover various expenses involved in the operation and give the bank some profit which is part of the incentive for the operation.

[6]This is an oversimplication intended only for illustration purpose. In real life, there is, of course, a variety of interest rates associated with, say, Treasury bills and other obligations of different maturities.

It can be seen from the above example that so long as the discount of the forward sterling from the spot sterling is less than the interest differential between London and New York it would pay holders of dollars to purchase spot sterling, invest sterling in London and sell sterling forward.[7] The increase in the demand for spot sterling and the supply of forward sterling would cause the spread between the spot and forward sterling rates to increase until it approaches the interest differential between New York and London. (What would be the movement of funds between New York and London should the discount of forward sterling be greater than the interest differential between New York and London? The reader is invited to work out this case). In actual practice, however, as a consequence of legal restrictions on capital flows and other limitations, the deviations of the forward rates from spot rates of currencies traded in the foreign exchange market differ substantially from interest rates differences.

BALANCE OF INTERNATIONAL PAYMENTS

Transactions which give rise to the demand for and supply of foreign exchange in the U.S. are shown in the U.S. balance of international payments. It is nothing more than a summary statement of total receipts of the United States from the rest of the world and total payments of the U.S. to the rest of the world over a given time period. Table 27-1 shows the balance of payments of the United States in 1967. The balance of payments is compiled on the basis of double-entry accounting. Hence total receipts or credit entries must equal total payments or debit entries, by definition. A credit entry represents a transaction which gives rise to a U.S. claim on the rest of the world. A transaction which results in a payment from the U.S. to the rest of the world is a debit entry. U.S. sales of merchandise abroad, foreigners' travel expenditures in the United States, transportation facilities provided by U.S. firms to foreigners, interest income and dividends received by U.S. residents for their foreign investments thus represent credit entries in the balance-of-payments statement. U.S. imports of goods, U.S. travel expenditures abroad, interest and dividends paid by U.S. firms to foreigners, on the other hand, are debit entries. Similarly, the purchase of foreign securities by U.S. residents is a debit entry, since U.S. residents "import" foreign securities which give rise to foreign claims for payments on the United States. The remittance of funds by U.S. residents to their relatives abroad is a debit entry, as it represents U.S. payments to foreigners. The purchase of U.S. securities by foreigners is a credit entry, since it represents the export of "promises to pay" by U.S. firms which consequently receive payments from foreign investors. The increase in deposit balances of foreign commercial banks and foreign residents with U.S. banks is a credit entry, as U.S. banks receive payments when these balances are built up. The sale of gold is a credit entry, since like the sale of goods it gives rise to U.S. receipts.

[7]The movement of funds between various market centers to take advantage of interest rate differences is commonly referred to as "interest arbitrage."

TABLE 27-1
United States Balance of Payments, 1967
(millions of dollars)*

Item	Amount
Exports of goods and services	45,693
Imports of goods and services	-40,893
Remittances and pensions	- 1,284
U. S. Government grants and capital flow, net	- 4,127
U. S. private capital flow, net	
Direct investments	- 3,027
Foreign securities and other long-term claims	- 1,269
Short-term claims	- 1,150
Errors and unrecorded transactions	- 595
Foreign capital flow, net	
Long-term investments	2,235
U. S. corporate securities and other claims	- 432
U. S. nonliquid liabilities to foreign official agencies	1,274
U. S. liquid liabilities to foreigners	
Commercial banks	1,265
Others†	186
Foreign central banks and governments	2,072
Changes in U. S. official reserves (decrease +)	
Gold	1,170
Convertible currencies	- 1,024
IMF reserve position	- 94
Total	53,895 - 53,895 = 0

Source: *Federal Reserve Bulletin*, April 1968.
*Minus sign indicates debit and absence of sign indicates credit.
†These include U.S. liquid liabilities to other private holders as well as to international and regional organizations.

Transactions in goods and services are referred to as "current account" transactions. The current account is an international income account representing income receipts by U.S. residents from foreigners and income payments of U.S. residents to foreigners. The current account for 1967 showed a surplus (excess of current receipts over current payments) of $4.8 billion which means that foreign trade added to the income flow at an annual rate of $4.8 billion. Gifts of private U.S. residents to foreigners, and U.S. government grants to foreign countries, which have become almost a permanent institution, may be considered as current account transactions; they constitute practically a regular source of income for foreign recipient. In many cases, there are no monetary payments to foreign countries in connection with U.S. government grants, but they are recorded as "debits" offsetting "credits" nominally accruing from the exports covered by grants. A grant in kind thus can be looked at as a grant in money which is used by the recipient country to import the goods.

In addition to transactions in goods and services and unilateral transfers in the form of gifts and grants from U.S. official and private sources, there are capital transactions which include both short- and long-term loans and investments, changes in bank balances, and changes in U.S. official reserve assets (such as gold and convertible currencies). U.S. private capital flow includes the purchase of foreign securities by U.S. individuals and businesses, direct investments of U.S. firms in foreign countries, and U.S. bank loans abroad. The net U.S. capital outflow or "export" amounted to $5.446 billion in 1967. Foreign capital flow includes foreign direct investments in the U.S., the acquisition of U.S. corporate securities by foreigners, and changes in their holdings of liquid claims in the United States, namely banks' demand and time deposits, U.S. Treasury bills and certificates, bankers' acceptances, and other short-term assets. The net foreign capital inflow, both official and private, was $6.6 billion. The net decreases in U.S. official reserve assets ($52 million) and increases in the holdings of bank deposits and other liquid assets in the United States by foreigners helped balance the excess of payments over receipts in some other accounts of the balance of payments.

SUMMARY

International trade and payments involve different national currencies. In the course of trading activity, many individuals and enterprises receive foreign currencies for the goods and services which they sell abroad, while others have to make payments in foreign currencies for the goods and services which they purchase from foreigners. The foreign exchange market provides the facilities which bring together users and suppliers of foreign currencies. The bulk of foreign-exchange transactions in the United States is handled by a number of commercial banks, mostly banks in New York City. They buy and sell foreign exchange for the accounts of their customers as well as for the customers of their customer banks throughout the country.

Transactions in the foreign-exchange market are effected through specialized instruments, namely cable and airmail transfers and bills of exchange. A cable transfer is a transfer order effected by cable, and airmail transfer, a transfer order effected by air mail. A bill of exchange is an order to pay drawn by the maker ordering the person to whom the bill is addressed to pay a specified sum of money. A bill requiring payment on sight is a sight bill. A bill that demands payment after a specified time period is a time bill.

The rate of exchange in the New York foreign exchange market is the dollar price of a foreign currency unit. The exchange rate on a contract for the sale or purchase of a foreign currency for immediate delivery is the "spot" exchange rate, and the rate on a contract calling for future delivery of a foreign currency is the "forward" rate of exchange. Through the forward-exchange market, expected users of foreign currencies may cover the risk of exchange appreciation by purchasing forward exchange, and expected recipients of foreign currencies may cover the risk of exchange depreciation by selling exchange forward. The spot-exchange rate is determined by the demand for and supply of spot exchange, and the forward-exchange rate by the supply of and demand for forward exchange. Demand arises from imports and supply from exports. The spot- and forward-exchange rates tend to move in the same direction, but the forward rate may be higher or lower than the spot-exchange rate. According to the theory of forward exchange, given the free movement of currency between two money centers, say, New York and Toronto, the forward rate of the Canadian dollar would fall (rise) to a discount (premium) from the spot rate if the rate of interest in Toronto is higher (lower) than the rate of interest in New York, and the spread between the spot and forward rates tends to approach the interest differential between the two money centers under the influences of the movement of funds between the two centers to take advantage of interest differences.

Transactions which give rise to the demand for and supply of foreign exchange are shown in the balance of international payments, which is a summary statement of total receipts and payments between a country's residents and the rest of the world over some period of time. The statement shows transactions in goods and services, unilateral transfers, as well as capital transactions. A transaction which gives rise to a claim on foreigners is a credit entry. A transaction which gives rise to a payment to foreigners is a debit entry. Since double-entry accounting is used in compiling the balance of payments, total receipts or credits are necessarily equal to total debits or payments—that is, the balance of payments as a whole shows neither a surplus nor a deficit.

PROBLEMS

1. In what respect does the New York foreign exchange market differ from the New York stock exchange? What are participants in the New York foreign exchange market? Would there be a need for a foreign exchange market in the U.S. should payments between the U.S. and the rest of the world be all effected in U.S. dollars? Explain.

2. What is the spot-exchange rate? The forward-exchange rate? What are their determinants? Give some examples regarding the covering of exchange risk through the forward-exchange market. What are relationships between the spot- and forward-exchange rates?

3. Explain briefly some of the instruments used for international payments. Give some examples regarding the uses of these instruments.

4. Assume that the Belgian franc was bid in New York at \$0.0205 to the franc. The U.S. dollar was offered at 4 marks in Frankfurt. And the mark was offered at 12.240 Belgian francs in Brussels. What would you expect the movement of the funds between these foreign exchange centers? What would happen to the value of the U.S. dollar vis-à-vis the German mark and the Belgian franc as a consequence of arbitrage operations?

5. For a certain year, the U.S. exported \$37.099 billion of goods and services and imported \$28.637 billion. U.S. government grants to foreign countries

were valued at $3.560 billion, and gifts given by U.S. residents to their relatives abroad at $896 million. U.S. residents purchased $4.250 billion of foreign corporate securities and other claims and reduced their deposit balances with foreign banks by $400 million. U.S. direct investments abroad were $3.418 billion. For the same period, foreigners increased their deposits with U.S. banks by $1.620 billion, purchased $500 million of U.S. Treasury bills, and reduced their long-term investments in the U.S. by $150 million. The U.S. Treasury sold $850 million of gold to foreign central banks and reduced its holdings of foreign exchange by $392 million.

Arrange these items into a proper balance-of-payments statement.

chapter 28

Balance of Payments Equilibrium and Exchange Rate Systems

The value of the currency of a country in international transactions may be strengthened, weakened, or remain stable over the long-run depending upon the long-run changes in its payments position vis-à-vis the rest of the world. The external value of its currency would remain stable if it can achieve some long-run equilibrium in its balance of payments. A persistent payments deficit, on the other hand, would weaken its currency in relation to foreign currencies in international transactions. But what do we mean by equilibrium in the balance of payments? What do we mean by a payments deficit or surplus? What are the mechanics of balance of payments adjustment under different exchange rate systems? We shall answer these and other questions in this chapter.

THE MEASUREMENT OF PAYMENTS IMBALANCES

An individual covers his expenditures with the income he earns. Should his expenditures exceed income, he could make up for the deficit by running down savings that he has accumulated and/or borrowing. But this is not sustainable indefinitely. Should his expenditures continue to exceed income, he would eventually come to a point where his savings are exhausted and creditors would refuse to grant him new loans. It is clear that he would have to establish some balance between his income and expenditure over the long run.

The same can be said for a country engaged in international trade. It pays for what it purchases from the rest of the world with what it earns from the rest of the world. If it spends abroad more than it earns from abroad, it may cover the deficit by borrowing from foreigners, running down its international reserves such as gold and foreign exchange, and/or relying on international gifts. The deficit obviously cannot be permitted to go on indefinitely. Persistent payments deficits eventually would result in the exhaustion of international reserves and the refusal of new credit on the part of foreign creditor countries. It follows that if foreign confidence in the safety and stability of a country's currency in international transactions is to be maintained, the country would have to achieve some equilibrium between what it "earns" from abroad and what it "spends" abroad over the long run—that is, some equilibrium in its payments position in reference to the rest of the world.

It is difficult to determine the equilibrium position of a country's balance of payments. But continued losses of its international reserves and decreases in the external value of its currency indicate that it is subject to persistent payments disequilibrium—"living beyond its means." The concept of payments deficit or surplus is used as a measure of the extent of disequilibrium in a country's balance of payments. Measuring a payments deficit or surplus is a problem. As we have seen, the balance of payments as a whole shows neither a deficit nor a surplus as it is compiled on the basis of double-entry accounting. But while the net balance of all balance of payments transactions is zero, the net balance of certain groups of transactions in the balance of payments may be positive or negative. For instance, the transactions in goods and services in the U.S. balance of payments in 1967 showed a surplus or positive balance of $4.8 billion, while government grants and capital flow showed a negative balance or deficit of $4.1 billion. It follows that a payments deficit or surplus refers to the negative or positive balance of some selected groups of transactions in the balance of payments.

The general approach to measuring the deficit or surplus in the balance of payments is to classify balance of payments transactions into two groups: "autonomous" transactions and "balancing" transactions. Autonomous transactions are those that arise independently of balance-of-payments considerations. Balancing transactions are those that arise to accommodate autonomous transactions. A deficit or surplus in the balance of payments refers to the negative or positive sum of autonomous transactions. The deficit or surplus is settled (balanced) by the positive or negative sum of the balancing transactions. But the difficulty is that while some transactions in the balance of payments such as imports and exports of goods and services and unilateral transfers are clearly autonomous transactions, the same cannot be said for capital transactions, both short- and long-term. Some short- and long-term capital transactions are autonomous in nature and others are balancing transactions. There is no clear-cut way to separate autonomous capital transactions from balancing transactions, because of unknown motives behind capital movements. Measuring a balance-of-payments deficit or surplus is therefore somewhat arbitrary because of arbitrary decisions involved in the classification of capital transactions. The transfer of certain capital transactions from one category to the other category will affect the size of the payments deficit or surplus.

The classification of transactions in the balance of payments in order to obtain some measure of a payments deficit or surplus should be related to the purpose for which the deficit or surplus is estimated. The general purpose of a payments deficit or surplus is that it serves as an indicator of the extent of imbalance or disequilibrium in a country's international economic position, a guide to economic policy aimed at maintaining a stable value of its currency in international markets among other things. The United States, for example, is committed to maintain the exchange rate of the dollar by standing ready to sell gold against dollars as may be requested by foreign monetary authorities at the fixed price of $35 per ounce as part of its obligations with the International Monetary Fund. The ability of the United States to maintain the external value of the dollar therefore reflects its holdings of monetary gold (and other international reserve assets).

But the U.S. dollar, unlike other foreign currencies, is an international reserve currency. It is widely held by foreign central banks and governments as well as private foreigners. Inasmuch as part of these foreign dollar assets may be exercised as claims against U.S. reserves, a measure of the U.S. international economic position (deficit or surplus) consequently would have to take into consideration not only changes in U.S. official reserves, but also changes in those U.S. liabilities to foreigners that may be exercised as claims on U.S. reserves. But which of these dollar claims are to be treated as such? There is disagreement in this regard.[1] To take account of divergent views on this issue, the United States has used two alternative measures to evaluate its balance of payments performance: the balance on liquidity basis and the balance on basis of official reserve transactions.

Balance on Liquidity Basis

The balance on liquidity basis is a measure of changes in the U.S. international liquidity position. Since privately held foreign liquid dollar assets may be sold to foreign central banks, thereby constituting claims which may be indirectly exercised against U.S. reserves, the liquidity balance treats changes in U.S. liquid liabilities to all foreigners, both official and private, as balancing transactions—just like changes in U.S. official reserve assets. Nonliquid U.S. liabilities to

[1] It should be noted that these are special problems of reserve-currency countries. In regard to nonreserve-currency countries, the major problem in measuring international payments imbalances is to determine which capital transactions should be treated as compensatory or balancing transactions. One approach to the problem is to treat as autonomous transactions those transactions which respond to long-run economic forces. This measure, frequently referred to as the "basic" balance, treats transactions in goods and services, unilateral transfers, and long-term capital flows as autonomous transactions, and all other transactions, including short-term capital movements and changes in official gold and foreign exchange reserves, as balancing transactions. A difficulty with this approach is the separation of capital transactions that respond to "long-run" forces and those that do not, since certain capital transactions classified as long-term may be of the short-term variety and vice versa.

Another measure which is consistent with the policies of governments to insulate the domestic economies from fluctuations in international economic activity, and to maintain the external value of their currency (in accordance with the Fund's Articles of Agreement) consists of the funds available to them to make international payments and to maintain the stability of the exchange rate of their currency. For most countries, these funds consist of gold and foreign exchange reserves, their reserve position with the IMF, and foreign exchange holdings of commercial banks to the extent that they have control over these holdings.

TABLE 28-1
U.S. Balance of Payments, 1967
(millions of dollars)*

	Balance on Liquidity Basis		Balance on Basis of Official Reserve Transactions	
	Autonmous Transactions (1)	Balancing Transactions (2)	Autonmous Transactions (3)	Balancing Transactions (4)
Exports of goods and services	45,693		45,693	
Imports of goods and services	-40,893		-40,893	
Remittances and pensions	-1,284		-1,284	
U.S. Government grants and capital flow, net	-4,127		-4,127	
U.S. private capital flow, net				
Direct investments	-3,027		-3,027	
Foreign securities and other long-term claims	-1,269		-1,269	
Short-term claims	-1,150		-1,150	
Errors and unrecorded transactions	-595		-595	
Foreign capital flow, net				
Long-term investments	2,235		2,235	
U.S. corporate securities and other claims	-432		-432	
U.S. nonliquid liabilities to foreign official agencies	1,274			1,274
U.S. liquid liabilities to foreigners				
Commercial banks		1,265	1,265	
Others†		186	186	
Foreign central banks and governments		2,072		2,072
Changes in U.S. official reserves (decrease +)				
Gold		1,170		1,170
Convertible currencies		-1,024		-1,024
IMF gold tranche position		-94		-94
Total	-3,575	3,575	-3,398	3,398

Source: *Federal Reserve Bulletin*, April 1968.
*Minus sign indicates debit and absence of sign indicates credit.
†These include U.S. liquid liabilities to other private holders as well as international and regional organizations other than IMF.

foreigners are treated as autonomous transactions, just like transactions in goods and services, unilateral transfers, and U.S. government and private capital flows. The liquidity balance thus measures the U.S. overall deficit or surplus in terms of (a) changes in U.S. official reserves which include U.S. monetary gold, U.S. official holdings of convertible foreign currencies, and U.S. "gold tranche" claims on the International Monetary Fund,[2] and (b) changes in U.S. liquid liabilities to all foreigners regardless of whether they are held by foreign official agencies or by private individuals and organizations. An increase in U.S. liquid liabilities to all foreigners and a decrease in U.S. official reserve holdings mean an increase in the U.S. payments deficit and a decrease in the U.S. liquidity position.

Column 1 of Table 28-1 shows the liquidity deficit in the U.S. balance of payments in 1967 and column 2 shows how the deficit was settled. The deficit of $3,575 million was settled by a net increase in U.S. liquid liabilities to all foreigners of $3,523 million—increase in U.S. short-term borrowings from foreigners, (made up of increases in liquid dollar holdings of foreign commercial banks by $1,265 million, of other private foreign holders by $186 million, and of foreign central banks and governments by $2,072 million) and a net decrease in U.S. official reserves of $52 million. (U.S. gold stock decreased by $1,170 million, but this was offset by an increase in U.S. holdings of convertible currencies of $1,024 million, and an increase in the U.S. gold tranche position with the IMF of $94 million.)

Balance on Basis of Official Reserve Transactions

The balance on basis of official reserve transactions measures the U.S. payment deficit or surplus in terms of (a) changes in U.S. official reserves, and (b) changes in U.S. liquid liabilities and certain nonliquid liabilities (mostly nonmarketable, nonconvertible U.S. Government securities) to foreign central banks and governments. The difference between the balance on liquidity basis and balance on basis of official reserve transactions thus lies in the treatment of U.S. liquid liabilities to private foreigners and certain nonliquid U.S. liabilities to foreign official agencies. The balance on basis of official reserve transactions treats any increase in foreign private liquid claims on the United States as an ordinary capital inflow whereas the balance on liquidity basis considers it as an increase in claims on U.S. reserves. On the other hand, while the liquidity balance considers any increase in U.S. nonliquid liabilities to foreigners (both official and private) as an ordinary capital inflow, the balance on basis of official reserve transactions treats the increase in certain nonliquid U.S. liabilities to foreign

[2] The U.S. "gold tranche" position in the International Monetary Fund represents the amount that the U.S. could draw in foreign currencies virtually automatically if needed to the extent that IMF holdings of dollars are less than the U.S. IMF quota. For example, at the end of March 1968, IMF holdings of dollars were $4,683 million. Since the U.S. quota has been increased to $5,160 million since February 1966, the U.S. gold tranche position was then $477 million.

monetary authorities as an increase in claims on U.S. official reserves. The difference between these measures can be seen in Table 28-1. The balance on basis of official reserve transactions shows a deficit of $3,398 million which was settled by an increase in U.S. liquid and nonliquid liabilities to foreign central banks of $3,346 million and a net decrease in U.S. official reserves of $52 million.

Under current international monetary arrangements, foreign official monetary agencies are committed to maintain the exchange rates of their currencies vis-à-vis the U.S. dollar by selling or buying U.S. dollars as part of their obligations with the International Monetary Fund. The sales or purchases of U.S. dollars by these official monetary agencies for exchange-rate stabilization would result in a decrease or increase in their holdings of dollar assets. Since these foreign official dollar holdings are convertible into gold at the U.S. Treasury, it is felt that the size of the net change in the dollar holdings of foreign monetary authorities along with the net change in U.S. official reserves is an indicator of the U.S. payment deficit or surplus, of the ability of the U.S. to sustain the value of the dollar in international transactions.

These measures, as we have mentioned, are only indicators of the extent of imbalances in the U.S. balance of payments, not definitions of equilibrium. They have limitations that arise mainly from the arbitrary classification of assets which are claims on U.S. reserves and those which are not. In a sense, the balance on liquidity basis may be said to overstate the extent of imbalance in the U.S. balance of payments. The U.S. dollar is an international means of payment. With the expansion of world trade, the volume of liquid dollar assets in the hands of private foreigners (and foreign official monetary agencies as well) is expected to increase. Consequently at least part of the increase in private foreign liquid dollar holdings reflects the greater need of reserve currency to sustain the growth of international trade and payments and should therefore be treated as an ordinary capital flow just like any increase in U.S. private liquid claims on foreigners. It is not readily available to foreign monetary authorities and does not constitute a threat on U.S. gold reserve. Moreover, certain liquid dollar claims held by foreigners arise from their dollar liabilities to U.S. residents and consequently can hardly be considered as claims that may be indirectly exercised against U.S. reserves as in the case in which foreign banks receive dollar deposits from U.S. residents and invest them in U.S. liquid assets. On the other hand, the liquidity balance may be said to underestimate the potential threat on U.S. reserves, since any marketable dollar asset, to a degree, can be indirectly exercised as a claim on U.S. reserve assets. The balance on basis of official reserve transactions, therefore, may be considered as understating claims on U.S. reserves, since part of the foreign liquid dollar assets privately held may be readily transferrable to official monetary agencies, especially where they have some degree of control over the foreign exchange holdings of private commercial banks.

While the long-run equilibrium in the U.S. balance of payments is difficult to ascertain, a continuous loss of U.S. gold reserve and deterioration in the position of the U.S. dollar in international markets is a sure indicator of persistent U.S. payments disequilibrium. And a persistent U.S. payment deficit has to be corrected if the U.S. dollar is to continue its dominant role in international trade and payments. What are various methods available for the adjustment of payments imbalances? We shall turn to these questions, but before doing so we shall discuss the relationship between international trade and the formation of income. As will be seen, the level of income is affected by international trade, and income changes influence trade and the balance of payments. Measures used to correct payments imbalances may influence the level of income and employment. For convenience, we shall define balance of payments as balance between the exports and imports of goods and services. A payments deficit is an excess of imports over exports, and surplus represents the opposite situation.

INCOME, TRADE, AND THE BALANCE OF PAYMENTS

Income Determination in an Open Economy

The various models of income determination presented in chapter 19 are for a closed economy. For an open economy—an economy with international trade activity, these models have to be extended to take accounts of the effects of the imports and exports of goods and services on the level of income. When U.S. firms sell goods and services to foreigners, they receive payments from them. These are paid out in wages, salaries, or fees, to those who contribute to the production of exported goods. Exporting of goods and services thus adds to the income flow, just as investment spending. On the other hand, when U.S. residents purchase goods and services from foreigners, it is the foreign producers who receive income payments. It follows that the imports of goods and services, like savings, are a leakage from the flow of income. The effect of foreign trade on the level of income therefore depends upon the excess of exports over imports, commonly referred to as net exports or net foreign investments. This, of course, may be positive, negative, or zero. Positive net export (which we also refer to as a payment surplus) is a net addition to the income flow, and a negative net export, a reduction in the flow of income.

A country's imports are determined mainly by the level of import prices relative to the level of prices of domestic products which may be substituted for imports, the preference of the public for imported goods, and the level of income. Given import prices and the prices of domestic substitutes for imports and import preferences, we can safely say that the level of imports in a country is an increasing function of income, or $M = M(Y)$; as the level of income increases, certain proportion of the increase in income can be expected to be spent on imports. Given the level of exports X, private domestic consumption $C(Y)$, and domestic investment I, we have the following expression for the equilibrium level of income in an open economy:[3]

$$Y = C(Y) + I + X - M(Y) \tag{1}$$

Income is in equilibrium when it is consistent with planned private domestic consumption and the sum of planned domestic and foreign investment (i.e., $I + X - M(Y)$. From Equation (1) we can also state the condition for the equilibrium level of income as:

$$S(Y) + M(Y) = I + X \tag{2}$$

where $S = S(Y)$ is saving. The level of income is in equilibrium when the sum of planned savings and imports is equal to the sum of planned investment and exports–that is, when the leakage from the flow of income through savings and imports is equal to the addition to the income flow through investment and exports. This approach is presented geometrically in Fig. 28-1. Since investment

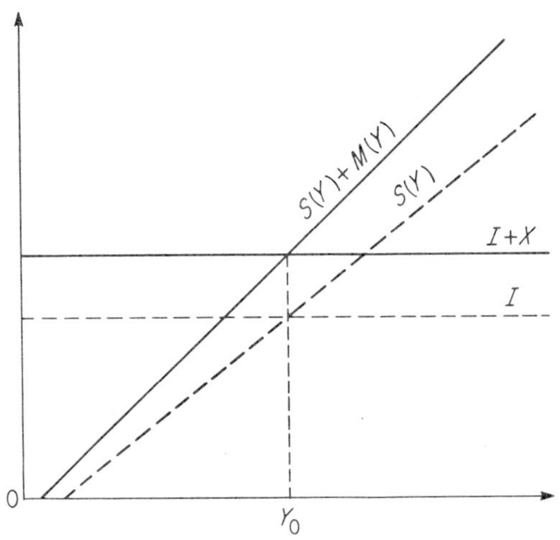

Fig. 28-1. Income equilibrium.

and exports are assumed to be constant, the investment plus export curve is a straight line parallel to the income axis. The savings plus import curve $S(Y) + M(Y)$ is positively sloped: both savings and imports rise as the level of income rises. The intersection between the investment plus export curve and the savings plus import curve determines the equilibrium level of income Y_0. It is only at the level of income Y_0 is there equality between the sum of planned savings and imports and the sum of planned investment and exports. For any level of income smaller than Y_0, the addition to the income flow through

[3]Note that government spending is abstracted for simplicity.

investment and exports exceeds the leakage from the flow of income through savings and imports. And this will cause the level of income to rise. Conversely, for any level of income higher than the equilibrium level Y_0, the leakage from the income flow through imports and savings exceeds the injection into the flow of income through exports and investment. Consequently, the level of income will decline.

For a numerical example, assume that we have the following consumption and import functions. $C = a + bY = 50 + 4/5Y$ and $M = p + mY = 2 + 5/100Y$, where $b = 4/5$ is the marginal propensity to consume and $m = 5/100$ is the marginal propensity to import ($m = \Delta M/\Delta Y$) that is, the change in imports resulting from a small change in income. ($m = 5/100$ means that as income increases by \$1, expenditure on imports would increase by 5 cents.) Suppose that investment is constant at $I = 40$, and exports, at $X = 32$. To obtain the equilibrium level of income, we substitute the value of $C(Y), M(Y), I$ and X in Equation (1) and solve for Y, we have

$$Y = 120 + 4/5Y - 5/100Y = 480$$

At this level of income, planned savings or $S(Y) = 46$, and imports or $M(Y) = 26$. The sum of planned savings and imports at that level of income is exactly equal to the sum of planned investment and exports ($S + M = I + X = 72$). At the equilibrium level of income $Y = 480$, there is a balance of payment surplus of 6 (i.e., $B = X - M = 32 - 26 = 6$). It follows that the equilibrium level of income is consistent with balance of payment equilibrium, surplus, or deficit. This can be seen from the expression for the equilibrium level of income. From Equation (2) we have

$$S(Y) - I = X - M(Y)$$

When $X - M(Y) = 0$, we have both equilibrium income and the balance of payments. When $X - M(Y) > 0$, we have income equilibrium with a payment surplus (the leakage from the flow of income through the excess of savings over investment is offset by the addition to the income flow by the excess of exports over imports, hence, income is in equilibirum). On the other hand, when $X - M(Y) < 0$, we have income equilibrium and a payment deficit.

Income Changes: The Multiplier

We have seen that the equilibrium level of income is equal to the sum of planned consumption, investment, and net exports of goods and services. An autonomous change in exports, other things being equal, therefore will cause the level of income to change. The question we wish to answer is, given an autonomous change in exports, how much would be the corresponding change in the equilibrium level of income? To show the extent of the change in the equilibrium level of income generated by a given change in exports, assume that $C = C(Y) = a + bY$ and $M = M(Y) = p + mY$. Given investment (I) and exports

(X), the equilibrium level of income is:

$$Y = (a + I + X - p)\left(\frac{1}{1 - b + m}\right) \tag{3}$$

Now, let us allow exports to change by a given amount ΔX, the new equilibrium level of income will be:

$$Y + \Delta Y = (a + I + X - p)\left(\frac{1}{1 - b + m}\right) + \Delta X\left(\frac{1}{1 - b + m}\right) \tag{4}$$

Subtracting (3) from (4), we have:

$$\Delta Y = \Delta X\left(\frac{1}{1 - b + m}\right)$$

The expression shows the extent of the change in the equilibrium level of income as a result of an autonomous change in exports; it is equal to the product of the change in exports and the multiplication factor $\left(\frac{1}{1 - b + m}\right) = \left(\frac{1}{s + m}\right)$ where $s = 1 - b$ is the marginal propensity to save. This multiplication factor is referred to as the export multiplier.[4] It is clear that the size of the export multiplier depends on the value of the marginal propensity to consume b and the marginal propensity to import m. The greater the value of b (the smaller the value of s) and the smaller the value of m, the greater the size of the export multiplier, and the greater the size of the export multiplier, the greater the change in the equilibrium level of income, given the autonomous change in exports. Figure 28-2 shows the export multiplier geometrically. Y_0 is the initial equilibrium level of income. As exports increase by ΔX, the investment plus exports curve shifts vertically upward by the same amount. Given the propensity to save $S(Y)$ and the propensity to import $M(Y)$, the increase in exports causes the level of income to increase by ΔY.

We know that the ratio $\Delta X/\Delta Y$ is the slope of the savings-plus-imports curve, which is the sum of the marginal propensity to save and the marginal

[4]Following is a more rigorous way to derive the export multiplier. By differentiating $Y = C(Y) + I + X - M(Y)$ with respect to X, we have:

$$\frac{dY}{dX} = \frac{dC}{dY}\frac{dY}{dX} + 1 - \frac{dM}{dY}\frac{dY}{dX}$$

Hence

$$\frac{dY}{dX} = \frac{1}{1 - \frac{dC}{dY} + \frac{dM}{dY}}$$

where dC/dY is the marginal propensity to consume and dM/dY is the marginal propensity to import.

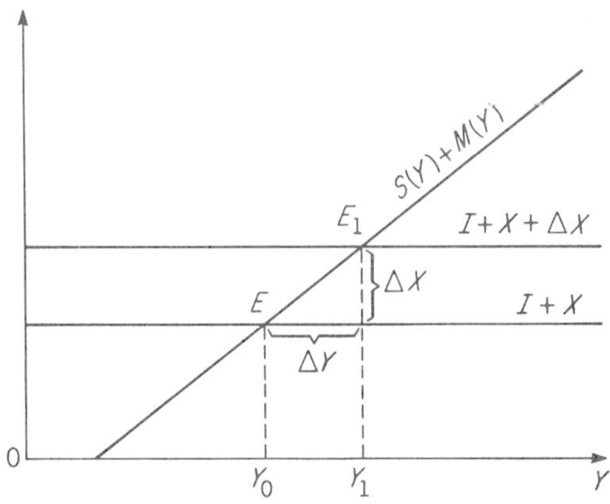

Fig. 28-2. The export multiplier.

propensity to import; that is $\Delta X/\Delta Y = s + m = 1 - b + m$, hence

$$\frac{\Delta Y}{\Delta X} = \frac{1}{s+m} = \frac{1}{1-b+m}$$

which is the export multiplier.

We have shown the effect of an autonomous increase in exports on the equilibrium level of income. But what about the effect of this on the balance of payments? Since $B = X - M(Y)$, we have:

$$\Delta B = \Delta X - \Delta M = \Delta X - \mathrm{m}\,\Delta Y = \Delta X\left(\frac{1-b}{1-b+m}\right) = \Delta X\left(\frac{s}{s+m}\right)$$

As $\dfrac{s}{s+m} > 0$, an autonomous increase in exports always improves the balance of payments. It can be seen from the expression that for the payments position to remain unchanged, the marginal propensity to save would have to be zero. Since $s > 0$, the leakage of income through savings prevents the increase in the level of income generated by the increase in exports to reach a level which would induce sufficient increase in imports to catch up with the increase in exports.

In the numerical example presented in the preceding section, since $b = 4/5$ and $m = 5/100$, the export multiplier is equal to 4. Assume that there is an autonomous increase in exports by 5. This will cause the equilibrium level of income to increase by 20 $\left[\text{i.e., } \Delta Y = \Delta X\left(\frac{1}{1-b+m}\right) = 5 \times 4 = 20\right]$, and the payments surplus to increase by 4 i.e., $\Delta B = \Delta X\left(\frac{s}{s+m}\right) = 5(0.8) = 4$.

From Equation (3), it is clear that the effect of an autonomous change in imports (Δp) on the level of income differs from that of an autonomous change in exports only in the algebraic sign:

$$\Delta Y = -\left(\frac{1}{1 - b + m}\right)\Delta p$$

An autonomous increase in imports, other things being equal, will cause the level of income to decline. The change in the balance of payments resulting from a given autonomous increase in imports is:

$$\Delta B = \Delta X - \Delta p - m\Delta Y = \Delta p\left(\frac{m}{s + m} - 1\right)$$

$\Delta X = 0$ as exports are assumed to remain unchanged. Since $\frac{m}{s + m} < 1$, the deficit generated by an autonomous increase in imports is less than the initial increase in imports as a consequence of the decrease in imports demand induced by the contraction of income following the autonomous increase in imports. It can also be seen from Equation (3) that the effect of an autonomous increase in investment on the level of income is the same as that of an autonomous increase in exports:[5]

$$\Delta Y = \left(\frac{1}{1 - b + m}\right)\Delta I$$

An autonomous increase in investment, however, would cause a deterioration in the balance of payments by:

$$\Delta B = \Delta X - \Delta M = -\left(\frac{m}{1 - b + m}\right)\Delta I = -\left(\frac{1}{1 + \frac{s}{m}}\right)\Delta I$$

Trade and the Propagation of Income

The imports of goods and services of the United States from the rest of the world is the rest of the world's exports to the United States, and the exports of the United States to the rest of the world is the rest of the world's imports. The addition to (leakage from) the U.S. income flow as a result of U.S. exports (imports) corresponds to the contraction (addition to) in the flow of income of the rest of the world. Thus an autonomous increase in U.S. exports will cause the level of income in the United States to rise and the level of income in the foreign countries which increase their imports from the United States to fall. The expansion of income in the United States in turn will cause U.S. imports (foreign exports) to rise. This will cause income in the United States to contract

[5]Note that the multiplier effect in an open economy is smaller than that in a closed economy since in an open economy, there are two sources of leakage from the income flow–savings and imports.

and that of the foreign exporting countries to expand, and these income changes then would induce changes in U.S. and foreign imports and exports and so on. The level of income in a country is closely related to the level of income of other trading countries. Changes in the level of income in a country would cause the level of income in other countries to change as well through changes in imports and exports induced by income changes. The repercussion of income changes between trading countries is illustrated in the following simplified model of two trading countries: country 1 and country 2. The imports of country 1 are of course the exports of country 2 and the imports of country 2 are the exports of country 1. Assume that we have the following linear consumption, import, and export functions of the two countries.

Country 1	Country 2
$C_1(Y_1) = a_1 + b_1 Y_1$	$C_2(Y_2) = a_2 + b_2 Y_2$
$M_1(Y_1) = X_2(Y_1) = p + m_1 Y_1$	$M_2(Y_2) = X_1(Y_2) = q + m_2 Y_2$
$X_1(Y_2) = M_2(Y_2) = q + m_2 Y_2$	$X_2(Y_1) = M_1(Y_1) = p + m_1 Y_1$

Given autonomous investments I_1 and I_2 in the two countries, the equilibrium level of income in country $1(Y_1)$ and country $2(Y_2)$ is then

$$Y_1 = (a_1 + I_1 + q - p)\left(\frac{1}{1 - b_1 + m_1}\right) + \left(\frac{m_2}{1 - b_1 + m_1}\right)(Y_2) \tag{5}$$

$$Y_2 = (a_2 + I_2 + p - q)\left(\frac{1}{1 - b_2 + m_2}\right) + \left(\frac{m_1}{1 - b_2 + m_2}\right) Y_1 \tag{6}$$

The equations show that the level of income in country 1 depends on the level of income of country 2, and vice versa. To find the equilibrium level of income in the two countries, we can solve (5) and (6) simultaneously for Y_1 and Y_2. For a numerical example, assume that $C_1 = 40 + 4/5Y_1$; $M_1 = X_2 = 2 + 5/100Y_1$; $X_1 = M_2 = 3 + 1/10Y_2$; $C_2 = 50 + 7/10Y_2$; $I_1 = 20$, and $I_2 = 25$, We then have:

$$Y_1 = 244 + 4/10Y_2$$

$$Y_2 = 185 + 12.5/100Y_1$$

Solving these equations for Y_1 and Y_2, we obtain

$$Y_1 = 335$$

$$Y_2 = 226$$

From Equations (5) and (6) it can be seen that an autonomous change in either country 1 or country 2 export functions (i.e., Δq or Δp) would cause the level of income in both countries to change. But what is the extent of income change? Assume that the export function of country 1 shifts upward by Δq, the change in the equilibrium level of income of both countries, from Equations (5) and (6), will be:

$$\Delta Y_1 = \Delta q \left(\frac{1}{1 - b_1 + m_1}\right) + \left(\frac{m_2}{1 - b_1 + m_1}\right) \Delta Y_2$$

$$\Delta Y_2 = -\Delta q \left(\frac{1}{1 - b_2 + m_2}\right) + \left(\frac{m_2}{1 - b_2 + m_2}\right) \Delta Y_1$$

Solving for ΔY_1 and ΔY_2 in terms of Δq, we have:

$$\Delta Y_1 = \frac{1 - b_2}{(1 - b_1 + m_1)(1 - b_2 + m_2) - m_1 m_2} \cdot \Delta q = \frac{1}{m_1 + s_1 + m_2 \dfrac{s_1}{s_2}} \cdot \Delta q$$

$$\Delta Y_2 = \frac{1 - b_1}{(1 - b_1 + m_1)(1 - b_2 + m_2) - m_1 m_2} \cdot (-\Delta q) = \frac{1}{m_2 + s_2 + m_1 \dfrac{s_2}{s_1}} (-\Delta q)$$

Where $s_1 = 1 - b_1$ and $s_2 = 1 - b_2$ are the marginal propensities to save in country 1 and country 2 respectively. An autonomous increase in the export function of country 1 thus causes the equilibrium level of income in this country to rise, and that in country 2 to decline. The extent of income changes is indicated by the export multiplier $\dfrac{1}{m_1 + s_1 + m_2 \dfrac{s_1}{s_2}}$ for country 1 and $\dfrac{1}{m_2 + s_2 + m_1 \dfrac{s_2}{s_1}}$ country 2. In the above numerical example, assume that $\Delta q = 5$. This will cause the equilibrium level of income of country 1 to increase by 15.6 and that of country 2 to decrease by 24.5. This autonomous increase in country 1 exports improves its balance of payments by $\Delta B_1 = 1.77$ [i.e., $\Delta B_1 = \Delta X_1 - \Delta M_1 = \Delta q + m_2 \Delta Y_2 - m_1 \Delta Y_1 = 5 + 1/10(-24.5) - 5/100(15.6) = 1.77$].[6] The surplus in country 1 balance of payments is much smaller than the initial surplus (gen-

[6]Note from Equations (5) and (6) that an autonomous increase in country 1 investment would cause its income to rise by

$$\Delta Y = \frac{1}{s_1 + \dfrac{m_1 s_2}{s_2 + m_2}} \Delta I_1$$

and the level of income in country 2 to increase by

$$\Delta Y_2 = \frac{1}{s_2 + \dfrac{s_1 (s_2 + m_2)}{m_1}} \Delta I_1$$

This, however, would cause a deterioration in country 1 balance of payments by

$$\Delta B_1 = m_2 \Delta Y_2 - m_1 \Delta Y_1 = -\frac{1}{\dfrac{s_1 (s_2 + m_2)}{m_1 s_2} + 1} \Delta I_1$$

erated by the autonomous increase in its exports). This reflects the repercussion of income changes and subsequently induced changes in the imports and exports in the two countries which operate to narrow the initial deficit of country 2 or surplus of country 1.

The repercussion of income changes in a country on the level of income of the rest of the world depends upon the level of income and trade in the country in which income changes relative to world trade and income. For a very important country like the United States whose income and trade represent a dominant component of world trade and income, income changes in the United States carry important repercussions on the rest of the world. A decline in the level of income in the United States as a consequence of a recession or depression would cause U.S. import demand to decline and the decline in U.S. import demand may cause severe decline in income and employment in foreign countries. It is therefore not difficult to see why maintaining a high level of income and employment in the United States is not only for its own good but also for the good of the world community as a whole.

BALANCE-OF-PAYMENTS ADJUSTMENT

Income changes which induce changes in the demand for imports and exports constitute a channel through which imbalances in a country's balance of payments are adjusted. We have seen that an increase in income in country 1 would cause its imports to rise. Starting from an initial equilibrium in its balance of payments, the induced increase in import demand would result in a payment deficit. The increase in imports would cause income in country 1 to contract and income in the foreign exporting countries to expand. The contraction of income in country 1 in turn would cause its imports to decline and the expansion of income in foreign countries would cause their imports from country 1 to rise. Import and export changes induced by income changes thus operate to reduce country 1 payments deficit or the rest of the world's payments surplus. But in addition to income changes, changes in the prices of imports and exports represent another important channel for the adjustment of payments imbalances. A decrease in the prices of a country's exports can be expected to give rise to greater foreign demand for its exports, and an increase in the prices of imports tend to reduce its import demand.

Now the prices of imports and exports are made up of two components: (a) the domestic prices of imports and exports, and (b) the foreign exchange rates. The price of an exported product may change either because of changes in the domestic price of the product or because of changes in the value of the currency of the exporting country vis à vis foreign currencies or a combination of both. As an example, suppose that the Renault Company in France sells its cars to a New York importer at the price of 10,000 francs each. If the exchange rate between the U.S. dollar and the French franc is 5 francs to the dollar, then the cost of the car to the U.S. buyer will be $2,000. The dollar price of the Renault car thus reflects both the French price and the dollar-franc exchange rate. Now, assume that as a consequence of productivity increases, the franc price of the Renault is reduced to 9,000 francs. Given the exchange rate of 5 francs to the dollar, the dollar price of the Renault is now only $1,800. It is clear that price decreases in France (e.g., as a result of productivity improvements or deflationary domestic economic policy) would make France a better place for foreigners to buy—that is, they would stimulate France's exports. On the other hand, given the franc price of the Renault, its dollar price may be reduced to $1,800 if France reduces the value of the franc in relation to the U.S. dollar from 5 francs to the dollar to about 5.5556 francs to the dollar—that is, by devaluing the franc in terms of the dollar. With the lower dollar price of the Renault, France would probably be able to sell more of it to the United States. But while the increase in the exchange rate of the franc vis-à-vis the dollar makes French products cheaper to U.S. buyers (thereby encouraging U.S. imports from France), it makes U.S. goods more expensive to the French buyers (since given the dollar prices of U.S. products, their prices in francs increase as a result of devaluation of the franc), thereby discouraging French imports from the United States. It follows that a country with a payments deficit may correct the imbalance by resorting to deflationary monetary and fiscal policies to reduce domestic income and prices, and/or raise the exchange rate of its currency in reference to foreign currencies in order to reduce import demand and stimulate exports. Whether changes in domestic income and prices or exchange rate changes are used as measures to adjust payments imbalances depending upon the exchange rate system in effects. Should neither of these methods be considered desirable under certain circumstances, then the adjustment could be effected through controls over international transactions.

Adjustment under the Gold Standard

The monetary unit of a country "on gold," as already noted, is defined in terms of a given weight of gold and circulating currency is freely convertible into gold and vice versa at a legally fixed rate. Since the currencies of countries on gold are defined in terms of gold, their exchange rates can fluctuate around the mint parities within very narrow limits represented by the gold export and import points. The gold-export point is the exchange rate at which it would be advantageous for gold arbitrageurs to sell gold abroad for foreign exchange to supply their foreign exchange markets, and the gold-import point, the exchange rate which induces gold inflows as gold arbitrageurs would buy gold from foreigners in return for their own currency. Since under the gold standard, the exchange rate can fluctuate only within narrow limits, the adjustment of payments imbalances is effected largely through the mechanism of income and price changes.

Starting from a payments equilibrium, suppose that there is an autonomous increase in country A's import demand. The consequent increase in the demand for foreign exchange in country A would cause the foreign exchange rate to rise. When the gold-export point is reached, gold arbitrageurs would purchase gold from the central bank and sell it abroad for foreign exchange with which to supply their exchange market. The sale of gold by the central bank would cause bank reserves and the supply of money and credit to decline (there may be a multiple contraction in credit and deposit money, depending upon the reserve position of the banking system). The decrease in the supply of money and credit is expected to cause interest rates to rise and the level of prices to decline. Lower domestic prices would stimulate exports which are also promoted by higher prices in the gold-receiving countries as a result of the expansion of the supply of money and credit in these countries following gold inflows. Higher interest rates would also help attract capital inflows. The contraction in country A's income caused by the autonomous increase in its imports (and decrease in its investment spending due to higher rates of interest) on the other hand, would work to reduce its imports. The increase in exports and decrease in imports in country A induced by price and income changes (and induced capital inflows) would help restore its payments imbalance.

The adjustment mechanism under the international gold standard is supposed to be automatic. A payments deficit would automatically cause gold reserve, the supply of money and credit, and the level of money income and prices to decline; lower income and prices would promote exports and discourage imports and help remove the payments imbalance.

Adjustment under the Freely Fluctuating Exchange-Rate System

Under a freely fluctuating exchange-rate system, the rate of exchange is determined by the free play between the demand for and supply of foreign exchange. Under this exchange-rate system the adjustment of payments imbalances is effected automatically through exchange-rate changes. An autonomous increase in import demand would cause the demand curve for foreign exchange to shift upward and the foreign exchange rate to rise. Increases in the foreign exchange rate in turn would work to restore equilibrium by promoting exports and the supply of foreign exchange and moderating import demand. Conversely, an autonomous increase in exports would cause the supply curve of foreign exchange to shift downward and the foreign exchange rate to decline. The decline in the foreign exchange rate would cause import demand and the demand for foreign exchange to rise. This again would help restore payments equilibrium. The adjustment of imbalances under a freely fluctuating exchange-rate system is illustrated in Fig. 28-3. The horizontal axis represents the quantity of foreign exchange and the vertical axis the rate of exchange—that is, the price in domestic currency of a unit of foreign exchange.

R_0 is the initial equilibrium rate of exchange—that is, the rate at which the demand for foreign exchange is just equal to the supply of foreign exchange

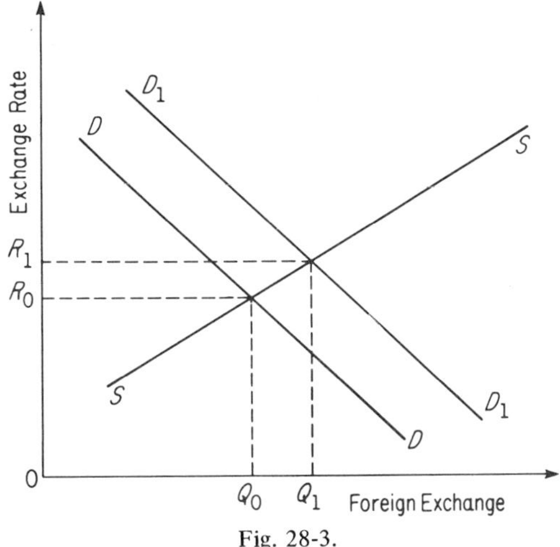

Fig. 28-3.

OQ_0. Now, assume that there is an increase in the demand for foreign exchange from DD to D_1D_1 as a result of, say, an autonomous increase in import demand. At the prevailing rate of exchange R_0, there is an excess of demand over supply of foreign exchange. This causes the foreign exchange rate to rise. The rise in the rate of exchange stimulates exports and the supply of foreign exchange. When the exchange rate rises to R_1, payments equilibrium is again restored: the value of imports is again equal to the value of exports (OQ_1 in terms of foreign exchange and $OQ_1 \times OR_1$ in terms of domestic currency).

Adjustment under Limited Flexible Exchange Rates

Under a "limited" flexible exchange-rate system, the rate of exchange is left to be determined by free market forces but the monetary authorities seek to limit the fluctuations in the exchange rate by undertaking stabilization operations—that is, by selling or buying foreign exchange against domestic currency, depending upon supply-and-demand conditions in the foreign exchange market. When the demand for foreign exchange is such that it tends to cause the exchange rate to rise above certain desired upper limit, the monetary authority can prevent that by selling foreign exchange. On the other hand, when the supply of foreign exchange is strong relative to demand and causes the exchange rate to fall, to prevent it from declining further, the monetary authority can purchase foreign exchange.

Under this exchange-rate system, if the authority is committed to stabilize the foreign exchange rate, then the adjustment of payments deficits would have to be effected through domestic income and price deflation, essentially the same as under the gold standard. On the other hand, to avoid income and price deflation, the deficits would have to be adjusted through devaluation—that is, through raising the exchange rate of the domestic currency vis-à-vis foreign currencies. Maintaining stable exchange rates in the face of persistent payments deficits without income and price deflation would eventually exhaust foreign exchange reserves (and international credits) available to the monetary authority for stabilization operations. At this point the choice has to be made of either income and price deflation or devaluation or a combination of both. If no choice is made, then exchange controls have to be imposed.

Adjustment Through Exchange Controls

Payments imbalances may also be adjusted by substituting exchange controls for the operations of market forces. Under exchange controls, exporters and other recipients of foreign exchange are required by law to surrender foreign exchange to the control authority at the officially fixed exchange rate which is typically below the rate that would be established if free-market forces were allowed to function. Importers and other users of foreign exchange, on the other hand, may obtain foreign exchange by applying to the control authority. Since the official exchange rate is fixed below the free-market rate, the excess demand for foreign exchange at the official rate is suppressed by the exchange control agency through granting foreign exchange only for authorized imports. Whether or not this kind of controlled equilibrium can be sustained depends on the efficiency of the exchange control mechanism and the degree of currency overvaluation, among other things. Extensive black-market operations which usually result from a high degree of currency overvaluation may render ineffective exchange controls.

EXCHANGE-RATE SYSTEMS: STRENGTH AND WEAKNESSES

The various exchange-rate systems which we have discussed in connection with the adjustment of payments imbalances have been adopted at one time or another by various countries in the world. They all have advantages and disadvantages.

Fixed versus Flexible Exchange Rates

The relative strength and weaknesses of fixed exchange rates and flexible exchange rates, hence, the choice between these alternative systems, has been a subject of much controversy.

Up to the early 1930's, the fixed-exchange-rate system which was widely adopted throughout the world was the gold standard system. Gold, however, was abandoned wholesale following the Great Depression. One of the outstanding advantages of the gold standard is that it provides for exchange-rate stability. Stable exchange rates promote the expansion of international trade and investments, as there is little or no exchange risk involved; they enable more reliable planning and forecasting on costs, prices, and profits for business firms specializing in foreign trade and investments. Another important advantage of the gold standard, according to its advocates, is that it provides for an automatic mechanism for the adjustment of international payments imbalances. The supply of money and credit, the level of income, expenditure, and prices are supposed to increase or decrease in accordance with gold inflows or outflows generated by payments surpluses or deficits, thereby promoting imports and deterring exports, or stimulating exports and discouraging imports to restore payments equilibrium. The correction of payments disequilibrium under the gold standard implies complete dependence of monetary policy on balance-of-payments consideration. Monetary expansion in the case of surplus and contraction in the case of deficit.

The gold standard did work quite well during the pre-1914 period. The objective of economic policy was then the free convertibility of currency into gold and exchange-rate stability. Prices and wages were then rather flexible upward as well as downward, so that the adjustment of payments imbalances through gold movements and price and income changes did not generate any significant change in employment. Economic conditions, however, have changed. The gold standard, in its classical form is believed by many to be unworkable under present-day conditions. With the emphasis of modern economic policy on full employment and high rates of economic growth, and with the power of strong labor unions to resist wage cuts and the ability of oligopolistic enterprises to "fix" prices, deflationary fiscal and monetary measures required for the adjustment of payments deficits under the gold standard would result in intolerable unemployment. Furthermore, even during the heyday of the international gold standard, the gold standard game was not "fairly" played. Although the adjustment of payments deficits through income and price deflation in the deficit country was supposed to be reinforced by the expansion of money, income, spending, and prices in the surplus countries, this did not always happen. While the deficit country was anxious to remove the deficit, the surplus country might not be so disposed to reduce the surplus particularly when such measures would result in inflationary pressures. Various countries under gold indeed did take restrictive monetary measures to sterilize the expansionary effects of gold inflows generated by payments surpluses, and this would make harder for deficit countries to correct payments imbalances.

Under the gold standard, or any form of fixed exchange system, the maintenance of fixed exchange rates implies subordination of domestic economic policy to balance-of-payments considerations. In the face of payments deficits, it would not be possible for a country to maintain fixed exchange rates and at the same time follow an independent course of monetary and fiscal actions to foster full employment and economic growth. Because such a course of action would allow payments deficits to persist, the country would suffer losses of international reserves and a weakening of its currency in international markets. The correction of payments deficits would either require deflationary monetary and fiscal policies (with some measure of unemployment when wages and prices are downwardly rigid) or devaluation or a combination of both, or some forms of direct and indirect controls over international transactions. The attempt of the United Kingdom, for instance, to maintain the exchange rate of the pound sterling vis à vis the U.S. dollar at approximately $2.80 to the pound in the face of persistent payments deficits had resulted in continuous losses of reserves and so weakened the pound in international markets that the British government finally had to devalue the pound from $2.80 to $2.40 to the pound in late 1967 and embark on a program of "economic austerity," hoping that this would help restore payments equilibrium. The United States in the 1960's faced the same problem. The commitment of the United States to maintain the exchange rate of the dollar by selling gold to foreign official holders of dollars at a fixed price and the pursuit of domestic economic policy to promote high-level employment and growth in the face of persistent payments deficits (generated partly by rising expenditures required to sustain U.S. economic and military commitments abroad) have led to continuous losses of U.S. gold reserves and undermined to some extent the dollar in international transactions. The United States, however, has refrained from both drastic deflationary monetary and fiscal policies and devaluation. It has elected to let its gold reserves dwindle. But U.S. reserves are not inexhaustible. Eventually the United States would have to put its international economic position in order either by changing the exchange rate of the dollar, or "deflationary" economic policy, and imposing certain voluntary as well as legal controls over international transactions (some of which have in fact been in effect),[7] if the dollar is to continue its role as an international reserve currency.

Under a freely fluctuating exchange-rate system, just as under the gold standard, the adjustment of international payments imbalances is supposed to be automatic. But whereas under the gold standard the adjustment is effected through domestic income and price changes, under a freely fluctuating exchange-rate system the adjustment is made through exchange-rate changes as noted earlier. Under a freely fluctuating exchange-rate system, since the shocks generated by the adjustment of payments imbalances are absorbed by exchange-rate changes, the adjustment process does not affect domestic income and employment. An increase in the demand for foreign exchange generated by, say, an increase in the demand for imports would cause the foreign exchange rate to rise. But the rise in the exchange rate in turn would promote exports.

It follows that under a freely fluctuating exchange-rate system the public authority can pursue an independent course of monetary and fiscal policies and leave the operations of free-market forces to take care of payments imbalances

[7]More on this in Chapter 30.

by letting the exchange rate find its own equilibrium position in the foreign exchange market.

However, if stable exchange rates are conducive to the expansion of foreign trade and investments, then frequent and wide fluctuations in exchange rates which may be generated under a freely fluctuating exchange-rate system would reduce the flow of trade and investments between nations. The extent of changes in the exchange rate under a freely fluctuating exchange-rate system resulting from the adjustment of payments imbalances depends on the degree of responsiveness of the supply of and demand for foreign exchange. If the demand for and supply of foreign exchange are relatively irresponsive to exchange-rate changes, then the change in the exchange rate caused by an increase or decrease in the supply of and demand for foreign exchange may be large enough to adversely affect international trade and payments. Exchange-rate changes under a freely fluctuating exchange-rate system, moreover, may under certain circumstances be "destabilizing" in that they may lead to one-way movement in the exchange rate which would be disruptive to international transactions.

Suppose that certain demand pressures cause the exchange rate to rise, and this leaves exchange speculators and others to expect that the rate of exchange will continue to rise. This would give rise to speculative purchases of foreign exchange by exchange speculators. Importers would try to speed up import orders to avoid expected rising costs of imports, and at the same time foreign importers might slow down their import orders, hoping to obtain imports at lower foreign exchange costs. These activities would cause the excess demand for foreign exchange to widen as the exchange rate rises. This consequently would cause the rate of exchange to rise further and further. Stopping this kind of destabilizing speculative operations in the foreign exchange market may require controls over foreign exchange transactions.

The evidence from history regarding the operations of the freely fluctuating exchange-rate system was not conclusive either in favor or against it. The system was adopted by a number of countries in the early 1920's and showed a high degree of instability. It should, however, be borne in mind that this was a period of international monetary chaos. The experience of Canada which adopted a floating exchange-rate system in the 1950's indicated that the system was capable of remarkable stability. But again this was not a conclusive testimony to the stability of the system as the Canadian dollar was closely tied to the U.S. dollar. Moreover, the system was abandoned by Canada in the early 1960's in favor of the fixed-par-value system under the Articles of Agreements of the International Monetary Fund.

Exchange Controls

As we have mentioned when exchange controls are imposed in a country, residents of that country are required by law to surrender foreign exchange receipts against domestic currency at the official rate of exchange, and are permitted to buy foreign currencies only through the authorization of the control authority. An artificial equilibrium between the supply of and demand for foreign exchange is maintained by substituting control regulations for market forces.

If trade promotes the expansion of real income of trading nations, then exchange controls which restrict the international flow of goods and services would tend to reduce real income of trading nations. In order for a country to sell goods and services to foreign countries it would also have to buy goods and services abroad. A country which imposes restrictions on the goods and services that its residents wish to purchase from foreigners would also reduce the ability of foreigners to purchase goods and services from its own residents. Yet under certain circumstances exchange controls are necessary. For instance, they are necessary to prevent destabilizing capital outflows as a consequence of speculative operations, or to stop massive capital flight generated by political upheavals. Exchange controls are necessary during wartime periods to use the available supply of foreign exchange in the acquisition of defense material and equipment, and during postwar periods to channel foreign exchange to the imports of necessities and capital goods required for reconstruction; to avoid excessive exchange depreciation which would take place in the absence of controls since in a country devastated by war, the demand for foreign exchange far exceeds its ability to earn foreign exchange. This was the experience of Western Europe, for example, during and after World War II. Ravaged by the war, these countries needed U.S. dollars for the imports of necessities and capital goods for economic reconstruction—and had little to offer in exports. In view of the then enormous demand for U.S. dollars, the currencies of these countries would have drastically depreciated vis-à-vis the U.S. dollar had exchange controls not been imposed. Exchange controls were not liberalized in Western European countries until the late 1950's when they sufficiently recovered from the devastations of the war and regained their competitiveness in relation to the United States in world markets.

Exchange controls, however, are still prevalent in most developing and underdeveloped countries. The demand for hard currencies in these countries is strong relative to their supply ability. Exchange controls are consequently needed to prevent undesirable depreciation of their currencies, and to channel their limited foreign exchange receipts to the imports of basic necessities and capital equipment for development purposes, among other things.

SUMMARY

The concept of deficit or surplus is used as an indicator of balance-of-payments disequilibrium. The general approach to measuring payment deficit or surplus is to separate balance-of-payments transactions into two groups: "autonomous" transactions and "balancing" transactions. Autonomous transactions are those carried on independently of balance-of-payments consideration, and balancing transactions those that arise to accommodate autonomous transactions. A payments deficit or surplus refers to the negative or positive sums of autonomous transactions. Since there is no clear-cut way to know whether certain transactions are autonomous or balancing, the measurement of payments deficit or surplus is somewhat arbitrary. In the United States, two alternative measures have been used to evaluate U.S. balance of payments performance—the balance on liquidity basis and the balance on basis of official reserve transactions. The balance on liquidity basis is an indicator of changes in the U.S. liquidity position measured by changes in U.S. liquid liabilities to all foreigners and changes in U.S. official reserves. The balance on basis of official reserve transactions differs from the liquidity balance in that it treats all balance-of-payments transactions except for changes in U.S. official reserves and changes in U.S. liquid and certain nonliquid liabilities to foreign official monetary agencies as autonomous transactions.

International trade influences the level of income and employment. The exports of goods and services, like investment spending, add to the income flow, while the imports of goods and services, like savings, constitute a leakage from the flow of income. Given the propensity to save $S(Y)$, the propensity to import $M(Y)$, investment I and exports X, we have the following condition for equilibrium income:

$$S(Y) + M(Y) = I + X$$

Income is in equilibrium when the leakage from the income flow through savings and imports is exactly equal to the injection into the flow of income by investment and exports. Income changes as exports (or for that matter, investment, the propensity to import, the propensity to save or to consume) change. Given an autonomous change in exports, the change in the equilibrium level of income is equal to the product of the autonomous change in exports and the export multiplier, or

$$\text{Export Multiplier} = \frac{1}{\begin{matrix}\text{Marginal} \\ \text{Propensity} \\ \text{to save}\end{matrix} + \begin{matrix}\text{Marginal} \\ \text{propensity} \\ \text{to import}\end{matrix}}$$

Income, price, and exchange-rate changes are channels through which payments imbalances are adjusted. Which channel is operative depends upon the exchange-rate system in effect. Under the gold standard, which is a special form of fixed exchange-rate system, the adjustment is supposed to be effected automatically through domestic income and price changes generated by gold movements. This adjustment mechanism, however, would give rise to unemployment if wages and prices were downwardly inflexible. Under a freely fluctuating exchange-rate system, the adjustment is effected through exchange rate changes. The level of income and employment is not affected by this adjustment process. Frequent and wide fluctuations in exchange rates which may be generated under this exchange-rate system, however, would impair the flow of international payments. If none of these adjustments methods is deemed operative, then adjustment may be forced through exchange controls which may be necessary to avoid capital flight or excessive exchange depreciation.

PROBLEMS

1. If the balance of payments as a whole shows neither a deficit nor surplus, then what do we mean when we talk about a balance of payments deficit or surplus? What are problems involved in measuring a payments deficit or surplus? What are alternative measures of balance of payments performance in the United States? What is the rationale of these alternative measures?

2. Explain the process of balance-of-payments adjustment under the gold standard. What are advantages and disadvantages of this system of fixed exchange rates?

3. What is a freely fluctuating exchange-rate system? How are payments imbalances supposed to be adjusted under this system? What are its relative strength and weaknesses?

4. Discuss some of the circumstances in which you would consider exchange controls necessary.

5. You are given the following information on balance of payments transactions of the United States in a certain year (in millions of dollars): Exports of goods and services, $43,039. Imports of goods and services, $37,937. Increase of U.S. government grants and capital flow, net, $3,446. Increase in remittances and pensions, net, $1,010. Increase in U.S. direct investments abroad, $3,543. Increase in U.S. purchases of foreign short and long-term obligations, $670. Increase in long-term foreign investments in the United States, $1,710. Increase in foreign central banks' holdings of U.S. nonmarketable, nonconvertible government securities, $802. Increase in foreign commercial banks' demand and time deposits with U.S. banks, $2,697. Foreign central banks and governments reduce their holdings of U.S. short-term assets by $1,908. (a) What would be the net change in U.S. official reserves? (b) What is the size of the deficits (or surplus) on liquidity basis and on basis of official reserve transactions?

6. You are given the following information on consumption, investment, imports, and exports of a certain country:

$$C = 60 + 3/5Y$$
$$M = 2 + 1/10Y$$
$$X = 15$$
$$I = 25$$

(a) Find the equilibrium level of income. What is the payments position of this country at that level of income?

(b) Suppose that exports X increase by 5, what would be the change in the equilibrium level of income? What is the change in the balance of payments of this country? What is the size of the export multiplier?

(c) Instead of exports increasing by 5, assume that investment I increases by 5. Would the effect of the increase in investment on the level of income and the balance of payments be the same as that of an equal increase in exports?

APPENDIX

NOTES ON THE BALANCE-OF-PAYMENTS EFFECTS OF EXCHANGE-RATE CHANGES[8]

We have seen that changes in the rate of exchange are a channel through which international payments imbalances may be corrected. Here we shall discuss this in more details.

Assume that the rate of exchange of a country's currency is fixed and it is now changed. How would this affect this country's balance of payments? The effect of a change in the rate of exchange on the balance of payments depends on its effect on the rate of change of the value of imports and the value of exports. Changes of the value of imports and exports depend on changes of the quantities and prices of imports and exports. In what follows we shall consider the effects of a devaluation of country A's currency (i.e., a reduction in the value of its currency vis-à-vis foreign currencies) on the changes in the value of its imports and exports in terms of its own currency.

In Fig. 28-4, the curve DD represents the foreign demand for country A's exports, and SS is country A's supply of exports before the rate of exchange is changed. They are both functions of prices expressed in terms of country A's

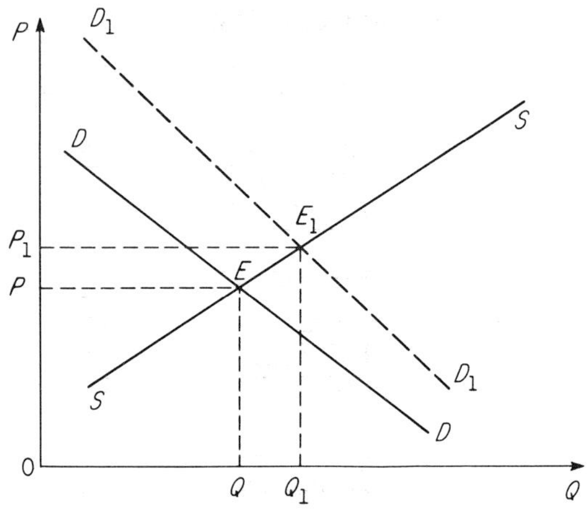

Fig. 28-4. Exports.

[8]Drawn mostly from Charles P. Kindleberger, *International Economics* (Homewood, Ill.: Irwin, 1963).

currency.[9] Assume now that country A devalues its currency by a given percentage. The supply curve of exports, as a function of prices in domestic currency, remains unchanged. But the foreign demand curve for country A's exports will shift upward (D_1D_1) as the price of country A's exports is reduced by the devaluation (the same quantity of country A's exports is now demanded by foreigners at a higher price in country A's currency).[10] As a consequence of the upward shift of the foreign demand for exports curve, the quantity of country A's exports and the exports price in local currency increase. Hence the value of exports in local currency increases (represented by the difference between the areas $OQ_1E_1P_1$ and $OQEP$). This is normally the case. Only in the limiting case of a completely inelastic foreign demand for country A's exports (i.e., DD is parallel to the price axis) does the value of exports in terms of local currency remain unchanged.

Figure 28-5 shows country A's demand curve for imports (DD) and the

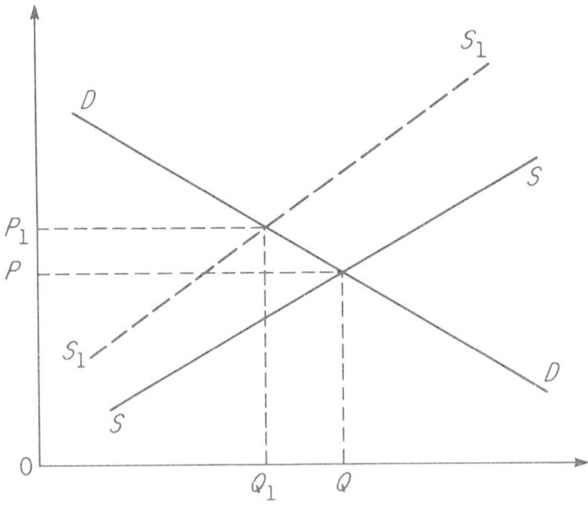

Fig. 28-5. Imports.

foreign supply curve of imports (SS) before the exchange rate is changed. They are functions of prices expressed in terms of country A's currency. The devaluation of country A's currency will leave its demand curve for imports unchanged. The supply curve of imports, however, will shift upward (S_1S_1) since a given quantity of foreign exports will now be supplied to country A at a higher price

[9]It should be noted that at a given rate of exchange, the price in terms of domestic currency is equal to the price in foreign currency times the rate of exchange. The demand and supply curves therefore can be expressed as functions of domestic prices or foreign prices.

[10]Note that the shift represents a constant percentage, hence D_1D_1 is not parallel with DD. For example, if country A's currency is devalued by 50 percent, the upward shift of the ordinates of the foreign demand curve for exports will be 100 percent.

in terms of country A's currency. The upward shift of the supply curve of imports causes the local currency price of imports to rise and the quantity of imports to fall. It follows that the value of imports in terms of local currency will rise, remain unchanged, or fall, following a devaluation, depends on whether the elasticity of country A's demand for imports is less than one, equal to one, or greater than one.

It is clear from Figs. 28-4 and 28-5 that a change of the rate of exchange normally causes both the value of imports and the value of exports to change. The balance of payments is said to react favorably to a devaluation when the increase in the value of exports is greater than the increase in the value of imports. Starting from a balance-of-payments equilibrium, it can be shown that that is the case when the sum of the elasticities of a country's demand for imports and of foreign demand for its exports is greater than one.[11] Consider for instance the limiting case of a completely inelastic foreign demand for country A's exports. We know that in this case the value of exports in local currency remains unchanged. But if the sum of the elasticities is greater than one, the elasticity of country A's demand for imports is greater than one; hence the value of imports in local currency falls following a devaluation. On the other hand, in the case of a complete inelasticity of country A's demand for imports, the value of imports in local currency will rise to the extent of the devaluation. But if the sum of the elasticities is greater than one, the elasticity of foreign demand for country A's exports is greater than one, which means that the increase in the local currency value of exports is greater than the increase in the local currency value of imports.

[11] This is commonly referred to as the Marshall-Lerner condition.

chapter 29

International Financial Cooperation and Institutions

The demise of the international gold standard in the early 1930's as a consequence of the depression was followed by international monetary chaos. Unilateral actions on trade and payments were taken by various nations to alleviate the effects of the depression with little or no regard to their consequences on trade and income of other nations. A number of countries resorted to devaluation as a means to improve domestic income and employment. But since other countries did the same to prevent their trade and payments positions from further deteriorating, the resulting competitive exchange depreciation led to nowhere but a drastic contraction in world trade and income. And this was aggravated by exchange controls, import restrictions and multiple-currency practices among other things (practices under which various import and export transactions are subject to a variety of exchange rates) imposed by other countries. It soon became apparent that world trade and payments could be promoted only through the concerted actions of trading nations. But the international political situation was then hardly conducive to international economic and monetary cooperation. With the outbreak of the war, international economic relationships were cut off. Exchange controls became world-wide (and continued throughout the postwar period). While the war raged on, financial leaders of the world, aware of the curse of competitive exchange depreciation and exchange restrictions, decided to meet at the International Conference of Bretton Woods in New Hampshire in 1944 to consider plans for international cooperation for the postwar period. The outcome of the Conference was the establishment of two international financial institutions: the International Monetary Fund and the International Bank for Reconstruction and Development; the former, to promote cooperation between nations to assist members with international payments difficulties, and the latter, to contribute to the economic reconstruction of countries devastated by the war, and to the economic development of the underdeveloped world.

THE INTERNATIONAL MONETARY FUND (IMF)

The International Monetary Fund began operations in 1946. Its membership which initially numbered 39 countries rose to 107 in 1968. The Fund's members range from the most important industrial powers of the world such as the United States, the United Kingdom, the Republic of Germany, and Japan to small and underdeveloped countries such as Laos and Panama.[1] The basic objectives of the Fund are (a) to promote international monetary cooperation and the expansion and balanced growth of international trade, (b) to maintain exchange-rate stability and orderly exchange-rate adjustments whenever such adjustments are necessary, (c) to assist members in temporary payments difficulties, and (d) to promote free trade and eliminate exchange restrictions. The Fund is an attempt to combine some of the advantages of exchange-rate systems in effect in the past. The commitment of member countries to maintain stable exchange rates would provide a firm foundation for the expansion of international trade and payments. Countries which are in temporary balance of payments difficulties would be able to draw on the Fund's resources so that they may have time to take necessary adjustment measures without resorting to unduly deflationary policies which could depress domestic income and employment or to exchange restrictions which would stifle trade and payments. In the case of persistent payments disequilibrium, a member country may adjust the exchange rate of its currency, but exchange-rate adjustments are to be conducted in an orderly manner so as to minimize adverse effects of such changes on world trade.

Par Value

In terms of the Articles of Agreement of the Fund, "a member country agrees with the Fund to establish an exchange rate for its currency in terms of gold or the U.S. dollar, which is referred to as "par value." Once the par value of its currency is established, a member country is under obligation to maintain the fluctuations of the spot-exchange rates of its currency to within 1 percent on either side of the par value. Changes in the par value of a currency have to be agreed by the Fund and this is permissible only for correcting "fundamental" payments disequilibrium. What constitutes fundamental disequilibrium, however, is yet to be defined by the Fund.

The initial par values of the currencies of some major trading nations were established at a time when international trade relations were badly distorted. These initial par values were soon proved to be unrealistic. They were substantially overvalued vis-à-vis the U.S. dollar. This was reflected in the substantial discounts of some currencies, particularly the pound sterling, in various free foreign-exchange markets in the world. The overvaluation of the pound led to British payments deficits. To cover payments deficits, the United Kingdom had to dip into its gold and foreign exchange reserves. This caused the position of the pound to weaken further in international markets. Holders of pound sterling, afraid that the United Kingdom would soon devalue the pound which would mean losses in the foreign exchange value of their sterling holdings, began to

[1]The Soviet Union, the People's Republic of China, and other communist-bloc countries are not members of the Fund. Yugoslavia, however, is a member. Czechoslovakia was a member but was voted out of membership in 1948.

unload sterling balances for foreign exchange and gold. The consequent run on the pound caused the currency crisis in Western Europe in late 1949. The need for adjustment of the exchange rate of the pound sterling and some other currencies was then obvious. Consequently the Fund consented to the devaluation of the pound and a number of other currencies including the Belgian franc, the Danish krone, and the Indian rupee. The pound sterling was readjusted from \$4.03 U.S. to the pound to \$2.80 to the pound. The pound sterling was again revised downward to \$2.40 to the pound in late 1967 in the face of persistent payments deficits and continuous losses of reserves. Upward revision of exchange rates, however, has also taken place. Such an instance was the 5 percent appreciation of the Deutsche mark and the Netherlands guilder by the Federal Republic of Germany and the Netherlands respectively in early 1961 as a means to relieve domestic inflationary pressures. Occasional exchange rate adjustments by individual members are of course to be expected as a result of domestic and foreign economic changes and developments which shift their competitive positions in world markets.

Although members of the Fund are required, in principle, to establish par values for their currencies, but a number of countries are yet to establish par values. This is due largely to the fact that in most of these countries, economic conditions are such that the establishment of realistic par values would be difficult. Also, there are member countries which had established par value for their currency abandoned it and later returned to the par value system. France, for instance, which abandoned par value in 1948 and was consequently declared ineligible to the Fund's credit facilities, reestablished a new par value for the franc in 1958. Canada, in 1950, gave up par value in favor of a freely floating exchange-rate system as a consequence of domestic inflationary pressures generated partly be heavy capital inflows reestablished a new lower par value for the Canadian dollar in 1962.

Fund Resources

The resources of the Fund consist mainly of quotas or subscriptions of members. The quota of each member is determined on the basis of an agreed formula which reflects its national income, its gold and dollar reserves, and its volume of trade, among other things. In terms of the Articles of Agreement of the Fund, each member is to pay a minimum of 25 percent of its quota in gold and the remaining balance, in its own currency, calculated on the basis of the par value of its currency.[2] The Federal Reserve Bank of New York, the Bank of England and a few other major central banks serve as the Fund's gold depositories. The currency portion of the quota is paid by each member to the Fund's account with the member's central bank. For example, the quota for Belgium, in

[2]For a member which has not established a par value for its currency, the payment of its subscription is effected on the basis of an agreed accounting rate.

U.S. dollars, in 1967 was $422 million of which $105.5 million would be paid in gold and $316.5 million would be credited to the Fund's account with the National Bank of Belgium.

General increases in the quotas of all members may be made by decisions of the Fund's Board of Governors when the growth in world trade and payments warrants such quota increases to improve the adequacy of the Fund's resources. Additional quota increases for individual members may also be made as a consequence of the growth in their income and trade relative to the growth of world trade and income. Members' quotas have indeed been increased a number of times. In 1958 there was a general increase in members' quotas by 50 percent. This, coupled with additional quota increases for Canada, Germany, and Japan, raised the Fund's quotas from $9.2 billion at the end of 1958 to $15 billion in 1961. A general quota increase of 25 percent and special increases for 16 members were again approved in 1965. The Fund's quotas, consequently, were raised to approximately $23 billion.

Although the resources of the Fund are made up of a large number of national currencies (in addition to gold), those which have been actively used in Fund transactions have been largely the U.S. dollar, the pound sterling, and the currencies of some other major trading nations in Europe. With the freer flow of capital between major trading countries, there is a danger of speculative runs on some of these currencies particularly when there is suspect on the part of holders of these currencies regarding their possible devaluation. In order to provide emergency assistance to a member country subject to heavy reserve losses as a consequence of speculative attacks on its currency, the Fund in 1962 made arrangements to borrow, with obligation to repay within five years, up to $6 billion in currencies of ten major trading nations,[3] which might be needed for emergency assistance. This General Agreement to Borrow (GAB), effective for four years, was renewed for a second four-year term, until late 1970. In addition, the Fund may increase its holding of a member's currency by entering into bilateral agreement to borrow with it. Thus in late 1966 the Fund borrowed from Italy $250 million lira in order to replenish its lira holdings depleted by lira drawings by other members. The Fund may also increase its holdings of a member's currency needed for transactions by offering part of its gold reserve for sale to this member country.

Drawing

The primary source of reserves available to a country to cover its payments deficits is its holdings of gold and foreign exchange. Should its gold and foreign exchange reserves be inadequate to settle its payments deficits, it could borrow from other countries and from the Fund. Borrowing from the Fund is in the form of an exchange of currency. When a member country "draws" or "pur-

[3]These countries are: Belgium, Canada, France, Germany, Italy, Japan, the Netherlands, Sweden, the United States and the United Kingdom.

chases" from the Fund a given amount of foreign currency it needs, it pays the Fund in return an equivalent amount of its own currency (calculated at the established par value or some agreed accounting rate). Suppose a member wishes to purchase a given sum of U.S. dollars from the Fund. The transaction is effected by the Fund instructing the Federal Reserve Bank of New York to debit its account and credit the account of the drawing member or that designated by it, the stated amount of dollars. The drawing member, in turn, instructs its central bank to credit the account of the Fund with an equivalent amount in local currency.

The ability of a member to draw on the Fund's resources is both conditional and unconditional. The drawing on the Fund by a member which does not cause the Fund's holding of the member's currency to exceed its quota is granted virtually automatically. As we have explained, this is "gold tranche" drawing—that is, drawing not in excess of that portion of the member's quota paid in gold. Drawing which causes the Fund's holding of the member's currency to exceed its quota is referred to as "credit tranche" drawing. This is conditional drawing. The attitude of the Fund has been liberal in regard to a member drawing not in excess of an additional 25 percent of its quota (first credit tranche) provided it makes efforts to correct its payments difficulties. For higher "credit tranche" drawing, drawing members are expected to implement comprehensive monetary and fiscal programs to overcome their difficulties.

A member wishing assurance of financial assistance from the Fund when needed instead of immediate drawing may enter into a stand-by agreement with the Fund. It is an agreement by which the Fund authorizes a member to draw up to a specified amount over a specified period.[4] In terms of the Fund's Articles of Agreement, a member is not to draw on the Fund which would increase the Fund's holding of its currency by more than 25 percent of its quota for any 12-month period or in excess of 200 percent of its quota. Drawing beyond these limits requires a special waiver from the Fund.

In addition to drawing under the Fund's ordinary arrangements, a member country which experiences temporary short falls in its export earnings due to circumstances beyond its control (such as major emergencies or disasters and sharp declines in export prices) may apply for special drawings under the Fund's compensatory financing facility to compensate for the decrease in export earnings. In terms of the Fund's compensatory financing facility, introduced in 1963 and modified in 1966, a member adversely affected by decreases in export earnings may be granted special drawings up to 50 percent of quota even if this would bring its drawings above the limits prescribed by the Articles of Agreement. However, except for the case of major emergencies or disasters, outstanding compensatory drawings of a member may not exceed 25 percent of quota in any 12-month period. These drawings are separate from other drawing

[4]Stand-by agreements were introduced by the Fund in 1955 and since then a large number of members have resorted to these facilities.

facilities in the sense that they will not be taken into account in determining a member's ability to draw under the normal policies governing the use of the Fund's resources. Since its introduction, a number of members have requested drawings under this facility.[5] This, coupled with the Fund's ordinary facilities, would undoubtedly help mitigate the effects of instability of export earnings of primary producing countries.

A member drawing on the Fund's resources is under obligation to repurchase from the Fund some of its holdings of the member's currency to the extent that the Fund's holdings of the member's currency is in excess of 75 percent of quota; and the repurchase is to be made in gold or a convertible currency of a member country to the extent that the holdings of the Fund of this member's currency is less than 75 percent of quota.[6] The Articles of Agreement provides that a member shall have to repurchase annually an amount of its currency held by the Fund in excess of 75 percent of quota equivalent to one half of any increase in the Fund's holdings of its currency which has taken place during the fiscal year, plus or minus one half of any increase or decrease in its monetary reserves during the same period.[7] This provision insures that no member will be able to draw on the Fund's resources to finance more than one half of its payments deficits or to increase its monetary reserves. For example, suppose a member incurs a payments deficit of 50. To cover that deficit, assume that it draws 30 from the Fund and reduces its foreign exchange reserves by 20. The repurchase obligation of the member is then 5 for the period (one half of the increase in the Fund's holdings of its currency minus one half of the decrease in the member's reserves). A member, however, may request a postponement of payment of its repurchase obligation if it can make a case out of such a request.

Payments Restrictions

One of the purposes of the establishment of the Fund, as provided by the Articles of Agreement, is to "assist in the establishment of a multilateral system of payments in respect of current transactions between members and in the elimination of foreign exchange restrictions which hamper the growth of world trade." Article VIII therefore requires member countries to refain from "imposing restrictions on the making of payments and transfers for current international transactions . . . " without the approval of the Fund, and to "engage in

[5]For instance, in 1967 Ceylon, Colombia, the Dominican Republic, New Zealand, and Ghana, as a consequence of unfavorable development in their export earnings, requested compensatory drawings from the Fund totaling more than $90 million.

[6]The U.S. dollar was the popular currency used by member countries to repurchase their currencies held by the Fund. However, in the mid 1960's, as a consequence of U.S. heavy drawings on the Fund which resulted in the Fund holding U.S. dollars in excess of 75% of the U.S. quota, the Fund at times refused to accept U.S. dollar for repurchase purposes.

[7]Monetary reserves of a member country are defined by the Fund to include gold and short-term claims on convertible currencies of members minus the holdings of its currency by specified institutions of other members.

discriminatory currency arrangements or multiple currency practices except . . . as approved by the Fund." However, aware of the fact that in many countries conditions in the postwar period were such that it would not be possible for them to lift restrictions on payments and transfers for current international transactions without suffering from severe losses of reserves, Article XIV of the Fund Agreement provides for members to continue payments restrictions which had been imposed during the war for a transitional period without seeking Fund approval, with the understanding that restrictions are to be reduced or removed when circumstances are favorable for such action.

When the Fund began its operations, only a handful of countries were prepared to accept the obligation of Article VIII. These included Canada, Cuba, Honduras, Mexico and the United States, all in the Western Hemisphere which was hardly touched by the war. All other members continued to impose payments restrictions as authorized by Article XIV. These restrictions take a variety of forms, including exchange rationing, multiple exchange rates, and bilateral payments agreements. Members accepting Article VIII obligations have increased, however. In late 1950's, as Western European countries sufficiently recovered from the damages of the war and regained their competitive position in relation to the United States in world markets (thanks largely to massive U.S. unilateral assistance under the Marshall Plan), they began to liberalize payments restrictions. Some of these countries established nonresident convertibility for their currency (currency of a country held by all holders resident outside that country is convertible into other currencies). In early 1961 Belgium, France, The Federal Republic of Germany, Italy, the Netherlands, Sweden, the United Kingdom and some other countries accepted the obligations of Article VIII. Austria joined the "convertible" club in 1962, and Japan in 1964. As of 1967, 31 members of the Fund operated under Article VIII, about one half of which were less developed countries. Efforts have been made by a number of countries to either eliminate or simplify multiple exchange rates. Finland, Spain, Israel, and Turkey, for instance, abolished multiple exchange rates in the late 1950's. Iran, Jordan, and Yugoslavia, among others, planned to gradually eliminate multiple exchange rates practices. Some of these countries, however, reintroduced multiple exchange rates in the form of export and import subsidies and taxes which are tantamount to multiple exchange rates.

Member countries operating under Article XIV are under obligation to consult with the Fund regarding the future retention or abolition of restrictions. In the course of consultation, the Fund may give advices on policy measures which could be implemented to remove or alleviate problems which require the imposition of payments restrictions. When conditions are favorable for a member to lift restrictions and is ready to do so, it can always rely on the Fund for financial assistance should the removal of payments restrictions result in temporary payments difficulties.

Administrative Structure

The highest policy-making body of the Fund is the Board of Governors whose members are appointed by member countries. Each member country appoints a governor and an alternate governor. The Board of Governors decides on the admission of new members, the revision and changes of quotas, the establishment and readjustment of the par values of members' currencies, among other things. The Board of Governors meets once a year around September or October to review the operations of the Fund in the past fiscal year and consider policies for the future.

The general direction of the Fund's operations is delegated by the Board of Governors to the Executive Board made up of 19 executive directors appointed by individual members or groups of members. Five members which have the largest quotas in the Fund–The United States, the United Kingdom, France, the Federal Republic of Germany, and India–each appoints an executive director, and the remaining 14 executive directors are elected for two-year terms by all other members grouped into 14 groups. The voting power of a member or groups of members reflects their quotas. The United States, for example, has slightly more than 23 percent of the total number of votes. The five members with largest quotas have almost one half of the total number of votes (47 percent). The Executive Board meets regularly, practically on a weekly basis.

The Fund's day-to-day business is run by the Managing Director who also serves as chairman of the Executive Board. He heads the Fund's international staff with the assistance of a Deputy Managing Director. It is through the international staff that the Fund undertakes studies on international economic and financial problems, and provides members with advice and recommendations on general and specific economic and financial problems and policies.

Performance and Problems

The scope of the Fund's operations during the formative years was limited not only because it would take some time for the Fund to acquire the necessary experiences but also because of the massive financial assistance granted by the United States to Western Europe which consequently did not rely on the Fund's assistance. With the economic recovery of Western Europe, the liberalization of payments restrictions, and the growth in world trade and payments, the scope of the Fund's operations with members has been remarkably widened. Thus, of the cumulative drawings of the Fund's members of more than $18 billion since its inception to mid 1969, $14.5 billion were drawn after 1960. The establishment of the Fund has undoubtedly been an important contributing factor in the expansion of world trade and payments, in the relative stability of exchange rates and the remarkable economic progress achieved by the world community in the postwar period.

There are problems, however, inherent in the international monetary system as instituted by the Articles of Agreement of the Fund. The system is based on gold and a number of key national currencies serving as reserve currencies, namely the U.S. dollar, and to a much lesser extent the pound sterling. The system can be expected to operate smoothly so long as holders of these reserve currencies have confidence in their safety and stability. But this confidence may be undermined by some deterioration in the position of a reserve currency in world markets as a consequence of continuous international payments deficits of the reserve-currency country. A loss of confidence in these reserve currencies may generate currency crises serious enough to wreck the existing international monetary system.

Currency crises indeed have been somewhat frequent reflected by frequent runs on the pound sterling weakened in international markets by persistent British payments deficits that led to the devaluation of the pound in late 1967. And this caused a crisis which was overcome by massive assistance from the Fund and other central banks to the Bank of England. The rescue of a reserve currency in trouble has been in the form of loans in other key currencies, namely the German mark, the U.S. dollar, and the French franc. Yet the dollar and the French franc were recently in trouble. The U.S. dollar was subject to speculative attacks only four months after the devaluation of the pound. Foreign holders of dollar balances, fearing the devaluation of the dollar, attempted to unload their dollar holdings for foreign exchange and gold. This resulted in a loss of more than $1 billion in U.S. gold reserve and in the abandonment of the London Gold Pool, an agreement between the Federal Reserve Bank of New York and some central banks in Western Europe to pool part of their gold reserves for the stabilization of gold prices. The gold market became a two-tier market, an official market and a private market. In the private market, the price of gold is left to the free play between the demand for and supply of gold.[8] The French franc, in mid-1968, was a subject of speculative attacks resulting from economic difficulties generated by strikes and social disorders. The rescue of the franc did cost the Bank of France more than $2 billion of reserves. Yet this was not enough. The continued weakening of the franc in late 1968 and in the first half of 1969 finally led to its devaluation in August 1969. This, coupled with the revaluation of the German mark in October of the same year, helped restore some measure of stability in the international monetary system. But confidence crises may be expected to take place again should the confidence of holders of reserve currencies in their safety and stability be somehow impaired.

The present international monetary system intended to be flexible in that it enables a member country to adjust the exchange rate of its currency to correct "fundamental" payments imbalances, is somewhat rigid in regard to an im-

[8]More on this in the next chapter.

portant reserve-currency country like the United States. The devaluation of the dollar as a means for the United States to correct payments imbalances could indeed deal an irreparable blow to the system. The avenue which is available to the United States to remove or reduce its payments deficits is therefore deflationary domestic economic policies or payments restrictions or both. But while deflationary domestic economic policies are desirable at times of heavy inflationary pressures and overfull employment, they are hardly tolerable at times of declining income and employment. Payments restrictions, of course, may be imposed but considering the size of U.S. income and trade relative to world trade and income, severe trade and exchange restrictions by the United States would cause drastic contractions in world trade and income. This is what the Articles of the Fund's Agreement sought to eliminate. It is true that the availability of short-term financial assistance from the Fund enables a member with payments difficulties to put its financial house in order, but the fact that it may draw on the Fund's facilities could make it complacent in taking timely corrective measures and this delay could so aggravate its payments problems that to correct them is much more difficult and requires much more drastic actions.

Another problem which may be faced by the present international monetary system is the "inadequacy" of international reserves. Some rate of growth of international reserves is required to sustain growing world trade and payments. As we know, international reserves consist of gold supplemented by foreign-held dollar and sterling balances and some other convertible currencies. But where is this source of supply of dollar and sterling reserves? The payments deficits of the United States and the United Kingdom. We have a problem here. As the supply of official gold reserves does not increase significantly over time, growth in world trade and payments can be sustained only through increases in reserves which are national currencies. But increases in these currency reserves can be provided only through continuous payments deficits of these reserve-currency countries. Continuous deficits of these reserve-currency countries, however, could result in some surplus countries holding more reserve currencies than they need for reserve purposes. They may elect to convert part of their excess reserves into gold or other foreign currencies. This could undermine the value of these currencies in world markets and bring about damaging speculative attacks on these currencies. On the other hand, the elimination or reduction in the payments deficits of reserve-currency countries would enhance foreign confidence in their stability and safety. But this would reduce the aggregate reserves available for international trade and payments. And inadequate international reserve would stifle the flow of world trade. It follows that under the present international monetary system, to maintain the stability of reserve currencies while at the same time providing adequate reserves to sustain the growing volume of international trade and payments requires supplementing gold and reserve currencies with some internationally created reserves acceptable to all trading nations. We shall discuss in more details the problem of international reserves and the plan for the creation of a new international reserve, the "special drawing rights" plan, in the next chapter.

THE INTERNATIONAL BANK FOR RECONSTRUCTION AND DEVELOPMENT (IBRD)

The International Monetary Fund, conceived by the Bretton Woods Conference, was intended to be an international institution through which members pool up resources to assist member countries in temporary payments difficulties. Considering, however, the enormous need for long-term capital by war-torn countries and less developed nations for economic reconstruction and development during the postwar period, it was feared that in the absence of an international institution to make long-term funds available to these capital-hungry nations they would be tempted to avail themselves of the Fund's resources for reconstruction and development, and this would put the Fund in serious jeopardy. Consequently, in addition to the IMF, the Bretton Woods Conferees decided to establish an international development bank to assist in the reconstruction of war-devastated nations and in the economic development of the underdeveloped world. This is the International Bank for Reconstruction and Development, popularly known as the World Bank. As implied by its name, the primary objective of the Bank is the promotion of economic reconstruction and development of members. This it intends to attain by guaranteeing, participating in, or making direct loans where private capital is not available with "reasonable" terms and conditions.

The Bank began operations in mid-1946. Its administrative organization is essentially the same as that of the Fund. The powers over the operations of the Bank are vested in the Board of Governors whose members are appointed by member countries. The Board meets once a year. Most of the Board's responsibilities are delegated to the Board of Executive Directors of 19 members, five of whom represent the five largest contributors to the Bank's capital (the United States, the United Kingdom, France, Germany and India), and the remaining representing other groups of member countries. The daily business of the Bank is run by the President (elected by the Executive Board) who heads the Bank's international staff.

Lending

During the early years, most of the Bank's loans were directed to the economic reconstruction of Western Europe. Following the institution of the Marshall Plan for the economic recovery of Europe, the Bank began to direct its credit facilities to developing and underdeveloped members. Most of the Bank's loans have been made for specific "infrastructure" projects—projects considered to provide the foundation for development and growth. Thus more than two-third of the credit facilities of the Bank have been devoted to projects for the development of electric power and transportation, and less than a third to the financing of agriculture (namely flood control or irrigation projects), industry (particularly such heavy industries as mining, iron and steel) and education. Although relatively greater emphasis has recently been shifted to the development of education, industry, and agriculture, the lion share of the Bank's loans has remained committed to transportation and power supply.[9]

The Bank may guarantee, participate in, or make direct loans to member-countries' governments, political subdivisions, or private borrowers. When the borrower is not the government of a member country or a governmental agency, the government of the member in which the project is located is under obligation to fully guarantee the repayment of principal and interest. Loans made by the Bank have no strings attached in that borrowers may use the loan proceeds in any member countries where they may secure necessary material and equipment at lowest possible prices.[10] Loans granted by the Bank are to provide for the foreign exchange required by the project. The local currency expenditure connected with the project is supposed to be provided by the borrower, "unless in exceptional circumstances when local currency required for the purpose of the loan cannot be raised by the borrower on reasonable terms, the Bank may provide the borrower as part of the loan with an appropriate amount of that currency." A loan is made by the Bank only after a careful and thorough study of the technical and financial feasibility of the proposed project, the merits of the project in terms of its potential contribution to the economic development and growth of the member country, and when the borrower is not able to secure financing from private sources with reasonable terms. The last provision would assure that the Bank would not compete with private capital the expansion of which the Bank seeks to promote in the first place.

Lending Funds

The lending funds of the Bank come from several sources. Part of these represents the capital subscriptions of member countries the determination of which is based essentially on the same basis as that for the determination of the quotas of the International Monetary Fund. In terms of the Articles of Agreement of the Bank, each member is to pay in 2 percent of its subscription in gold or U.S. dollars, and 18 percent, in the currency of the subscribing member. While the gold subscriptions are at the free disposal of the Bank, the local currency payments can be used by the Bank only with the consent of the member country whose currency the Bank proposes to use. The Bank may call on members to pay the remaining 80 percent of their subscriptions or part of

[9]For 1966-67, for example, of the total Bank's loans of $715 million, $540 million went to transportation and electric power, and $175 million, to industry, agriculture and education.

[10]This is different from requirements under most bilateral loans and aid programs between individual countries where borrowers or grant recipients are required to use the proceeds to purchase goods and services from the lending or aid-granting countries.

them either in gold, U.S. dollars, or other currencies which the Bank may need to discharge its obligations. This then is basically a "guarantee fund," a capital cushion on which creditors of the Bank can fall when the Bank is in financial difficulty. By decisions of the Bank's Board of Governors, the capital subscriptions of members may be increased. And they have been increased. Thus in 1959 the capital subscription of each member was doubled. This, coupled with the subscriptions of new members, raised the authorized capital stock of the Bank from an initial amount of $10 billion to about $23 billion in 1967 of which about $2.3 billion was paid in.

Another important source of lending funds of the Bank is borrowings through the flotation of World Bank bonds in various capital markets of the world, namely in the United States and some Western European countries. This indeed has been the major source of the Bank's Funds. World Bank bonds are denominated in some 8 currencies, including U.S. dollars, pound sterling, Swiss franc,[11] and Deutschemark, and are held by investors in some 50 countries throughout the world. The Bank's bonds, initially met with some reluctance and skepticism on the part of investors, have enjoyed the highest rating possible in various capital markets as investors came to realize the safety record of the Bank's operations and the enormous amount of funds which the Bank may call upon members to pay for it to discharge its obligations. In addition to borrowings and capital subscriptions, earnings constitute another though less important source of lending funds. The Bank also can rely on the replenishment of its resources through the sale of part of its loan portfolio to financial institutions and other investors and cash inflows from loan repayments.

Apart from credit facilities, the Bank, with its expert staff, also provides member countries with technical assistance in preparing specific projects for financing, with advices and recommendations on the preparation of development plans which also serve as bases for the Bank to consider the merits of proposed projects in the light of their priorities within the framework of the member country's overall development program.

Evaluation

The Bank is an illustration of international cooperation through an institution in which rich members put up resources to assist in the economic development of less developed members. The credit facilities made available by the Bank to members, which totaled some $10.5 billion as of 1967—though very modest relative to the development capital needed by members—have undoubtedly assisted some members in gaining some head start in their development efforts. The technical assistance provided by the Bank to member countries in establishing development plans, in setting up training programs in economic development

[11] Switzerland is not a member of the Bank, but has opened its capital markets for the Bank to raise funds.

problems, is certainly a contribution to the development potential of members; as they gain greater knowledge in development planning, they would be in a position to set up more realistic development programs that would enable them to allocate more effectively their own resources as well as resources from bilateral loans and international lending institutions.

The Bank's operations, however, have limitations. They are somewhat "conservative" not only in regard to the terms and conditions of loans but also in terms of the purposes for which loans are made. The maturity terms of the Bank's loans to some members are unfavorably short, especially to those countries which are subject to a substantial degree of instability in export earnings. The servicing of such a structure of debts to a country suffering from adverse developments in export earnings is indeed a heavy burden. The use of exchange resources needed for development purposes to service its debts would adversely affect its development efforts. On the other hand, by defaulting its obligation, it would not be able to secure credit facilities in the future. The Bank has been mainly concerned with the financing of projects which are more or less "self-liquidating" in view of safeguarding its resources. And inadequate attention has been given to areas of activity which are potentially of great importance to economic development, yet their contribution to national output is somewhat intangible. The Bank has found, through experiences, that the ability of less developed countries to absorb capital is rather limited. And one of the causes of this limited capital-absorption capacity is undoubtedly the lack of an important cooperating factor: technical skills and know-how. Yet, the volume of loans made by the Bank to education—the major source of acquiring technical skills—has been relatively very small as compared to loans directed to so-called infrastructure projects.[12]

The Bank has made little or no progress in its efforts to promote private investment, which is one of the primary purposes of the establishment of the Bank. Many factors appear to be at work to limit the flow of private capital to less developed countries. The unprecedented economic prosperity of Western industrial nations during the postwar period offer plenty of profitable investment opportunities to private enterprises. It is only understandable that they would not venture to less developed countries where risks are too great and the future is too uncertain. The provision of the Bank's Articles of Agreement requiring a member country to fully guarantee loans made to private borrowers located within its territories provides no incentive for private borrowers to borrow for fear that their government, acting as guarantor, would unduly interfere with the running of their businesses. In a number of less developed countries the establishment of governmental enterprises in areas of activity which are potentially attractive to private capital because of high prospective yields leaves little room to private investments. The kind of infrastructure projects sponsored by

[12] Thus, of the cumulative total of the Bank's loans of $10.5 billion as of June 1967, only $26.3 million was made for educational projects.

the Bank are generally not attractive to the participation of private capital because of inadequate profitability and long recoupment times.

Efforts to remove some of these limitations have been made. This is reflected by some degree of liberalization of the Bank's lending policies—loans made for purposes which had little or no access to the Bank in the past, relatively longer maturity terms, greater provisions for local currency expenditures in connection with loans, among other things, and by the establishment of two affiliates: The International Development Association and the International Finance Corporation. These two institutions, together with the Bank, are popularly referred to as the World Bank Group.

THE INTERNATIONAL DEVELOPMENT ASSOCIATION (IDA)

The IDA was established in 1960. It is basically a special fund of the World Bank. The primary function of the IDA is to make long-term loans to less developed countries at minimum interest cost in view of alleviating their burden of servicing the debts. Loans made by IDA may run up to 50 years and the borrower's repayment obligation begins only after 10 years. The cost to the borrower on IDA loans has been less than 1 percent charged largely to cover administrative expenses. The resources of the Association come from contributions of member countries and grants made by the World Bank from its net earnings. Additional subscriptions may be made when needed for IDA to undertake new loan commitments. Since the interest charged by the IDA on its loans is low, it is not in a position to raise funds by borrowing in capital markets. In regard to capital contributions, IDA's members which numbered some 97 in 1967 are divided into two groups: Part I group and part II group.[13] The former is made up of some 18 developed countries, and the latter of undeveloped members. The contributions of part I members are paid entirely in gold or convertible currencies. Part II members pay only 10 percent of their contributions in convertible currencies, and the remaining in their own currencies, which can be released for IDA's uses only with the consent of the member whose currency is to be lent. The bulk of IDA's subscriptions comes from Part I members, of which the United States, as usual, accounts for the lion share.[14]

Most of IDA loans have been made to underdeveloped members in Asia and the Middle East. Apart from loans to projects which are popular to the World Bank (such as transportation and power supply) IDA has ventured in areas which have limited access to the Bank's funds, especially education. Thus loans made by IDA for educational projects totaled $113.5 million as of June 1967 as

[13] The great majority of IDA's members are also members of the World Bank.

[14] Thus, of the total subscriptions of IDA of $1.773 billion in 1967 (both initial and supplementary subscriptions), $1.524 billion was subscribed by part I members (of which $633 million was subscribed by the United States), and $249 million by Part II members, a sizable portion of which has not been released for IDA's uses.

compared with $24.3 million made by the Bank. Like the Bank, loans are granted by IDA only after careful investigation of the economic merits of the proposed projects as well as the general economic and financial policies of the borrowing member.

THE INTERNATIONAL FINANCE CORPORATION (IFC)

The International Finance Corporation was established in 1956 for the purpose of promoting economic development in member countries by stimulating private investment. To this effect the IFC is engaged in operations which are not undertaken by the Bank. The IFC operates exclusively in the private sector. It underwrites offerings or placements of securities by new or expanding enterprises, invests in share capital, makes loans to private borrowers without government guarantees, and assists in the establishment of business, especially development finance companies established in less developed countries for the mobilization of private capital for economic development.

The resources of the IFC come from the capital subscriptions of members which are also required to be members of the World Bank. The scope of the operations of the IFC has been limited, which reflects its small authorized capital of $110 million and its total loan and investment commitments of some $200 million as of 1967.

REGIONAL FINANCIAL INSTITUTIONS

In addition of the IMF and the World Bank Group which are truly international financial institutions, there are regional lending institutions such as the Asian Development Bank, the African Development Bank, and the Inter-American Development Bank established to promote regional growth and development. The administrative structure of these institutions and their operations are closely patterned on those of the World Bank and the International Development Association.

The Asian Development Bank (ADB)

The Asian Development Bank, conceived by the United Nations Economic Commission for Asia and the Far East (ECAFE), began operations in December 1966. The ADB is in fact more than a regional institution as its membership includes quite a few nonregional member countries. Thus of the 32 countries which are members of the ADB, 19 are ECAFE countries and 13 are nonregional members from Europe (The Federal Republic of Germany, Italy, Belgium, Switzerland, Sweden, and Finland) and North America (Canada and the United States).

The Bank was established for the purpose of lending funds, promoting investment, and providing technical assistance to member countries, and generally for fostering economic growth and cooperation in the Asian region. The ADB can guarantee, participate in, or make direct loans to member governments, any of their agencies or political subdivisions, and to both public and private enterprises operating in member countries. Like the World Bank, the ADB concentrates largely on the financing of specific projects in the areas of industry, agriculture, power supply, and transportation. In making loans or participating in loans, the ADB provides the borrower with foreign exchange to cover the foreign exchange cost of the project and local currency to meet local currency expenditures connected with the project where this can be done without the ADB selling any of its holdings of gold or convertible currencies.

The lending operations of the ADB consist of two separate categories: ordinary operations and special operations. Ordinary operations are those financed from the ADB's ordinary funds which consist of members' capital subscriptions, borrowings in international capital markets, and earnings. Special operations are those financed from the ADB's special funds which represent special contributions by members and up to 10 percent of paid-in capital which could be earmarked as special funds by decisions of the Board of Governors. While projects financed by ordinary funds are commercial-type projects, special operations are concerned with assistance for projects of high development priority and calling for loans of longer maturities, longer deferred commencement of repayment and lower interest rates than those established for ordinary operations. (It is obvious that the special operations of the ADB are similar to those of the IDA of the World Bank Group).

The ADB has an authorized capital of \$1.1 billion of which \$970 million has been subscribed. Of the subscribed capital, one half is to be paid in and the remaining are "callable" shares serving as security for the ADB's obligations. The paid-in portion is to be paid in five installments, one half of each installment being in gold or convertible currencies, and the other half in local currency. The capital of the ADB may be increased if necessary by decisions of the Board of Governors.

The Board of Governors is the highest policy-making body of the institution. Each member appoints a governor and an alternate governor. The Board of Directors which is responsible for the general direction of the ADB exercises powers delegated to it by the Board of Governors. There are 10 directors of whom seven represent regional members, and three nonregional members. The President, who is the chairman of the Board of Directors, is in charge of the international staff and runs the day-to-day business of the institution.

The Inter-American Development Bank (IDB)

The Inter-American Development Bank was established in 1960 for the purpose of fostering economic growth and development in the Latin American region. Like the ADB, the IDB combines the operations principles of the World

Bank and the IDA. There are ordinary operations and special operations. The former are financed out of ordinary funds which, like those of the ADB, consist of capital subscriptions of members, borrowings, and earnings and the latter, out of special funds which are made up mainly of members' contributions. In 1968 the IDB had a total capital of $3.150 billion, of which $475 million were paid in and the remaining was callable shares. In addition, the IDB borrowed more than $513 million through the flotation of bonds in various capital markets of the world. The total net cumulative loans made by the IDB under ordinary operations was slightly more than $963 million most of which went to agriculture, industry, water supply, and infrastructure projects. The IDB's special contributions by members amounted to $2.321 billion as of 1968. Loans made from these special funds, which totaled more than $967.5 million since inception up to 1967, are for longer maturities and minimum interest rates and their repayment begins only after a period of deferment.

These regional financial institutions which offer regional cooperation and assistance may deal effectively with problems and interest peculiar to these regions. But regionalism may weaken efforts toward greater international economic coordination and cooperation. Moreover, since these regional institutions have been concerned with lending activities which also have been the main concern of the World Bank Group—namely in the areas of power supply, transportation, agriculture and industry—one may question whether these funds could not be more effectively administered and allocated if instead of being vested in these new institutions they were made available to the World Bank Group as earmarked funds for promoting regional growth and development. At any rate, these are new development institutions. Their contribution to the advancement of regional development and growth can only be told by time.

SUMMARY

The monetary and financial cooperation and assistance between nations is embodied in two international institutions: the International Monetary Fund and the World Bank Group. The former designed to assist members in temporary payments difficulties, and the latter, to promote economic growth and development through guaranteeing, participating in, or making direct long-term loans to members. The availability of the Fund's resources enables members with temporary payments deficits to adjust these imbalances either through changes in domestic economic and financial policies or orderly changes in the exchanges rates of their currencies or both. But there are problems inherent in the present international monetary system. It is built on gold and a number of national currencies serving as reserve currencies. The working of the system thus depends on the confidence of holders of these reserve currencies on their safety and stability. A serious loss of confidence in these reserve currencies could plunge the system in an irrecoverable crisis. The system does not provide for a payments adjustment mechanism which is consistent with both external payments equilibrium and internal stability in growth and employment. Inadequacy of international reserves is another problem which the present system may encounter. International reserves consist of gold supplemented by national reserve currencies which are provided by reserve-currency countries through their payments deficits. Efforts made by these countries to reduce their payments deficits in order to avoid weakening their currency in international markets would dry up this source of supply of international reserves. Reserves so reduced, unless replaced by new forms of reserves, would stifle the flow of world trade and payments.

The World Bank, together with its two affiliates the International Development Association and the International Finance Corporation, has contributed to some extent to the development efforts of less developed countries through both financial and technical assistance. But assistance from these international institutions is somewhat modest relative to the immense need for capital of the underdeveloped world. In addition to these international institutions, there are also regional institutions such as the Asian Development Bank and the Inter-American Development Bank established for promoting regional economic growth and development. They operate along the lines of the World Bank and the International Development Association.

The degree of cooperation which has been achieved between nations has been remarkable. But this cooperation is by no means global. The Soviet Union, the People's Republic of China (the most populous nation on earth) and other Communist-bloc countries, due to economic and political ideological differences, remain pretty much a world apart from the so-called free world. World trade and income would indeed be immensely promoted by economic and monetary cooperation and assistance among nations of the globe. Nationalistic feelings, and differences in economic and political ideologies are major hurdles in the road toward this kind of global cooperation and integration. But recent establishment of economic and trade relations between some countries of the West and some Communist-bloc countries could constitute a first step toward some political détente and economic and monetary cooperation which is essential to the development and growth of the world community as a whole.

PROBLEMS

1. What are major functions of the International Monetary Fund? In what sense would you consider the Fund to be the central bank of central banks?

2. Explain the major sources of Funds available to the Fund for financial assistance to members.

3. Discuss some of the problems inherent in the present international monetary system.

4. What is the *raison d'être* of the World Bank? What are the major sources

of funds available to the Bank for its operations? In what respects do the operations of the Bank differ from those of the International Development Association?

5. What are factors which account for the failure of the World Bank in promoting private investments in less developed countries?

6. In what respects do regional financial institutions such as the Asian Development Bank and the Inter-American Development Bank resemble those of the World Bank Group? Is the existence of these regional institutions justifiable on economic grounds? Give your opinions.

chapter 30

Recent International Financial Problems

We have discussed in the preceding chapter the financial cooperation and assistance between nations and international financial institutions. In this chapter we shall discuss some international financial problems the solution of which requires further international economic and financial cooperation and coordination.

CURRENCY CONVERTIBILITY

The convertibility of a currency is its exchangeability for other currencies for international payments purposes. Currency convertibility may be limited or unlimited. Unlimited or full convertibility prevails when a currency is freely convertible into other currencies in all circumstances. But convertibility may be limited only to certain categories of holders or certain types of transactions. For instance, convertibility may be limited to holders resident outside the country issuing the currency, in which case is referred to as nonresident convertibility. Or it may be confined only to current-account transactions while capital transactions are subject to controls. The latter type of limited convertibility, as we have seen, is promoted by the Articles of Agreement of the International Monetary Fund.

Currency convertibility is essential to the development of multilateral trade. International trade would be greatly increased when residents of a country holding currency of another country were able to use it in the purchases of goods and services from other countries. Although the scope of currency convertibility at present is still limited, it is a remarkable improvement over the situation that prevailed during the war years and the postwar period. During this time international trade was carried out mostly under bilateral agreements. Foreign exchange earned by exporters in country *X* from importers in country *Y* could be used only for the purchases of goods and services from country *Y*. International trade was drastically reduced nuder bilateral agreements, since each country had to balance its imports and exports individually with other countries and the volume of trade between any pair of countries was determined by the country which wished to purchase the smaller amount of imports. Currency convertibility during this period was confined largely to currencies of countries which belonged to the same currency area such as the franc area (made up of France and French colonies and protectorates and former colonies which regained independence and elected to remain in the franc area) and the sterling area (made up of the United Kingdom and some countries both inside and outside the Commonwealth except Canada). Thus in the franc area, for example, currencies of area members were convertible into French franc. U.S. dollars and other hard currencies earned by area members were sold to the French Treasury against franc balances held in France. Area members could draw on these balances to pay for dollars and other currencies from the pool in payments for imports from nonfranc-area countries. But even within the same currency area, convertibility, in some members, was subject to limitations and controls.

In an effort to promote the expansion of intra-European trade and payments and the free convertibility of Western European currencies, the European Payments Union (EPU) was established in 1950 by a number of countries of Western Europe. The Union provided for the monthly multilateral clearings of transactions between members, for the extension of credit by surplus to deficit members, and for the convertibility of members' currencies. Transactions between members were carried on in terms of the U.S. dollar as a unit of account. The Union started with an initial reserve of $350 million provided by the United States. Each member of the EPU was assigned a quota (on the basis of its trade and income) which served as a basis for the determination of the extent of credit balance to be extended by a surplus member to the Union and the ability of a deficit country to draw on the Union for payments purposes.[1] Mutual claims between members were offset and the net balances were settled by the Union. A surplus country would receive part of its surplus balance in gold and part in the form of a credit balance with the Union. A deficit member, on the other hand, would pay part of its deficits in gold and assume a debit balance with the Union for the remaining. Initially, a creditor country would agree to grant the Union credit up to 20 percent of its quota and also half of any excess of this amount, the remaining being paid in gold (that is, up to the extent of its quota, the creditor country would receive in settlement 40 percent of its quota in gold and 60 percent in the form of credit with the Union). The deficit country, on the other hand, was permitted to draw on the Union up to 10 percent of its quota, and for amounts in excess of this, part had to be paid in gold. In 1954 members' quotas were increased and also the gold payment obligation of a deficit member. The latter could borrow from the Union up to 50 percent of its quota to cover its deficits and the rest would be paid in gold. In 1956, the gold payment obligation was again increased to 75 percent of quota. In 1959, as Western European countries sufficiently recovered from war damages and regained their competitive position in world markets, they declared nonresident convertibility for their currencies. Foreign holders of these currencies were free to convert

[1] It can be seen that the Union applied the principles of the IMF on a smaller scale.

their holdings into U.S. dollar and other currencies as they wished. The EPU was then terminated and its outstanding credit and debit balances were dealt with by the European Monetary Agreement. In the early 1900's, Western European countries and Japan made their currencies convertible for current account transactions. While capital transactions remain under controls, efforts have been made by these nations toward greater liberalization of controls over capital flows.

The progress toward freer currency convertibility during the last few decades was thus represented by the movement from bilateralism to regional convertibility to the present stage of limited multilateralism. The road toward full convertibility and complete multilateralism is a long one. A large number of countries, particularly undeveloped countries, remain firmly under exchange controls as their ability to earn foreign exchange is limited. Greater contributions of developed nations to the economic development and growth of underdeveloped countries would help toward greater currency convertibility in the long run. But while full convertibility is an essential requirement for maximum world trade and investments, the free international movements of funds under a system of free convertibility could at times interfere with efforts to promote economic growth, stable prices, and full employment. With high priority granted to economic growth and employment by national economies, free trade and currency convertibility would be promoted to the extent that they were consistent with the pursuit of domestic economic goals. To maintain currency convertibility and free trade, and full employment with stable prices simultaneously requires substantially greater cooperation and coordination between nations in their domestic and international economic and financial policies than hitherto prevalent.[2]

GOLD, THE DOLLAR, AND THE U.S. BALANCE OF PAYMENTS

Gold Flows and Payments Imbalances

Gold and the U.S. dollar are international reserves. They are close substitutes as dollar reserves held by foreign central banks and governments are convertible into gold at the U.S. Treasury at the fixed price of $35 per ounce. The willingness of foreign monetary authorities to hold dollar reserves depends in part on their confidence in the ability of the U.S. to redeem these dollars in gold. And the ability of the U.S. to make gold payments depends on its gold stock relative to its liabilities that are redeemable in gold. The gold stock of the United States and its liabilities to foreign monetary authorities change as the payments posi-

[2]It should be noted that while progress is being made by the free world community toward greater currency convertibility, trade and payments between nations of the Communist bloc and between them and free-world countries remain largely on a bilateral basis. The control over international exchanges in these countries is only part of a centrally controlled system. Currency convertibility cannot exist as long as both domestic and international economic activities are controlled by the state.

tion of the United States relative to the rest of the world changes. A deficit in the U.S. balance of payments would result in an increase in the liquid claims of foreign monetary authorities on the United States, and to the extent that they elect to convert these dollar claims into gold, the U.S. gold reserves will decline. A surplus in the U.S. balance of payments, on the other hand, will increase U.S. gold reserves and U.S. liquid claims on foreigners, or reduce foreign liquid claims on the United States.

The last few decades have witnessed some dramatic changes in the U.S. international payments position. When Europe was prepared for war and during the war and early postwar years, Western Europe (as well as other parts of the world) depended almost entirely on U.S. imports which were needed to sustain the war efforts and for economic reconstruction during the postwar period. Apart from massive U.S. government grants and loans, Western European countries had to draw down their gold and foreign exchange reserves to cover their payments deficits. This resulted in an enormous accumulation of gold reserves by the United States, which increased from slightly more than $6 billion in 1929 to more than $24.5 billion in 1949. To the rest of the world, the dollar was then indeed better than gold. Gold was sought after precisely because it could be sold for U.S. dollars to pay for U.S. imports. It is not far from the truth to say that gold was then on the dollar standard.

Beginning with 1950, the U.S. balance of payments changed from surplus to deficit that has remained persistent ever since. From 1950 to 1956 the payments deficits could be said to have been consciously planned by the United States for the redistribution of reserves to the rest of the world since an increase in the reserves of the rest of the world was essential to the promotion of free world trade and payments (which were then subject to strict controls, particularly trade with the dollar area). Thus during this period, the United States ran a cumulative deficit of about $10.7 billion. This enabled the rest of the world, particularly Western Europe, to increase gold reserves by $1.7 billion, and short-term dollar claims by about $9 billion. Beginning with 1958, the U.S. payments position took a sharp turn for the worse. In that year, the liquidity deficit rose to $3.365 billion as compared with a deficit of $975 million in 1956 and a small surplus of $578 million in 1957 (following the Suez crisis). During the 1958-67 period the U.S. payments deficit averaged to almost $3 billion as compared to an average of about $1.4 billion for the period from 1950 to 1956. If the U.S. deficits incurred in the early 1950's were somewhat designed for the redistribution of world reserves, the deficits in the late 1950's and the 1960's were indeed anything but planned.

The heavy and persistent deficits in the U.S. balance of payments throughout the 1960's resulted in a steady increase in the gold and dollar reserves of foreign central banks and governments, especially those of Western Europe, as they converted their excess dollar holdings into gold. For instance, during the 1963-66 period, France alone had purchased more than $2.3 billion in gold from the United States. From 1958 to 1968, the U.S. net sales of gold to foreign countries amounted to $11.6 billion, of which about $11 billion went to Western Europe. Figure 30-1 shows the depletion of the U.S. gold stock and the

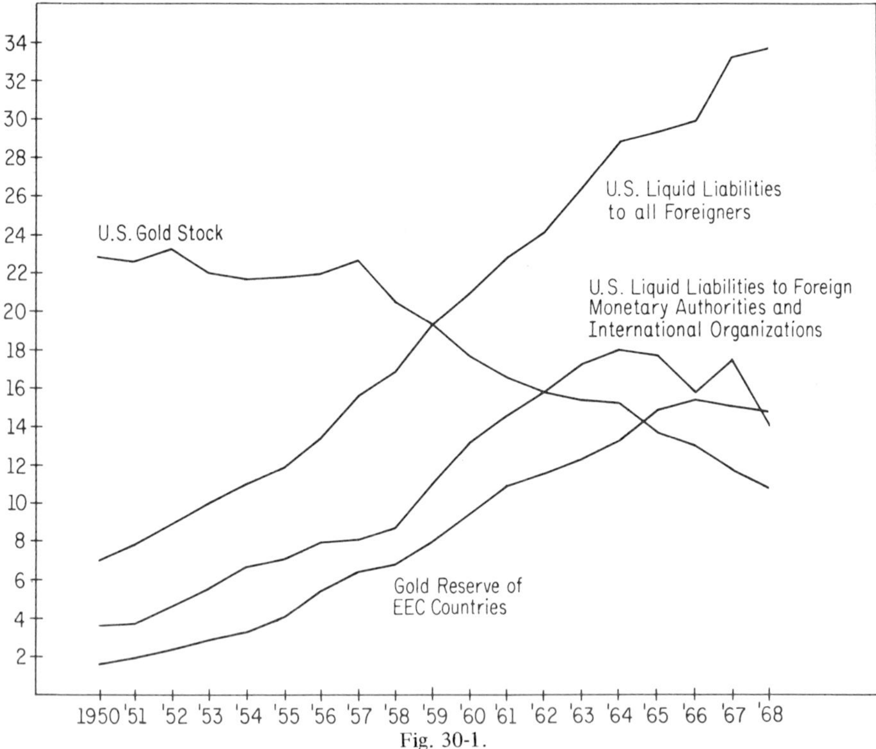

Fig. 30-1.

increase in U.S. liquid liabilities to foreign monetary authorities, international financial institutions and organizations, and private foreigners, and the increase in the gold reserve of the countries of the European Economic Community. The decrease in the U.S. gold stock and the increase in foreign liquid claims on the United States indicate the decrease in the liquidity position of the United States toward the rest of the world.[3] While in the late 1950's, U.S. liquid liabilities to

[3]This liquidity problem should not be confused with the question of solvency. In regard to solvency, the United States is more solvent vis-à-vis the rest of the world than ever before. Its assets abroad have risen faster than foreign assets in the United States. For example, during the 1956-66 period, U.S. assets abroad increased by 126 percent to more than $112 billion compared with a 91 percent increase to $60 billion of foreign assets in the United States. The trouble is that foreign liquid claims on the United States have risen more sharply relative to the increase of U.S. liquid claims on foreigners.

foreigners was about equal to the U.S. gold stock, in 1968, foreign liquid claims on the United States was more than 3 times the U.S. gold reserve. Short-term dollar balances held by foreign central banks and governments alone exceeded the U.S. gold reserve since the early 1960's. The potential claims on U.S. gold were even greater than this, since certain portions of U.S. liquid liabilities to private foreigners may be transferrable to foreign monetary authorities. It is obvious that if foreign official monetary agencies were to convert all their dollar claims into gold, the United States would not be in a position to honor all of them in gold.

The continuous loss of U.S. gold reserves which reduces its ability to pay gold could weaken the dollar in international markets and undermine the confidence of foreign authorities in the dollar as a reserve asset. And the impairment of the confidence of foreigners in the safety and stability of the dollar could generate severe international monetary crisis as they would attempt to reduce their dollar holdings for foreign exchange and gold. Crisis did indeed take place as recently as early 1968. Following the devaluation of the pound, speculators and holders of dollars, fearing that the dollar would also be devalued, unloaded their holdings for foreign currencies and gold in the free gold markets of London, Paris, and Zurich. This caused the price of gold to rise substantially above the selling price of gold by the U.S. Treasury of $35.0875 per ounce. To prevent sharp increases in the price of gold which it was believed would jeopardize the stability of the existing international monetary structure, the United States contributed more than $1 billion of gold to the London Gold Pool[4] (in addition to contributions by other members of the Pool such as the central banks of Belgium, Italy, the Netherlands, Switzerland, and the Federal Republic of Germany) to increase the supply of gold in the London market in an effort to halt the increase in the price of gold. This, however, was not materialized. Consequently, to avoid further losses of gold reserves to private speculators, the London Gold Pool was abandoned. As we have mentioned, this resulted in a two-tier market for gold: an official market and a private market. This arrangement appeared to have worked quite well. In the official market, the

[4]The origin of the London Gold Pool dated back to late 1960 following the London gold crisis which was overcome by large scale gold sales by the Bank of England with assistance from the U.S. Federal Reserve. The Pool was nothing more than a gentlemen's agreement between a number of European central banks (Belgium, the Federal Republic of Germany, Italy, the Netherlands, Switzerland, the United Kingdom, and France. The latter withdrew from the Pool in early 1968) and the Federal Reserve Bank of New York to stabilize the price of gold in the London gold market by either buying or selling gold, since sharp fluctuations in the price of gold in the free market could undermine the stability of the exchanges. The Bank of England acted as operating agent of the Pool. The sales of gold were made from gold contributed by participants. The contribution of each participant was determined by its quota, the U.S. quota being 50 percent of total. Gold was sold when its price rose above the U.S. selling price plus the shipment cost of gold from New York to London and was purchased whenever it was available at or below the U.S. selling price, and gold so acquired was distributed among interested participants. The agreement, however, had to be abandoned because of the severity of the gold crisis in early 1968.

United States continues its commitment to sell gold to foreign monetary authorities at the price of $35.0875 per ounce for monetary purposes. To boost the confidence of foreign official institutions in the gold convertibility of their dollar reserves, the U.S. Congress in mid-1968 passed a bill exempting the notes liabilities of the Federal Reserve banks from the 25 percent gold certificate reserve requirements thereby making the whole U.S. gold stock available to the Treasury to honor its international obligations in gold.

In the private market, the price of gold was left to find its own level through supply and demand conditions. The supply of gold would come from new gold output (namely South Africa), private holders, and gold sales by the Soviet Union and the like. The fever of speculation caused the price of gold in the private market to rise sharply, reaching a peak of $43.80 per ounce in early 1969. But the agreement of the United States and European central banks not to acquire gold from South Africa which was consequently forced to sell more gold in the private market (South Africa initially elected to stockpile gold instead of selling it in the free market) caused the supply of gold in this market to increase. This coupled with the uncertainty of the U.S. policy regarding the future purchase of gold, hence the uncertainty in the future of gold, among other things, drove down the price of gold in the private market. In late 1969, the price of gold in this market dipped to a low of $34.80 per ounce. This low price of gold again caused concern on the part of European central bankers for the value of their own gold reserves. In addition, they would want to increase the official gold reserves thereby lessening the dependence on the dollar as a reserve currency. This resulted in an agreement between the United States, European countries, and South Africa allowing the latter to sell a certain amount of gold to the IMF at $35 per ounce in case of payments deficits or a drop of the free price of gold to $35 or less. The IMF would in turn resell gold to member countries. This would put a floor to the price of gold and again eliminate the risk from gold speculation. It would seem that this is a step backward in the progress toward reducing the use of gold as a monetary reserve.

The persistent deficits in the U.S. balance of payments were mainly at the root of the recent trouble of the dollar and the crisis on gold. To prevent erosion of the U.S. gold reserve and the position of the dollar in international market requires a direct attack on the U.S. payments imbalances. What caused the U.S. payments deficits? What measures have been taken to reduce payments deficits? And once the U.S. payments deficits are reduced or eliminated, what kind of problems can the existing international monetary system be expected to face?

Causes of U.S. Payments Deficits

The deficit in the U.S. balance of payments has been the result of the excess of deficits on capital accounts over the surplus on current transactions. This can be seen in Fig. 30-2 showing the U.S. liquidity deficits for the 1960-67 period.

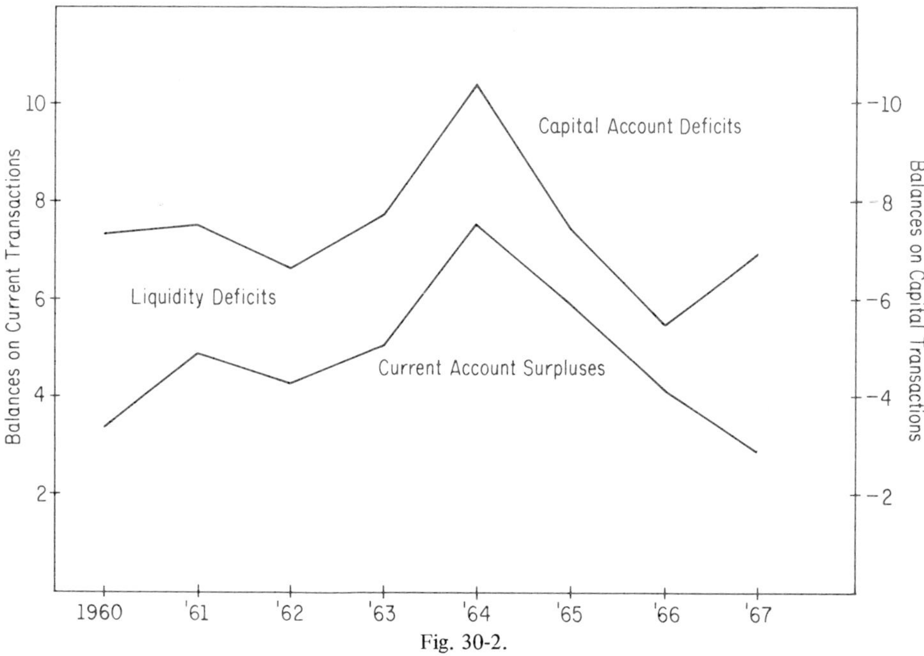

Fig. 30-2.

From 1960 to 1964 the current account surplus increased from slightly more than $3 billion to $7.5 billion. This was generated by the stable expansion in the United States while other industrial nations were under inflationary pressures. But during the same period there were increases in U.S. government grants and loans and in U.S. capital outflows attracted by profitable investment opportunities in foreign countries, particularly those of Western Europe that offer stiff competition to the United States in both American and world markets. As a result, the deficits on capital accounts increased from $7.2 billion to more than $10 billion, leaving a cumulative liquidity deficit of almost $14 billion for the period.

After 1964 the current account surplus took a downward plunge caused by sharp increases in imports of goods and services following domestic expansion, inflationary pressures, rising U.S. foreign travel spending, and rising expenditures required for the Vietnam war. During the period 1964-67 import demand increased at an average annual rate of 14 percent, twice the average rate for 1960-61 to 1964-65, while the average annual rate of increase of exports remained at 8 percent for the 1960-61 to 1966-67 period. The decrease in the deficits on capital accounts during the 1964–66 period did reduce the liquidity deficits. But after 1966 the capital account deficits increased again as U.S. government grants and loans and U.S. private capital outflows continued to rise and the inflows of foreign capital decreased. This caused the liquidity deficits to increase from $1.357 billion in 1966 to $3.571 billion in 1967. Stiffer foreign competition, domestic inflationary pressures, rising military spending, and increases in U.S. government grants and loans as well as in U.S. private capital outflows are thus among major factors that have been at work to generate the U.S. payments deficits.

Corrective Measures

Until early in 1968, measures that were taken by the United States to correct its payments imbalances were largely stop-gap measures. For instance, to reduce U.S. private capital outflows and the deficits on capital accounts, an interest equalization tax was levied on the purchases by American investors of foreign securities. This was designed to increase the interest costs of those foreigners subjects to the tax who raised funds in U.S. financial markets.[5] Voluntary restraint programs were established by the Federal Reserve and the Department of Commerce urging banking institutions to limit their foreign lending and business firms to restrain their direct investments abroad. The latter were encouraged to borrow from foreign capital markets to finance their foreign expansion. An Executive order of June 1, 1968 prohibited persons owning 10 percent or more of a foreign business venture from engaging in transfers of capital abroad except as authorized by the Department of Commerce. The latter was also authorized to require such persons to repatriate to the United States their earnings from such foreign business ventures and their short-term assets, including bank deposits. Domestic banks were authorized to pay higher interest rates on foreign time deposits than those payable on domestic time deposits in view of encouraging foreigners to keep dollar balances in the United States. In addition, in an attempt to curtail tourist expenditures abroad, limits were put on the value of foreign goods which could be brought home duty-free by returning American tourists.

Few of these measures appeared to work effectively, however. Net U.S. private capital outflows continued to rise from $3.8 billion in 1965 to $5.5 billion in 1967. The effect, if any, of voluntary restraint programs on U.S. private foreign lending and direct investments would be likely to wear off as profitable investment opportunities in foreign industrial countries continue to beckon U.S. capital. With regard to the interest equalization tax, whether it would work or not depends largely on the difference between the interest costs in foreign financial markets relative to the interest costs (tax included) in U.S. markets to foreign borrowers. Lower interest rates in the U.S. relative to interest rates abroad would not deter foreign borrowers from raising funds in U.S. markets but would encourage U.S. firms to ship capital overseas instead of borrowing abroad for their foreign business undertakings. With rising income in the United States, American travel spending in foreign countries continued to rise (from $2.4 billion in 1965 to $3.2 billion in 1967) despite measures designed to curb foreign travel expenditures.

[5] Canadian securities, securities of less developed countries, and certain other foreign securities, however, were exempted from the tax.

The improvement in the balance of payments may come from an improvement in the trade balance, the capital balance, or both. A deterioration in the trade balance that is more than offset by the improvement in the capital balance will improve the balance of payments. The same thing holds when the improvement in the trade balance more than offsets the deterioration in the capital balance. In regard to the U.S. balance of payments, the trade balance has deteriorated; and, except for 1968, there was no marked improvement in the capital balance. The 10 percent surcharge on corporate and individual income taxes imposed in mid-1968, and the slowdown in government spending, designed to hold down domestic expansion and inflationary pressures, and restrain domestic demand and imports, did not appear to have generated the expected results. As we have seen, as of late 1969, inflationary pressures continued heavy, and prices continued to accelerate. The current account surplus in the U.S. balance of payments decreased from $3.981 million in 1967 to $1,357 million in 1968. But in view of the sharp increase in foreign capital flow (induced by attractive financial investment opportunities in the United States, the restored confidence in the U.S. dollar following the French franc crisis, and restrictive economic policy in the United States), there was a liquidity surplus of some $168 million in 1968. This, however, was changed in early 1969. The continued deterioration in the current account and the decrease in foreign capital flow generated a liquidity deficit of some $5.4 billion in the first half of 1969.

The correction of the U.S. payments imbalances without resorting to unduly restrictive measures which would exert unhealthy influences on both domestic income and employment and on world trade and investments would call for some cooperation and assistance from surplus countries, particularly creditor countries of Western Europe. These surplus countries could assist in pursuing expansionary fiscal and monetary policies for a steady expansion of their domestic economies. They could relax restrictions on certain imports for which the United States has competitive advantage such as wheat, tobacco, poultry, other agricultural products, and on manufactured products such as computers, automobiles, heavy electrical equipment, and drugs. The relaxation of obstacles to trade and domestic expansion in continental Europe with payments surpluses would contribute substantially to restoring equilibrium in the U.S. balance of payments. But the restoration of U.S. payments equilibrium would give rise to problems which, if not timely solved, would work to reduce world trade and income.

INTERNATIONAL RESERVES

The Need of International Reserves

An individual business firm needs to have adequate liquid reserves on hand for working balances as well as for emergency expenditures. So does a nation. As we have seen, a member of the International Monetary Fund is under obligation to maintain the fluctuations in the exchange rates of its currency to within 1 percent on either side of the established par value. This is achieved by buying or selling foreign exchange. Central banks and governments need reserves on hand as working balances to intervene in the exchange market. But the bulk of reserve assets held by central banks and governments is not held for working balances but rather for guarding against adverse developments that would undermine the stability of exchange rates, such as speculative runs on their currencies, and for covering balance of payments deficits while taking measures to correct payments imbalances.

International reserves consist of all assets available to the monetary authorities of countries for the purpose of meeting the above problems. They consist of gold reserves and foreign exchange holdings, reserve position in the IMF, IMF's credit tranche facilities, and central bank credit facilities under "swap" agreements–arrangements by which a central bank makes a given amount of its currency available to another central bank for a given amount of the latter's currency for a specified time period. International reserves may be classified into unconditional reserves and conditional reserves. Unconditional reserves are those automatically accessible to a country without prior conditions. These are generally defined to include owned gold and foreign exchange reserves and reserve positions in the IMF. Other types of reserves such as credit tranche drawings on the Fund and central bank credit facilities are referred to as conditional reserves as their availability involves some prior conditions. We shall refer to international reserves as unconditional reserves, bearing in mind the fact that the classification in somewhat arbitrary; credit facilities under bilateral mutual credit or swap agreements are practically as liquid as gold tranche claims on the IMF or owned foreign exchange holdings.

Gold is the basic reserve under the existing international monetary system. Official gold reserves can be increased through the absorption of newly mined gold, the dishoarding of gold by private holders, or the sales of gold by the Soviet Union and mainland China. The increase in the gold subscriptions of member countries of the IMF does not represent an increase in world reserves, since this is offset by an equivalent decrease in the gold reserves of member countries paying gold to the Fund. Foreign exchange reserves which consist largely of U.S. dollars and to a lesser extent sterling balances held by countries other than the United States and the United Kingdom–the reserve-currency countries–increase as a result of increases in U.S. and U.K. payments deficits and to the extent that surplus countries hold dollars as reserves instead of converting them into gold at the U.S. Treasury. Should surplus countries elect to purchase gold from the United States with dollars, world reserves would decrease accordingly as this would reduce the foreign exchange component of world reserves.

Figure 30-3 shows the composition and growth of world reserves during the 1950-68 period. Gold constitutes the most important component. But its rela-

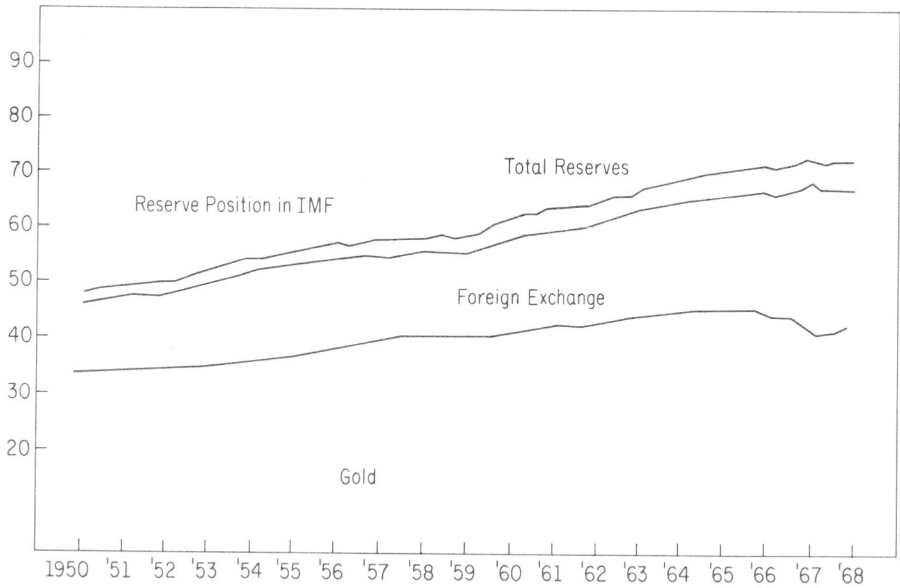

Source: International Financial Statistics, January 1969 and *Supplement* to 1966/67 issues.

Fig. 30-3. Composition of world reserves, 1950–68 (billions of dollars).

tive share of total reserves had declined from more than 70 percent in the late 1940's to about 50 percent at the end of 1968. Official gold holdings which grew at an average annual rate of about 1.5 percent for the 1950-64 period, remained practically unchanged at about $40 billion in 1964-66 and then declined to about $39 billion in late 1967 and slightly more than $37.5 billion in early 1968 as a consequence of gold reserve losses following the sterling and dollar crisis. The growth in world reserves was thus largely in the form of reserve position in the IMF and foreign exchange, namely dollars which were attributable to the payments deficits of the United States. For instance, from 1962 to 1968, the reserve position in the IMF increased by $2.7 billion, and foreign exchange, by $10.2 billion (while gold reserve declined by $360 million).

The growth of world reserves, as shown in Fig. 30-4, was somewhat slow relative to the growth of world imports. World reserves, as a percentage of imports, declined substantially from 70 percent in 1953 to about 34 percent in 1968. For the 1950-66 period the average annual rate of growth of world reserves was 2.4 percent as compared with an average annual rate of growth of world imports of 8 percent. World reserves in the late 1960's remained practically unchanged. But while the supply of reserves was slowing down, the demand for international reserves was expected to continue to increase as the expansion of world trade and free movements of capital would probably cause greater payments imbalances for which the bulk of world reserves is needed. It is be-

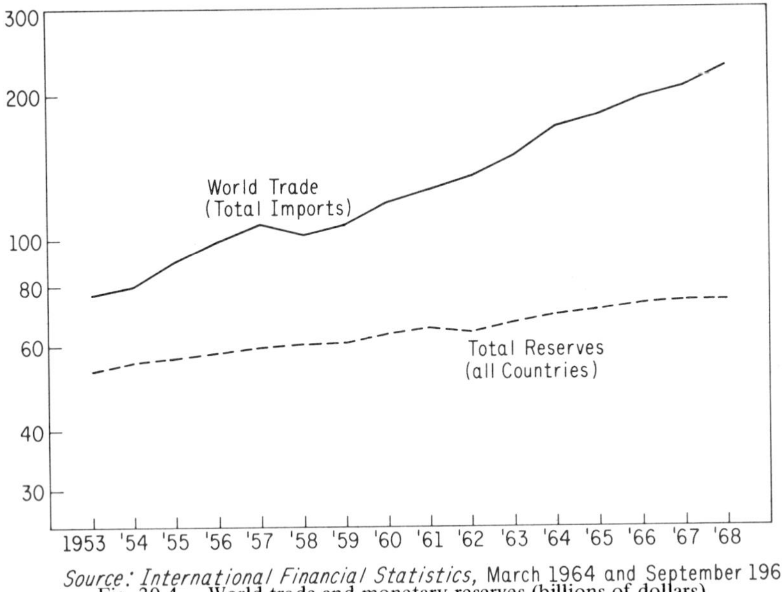

Source: International Financial Statistics, March 1964 and September 1969

Fig. 30-4. World trade and monetary reserves (billions of dollars).

lieved by many that the future need of international reserves could not be adequately met by the traditional sources of supply. The role of monetary gold supply in providing for world reserve growth has dwindled in the light of events in the late 1960's. Foreign exchange reserves provided by the payments deficits of reserve-currency countries would likely decrease, inasmuch as the United States (and the United Kingdom) could not sustain indefinitely its payments deficits without suffering further gold losses and impairing the position of the dollar in world markets. But the elimination of the U.S. payments deficits—hitherto a major source of supply of international reserves—would create a reserve gap which, if not filled by the creation of new reserve assets, would stifle the flow of world trade and investments, as nations with insufficient reserve facilities to ride through balance-of-payments difficulties would resort to restrictive measures to correct their payments imbalances.

The President of the United States, in his message to Congress on the balance of payments in 1965, stated: "Healthy growth of the free world economy requires orderly but continuing expansion of the world's monetary reserves. . . . Through the past decade, our deficits have helped meet that need. The flow of deficit dollars into foreign central banks has made up about half of the increase in free world reserves. As we eliminate that flow, a shortage of reserves could emerge. We need to continue our work on the development of supplementary sources of reserves to head off that threat."

How and what kinds of reserves were to be created if existing reserve facilities were inadequate to sustain the rising volume of world trade and investments?

Plans To Increase World Reserves

Many plans were proposed to increase international reserves. Some of these proposed to replace existing reserve currencies with internationally created reserves. Others were designed to supplement existing reserve assets with new international reserves. Perhaps the plan most widely discussed was that offered by Professor Triffin of Yale. Triffin proposed to convert the IMF into a truly international central bank to create international reserves the same way as a central bank creates monetary assets through loan and investment operations. The role of the dollar and sterling as reserve currencies would be gradually eliminated. Quotas of members of the IMF would be abolished and the net credits and debits of individual members would be credited and debited to their accounts with the international central bank and would be settled over some specified time period. The amount of international reserves created by the international central banks would be dictated solely by the need of reserves of the world economy. One of the main difficulties of the proposal is that its execution would require a degree of international economic and monetary cooperation and integration that would hardly be acceptable to individual nations under prevailing international economic and political conditions and relations.

A plan advocated by Jacques Rueff, advisor to President de Gaulle and others, called for a return to the pure gold standard. Only gold would serve as international reserve and payments deficits would be settled entirely in gold. But a return to the pure gold system would sharply reduce world reserves, because the conversion of existing dollar reserves into gold would cause U.S. gold reserves and world reserves to decline by the same amount. This could generate heavy deflationary pressures on the world economy. To avoid deflationary effects, the return to gold would be coupled with doubling the price of gold. The United States would redeem its liabilities to foreign monetary authorities in gold at the new price of gold. This would enable it to retire its official liabilities with no substantial losses of gold reserves.

The plan would obviously have a great appeal to such important gold-producing countries as South Africa, those surplus countries of continental Europe which hold a sizable portion of their reserves in gold, and private gold hoarders. The plan would discriminate against those countries which have helped finance part of the U.S. payments deficits by holding dollar reserves. It would again tie the international monetary system to the supply of a commodity whose changes are not reflective of the changing reserve requirements of a growing world economy but rather of production costs, the availability and accessibility of new gold resources, the gold sales of the USSR and mainland China, and the unpredictable behavior of gold hoarders and speculators. The increase in the price of gold would probably stimulate greater gold output. But the increase in gold output may be too much or too little. Too much gold output may generate world-wide inflationary pressures. Inadequate gold production, on the other hand, would mean inadequate international reserves and deflationary pressures. Further gold-price increases would then become necessary. The anticipation of gold-price increases would tend to reduce the flow of new gold into official reserves, as most of new gold output would likely go to private hoarders and speculators. There would be need of additional international reserves to meet the future growth of the world economy, but this could be satisfied by the creation of international reserves which can be controlled to meet the changing reserve needs of the world economy instead of going back to the vagaries of gold production.

A number of other plans represent essentially an extension of the gold standard system. They called for the creation of a composite reserve unit based on the deposits of currencies of major trading nations to supplement gold, or gold and foreign exchange reserves. By agreement between participating countries, the reserve unit would assume the nature of gold and would be automatically accepted by participants under stipulated conditions. One proposed variant which won the support of France called for the issuance of reserve units to a group of participants through the deposits of their currencies with the Bank for International Settlements in some proportion to their gold reserves. The reserve unit would be a truly international fiduciary money representing U.S. dollar, Canadian dollar, pound sterling, French franc, German mark, Japanese yen, Swiss franc, etc., in specified proportions. Gold and reserve units would replace U.S. dollar and other national reserve currencies. Payments deficits among participants would be settled in gold and reserve units in predetermined proportions.

The operation of this system would essentially be the same as that of the pure gold system. The supply of reserve units would be tied to the monetary supply of gold. If reserve units were issued to participating countries in proportion to their gold reserves, the effect would be the same as doubling the price of gold. Since the U.S. dollar would be only a fractional component of the reserve unit, the replacement of official dollar reserves with reserve units would cause heavy losses of reserves to the U.S. and the world economy.

Another variant also called for the creation of composite reserve units based on a portfolio of the currencies of the Group of Ten and Switzerland to supplement gold and foreign exchange reserves. Reserve units would be issued to the account of each participant with the IMF in return for an equivalent amount of its currency deposited with the Fund. As supplement to gold and foreign exchange reserves, reserve units would be issued when the growth of gold and foreign exchange reserves fall short of some rate considered as appropriate for the steady growth of world trade. The settlement of payments deficits would be in gold, reserve units as well as foreign exchange. Nonparticipating as well as participating countries could hold reserves in either form but in the case of participating countries, if they hold reserves in gold they would have to match gold holdings with reserve units at a predetermined ratio. The convertibility of the currencies of participating countries held by the official authorities of other participating countries into gold and reserve units would be undertaken at the agreed conversation ratio.

These plans which were to be confined to the Group of Ten and Switzerland clearly would be beneficial only indirectly to nonparticipating countries. Their execution would involve some practical problems such as the determination of the components of the portfolio of the currencies of participants on which reserve units were to be created, and the determination of the conversion ratio between gold and reserve units. Perhaps the most important problem would be the manner in which decisions were to be made to increase or reduce reserve units. The plans would require the unanimous agreement of participating countries to issue new reserve units. But while deficit countries which have exhausted their allocation of reserve units and have low gold reserves would favor the creation of additional reserve units, creditor countries with ample reserves would not be anxious to agree to the creation of new reserves particularly when this would threaten their domestic stability.

Apart from the above plans, there are of course several other ways to increase international reserves. One way is to make some part of credit tranche drawings on the IMF as automatic as gold tranche drawings. Another way is to grant the IMF the authority to purchase securities issued by member countries against its currency holdings thereby making them available to member countries which need reserves for their payments deficits.

The "Special Drawing Right" (SDR) Plan. To increase world reserves, a plan to create a new international reserve asset referred to as "special drawing right" in the IMF was approved at the annual meeting of the Board of Governors of the Fund at Rio in September 1967. After two years of arduous technical discussion and negotiations, the plan was finally adopted by the Fund's members in July 1969 (three-fifths of the Fund's members representing four-fifths of the total voting power as required under the Articles of Agreement).[6]

The plan in some respects is similar to the plans for the creation of composite reserve units which we have disucssed above. The SDR will be a truly international fiduciary money created by deliberate international decisions within the framework of the IMF. It will be "paper gold" representing the gold value of the U.S. dollar (0.888671 gram of fine gold). Member countries will accept it as gold and pay convertible currencies in return.

Proposals regarding the creation of SDR, the amount to be created, the basic period during which SDR will be allocated and the rate or rates at which SDR will be allocated during the allocation period would be initiated by the Fund's

[6]In regard to the United States, the Congress, through Public law 30-349 (June 19,1968) authorized the President to accept the amendment to the Fund's Articles of Agreement regarding the creation of SDR and the United States to participate in the Special Drawing Account and to accept obligations resulting from such participation.

Managing Director after careful consideration of such relevant variables as the growth of gold and foreign exchange reserves, the rate of growth of world trade and payments, policies of member countries regarding domestic and balance of payments problems, and so on. These proposals will be put into operation upon approval of the Fund's governors with an 85 percent majority of voting power.

The SDR plan is opened to all members. The allocation of SDR to members will be in proportion to their quotas in the form of entries in the Fund's Special Drawing Account (as distinguished from the Fund's General Account which is concerned with the Fund's present operations). A member may acquire a convertible currency by having SDR transferred from its account to the account of the country providing the currency. A member's obligation to provide currency in return for SDR however, will be limited to the difference between its actual holding of SDR and three times its cumulative allocation.[7] (A member of course may agree to provide currency in excess of the prescribed limit.) As SDR is intended to be used only for balance-of-payments needs, a member country will not be allowed to use SDR as a means to increase the gold component of its reserves by obtaining dollars with SDR and converting dollars into gold.

The SDR position of a member country in the Fund would change with changes in its international payments position, increasing with payments surpluses and decreasing with deficits. For the initial period a member country would be under obligation to reconstitute its SDR position should its average net use of SDR during the most recent five years be in excess of 70 percent of its average net cumulative allocation during the period. And reconstitution would be effected by the Fund transferring SDR to the account of the country with reconstitution obligation, with the latter paying convertible currencies to other users. For each subsequent period of SDR allocation, reconstitution rules may be left unchanged, modified or abolished by decisions of the Fund's governors with 85 percent of voting power.

The SDR plan is a landmark in the history of international monetary cooperation. The plan will assure that the future supply of world reserves would be adequate to meet the reserve needs of the expanding world economy. The agreement is a step toward a more rational foundation for the international monetary system. The creation of SDR is a permanent addition to world reserves. With the foreign exchange component of world reserves expected to slow down or decrease particularly when the U.S. payments deficits are reduced or eliminated, and the slow rate of growth of official gold reserves, SDR would

[7]As an illustrative example, assume that the Fund's Governors decide to create SDR at the rate of $1 billion a year for five years. The yearly SDR allocation to the United States will be $246 million (the United States has 24.6 percent of total Fund's quotas) and its cumulative allocation for the period will be $1.230 billion. Suppose that the United States actually held $1.8 billion of SDR. Its potential acceptance obligation would be $1.89 billion. The reasons for the limit to the acceptance obligation is rather pragmatic. SDR is a new reserve asset, and while member countries get used to it, a limit to their acceptance obligation would assure wide acceptance of this new asset. Once SDR becomes widely used, the limit would probably be abolished.

likely increase with the growth of the world economy and become the dominant component of international reserves. As the relative importance of gold and foreign exchange reserves decline, they could eventually be replaced altogether by SDR. The relief of the U.S. dollar from its status as an official reserve asset of course would not undermine its role in private international transactions. The dollar, supported by the tremendous capacity of the United States to produce goods and services and its enormous money and capital market facilities, would certainly continue to play a key role in private international transactions.

Certain members of the European Economic Community initially appeared reluctant in regard to the activation of the plan. These countries had accumulated large amounts of foreign exchange reserves. To these countries, unless the balance of payments deficits of reserve-currency countries are reduced or eliminated, the activation of the plan would simply be a means for them to finance payments deficits and would delay the adjustment of their balance of payments imbalances. This position however appeared to have been changed as a consequence of recent international monetary difficulties–the U.S. dollar and the French franc crises. Thus in the 1969 Fund annual meeting in Washington D.C. from September 29 to October 3, the Governors activated and approved the proposal of the Managing Director to allocate $9.5 billion of SDR for the basic period 1970-72, with $3.5 billion for 1970, $3 billion for 1971, and $3 billion for 1972.

We have been concerned with meeting the need of international reserves through plans to increase world reserves. But the problems of reserves can also be met through instituting alternative exchange rate systems which would require less international reserves than does the existing system. We know that the bulk of international reserves is needed to meet balance of payments deficits while measures are taken to adjust the imbalances. Since the greater the speed with which payments deficits are corrected, the smaller the need for international reserves, the need of international reserves may be reduced by adopting an exchange rate system which speeds up the adjustment process.

THE PAYMENTS-ADJUSTMENT PROBLEM

The existing IMF system, intended to be flexible in that it would allow payments imbalances to be adjusted through exchange rate changes in the case of "fundamental disequilibrium" is rather rigid particularly in regard to an important reserve currency country like the United States. The United States, with its commitment to stabilize the exchange rate of the dollar by selling gold to official monetary authorities against dollars at the fixed price of $35 per ounce, would not be in a position to adjust its payments deficits by changing the rate of the dollar without generating severe international monetary crisis. With the practical preclusion of payments adjustment through exchange rate changes, the United States would have to correct its payments imbalances either through deflationary domestic economic policies or some forms of exchange control or both. Yet with high priority given to full employment and high rates of economic growth as national economic goals, deflationary fiscal and monetary measures are hardly acceptable alternatives, especially when these measures would result in slower economic growth and high unemployment rates. The imposition of exchange controls is likewise undesirable, as it would lead to a severe contraction in the flow of world trade and payments. Furthermore, controls if imposed on current transactions would represent a violation to the IMF's Articles of Agreement. These payments adjustment alternatives are thus practically inoperative to the United States in view of its commitment to full employment and maximum economic growth at home, and the maintenance of exchange-rate stability as required under the existing international monetary system. Yet the persistent U.S. payments deficits will have to be removed. The United States cannot rely indefinitely on creditor countries to continue financing its deficits by accumulating dollar reserves which in some countries already prove more or less excessive. If priority were given to the pursuit of domestic economic objectives, then the external-payments problem would have to be solved by either modifying the existing international monetary system or by substituting it with alternative systems, which would allow greater room for market forces to operate in the adjustment process. In this regard a number of alternatives have been advanced. One alternative which is attractive to a number of leading academic economists is the adoption of a system of floating exchange rates. Under this system, payments imbalances would be automatically corrected through exchange-rate variations. With external imbalances taken care of by the supply and demand forces in the foreign exchange market, monetary and fiscal policies could be devoted entirely to domestic economic problems. Bankers, businessmen, and many economists object to such a system. One main objection is that the uncertainty created by a constantly changing monetary yardstick which would prevail under this system would severely reduce the international flow of both trade and capital.

Another alternative proposal is basically a modification of the IMF system; it is a compromise between a system of rigidly fixed exchange rates and a system of floating exchange rates. This alternative proposes to establish fixed par values for currencies (like IMF par values) but allows greater limits for exchange rate variations around the par values, say, 5 percent on either side (instead of 1 percent as under the existing system).[8] Official intervention in the exchange market would be called for only to iron out variations which are believed to be generated by disequilibrating speculation or to prevent exchange rate changes from exceeding the predetermined limits.

[8]This proposal has several versions. For a detailed discussion, see George H. Halm, "The "Band" Proposal: The Limits of Permissible Exchange Rate Variations," *International Finance Section* (Princeton, N.J.: Princeton U. P., 1965), reprinted in *Guidelines for International Monetary Reforms*, Hearings, Joint Economic Committee, U.S. Congress, 89th Cong., 1st sess., 1965.

Under this system, there would be greater room for supply and demand forces in the exchange market to operate to correct payments imbalances. The pursuit of domestic economic policy is of course not entirely independent of balance of payments considerations. The correction of a severe external disequilibrium may require some changes in monetary and fiscal policies. But this system would allow greater freedom of domestic economic policy from external considerations. The monetary authority of a deficit country, for example, may pursue an easy-money policy and maintain low rates of interest to stimulate economic growth and employment with little to worry about disequilibrating capital movements. Relatively low rates of interest in this country would induce outflows of capital to foreign money centers with relatively higher rates of interest. But the increase in the rate of exchange of the deficit country vis-à-vis foreign currencies would reduce the interest differential and discourage disequilibrating capital outflows.

Under this system there would be uncertainty which would arise from frequent exchange rate changes but this could be minimized through active forward exchange markets which would provide opportunities for hedging against losses resulting from exchange rate variations. The need for international reserves under this system would be greater than under a system of floating exchange rates, as the monetary authority would have to sell foreign exchange in the exchange market to prevent the exchange rates from rising above the predetermined upper limit. Yet it would be substantially less than under the existing system, since the greater limits of exchange rate changes would tend to reduce the gap between the supply of and demand for foreign exchange which would have to be filled to keep exchange-rate changes within set limits—not to speak of the greater speed of the adjustment process. An important practical problem regarding this alternative is the determination of the range within which exchange rates are permitted to vary. It will operate like a system of floating exchange rates when the limits are wide. It will approach a system of fixed exchange rates when these limits are narrow. This system, to strict adherents to a system of floating exchange rates is at most a second-best solution to the present adjustment problem.

SUMMARY

Currency convertibility, which is essential to the expansion of international trade and investments, is the exchangeability of a currency into other currencies. Full convertibility refers to the convertibility of a currency into others under any circumstances, while limited convertibility prevails when it is confined to certain types of transactions or certain categories of holders. The scope of currency convertibility at present remains limited. Yet it is a substantial improvement over the situation in the 1930's and 1940's when exchange controls and bilateral agreements were predominant. Progress toward greater currency convertibility requires greater cooperation and coordination between nations in their domestic and international economic and financial policies.

The U.S. balance of payments during the last few decades has changed from persistent surpluses to persistent deficits. And this has been caused mainly by large-scale U.S. government grants and loans to foreign countries, U.S. private capital outflows attracted by profitable investment opportunities in other industrial nations which offer steeper competition to the United States in world markets, domestic economic expansion, inflationary pressures, and rising defense expenditures. These deficits have resulted in continuous losses of U.S. gold reserves and steady accumulation of foreign claims on the United States, a sizable portion of which is convertible into gold on demand. The U.S. payments problem requires correction, for the United States cannot count on creditor countries to finance its deficits by continuing to accumulate dollar reserves. But the restoration of equilibrium in the U.S. balance of payments could substantially reduce the supply of international reserves a significant portion of which has been provided by the U.S. deficits. To assure that the supply of world reserves would be adequate to sustain high rates of growth of world trade and payments, a plan to create a new international reserve within the framework of the IMF has been approved and activated by member countries. The new reserve consists of special drawing rights or deposits in the Fund assigned to member countries in accordance with their quotas. They will be transferred between accounts of members for payments purposes.

Another problem which needs solution is the balance-of-payments adjustment problem. In regard to the adjustment of payments imbalances, the existing exchange rate system is rather rigid for an important reserve-currency country like the United States, as it could hardly resort to exchange rate changes as a means to correct payments imbalances without undermining the stability of the system. Nor could it employ deflationary monetary and fiscal policies or exchange controls because of their adverse domestic and international economic implications. Alternative systems thus have been advanced to allow for greater operating room to the adjustment process. One alternative is the adoption of a system of floating exchange rates which would automatically correct external disequilibrium and allow complete freedom to the pursuit of domestic economic objectives. The uncertainty created by constantly changing exchange rates is one of the main objections leveled against this system. Another alternative proposes to modify the existing system to provide for wider limits within which exchange rates could vary around par values. It is believed that such a system would allow greater market forces to operate to correct payments imbalances, yet the uncertainty generated by exchange-rate changes could be minimized through active forward-exchange operations.

PROBLEMS

1. What is currency convertibility? Why is it that currency convertibility is essential to the expansion of international trade and investments? In what ways

could the promotion of currency convertibility be inconsistent with the pursuit of domestic economic goals?

2. Discuss some of the factors which caused the U.S. payments deficits. What were consequences of the U.S. payments deficits? What would you do to correct the U.S. payments imbalances?

3. What do you understand by international reserves? What are purposes for which international reserves are needed? What kind of problems would you expect to arise once the U.S. payments deficits are eliminated?

4. What is the major purpose of the "special drawing rights" plan? Discuss some major features of this plan. What are alternatives which could be used to increase international reserves? Discuss the strength and weaknesses of these alternatives.

5. In the 1950's, if creditor countries of continental Europe insisted on gold payments from the United States instead of holding dollar reserves, what would be the effects of such a policy on the volume of world trade, investments, and income?

6. In what sense would you say that from the late 1930's to the late 1950's, gold was on the dollar standard, and that after the late 1950's the dollar was on the gold standard?

7. Why is it that under the existing international monetary system, the United States is faced with a difficult balance-of-payments adjustment problem? How would you propose to solve this problem?

Bibliography

Ackley, Gardner. *Macroeconomic Theory*. New York: Macmillan, 1961.

Ahearn, Daniel S. *Federal Reserve Policy Reappraised, 1951-1959*. New York: Columbia U. P., 1963.

Alhadeff, David A. *Monopoly and Competition in Banking*. Berkeley: U. of California Press, 1954.

American Bankers Association. *The Commercial Banking Industry*. Englewood Cliffs, N.J.: Prentice-Hall, 1962.

Anderson, Clay J. *A Half-Century of Federal Reserve Policy Making, 1914-1964*. Philadelphia: Federal Reserve Bank of Philadelphia, 1965.

Aufricht, Hans (ed.). *Central Banking Legislation: A Collection of Central Bank, Monetary, and Banking Laws*. Washington, D.C.: International Monetary Fund, 1961.

Balassa, Bela. *Changing Patterns in Foreign Trade*. New York: Norton, 1964.

Ball, R. J. *Inflation and the Theory of Money*. Chicago: Aldine, 1964.

Barger, Harold. *The Management of Money*. Chicago: Rand McNally, 1964.

Baumol, William J. *Economic Dynamics*. New York: Macmillan, 1964.

———. *Economic Theory and Operations Analysis*. Englewood Cliffs, N.J.: Prentice-Hall, 1965.

Bernstein, Peter L. *The Price of Prosperity*. New York: Vintage Books, 1966.

Biven, W. Carl. *Economics and Public Policy*. Columbus, Ohio: Merrill, 1966.

Bloomfield, Arthur I. *Monetary Policy Under the International Gold Standard, 1880-1914*. New York: Federal Reserve Bank of New York, 1959.

Board of Governors of the Federal Reserve System. *The Federal Reserve System: Purposes and Functions*. 5th ed., New York, 1963.

Bronfenbremer, M., and F. D. Holzman. "Survey of Inflation Theory," *American Economic Review* (September 1963).

Brunner, Karl. *Targets and Indicators of Monetary Policy*. San Francisco: Chandler, 1967.

Burns, A. R. *Money and Monetary Policy in Early Times*. New York: Knopf, 1927.

Burnstein, Meyer. *Money*. Cambridge, Mass.: Schenkman, 1965.

Carson, Deane (ed.). *Money and Finance*. New York: Wiley, 1966.

Carothers, Neil. *Fractional Money*. New York: Wiley, 1930.

Cauley, Troy J. *Public Finance and the General Welfare.* Columbus, Ohio: Merrill, 1960.

Caulhorn, W. A. L. *A Discussion of Money*. London: Longmans, 1950.

Chandler, Lester V. *The Economics of Money and Banking.* 5th ed. New York: Harper, 1969.

Chase, Stuart. *Money to Grow On.* New York: Harper, 1965.

Clapham, Sir John Harold. *The Bank of England.* 2 vols. New York: Macmillan, 1944.

Clark, J. M. *The Wage-Price Problem.* New York: American Bankers Association, 1960.

Clifford, J. *The Independence of the Federal Reserve System.* Philadelphia: U. of Pennsylvania Press, 1964.

Cochran, John A. *Money, Banking and the Economy.* New York: Macmillan, 1967.

Cohen, Kalman J., and Frederick S. Hammer (eds.). *Analytical Methods in Banking.* Homewood, Ill.: Irwin, 1966.

Commission on Money and Credit. *Money and Credit: Their Influence on Jobs, Prices, and Growth.* Englewood Cliffs, N.J.: Prentice-Hall, 1961.

———. *The Federal Reserve and the Treasury: Answers to Questions from the Commission on Money and Credit.* Englewood Cliffs, N.J.: Prentice-Hall, 1963.

———. *Stabilization Policies.* Englewood Cliffs, N.J.: Prentice-Hall, 1963.

———. *Federal Credit Agencies.* Englewood Cliffs, N.J.: Prentice-Hall, 1963.

———. *Private Financial Institutions.* Englewood Cliffs, N.J.: Prentice-Hall, 1964.

———. *Private Capital Markets.* Englewood Cliffs, N.J.: Prentice-Hall, 1964.

———. *Inflation, Growth, and Employment.* Englewood Cliffs, N.J.: Prentice-Hall, 1964.

Committee for Economic Development. *The Dollar and the World Monetary System.* Washington, D.C., 1966.

Conard, Joseph W. *An Introduction to the Theory of Interest.* Berkeley: U. of California Press, 1959.

Copeland, Morris A. *A Study of Money Flows in the United States.* New York: National Bureau of Economic Research, 1952.

Crosse, Howard D. *Management Policies for Commercial Banks.* Englewood Cliffs, N.J.: Prentice-Hall, 1962.

Culbertson, John M. *Full Employment or Stagnation.* New York: McGraw-Hill, 1964.

Day, A. C. L., and S. T. Beza. *Money and Income.* Fair Lawn, N.J.: Oxford, 1960.

Davies, S. Gethyn (ed.). *Central Banking in South and East Asia.* Hong Kong: Hong Kong U. P., 1960.

Dean, Edwin (ed.). *The Controversy over the Quantity Theory of Money.* Boston: Heath, 1965.

Dekock, M. H. *Central Banking.* rev. ed. Staples Press Limited, 1946.
Edwards, Edgar D. (ed.). *The Nation's Economic Objectives.* Chicago: U. of Chicago Press, 1964.
Einzig, Paul. *Primitive Money.* London: Eyre Spottiswoode, 1949.
______. *Monetary Policy: Means and Ends.* Baltimore: Penguin Books, 1964.
Elderer, R. J. *The Evolution of Money.* Washington, D.C.: Public Affairs Press, 1964.
Ellsworth, P. T. *The International Economy.* London: Macmillan, 1969.
Entine, Alan D. (ed.). *Monetary Economics: Readings.* Belmont, Calif.: Wadsworth, 1968.
Federal Reserve Bank of Boston. *The Federal Funds Market: Its Origin and Development.* Rev. ed. Boston, 1964.
Federal Reserve Bank of Chicago. *Modern Money Mechanics: A Workbook on Deposits, Currency, and Bank Reserves.* Chicago, 1961
Federal Reserve Bank of New York. *Essays in Money and Credit.* New York, 1964.
Federal Reserve Bank of Philadelphia. *Fifty Years After the Federal Reserve Act.* Philadelphia, 1964.
Fisher, Irving. *The Purchasing Power of Money.* New York: Macmillan, 1911.
______. *The Theory of Interest.* New York: Macmillan, 1930.
Fleming, J. Marcus. *The International Monetary Fund: Its Form and Functions.* Washington, D.C.: International Monetary Fund, 1964.
______. *Guidelines for Balance of Payments Adjustment Under the Par-Value System.* International Finance Section. Princeton University, May 1968.
Ford, A. G. *The Gold Standard, 1840-1914.* Oxford: Clarendon, 1962.
Fousek, Peter G. *Foreign Central Banking: The Instruments of Monetary Policy.* New York: Federal Reserve Bank of New York, 1957.
Friedman, Milton. *A Program for Monetary Stability.* New York: Fordham U. P., 1960.
______ (ed). *Studies in the Quantity Theory of Money.* Chicago: U. of Chicago Press, 1956.
Friedman, Milton, and Anna Jacobson Schwartz. *A Monetary History of the United States, 1867-1960.* Princeton, N.J.: Princeton U. P., for the National Bureau of Economic Research, 1963.
Frazier, William J., and William P. Yohe. *Introduction to the Analytics and Institutions of Money and Banking.* Princeton, N.J.: Van Nostrand, 1966.
Gaines, T. C. *Techniques of Treasury Debt Management.* New York: Free Press, 1962.
Garcia, F. L. *How to Analyze a Bank Statement.* Boston: The Bankers Publishing Company, 1964.
Gramley, Lyle E. *A Study of Scale Economies in Banking.* Kansas City: Federal Reserve Bank of Kansas City, 1965.
Gray, H. Peter (ed.). *The Dollar Deficit: Causes and Cures.* Boston: Heath, 1967.

Gurley, J., and E. S. Shaw. *Money in a Theory of Finance.* Washington, D.C.: Brookings Institution, 1960.

Guttentag, Jack M., and Edward S. Herman. *Banking Structure and Performance,* New York: New York University Graduate School of Business Administration, 1967.

Haggar, A. J. *The Theory of Inflation: A Review.* London: Cambridge U. P., 1964.

Hahn, F. H., and F. P. R. Brechling (eds.). *The Theory of Interest Rates.* Proceedings of a Conference held by the International Economic Association. New York: St. Martin's 1965.

Halm, George N. *Monetary Theory*. 2d ed. New York: McGraw-Hill, 1946.

Hamovitch, William (ed.). *The Federal Deficit: Fiscal Imprudence or Policy Weapon?* Boston: Heath, 1965.

Hansen, Alvin H. *Monetary Theory and Fiscal Policy.* New York: McGraw-Hill, 1949.

Harrod, Roy F. *Policy Against Inflation.* New York: St. Martin's, 1958.

Heilbroner, Robert. *The Quest for Wealth.* New York: Simon and Schuster, 1965.

Hodgman, Donald R. *Commercial Bank Loan and Investment Policy.* Urbana, Ill.: Bureau of Economic and Business Research, University of Illinois, 1963.

Holmes, Alan, and Francis H. Schott. *The New York Foreign Exchange Market.* New York: Federal Reserve Bank of New York, 1965.

Horvitz, Paul M. *Monetary Policy and the Financial System.* Englewood Cliffs, N.J.: Prentice-Hall, 1964.

Horwich, George (ed.). *Monetary Process and Policy: Symposium.* Homewood, Ill.: Irwin, 1967.

———. *Money, Capital, and Prices.* Homewood, Ill.: Irwin, 1964.

Hutchinson, Harry D. *Money, Banking, and the United States Economy.* New York: Appleton, 1967.

International Monetary Arrangements: The Problem of Choice. Report on the Deliberations of an International Study Group of 32 Economists. International Finance Section, Princeton University, 1964.

International Payments Problems. A symposium sponsored by the American Enterprise Institute for Public Policy Research. Washington, D.C., 1966.

Jacobsson, Per. *International Monetary Problems.* Washington, D.C.: International Monetary Fund, 1964.

Johnson, Harry G. *The World Economy at the Crossroads: A Survey of Current Problems of Money, Trade, and Economic Development.* Oxford: Oxford U. P., 1965.

Kemmerer, Edwin. *Gold and the Gold Standard.* New York: McGraw-Hill, 1944.

Kemp, Arthur. *The Legal Qualities of Money.* New York: Peagant, 1956.

Ketchum, Marshall D., and L. T. Kendall (eds.). *Readings in Financial Institutions.* Boston: Houghton, 1965.

Keynes, J. M. *The General Theory of Employment, Interest and Money.* New York: Harcourt, 1936.

_______. *Treatise on Money.* 2 vols. New York: Harcourt, 1930.

Kindleberger, Charles P. *International Economics.* Homewood, Ill.: Irwin, 1968.

Klein, John J. *Money and the Economy.* New York: Harcourt, 1965.

Klein, Lawrence R. *The Keynesian Revolution.* New York: Macmillan, 1950.

Larry, H. B. *Problems of the United States as a World Trader and Banker.* New York: National Bureau of Economic Research, 1963.

Lindauer, John (ed.). *Macroeconomic Readings.* New York: Free Press, 1968.

Machlup, Fritz. *The International Monetary System: The Rio Agreement and Beyond.* Baltimore: John Hopkins Press, 1968.

Madden, Carl H. *The Money Side of the "Street."* New York: Federal Reserve Bank of New York, 1963.

Marcus, Edward, and Mildred Rendl Marcus. *International Trade and Finance.* New York: Pitman, 1965.

_______. *Monetary and Banking Theory.* New York: Pitman, 1965.

Mayer, Martin. *Wall Street: Man and Money.* New York: Collier, 1966.

Mayer, Thomas. *Monetary Policy in the United States.* New York: Random House, 1968.

McKay, George L. *Early American Currency.* New York: The Typophiles, 1944.

Mckenna, Joseph P. *Aggregate Economic Analysis.* New York: Holt, 1965.

Meek, Paul. *Open Market Operations.* New York: Federal Reserve Bank of New York, 1963.

Mints, Lloyd W. *A History of Banking Theory.* Chicago: U. of Chicago Press, 1945.

Mund, V. A. *Government and Business.* New York: Harper, 1965.

Musgrave, Richard A. *The Theory of Public Finance.* New York: McGraw-Hill, 1959.

Nadler, Marcus. *New Tools for Credit Control.* New York: C. J. Devine Institute of Finance, New York University, 1964.

Nadler, Paul S. *Commercial Banking in the United States.* New York: Random House, 1968.

Newlyn, W. T. *Theory of Money.* Oxford: Clarendon Press, 1962.

Niebyl, Karl H. *Studies in the Classical Theories of Money.* New York: Columbia U. P., 1945.

Nussbaun, Arthur. *A History of the Dollar.* New York: Columbia U. P., 1957.

Okun, Arthur M., *The Battle Against Unemployment.* New York: Norton, 1965.

Organization of European Cooperation and Development. *The Balance of Payments Adjustment Process.* Working Party No. 3, Paris, 1966.

Patinkin, Don. *Money, Interest, and Prices.* 2d ed. New York: Harper, 1965.

Pesek, Boris P., and Thomas R. Saving. *The Foundations of Money and Banking,* New York: Macmillan, 1968.

Phelps, Edmund S. *The Goal of Economic Growth.* New York: Norton, 1962.

President's Commission on National Goals. *Goals for Americans.* Englewood Cliffs, N.J.: Prentice-Hall, 1960.

Pritchard, Leland J. *Money and Banking.* Boston: Houghton, 1964.

Reed, Edward W. *Commercial Bank Management.* New York: Harper, 1963.

Richards, Richard D. *The Early History of Banking in England.* London: Cass, 1958.

Ritter, Lawrence S. (ed.). *Money and Economic Activity.* Boston: Houghton, 1967.

Robertson, D. H. *Money.* Chicago: U. of Chicago Press, 1962.

Robinson, Roland I. *The Management of Bank Funds.* New York: McGraw-Hill, 1962.

———. *Money and Capital Markets.* New York: McGraw-Hill, 1964.

Roosa, Robert V. *Monetary Reform for the World Economy.* New York: Harper, 1965.

———. *Federal Reserve Operations in the Money and Government Securities Market.* New York: Federal Reserve Bank of New York, 1956.

Ruggles, Richard. *An Introduction to National Income and Income Analysis.* New York: McGraw-Hill, 1949.

Sayers, R. S. *Central Banking After Bagehot.* Oxford: Clarendon, 1961.

Schneider, Erich. *Money, Income, and Employment.* New York: Macmillan, 1962.

Scitovsky, Tibor. *Money and the Balance of Payments.* Chicago: Rand McNally, 1969.

Schultze, Charles L. *Recent Inflation in the United States.* Study Paper No. 1, Joint Economic Committee, 86th Congress, Washington, D.C., 1959.

Sen, S. N. *Central Banking in Underdeveloped Money Markets.* Calcutta: Bookland, 1952.

Shannon, I. *International Liquidity: A Study in the Economic Function of Gold.* Melbourne, Australia, 1964.

Shapiro, Eli, Ezra Solomon, and William L. White. *Money and Banking.* New York: Holt, 1968.

Sherman, Howard J. *Macrodynamic Economics.* New York: Appleton, 1964.

———. *Growth, Employment, and Inflation.* New York: Appleton, 1964.

Sirkin, Gerald. *Introduction to Macroeconomic Theory.* Homewood, Ill.: Irwin, 1962.

Slesinger, R. E. *Business, Government, and Public Policy.* Princeton, N.J.: Nostrand, 1968.

Smith, Warren L. *Debt Management in the United States.* Study Paper No. 19, Prepared for the Joint Economic Committee, Washington D.C.: Government Printing Office, 1960.

______ and Ronald L. Teigen (eds.). *Readings in Money, National Income, and Stabilization Policy.* Homewood, Ill.: Irwin, 1965.

Snider, Delbert A. *International Monetary Relations.* New York: Random House, 1966.

Strayer, Paul J. *Fiscal Policy and Politics.* New York: Harper, 1958.

Studenski, Paul, and H. E. Krooss. *The Financial History of the United States.* New York: McGraw-Hill, 1963.

Tamagna, Frank. *Central Banking in Latin America.* Mexico City: Centro De Estudios Monetarios Latinoamericanos, 1965.

Tew, Brian. *International Monetary Cooperation: 1945-1965.* London: Hutchinson University Library, 1965.

Thorn, Edward S. (ed.). *Monetary Theory and Policy.* New York: Random House, 1966.

Thorp, Willard L., and Richard Quandt. *The New Inflation.* New York: McGraw-Hill, 1959.

Timberlake, Richard H., Jr. *Money, Banking, and Central Banking.* New York: Harper, 1965.

______. "Mr. Shaw and his Critics: Monetary Policy in the Golden Era Reviewed," *Quarterly Journal of Economics* (February 1963).

______. "The Specie Standard and Central Banking in the United States Before 1860," *Journal of Economic History* (September 1961).

Trescott, Paul B. *Money, Banking, and Economic Welfare.* New York: McGraw-Hill, 1965.

Triffin, Robert. *Our International Monetary System.* New York: Random House, 1968.

U.S. Congress. *Employment, Growth, and Price Levels.* Hearings, 86th Cong., Part IV. Washington, D.C., 1959.

______. *Factors Affecting the United States Balance of Payments.* Compendium. Prepared for the Subcommittee on International Exchange and Payments, December 1962.

______. House Committee on Banking and Currency. *Federal Credit Programs.* 2 vols. Washington, D.C.: Government Printing Office, 1964.

______. *Fiscal Policy Issues of the Coming Decade: Statements by Individual Economists and Representatives of Interested Organizations,* Subcommittee on Fiscal Policy, February 1965.

______. *Guidelines for International Monetary Reform.* Subcommittee on International Exchange and Payments, Hearings, 89th Cong. Part II (Supp.). Washington, D.C., 1965.

______. *Inflation and the Price Indexes.* Monograph submitted to the Subcommittee on Economic Statistics by the National Industrial Conference Board, June 1966.

______. *Government Price Statistics.* Hearings before the Subcommittee on Economic Statistics, 89th Cong. Washington, D.C., 1966.

———. *U.S. Economic Growth to 1975: Potentials and Problems.* Staff study prepared for the Subcommittee on Economic Progress, December 1966.

———. *The Future of U.S. Foreign Trade Policy.* Hearings before the Subcommittee on Foreign Economic Policy, 90th Cong. Vols. I and II. July 1967.

———. *Next Steps in International Monetary Reform.* Hearings before the Subcommittee on International Exchange and Payments, 90th Cong. September 1968.

———. *On Linking Reserve Creation and Development Assistance.* Staff study prepared for the Subcommittee on International Exchange and Payments, April 1969.

———. *A Review of Balance of Payments Policies.* Hearings before the Subcommittee on International Exchange and Payments. Washington, D.C., January 1969.

Ward, Richard A. (ed.). *Monetary Theory and Policy*. Scranton, Pa.: International Textbook, 1966.

Whittlesey, Charles R., Arthur M. Freedman, and Edward S. Herman. *Money and Banking: Analysis and Policy.* New York: Macmillan, 1964.

Weldon, Welfling. *Bank Investments.* New York: American Institute of Banking, 1963.

Weintraub, Sidney. *An Approach to the Theory of Income Distribution.* Philadelphia: Chilton, 1958.

———. *A General Theory of the Price Level, Output, Income Distribution, and Economic Growth.* Philadelphia: Chilton, 1959

———. *Classical Keynesianism, Monetary Theory, and the Price Level.* Philadelphia: Chilton, 1961.

Wicksell, Knut. *Lectures on Political Economy.* London: Macmillan, 1934.

———. *Interest and Prices.* London: Macmillan, 1936.

Wolf, Harold A. *Monetary and Fiscal Policy.* Columbus, Ohio: Merrill, 1966.

Wolf, Harold A., and R. Conrad Doenges (eds.). *Readings in Money and Banking.* New York: Appleton, 1968.

Woodworth, Walter G. *The Money Market and Monetary Management.* New York: Harper, 1965.

Yeager, Leland B. (ed.). *In Search of a Monetary Constitution.* Cambridge: Harvard U. P., 1962.

Answers to Selected Problems

CHAPTER 4

6. (a) \$705.41; (b) \$885.30; (c) \$1,133.92; (d) through the "accumulation of the discount" or the "amortization of the premium."
7. (a) \$2,500; (b) \$5,000; (c) not applicable.
8. (a) \$99.01 for the bill and \$805.79 for the bond; (b) the price of the bill will increase to \$99.50 and that of the bond, to \$1,119.42; (c) the longer the maturity, the greater the price variation, given the change in the rate of interest. This is important to investors; investors in long-term securities are assured of a fixed stream of income (income certainty) but they face greater risk of capital losses (capital uncertainty). Investors in short-term securities, on the other hand, face income uncertainty (i.e., reinvestments are to be made at varying rates of interest) but there is little risk of capital losses (capital certainty).

CHAPTER 6

7. Here we shall show changes in the assets and liabilities of banks and the Federal Reserve only.

(a)

Bank A

Investment	Demand deposits
+1,000	+1,000

(c)

Bank C

Cash	Demand deposits
-1,000	-1,000

(d)

Bank D

Deposits at	Borrowings at
Fed. +1	Fed. +1

Federal Reserve

Loans to	Deposits of
banks +1	banks +1

(g)

Bank G

Loans	Demand deposits
-1,000	-1,000

8.

Houston Bank	
Deposits at Fed. −1,000	Demand deposits −1,000

Dallas Third National	
Deposits at Fed. +1,000	Demand deposits +1,000

Reserve Bank of Dallas	
	Balance of H. Bank −1,000 Balance of D. Bank +1,000

9. Follow the example in the text.

10. It should be noted that "acceptance outstanding" is a liability item, and "customers' acceptance liability" is an asset item. Federal Reserve Bank stock is also an asset item. Total assets = Total liabilities + Net Worth = $222,500.

CHAPTER 7

8. (a)

Bank A	
Investments −1 Deposits at Fed. +1	

Bank B	
Investments +1 Deposits at Fed. −1	

Federal Reserve	
	Balance of A +1 Balance of B −1

(b)

Bank A	
Deposits at B −100,000 Deposits at Fed. +100,000	

Bank B	
Deposits at Fed. −100,000	Balance of A −100,000

Federal Reserve	
	Balance of A +100,000 Balance of B −100,000

(c)

Bank A	
Cash + Deposits at Fed. −	

Federal Reserve	
	Deposits of banks − Fed. notes +

(d)

Bank A	
Investments −1 Deposits at Fed. +1	

Federal Reserve	
	Deposits of Treasury −1 Deposits of banks +1

(e) Except for (d) where the reserves of the banking system increase, bank reserves R remain unchanged in other cases.

CHAPTER 8

6. (a) $10,000

(b) Banking System

Required reserves +1,000	Demand deposits +10,000
Loans +9,000	

(c) The money supply M increases by $9,000.

7. (a) $4,000;

(b) Banking System

Required reserves +440	Demand deposits +4,000
Loans +4,360	Time deposits +800

(c) about $4,170;

(d) Banking System ($\Delta T = 0$)

Required reserves +417	Demand deposits +4,170
Loans +3,753	

8. (a) −10 million;
   (b) the process of multiple deposit contraction would not operate as the acquisition of $900,000 of reserves (through the sale of securities to the Federal Reserve) would help remove the reserve deficiency of $900,000.

Banking System

Cash −1 million	Demand deposits −1 million
Securities −900,000	
Deposits at Fed. +900,000	

CHAPTER 9

8. Bank A is insolvent. Its loss is 260. Since the capital account is 80, a loss of 180 would be suffered by (time) depositors. Bank B is solvent but its capital is impaired as the loss of 5 is charged off the capital account, thereby reducing it to 5.

CHAPTER 11

6. (a)

Bank A

Cash +1,000	Demand deposits +1,000

S & L Association

Cash +1,000	S+L share +1,000
Loans +1,000	
Cash −1,000	

(b) No change in M; the increase in demand deposits is offset by the decrease in currency in circulation of like amount. But if we define M to include savings and loan share accounts, then we can say that M increases by 1000; (c) the activation of idle balances would cause the expenditure flow to rise.

7. (a)

Bank B		Savings Bank	
	Demand deposits of Y −500 Demand deposits of savings banks +500	Deposits at bank B +500	Savings deposits +500

(b) No change in M. (It should be noted that the demand liability of the commercial bank vis-a-vis the savings bank is part of M.) If we include savings deposits in the savings bank as part of M, then the latter will increase by 500.
(c) Increase by 500.

CHAPTER 12

5. (a) (i)

Federal Reserve		Member Banks	
	Member bank deposits −10 Federal Reserve notes +10	Cash −10	Demand deposits −10
		Deposits at Fed. −10 Cash +10	

(ii)

Federal Reserve	
Treasury currency −5	Member bank deposits −10 Fed. notes +5

M is not immediately affected. R decreases and this could lead to some contraction in M.

6. (a)

Treasury		Federal Reserve		Member Banks	
Deposits at Fed. +10 Deposits at banks −10			Deposits of Treasury + 10 Member bank deposits −10	Deposits at Fed. −10	Deposits of Treasury −10

(b) No immediate change in M, but R decreases.

7. The process is the same as the inter-district collection of a check.

CHAPTER 13

7. (a)

Federal Reserve	
Securities −10	Deposits of banks −10

Commercial Banks	
Deposits at Fed. −10	Demand deposits −10

M and R decrease.

(c)

Treasury	
Gold −10	
Deposits at Fed. +10	
Deposits at Fed. −10	Gold certificates −10

Reserve Bank of N.Y.	
	Deposits of Treasury +10
	Foreign deposits −10
Gold cert. −10	Deposits of Treasury −10

Bank of France	
Gold +10	
Deposits at N.Y. Fed. −10	

M, as defined by the Federal Reserve, decreases. R remains unchanged.

(g)

Federal Reserve	
	Deposits of banks −5
	Capital stock +5

Member Banks	
Deposits at Fed. −5	
Reserve Bank stock +5	

R decreases.

CHAPTER 16

5. (a) 1960 = 100; 1961 = 107; (b) 1960 = 100; 1961 = 108; (c) same as in (b) since the weighted aggregative index using base-year quantities as weights is the same as the weighted average of price relatives using base-year values as weights.

6. (a) $\dfrac{\Sigma p_1 q_0}{\Sigma p_0 q_0} \cong 111.4$; (b) $\dfrac{\Sigma p_1 q_1}{\Sigma p_0 q_1} \cong 114.0$; (c) $\left[\dfrac{\Sigma p_1 q_0}{\Sigma p_0 q_0} \times \dfrac{\Sigma p_1 q_1}{\Sigma p_0 q_1}\right]^{1/2} \cong 112.8$

CHAPTER 17

6. (a) $M_d = k \cdot P_y Y_r = 50$; (b) Since $M = 100$, there is an excess supply of money at that price level; (c) the equilibrium price level would be \$2; and this is brought about by attempts of the public to reduce excess money supply by spending; given $Y_r = 200$, the pressure of demand would drive up the price level until it reaches \$2; at that level, $M_d = M = 100$.

CHAPTER 18

5. (a) GNP = 140 + 30 + 120 = 290; (b) GNP = 210 + 80 (profits before taxes) = 290; (c) GNP = 230 + 60 = 290 (230 = value added by business; and 60 = value added by government).

6. (a) (1) GNP as sum of expenditures = 200 + 50 + 170 = 420; (2) GNP as sum of value added = 350 + 70 = 420.

   (b) Total savings = Household savings + Business savings + Government savings = 30 + 30 - 10 = 50; total investment = 50 (equipment + inventory); Household surplus = 30; Business deficit = -20; Government deficit = -10; the Business sector saved 30 but invested 50; it borrowed 40 (10 from Household and 30 from Banks) to cover the deficit of 20 and build up money balances of 20; the Government borrowed 30 (20 from Household and 10 from Banks) to cover its deficit of 10 and build up money balances of 20. Household saved 30 and borrowed 10 (from Banks) of which 20 was used in the purchase of government securities, 10, in the purchase of corporate bonds, and 10, to build up money balances.

CHAPTER 20

1. (a) $Y = 300$; $Y + \Delta Y = 325$; $k = 5$; the change would be the same i.e. $\frac{dY}{da} = \frac{dY}{dI} = \frac{1}{1-b}$

   (b) $Y = 350$; $Y + \Delta Y = 322$; $k = 7$

   (c) The equilibrium equation contains 2 unknowns, Y and i; we can solve it for Y only when the value of i is given. For each given value of i, an equilibrium level of income is determined. Suppose that $i = 0.05$, then $Y = 462$

2a. (i) $Y = 390$; $Yd = 375$; $C = 340$; $S = 35$; (ii) $\Delta Y = 10$; (iii) $\Delta Y = -20$; (iv) $\Delta T = 2.5$

2b. (i) $Y = 270$; $T = 45$; $Yd = 225$; $C = 220$; $S = 5$; (ii) $\Delta Y = 15$

CHAPTER 21

6. (a) $i_0 = 0.02$; (b) $i_1 = 0.023$
7. (a) $i_0 = 0.05$; (b) $i_1 = 0.10$

CHAPTER 22

5. (a) $Y = 100; i = 0.05$
   (b) $\Delta Y = 5.7; \Delta i = -0.006$; given $Y = 100$, then $\Delta i = 0.02$
   (c) $\Delta Y = 5.7$ and $\Delta i = 0.0142$

CHAPTER 25

8. Here, we shall show changes in the assets and liabilities of commercial banks and the Federal Reserve only.

(a)

Federal Reserve	
	Deposits of banks −1 Deposits of Treasury +1
U.S. Gov't. securities −1	Deposits of Treasury −1

Commercial banks	
Deposits at Fed. −1	Deposits of Treasury −1

R decreases and this could lead to contraction in *M*.

(b)

Federal Reserve	
	Deposits of Treasury +1 Deposits of Banks −1
	Deposits of Banks +1 Deposits of Treasury −1

Commercial Banks	
Deposits at Fed. −1	Deposits of Treasury −1
U.S. Gov't. Securities −1 Deposits at Fed. +1	

M and *R* unchanged. But note that the decrease in the banks' demand liabilities would release excess reserves for loan and deposit expansion.

(c)

Federal Reserve		Commercial Banks	
	Deposits of Treasury +1 Deposits of Banks −1	Deposits at Fed. −1	Deposits of Treasury −1
	Deposits of Treasury −1 Deposits of Banks +1	Deposits at Fed. +1	Demand Deposits (pub.) +1

No change in R; M increases.

9. (a)

Federal Reserve		Commercial banks	
	Deposits of banks −2 Deposits of Treasury +2	Deposits at Fed. −2	Demand deposits −2
	Deposits of Treasury −2 Deposits of banks +2	Deposits at Fed. +2	Demand deposits +2

R and M initially decline; But the disposition of borrowed Funds by the Treasury (payments to the public) will cause R and M to increase again.

(b)

Federal Reserve		Commercial banks	
		U.S. Gov't. Securities +2	Deposits of Treasury +2
	Deposits of Treasury +2 Deposits of banks −2	Deposits at Fed. −2	Deposits of Treasury −2
	Deposits of Treasury −2 Deposits of banks +2	Deposits at Fed. +2	Demand Deposits +2

No change in R; M increases following payments made by the Treasury to the public

(c)

Federal Reserve		Commercial banks	
U.S. Gov't. Securities +2	Deposits of Treasury +2		
	Deposits of Treasury −2 Deposits of banks +2	Deposits at Fed. +2	Demand Deposits +2

R and M increase.

CHAPTER 27

4. On the basis of the dollar-franc rate in New York and the dollar-mark rate in Frankfurt, the cross-rate between the mark and the (Belgian) franc is about 1 mark = 12.195 francs. Since the mark-franc rate in Brussels is 1 mark = 12.240 francs, a New York banker, for instance, could make a profit by offering dollars for marks in Frankfurt, marks for francs in Brussels, and francs for dollars in New York. Consequently, the value of the dollar vis-a-vis the mark will decline in Frankfurt, and increase vis-a-vis the Belgian franc in New York (The value of the mark vis-a-vis the franc will decline in Brussels).
5. In answering this question, it should be noted that the reduction of U.S. residents' deposits balances with foreign banks is a credit entry. On the other hand, the reduction of foreign long-term investments in the U.S. is a debit entry. The reduction of foreign exchange holdings of the Treasury, like its sale of gold, represents a credit entry. There should be an "errors and unrecorded transactions" of 50 to make total credits equal to total debits.

CHAPTER 28

5. (a) U.S. official reserves decrease: −$266 million
   (b) liquidity balance: −$1,055 million; Balance on basis of official reserve transactions: $840 million.
6. (a) $Y = 196; B = X - M = -6.6$; (b) $\Delta Y = 10$; $\Delta B = \Delta X - \Delta M = 4$; multiplier = 2; (c) effect of income is the same: $\Delta Y = 10$; but balance of payment deficit worsened, $\Delta B = -1$.

Index